Software Engineering:
Effective Teaching and Learning Approaches and Practices

Heidi J. C. Ellis
Trinity College, USA

Steven A. Demurjian
University of Connecticut, USA

J. Fernando Naveda
Rochester Institute of Technology, USA

INFORMATION SCIENCE REFERENCE

Hershey · New York

Director of Editorial Content:	Kristin Klinger
Director of Production:	Jennifer Neidig
Managing Editor:	Jamie Snavely
Assistant Managing Editor:	Carole Coulson
Typesetter:	Kim Barger
Cover Design:	Lisa Tosheff
Printed at:	Yurchak Printing Inc.

Published in the United States of America by
Information Science Reference (an imprint of IGI Global)
701 E. Chocolate Avenue, Suite 200
Hershey PA 17033
Tel: 717-533-8845
Fax: 717-533-8661
E-mail: cust@igi-global.com
Web site: http://www.igi-global.com

and in the United Kingdom by
Information Science Reference (an imprint of IGI Global)
3 Henrietta Street
Covent Garden
London WC2E 8LU
Tel: 44 20 7240 0856
Fax: 44 20 7379 0609
Web site: http://www.eurospanbookstore.com

Library of Congress Cataloging-in-Publication Data

Software engineering : effective teaching and learning approaches and practices / Heidi J.C. Ellis, Steven A. Demurgian, and J. Fernando Naveda, editors.

p. cm.

Includes bibliographical references and index.

Summary: "This book presents the latest developments in software engineering education, drawing contributions from over 20 software engineering educators from around the globe"--Provided by publisher.

ISBN 978-1-60566-102-5 (hardcover) -- ISBN 978-1-60566-103-2 (ebook)

1. Software engineering--Study and teaching. 2. Computer software--Development--Study and teaching. I. Ellis, Heidi J. C. II. Demurjian, Steven A. III. Naveda, J. Fernando.

QA76.758.S646254 2008

005.1'07--dc22

2008022554

British Cataloguing in Publication Data
A Cataloguing in Publication record for this book is available from the British Library.

All work contributed to this book set is original material. The views expressed in this book are those of the authors, but not necessarily of the publisher.

If a library purchased a print copy of this publication, please go to http://www.igi-global.com/agreement for information on activating the library's complimentary electronic access to this publication.

Table of Contents

Section I
Introduction

Section II
Student Learning and Assessment

Section III
Innovative Teaching Methods

Section V
Educational Technology

Section VI
Curriculum and Education Management

Section VII
Professional Practice

Detailed Table of Contents

Section I
Introduction

Chapter I

    Gregory W. Hislop, Drexel University, USA

There is a strong and growing global demand for skilled software engineers. The institutions that educate software engineers are evolving and changing to meet this need. This chapter provides an overview of this effort to develop software engineering education. It discusses the historical development of software engineering education, provides some perspective on current status, and identifies some of the challenges faced by software engineering educators. The intended audience for this chapter is anyone interested in software engineering education who has not participated in the developments to the present time. The goal is to provide a summary background of how the discipline has evolved and pointers to key publications that are part of that history. Since this chapter surveys foundational topics in software engineering education, many of the topics touched on in this chapter are covered in more detail in other chapters of this volume.

Section II
Student Learning and Assessment

Chapter II

    Jocelyn Armarego, Murdoch University, Western Australia

Practitioner studies suggest that formal IT-related education is not developing the skills and knowledge needed by graduates in daily work. In particular, a shift in focus from technical competency to the soft and metacognitive skills is identified. This chapter argues that a framework for learning can be developed that more closely models the experiences of practitioners, and addresses their expectations of novice Software Engineers. Evaluation of a study incorporating three Action Research cycles shows that what is needed is a mapping between the characteristics of professional practice and the learning model that is applied. The research shows that a relationship also exists between learner and learning model, and that this relationship can be exploited in the development of competent discipline practitioners.

Chapter III

Learning theories describe how people learn. There is a large body of work concerning learning theories on which to draw, a valuable resource of which the domain of software engineering educational research has thus far not taken full advantage. In this chapter, the authors explore what role learning theories could play in software engineering education. The authors propose that learning theories can move the field of software engineering education forward by helping us to categorize, design, evaluate, and communicate about software engineering educational approaches. They demonstrate this by: (1) surveying a set of relevant learning theories, (2) presenting a categorization of common software engineering educational approaches in terms of learning theories, and (3) using one such approach (SimSE) as a case study to explore how learning theories can be used to improve existing approaches, design new approaches, and structure and guide the evaluation of an approach.

Section III
Innovative Teaching Methods

The field of software engineering is multifaceted. Accordingly, students must be educated to cope with different kinds of tasks and questions. This chapter describes a collection of tasks that aim at improving students' skills in different ways. The authors illustrate their ideas by describing a course about human aspects of software engineering. The course objective is to increase learners' awareness with respect to problems, dilemmas, ethical questions, and other human-related situations that students may face in the software engineering world. The authors attempt to achieve this goal by posing different kinds of questions and tasks to the learners, which aim at enhancing their abstract thinking and expanding their analysis perspectives. The chapter is based on the authors' experience teaching the course at Carnegie-Mellon University and at the Technion – Israel Institute of Technology.

Ann Brady, Michigan Technological University, USA
Marika Seigel, Michigan Technological University, USA
Thomas Vosecky, Michigan Technological University, USA
Charles Wallace, Michigan Technological University, USA

In this chapter, the authors describe their recent efforts to generate and use case studies to teach communication skills in software development. They believe their work is innovative in several respects. The case studies touch on rhetorical issues that are crucial to software development yet not commonly associated with the field of software engineering. Moreover, they present students with complex, problematic situations, rather than sanitized post hoc interpretations often associated with case study assignments. The case study project is an interdisciplinary collaboration that interweaves the expertise of software engineers and technical communicators. Their software engineering and technical communication curricula have been enhanced through this cross-fertilization.

Nancy R. Mead, Software Engineering Institute, USA
Dan Shoemaker, University of Detroit Mercy, USA

This chapter describes methods of incorporating security requirements engineering into software engineering courses and curricula. The chapter discusses the importance of security requirements engineering and the relationship of security knowledge to general computing knowledge by comparing a security body of knowledge to standard computing curricula. Then security requirements is related to standard computing curricula and educational initiatives in security requirements engineering are described, with their results. An expanded discussion of the SQUARE method in security requirements engineering case studies is included, as well as future plans in the area. Future plans include the development and teaching of academic course materials in security requirements engineering, which will then be made available to educators. The authors hope that more educators will be motivated to teach security requirements engineering in their software engineering courses and to incorporate it in their curricula.

Section IV
Project-Based Software Engineering

Kevin A. Gary, Arizona State University, USA

This chapter describes the development of a learning-by-doing approach for teaching software engineering called the Software Enterprise at the Polytechnic Campus of Arizona State University. The Capstone experience is extended to two one-year projects and serves as the primary teaching and learning vehicle for best practices in software engineering. Several process features are introduced in an attempt to make projects, or more importantly the experience gained from project work, more applicable to industry expectations. At the conclusion of the Software Enterprise students have an applied understanding of how to leverage software process as a tool for successful project evolution. This chapter presents the Software Enterprise, focusing the presentation on three novel aspects: a highly iterative, learner-centered pedagogical model, cross-year mentoring, and multiple projects as a novel means of sequencing learning objectives.

This chapter describes a two-semester software engineering course that is taught in a computer science program at the University of Texas at El Paso. The course is distinguished from other courses in that it is based on the Affinity Research Group (ARG) philosophy that focuses on the deliberate development of students' team, professional and technical skills within a cooperative environment. To address the challenge of having to teach professional and team skills as well as software engineering principles, approaches, techniques, and tools in a capstone course, the authors have defined an approach that uses a continuum of instruction, practice, and application with constructive feedback loops. The authors hope that the readers will benefit from the description of the approach and how ARG components are incorporated into the course.

Chapter IX

This chapter demonstrates the importance of Real Projects for Real Clients Courses (RPRCCs) in computing curricula. Based on the authors' collective experience, advice for setting up an effective support infrastructure for such courses is offered. The authors discuss where and how to find clients, the types of projects that they have used, and how to form and train teams. The authors also investigate the variety of standards and work projects that they have used in their courses and explore issues related to assessment and evaluation. Finally, the chapter considers the benefits of an RPRCC-centric approach to computing curricula.

Chapter X

Steven A. Demurjian, University of Connecticut, USA
Donald M. Needham, United States Naval Academy, USA

Project-based capstone software engineering courses are a norm in many computer science (CS) and computer science & engineering (CS&E) accredited programs. Such cap-stone design courses offer an excellent vehicle for educational outcomes assessment to support the continuous improvement process required for accreditation. A project-based software engineering capstone course near the end of a student's program can span the majority of CS and CS&E program objectives, providing a significant means to assess attainment of these objectives in a single course location. One objective of this chapter is to explore the role of a project-based, software engineering course in accreditation. An additional objective is to relate over twelve combined years of experience in teaching such a course, and in the process, highlight what works and what does not. The authors candidly examine both the successes and the failures that they have encountered over the years, and provide a roadmap for other instructors and departments seeking to institute such courses.

Section V
Educational Technology

Chapter XI

Christian Bunse, International University in Germany, Germany
Christian Peper, Fraunhofer Institute Experimental Software Engineering, Germany
Ines Grützner, Fraunhofer Institute Experimental Software Engineering, Germany
Silke Steinbach-Nordmann, Fraunhofer Institute Experimental Software Engineering, Germany

With the rapid rate of innovation in software engineering, teaching and learning of new technologies have become challenging issues. The provision of appropriate education is a key prerequisite for benefiting from new technologies. Experience shows that typical classroom education is not as effective and efficient as it could be. E-learning approaches seem to be a promising solution but e-learning holds problems such as a lack of social communication or loose control on learning progress. This chapter describes a blended learning approach that mixes traditional classroom education with eLearning and that makes use of tightly integrated coaching activities. The concrete effects and enabling factors of this approach are discussed by means of an industrial case study. The results of the study indicate that following a blended learning approach has a positive impact on learning time, effectiveness and sustainability.

Chapter XII

Daniel Bolanos, Universidad Autonoma de Madrid, Spain
Almudena Sierra, Universidad Rey Juan Carlos, Spain

Due to the increasingly important role of software testing in software quality assurance, during the last several years, the utilization of automated testing tools, and particularly those belonging to the xUnit family, has proven to be invaluable. However, as the number of resources available continues increasing, the complexity derived from the selection and integration of the most relevant software testing principles, techniques and tools into an adequate learning environment for training computer science students in software testing, increases too. This chapter introduces an experience of teaching Software Testing for a senior-level course. In the elaboration of the course a wide variety of testing techniques, methodologies and tools have been selected and seamlessly integrated. An evaluation of students performance during the three academic years that the course has been held show that students' attitudes changed with a high or at least a positive statistical significance.

Section VI
Curriculum and Education Management

Chapter XIII

This chapter provides a brief history of the accreditation of software engineering programs in the United States and describes some of the experiences encountered by programs in achieving their accreditation and by program evaluators in reviewing those programs. It also describes how the accredited programs have addressed the most difficult issues that they have faced during the accreditation process. The authors have served as leaders of the accreditation efforts at their own institutions and as ABET program evaluators at several other academic institutions that have achieved accreditation. The objective of this chapter is to provide those software engineering programs that will be seeking accreditation in the future with some of the experiences of those who are familiar with the process from both the programs' and the evaluators' points of view. Leaders of programs that are planning to request an accreditation review will be well prepared for that review if they combine the information contained in this chapter with the recommendations contained in Chapter XVI of this text.

Chapter XIV

In 1996, a new Software Engineering curriculum was launched at Universität Stuttgart. It was based on many years of practical experience teaching computer science and also on experience in industry where most of our graduates will find jobs. While the topics of this curriculum are not very different from those of computer science, there is much more emphasis on problem solving, software construction, and project work. In 2009, our traditional curriculum leading to the so called diploma (equivalent to a master's degree) will be replaced by a new curriculum according to the bachelor and master concept. This chapter describes both the old and the new curriculum, and discusses problems and achievements.

Chapter XV

Daniela Rosca, Monmouth University, USA
William Tepfenhart, Monmouth University, USA
Jiacun Wang, Monmouth University, USA
Allen Milewski, Monmouth University, USA

The development, maintenance and delivery of a software engineering curriculum present special challenges not found in other engineering disciplines. The continuous advances of the field of software engineering imposes a high frequency of changes reflected in the curriculum and course content. This chapter describes the challenges of delivering a program meeting the needs of industry and students. It presents the lessons learned during 21 years of offering such a program, and dealing with issues pertaining to continuous curriculum and course content restructuring, and the influence of the student body on the curriculum and course content. The chapter concludes with the authors' recommendations for those who are seeking to create a graduate program in software engineering, with a special note on the situations where an undergraduate and graduate program will need to coexist in the same department.

Chapter XVI

Stephen Frezza, Gannon University, USA
Mei-Huei Tang, Gannon University, USA
Barry J. Brinkman, Gannon University, USA

This chapter presents a case study in the development of a Software Engineering (SE) Bachelor's Degree program. It outlines issues in SE program development, various means to address those issues, and explains how the issues were addressed in the initial and ongoing development of an undergraduate SE program. By using SEEK and SWEBOK as requirements sources to define what an undergraduate software engineer needs to know, the authors walk through the creation of a sample curriculum at a small, comprehensive university in the United States. Both the current and initial curricula are presented. The chapter discusses many items to consider in the process of planning and launching a new BSSE program, such as accreditation, curriculum guidelines, sources of information, and potential problems.

Section VII
Professional Practice

Chapter XVII

J. Barrie Thompson, University of Sunderland, UK

The teaching and learning of aspects related to ethics and professional practice present significant challenges to both staff and students as these topics are much more abstract than say software design and testing. The core of this chapter is an in-depth examination of how ethics and professional practice can be addressed in a very practical manner. To set the scene and provide contextual information the chapter commences with information on an international model of professionalism, a code of ethics for Software Engineers, and different teaching and learning approaches that can be employed when addressing ethical issues. The major part of the chapter is then devoted to detailing a particular teaching and leaning approach, which has been developed at the University of Sunderland in the UK. Finally conclusions, views on the present situation and future developments, and details of outstanding challenges are presented.

Chapter XVIII
Stephen B. Seidman, University of Central Arkansas, USA

This chapter provides an international perspective on professional software engineering credentials. It distinguishes between professional licensing, certification, and other forms of credentials. It compares and contrasts several major approaches to professional credentials: broad-based certifications, national examinations, and job frameworks. Examples of credentials in each category are discussed in detail. The chapter also discusses efforts to develop international standards for these credentials. The chapter concludes with a brief description of the current landscape of professional software engineering credentials.

Foreword

"It is not enough to aim; you must hit." - *Italian Proverb*

"Software engineering – the "engineering" of software – is part process, part technology, part resource management, and, debatably, until recently, part luck – which make interesting challenges for educators at the undergraduate or graduate level. Learning to be a software engineer – learning about software – learning about engineering (the former, a nebulous topic, the latter an equally nebulous attitude of professionalism) form the target that educators are aiming to hit. Unfortunately, with constant "innovations" in methodologies, technologies, and programming languages, this is a moving target.

"The great aim of education is not knowledge but action." Herbert Spencer (1820-1903)

Simply put, the aim of this book is to better prepare educators to better prepare students to be better software engineers. The material in the 18 chapters of this book hits the mark by providing proven ammunition for student learning and assessment, curriculum development, innovative teaching methods, and project approaches that solidify classroom concepts, as well as instill an engineering mindset with respect to responsibility, ethics, certification and licensing. It provides a synergistic experience base that can serve the ongoing and future needs of software engineering educators.

"Nothing can add more power to your life than concentrating all your energies on a limited set of targets." Nido Qubein

To paraphrase Yogi Berra, "Software engineering is 90% aptitude, and the other half attitude." In my opinion, one of the main challenges facing software engineering educators today is finding a formula for a curriculum that balances theory and application – that channels a student's aptitude and enhances their ability and capability to be a software engineer. As stated earlier, software is a nebulous topic – not all software applications require the same engineering tradeoffs, but there are key engineering concepts that can be distilled from the experience of others, as captured in the chapters of this book, which will help guide educators in defining and refining software engineering curriculum.

"Aim for success, not perfection. Never give up your right to be wrong, because then you will lose your ability to learn new things and move forward with your life." Dr. David M. Burns

Perfection is the seductive goal of all software engineering projects - yet perfection has a price that can stand in the way of a successful software solution. The readers of this book will clearly learn new things that I am convinced will lead to success in the classroom that will, in turn, lead to more successful engineering graduates, that will, in turn lead to more successful engineering projects.

In closing, there is one phrase that I first heard used jokingly when I entered the job market only 4 years after the term "Software Engineering" was coined – "*Ready, Fire, Aim.*" At the time, I did not appreciate its profound applicability to the real world. Software Engineering is the real world. Academia is not, and there lies the challenge that this book addresses. Metaphorically speaking, the material in this book will help educators get ready for software engineering students to learn as well as the educators themselves to teach (by providing a survey of existing learning theories and blended learning approaches as they apply to software engineering education), it will help give educators the ammunition they need to build their software engineering programs and capstone projects (leading to accreditation and more "experienced" students, who can better communicate and work in teams), and finally, it better prepares the students to successfully hit the (moving) target (by giving them an appreciation of ethics and professionalism that they can take outside the classroom).

Will Tracz, PhD
Lockheed Martin Fellow
Editor ACM Software Engineering Notes

Preface

Software plays an ever increasing role in society today. In fact, software is a factor in almost all aspects of life including health care, entertainment, transportation, communications, and finance, among others. Our dependency on software today is such that the spread of a computer virus can bring our way of life to a standstill for a significant period of time. Demand for an increasing number of software professionals has been cited in business and government circles for at least two decades, with no leveling in sight. In addition, the methods, approaches and tools used to produce the software on which we so much depend are also undergoing rapid expansion. As a result, academic institutions are facing an increasing pressure to produce a greater number of students that are competent software developers.

Software engineering and software development education currently face many challenges. The ever expanding area of software engineering knowledge makes educating the next generation of software engineers a challenge. In addition, the current generation of students has very different interaction patterns than prior generations, making assessing learning difficult. The increasing role that software plays in our lives today (e.g., grid computing, ubiquitous computing, wearable computing, bioinformatics, etc.) requires educators to adapt their education coverage to include these new applications. In addition, many academic institutions must face these challenges within the constraints of program accreditations, university mission, demographics, and even political environments. Clearly, identifying successful approaches to handling these problems is essential to aid software engineering educators. This book contains a generous collection of approaches that represent best practice for software engineering education including student assessment and learning, innovative teaching methods, project-based software engineering, professional practice and ethics, curriculum management and certification and licensing.

This book will be useful to both academicians and practitioners. Academic readers will gain an understanding of proven practices used in software engineering education that could be employed at their institutions. Industry readers will benefit from an understanding of the synergies between educational practices and real-world software development. All readers will gain an international view of software engineering education. Educators can use the book as a reference for adopting novel teaching techniques and for improving their teaching across a variety of computing courses.

The book is organized into seven sections that cover student learning and assessment, innovative teaching methods, project-based software engineering, educational technology, curriculum and education management, and professional practice. Below we provide a brief summary of the chapters.

I. Hislop

In order to provide context for the remainder of the book, the introductory chapter by Dr. Hislop provides an overview of the history and current state of software engineering education. Software engineering is a relatively new discipline and software engineering education is even newer. Dr. Hislop discusses the issues that have shaped the development of software engineering education including the genesis of a new discipline, the organizational location of software engineering, licensing, certification, and accreditation. The issue of community where software engineering educators can exchange ideas and collaborate is also discussed. In addition, the development and state of curriculum is presented including a discussion of a range of educational venues from entire software engineering programs to individual software engineering courses in other computing degrees.

II. Armarego

An appreciation of learning theory is vital to understanding how best to educate students. In fact, experience has shown that an organized and controlled approach to educating software engineers is more successful than ad hoc approaches. However, the software engineering education community has been slow to explore the application of various learning theories to education. Correctly applied, learning theories could improve the state of software engineering education by allowing educators to design, evaluate and communicate about educational approaches, allowing the best approaches to be identified.

In the first chapter of the section on **Student Learning and Assessment**, *"Constructive Alignment in SE Education: Aligning to What?"*, Dr. Armarego argues that learning should fit both the learner as well as the discipline being learned. The chapter explores the alignment between the practices utilized in the software engineering discipline and the models of learning that are used by students to absorb software engineering knowledge in academic institutions. Dr. Armarego discusses the development of a framework for learning that models experiences of software practitioners and suggests that the learning model used for education be characterized and mapped to fit the professional practice. The chapter includes the results of a study which indicates that tailoring the learning models used in academia today holds the potential for improving student software engineering learning.

III. Navarro

Continuing on the role of learning theory in software engineering education, Chapter III *"On the Role of Learning Theories in Furthering Software Engineering Education"*, by Drs. Navarro and van der Hoek discusses the possible uses of learning theory in software engineering education. This chapter provides a survey of existing learning theories and comments on their use in software engineering education. The authors categorize the current educational approaches in software engineering according to the theories. An example approach which uses an interactive, graphical game to teach software engineering process is used to demonstrate how learning theories can successfully be applied to software engineering education.

IV. Hazzan

The section on **Innovative Teaching Methods** begins with a discussion of one of the aspects of software engineering that is perhaps most difficult to convey to students, that is, the human perspective including teamwork, conflict resolution, and problem solving from different perspectives. Hazzan and Tomayko present an approach to educating students to the human aspects of software engineering in Chapter IV titled *"Tasks in Software Engineering Education: The Case of a Human Aspects of Software Engineering Course"*. The approach enhances abstract thinking and expands analysis perspectives of students using a question and task-based approach. The chapter presents a categorization of ten different types of tasks that can be used throughout a course in order to make students more aware of the human-related problems, dilemmas, ethical questions, and other situations that students may face in the software engineering world. The categorization of tasks is based on the authors' experience in teaching a Human Aspects of Software Engineering course at two different institutions, one located in the United

States and one located in Israel. The chapter presents examples of each category of task and describes the use of the example within a course.

V. Brady

Chapter V titled *"Speaking of Software: Case Studies in Software Communication"* also addresses the human aspect of software engineering education, specifically both oral and written communication. Typically, communication is given little direct attention in software engineering courses and programs. Teaching communication is difficult and communication in the software workplace is very complex and fraught with subtlety.

Drs. Brady, Seigel, Vosecky, and Wallace are an interdisciplinary team containing both technical writers and software engineering educators that has created an approach to teaching communication skills to software engineering students using case studies. The case studies are based on experiences of software engineering students in a capstone course and are used in the pedagogical sense. These real case studies provide students a complex situation in which to learn and understand communication.

VI. Mead

In this final chapter for **Innovative Teaching Methods**, titled *"Novel Methods of Incorporating Security Requirements Engineering into Software Engineering Courses and Curricula,"* Drs. Mead and Shoemaker explore the inclusion of security requirements engineering into software engineering courses and curricula. Security engineering has emerged as a vital national and international concern, part of almost every application designed and developed. These authors explore the integration of security into the earliest stage of the process, namely requirements engineering. The authors identify that security is often considered at either the system level (e.g., authentication, firewalls, etc.) or in isolation from overall system requirements elicitation. To bolster this assertion, the authors provide a careful and detailed analysis of *Computing Curricula 2005: The Overview Report*, trying to understand the way that security can mesh with the desired outcomes of CC2005. The authors propose and discuss the inclusion of security into curricula, ranging from undergraduate project-based courses to graduate courses on secure systems development to usage of processes such as comprehensive, lightweight application security process (CLASP) and security quality requirements engineering (SQUARE). The bulk of the chapter presents a detailed approach using SQUARE, detailing specific curricula, course content, projects, and so on.

VII. Gary

The fourth section of the book, **Project-Based Software Engineering,** supports the old undisputable proverb that states that "Experience is the best teacher." Academics and industry professionals agree that students that graduate with a better understanding of the real world have a better chance of early success in their careers. With the increasing popularity of software engineering course offerings embedded in a variety of computing degrees, inevitably, one must wonder how someone in a classroom could teach students how the real world works. While it is impossible to teach experience, it is possible to teach through experience. This observation has guided the development of many software engineering courses being taught today.

In Chapter VII titled *"The Software Enterprise: Preparing Industry-Ready Software Engineers"* Arizona State University's Dr. Gary, describes an innovative approach to learning-by-doing called the Software Enterprise. Under this model, students enroll in two consecutive yearlong software development capstone courses where they learn through experience software engineering's best practices. At the completion of the software enterprise students have an experiential understanding of how software process can be used to manage the evolution of software artifacts. While this chapter may be quite helpful to those new to teaching software engineering, due to the interesting way in which the software enterprise brings together so many aspects of the software development lifecycle in two consecutive courses, even experienced instructors may learn a thing or two.

VIII. Roach

In the second chapter for **Project-Based Software Engineering**, titled *"Using the Affinity Model in the Capstone Project Course: Teaching Software Engineering in a Computer Science Program,"* Drs. Roach and Gates describe their approach for a two-semester software engineering sequence that uses an approach that stresses cooperative (team-based) learning of professional and technical skills. This sequence, underway at University of Texas at El Paso (UTEP), offers a combined two-course sequence taken by students in their final year of study, combining fundamental software engineering topics with the development of communication and team skills, which includes a practical exposure to the software engineering code of ethics and professional practice. Unlike the approach as given in Chapter X, where the capstone project succeeds a much earlier exposure to software engineering principles and practices, this course offered in the Computer Science department at UTEP assumes the opposite – coupling the first exposure of software engineering with the capstone project experience. The authors explore their approach by detailing the curricula, student and faculty responsibilities, project and course requirements, project management, course deliverables, and so on. The authors have evaluated their unique sequence through a combination of surveys that has collected data from alumni and employers; they have had many positive results and feedback. The authors conclude with a discussion of future trends ranging from the high-level (The President's Council of Advisors on Science and Technology reports on the importance of networking and information technology (NIT) systems and the workforce required to support them) to emerging technology trends (service-oriented architectures) and their impact on curricula.

IX. Klappholz

Clearly, the software industry prefers to hire students who have real-world experience as such students are well-rounded and can more quickly contribute to a project. The presence of an actual client can motivate students and provide direction for a project. However, involving students in projects with real-world clients can pose problems such as locating clients, client communication issues, setting reasonable scope for a project, creating functional teams, assessing the project and more.

Drs. Klappholz, Almstrum, Modesitt, Johnson and Condly present advice for involving students in projects with real clients in Chapter IX *"A Framework for Success in Real Projects for Real Clients Courses"*. The authors discuss the importance of using real-world projects and present a taxonomy of issues related to involving students in real projects for real clients courses. The authors discuss issues related to client interactions including locating appropriate clients, project-related issues including appropriate projects and scope, team-related issues including team formation and operation, product-related issues including deliverables, and issues related to assessment and evaluation. The approach was developed based on experiences with real-world projects with real customers at a wide variety of U.S. institutions.

X. Demurjian

Continuing in the project area, Drs. Demurjian and Needham discuss the successful and unsuccessful characteristics of a project-based capstone software engineering course in Chapter X, *"Experiences in Project-Based Software Engineering: What Works, What Doesn't"*. The authors present the results of 12 combined years of experience in offering project-based courses at two different U.S. institutions. They demonstrate how such courses can be used to support ABET accreditation by providing educational outcomes assessment. Understanding that obtaining accreditation assessment data can be time consuming, the authors offer guidance to instructors to help manage the assessment data collection. In addition, the authors discuss project attributes and suggest that projects be flexible in order to allow them to be adapted to instructor background. Team size and communication is also addressed and the authors provide a rubric for assessing individual student effort within a team. Future plans include using mixed teams of CS and IT majors.

XI. Bunse

In this first chapter in the **Educational Technology** section of this book, titled *"Applying Blended Learning in an Industrial Context: An Experience Report,"* the authors Drs. Bunse Peper, Ochs, Grützner, and Steinbach-Nordmann, explore the usage of blended learning in software engineering education, continuing the investigation of practice-based software engineering in a classroom setting. Blended learning is a technique that combines multiple teaching methods into a single setting, providing a unique perspective and learning experience for students. In this chapter, the authors report on their efforts in blended learning for model-based and object-oriented development with UML, providing an experience which combines self-directed study, collaborative learning, learning with an on-line tutor, social learning, and traditional classroom delivery. The unique aspect of this chapter is that these experiences are related for both an academic and an industrial setting. The work includes a strong case study (questionnaire), data collection, and data analysis of blended learning, offering conclusions based on these results, and exploring future trends such as the use of wikis, podcasts, Weblogs, and virtual learning environments.

XII. Bolanos

Chapter XII, titled *"Integrated Software Testing Learning Environment for Training Senior-Level Computer Science Students,"* completes the **Educational Technology** section, Drs. Bolanos and Sierra explore a methodology for software testing that targets senior-level computer science students. The educational technology component in this chapter is to establish an environment that allows actual testing, including: test plans, test case designs, a suite of testing automation tools, analysis and reporting of test results, software configuration management tools (for multiple testing iterations), and a software execution and deployment tool. This is accomplished via an actual, custom, multi-tiered, client server software application developed for this purpose, allowing for a full range of testing (e.g., unit testing, integration testing, functional testing, etc.). As with the prior chapter, the authors rely on a voluntary evaluation survey (93% surveys returned for an average of 150 students taking the course per year) to assess their course, and feed back results into future offerings. In the future, the authors expect constant change, as the underlying development technologies evolve, and more and more testing tools become available.

XIII. McDonald

The history of undergraduate software engineering education in the US reached a critical milestone when the first baccalaureate programs received ABET accreditation in 2001. Since then an increasing number of undergraduate software engineering programs are seeking ABET's recognition. But for many program leaders, accreditation is still an intimidating event.

For many program leaders and their faculty, a program accreditation exercise goes more or less like this: About a year prior to the accreditation visit, the program leader must first get the faculty to understand why self-assessment should not be an activity that is counted in 5-year cycles but rather, an activity that happens almost daily, and is a natural part of teaching. Then, one lucky faculty member is sent to at least one ABET workshop to learn about accreditation. Upon returning, the terrified faculty member, now the in-house accreditation expert, calls an emergency meeting no one wants to attend, but everyone attends for fear of being assigned to a laborious (and unfair) accreditation task. The race is then set and faculty and staff rush to collect data and make some sense of it. The accreditation expert earns a couple of course releases to help the program documents in order. About a month or so prior to the visit there are numerous faculty meetings spiced up with incredibly long and fruitless arguments, and endless visits to the department's copier. The week before the ABET team arrives, tempers run high as the program leader and the accreditation expert put the final touches on what they hope will be a great event.

But preparing for an accreditation visit does not have to be an ordeal. In Chapter XIII, the first in the **Curriculum and Education Management** section of the book, titled "*Software Engineering Accreditation in the United States*", McDonald, Sebern and Vallino explain in simple terms many of the issues involved in an accreditation. The authors cover issues such as making sense of ABET's criteria, outcomes and objectives, and data collection. One of the most valuable features of this chapter is the way in which the authors, who collectively account for years of experience as program evaluators, program leaders, and in-house accreditation experts; present numerous topics of interest combining their viewpoints succinctly and straightforwardly.

XIV. Ludewig

Software Engineering curricula can resemble vanilla ice cream: they all are called by the same name, but their flavors are quite different. The history of software engineering education is crowded with curricula whose flavors range from strong computer science with nuances of software engineering, to software engineering smeared with heavy blobs of computer science caramel, to the purest unadulterated software engineering. Regardless of their structure, these curricula serve their intended audiences and meet the academic mission of their respective universities.

In Chapter XIV "*Software Engineering at Full Scale: A Unique Curriculum*", Dr. Ludewig describes the evolution, content and structure of a software engineering curriculum developed at Universität Stuttgart. The software engineering program Dr. Ludewig describes is somewhat unique in Germany in that, according to his account, no other university in his native Germany has a complete software engineering curriculum. It is based on a principle of individual responsibility and consists of a defined set of initial courses followed by allowing the student great flexibility in the latter courses. In addition, there is only a single set of exams per semester and students are allowed to attend the course in one semester and take the exam for that course the next year or even later.

XV. Rosca

Anyone who has had the opportunity to build an academic program from scratch can identify themselves with the challenges of building the program, and the thrill of seeing its student body grow over the years. While creating a graduate level software engineering program is a formidable task, keeping it up-to-date and maintaining its integrity are essential to ensuring the program's success over the years. Dedicated faculty must constantly weigh market needs against academic and technical developments such as changes in technology, innovations in software development and maintenance processes, or new software design trends. Then, they must determine how to bring about change to the graduate program.

In Chapter XV titled "*Continuous Curriculum Restructuring in a Graduate Software Engineering Program*", Drs. Rosca, Tepfenhart, Wang, and Milewski share with the reader their extensive experience maintaining a master's level program at Monmouth University over the program's 21 year history. Due to continuous advances in the engineering of software, the authors assert that maintenance of a software engineering graduate program offers challenges not found in other engineering programs. In addition, the authors discuss their experience maintaining their graduate program factoring in student input while coexisting with their department's baccalaureate program in software engineering. Readers of this chapter will benefit from the authors experience maintaining Monmouth University's graduate software engineering degree over its 21-year history.

XVI. Frezza

It was at a NATO conference in 1968 in Garmisch, Germany, where the term Software Engineering was first mentioned in a formal setup. At the time, the term was more a statement of aspiration than a fact. The field of computing as we know it today was still in gestation. Sixteen years later the U.S. Department of Defense awarded Carnegie Mellon University the contract to establish the Software Engineering Institute (SEI) with the intent to "Advance the practice of software engineering because quality software that is produced on schedule and within budget is a critical component of U.S. defense systems." One of the ways in which the SEI accomplished its mission was to enable universities to develop masters degrees in software engineering. But no one was yet talking of undergraduate degrees in software engineering. It was not until 1996 when the first undergraduate degrees in software engineering were born in the US. Since then an increasing number of schools are taking a serious look at undergraduate software engineering.

In Chapter XVI, Frezza and his colleagues describe in great detail the many issues that surrounded the development of a "Credible Software Engineering Bachelors Program." The intriguing use of the word "Credible" should spike the reader's interest in this chapter because, with declining enrollments in computer science in the US and Canada, schools are being tempted with the concept of re-baptizing existing computer science programs as software engineering hoping to capitalize on the upward trend of enrollments in software engineering. As Frezza and his colleagues explain, building a credible undergraduate degree in software engineering requires effort, compromise, and dedication. But more importantly, it requires academic integrity.

XVII. Thompson

The final section of the book is titled **Professional Practice**. Ethics is one important component of the aspect of professional practice for software engineers. The topic of ethics is especially important to software engineering students who will enter a global environment of software development. Upon graduating from an academic program, students must understand their responsibilities with respect to professional practice as well as the role of ethics.

Dr. Thompson addresses the issue of teaching ethics in software engineering education in Chapter XVII, "*Ensuring Students Engage with Ethical and Professional Practice Concepts*". Dr. Thompson provides an overview of two widely used codes of ethics, the IFIP Harmonization of Professional Standards and the ACM and IEEE-CS software engineering code of ethics and professional practice. The author then presents an approach to teaching ethics and professional practice in a practical manner which has resulted in increased enthusiasm on the part of students. Dr. Thompson provides insights into effective teaching of ethics including that the education be relevant to the students' discipline, all instructors should be competent to teach ethics, teaching should respect the values of different people groups and that the teaching of ethics should be pervasive throughout the curriculum.

XVIII. Seidman

The final chapter of the book, titled "A*n International Perspective on Professional Software Engineering Credentials*", supplies an international perspective on professional software engineering credentials. Dr. Seidman provides an overview of forms of credentialing including professional licensing, certification and more. The chapter explains approaches to professional credentialing used world-wide including broad-based certifications, national examinations, and job frameworks and discusses international efforts to develop standards for these credentials. Dr. Seidman concludes that credentialing software engineering professionals should be distinct from a specific product or tool and that credentialing will become increasingly important as the role of software in society continues to grow.

This book is an aggregation of classroom techniques and experiences garnered from around the world that have been proven successful in educating software engineers. It contains a collection of best practices in the field of software engineering teaching and learning, providing an understanding of the effective educational approaches used in software engineering education. It provides guidance to educators who are already teaching software engineering education or are considering establishing or expanding software engineering education within their institutions. In addition, the book can be used as a resource by software engineering educators to learn and adopt new educational practices to improve education. The diversity of topics and approaches presented provides a broad and international perspective on software engineering education.

Acknowledgment

We would like to acknowledge and thank the following list of reviewers:

Name	Affiliation	Country
Almstrum, Vicki	University of Texas at Austin	USA
Armarego, Jocelyn	Murdoch University	Australia
Bolanos, Daniel	Autonoma University of Madrid	Spain
Bourque, Pierre	University of Quebec	Canada
Brinkman, Barry	Gannon University	USA
Carrington, David	University of Queensland	Australia
Condly, Steve	University of Central Florida	USA
Duggins, Sheryl	Southern Polytechnic State University	USA
Dupuis, Robert	University of Quebec	Canada
Hazzan, Orit	Technion - Israel Institute of Technology	Israel
Henderson, Pete	Butler University	USA
Horton, Tom	University of Virginia	USA
Kaner, Cem	Florida Institute of Technology	USA
Klappholtz, David	Stevens Institute of Technology	USA
Lethbridge, Tim	University of Ottawa	Canada
Liu, Chang	Ohio University	USA
Ludewig, Jochen	Universität Stuttgart	Ger
Lutz, Mike	Rochester Institute of Technology	USA
James McDonald	Monmouth University	USA
Murphy, Mike	Southern Polytechnic State University	USA
Navarro, Emily	University of California Irvine	USA
Owen, Cherry	University of Texas of the Permian Basin	USA

Phat, Vinh	Cogswell Polytechnical College	USA
Roach, Stephen	University of Texas at El Paso	USA
Rosca, Daniela	Monmouth University	USA
Seidman, Steve	University of Central Arkansas	USA
Shoemaker, Dan	University of Detroit Mercy	USA
Sobel, Ann	Miami University	USA
James R. Vallino	Rochester Institute of Technology	USA
Wallace, Charles	Michigan Technological University	USA

Section I
Introduction

Chapter I
Software Engineering Education:
Past, Present, and Future

Gregory W. Hislop
Drexel University, USA

ABSTRACT

There is a strong and growing global demand for skilled software engineers. The institutions that educate software engineers are evolving and changing to meet this need. This chapter provides an overview of this effort to develop software engineering education. It discusses the historical development of software engineering education, provides some perspective on current status, and identifies some of the challenges faced by software engineering educators. The intended audience for this chapter is anyone interested in software engineering education who has not participated in the developments to the present time. The goal is to provide a summary background of how the discipline has evolved and pointers to key publications that are part of that history. Since this chapter surveys foundational topics in software engineering education, many of the topics touched on in this chapter are covered in more detail in other chapters of this volume.

INTRODUCTION

The demand for skilled software developers is growing at an extraordinary rate as software is being used in an ever widening set of domains. The increase in the use of the internet, the phenomenal rate of growth of available data, and new developments such as biosensors, grid computing, and cognitive machines require software engineers who can correctly engineer and modify these kinds of systems within budget and at a reason-able cost. As a result, educational institutions are under increasing pressure to produce educated and capable software engineers. However, educational institutions face many challenges in producing these software engineers that extend far beyond curriculum issues. Software engineering is still a discipline trying to define itself and find a place among the set of computing and engineering disciplines. As such, this chapter will address a mix of issues related to three themes:

- **Context:** The external issues that have influenced the development of software engineering education including the issue of organizational location of software engineering within a college or university, politics related to emergence of a new discipline, licensing, certification, and accreditation.
- **Community:** The collaboration, cooperation, and sharing of information among software engineering educators.
- **Curriculum:** The content and organization of degree programs and individual software engineering courses in other computing degrees.

The chapter is organized by looking at these issues historically, in the present, and for the future.

The intended audience for this chapter is anyone interested in software engineering education who has not participated in the developments to the present time. The goal is to provide a summary background of how the discipline has evolved and pointers to key publications that are part of that history.

DEVELOPMENT OF SOFTWARE ENGINEERING AS A DISCIPLINE

The problems of developing software were noticed as soon as significant software development activities began. The notion of software engineering as a solution to this problem is commonly dated to the NATO conference on this topic held in 1968 (Naur & Randell, 1969). Versions of the conference report and the report of a second conference held a year later are available at http://homepages.cs.ncl.ac.uk/brian.randell/NATO/.

This conference is noteworthy for the extent to which the range of topics currently recognized as central to software engineering were clearly identified even in this early effort. Organization of software development activities was clearly

understood, at least from a waterfall model perspective. Key software engineering problems such as scale and complexity were clearly recognized, as were difficulties in estimation, and even the potential for things like construction of software from components.

A review of this material is helpful to make the point that software engineering has a core set of issues and problems that are stable over some extended period of time, and across very substantial technology changes. On the other hand, this same review is striking in indicating how modest progress has been in addressing software engineering issues decisively.

Although there is broad agreement on the need for solutions to the issues software engineering addresses, the question of whether software engineering should be a discipline has been a more divisive question. Almost 40 years after the NATO conference, computing professionals have not reached consensus on how to organize computing knowledge or the computing professions.

In academic discussions of the disciplines, the key issue for software engineering has been the relationship of software engineering to computer science. This debate has often been described using Venn diagrams to question whether the two disciplines intersect, are disjoint, or whether one is a subset of the other. A more recent set of diagrams in Computing Curricula 2005: The Overview Report (ACM & IEEE, 2005) clearly shows the disciplines as distinct but with substantial intersection.

Beyond academic circles, the separation of computing disciplines is generally ignored. The use of job titles and professional designations is almost completely ad hoc. With regard to software engineering, there is "no standard definition for this term when used in a job description. Its meaning varies widely among employers." (ACM & IEEE, 2005, p. 15) Like any computing profession label, the term is applied with no particular concern for formal education or certification of the person involved. While the

Table 1. Infrastructure elements of a mature profession

Initial Professional Education
Accreditation
Skills Development
Certification
Licensing
Professional Development
Code of Ethics
Professional Society

designation of someone as a "systems analyst" or "systems administrator" might be expected to be a flexible choice, the designation of someone as an "engineer" is generally much more restricted due to the licensing implications associated with engineering. This sense of restriction clearly does not apply to "software engineer" as the term is commonly used today.

Although there is still variation in approach to organizing the computing disciplines, since the NATO conference, and particularly in the last 20 years, there has been great progress in establishing software engineering. A variety of authors have discussed this progress, with Ford and Gibbs (1996) providing a very complete discussion from the perspective of maturity as a profession. The infrastructure elements of the model they propose for characterizing a mature profession are shown in Table 1. By the measures of this model, software engineering has made substantial progress but still has considerable room to develop.

This combination of substantial accomplishment with continuing need for development and lingering resistance to the very idea of software engineering as a separate discipline may simply be a reflection of the relative newness of software engineering. A discussion of software engineering from the perspective of the history of science by Mahoney notes that "its practitioners disagree on what software engineering is, although most

of them freely confess that, whatever it is, it is not (yet) an engineering discipline." (Mahoney, 2004, p. 8).

Mahoney concludes his analysis with the observation that "software may be fundamentally different from any of the artifacts or processes that have been the object of traditional branches of engineering." He further suggests that perhaps architecture rather than engineering should be looked at more closely as a model for the software profession and notes that the same NATO conference recognized as a starting point for software engineering also contained a proposal for "software architecture" as the appropriate model for addressing the issues related to software.

To summarize, software engineering is built around a stable, well-defined set of issues. Over recent decades, software engineering has come to exhibit many of the characteristics of a mature profession. At the same time, the set of computing disciplines continues to evolve, and a lively and sometimes contentious discussion about software engineering is part of that evolution.

DEVELOPMENT OF SOFTWARE ENGINEERING EDUCATION PROGRAMS

Software engineering was already a curriculum topic by the late 1960's, and over time, many computer science programs developed single courses related to software engineering either in the form of team project courses or survey courses of software engineering topics. These individual courses have continued to be a staple of computer science programs and many are still offered today.

It was about 10 years after the NATO conferences before the first software engineering degree programs began to appear. The first programs in the U.S. appeared at the Masters level, with early efforts including degrees at Seattle University, Texas Christian University, and the Wang Institute. Tomayko (1998) provides a good summary of the early years of software engineering education in the U.S, and notes that the first efforts were largely triggered by a response to local industry need.

The next growth phase for software engineering education was precipitated by the funding of the Software Engineering Institute (SEI) at Carnegie Mellon University by the U.S. Department of Defense. The SEI started an initiative on software engineering education almost immediately. This was a powerful catalyst since it provided funding specifically focused on SE education. More generally, the Department of Defense is an important source of funding for research unrelated to education across a variety of science and engineering areas. Any interest in software engineering education by the SEI was bound to attract substantial attention.

The results of the SEI effort included a curriculum model for a Master of Software Engineering degree, a variety of reports on software engineering as a profession, and a fairly extensive set of curriculum modules that were made publicly available (Ardis & Ford, 1989). The SEI also organized a variety of meetings and workshops that allowed people from different institutions to compare notes and share ideas on software engineering education. Two of these efforts evolved into the Working Group on Software Engineering Education and Training and the Conference on Software Engineering Education and Training, both of which continued long after the SEI had ceased its education initiative around 1994.

Development of undergraduate programs significantly lagged development of Masters programs in the U.S. Development of undergraduate programs proceeded much more quickly in other places, particularly in the U.K and Australia. Cowling (1998), for example, provides a detailed discussion of the development and evolution of one such program. In part, this more rapid growth seems to have been a result of differences in the approach to licensing engineers, which is a key question for an undergraduate degree with a title including "engineering." In particular, the U.S. system is heavily dependent on having appropriate exams, while the U.K. and Australia place more emphasis on completion of a degree. This latter approach makes it easier to accommodate a substantially different kind of engineering such as software engineering that deals with non-physical artifacts.

The slower development of undergraduate programs may have been influenced by the SEI focus on Master's level education. While the SEI applied some effort toward development of undergraduate education (Ford, 1991a, 1994), not much progress had been made at the time the SEI education initiative ended. Interested faculty members picked up the undergraduate issues in a volunteer continuation of the SEI software engineering working group. This effort resulted in an early set of curriculum guidelines (Bagert et al, 1999), and many of the participants were key contributors to the SE 2004 curriculum model (ACM & IEEE, 2004).

The first U.S. BSSE program began in 1996 at Rochester Institute of Technology as described by Lutz and Naveda (1997). Others soon followed and the number of U.S. programs has continued to grow. There are currently over 30 U.S. BSSE programs. While growth has not been explosive, it has been steady even during the recent years of substantial downturn in the number of students majoring in computing disciplines. The chapter in this volume by McDonald, et al provides some details of this growth in the context of accreditation.

It has been common for the U.S. institutions to encounter organizational difficulties or other road blocks in establishing SE degree programs. For many years, this has been a regular discussion topic at meetings of faculty interested in software engineering. It also appears repeatedly in various surveys and discussions of software engineering education. For example, Fairley (1986) notes several examples where graduate programs in software engineering could not be established due to various clashes of perspective or interests of relevant stakeholders.

In this text, the chapter by Frezza, et al includes a discussion of some of the typical political issues that arise in establishing undergraduate software engineering degree programs.

THE COMMUNITY OF SOFTWARE ENGINEERING EDUCATORS

Software Engineering is still a new discipline, but substantial results have been achieved already. Degree programs are in place, undergraduate and graduate curriculum models have been developed. In the U.S., ABET accreditation criteria for Software Engineering have been approved and 13 degree programs have been accredited.

Such activity requires sustained, coordinated effort across multiple institutions as well as involvement of professional societies. During much of this development, the software engineering education community was quite cohesive, with a cadre of active members that provided infrastructure and guidance during the maturation process of software engineering education. Some of the more effective activities and community support mechanisms have been:

- **CSEET**, The Conference on Software Engineering Education and Training. The first SEI Conference on Software Education was held in April 1987. This conference series continued after the SEI education initiative ended and it is still held annually. Attendance has always been modest, but that reflects the relatively small community of SE educators. The conference provides a significant gathering place for institutions offering SE programs. Other conferences, notably IEEE Frontiers of Education, SIGCSE, and the annual ASEE Conference also provide outlets for software engineering education publications. Some SE conferences including the International Conference on Software Engineering also include education tracks in some years.

- **WGSEET**, the Working Group on Software Engineering Education and Training. Started in early 1990s, as part of the SEI software engineering education initiative (the "and Training" was appended to the name some years after the start). This group continued to meet after active SEI support ended. Volunteers met twice a year, usually before the CSEET and IEEE Frontiers in Education conferences to address development of software engineering education. The WGSEET meetings produced an early version of a software engineering undergraduate curriculum model, and reports on successful academic-industry collaborations.

More importantly, the WGSEET provided a general forum for community development and exchange of ideas. This forum created common understanding and fostered interactions that were instrumental in producing many publications on software engineering education. The WGSEET activity also provided a key feed into curriculum modeling and accreditation activities, and facilitated creation of other projects such as

SWENET, the Network Community for Software Engineering Educators.

- **SWEEP:** In 1998-1999, the ACM and IEEE-CS sponsored the Software Engineering Education Project (SWEEP). This group worked to create guidelines for undergraduate Software Engineering curricula and a draft set of accreditation guidelines for undergraduate software engineering programs. Members of SWEEP started work that evolved into the Software Engineering curriculum model (ACM & IEEE, 2004).

- **SWECC:** The Software Engineering Coordinating Committee was part of a joint effort by the ACM and IEEE-CS to promote SE as a profession. This effort provided the starting point for development of an SE Code of Ethics, and an SE Body of Knowledge project. The ACM withdrew from the group as part of the decision to take a position against licensing of software engineers.

- **SE 2004:** The undergraduate SE Curriculum Model grew out of some of the earlier efforts mentioned above. But it was a clear step beyond those efforts in having endorsement of the IEEE-CS and the ACM. In addition, it benefited from the more formal and more broadly based development process that has evolved over the history of the computing curricula volumes.

- **SWEBOK:** The Guide to the Software Engineering Body of Knowledge, was started as a project by SWECC in 1998. The intention "is to provide a consensually validated characterization of the bounds of the software engineering discipline and to provide a topical access to the Body of Knowledge supporting that discipline." (SWEBOK, 2004, p. xvii). To provide a starting point, the SWEBOK drew on prior SE standards efforts supported by the IEEE. In addition, the SWEBOK is notable for the effort to be

transparent and provide a consensus result based on broad participation.

- **FASE:** The Forum for Advancing Software Engineering, is an online newsletter that includes announcements, reports, and short articles of interest to software engineering educators. It was published monthly for many years, and archived articles are maintained online.

- **SWENET:** The Network Community for Software Engineering Education, was an NSF project that produced a repository of publicly available software engineering course modules (Hislop, Lutz & Sebern, 2006). SWENET also supported several workshops that were effective community building exercises for software engineering educators. The project ended in 2005, but the repository is still supported.

The list above represents an impressive effort given the modest size of the software engineering community. At the same time, it is clear that some of the mechanisms that served well in the past have not kept up with the changes and growth in the software engineering community.

For example, WGSEET, The Working Group on Software Engineering Education and Training has ceased to exist. An effort to replace WGSEET with SEECo, an Education Community within the IEEE CS Technical Council on Software Engineering, has not been a success. Similarly, SEPLA, the Software Engineering Program Leaders Association, was started as a spin-off of WGSEET to allow department chairs and program directors to interact. The group has a low activity listserv, but has never really been active. Finally, FASE, the online software engineering education newsletter, was published regularly for over 10 years. But FASE has been largely inactive for the last several years because few people are choosing to submit any material for distribution.

These changes can be taken as reflections of the success of software engineering. Many of the original goals of SE educators such as creating curriculum models and developing accreditation standards have been accomplished. These efforts now have mainstream support of the major computing professional societies. As such, the efforts will be widely visible, and maintained over time.

On the other hand, it seems that the community of software engineering educators has lost some of the supporting structure that mechanisms like WGSEET and FASE once provided. The opportunity for informal interaction among interested faculty members was a valuable side effect of those efforts. Given that the total number of SE degree programs worldwide is still not very large, it seems that looking for additional opportunities for informal community interaction might be valuable in the future too.

ACCREDITATION, CERTIFICATION, AND LICENSING

Accreditation has been a clear success for software engineering in the U.S. Accreditation criteria were developed in 1998-1999 and the first degree programs were accredited in 2003. At present 13 programs are accredited, and more are expected to complete this process over the next several years.

SE accreditation is handled by the Engineering Accreditation Commission (EAC) of ABET, the accrediting body for engineering and technology in the U.S. After the SE accreditation effort began, ABET merged with CSAB, the accrediting body for computer science. With the merger of CSAB, ABET created a Computing Accreditation Commission (CAC). The CAC currently handles accreditation of computer science, information systems, and information technology.

By curricular content, software engineering clearly has strong overlap with the CAC disciplines. On the other hand, it makes sense to place software engineering with the other engineering disciplines in the EAC. As it happens, this issue was decided simply by the sequence in which the events happened to occur (accreditation criteria development followed by the merger).

Licensing has been and remains a controversial issue for software engineering. Although licensing (or chartering in the U.K.) has proceeded relatively smoothly in the U.K. and Canada, there has been little progress in the U.S. Without regard to the question of whether software engineers should be licensed, there are several difficult issues associated with licensing.

Perhaps the most important question overall is the body of knowledge that provides the basis for license. Opinions diverge on whether software engineering knowledge is mature enough to support licensing in a meaningful way. That is, will a licensed practitioner in software engineering have the knowledge needed to protect the public from software risks, or, is the body of software engineering knowledge not mature enough to support meeting this responsibility? Shaw (1990) discusses this issue with a broad perspective of how a software engineering discipline might emerge. In a more recent discussion Shaw reiterates this argument with the comment: "…professional licensing carries a commitment to the public that we can achieve a level of practice that provides certain safety and utility properties of the product, but such a level of practice is not yet routinely achieved" (Shaw, 2000, p. 375).

It is also important to note that much of the attention to licensing has revolved around the difficulty of bringing the software community into the engineering community. This plays out in a variety of ways, including the following:

- Software engineering is not accepted by many engineers in traditional engineering disciplines as being a "real" engineering discipline
- Traditional engineering disciplines deal with engineering of physical products, and core knowledge of traditional engineering is built

on the assumption that all engineers need to deal with aspects of chemistry and physics and a fundamental set of engineering topics such as statics and dynamics. For the U.S., where licensing relies in part on examination, this means that existing exams focus on content that is not part of the software engineering curriculum

- Software engineering education has largely grown from computer science and other computing programs. Most of the faculty members in these programs are not engineers by training, and many of the computing programs are not housed in colleges of engineering. In fact, many computing programs are at institutions that do not offer any engineering programs. The notion of an engineering license that might limit ability of graduates to develop software is at least a potential threat to these other computing programs.

A good discussion of these issues in the Canadian context is provided by Parnas (2002). A companion piece by McCalla (2002) provides some contrasting coverage of the Canadian situation.

The licensing issue has been a difficult one for the computing professional societies too. The ACM in particular has adopted a clear position opposing licensing of software engineers at the present time. Details of this position are contained in White and Simons (2002) and Knight and Leveson (2002).

In recent years, the issue of licensing has been relatively quiet. Within the U.S, only Texas has allowed licensing for software engineers. Other states have not followed this lead. However, the promise of ubiquitous software, the ever increasing integration of software in engineered products, and the broad economic dependence on software clearly indicate that the issues that have raised the question of licensing will become more pressing

not less. At present, it is not clear how these questions will be addressed.

Somewhat connected to the licensing issue is the question of broad certifications for software engineering. There have been a variety of efforts of this sort, including the IEEE-CS Certified Software Development Professional program. Certifications such as this seem likely to expand in the future as one approach to helping employers understand the knowledge and skills of potential employees.

The chapter by Seidman in this text provides an international perspective on the development and status of certification and licensing for software engineering.

TEACHING SOFTWARE ENGINEERING

Software engineering degree programs share many topics with CS and as such, share many of the challenges in teaching and learning. At the same time, many of the areas that make SE unique also present different challenges in teaching. These factors include software scale and complexity, engineering notions of design under cost and quality constraints, and substantial human issues that affect various parts of SE.

Many problems and best practices in SE are driven by the large scale and great complexity in software systems. This creates particular challenges in teaching SE since it is difficult to give students exposure to large systems in an academic program. The number of hours and intense immersion required to grasp a large system is beyond many students in the early years of a program, and difficult to fit in the limited hours and term schedules throughout a degree program. Until students gain some understanding of scale and complexity, it is difficult for them to really appreciate the problems that SE attempts to address. The chapter by Ludewig in this volume presents one approach that helps students gain experience with larger software systems.

Software engineering focuses heavily on group-based work. This is reflected by an emphasis on team work and team projects in SE education. Section IV of this text includes a series of chapters that address various aspects of project-based work. The team emphasis is one mechanism to allow students to get experience with larger software systems.

Team projects are one example of a broader emphasis on preparing students for practice. As an engineering discipline, SE has a strong emphasis on application of knowledge, and preparation for professional practice. The chapter by Armarego in this volume explores one approach to ensuring that SE education lines up with practice. Other chapters in Section VI discuss issues of professionalism and preparation for professional practice.

Software engineering also involves a variety of human issues that range well beyond working in teams. In this volume, the chapter by Brady et al focuses particularly on the issue of communication about software. The chapter by Hazzan and Tomayko provides a survey of SE activities and topics with an emphasis on the human component. The broad sweep of topics addressed by these chapters plus the chapters on project-based work clearly shows that SE has a human component different from most of the traditional engineering disciplines.

The challenges in teaching SE are being worked on as research projects by many SE faculty members. Funding for these efforts is competitive, but available from several sources. The most important funding source in the U.S. is the National Science Foundation, primarily through funding for research and development related to undergraduate education. As mentioned earlier, the focused funding once provided by the Department of Defense through the SEI is no longer available, although the Department of Defense did recently fund an effort to create a new Masters level curriculum model for Software Engineering. Various other federal agencies and foundations provide occasional grants that impact software engineering education.

The combination of technical foundations and the emphasis on the issues outlined above makes teaching of SE particularly challenging. It also implies that qualifications for SE faculty members have distinct requirements, particularly with regard to the importance of having faculty with professional experience. This is a difficult issue since the pool of candidates with academic credentials and professional experience is relatively limited. The chapter by McDonald discusses this issue from an accreditation perspective, and Rosca et all address the issue of hiring and retaining faculty members with the right combination of qualifications.

ASSESSMENT OF THE CURRENT STATUS OF SOFTWARE ENGINEERING EDUCATION

There is no regular census of software engineering programs worldwide, although there have been a variety of efforts to track the degree programs at both the undergraduate and master's level including Knoke (1998), Modesitt, et al (2000), and Bagert (Bagert & Ardis, 2003; Bagert & Chenoweth 2005). As of 2007, there were at least 32 undergraduate software engineering programs and 53 MSSE programs in the U.S. alone. The worldwide numbers would at least double these counts. There are also 3 Ph.D. programs in software engineering in the U.S.

Software engineering programs in the U.S. have not been immune to the downturn in student enrollment experienced by computing programs since about 2000. There are no reliable numbers to measure the extent of downturn for software engineering, but there is extensive anecdotal evidence that it has been substantial, although perhaps not as great as for computer science. It would be difficult to know how to interpret enrollment data in any case since fully two thirds of the BSSE programs have been started in the years since 2000. The more interesting question

Table 2. BSSE degree programs at U.S. institutions

Auburn University	Milwaukee School of Engineering
Butler University	Mississippi State University
California Poly – San Luis Obispo	Missouri Tech
Capitol College	Monmouth University
Champlain College	Montana Tech
Clarkson University	Penn State University – Erie
Cogswell College	Rochester Institute of Technology
Colorado Tech	Rose-Hulman Institute of Technology
Drexel University	San Jose State University
Embry-Riddle Aeronautical Univ.	South Dakota State University
Fairfield University	Southern Polytechnic State Univ.
Florida Institute of Technology	University of Michigan-Dearborn
Gannon University	University of Texas at Arlington
Indiana Wesleyan University	University of Texas at Dallas
Iowa State University	University of Wisconsin-Platteville
Michigan Tech	Vermont Technical College

is how the BSSE programs will fare after the inevitable upswing in number of students seeking computing majors occurs. It is also a positive sign that institutions have continued to start BSSE programs during this period of lowered student interest in computing majors.

The set of U.S. institutions currently known to offer BSSE degrees is presented in Table 2. It is interesting to consider some of the overall characteristics of this group of institutions that might have made them early adopters in development of the BSSE.

For example, over a third of these institutions are technology focused colleges or universities. On the one hand, this might make a BSSE an easy fit. On the other hand, most of these institutions already have multiple computing degrees, which could make for sharp differences of opinion about the wisdom of adding yet another computing degree.

A second characteristic is that a number of these institutions have close connections with businesses in their local market. This is certainly true of some of the technical institutes, but also true of institutions like Monmouth and some of the branch campuses of the public institutions.

It is also interesting to note that the list has a mix of institutional types in terms of the Carnegie Foundation's classification scheme (Carnegie 2007). For example, there are four BSSE institutions (Auburn, Drexel, FIT, and Iowa) in one of the "Research University" categories and a good selection of institutions across the range of Master's and Baccalaureate categories.

While there is a relatively broad set of institutional types, institutions with highly ranked computer science departments are not present. For example, in considering the top 36 computer science departments according to the Taulbee Survey (Zweben 2007), none of the host institutions for those departments offer BSSE degrees, even though several of them, including Carnegie-Mellon and the University of Maryland, have very active software engineering research groups. Since the strong reputation of these institutions generally gives them freedom to enter new areas, the absence of BSSE programs probably results from a choice rather than constraints that prevent pursuing the BSSE.

FUTURE OF SOFTWARE ENGINEERING EDUCATION

In thinking about what lies ahead for software engineering education, there are several perspectives that might be taken. For example, one set of challenges has been outlined by Lethbridge, et al (2007) as follows:

1. Making programs attractive to students,
2. Focusing education appropriately,
3. Communicating industrial reality more effectively,
4. Defining curricula that are forward-looking,
5. Providing education for existing practitioners,
6. Making software engineering education more evidence-based,
7. Ensuring that software engineering educators have the necessary background, and
8. Raising the prestige and quality of software engineering educational research.

This is an excellent list, and clearly contains a variety of important challenges for software engineering education. It is interesting to note though, that most of the items in this list apply fairly well to all, or at least several, of the computing disciplines. This is particularly true if viewed in terms of not just computer science but also the newer disciplines like information technology. Even items 6, 7, and 8 apply more broadly if the words "software engineering" are removed. (For example, in IS for item 6 and IT for item 7.)

One possible conclusion from this set of challenges is that the future of software engineering education is unavoidably linked to the other computing disciplines. To a large extent the group shares common challenges, and all will rise or fall depending on how well those challenges are addressed. In spite of a history of tensions among the computing disciplines, cooperation, where possible, is much more likely to result in advances for all.

Another perspective on the future would be to look at the model proposed by Ford shown in Table 1. While there is substantial reason to look favorably on the progress made against this framework, there is still much to be done in most of these categories. Software engineering clearly has not reached the level of a "mature" profession as defined by the Ford model. It seems that this should be viewed as a comment on the relative newness of the discipline, and certainly not as a sign of failure. At the same time, it implies that the SE education community needs to keep advancing the discipline and not be content with the accomplishments thus far achieved.

A more difficult perspective to assess is the ongoing evolution and tension among disciplines, particularly between computer science and software engineering. The continuing skirmishes that seem typical as new software engineering programs begin, and the absence of BSSE programs in institutions with highly ranked computer science programs, are two good indicators that this evolution is not complete. One root issue is the fact that a large percentage of CS graduates go on to careers as practitioners rather than scientists. This raises the question of whether growth in SE programs will come largely at the expense of CS programs. That possibility would present difficulties for both disciplines.

Within the community of software engineering educators, the sense of cohesion maintained during the 1990's seems to be substantially diminished. In part that reflects success in achieving initial goals such as accreditation. However, for a community that is still quite small this is cause for concern. As additional institutions offer software engineering degree programs, it is important that they have a community to join. Without that, it is difficult to see how software engineering will continue to evolve as a cohesive academic discipline.

Finally, in spite of good progress on the curriculum front, the world continues to change. SE 2004 is already over 3 years old and a round of updates will need to begin soon. For example, the chapter by Mead in this volume discusses aspects of system security that require increased attention in SE programs. Other issues that need to be addressed include changes in the way software systems are constructed, growth of various forms of parallel and distributed processing, and the expanding range of devices that contain software. Approaches to software process continue to expand as does the range of application domains with special considerations. There is also an increasing demand that students have better non-technical skills including communication and group interaction skills. Addressing this range of issues will require concerted effort of the community of SE educators for years to come.

REFERENCES

ACM & IEEE (2005). *Computing Curriculum 2005: The Overview Report.* IEEE Computer Society and Association for Computing Machinery. Piscataway, NJ: IEEE CS Press

ACM & IEEE (2004). *Computing Curricula, Software Engineering 2004: Curriculum Guidelines for Undergraduate Degree Programs in Software Engineering.* IEEE Computer Society and Association for Computing Machinery. Piscataway, NJ: IEEE CS Press

Ardis, M. A., & Ford, G. A. (1989). *SEI Report on Graduate Software Engineering Education.* TR CMU/SEI-89-TR-21. Pittsburgh PA: Carnegie Mellon University.

Bagert, D. J. & Ardis, M. A. (2003). Software engineering baccalaureate programs in The United States: An Overview. *Proceedings, Frontiers in Education Conference,* pp. S3C-1 to S3C-6. Piscataway, NJ: IEEE CS Press.

Bagert, D. J., & Chenoweth, S. V. (2005). Future growth of software engineering baccalaureate programs in the United States, *Proceedings, ASEE Annual Conference.* Portland, Oregon.

Bagert, D. J., Hilburn T. B., Hislop, G. W., Lutz, M., McCracken, M., & Mengel, S. (1999). *Guidelines for Software Engineering Education Version 1.0* Technical Report CMUISEI-99-TR-032. Pittsburgh PA: Carnegie Mellon University.

Carnegie (2007). *The Carnegie Classification of Institutions of Higher Education.* Stanford, CA: The Carnegie Foundation for the Advancement of Teaching. Retrieved January 15, 2008 from http://www.carnegiefoundation.org/classifications/

Cowling, A.J. (1998). The First Decade of An Undergraduate Degree Programme in Software Engineering. *Annals of Software Engineering,* 6(1-4), 61-90.

Fairley, R. (1986). *The role of academe in software engineering education.* Proceedings of the 1986 ACM Fourteenth Annual Conference on Computer Science. p. 39-52. New York: ACM Press.

Ford, G. & Gibbs, N. (1996) *A Mature Profession of Software Engineering.* Software Engineering Institute. Technical Report CMU/SEI-96-TR-04. Pittsburgh, PA: Carnegie Mellon University.

Ford, G. A. (1994). The Progress of Undergraduate Software Engineering Education. *SIGCSE Bulletin.* 26,4. New York: ACM Press.

Ford, G. A. (1991a). The SEI Undergraduate Curriculum in Software Engineering. *Proceedings, 22nd SIGCSE Technical Symposium on Computer Science Education.* pp. 375–385 New York: ACM Press.

Ford, G. A. (1991b) *SEI Report on Graduate Software Engineering Education.* CMU/SEI-91-TR-2. Pittsburgh, PA: Carnegie Mellon University.

Hislop, G. W., Lutz, M. J., & Sebern, M. J. (2006). Sharing Software Engineering Curriculum Materials. *Proceedings, ASEE 2006.*

Knoke, P. J. (1998). *Graduate SE Program Survey Results And Evaluation*, Forum for Advancing Software engineering Education (FASE), Vol. 8, No. 9. (electronic newsletter) <http://www.cs.ttu.edu/fase/v8n09.txt>

Knight, J. & Leveson, N. (2002). Should Software Engineers be Licensed? *Communications of the ACM.* 45(11), 87-90. New York: ACM Press.

Lethbridge, T. C., Diaz-Herrera, J., LeBlanc, R. J., & Thompson, J. B. (2007). Improving software practice through education: Challenges and future trends. *In 2007 Future of Software Engineering. International Conference on Software Engineering.* pp. 12-28. Piscataway, NJ: IEEE CS Press.

Lutz, M. J. & Naveda, J. F. (1997). The Road Less Traveled: A Baccalaureate Degree In Software Engineering. *Proceedings, SIGCSE Technical Symposium.* p. 287-291. New York: ACM Press.

Mahoney, M.S. (2004) Finding a History for Software Engineering. *IEEE Annals of the History of Computing.* p. 8-19. Piscataway, NJ: IEEE CS Press.

McCalla, G. (2002). Software Engineering Requires Individual Professionalism. *Communications of the ACM.* 45(11), 98-101. New York: ACM Press.

Modesitt, K. L., Bagert, D. J., Werth, L., & Knoke, P. J. (2000). *Annual Survey of International Software Engineering Academic Programs - Progress Report Number 2.* Forum for Advancing Software engineering Education (FASE), Vol. 10, No. 11. (electronic newsletter) <http://www.cs.ttu.edu/fase/v10n11.txt>

Naur, P. & Randell, B. eds. (1969) *Software Engineering: Report on a Conference Sponsored by the NATO Science Committee, Garmisch, Germany, 7th to 11th October 1968.* Scientific Affairs Division, NATO.

Parnas, D. L. (2002). Licensing Software Engineers in Canada. *Communications of the ACM.* 45(11), 90-98. New York: ACM Press.

Tomayko, J. E. (1998). Forging a Discipline: An Outline History of Software Engineering Education. *Annals of Software Engineering,* 6(1-4), 3-18.

Shaw, M. (1990). Prospects for an Engineering Discipline of Software. *IEEE Software.* 7(6), 15-24. Piscataway, NJ: IEEE CS Press.

Shaw, M. (2000). *Software Engineering Education: A Roadmap. Proceedings of the Conference on The Future of Software Engineering.* 373-380.

SWEBOK. (2004). *Guide to the Software Engineering Body of Knowledge.* Piscataway, NJ: IEEE CS Press.

White, J. & Simons, B. (2002). ACM's Position on Licensing of Software Engineers. *Communications of the ACM.* 45(11), 91-92. New York: ACM Press.

Zweben, S. (2007). *2005-2006 Taulbee Survey.* Computing Research News. pp. 7-22.

Section II
Student Learning and Assessment

Chapter II
Constructive Alignment in SE Education:
Aligning to What?

Jocelyn Armarego
Murdoch University, Western Australia

ABSTRACT

Practitioner studies suggest that formal IT-related education is not developing the skills and knowledge needed by graduates in daily work. In particular, a shift in focus from technical competency to the soft and metacognitive skills is identified. This chapter argues that a framework for learning can be developed that more closely models the experiences of practitioners, and addresses their expectations of novice software engineers. Evaluation of a study incorporating three action research cycles shows that what is needed is a mapping between the characteristics of professional practice and the learning model that is applied. The research shows that a relationship also exists between learner and learning model, and that this relationship can be exploited in the development of competent discipline practitioners.

INTRODUCTION

In the late 1960s those involved in the development of software agreed that one mechanism for dealing with intrinsic difficulties (eg complexity, (in)visibility, and changeability (Brooks, 1986)) was to embed its production within an applied science environment. Royce (1970) was the first to note explicitly that an engineering approach was required. The implication of this alignment

was that, like other engineering endeavours, methods, tools and procedures must be applied in a systematic way to contribute to the overall purpose of the process, control it and enable the development of a quality product.

This interest in engineering is mirrored in the education of software developers, with initially an exponential growth in offerings of undergraduate software degrees within an engineering environment. Increasingly, education for software development focuses on process and repeatability, modelling scientific and engineering methodologies. The underlying assumption of this approach is that 'good' software development is achieved by applying scientific investigative techniques (Pfleeger, 1999).

Practitioner-based studies (eg., Trauth, Farwell, & Lee, 1993; Lethbridge, 2000; Lee, 2004) assist us in building a profile of a practicing IT professional. The synthesis of these is that the skills and knowledge required to be active as competent practitioners are multidisciplinary: industry requires professionals who integrate into the organisational structure, and, rather than cope specifically with today's perceived problems, have models, skills and analytical techniques that allow them to evaluate and apply appropriate emerging technologies and to manage the process of delivering solutions. More broadly, software technology is seen as a rapidly shifting landscape: new methods, tools, platforms, user expectations, and software markets underscore the need for education that provides professionals with the ability to adapt quickly.

Developing Education-Learner-Practitioner Alignments[1]

Freed (1992) coined the term 'relentless innovation' to describe the capacity to invent and implement new ideas that will impact on every facet of life. Oliver (2000) suggested the rate of innovation is so prolific that most of the knowledge which will be used by the end of the first decade of the twenty-first century has yet to be invented. The speed with which technology evolves, the multiplicity of its impact on society and the ramifications of that impact mean that metacognitive and knowledge construction skills as well as adaptability become vital for professionals working with technology. Professional practitioners with such skills become *agents of change* (Garlan, Gluch, & Tomayko, 1997).

However, the basic features of most engineering training programmes have hardly been challenged since engineering schools were established (Mulder, 2006). In general this education is based on a normative professional education curriculum, in which students first study basic science, then the relevant applied science (Waks, 2001), so that learning may be viewed as a progression to expertise through task analysis, strategy selection, try-out and repetition (Winn & Snyder, 1996). The risk is that strict adherence to engineering and science methodologies hampers the quintessential creativity of the design process for software (Lubars, Potts, & Richer, 1993; Maiden & Gizikis, 2001; Maiden & Sutcliffe, 1992; Thomas, Lee, & Danis, 2002).

The aim of this chapter therefore is to explore the degree of alignment between the actuality of practice in the discipline and the models of learning provided in formal education for software development. An overview of both the dominant pedagogy for formal education in IT disciplines, and practitioner studies undertaken over the last 15 years establishes a base for this exploration.

An Action Research project, undertaken within Murdoch University's Software Engineering (SE) programme, provided the context for developing a model for alignment between formal education for SE and industry requirements. In order to achieve this, several techniques, including curriculum mapping and discipline decoding, were applied during the project to establish and then evaluate the alignments identified. The chapter continues by exploring the importance of alignment between student and learning environment, so that the eventual outcome, affinity between discipline, learning environment and graduate practitioner may be achieved.

CONTEXT

The context for the Action Research[2] project was the SE programme within the School of Engineering. In an attempt to align the characteristics of the discipline with appropriate learning environments, and to address knowledge gaps identified by practitioners, interventions based on different learning models were embedded in the curriculum over three cycles:

- **Cycle 1:** The Cognitive Apprenticeship (Brown, Collins, & Duguid, 1989) model as a mechanism for enabling authentic learning and facilitating knowledge transfer.
- **Cycle 2:** Problem-based learning (PBL) (Barrows & Tamblyn, 1980) as the basis for a model that focuses on students dealing with ill-structured problems by taking control of their learning. The model developed and applied in this cycle also addresses issues of enabling creativity within a supportive learning environment (Armarego, 2005).
- **Cycle 3:** A hybrid model developed on the basis of reflection on the interventions of the previous two cycles. Based on the constructivist paradigm, this Studio Learning model exploits the reflective practitioner (Schön, 1983) concept of professional learning by incorporating some elements of Cognitive Apprenticeship with components of problem-based learning and creativity-enhancing strategies. The focus is on the longer-term success of the learning strategies identified as appropriate for SE education (Armarego, 2007a; Armarego & Fowler, 2005).

The SE curriculum at Murdoch is an integrated one – all courses are prescribed, therefore a very precise understanding of what knowledge students have constructed is available. As Armarego (2002) indicates, initial changes were made only to the 'capstone' course. However, issues identified in the evaluation (see Armarego, 2004) indicated changes were required earlier in the curriculum. Cycles 1 and 2 of the project addressed this aspect by focussing on changing student perception of 'appropriate' learning of SE. Cycle 3 consolidated

the evolved learning model and extended it, not only to all SE learning within the curriculum, but to the final years of all engineering learning (Armarego & Fowler, 2005) in the School.

CHARACTERISTICS OF THE DISCIPLINE

The Engineering of Software

The alignment of software development with science and engineering has been seen as a means to leverage from the 'status' of these domains: the profession of scientifically trained engineer came into existence in the 18th and 19th centuries as a product of the Enlightenment[3]. For engineers it meant rethinking traditional technologies in order to rationalise and optimise them. However, Mulder (2006) notes that engineers sometimes failed to recognise that the issue at stake was not always a scientifically-/mathematically-solvable optimisation problem, but a choice between irreconcilable norms and values.

The implication of the alignment of software development with science and engineering is that, like other engineering endeavours, methods, tools and procedures must be applied in a systematic way to contribute to the overall purpose of the process, control it and enable the development of a quality product.

However, by the late 1960s philosophers such as Habermas (1972) criticised the ideological character of science-based technology – successful technologies were seen to challenge society and affect it as a whole. A deep understanding of the motives and desires of people who would be relating to the new technology, developed through interaction, was critical.

The Crafting of Software

Software development has also been described as a 'craft'. The negative connotations of this label include an inability to consistently guarantee a quality product, fit for the purpose for which it was developed, produced on time and within budget. The rates of successful projects reported in the mid 1990s are not significantly higher than those reported in the 1970s and 1980s (Mann, 1996), and continue to be low in the 2000s.

There are positive implications as well for the label 'craft'. Each system is considered a unique synergy between the hardware, software and organisational context in which it will be used. This viewpoint suggests that the development process cannot be repeatable, as the forces at play will differ for each context: continually changing as understanding of the characteristics of the developing system grows in all stakeholders. From this perspective software is a collaborative invention. Its development is an exploratory and self-correcting dialogue (Bach, 1999), based on insight-driven knowledge discovery (Guindon, 1989) facilitated by opportunistic behaviour (Guindon, 1990; Visser, 1992).

EDUCATION FOR THE DISCIPLINE

Hannafin (1997) and Reeves (1994) suggest that several dimensions are relevant in the description of learning systems:

- *Epistemological* foundations: Are concerned with theories about the nature of knowledge, and describe the world view to be disseminated. At one extreme (objectivism), content aims to be comprehensive and accurate, and based on advice from experts in the field. At the other (constructivism), content reflects the spectrum of views in the domain, providing multiple perspectives/options for constructing knowledge.
- *Psychological* foundations: Represent beliefs about how individuals think and learn. On this continuum, shaping desirable behaviours via stimuli, feedback, reinforcement

etc at one pole contrasts with a cognitivist emphasis on mental models and the connections between them. The type of knowledge to be constructed is seen to drive the learning strategy employed.
- *Philosophical* foundations: Emphasise how to-be-learned domains are represented and affordances provided to support learning. An instructivist foundation stresses the importance of goals and objectives drawn from the domain. Constructivist foundations, on the other hand, stress the primacy of learner intentions, experience and metacognitive strategies through a rich environment that can be tailored to individual needs.

These dimensions describe the nature of learning, the methods and strategies employed, and the ways in which the discipline should be organised and made available to the learner.

Although any software development project is acknowledged as knowledge-intensive, with many concepts developed to ease or guide the processing of knowing (Robillard, 1999), and learning (Klemola & Rilling, 2002), what is actually taught within a discipline is a complex synthesis deriving from the ideology of the discipline, the context of the learning and the 'tools' used to facilitate that learning, all, in theory, influenced by the needs of practitioners in the discipline. Figure 1 describes a conceptual framework that identifies the elements of this synthesis: the bodies of knowledge (BoKs) and model curricula are a distillation of expert opinion and domain-specific texts. The breakdown is seen to cover the areas discussed in texts and standards, either identically, or, as noted in the **S**oft**W**are **E**ngineering **B**ody of **K**nowledge (SWEBoK), derived from these and other sources to reflect a consensus and identify mature and stable concepts (Sawyer & Kotonya, 2000) in the discipline.

At the same time, a perspective (composed of the epistemological, psychological and philosophical foundations noted above) also exerts

Figure 1. Influences on the learning environment for SE

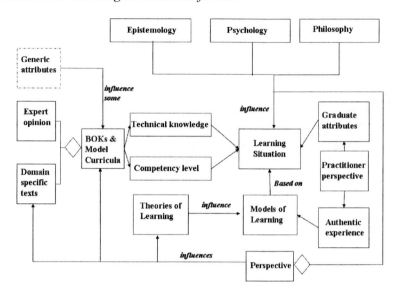

influence on each of the domain, BoKs etc and theories of learning. Within the IT disciplines this has led to multiple approaches to its definition and study: the work of Iivari (1991) and Glass (1992) identified and categorised these, based on epistemological and ontological positions taken. The implication of this is a different understanding of the discipline and education for it dependent on the stance (perspective) adopted. This poses a serious challenge for the learning of software development practice.

The accepted view, that a science/engineering approach will ensure quality, influences the learning of SE: by implication a scientific/engineering education is seen as the mechanism to train students to be competent practitioners. The same is true outside the science/engineering academic faculties: Benson (2003) notes that within the emerging information systems (IS) discipline of the 1970s, academics were migrants to the discipline, with an overwhelming majority having qualifications in other areas, most often computer science. Practitioners also relied heavily on scientific, mathematic and engineering disciplines, many with engineering and manufacturing backgrounds.

These influences are mirrored in attempts at developing model curricula, with the occasional addition of guidelines addressing generic attributes. Shackelford (2005) provides an overview of what might be considered computing today (the space for SE is illustrated in Figure 2). At a fundamental level, the assumptions made on, for example, the nature of the system or the importance of its context, and the nature of knowledge, influence the perspective taken and how the work is undertaken. However, each of the volumes of the Computing Curriculum (CC-CS (Engel & Roberts, 2001), CC-IS (Gorgone et al., 2002) and CC-SE (LeBlanc & Sobel, 2004)), which help determine the learning situation for a discipline, applies the same model and draws on the same types of sources.

Within the broad IT specialisations in general, the underlying assumption is that the world works rationally and that therefore 'good' software development is achieved by applying (from a choice of) scientific investigative techniques. In this positivist approach, borrowing from the physical sciences, software developers build models based on: *theoretical* and *scientific* knowledge; *engi-*

Figure 2. SE computing space (Shackelford, 2005) [©2005 ACM and IEEE. Reprinted by permission]

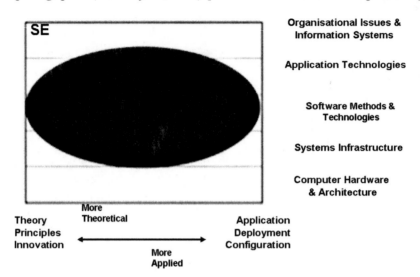

neering knowledge – experiential and including what skills are needed, how tools work together, what has/has not worked in the past; *biomedical* and *epidemiological* knowledge – experiential, this captures evidence about causation and *social, economic* and *institutional* knowledge – who and what are involved in what we are observing (Pfleeger, 1999). By these means the 'scientific' software developer seek relationships that add to an understanding of what makes software good. These are applied to increase the number of times good software is produced, based on a cause-effect search: if s/he can find out what process activities, tools, measurements cause good software s/he can build an effective software process that will produce good software every time (Pfleeger, 1999).

Also applied within IS education such approaches lean towards project management-based methods, techniques and tools, and, while successful in creating a range of artefacts, do not succeed in the development of management information systems (Banks, 2003). Banks concludes that the weakness inherent in approaches which lend themselves to 'cookbooks' with clearly defined

problems, rigid method and limited range of outcomes but tangible skills in students is the lesser regard for real-world influences and pressures.

Therefore, while a review of major model curricula for software development (ie IS, CS and SE) shows that, in general terms, a graduate should emerge from formal education with knowledge of the basic software development processes (and therefore, in theory be able to produce successful software), this does not acknowledge either the multi-disciplinary skills highlighted by practitioners as missing in formal education[4] or the generic intellectual abilities and skills which, although highly valued by employers, are sometimes given only 'lip service' in tertiary education curricula (Bentley, Lowry, & Sandy, 1999).

DISCIPLINE DECODING

One of the primary motivations for the development of models of teaching and learning in which practitioners can be more involved in the research on how people think and how students learn has been a concern with the disciplinary nature of learning. The result of the decoding process is a model of the skills identified as necessary within a discipline.

Disciplines differ in the strategies and the 'ways of thinking' practitioners apply. However, although these are essential for both understanding the discipline and acting within it, they are not usually presented to students explicitly. Parnas and Clements (1986) suggest that, given an irrational design process (ie all design processes), the documentation should make it appear as though it were rational. They justify this *faking* of the appearance of rationality through the need to make the eventual maintenance task easier, as well as enabling new members of the design team to absorb knowledge about the project more easily. However, as some research (eg., Nguyen & Swatman, 2000) suggests, the process to such simplification is hidden and leads to unreal expectations in novice undertakings. According to Middendorf and Pace (1986), this dichotomy has led to a gap between strategies for learning and the skills necessary in specific disciplines.

Therefore, although practitioner studies agree that the base case of *content* knowledge is covered in models used in university programmes, a closer look reveals the depth of the mismatch between practitioner needs and formal education for software development.

Practitioner Perspectives

In his *Point/Counterpoint* discussion, Bach (1997) stated that one reason SE is not more seriously studied is the common industry belief that most of the books and classes that teach it are *impractical* An overview of the studies undertaken to gain a practitioner perspective indicates that such an indictment is not too far from the mark.

Most of the studies noted below address the requirements for software development activities by examining the general importance of specific topics, as perceived by different stakeholders. Since different approaches are taken in gaining

this knowledge from different target groups: surveys, focus groups, fora or interviews applied to experienced practitioners, managers, recruitment staff, students and recent graduates, as well as examination of job advertisements over the disciplines of IS, CS and Engineering, some insight into the practitioner perspective is possible.

In IS practitioner studies since the early 1990s (eg., Trauth et al., 1993; Parker et al., 1999; Lee, 2004) a long term shift from programming and other technical subjects to business analysis and people-oriented skills is significant – a change in emphasis to both generic attributes and managerial knowledge. From the student perspective, awareness of the need for 'career resilience' has surfaced (Waterman, Waterman, & Collard, 1994), while a technology-relevant degree is less necessary. Lee (1999) concluded that academic programmes should emphasise information searching and problem formulation (as opposed to problem solving alone) so that students can deal more effectively with the challenges of industry. He noted that interpersonal communication accounts for the most important means of knowledge transfer in technological work, with team members as the most utilised inter-personal information source.

From a later study Lee found that one of the *reality shocks* involved in the socialisation of new graduates to work was the onus of teaching themselves what they needed to know in order to perform the task successfully. He concludes

...educators should also help students to develop their initiatives and abilities to deal with ill-structured problems. This would require approaches which emphasize independent learning and collaborative teamwork. (Lee, 2004, p 135)

Fewer studies address the skills and knowledge needed in SE and CS. Turley and Bieman (1995) examined professional Software Engineers in an attempt to identify the competencies and demographics that contribute to 'excellence' in performance. They provide a set of thirty eight competencies that express a broad range of behaviours required of an IT professional engaged in *the creation of software products* (as opposed to maintenance, management etc). They identify four categories of competencies which differentiate between exceptional (XP) and non-exceptional (NXP) performers (see Table 1). Of the statistically significant competencies associated with exceptional performance most are seen to cluster around the theme of external focus, with only *Mastery of Skills and Techniques* as a self-directed (internal) skill. Earlier Turley (1991) concluded that education needed to support the development of differential skills (namely interpersonal skills and personal attributes) through the creation of learning situations that stress these. Lethbridge (2000) also examined the industry perception: his aim was to gain a practitioner ranking of the usefulness of specific topics compiled from the curricula of (emerging) SCE (Software and Computer Engineering) and CS, the influence of these on respondents' career and how much they had learned formally compared to what

was required as a professional. Of relevance to our consideration, Lethbridge computed overall importance of topics, based on the average of both importance of details and influence. The results of his work indicate the existence of significant gaps between formal learning and importance on the job. Of the top ten topics exhibiting considerable gap, 50% reflect 'soft' knowledge (eg negotiation (84% gap), leadership (73%), ethics and professionalism (62%)).

Studies in the Australian context support these findings. Respondents to a study by Scott and Yates (2002) noted that learning profession-specific content provides the 'scaffold' for the important task of career-long professional learning: the skills to undertake this are of great importance, with the ability to know when and when not to deploy technical expertise, and how to continuously update it, the keys to successful professional practice.

From Scott and Wilson (2002)'s work, the finding is that, while the successful professional must possess a high level of profession-specific

Table 1. Turley rankings: Competencies by participant category

Competency	XP Rank	NXP Rank
Task Accomplishment Mastery of Skills & Techniques	4	
Personal Attributes Driven by a desire to contribute Perseverance Maintains 'Big Picture' view Desire to do/bias for action Driven by a sense of mission *Exhibits and articulates strong beliefs and convictions* Proactive role with management	 5 XP XP *3* 2	 3 NXP
Situational Skills *Responds to schedule pressures by sacrificing parts of the design process*		2
Interpersonal Skills Seeks help from others *Helps others* *Willingness to confront others*	 *1* 	1 4

Numbers indicate ranking based on statistical significance results of a t-test. Items not numbered are the result of a discriminant analysis based on Q-sort results. Competency element in italics indicates both tests identify this as significant.

technical expertise, such skills have little value without other skills:

...when the unexpected occurs, what is most telling is being able to tolerate the uncertainty and ambiguity of the situation, having well developed reciprocal networks upon which to call to identify potentially relevant solutions, being able to 'read' the total technical and social components of a troubling situation, and then being able to apply a high level of appropriate technical skill in partnership with other team members to resolve the situation. (Scott & Wilson, 2002, p 6)

The synthesis of these studies implies a need to enable students to not only learn to use past experience on a general level, but to also be able to deal with each new problem situation in its own terms, requiring certain generic intellectual abilities and skills. Gott et al (1993) posit that this adaptive/generative capability suggests the performer not only knows the procedural steps for problem solving but also understands when to deploy them and why they work. The implication of this is effort spent on higher (metacognitive) learning skills, including abstraction and reflection. However, merely applying knowledge has been identified as the aim of undergraduate education, so that generally only the lower three (ie foundational) levels of Bloom (1956)'s taxonomy of cognitive learning have been chosen as educational objectives, since they represent

what knowledge may be reasonably learned during an undergraduate education, (Sobel, 2003, p 6),

effectively ignoring the development of higher level skills (analysis, synthesis, evaluation) in formal (undergraduate) education. This runs counter to Thomas et al (2002)'s suggestion of a (critically) widening gap between the degree of flexibility and creativity needed to adapt to a changing world and the capacity to do so.

ALIGNING EDUCATION TO PRACTICE

Reigeluth (1997) argues that the current paradigm of education is based on standardisation, conformity and compliance, geared to the mass production of industrial age manufacture. This does not equate with the needs of the late 20th/early 21st century job market, which revolves around problem solving, teamwork, communications, initiative taking and diverse perspectives. What this implies is a lack of coincidence between the actuality of practice in the discipline and the instructional design supposed to model it – suggesting the need for a new paradigm, based on customisation, diversity and initiative, to suit the needs of the information age.

Felder and Brent (2005) assert that traditional engineering education does little to provide students with the systemic perspective on individual subjects (a global perspective) they need to function effectively, and the ones who take too long to get it by themselves are at risk academically. They see most engineering instruction oriented toward students with specific traits – *introverts* (favouring lecturing and individual assignments rather than active class involvement and cooperative learning), *intuitors* (preferring emphasis on science and math fundamentals rather than engineering applications and operations), *thinkers* (favouring objective analysis rather than interpersonal considerations in decision-making), and *judgers* (preferring emphasis on following the syllabus and meeting assignment deadlines rather than on exploration of ideas and creative problem solving). Holt and Solomon (1996) point out that, while engineering education relies heavily on problem solving and engineering science, it limits the opportunities of all learners to develop the skills required for proficiency in two key areas: design and invention (requiring a *divergent* approach), and business management (requiring *accommodative* skills). The work of Lumsdaine and Lumsdaine (1995) suggests that between 20%

and 40% of student intake to engineering is lost through not catering for students with strengths in communications and team work or creative problem solving, synthesis and design.

In SE, Glass (1995) suggests that *discipline* and *creativity* are the odd couple of software development – the discipline imposed by methodology, for example, forms a frame for the opportunistic creativity of design. The educational dilemma becomes one of providing a base that enables software developers to both create and engineer the systems they build: to be adaptable to the changing environment that is inevitable in their chosen discipline. However, criticism has arisen regarding engineering graduates' ability to be creative (Cropley & Cropley, 1998). The need for flexibility, fluency and originality in day-to-day dealings, which typically define the creative effort (Guilford, 1967), is seen as lacking from their education.

The inadequacy of formal education in training competent practitioners, then, may be partly explained by the 'incorrect' learning environment that results from the poor fit between the characteristics of the discipline identified by practitioners and those of the learning model. A solution can be proposed through the development of a new framework for SE education. This framework should:

- Be based on constructivist theory (as more suitable for learning in domains involving ill-structured problems (Spiro, Feltovich, Jacobson, & Coulson, 1991) with a focus on strategic knowledge to enhance knowledge construction and transfer. This includes metacognitive strategies for directing, monitoring and evaluating learning.

- Be placed within a situated experiential learning environment where authenticity (with rich contextual information) is exploited (Dreyfus & Dreyfus, 1986). Focusing on the solution of authentic problems as a context for learning provides students with entry to the community of practice to which they will belong.

- Provide the student with a learning environment that has an emphasis on modelling practice, making tacit knowledge explicit and thus empowering students to think independently.

Several learning models apply these concepts. As noted previously, the project looked specifically at Cognitive Apprenticeship and problem-based learning as exemplars. However, there is a suggestion in the literature that efforts to help students learn at Bloom's higher-order levels may be impeded by a mismatch between the kinds of thinking actually required in specific disciplines and generic formulae for encouraging higher-order thinking (Middendorf & Pace, 1986). In the final analysis, applying generic learning models (even non-traditional ones) for situated, higher-order learning that is student-centred may run counter to an important strand in the current thinking about teaching. This stresses the disciplinary nature of knowledge. As a tool for learning, the model must be adapted to the discipline. The development of a curriculum map aligns the needs of the discipline with the educational strategies to address these concerns.

Curriculum Mapping for Constructive Alignment

As both curriculum development and learning theory move away from behavioural to cognitivist and constructivist approaches in order to address the needs of both the discipline and changing context for the discipline, the value of alignment is enhanced.

The basis of a framework for a learning environment is a 'constructive alignment' (Biggs, 1999) of objectives, teaching context and assessment tasks. Based on the discussions of Brown, Bull, and Pendlebury (1997), aligning these components achieves the following aims: the educational expectation (learning objective) is mapped to learning activities likely to achieve these (teaching context) while assessment tasks focus on the quality of the learning process. A model of alignment, based on the work of the engineering subject centre of the learning and teaching support network (LTSN, 2002), was applied within the research project (see Figure 3).

In order to facilitate all the alignments required, a map of the curriculum for SE at Murdoch University was constructed. Curriculum mapping, as an evaluative tool attributed to English (1978), has been used primarily in schools, with limited use in higher education. English advocated the use of mapping to ensure that the constructive alignment described above - alignment of declaration, delivery, learning and assessment of individual skills - is achieved.

The outcome of these initial phases, examining curricula and learning models, and decoding the discipline through a meta-analysis of practitioner perspectives, was to confirm the need to build into the curriculum a focus on generic and soft skills as part of the outcomes of each course within the programme, to address both practitioner and discipline needs. To maximise effectiveness, these had to be embedded into

the knowledge base constructed by the students during their learning. This has the advantage of enabling students to develop the requisite skills situated within the learning context but, of course, required extensive adaptation of the existing learning environment.

Within the project undertaken, curriculum mapping was tackled course by course, commencing with the initial SE course offered (identified as ENG260), which addresses Requirements Engineering. This was categorised firstly by the broad area of curriculum and then by the learning outcomes to be addressed. The map was based on scrutiny of documentation related to the course; in particular syllabus and course outline information provided to students at the commencement of the semester. These detail topics to be covered, assessment elements and criteria and expected demonstrable outcomes. The data gleaned from all of these were initially mapped to Murdoch's generic graduate outcomes, and then, as progress was made in developing the activities to address the learning outcomes identified, to these as well. Figure 4 shows the mapping necessary for alignment. The *Learning Objectives* are determined from the appropriate BoKs and model curricula, tempered by our understanding of the needs of

Figure 3. Alignment between outcomes and assessment (adapted from LTSN, 2002)

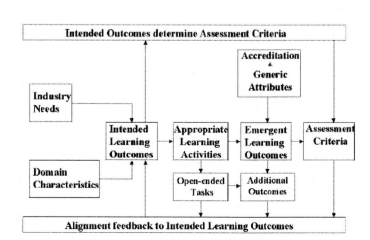

practitioners in our context. The topics addressed (indicated as *Domain*) are mapped to Murdoch's *Graduate Attributes*. The *Problem*(s) identify the activity that will address these objectives. Because the course has been presented within a PBL environment (and hence problem-driven) these are never lectures nor simply assessment items or tutorial/laboratory exercises. Students engage with the required content through identifying, exploring and subsequently solving specific problem scenarios. These scenarios are exposed progressively by means of triggers (Figure 5 is one example – at this point students have no prior knowledge of SE estimation techniques).

Figure 4. (excerpt from) Learning objectives - ENG260

Requirements Engineering

	Objective	Domain	Graduate Attributes	Problem
	To incrementally build knowledge on:			
1	Requirements Engineering	Concepts	Professional Knowledge	1, 2 6
2	Elements of the SDLC, both classical and object-oriented	Requirements Engineering Process	Professional Knowledge	2, 6
	To identify:			
3	Components of Requirements Specification	Concepts	Professional Knowledge	2
4	SDLC Process Models (classical and OO)	Requirements Engineering Process	Professional Knowledge	6, 2
	To be aware of:			
5	Group Dynamics and collaboration in the Software Development process (Team and Stakeholder)	People Issues/Teamwork	Interdisciplinarity/ Social Interaction	3 +
6	Historical issues in Software Development	History	Professional Knowledge	2 +
	To develop skills in:			
7	Creating and evaluating deliverables of the Requirements Phase (complementary models, documentation)	Requirements Engineering Process	Analysis & Problem Solving/ Communications	2 +
8	Group Collaboration	People Issues/Teamwork	Social Interaction	3

Curriculum mapping may therefore be considered a traceability exercise: each 'requirement' (learning objective) is designed for (triggering one or more problem component/learning object) and may lead to an artefact (an assessment element). The appropriate learning environment is determined by the 'fit' of all components to the course and ultimately the overall programme (thus placing emphasis on alignment of elements identified in Figure 1 with those in Figure 3).

It should be noted that the development of the learning environment was continuing throughout the project: the initial model – based on *Cognitive Apprenticeship*, evolved to a model based on PBL (*CreativePBL*) and finally to *Studio Learning*. As Figure 3 indicates, alignment feedback informs the refining of the intended learning outcomes, and hence the learning activities, for subsequent offerings of the course. In this context, ongoing project evaluation indicated the process-oriented approach advocated in PBL acted as an alignment inhibitor by reinforcing the perception of RE is a smooth process of sequential stages – the contingency measures advocated by Andresen, Boud, and Cohen (1995) as needing to be available in the creative nature of design, could not be easily incorporated.

A learning model based on the 'studio' approach (itself modelled on the 19th century atelier-based training at the Parisian *Ecole des Beaux-Arts*), that also emphasised the development of reflective skills and sensibilities (Schön, 1983) was implemented as the learning environment of choice. This *Studio Learning* model incorporates some elements of *Cognitive Apprenticeship* with components of problem-based learning and creativity-enhancing strategies. The model supports the idea that learning is defined in terms of dynamic sets of relationships whose interactions and interdependencies create and control conditions that are supportive of specified concepts within a discipline.

Developing a Student-Education Alignment

Student approaches to both learning and the learning environment can be investigated through several diagnostic instruments. Within the study, learning styles (Kolb, 1984; Soloman & Felder, 1999), temperament (Keirsey & Bates, 1984), study approaches (Entwistle & Ramsden, 1983) and relationship to learning activities (Meyer & Boulton-Lewis, 1997) were all incorporated. The results of these instruments help build several profiles of the student cohorts. Important in this context was the individual learning styles[5] and individual approaches to learning. The results confirmed other research (Entwistle & Tait, 1990, 1995; Tynjälä, Salminen, Sutela, Nuutinen, & Pitkänen, 2005) about students with specific learning styles having a preference for surface

Figure 5. Trigger for investigation of estimation techniques

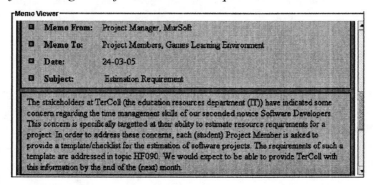

learning and 'being taught', and indicated that students conceptions of the characteristics of their learning environments were related to their study orientations and strategies.

Other research within this School (Armarego, Fowler, & Roy, 2001) indicates that engineering students' motivation and success can be adversely affected if their learning styles, and the learning styles of the staff teaching them, are not taken into account. There is considerable evidence that a mismatch, between lecturers' expectations of the way students learn and students' own individual preferred learning styles, disadvantage students. Research suggests that these mismatches lead to lack of motivation and interest in students and affect their success (Felder, 1996; UWA, 1996; Zywno & Waalen, 2001).

These findings were supported by the project discussed in this chapter, strengthening indications of the importance of additional alignments – teacher and learning environment to student. Learning styles instruments, when applied to engineering academic staff, also indicated a strong Converger approach to teaching. The implication of this was that the dominant teaching style did not exhibit the adaptability and flexibility required by either the characteristics of the discipline or the learning environment being developed.

The term constructive alignment, therefore, goes beyond the need to ensure that teaching, assessment and every aspect of the teaching-learning environment are aligned to the main aims or intended learning outcomes of a course. When the course is not aligned with learner interests or the situation constrains the student's approach to learning, the dependent learner mode will tend to dominate – control of the learning process is relinquished to the teacher, while the student will demand carefully articulated structure, clear guidance and clearly-defined assessment (Armarego, 2007b). A dependent learner, therefore, does not align with the discipline characteristics described earlier in this chapter. Staff development, to introduce experiential learning models

and 'teaching around the learning cycle' (Felder, 1996) are advocated (Armarego & Fowler (2005) also discusses the staff development implemented in this project).

CONCEPTUAL MODEL OF ALIGNMENT

The result of the investigation described here, and the Action Research project that underpins it, is the development of a complex model that aligns discipline competencies with student characteristics with learning environment, as illustrated in Figure 6.

This chapter argues that traditional formal education does not meet the competency expectations of industry. Practitioner dissatisfaction with formal education focuses on non-technical components of competency: they look for graduates who are flexible, adaptable in the organisational environment and can continue learning. These have been identified as cognitive skills related to higher order learning, strategies to enable opportunism and creativity and the development of emotional intelligence.

The three cycles of this project explored alternate learning models to evaluate their appropriateness for addressing these issues. A shift in focus from technical competency to the soft and metacognitive skills that enable the competent practice of SE was achieved. Each intervention strategy addressed specific concerns and, through evaluation of and reflection on the intervention, strategies are refined for the next cycle to address additional issues identified:

- **Cycle 1 – Cognitive Apprenticeship:** Focus on authenticity and transfer of skills acquired to other courses and, eventually, to the profession. This cycle highlighted student problems in generalising their learning, and in willingness to apply previous knowledge to the 'new' learning. In effect they were

Figure 6 Conceptual model of discipline-learning- environment-student characteristics alignment

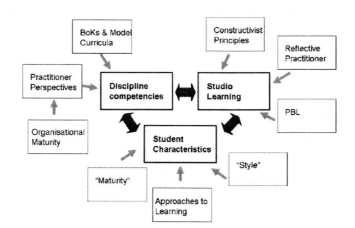

constrained by the 'apprenticeship' nature of the model. A significant finding of this cycle related to student emphasis on 'correct' answers to problem solving undertaken. Students focussed on learning the tools and techniques of SE at the expense of a broader (and more abstract) understanding within the discipline

- **Cycle 2 – CreativePBL:** Focus on student-centred learning; creativity and adaptability. This model was developed to address the deficiencies of the Apprenticeship model that were identified in Cycle 1. It was developed to focus on creativity and divergent thinking, so that, instead of students aimed at finding the single, best, correct answer to a standard problem in the shortest time (convergent thinking) they aimed at redefining or discovering problems and solving them by means of branching out, making unexpected associations, applying the known in unusual ways, or seeing unexpected implications. However, process itself acted as a deterrent to student motivation to study and to exploit the creativity being nurtured – opportunism was difficult within the process and

hence flexibility inhibited; here a focus on process detracted from the 'authenticity' of the environment

- **Cycle 3 – Studio Learning:** Focus on deep learning; opportunism and metalearning. This model was developed to gain leverage from the positive elements of the models previously applied. Here the strategy was to reach all types of learners by 'teaching around the cycle'[6], thus enabling students to develop the mental dexterity required in professional practice, and introducing the importance of contingency measures and opportunistic creativity. The Studio environment also provided the opportunity for students to adopt expert strategies – the teacher acts as guide or 'consultant' in these processes and helps students to reflect critically on their effectiveness in specific contexts.

This research shows the gap between practitioner expectations of formal education for SE can be reduced through fine-grained alignment of the learning environment with the characteristics of the discipline. While technical knowledge acquired by students is important in that it acts as a 'filter' for graduate employment, of greater impact on the professional competence is the focus on soft and metacognitive skills. These are learnable within a formal education environment, albeit through the application of non-traditional learning models. The final model developed and applied in the research project, *Studio Learning*, appeared to be effective in addressing issues raised in studies of discipline practitioners and the education literature. The application of *Studio Learning* within the Murdoch SE programme is discussed in greater detail elsewhere (Armarego, 2007a).

The results of the alignment of this model with the discipline/educational issues highlighted earlier in this chapter can be summarised as the need to:

- *Provide students with authentic experiences which address competencies additional to specific discipline knowledge*: students were exposed to learning both as a 'generic' metacognitive activity, and as a skill to be continually adapted and utilised within a discipline context. Flexibility in thinking - addressing creativity, opportunism and divergency/convergency - was made explicit and strategies to exploit it developed

- *Provide learners with a deep understanding of self and others in complex human activity systems in a collaborative environment*: students became aware of and learnt to utilise each other's strengths and weaknesses in achieving the learning outcomes. They learnt how to 'jell', what to do if they did not, and to be empathetic to the contexts of other students. They learnt to value and exploit alternate perspectives brought to a problem by different stakeholders (client, teacher/consultant, other team members) to enrich their learning. They became aware of the need to be self-motivated and learn independently - students were confident in

questioning their own and others' assumptions within the learning environment

- *Allow time to explore new ideas and to reflect on possible processes and outcomes*: students were willing to 'trust' each other's knowledge (implicit or not, technical or not), accepting the multi-disciplinary nature of the skills and knowledge required to achieve the learning objectives

- *Be challenged*: students were motivated by the (increasing) complexity of the tasks assigned, and were able to focus on cognitive and interpersonal skills to adapt to the changes imposed.

Techniques applied included: providing students with information about learning theory (PBL, situated learning, life-long learning), ensuring 'higher order learning' was addressed with greater emphasis on *analysis* and *synthesis* rather than *application* of knowledge within courses, embedding reflective practices within each course (eg journals, performance and team-work reviews), emphasising alternative approaches to problems and 'rewarding' diversity of (feasible) solutions, embedding change in all aspects of the problems tackled (changing requirements, scenarios, deliverables, team composition, client contact, etc) to highlight the importance of opportunism, flexibility and adaptability (Armarego, 2007c).

Not only was student feedback positive, and a significant improvement in their assessment marks discernable, but observation and analysis of subsequent learning (Armarego, 2007c) showed strong indications of willingness to transfer knowledge gained, to take control of their learning, and indicated motivation to deeper learning, as indicated by the work of Entwistle and Ramsden (1983).

However, what both practitioner studies (especially the work of Minor (2004)) and this research hint at is the importance of individual characteristics and abilities. Minor's participants indicated a *Personality* component to competent practice. Examination of student reflective comments, in conjunction with data regarding student learning, adds another dimension to the issue of education for competent practice.

This research suggests that an alignment between the learner and the (discipline-aligned) learning model enhances student learning of that discipline. However, further research is required to test these findings in the context of student transition to the workplace: at this time, reporting of graduate success (although very encouraging) is only anecdotal.

IMPLICATIONS FOR THE FUTURE

An increasing shortage in IT practitioners both through disengagement with the discipline and decreasing enrolments in tertiary institutions suggest an imperative to address the needs of industry and provide graduates with appropriate competency. The implication for education is that it is no longer adequate for academics to only be discipline experts – knowledge and understanding of the complete learning process is vital in achieving this goal, and implies resources committed to appropriate (educational) training. The implication for the learning environment is that it is no longer appropriate to rely on traditional teaching as the basis for the learning process – these methods do not align well with the requirements of the profession, and inhibit many (actual as well as potential) students from engaging with the discipline. This, too, requires resources to be dedicated to invigorating the learning environments provided. The implication for the students themselves is that dependent learning is contra-indicated for success in the IT professions. As learning becomes necessarily life-long, students must embrace the skills and knowledge outside the discipline content (the affective and soft skills) required for successful professional practice. From the educational perspective, these must be made explicit by, for example, moving towards student-centred experiential learning models; by

embedding higher order, soft and affective skills into the course; and ensuring – through mapping and constructive alignment - that these are a measurable outcome of the learning process.

CONCLUSION

This chapter describes a relationship between the characteristics of the discipline and established models of learning. These characteristics inform the development of a conceptual model for SE education, and a learning model that addresses more explicitly the gaps in formal education identified by practitioners. These gaps may be considered as a lack of alignment between the various elements which contribute to graduate competence as practicing professionals in the discipline.

The concept of alignment is well understood and is backed by a body of research literature: in an educational context constructive alignment (eg between objectives and assessment) is considered 'best practice'; as practitioner studies highlight, in industry alignment between IT practice and formal education is also considered best practice. However, shortfalls in IT professionals in industry, as well as decreasing enrolments and growing student attrition suggest other alignments; those between the discipline, the organisation and education should also be explored. Yet not much work has been published in this area.

The research that this chapter discusses confirms that there is a relationship between characteristics exhibited by learners and the learning environment provided. Students display aptitudes for specific learning environments; these should therefore exploit student learning characteristics since those whose approaches to learning align with the learning model appear to gain increased benefits. If that environment is also aligned with the characteristics of the discipline, it is suggested that students with specific characteristics, taught in a manner that is appropriate to the discipline, have greater potential to becoming competent practitioners: a case of the sum of the alignments being greater that its parts.

REFERENCES

Andresen, L., Boud, D., & Cohen, H. (1995). Experience-based learning. In G. Foley (Ed.), *Understanding Adult Education and Training* (pp. 207-215). Sydney: Allen and Unwin.

Armarego, J. (2002). *Advanced Software Design: a case in problem-based learning.* Paper presented at the CSEET2002 15th Conference on Software Engineering Education and Training, Covington (Ke).

Armarego, J. (2004). *Student perceptions of quality learning: evaluating PBL in Software Engineering.* Paper presented at the Seeking Educational Excellence: 13th Teaching Learning Forum, Perth.

Armarego, J. (2005). *Educating agents of change.* Paper presented at the CSEE&T2005 18th Conference on Software Engineering Education and Training, Ottawa.

Armarego, J. (2007a). *Beyond PBL: preparing graduates for professional practice.* Paper presented at the CSEET2007: 20th Conference on Software Engineering Education & Training, Dublin.

Armarego, J. (2007b). *Deconstructing student attitude to learning: a case study in IT education.* Paper presented at the CSITed2007: Computer Science and IT Education Conference, Mauritius.

Armarego, J. (2007c). *Educating Requirements Engineers in Australia: effective learning for professional practice.* Unpublished PhD, University of South Australia, Adelaide.

Armarego, J., & Fowler, L. (2005). *Orienting students to Studio Learning.* Paper presented at the Proceedings of the 2005 ASEE/AaeE 4th Global Colloquium on Engineering Education, Sydney.

Armarego, J., Fowler, L., & Roy, G. G. (2001). *Constructing Software Engineering Knowledge: development of a learning environment.* Paper presented at the In search of a Software Engineering Profession: CSEE&T2001 14th Conference on Software Engineering Education and Training, Charlotte (NC).

Bach, J. (1997). SE education: we're on our own. *IEEE Software, 14*(6), 26,28.

Bach, J. (1999). Reframing requirements analysis. *IEEE Computer, 32*(2), 120-122.

Banks, D. A. (2003). Belief, inquiry, argument and reflection as significant issues in learning about Information Systems development methodologies. In T. McGill (Ed.), *Current Issues in IT Education* (pp. 1-10). Hershey (PA): IRM Press.

Barrows, H. S., & Tamblyn, R. M. (1980). *Problem-based Learning, an Approach to Medical Education.* New York: Springer.

Bentley, J. F., Lowry, G. R., & Sandy, G. A. (1999). *Towards The Compleat Information Systems Graduate: a Problem based Learning Approach.* Paper presented at the Proceedings of the 10th Australasian Conference on Information Systems.

Biggs, J. (1999). *Teaching for Quality Learning at University: what the student does.* Buckingham (UK): Open University Press.

Bloom, B. S. (1956). *Taxonomy of Educational Objectives: the classification of educational goals Handbook 1: cognitive domain.* New York: David Mackay.

Brooks, F. P. (1986). *No silver bullet - essence and accidents of software engineering.* Paper presented at the Proceedings of Information Processing 86: the IFIP 10th World Conference, Amsterdam.

Brown, G., Bull, J., & Pendlebury, M. (1997). *Assessing Student Learning in Higher Education*. London: Routledge.

Brown, J. S., Collins, A., & Duguid, P. (1989). Situated cognition and the culture of learning. *Educational Researcher, 18*, 32-42.

Carr, W., & Kemmis, S. (1986). *Becoming Critical: education, knowledge and action research*. Lewes (UK): Falmer.

Cropley, D. H., & Cropley, A. J. (1998). *Teaching Engineering Students to be Creative - Program and Outcomes*. Paper presented at the Australasian Association of Engineering Education: 10th Annual Conference.

Dreyfus, H. L., & Dreyfus, S. E. (1986). *Mind over Machine*. New York: Free Press.

Engel, G., & Roberts, E. (Eds.). (2001). *Computing Curricula 2001: Computer Science --final report*: Joint Task Force on Computing Curricula, ACM and IEEE Computer Society.

English, F. (1978). *Quality control in curriculum development*. Arlington (VA): American Association of School Administrators.

Entwistle, N. J., & Ramsden, P. (1983). *Understanding Student Learning*. London: Croom Helm.

Entwistle, N. J., & Tait, H. (1990). Approaches to learning, evaluations of teaching, and preferences for contrasting academic environments. *Higher Education, 19*, 169-194.

Entwistle, N. J., & Tait, H. (1995). Approaches to studying and perceptions of the learning environment across disciplines. *New directions for teaching and learning, 64*, 93-103.

Felder, G. M., & Spurlin, J. (2005). Applications, reliability and validity of the Index of Learning Styles. *International Journal of Engineering Education, 21*(1), 1-3-112.

Felder, R. M. (1996). Matters of Style. *Prism: Journal of the American Society of Engineering Education, 6*(4), 18-23.

Felder, R. M., & Brent, R. (2005). Understanding student differences. *Journal of Engineering Education, 94*(1), 57-72.

Felder, R. M., & Silverman, R. L. (1988). Learning and teaching styles in engineering education. *Engineering Education, 78*(8), 674-681.

Freed, G. (1992). *Fifth generation innovation*. Sydney: Australian Centre for Innovation and International Competitiveness, University of Sydney.

Garlan, D., Gluch, D. P., & Tomayko, J. E. (1997). Agents of Change: Educating Future Leaders in Software Engineering. *IEEE Computer, 30*(11), 59-65.

Glass, R. L. (1992). A comparative analysis of the topic areas of Computer Science, Software Engineering, and Information Systems. *Journal of Systems and Software, 25*.

Glass, R. L. (1995). *Software Creativity*: Prentice-Hall.

Gorgone, J. T., Davis, G. B., Valacich, J. S., Topi, H., Feinstein, D. L., & Longenecker, H. E. (Eds.). (2002). *IS 2002: model curriculum for undergraduate degree programs in Information Systems*. Park Ridge (IL): ACM.

Gott, S. P., Hall, E. P., Pokorny, R. A., Dibble, E., & Glaser, R. (1993). A naturalistic study of transfer: adaptive expertise in technical domains. In D. K. Detterman & R. J. Sternberg (Eds.), *Transfer on Trial: intelligence, cognition and instruction* (pp. 258-288). Norwood (NJ): Ablex.

Guilford, J. P. (1967). *The Nature of Human Intelligence*. New York: McGraw-Hill.

Guindon, R. (1989). The process of knowledge discovery in system design. In G. Salvendy &

M. J. Smith (Eds.), *Designing and Using Human-Computer Interfaces and Knowledge Based Systems* (pp. 727-734). Amsterdam: Elsevier.

Guindon, R. (1990). Knowledge exploited by experts during software systems design. *International Journal of Man-Machine Studies, 33,* 279-304.

Habermas, J. (1972). *Theory and Practice* (V. J, Trans.). London: Heinemman.

Hannafin, M. J. (1997). *The case for grounded learning systems design: what the literature suggests about effective teaching learning and technology.* Paper presented at the Proceedings of ASCILITE '97, Perth.

Holt, J., & Solomon, F. (1996). Engineering Education - the way ahead. *Australasian Journal of Engineering Education,, 7*(1), 1-22; 83-98.

Iivari, J. (1991). A paradigmatic analysis of contemporary schools of IS development. *European Journal of Information Systems, 1*(4), 249-272.

Keirsey, D., & Bates, M. (1984). *Please Understand Me* (3 ed.): Prometheus Nemesis Book Company.

Klemola, T., & Rilling, J. (2002). *Modeling comprehension processes in software development.* Paper presented at the Proceedings of the first IEEE Conference on Cognitive Informatics (ICCI'02), Calgary (Canada).

Kolb, D. A. (1984). *Experiential Learning Experience as the Source of Learning and Development,* : Prentice-Hall.

Kolb, D. A. (1995). *Learning style inventory: technical specifications.* Boston: McBer & Company.

LeBlanc, R., & Sobel, A. E. K. (Eds.). (2004). *Software Engineering 2004: curriculum guidelines for undergraduate degree programs in Software Engineering.* Los Alamitos (CA): IEEE Computer Society Press.

Lee, D. M. S. (1999a). Knowledge/skill requirements and professional development of IS/IT workers: a summary of empirical findings from two studies. In *Panel on Workforce Needs in Information Technology, Computer Science and Telecommunications Board, National Academy of Sciences.* Milwaukee (WI).

Lee, D. M. S. (2004). Organizational entry and transition from academic study: examining a critical step in the professional development of young IS workers. In M. Igbaria & C. Shayo (Eds.), *Strategies for Managing IS/IT Personnel* (pp. 113-141). Hershey (PA): Idea Group.

Lethbridge, T. C. (2000). What knowledge is important to a software professional? *IEEE Computer, 33*(5), 44-50.

LTSN. (2002). *Constructive alignment and why it is important to the learner,* from http://www. ltsneng.ac.uk/er/theory/constructivealignment. asp

Lubars, M., Potts, C., & Richer, C. (1993). *A review of the state of the practice in requirements modeling.* Paper presented at the International Symposium on Requirements Engineering, San Diego.

Lumsdaine, M., & Lumsdaine, E. (1995). Thinking preferences of engineering students: implications for curriculum restructuring. *Journal of Engineering Education, 84*(2), 193-204.

Maiden, N. A. M., & Gizikis, A. (2001). Where do requirements come from? *IEEE Software, 18*(5), 10-12.

Maiden, N. A. M., & Sutcliffe, A. G. (1992). Exploiting reusable specifications through analogy. *Communications of the ACM, 34*(5), 55-64.

Mann, J. (1996). *The Role of Project Escalation in Explaining Runaway Information Systems Development Projects: A Field Study.* Georgia State University.

Meyer, J. H. F., & Boulton-Lewis, G. M. (1997). *The association between university students' perceived influences on their learning and their knowledge, experience, and conceptions, of learning.* Paper presented at the Proceedings of the 7th European Conference for Research on Learning and Instruction, Athens.

Middendorf, J., & Pace, D. (1986). Decoding the disciplines: a model for helping students learn disciplinary ways of thinking. *New Directions for teaching and learning, 98,* 1-12.

Minor, O. (2004). *Theory and Practice in Requirements Engineering: an investigation of curricula and industry needs.* Unpublished Master, University of Koblenz-Landau, Koblenz (Germany).

Mulder, K. F. (2006). Engineering curricula in Sustainable Development: an evaluation of changes at Delft University of Technology. *European Journal of Engineering Education, 31*(2), 133-144.

Nguyen, L., & Swatman, P. A. (2000). *Essential and incidental complexity in requirements models.* Paper presented at the Fourth International Conference on Requirements Engineering Education, Schaumburg (Il).

Oliver, R. W. (2000). *The coming biotech age: The business of bio material.* New York: McGraw-Hill.

Parnas, D. L., & Clements, P. C. (1986). A rational design process: how and why to fake it. *IEEE Transactions on Software Engineering, 12*(2), 251-257.

Pfleeger, S. L. (1999). Albert Einstein and empirical software engineering. *IEEE Computer, 32*(10), 32-37.

Reeves, T. C. (1994). *Evaluating what really matters in computer-based education,* from http://www.medicine.mcgill.ca/ibroedu/review/Reeves Evaluating What Really Matters in Computer-Based Education.htm

Reigeluth, C. M. (1997). Instructional theory, practitioner needs and new directions: some reflections. *Educational Technology, 37*(1), 42-47.

Robillard, P. N. (1999). The role of knowledge in software development. *Communications of the ACM, 42*(1), 87-92.

Rothman, R., Slattery, J. B., Vranek, J. L., & Resnick, L. B. (2002). *Benchmarking and Alignment of Standards and Testing* (CSE Report No. 566). Los Angeles: Center for the Study of Evaluation,

National Center for Research on Evaluation, Standards, and Student Testing, Graduate School of Education & Information Studies, UCLA.

Royce, W. W. (1970). *Managing the development of large software systems: concepts and techniques.* Paper presented at the IEEE WESCON.

Sawyer, P., & Kotonya, G. (2000). *SWEBOK: software requirements engineering knowledge area description* (Version 0.6 ed.): IEEE Computer Society/ACM.

Schön, D. A. (1983). *The Reflective Practitioner: How Professionals Think in Action.* New York: Basic Books.

Scott, G., & Yates, W. (2002). Using successful graduates to improve the quality of undergraduate engineering programs. *European Journal of Engineering Education, 27*(4), 60-67.

Shackelford, R. (Ed.). (2005). *Computing Curricula 2005: the overview report*: The Joint Task Force for Computing Curricula 2005.

Soloman, B., & Felder, R. (1999). *Index of Learning Styles (ILS),*, from http://www2.ncsu.edu/unity/lockers/users/f/felder/public/ILSpage.html

Somekh, B. (1989). Action research and collaborative school development. In R. McBride (Ed.), *The Inservice Training of Teachers: some issues and perspectives.* Brighton: Falmer Press.

Spiro, R. J., Feltovich, P. J., Jacobson, M., & Coulson, R. (1991). Cognitive flexibility, constructivism and hypertext: random access instruction for advanced knowledge acquisition in ill-structured domains. *Educational Technology, 31,* 24-33.

Thomas, J. C., Lee, A., & Danis, C. (2002). Enhancing creative design via software tools. *Communications of the ACM, 45*(10), 112-115.

Trauth, E. M., Farwell, D., & Lee, D. M. S. (1993). The IS expectation gap: industry expectation versus academic preparation. *MIS Quarterly, 17,* 293-307.

Turley, R. T. (1991). *Essential Competencies of Exceptional Professional Software Engineers.* Colorado State University, Fort Collins (CO).

Turley, R. T., & Bieman, J. M. (1995). Competencies of exceptional and non-exceptional software engineers. *Journal od Systems and Software, 28*(1), 19-38.

Tynjälä, P., Salminen, R., Sutela, T., Nuutinen, A., & Pitkänen, S. (2005). Factors related to study success in engineering education. *European Journal of Engineering Education, 30*(2), 221-231.

UWA. (1996). *Do male and female students differ in their preferred style of learning?* Perth: Institutional Research Unit, University of Western Australia.

Visser, W. (1992). Designers' activities examined at three levels: organisation strategies and problem-solving processes. *Knowledge-Based Systems, 5*(1), 92-104.

Waks, L. J. (2001). Donald Schon's Philosophy of Design and Design Education. *International Journal of Technology and Design Education, 11,* 37-51.

Waterman, R. H., Waterman, J. A., & Collard, B. A. (1994). Toward a career resilient workforce. *Harvard Business Review, 69,* 87-95.

Winn, W., & Snyder, D. (1996). Cognitive perspectives in psychology. In D. H. Jonassen (Ed.), *Handbook of Research for Educational Communications and Technology* (pp. 112-142). New York: Simon & Schuster Macmillan.

Zuber-Skerritt, O. (1995). Models for action research. In S. Pinchen & R. Passfield (Eds.), *Moving On: creative applications of action learning and action research* (pp. 3–29). Mt Gravatt (Qld): Action Learning, Action Research and Process Management Assn, Inc.

Zywno, M., & Waalen, J. (2001). *The effect of hypermedia instruction on achievement and attitudes of students with different learning styles.* Paper presented at the Proceedings of the 2001 American Society for Engineering Education Annual conference and Exposition Session 1330.

ENDNOTES

[1] When applied to education, alignment refers to the ongoing process of bringing congruence to the declared, learnt and assessed components to guide instruction design and ultimately, student learning. Authors on curriculum alignment agree content, depth, emphasis and cognitive activity match are required for sound alignment (Rothman, Slattery, Vranek, & Resnick, 2002). In the context of this chapter, alignment transcends the educational environment to include discipline, practitioner and student characteristics.

[2] Somekh (1989) defines Action Research as *the study of a social situation, involving the participants themselves as researchers, with a view to improving the quality of action within it.* This research applies the style described as the 'Deakin' (Carr & Kemmis, 1986) approach. This has merit in being adopted for studies in educational contexts (Zuber-Skerritt, 1995)

3   This implied rearranging political and administrative structures in a rationalist way in order to abandon superstition and injustice

4   For software development, Zucconi (1995) suggested the underlying disciplines of central importance are psychology, computer science and discrete mathematics, and suggests an IT professional needs to be well organised, able to work as a member of a multi-disciplinary team, and within the scope of the employer's policies and procedures and society's tenets

5   In general, students exhibited 'engineering' styles. As the work of the Felders and their colleagues (eg Felder & Spurlin, 2005; Felder & Brent, 2005; Felder & Silverman, 1988) indicate, engineering students are pragmatists with a tendency to narrow technical interests. Converger characteristic, to seek "single, correct answers or solutions to a question or problem" (Kolb, 1995) becomes the dominant learning style

6   Exploring the relevance of each new topic (Diverger); making available basic information and methods associated with the topic (Assimilator); providing opportunities to practice the methods (Converger) and encouraging exploration of the applications (Accomodator) (Felder, 1996)

Chapter III
On the Role of Learning Theories in Furthering Software Engineering Education

Emily Oh Navarro
University of California, Irvine, USA

André van der Hoek
University of California, Irvine, USA

ABSTRACT

Learning theories describe how people learn. There is a large body of work concerning learning theories on which to draw, a valuable resource of which the domain of software engineering educational research has thus far not taken full advantage. In this chapter, we explore what role learning theories could play in software engineering education. We propose that learning theories can move the field of software engineering education forward by helping us to categorize, design, evaluate, and communicate about software engineering educational approaches. We demonstrate this by: (1) surveying a set of relevant learning theories, (2) presenting a categorization of common software engineering educational approaches in terms of learning theories, and (3) using one such approach (SimSE) as a case study to explore how learning theories can be used to improve existing approaches, design new approaches, and structure and guide the evaluation of an approach.

INTRODUCTION

Learning theories are attempts to describe and understand the various ways in which people learn. They are an important resource for educational research, as they can both guide us in creating new educational approaches, and help us analyze and improve existing approaches.

In this chapter, we propose that learning theories, which have thus far been explicitly leveraged in software engineering education in only a minimal way, can actually play quite a significant role in this domain. Specifically, we believe that learning theories can serve to move the field of software engineering education forward by helping us to categorize, design, evaluate, and communicate about software engineering educational approaches. Categorizing approaches in terms of learning theories can help us to understand the approaches in relation to each other, understand how they fit together, and point out areas of untapped potential. New approaches can be designed to leverage certain theories whose potential is unfulfilled or known to be especially valuable in our domain. Learning theories can be used to evaluate approaches by helping structure experiments to look for the presence of these and other theories in the processes of learners. And, we can use our newfound knowledge to communicate in a common language—that of learning theories—about different approaches and our experience with them.

This chapter details this vision of principally using learning theories in the domain of software engineering education. We first briefly present a set of well-known (mainly constructivist) learning theories that are especially applicable. We then introduce a categorization of the major software engineering educational approaches to date in terms of the learning theories that they appear to have been designed around. Following this, we discuss the role learning theories can play in analyzing and improving the design of a software engineering educational approach (and designing new approaches), and focus on the analysis of one such approach (SimSE) as a case study. We then discuss how software engineering educational approaches can be evaluated in terms of learning theories, again using SimSE as a case study. We conclude with a summary in the final section.

BACKGROUND: LEARNING THEORIES

To provide some background for our discussion on the role of learning theories in software engineering education, in this section we will briefly introduce the set of learning theories that we surveyed for the purposes of our analysis. We do not include here an exhaustive list of all learning theories with significant detail. Instead, the purpose of this section is to simply introduce some of the ones we have seen software engineering educational approaches centered around most frequently, and provide pointers to where more information about each one can be found. In addition, we will also briefly touch on implications and typical or possible applications of each theory for software engineering education.

We chose the particular set of learning theories discussed here because of two criteria: relevancy to software engineering and orthogonality among the factors defining the theory. In other words, these theories are the ones we have seen to be most clearly and/or frequently embodied in the software engineering educational approaches that we surveyed. Furthermore, there exists a great deal of overlap among learning theories, and there are several learning theories that encompass a number of others. In these cases, we either group theories that have the same basic idea, and omit those that simply combine a number of theories.

We acknowledge that these theories fall mainly into the constructivist paradigm (rather than the behaviorist or cognitive categories), however, given that constructivism is the most recently-developed paradigm, and software engineering is a relatively new discipline, this is not surprising (it has been argued elsewhere, in fact, that the evolution of computer science education in the past decade or so has been significantly influenced by constructivism (Kolikant, 2001)). While it is certainly true that most delivery methods generally contain a mix of various theories that fall into each of the three camps (constructivist, behaviorist, and cognitive), because the constructivist aspects are the most focused on, we have chosen to scope this survey and analysis to focus primarily on these theories. Surely similar surveys and analyses could be done with cognitive and behaviorist theories that would yield interesting results, however, such exercises are outside the scope of the one presented here.

Nevertheless, some of the theories surveyed in this chapter do have elements of cognitive and/or behaviorist principles. For example, Learning through Failure involves a form of "punishment" (failure) meant to "extinguish" a certain behavior.

An additional issue that should be noted is the distinction between learning "theories," learning "models," and learning "methods," as well as their counterparts in the domain of instructional design (instructional design theories, models, and methods). Because the lines between these are blurred and often used interchangeably, it should be noted that in this chapter several of the "learning theories" we refer to can also be called by some of these other terms. When this is the case, we will point it out in our discussion of those theories. However, as is frequently done in the literature, we use the term "learning theory" broadly, as a term that covers all of these categories.

One of best-known learning theories is *Learning by Doing*, a theory based upon the premise that people learn a task best not by hearing about it, but by actually *doing* it (Dewey, 1916). The implication of this theory for instructional design is the following: the learner should be provided with ample opportunity to actually perform the activities they are meant to learn, rather than using passive mediums such as lectures and readings. In software engineering education, this translates to going beyond just lectures and reading assignments (although, for most any domain, a certain amount of such scaffolding is necessary to provide the learner with the required background knowledge to effectively participate in the Learning by Doing). Software engineering educators have recognized this, and now a standard component of nearly all software engineering courses is the class project—a small software engineering project that students must develop using some of the techniques learned in class.

Situated Learning (Lave, 1988) is an educational theory that builds upon the Learning by Doing approach. While Learning by Doing focuses on the specific learning activities that the student performs, the Situated Learning theory is concerned with the environment in which the Learning by Doing takes place. In particular, Situated Learning is based on the belief that knowledge is situated, being in large part a product of the activity, context, and culture in which it is developed and used. Therefore, the environment in which the student practices their newly learned knowledge should be "authentic", resembling, as closely as possible, the environment in which the knowledge will be used in real life. A popular application of this theory in software engineering education focuses on incorporating aspects of realism (or "authenticity") into the class project, such as using an industrial participant to play the role of the customer (Hayes, 2002), using maintenance- or evolution-based projects (McKim & Ellis, 2004), or using large teams of people that are distributed across geographical locations (Favela & Pena-Mora, 2001).

Like Situated Learning, *Keller's ARCS Motivation Theory* (Keller, 1983) also focuses on motivating students to learn. However, rather than focusing on the physical environment in which they learn, Keller's ARCS Motivation Theory concerns itself with producing certain feelings in the learner that are believed to promote learning. In particular, these feelings are attention, relevance, confidence, and satisfaction.

- **Attention:** The attention and interest of the learner must be engaged. Proposed methods for doing so are: introducing unique and unexpected events; varying aspects of instruction; and arousing information-seeking behavior by having the learner solve or generate questions or problems.
- **Relevance:** Learners must feel that the knowledge is relevant to their lives. The theory suggests that knowledge be presented and practiced using examples and concepts that are relevant to learners' past, present, and future experiences.

- **Confidence:** Learners need to feel personal confidence in the learning material. This should be done by presenting a non-trivial challenge and enabling them to succeed at it, communicating positive expectations, and providing constructive feedback.
- **Satisfaction:** A feeling of satisfaction must be promoted in the learning experience. This can be done by providing students with opportunities to practice their newly learned knowledge or skills in a real or simulated setting, and providing positive reinforcements for success.

Keller's ARCS is technically considered an instructional design model that is rooted in various learning theories. Two of the most directly contributing theories are Andragogy (Knowles, 1984) and Expectancy-Value Theory (Fishbein & Ajzen, 1975). Andragogy concerns adult learners in particular, and focuses on their need for self-directed, relevant, hands-on learning. Expectancy-value theory states that in order for a learner to put forth the effort required to learn, they must both value the knowledge/task/exercise and expect that they can succeed at it. Because Keller's ARCS combines these theories and provides more hands-on applicability than either theory alone, we have chosen to include it (rather than the theories it is based on) in our survey and analysis.

While Keller's ARCS could be applied in a number of different ways in software engineering education, in general it entails providing the students with attention-grabbing, realistic, hands-on assignments that pose a significant, yet doable challenge. One class of approaches that explicitly sets out to accomplish such goals is that in which the class project is made purposely open-ended and/or vague. This is done in two main ways: either by allowing the students to define their own requirements (giving students the pseudo-experience of new product development based on market research) (Navarro & van der Hoek, 2005b), or by allowing them to define their own

process (giving students experience in not only following a process, but in designing the process that they follow) (Groth & Robertson, 2001). The stated purpose of these open-ended approaches is to mimic common, less-structured (authentic) real-world software engineering situations, giving the students more ownership of the project and therefore more interest in it, as well as a greater feeling of confidence and satisfaction when the project is completed.

Model-Centered Instruction (Gibbons, 2001) (which is also considered an instructional design theory) says educators should center all learning activities around models of three types: models of environments, models of cause-effect systems, and models of human performance. Presentation of general concepts and theories should be kept to a minimum. Instead, Model-Centered Instruction believes that knowledge is best learned by exploration of these models. In software engineering education, this translates to simulating realistic situations, presenting case studies, and assigning realistic problems for the students to solve. One software engineering educational approach that embodies this theory is the practice-driven one, in which the curriculum is largely lab- and project-based, and lectures are used only as supporting activities (Ohlsson & Johansson, 1995).

The *Discovery Learning* theory (Bruner, 1967) takes a similar approach to model-centered instruction in that it believes that an exploratory style of learning is best. Discovery Learning is based on the idea that an individual learns a piece of knowledge most effectively if they discover it on their own, rather than having it explicitly told to them. This theory encourages educational approaches that are rich in exploring, experimenting, doing research, asking questions, and seeking answers. Educational software engineering simulation approaches (Drappa & Ludewig, 2000; Navarro & van der Hoek, 2005a) are specifically designed to facilitate this type of learning—no knowledge is made explicit in the simulation, as it is rather discovered by students experimenting with different approaches and seeing the effects of their decisions on the outcome of the simulation. These types of approaches are generally given as structured exercises and combined with other teaching methods (such as lectures, readings, and projects). Including this type of scaffolding has been found to be crucial in making Discovery Learning maximally effective (Kirschner *et al.*, 2006; Roblyer, 2005).

Along the same lines as the Discovery Learning theory is the *Learning Through Failure* theory (Schank, 1997). This theory is based on the assumption that the most memorable lessons are those that are learned as a result of failure. The theory argues that: (1) Learning through failure provides more motivation for students to learn, so as to avoid the adverse consequences that they experience firsthand when they do not perform as taught, and (2) Failure engages students, as they are motivated to try again in order to succeed. Proponents of the theory argue that students should be allowed to (and even set up to) fail to encourage maximal learning. Although Learning through Failure is usually applied to the realm of e-learning, there have also been some non-e-learning software engineering educational approaches in which the main avenue of learning is through failure. In these "sabotage" approaches, the instructor purposely sets the students up for failure by introducing common real-world complications into projects (e.g., crashing hardware just before a deadline), the rationale being that students will then be prepared when these situations occur in their future careers (Dawson, 2000).

The theory of *Learning through Reflection* is primarily based on Donald Schön's work suggesting the importance of reflection activities in the learning process (Schön, 1987). In particular, Learning through Reflection emphasizes the need for students to reflect on their learning experience in order to make the learning material more explicit, concrete, and memorable. Some common reflection activities include discussions, journaling, or dialogue with an instructor (Kolb, 1984).

One example of this in software engineering is (Tomayko, 1996), a practice-driven industrial partnership approach that incorporates weekly one-on-one mentoring sessions with a "coach" to discuss each student's performance and help them reflect on their experience. The game-based simulation described in (Drappa & Ludewig, 2000) and the industrial simulation described in (Nulden & Scheepers, 2000) also incorporate dialogue and reflection as post-simulation activities in which students analyze and discuss their simulation experience with a tutor or instructor, and reflect on what they have learned.

Finally, the theory of *Elaboration* (Reigeluth & Rodgers, 1980) states that, for optimal learning, instruction should be organized in order of complexity, from least complex to most complex. Simplest versions of tasks should be taught first, followed by more complicated versions. This is a theory that is generally inherent to most curricula (as well as most other learning theories), as courses and topics are usually introduced in order of increasing complexity. In software engineering educational approaches, applying this theory can sometimes be difficult, as there is oftentimes no natural way to organize the information in terms of complexity (e.g., how can one do this for a class project?). One approach that has been able to do this is the industrial simulation approach described in (Collofello, 2000). In this approach, students are assigned very simple simulations to begin with, and the complexity of the simulations is incrementally increased as the students progress in their knowledge.

As mentioned previously, what has been presented in this section is only a brief introduction to the relevant learning theories. There is much more detail to these theories than what we have discussed, detail which must be looked into further before one can effectively apply these theories to their educational approaches. Typically, subtleties are involved in each one, and care must be taken to pay attention to these details.

LEARNING THEORY-BASED CATEGORIZATION OF EXISTING APPROACHES

One of the main ways that learning theories can be used in software engineering educational research is to provide the field with a way to analyze and categorize existing approaches, both independently and in relation to each other. Such a categorization can serve to help us understand how the different approaches fit together and create a picture of the field as a whole, so that areas of strengths, weaknesses, and untapped potentials can be unearthed. We have done such a categorization, which we will present in this section.

Before creating this categorization, in order to organize our analysis we first surveyed the major software engineering educational approaches published in the past several years and found that they can be lumped into three broad groupings: *realism*, *topical*, and *simulation* (these groupings can be broken down further into sub-groupings, as shown in Table 1). Realism approaches are those that focus on making various aspects of

Table 1. Grouping of software engineering educational approaches

Realism	53	Topical	48	Simulation	8
Industrial Partnerships	16	**Formality**	3	**Industrial**	2
- Modify real software	1	- Formal methods	2	**Game-Based**	4
- Industrial advisor	1	- Engineering	1	**Group Process**	2
- Industrial mentor/lecturer	2	**Process (Specific)**	21		
- Case study	5	- PSP	14		
- Real project / customer	7	- TSP	2		
Maintenance/Evolution	9	- RUP	3		
- Multi-semester	4	- XP	2		
- Single-semester	5	**Process (General)**	6		
Team Composition	13	- Process engineering	3		
- Long-term teams	1	- Project management	3		
- Large teams	3	**Parts of Process**	3		
- Different C.S. classes	1	- Scenario-based req. eng.	1		
- Different majors	2	- Code reviews	1		
- Different universities	2	- Usability testing	1		
- Different countries	1	**Types of Software Eng.**	8		
- Team structure	3	- Maintenance/Evolution	3		
Non-Technical Skills	2	- Component-based SE	2		
Open-Endedness	7	- Real-time SE	3		
- Requirements	2	**Non-Technical Skills**	7		
- Process	5	- Social/logistical skills	3		
Practice-Driven	3	- Interact w/ stakeholders	1		
Sabotage	3	- HCI	2		
		- Business aspects	1		

the students' project experience more closely resemble one they would encounter in the real world. Some of these have included industry participation (Beckman *et al.*, 1997; Kornecki *et al.*, 2003; Wohlin & Regnell, 1999), emphasizing non-technical skills such as marketing and project management (Gnatz *et al.*, 2003; Goold & Horan, 2002), and focusing on making the nature and composition of the student teams that work on the project more realistic (e.g., making them very large (Blake, 2003) or composed of several sub-teams (Navarro & van der Hoek, 2005b)). Topical approaches aim to educate students in detail about a topic generally not covered in depth in mainstream textbooks and lectures. These approaches do not focus on specific delivery methods, but instead focus on the mere addition of the topic as a crucial component of an effective and complete education in software engineering. Some examples of such topics are formal methods (Abernethy & Kelly, 2000), real-time software engineering (Kornecki, 2000), and specific software processes such as the Personal Software Process (Hilburn, 1999) or the Rational Unified Process (Halling *et al.*, 2002). Finally, simulation approaches are those that have students practice software engineering processes in a (usually) computer-based simulated environment. Within the realm of software engineering simulations, there are three main types: industrial simulations brought to the classroom (Collofello, 2000; Pfahl *et al.*, 2000), game-based simulations (Drappa & Ludewig, 2000; Navarro & van der Hoek, 2005a), and group process simulations (Nulden & Scheepers, 2000; Stevens, 1989).

To categorize these approaches in terms of learning theories, we carefully studied each one to determine which learning theories appear to have been applied (whether intentionally or unintentionally), and which learning theories have clear potential to be employed. The resulting categorization is presented in Table 2 as a matrix of approaches and the learning theories that they leverage. (For a complete discussion of this categorization, see (Navarro, 2005)—here we present only the highlights.) The presence of three stars in the table indicates that the approach embodies the particular theory, or is centered around it. The presence of two stars represents that the theory appears to be involved in the design of that type of approach, but is perhaps not an intrinsic part of it, and may not be involved in all approaches that fall within that type. The presence of one star indicates that there is an obvious potential for that particular type of approach to employ that learning theory, but there have been very few, or no known cases of it.

Example: Simulation and Learning Theories

As an example of how we analyzed each approach in terms of learning theories, in this section we will focus on the simulation category and walk through how we determined the applicability of each learning theory for these approaches. First of all, all aforementioned educational software engineering simulations allow students to learn software processes by participating in them (Learning by Doing), albeit virtually. This theory is central to the paradigm of educational simulations (hence, the three stars in the table). These simulations also employ Situated Learning by adding realism to the learning environment, although in different ways: Industrial simulations add realistic factors in the form of real project data in the simulation model; Game-based simulations add realism by immersing the student in the role of a participant in a realistic game scenario; Group process simulations inject realism through the simulated characters that behave similarly to real-world participants. Because these realistic factors are artificial in that they are virtual (rather than in a real-life setting), we put two stars in the table for this theory.

Simulation approaches strongly fit with the Keller's ARCS model of learning. In particular, they are specifically designed to promote attention, relevance, confidence, and satisfaction (and

Table 2. Software engineering educational approaches and the learning theories they incorporate

	Learning by Doing	Situated Learning	Keller's ARCS	Model-Based Instruction	Discovery Learning	Learning Through Failure	Learning Through Reflection	Elaboration
Industrial Partnership – Real Project	**	***	**				*	
Maintenance/Evolution	**	***					*	**
Team Composition	**	***					*	
Open-Endedness	**	**	***		**	**	*	
Non-Technical Skills	**	**					*	
Practice-Driven	***			***	***	**	*	*
Sabotage	**	**				***	*	
Topical	**	*	*	*	*	*	*	*
Simulation	***	**	***	*	***	**	*	**

have been shown to do so in some cases) in the following ways:

- **Attention:** A number of studies done with educational software engineering simulations have repeatedly shown that students find these simulations enjoyable, engaging, and an interesting challenge they are happy to take on (Baker *et al.*, 2003; Dantas *et al.*, 2004; Navarro & van der Hoek, 2005a; Sharp & Hall, 2000; Stevens, 1989). This is particularly true for game-based simulations. Clearly this is the result of the elements of surprise, humor, challenge, and fun that are integral to many game-based simulations.
- **Relevance:** Because learners can experience firsthand how the knowledge they are learning is relevant in a real-world situation (the one that is portrayed in the simulation),

simulation promotes a feeling of relevance to students' future careers. This relevance can be enhanced by the usage of real-world data in the model to make the simulation more realistic. Furthermore, as the theory suggests, relevance is enhanced even further if the educational approach builds on previous and present knowledge. Simulations that are used to demonstrate concepts that have already been communicated to the students in another form (e.g., lecture or text) directly address this.

- **Confidence:** Simulations provide a non-trivial challenge that is also doable. As students are given the opportunity to succeed at a simulation, they will feel a sense of personal confidence in the learning material. This is especially true in game-based simulations, in which students have the additional benefit of feeling they have "won the game."

- **Satisfaction:** As students are able to practice their knowledge and skills in a realistic (yet simulated) setting, seeing the positive consequences of applying their knowledge correctly promotes a true feeling of satisfaction. Again, game-based simulations add to this if the student is also rewarded with a high score or some other game-relevant measure of success.

Model-based instruction has not been utilized at all in simulation, but has obvious potential to be. In particular, simulations could be used as the model (realistic situation, case study, *and* problem, simultaneously) that instruction is centered around. In such a case, students would practice a simulation (or series of simulations) for each concept (or set of concepts) being taught. Simulations would allow for ample exploration—one of the basic tenets of model-based instruction—as students could practice the same simulation multiple times, using a different approach each time, learning the consequences of various actions, and, as a result, learning a great deal about the process and concepts being simulated.

The exploratory quality of simulation in and of itself directly implements the Discovery Learning theory. The nature of simulation is highly conducive to allowing students to discover knowledge on their own, as they see phenomena played out in a simulation, and are encouraged to explore, experiment, do research, ask questions, and seek answers.

This type of exploratory learning is also inherently related to the Learning through Failure theory. As students explore the simulation and try different approaches, they are likely to fail at least a few times. In fact, one of the basic purposes of simulations is to allow students to "push boundaries", try different approaches, and fail without fear of the drastic and severe consequences that would occur in a real-world setting. For example, a student who fails in a simulated software project would only have to worry about

getting a low game score or seeing an unhappy simulated customer, while in the real world such a failure could cost millions of dollars or have even more serious consequences.

Learning through Reflection has also been incorporated into simulation approach, although only limitedly: with the game-based simulation SESAM (Drappa & Ludewig, 2000), and the industrial simulation described in (Nulden & Scheepers, 2000). As mentioned previously, dialogue and reflection sessions have been incorporated into these learning processes as post-simulation activities. Some dialogue activity is also an inherent part of Problems and Programmers (Baker et al., 2003), the educational software engineering card game simulation. The face-to-face, competitive nature of this physical card game has been shown to promote rich and useful discussion between student opponents, regarding such topics as why they took the approach they did, the reasons behind one person's win and another's loss, and their reactions to unexpected events.

Finally, the Elaboration theory has also been only limitedly incorporated into simulation-based software engineering educational approaches. In particular, Elaboration has only been leveraged in the process used with the industrial simulation described in (Collofello, 2000). This process consists of assigning students very simple simulations to begin with, and incrementally increasing the complexity of the simulations as the students progress in their knowledge.

Categorization Highlights

The first thing to notice in general from Table 2 is that, although learning theories are not often explicitly discussed in software engineering education research, they are indeed applicable in our domain. Whether consciously or unconsciously, people have been building approaches toward them in various ways. If we look at how the different learning theories fare with respect to the number of approaches that incorporate them, we can clearly see that our domain has focused the most on Learning by Doing and Situated Learning. This is not a surprise, given the strong emphasis on preparing students for the "real world" that is intrinsic to the field. In contrast, Learning through Reflection is the most under-explored theory, but also has the most potential for greater use—every category of approach has the potential to leverage (or better leverage) this theory.

If we then look at each approach with respect to the learning theories they incorporate, we can see that most of them apply multiple theories at once. The "topical" category has one star for each theory because, since these approaches focus on the topic rather than on delivery methods, they theoretically have the potential to apply all of the theories, depending on the way that topic is taught. Simulation, on the other hand, directly incorporates, or has the potential to directly incorporate all of the theories considered in some way or another. While it certainly is not the case that any teaching method that addresses more learning theories than another is better than that other method (consider a combination of strategies put together haphazardly in some teaching method versus one well-thought-out and tightly-focused method cleverly leveraging one very good strategy), an approach that naturally addresses factors and considerations of multiple learning theories is one that is most definitely worth exploring. Simulation is such an approach, but one that has been significantly underexplored in software engineering education (Navarro, 2005)—something that we are attempting to address with the approach described in the following section.

DETAILED ANALYSIS/DESIGN/ DEVELOPMENT OF AN APPROACH IN TERMS OF LEARNING THEORIES

In addition to providing the field with a way to categorize and analyze existing software engi-

neering educational approaches, learning theories can also help in developing new approaches and modifying existing approaches to be more effective. Categorizations such as the one presented in the previous section can help guide the design (or re-design) of such approaches, as areas for potential are highlighted.

Case Study: The Design of SimSE

In this section, we present a case study of a software engineering educational approach that was actually not explicitly designed with learning theories in mind. In looking back at our approach in light of learning theories, however, we can see that several of our key decisions made in its design are highly relevant to some of these theories. We can also see missed opportunities of ways we could have leveraged additional learning theories to make it more effective.

The approach is SimSE, an educational game-based software engineering simulation environment. SimSE is a computer-based environment that facilitates the creation and simulation of realistic software process simulation models—models that involve real-world components not present in typical class projects, such as large teams of people, large-scale projects, critical decision-making, personnel issues, multiple stakeholders, budgets, planning, and random, unexpected events. In so doing, it aims to provide students with a platform through which they can experience many different aspects of the software process in a practical manner without the overarching emphasis on creating deliverables that is inherent in actual software development.

The graphical user interface of SimSE is shown in Figure 1. SimSE is a single-player game in which the player takes on the role of project manager and must manage a team of developers in order to successfully complete an assigned software engineering project or task. The player drives the process by, among other things, hiring and firing employees, assigning tasks, monitoring progress, and purchasing tools. At the end of the game, the player receives a score indicating how well they performed, and an explanatory tool provides them with a visual analysis of their game, including which rules were triggered when, a trace of events, and the "health" of various attributes (e.g., correctness of the code) over time (see Figure 2).

To date, six SimSE game models exist: a waterfall model, an inspection model, an incremental model, an Extreme Programming model, a rapid prototyping model, and a Rational Unified Process model. For more information on SimSE, including its design, game play, and simulation models, see (Navarro, 2006).

The idea of SimSE was originally motivated by the hypothesis that simulation can bring to software engineering education many of the same benefits it has brought to other educational domains. Specifically, we believed that software

engineering *process* education could be improved by using simulation to allow students to practice managing different kinds of "realistic" software engineering processes. The constraints of the academic environment prevent students from having the opportunity to practice many issues surrounding the software engineering process in their course projects. Our approach therefore focused on providing this opportunity through the use of simulation.

To guide us in the design of SimSE, we performed two activities: (1) a study of the domain of software engineering education to discover what its unique needs are, and (2) a survey of well-known principles for successful educational simulations from the research literature. The result of this was a specific set of key decisions that are listed here and discussed in light of the learning theory (or theories) that we later discovered related directly to them:

Figure 1. SimSE graphical user interface

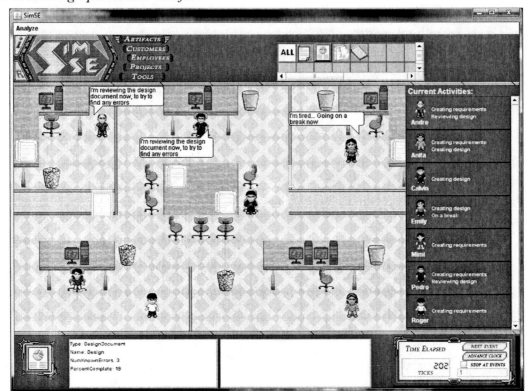

Figure 2. Graphical representation of a SimSE Game, generated by the explanatory tool

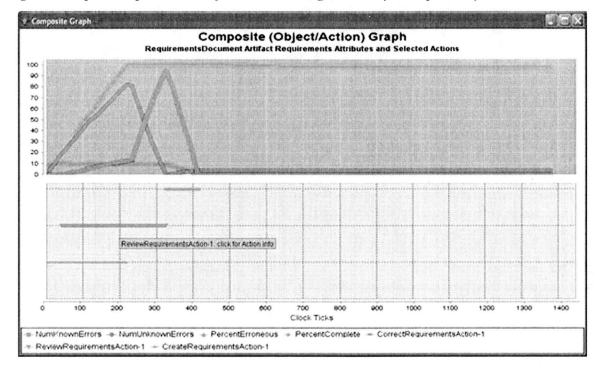

1. **Use of the game paradigm.** We could have chosen to base our simulation approach on the industrial simulation or group process simulation paradigms mentioned previously, but instead we chose the game paradigm. It has been shown that game-like features such as graphics, interactivity, surprising random events, and interesting, life-like challenges are known to hold a student's attention and promote a feeling of confidence and satisfaction as they succeed in the game (Ferrari *et al.*, 1999). This directly corresponds to the Keller's ARCS theory, which suggests that such qualities promote a highly effective learning experience.

2. **A fully-graphical user interface.** To make SimSE maximally engaging and visually realistic, we chose to design a fully graphical, rather than textual interface. As was shown in Figure 1, the focal point of this interface is a typical office layout in which the simulated process is "taking place", including cubicles, desks, chairs, computers, and employees who "talk" to the player through pop-up speech bubbles over their heads. In addition, graphical representations of all artifacts, tools, customers, and projects along with the status of each of these objects are visible. This decision to graphically portray simulated software engineering situations turned out to be strongly in line with the theory of Situated Learning—the learner is provided with a visual context that corresponds to the real world situations in which the learned knowledge would typically be used.

3. **A high level of interactivity.** Keeping the attention of the learner engaged is not only done by making a user interface visually appealing, but also by continuously involv-

ing the learner. Thus, rather than designing SimSE as a continuous simulation that simply takes an initial set of inputs and produces some predictive results, we designed it in such a way that the player must make decisions and steer the simulation accordingly throughout the entire process. SimSE operates on a step-by-step, clock tick basis, and every clock tick the player has the opportunity to perform actions that affect the simulation. Keeping the learner continuously engaged and giving them ample opportunity to practice their skills and tackle challenges are tactics suggested by the Keller's ARCS theory for promoting attention, relevance, confidence, and satisfaction.

4. **Customizable simulation models.** SimSE includes a model builder tool and associated modeling approach that allow an instructor to build simulation models and generate customized games based on these models. This feature adds the (unanticipated) potential for using SimSE in a way that follows the theory of Elaboration—instructors could build models of varying complexity and use them in order of increasing complexity with students. Although we have not yet built such models with SimSE, it is in our future plans to do so, as we now know that this potential for greater effectiveness is there.

5. **An explanatory tool.** An integral part of SimSE is its novel explanatory tool that provides players with a visual representation of how the simulated process progressed over time and explanations of the rules underlying the game. This feature promotes Learning through Reflection as it allows players to look back on their game and analyze their decisions and how those decisions affected the outcome. The explanatory tool output could also potentially be used as the focal point of a dialogue session between student and tutor/instructor.

6. **Complementary usage of SimSE.** Rather than design SimSE to be a standalone tool meant to replace standard course components such as lectures, readings, and projects, we instead designed it to be used complementary to them, and have used it in such a setting. The simulation models we have built require a basic set of knowledge and skills in order to play and learn from them effectively, knowledge that students conceivably obtain in lectures and readings. Thus, in essence, SimSE allows them to "Learn by Doing" by learning through experience the lessons communicated through reading and lectures, as well as other lessons that are simply not adequately teachable through passive means. Linking the knowledge learned in SimSE to existing knowledge also promotes the feeling that what a student is learning is of relevance to them, a major tenet of Keller's ARCS.

7. **Simulation models that provide a clear goal.** SimSE allows the modeler to compose a "starting narrative" for the player that appears at the start of a game, and to which the player can refer back at any time during a game. In the models we have built, we have used this starting narrative to provide the player with the exact goals of the simulation, criteria for completion of these goals, and any hints or special notes that might help them along the way. Precisely defined objectives not only guide students through a simulation, but also pose a challenge that many students find hard to resist. Achieving the goal becomes a priority and Discovery Learning is employed as creative thinking is sparked in coming to an approach that eventually achieves that goal.

8. **Simulation models that are adequately challenging.** We have built into our simulation models interesting situations that are adequately challenging (engaging students'

attention and making it likely that they learn through failure at times) but not impossible, promoting eventual success that leads to confidence in the learning material and satisfaction in the experience (central principles to Keller's ARCS).

Looking back on the design of SimSE in light of learning theories served to link some of our intuition in the design of SimSE to these theories, thereby increasing our confidence of being on the right path with our approach. In addition to this, it also revealed some missed opportunities that we could have taken advantage of, had we originally designed SimSE with learning theories in mind. For example, we could have better taken advantage of the Elaboration theory by designing our models in incrementally complex versions, and introducing them to students in order of increasing complexity. In our usage of SimSE in courses and in out-of-class studies, we also could have made reflection a more central and structured part of the approach by providing the student with explicit explanatory tool exercises to complete, exercises that would encourage the type of reflection that would help solidify the lessons learned in the simulation (currently, the student is simply given the explanatory tool, and decisions about how to use it are left up to them). As another example, we could have better incorporated aspects of authenticity (promoting Situated Learning) by including more random events (a characterizing feature of the real world) in our models. These types of events are only used sparingly in many of our models.

Like most software engineering educational approaches, SimSE was not designed with learning theories in mind. However, by looking back on its design in light of learning theories, we have learned a great deal about how SimSE promotes learning and how it can be improved to foster greater learning, as we have seen in this section.

LEARNING THEORY-CENTRIC EVALUATION

Although we did not explicitly use learning theories in SimSE's initial design, we did use them as a central guiding factor in designing a major part of its evaluation. Validating that the theories an approach was designed to employ (or appear to employ) are *actually* employed, as well as discovering if an approach incorporates aspects of any additional theories, can be highly useful exercises—such data can be used to make that and other similar approaches more effective as they are tailored to exploit the characteristics known to promote each theory (van Eck, 2006). Thus, as part of SimSE's evaluation, we performed an in-depth observational study that focused on investigating the learning processes of SimSE players to determine whether they exhibited behaviors indicative of various learning theories.

Case Study: SimSE Evaluation Setup

For this study, we used as subjects 11 undergraduate students who had passed the introductory software engineering course at the University of California, Irvine. This requirement was put in place so that they would have at least the basic understanding of software engineering concepts required to play SimSE. The study occurred in a one-on-one setting—one subject and one observer. Each subject was first given instruction on how to play SimSE, and was then observed playing SimSE for about 2.5 hours. In order to evaluate how well the explanatory tool achieves its goal of aiding Learning through Reflection, we had eight students play SimSE with the explanatory tool and three without. (Differences in the behavior, attitudes, and opinions of each group could then be compared, though clearly, not to the extent of being statistically significant.) While subjects were playing, their game play and behavior were observed and noted. Following this, the subject was interviewed about their experience for about

30 minutes. In addition to any spontaneous questions the observer formulated based on a particular subject's actions or behavior during game play, all subjects were asked a set of standard questions. Several of these questions were designed to specifically detect the presence of one or more learning theories in the subject's learning process. Some questions did not target a particular theory or set of theories, but were instead meant to evoke insightful comments from the subject from which various learning theories could be inferred, and from which general insights into the learning process could be discovered. Some samples from the standard set of questions are listed here, with the targeted learning theory (or theories) listed in parentheses afterwards when applicable.

- *To what do you attribute the change (or lack of) (improvement, worsening, fluctuation, steady state) of your score with each game?* (Discovery Learning, Learning through Failure)
- *Do you feel you learned more when you "won" or when you "lost"? Why? What did you learn from each "win" or "loss"?* (Discovery Learning, Learning through Failure)
- *When you lost, did you feel motivated to try again or not? Why?* (Learning through Failure)
- *On a scale of 1 to 5, how much did playing SimSE engage your attention? Why?* (Keller's ARCS)
- *How much has your level of confidence changed in the learning material since completing this exercise?* (Keller's ARCS)
- *Did you feel that you learned any new software process concepts from playing SimSE that you did not know before? If so, which ones?* (answer could be indicative of multiple theories)
- *If you feel you learned from SimSE, what do you believe it is about SimSE that facilitated*

your learning? (answer could be indicative of multiple theories)

There were also some questions primarily designed for comparison between the subjects who used the explanatory tool and those who did not. These questions were aimed at discovering how the player went about figuring out the reasoning behind their scores, as well as how well they understood this reasoning.

- *Where do you think you went wrong in game 1/2/x?* (Learning through Reflection)
- *Please describe the process that you followed to figure out the reasoning behind your score, or where you went wrong/right.* (Learning through Reflection)

Following the experiment, the interviewer's observations and interview notes were analyzed to try to discover which behaviors and comments were indicative of the various learning theories, and how, as well as to discover any other insights about SimSE as a teaching tool that could be gained from this data.

Evaluation Results

The learning theory that was most clearly involved in every subject's learning process was Discovery Learning. All subjects were able to recount at least a few lessons they learned from SimSE, and none of these lessons were ever told to them explicitly during their experience. Rather, they discovered them independently through exploration and experimentation within the game. Interestingly, although all subjects that played a model seemed to discover the same lessons (for the most part), no two subjects discovered them in the same way. Every subject approached the game with a different strategy, but came away with similar new knowledge, suggesting that SimSE can be applicable to a wide range of students that come from different backgrounds with different ideas and possibly, different learning styles. This is a central aspect of a student-centered theory like Discovery Learning. Since learning depends primarily on the learner and not the instructor, the learner is free to use their own style and ideas in discovering the knowledge, rather than being forced to adhere to a rigid style of instruction.

Learning through Failure also seemed to be widely evident. Every subject seemed to take a "divide and conquer" approach to playing SimSE, isolating aspects of the model and tackling them individually (or a few at a time). When subjects described the progression of their games in the interviews, it was clear that the way they conquered each aspect was by going through at least one or two rounds of failure in which they discovered what *not* to do, and from this discovering a correct approach that lead to success. When asked explicitly about learning through failure, every subject stated that they learned when they failed, but the amount of learning they reported varied. Five subjects said they learned more from failure than success, two subjects said they learned more when they succeeded, and four subjects said they learned equally as much from failure and success. All but one subject said that they were motivated to try again after they failed. This motivation was also evident in the behavior of several subjects, as some, after the completion of one failed game, hurriedly and eagerly started a new one. One subject even tried to start a new game when the time for the game play portion of the experiment was up and he was already informed that it would be the last game.

The Learning by Doing theory seemed to be involved in most of the subjects' learning experience. Eight out of the 11 subjects made comments about their experience playing SimSE that hinted at aspects of Learning by Doing. Some of their comments included:

- "[SimSE helped me learn because it] *puts you in charge of things. It's a good way of applying your knowledge.*"

- "[SimSE helped me learn because it is] *interactive, not just sitting down and listening to something.*"

Comments indicative of Situated Learning were also rather frequent, mentioned by seven out of the 11 subjects. Some of these included:

- "[SimSE helped me learn because] *it was very realistic and helped me learn a lot of realistic elements of software engineering, such as employees, budget, time, and surprising events.*"
- "[One of the learning-facilitating characteristics of SimSE was] *seeing a real-life project in action with realistic factors like employee backgrounds and dialogues.*"

Behaviors and comments suggestive of Keller's ARCS Motivation Theory were also evident, although certain aspects of the theory came out stronger than others. To explain, let us look at the four aspects of the theory (attention, relevance, confidence, and satisfaction) individually.

First, the attention of the subjects seemed to be quite engaged with SimSE. This was evident in their body language, the comments made both during game play and the interview, and their ratings of SimSE's level of engagement. Many of them spent the majority of their time during game play sitting on the edge of their seats, leaning forward and fixing their eyes on the screen. There were head nods, chuckles in response to random events and character descriptions, shouts of "Woo hoo!" after achieving a high score in a game, shaking of the head when things were not going so well for a player, and requests of, "Can I try this one more time?" when the experiment's allotted time for game play was coming to an end. Words some subjects used to describe SimSE in the interview were "challenging", "fun", "interesting", "addictive", and "amusing." When explicitly asked how much SimSE engaged their attention, the students rated it quite high—4.1 on average out of five.

Second, relevance was rated moderately high, but not as high as level of engagement. Five of the subjects rated SimSE's relevance to their future experiences as "pretty relevant" or "very relevant", five described it as "somewhat" or "partially" relevant and one said it was not relevant at all. Although not explicitly asked about SimSE's relevance to their past experiences, nearly all of the subjects mentioned that they used some of the knowledge they had learned in software engineering courses to come up with their strategies for playing the game, suggesting that there is also a relevance between their past experiences (learning the concepts in class) and their learning experience with SimSE.

Third, most subjects felt their level of confidence in the learning material (the software process model simulated and software process in general) had increased at least somewhat since playing SimSE. Four subjects reported their level of confidence had changed "a lot" or "very much", five said it had changed "somewhat", and two said it had not changed at all.

Fourth, satisfaction was rated quite high by the subjects. Nine out of the 11 subjects reported that they were "quite satisfied", "very satisfied", "fully satisfied", or "pretty satisfied", and three subjects stated they were "somewhat satisfied." Most of the reported factors that contributed to a feeling of satisfaction pertained to a subject's increasing success from game to game, although some also mentioned that the sheer fun and challenge of SimSE contributed to their satisfaction as well.

The explanatory tool did seem to promote Learning through Reflection, to some extent. Most of the subjects that had access to the explanatory tool did make use of it, the duration of its use after most games ranging from five to 25 minutes. It was obvious that the subjects who did not have the explanatory tool (to whom we will henceforth refer as "non-explanatory subjects") were significantly more confused and less confident about the reasoning behind their scores and how to improve than those who did have the explanatory tool (to whom

we will henceforth refer as "explanatory subjects"). All of the non-explanatory subjects expressed this, while only one explanatory subject stated such an opinion. The following are some of the comments made by the non-explanatory subjects:

- *"I was trying to guess what I was doing wrong, so I probably chose the wrong areas that I was doing wrong, and then I tried to switch back to my original way and then I kind of forgot what that was and once I started trying to improve it, all of my little details started changing and I didn't know what parts were causing my score to go lower."*
- *"I felt like I knew, oh, that's where I went wrong sometimes, like I should spend a little less time there, but a lot of times I was wrong about where it was I went wrong."*

On the other hand, most of the explanatory subjects' comments expressed that the explanatory tool did, indeed facilitate their learning:

- "[The explanatory tool] *showed me why I was doing poorly—because of certain events that were happening."*
- *"The rules* [described in the explanatory tool] *are really helpful—even if someone doesn't know anything about software engineering I think the rules can teach you how to play the game."*

Implications of Evaluation Results

Evaluating SimSE in terms of learning theories provided us with several valuable insights into how SimSE helps students learn. In addition, it also helped us to discover ways to potentially make SimSE more effective. In this subsection, we describe how focusing on some of the theories in our evaluation provided us with knowledge that will help us maximize SimSE's effectiveness.

Learning through failure: Overall, the challenge of receiving a "failing" score and trying to improve it seemed to be a significant avenue of learning and a strong motivating factor of SimSE. This reinforced our notion that simulation models should be made challenging enough that students are set up to fail at times. It is these failures that provide some of the greatest opportunities for learning. By focusing on this aspect in our observations, we also discovered that one of our models (Rapid Prototyping) was not quite challenging enough, and students could sometimes get a good score without really learning the lessons. Thus, we have since added more challenges to this model, and will continue to build simulation models in the future that have an adequate level of challenge.

Learning by doing: Several of the subjects' comments mentioned the ability to put previously learned knowledge into practice as a learning-facilitating characteristic of SimSE. This validates our choice to use SimSE complementary to other teaching methods, so that it can fulfill this important role of being an avenue through which students can employ Learning by Doing as they do the things they only heard about in class.

Situated learning: The realistic elements in SimSE seem to add significantly to its educational effectiveness. Thus, it is important that we continue to include elements of the real world in our models, in order to situate students' knowledge in a realistic environment.

Elaboration: It became clear from our observations that one of our models (waterfall) is much too large and complex for a "SimSE beginner." (Although the waterfall process is a simple one, the corresponding SimSE model is quite complicated, incorporating several non-technical, managerial aspects.) By giving such a complex model to a student who has never played SimSE before, we were clearly violating the principles of the elaboration theory. Thus, viewing this result in light of that theory taught us that such a model should not be introduced until the student has played other, simpler models first.

Keller's ARCS: Through this study we were able to discover what elements of SimSE and its models best hold students' attention by noting when students appeared to be most engaged, and what kinds of things they commented about favorably in the interviews. For example, several students mentioned that the random events in the models (e.g., the customer changing their mind and requiring the team to rework part of the code) added an element of surprise and realism that kept things entertaining. Thus, we will continue to build these elements into our future models, as well as try to maximize them in our current models. We also discovered which elements students found unengaging. For instance, several subjects thought the inspection model was boring and repetitive. Through the interviews, we were able to detect exactly what it was about the inspection model that made it this way, and have recently implemented changes that we anticipate will make it more interesting for future SimSE players.

Learning through reflection: The explanatory tool partially fulfills its goal of facilitating reflection, but it is clear that it needs to be improved. In particular, more help needs to be given to the user in generating meaningful, useful graphs, and the rule descriptions need to be more easily accessible. We have recently addressed these issues in our development by adding attributes to each model that are meant specifically for explanatory graphing purposes and by making the rule descriptions more accessible through the user interface.

Learning theories can help structure evaluations by providing ideas about what the researcher should be looking for in the learning processes of students. As we have seen with SimSE, this can be done even if the approach was not designed with learning theories in mind. A careful retro-analysis of the approach's design in terms of learning theories can reveal the aspects that a learning theory-centric evaluation should focus on. Conducting such an evaluation has the potential to both reveal the effectiveness of an approach, as well as guide future work in the area.

Certainly, not every aspect of an approach can be evaluated this way—an evaluation focused on learning theories should only be one part of an evaluation plan. In addition to the evaluation described here, SimSE's evaluation plan also included a pilot study, a comparative study, and in-class studies, each of which was designed to evaluate different aspects of SimSE to form a comprehensive picture of its ability as a teaching tool (see (Navarro & van der Hoek, 2007) for more information about these studies).

SUMMARY

Learning theories are an important educational resource of which the software engineering educational community has not yet taken full advantage. Learning theories can be used to categorize, design, evaluate, and communicate about software engineering educational approaches, providing a structured and informed way to move our domain forward with approaches that are effective and well-understood. We have shown one example of applying learning theories to software engineering education in our analysis and evaluation of SimSE. It is our hope that educators can take this example and apply it to other approaches and areas of software engineering education to create more effective teaching strategies that are rooted in educational theory.

MORE INFORMATION

More information about SimSE, including downloads, evaluations, and publications, are available at http://www.ics.uci.edu/~emilyo/SimSE/.

ACKNOWLEDGMENT

We would like to thank the reviewers of this chapter for their highly useful and constructive feedback. Effort partially funded by the National Science Foundation under grant number DUE-0618869.

REFERENCES

Abernethy, K., & Kelly, J. (2000). Technology transfer issues for formal methods of software specification. In S. A. Mengel & P. J. Knoke (Eds.), *Proceedings of the thirteenth conference on software engineering education and training* (pp. 23-31). Austin, TX: IEEE Computer Society.

Baker, A., Navarro, E. O., & van der Hoek, A. (2003). Problems and programmers: An educational software engineering card game. In *Proceedings of the 2003 international conference on software engineering* (pp. 614-619). Portland, Oregon.

Beckman, K., Khajenoori, K., Coulter, N., & Mead, N. R. (1997). Collaborations: Closing the industry-academia gap. *IEEE Software, 14*(6), 49-57.

Blake, B. M. (2003). A student-enacted simulation approach to software engineering education. *IEEE Transactions on Education, 46*(1), 124-132.

Bruner, J. S. (1967). *On knowing: Essays for the left hand.* Cambridge, Mass.: Harvard University Press.

Collofello, J. S. (2000). University/industry collaboration in developing a simulation based software project management training course. In S. Mengel & P. J. Knoke (Eds.), *Proceedings of the thirteenth conference on software engineering education and training* (pp. 161-168). Austin, TX: IEEE Computer Society.

Dantas, A. R., Barros, M. O., & Werner, C. M. L. (2004). A simulation-based game for project management experiential learning. In *Proceedings of the 2004 international conference on software engineering and knowledge engineering.* Banff, Alberta, Canada.

Dawson, R. (2000). Twenty dirty tricks to train software engineers. In *Proceedings of the 22nd international conference on software engineering* (pp. 209-218): ACM.

Dewey, J. (1916). *Democracy and education.* New York, NY: Macmillan.

Drappa, A., & Ludewig, J. (2000). Simulation in software engineering training. In *Proceedings of the 22nd international conference on software engineering* (pp. 199-208): ACM.

Favela, J., & Pena-Mora, F. (2001). An experience in collaborative software engineering education. *IEEE Software, 18*(2), 47-53.

Ferrari, M., Taylor, R., & VanLehn, K. (1999). Adapting work simulations for schools. *The Journal of Educational Computing Research, 21*(1), 25-53.

Fishbein, M., & Ajzen, I. (1975). *Belief, attitude, intention, and behavior: An introduction to theory and research.* Reading, Mass.: Addison-Wesley.

Gibbons, A. S. (2001). Model-centered instruction. *Journal of Structural Learning and Intelligent Systems, 14*(4), 511-540.

Gnatz, M., Kof, L., Prilmeier, F., & Seifert, T. (2003). A practical approach of teaching software engineering. In P. J. Knoke, A. Moreno & M. Ryan (Eds.), *Proceedings of the sixteenth conference on software engineering education and training* (pp. 120-128). Madrid, Spain: IEEE.

Goold, A., & Horan, P. (2002). Foundation software engineering practices for capstone projects and beyond. In M. McCracken, M. Lutz & T. C. Lethbridge (Eds.), *Proceedings of the fifteenth conference on software engineering education and training* (pp. 140-146). Covington, KY, USA: IEEE.

Groth, D. P., & Robertson, E. L. (2001). It's all about process: Project-oriented teaching of software engineering. In D. Ramsey, P. Bourque & R. Dupuis (Eds.), *Proceedings of the fourteenth conference on software engineering education and training* (pp. 7-17). Charlotte, NC, USA: IEEE.

Halling, M., Zuser, W., Kohle, M., & Biffl, S. (2002). Teaching the unified process to undergraduate students. In M. McCracken, M. Lutz & T. C. Lethbridge (Eds.), *Proceedings of the fifteenth conference on software engineering education and training* (pp. 148-159). Covington, KY, USA: IEEE.

Hayes, J. H. (2002). Energizing software engineering education through real-world projects as experimental studies. In M. McCracken, M. Lutz & T. C. Lethbridge (Eds.), *Proceedings of the fifteenth conference on software engineering education and training* (pp. 192-206). Covington, KY: IEEE.

Hilburn, T. (1999). PSP metrics in support of software engineering education. In H. Saiedian (Ed.), *Proceedings of the twelfth conference on software engineering education and training* (pp. 135-136). New Orleans, LA, USA: IEEE.

Keller, J. M. (1983). Motivational design of instruction. In C. M. Reigeluth (Ed.), *Instructional design theories and models: An overview of their current status.* Hillsdale, NJ: Erlbaum.

Kirschner, P. A., Sweller, J., & Clark, R. E. (2006). Why minimal guidance during instruction does not work: An analysis of the failure of constructivist, discovery, problem-based, experiential, and inquiry-based teaching. *Educational Psychologist, 41*(2), 75-86.

Knowles, M. (1984). *Andragogy in action: Applying modern principles of adult education.* San Francisco, CA: Jossey Bass.

Kolb, D. A. (1984). *Experiential learning: Experiences as the source of learning and development.* Englewood Cliffs, NJ, USA: Prentice-Hall International, Inc.

Kolikant, Y. B. (2001). Gardeners and cinema tickets: High school students' preconceptions of concurrency. *Computer Science Education, 11*(3), 221-245.

Kornecki, A. J. (2000). Real-time computing in software engineering education. In S. A. Mengel & P. J. Knoke (Eds.), *Proceedings of the thirteenth conference on software engineering education and training* (pp. 197-198). Austin, TX, USA: IEEE.

Kornecki, A. J., Khajenoori, S., & Gluch, D. (2003). On a partnership between software industry and academia. In P. J. Knoke, A. Moreno & M. Ryan (Eds.), *Proceedings of the sixteenth conference on software engineering education and training* (pp. 60-69). Madrid, Spain: IEEE.

Lave, J. (1988). *Cognition in practice: Mind, mathematics, and culture in everyday life.* Cambridge, UK: Cambridge University Press.

McKim, J. C., & Ellis, H. J. C. (2004). Using a multiple term project to teach object-oriented programming and design. In T. B. Horton & A. E. K. Sobel (Eds.), *Proceedings of the seventeenth conference on software engineering education and training* (pp. 59-64). Norfolk, VA: IEEE.

Navarro, E. O. (2005). *A survey of software engineering educational delivery methods and associated learning theories* (Technical Report No. UCI-ISR-05-5). Irvine, CA: University of California, Irvine.

Navarro, E. O. (2006). *SimSE: A software engineering simulation environment for software process education.* Ph.D. Dissertation, University of California, Irvine, Irvine, CA.

Navarro, E. O., & van der Hoek, A. (2005a). Design and evaluation of an educational software process simulation environment and associated model. In T. C. Lethbridge & D. Port (Eds.), *Proceedings of the eighteenth conference on software engineering education and training.* Ottawa, Canada: IEEE.

Navarro, E. O., & van der Hoek, A. (2005b). Scaling up: How thirty-two students collaborated and succeeded in developing a prototype software design environment. In T. C. Lethbridge & D. Port (Eds.), *Proceedings of the eighteenth conference on software engineering education and training.* Ottawa, Canada: IEEE.

Navarro, E. O., & van der Hoek, A. (2007). Comprehensive evaluation of an educational software engineering simulation environment. In H. Edwards & R. Narayanan (Eds.), *Proceedings of the twentieth conference on software engineering education and training.* Dublin, Ireland.

Nulden, U., & Scheepers, H. (2000). Understanding and learning about escalation: Simulation in action. In *Proceedings of the 3rd process simulation modeling workshop (prosim 2000).* London, United Kingdom.

Ohlsson, L., & Johansson, C. (1995). A practice driven approach to software engineering education. *IEEE Transactions on Education, 38*(3), 291-295.

Pfahl, D., Klemm, M., & Ruhe, G. (2000). Using system dynamics simulation models for software project management education and training. In *Proceedings of the 3rd process simulation modeling workshop (prosim 2000).* London, United Kingdom.

Reigeluth, C. M., & Rodgers, C. A. (1980). The elaboration theory of instruction: Prescriptions for task analysis and design. *NSPI Journal, 19*, 16-26.

Roblyer, M. D. (2005). *Integrating educational technology into teaching* (4th ed.). Upper Saddle River, NJ: Prentice Hall.

Schank, R. C. (1997). *Virtual learning.* New York, NY, USA: McGraw-Hill.

Schön, D. (1987). *Educating the reflective practitioner.* San Francisco, CA, USA: Jossey-Bass.

Sharp, H., & Hall, P. (2000). An interactive multimedia software house simulation for postgraduate software engineers. In *Proceedings of the 22nd international conference on software engineering* (pp. 688-691): ACM.

Stevens, S. M. (1989). Intelligent interactive video simulation of a code inspection. *Communications of the ACM, 32*(7), 832-843.

Tomayko, J. E. (1996). Carnegie Mellon's software development studio: A five year retrospective. In *Proceedings of the ninth conference on software engineering education and training* (pp. 119-129). Daytona Beach, FL, USA: IEEE.

van Eck, R. (2006). Digital game-based learning: It's not just the digital natives who are restless. *Educause Review, 41*(2), 17-30.

Wohlin, C., & Regnell, B. (1999). Achieving industrial relevance in software engineering education. In H. Saiedian (Ed.), *Proceedings of the twelfth conference on software engineering education and training* (pp. 16-25): IEEE Computer Society.

Section III
Innovative Teaching Methods

Chapter IV
Tasks in Software Engineering Education:
The Case of a Human Aspects of Software Engineering Course

Orit Hazzan
Technion - IIT, Israel

Jim Tomayko
Carnegie Mellon University, USA

ABSTRACT

The field of software engineering is multifaceted. Accordingly, students must be educated to cope with different kinds of tasks and questions. This chapter describes a collection of tasks that aim at improving students' skills in different ways. We illustrate our ideas by describing a course about human aspects of software engineering. The course objective is to increase learners' awareness with respect to problems, dilemmas, ethical questions, and other human-related situations that students may face in the software engineering world. We attempt to achieve this goal by posing different kinds of questions and tasks to the learners, which aim at enhancing their abstract thinking and expanding their analysis perspectives. The chapter is based on our experience teaching the course at Carnegie-Mellon University and at the Technion – Israel Institute of Technology.

INTRODUCTION

The complexity of software development environments is well known. This complexity includes technical aspects (such as IDEs and programming languages), cognitive aspects (for example, program comprehension) and social aspects of the profession (e.g., issues related to teamwork). As a result of this multifaceted nature, the discipline of software engineering requires that special attention be given to tasks executed by software engineering students.

This chapter presents a collection of tasks that can be integrated into software engineering education. The tasks presented here do not address software development activities (such as design or coding) but rather belong to peripheral topics related to the actual development of software. We suggest, however, that the discussion of these topics, when supported by students' engaging in a variety of tasks, has a direct influence on students' professional skills in general, and on their software development performance in particular.

We illustrate our ideas using a course on human aspects of software engineering. The course objective is to increase software engineering students' awareness of (a) the richness and complexity of various facets of the human aspect of software engineering and (b) problems, dilemmas, questions and conflicts that may arise with respect to human aspects of software engineering during the course of software development. The course is based on Tomayko and Hazzan (2004), and the tasks presented can be adapted to any software engineering course.

The Human Aspects of Software Engineering course is usually attended by senior undergraduate students or graduate students who already have some software development experience. Being an elective course, it is usually taught in a relatively small class setting. Indeed, as illustrated later on in the chapter, these course characteristics enable us to propose an interactive, hands-on and active teaching and learning style.

The importance attributed to active learning is based on the constructivist approach. Constructivism is a cognitive theory that examines the nature of learning processes. According to this approach, learners construct new knowledge by rearranging and refining their existing knowledge (cf. Davis, Maher and Nodding, 1990; Smith, diSessa and Roschelle, 1993). More specifically, the constructivism approach suggests that new knowledge is constructed *gradually,* based on the learner's existing mental structures and on feedback that the learner receives from the learning

environments. In this process, mental structures are developed in steps, each elaborating on the preceding ones; although, there may, of course, also be regressions and "blind alleys". This construction process is closely related to the Piagetian mechanisms of assimilation and accommodation (Piaget, 1977). One way to support such gradual mental constructions is by providing learners with a suitable learning environment in which they are *active*. The working assumption is that the feedback, provided by a learning environment in which learners learn a complex concept in an active way, supports mental constructions of the learned concepts.

In this chapter, we start by presenting the course structure and then focus on the ten kinds of tasks used throughout the course. We explain the nature of each kind of tasks and how it may improve students' skills as software engineers. We conclude with some suggestions for implementing our approach in other courses.

BACKGROUND: HUMAN ASPECTS OF SOFTWARE ENGINEERING-COURSE DESCRIPTION

This section describes the different topics addressed in the course on Human Aspects of Software Engineering by highlighting their importance from the learners' perspective.

Lesson 1—The Nature of Software Engineering: This lesson aims at increasing learners' awareness that the success or failure of software development stem mainly from people-centered reasons rather than from technology-related reasons. By inviting learners to analyze different development environments, we illustrate the effects of human interaction in software development processes.

Lesson 2—Software Engineering Methods: This lesson focuses on models of several software development methods including iterative, agile, and more. In this lesson, we highlight the human aspects of these software development methods.

Lesson 3—Working in Software Teams: Our aim in this lesson is to help learners comprehend the influence of team structures on the actual process of software development. In this lesson, we aim to expand learners' considerations when setting out to form software teams.

Lesson 4—Software as a Product: This lesson highlights the importance of the customers in software development environments and their significant role in discussions about human aspects of software development. Accordingly, special emphasis is put on different topics related to requirements (e.g., requirement management, gathering of requirements, and the understanding of requirements).

Lesson 5—Software Engineering Code of Ethics: In this lesson, learners are introduced to the concept of ethics in general, and to the Software Engineering Code of Ethics in particular. Our primary objective in this lesson is to teach students both how to identify situations in which ethical considerations should be integrated in software development processes (in addition to technical, financial and other considerations) and to perceive the Software Engineering Code of Ethics as a tool that can be used both in the identification of ethical dilemmas and in solving them.

Lesson 6—International and Cultural Perspectives on Software Engineering: This lesson highlights the potential influence of local events on the global high-tech industry, the influence of different cultures on software engineering processes, and the characteristics of software engineering processes in different places around the world. Diversity issues in the high-tech culture are addressed in this lesson as well.

Lesson 7—Different Perspectives on Software Engineering: The goal in this lesson is to increase learners' awareness to different perspectives on the discipline of software engineering, each of which emphasizes different aspects of the field. To this end, learners are introduced to different perspectives towards software engineering and are requested to examine which elements from each perspective fit their own perception of software engineering. The human aspect of software engineering is expressed by the fact that different practitioners in the field perceive the profession differently.

Lesson 8—The History of Software Engineering: It is important to introduce students to the history of software engineering since the nature of this historical process in some way reflects the nature of the field itself. Indeed, such connections are made during the course and on various occasions learners are asked to examine the influence of different events in the history of software engineering on the current status of the field. The main milestones of this history are highlighted, as are the interconnections among them.

Lesson 9—Program Comprehension, Code Inspections, and Refactoring: This lesson highlights the importance of programming style and its influence on program comprehension. Specifically, in this lesson, learners are encouraged to observe connections between programming style and the daily life of software developers, for example, with respect to code inspections and refactoring processes.

Lesson 10—Learning Processes in Software Engineering: In this lesson, software development processes are examined from a cognitive perspective with the intention of increasing learners' attention to learning processes in software engineering in general, and to a reflective mode of thinking in particular.

Lesson 11—Heuristics of Software Development: In this lesson, learners become aware of heuristics that can guide the performance of different activities throughout the process of software development. Specifically, the concept of abstraction and its relevance and contribution to software development processes are examined.

Lesson 12—Software as a Business: This lesson discusses several business-related issues in software engineering. Due to the significant influence of the Internet as a software-based system on world economy, this lesson also addresses connections between the Internet and the human aspects of software development.

Lesson 13—Case Studies in Software Engineering: In this lesson, students are presented with case studies which they are requested to examine according to the different theories presented thus far in the course. Similar to other disciplines that integrate case study analysis in the learning process, the target of this task is to use and apply theories in real-life situations.

Lesson 14—Students' Summary Projects and Presentations: In this lesson, students present case studies that they have constructed, reflect on the construction process of these case studies and present questions for discussion based on the case studies they have developed.

MAIN THRUST OF THE CHAPTER: KINDS OF QUESTIONS

As can be seen in the course description, the course addresses many topics related to the different human aspects of software engineering. It is, however, clearly impossible to cover all of the material cited in each topic within the framework of such a course. Indeed, it is not our intention to go into detail with respect to all of these topics. Rather, we aim to increase learners' awareness of these topics and to provide them with tools that will enable them to further their study of those subjects that they find interesting and relevant. One way to achieve this target is by giving the learners different kinds of tasks.

In what follows, we present ten kinds of questions we use for this purpose. For each category, we present its nature and illustrate it with several questions. For each illustrative question we indicate the learning stage at which it is presented (as a preparation question, during the learning process, or as a summary question) and explain how it may improve students' skills as software engineers in general, and their understanding of the human aspect of software engineering in particular.

Illustrative example: Before we present the ten kinds of questions, we present an illustrative example that comprises several kinds of questions. The question is presented first as a preparation question in Lesson 4, which examines software as a product and later on, the question is continued as a summary question in Lesson 12, which discusses software as a business. The students are given additional tasks with respect to each topic. The question is presented in Table 1.

This two-step task invites students to examine the process of requirement gathering from different perspectives by executing various kinds of tasks. First, the students are asked *to take the customer's perspective* – a perspective that they usually are not requested to adopt. As explained in the question and as explicitly explained to the students, such an experience has a value of its own. Second, the students are asked, as software developers, *to examine* the requirements they listed when acting as customers and to analyze their nature. Then, the students are asked *to compare* the list they generated with features of real, available, similar software tools. The aim of this experience is to illustrate, first, that a lot of information is available for the purpose of requirement elicitation and, second, that requirement gathering is a complex and multi-faceted process.

Table 1. Illustrative example

Step A: The question starts out as a preparation question for Lesson 4 – Software as a Product:

Question formulation:

1.   Students are usually given a list of requirements and are asked to develop a software system that meets these requirements. This task may help you reveal some of the problems involved in defining software requirements. For this purpose, you are asked to assume that you are a customer who needs a software system for web-based surveys.

   First, determine the kind of business you have. Based on this decision, define your requirements for the web-based system. Write these requirements as would a person who is not a software developer.

   After you finish listing the requirements, analyze them:
   - What kinds of requirements did you list (user-oriented, technical-oriented, performance-oriented, others)?
   - Compare your list with real web-based survey tools. Can you use existing tools as a resource for gathering requirements?

   This exercise is important for at least two reasons. First, you may at some time be a customer of software systems and will have to define the requirements of the software systems you need. Second, as a software developer, when you have real customers, such an experience may help you see the situation from the customer's point of view.

2.   .Based on your experience in §1, explain why requirement changes are so predominant in software engineering.

3.   Data indicate that the percentage of software tools that actually meet customers' needs is relatively low. Based on your experience in §1, explain this phenomenon.

Step B: The question continues as a summary question for Lesson 12 - Software as a Business:

Question formulation:

   This question continues the task presented in Lesson 4 - Software as a Product, in which you were asked to list requirements for an application that supports on-line surveys.

   - Expand the requirements list you constructed for the on-line survey so that it also includes a means for e-commerce.

   - How might the addition of these requirements influence the development process of the on-line survey tool?

In the second part of the task, the students are asked *to expand* the list that they originally generated. The idea is to illustrate that products can evolve in a gradual process, when customers either improve their understanding of their needs or when customer needs are expanded, and that additional features can be added to a software product as long as the development process supports the gradual addition of features. When the students add features, they are asked *to analyze* potential influences of this addition on the software development process.

In summary, throughout this task, the students *take the customer perspective*, *examine* and *ex-pand their own requirements list*, and *analyze* the connection between the process of requirement gathering and software development processes. It is reasonable to assume that such a collection of activities and perspectives that students take while working on this task, expand their perspective on software development processes in general, and increase their awareness of the human aspects of software engineering in particular.

We now present ten kinds of questions presented to the students during the course. Their contribution to student learning is illustrated by specific examples of questions taken from different course lessons. Questions that can be categorized into more than one kind of questions are presented in the category they best illustrate. We note that all kinds of questions can be presented at any stage of the course.

I. Review Questions

This kind of questions asks learners to examine and analyze the literature on a specific topic and to summarize their findings. Such a task has several purposes: First, when working on such tasks, learners develop a sense of the huge extent of resources available to them when they wish to learn about an unfamiliar topic. Second, learners realize that when they are stuck, with no idea of how to proceed, they can just look for information; as soon as they see what is available on the problem topic, the picture becomes clearer. Third, as opposed to passively sitting in a lecture hall listening to a lecture, the mental constructions built during such a process are significant for the learning process of the topic about which information is sought.

Example 1: Lesson 2
Software Engineering Methods,
Summary Question

There are several inherent problems in software development. If you are not familiar with them, just search the web using a phrase such as "problems with software development". Select the five problems that are, in your opinion, the most critical problems in software development and explain how each of the software development methods discussed in this lesson helps solve them.

We will address this question on three levels: On the first level, it is clear that even a brief search will highlight the fact that there are many problems in software development. On the second level, addressing this question may illustrate to students that the problems they face are common in the community of software engineering

professionals. Finally, they may observe that most of the problems are related to human aspects of software engineering and that, if they increase their awareness of this characteristic, they can improve their understanding and performance in the field.

Example 2: Lesson 1
The Nature of Software Engineering,
Preparation Question

How did the term "software engineering" come into being?

When students are asked to answer such a question before hearing the answer in the lecture, their awareness might increase with respect to several facts. First, they may observe that the concept of software engineering was not invented in one day, but rather, it was a process that led to the establishment of the field. Second, when delving into the details, students may recognize that many of the same problems that characterized the field in its early days still exist today. Such an acknowledgment reflects very clearly the complexity of the problems with which the field deals. Third, the students are required to examine the field of software engineering as a profession with its own life cycle. We suggest that a task of this kind enriches students' perspective of their profession, and that this perspective is broader than the perspective students form if they passively hear about the establishment of the field of software engineering from their instructor in class.

II. Concept-Exploration Questions

In these questions, students are asked to explore new terms and to examine their connection to software engineering. Such an examination, we suggest, may increase learners' awareness of both the uniqueness of the field of software engineering and its dynamic nature. In addition, such understanding may enrich the students' perspective with respect to their own professional development in the field.

Example 3: Lesson 10
Learning Processes in Software
Engineering, Preparation Question

Search the Web for the concept "learning organization". Describe the essence of this concept in a few sentences. What direct implications does it have for software engineering processes?

In this question, students are asked to learn a new topic (in this case "learning organization") and to analyze its connection to the profession of software engineering. It is suggested that this skill (that is, the ability to analyze how a new topic is connected to one's profession) is extremely important in the case of software engineering since software engineering is a relatively young field with many buzzwords whose meaning and targets are not always clear. Thus, one's ability to recognize potential connections (as well as the ability to decide that no relationships exist) is particularly important in our profession.

III. Opinion Questions

These questions require the students to give their opinion about a specific concept or situation. Usually, such questions are presented as preparation questions that aim at fostering learners' thinking about the topic to be learned.

Example 4: Lesson 5
Code of Ethics of Software
Engineering, Preparation Question

In your opinion and based on your familiarity with the notion of ethics, does the community of software engineering need a code of ethics? If "yes" - explain why. What principles should it be based on? What topics should it address? If "no" - explain and defend your opinion.

This question is presented to the students before they are introduced to the software engineering code of ethics, but after they have been exposed to the concept of ethics. Thus, on the one hand, they can ponder the application of the concept with respect to software engineering, while, on the other hand, not being influenced by the details of the code, to which they will be exposed later. We suggest presenting this question at this stage (that is, before the students become familiar with the software engineering code of ethics itself) for at least three reasons. First, at this stage, students can examine, for themselves, what values they, as individuals, appreciate in the context of software engineering. Second, at a later stage, they will be able to compare their personal perspective with that which is reflected in the software engineering code of ethics that was formulated by a committee representing the community of software engineers. Third, working on such an activity opens the students up to the idea that they are part of a professional community, which, perhaps, needs additional documents to unify its members. Thus, they may enhance their personal perception as software engineering professionals.

IV. Reflective Questions

Being a reflective practitioner (Schön, 1983, 1987) is an important advantage for software engineers, since a reflective mode of thinking can increase one's performance in the field beyond the application of previous experience. This mode of thinking has already been pursued in the context of software engineering (cf. Cockburn, 2001; Hazzan, 2002; Kerth, 2001). We illustrate here how it can be integrated into software engineering *education*.

Example 5: Lesson 4
Software as a Product,
Summary Question

Visit a company (a software house or any other company). Observe how people communicate and behave in that company. Identify a situation in the company workflow that can be improved by a computational tool. Create a requirements list for this tool. Interview different people in the organization about this list of requirements.

Analyze and reflect: Are their impressions consistent with yours? Have they suggested any improvements? How would you improve the requirements list based on these interviews?

This question aims at increasing the students' awareness that there multiple opinions exist with respect to software products. Accordingly, this question suggests the option of asking different peoples' opinion before making final decisions. The reflective task that concludes the question invites the students to rethink the entire process and see how its outcome can be used to improve their product. Such a task, if conducted (and reflected on) properly, shows the students that being a reflective practitioner can improve one's professional performances.

V. Analysis Tasks

In these tasks, learners are requested to analyze vast information related to software development processes. The questions aim at increasing learners' awareness to the availability of this information as well as to different ways in which its analysis may be useful to them as software engineers.

Example 6: Lesson 6
International Perspective on Software Engineering, In-Process Question

The following tasks examine the NASDAQ (National Association of Securities Dealers Automated Quotation) during the decade 1997-2007.

1. Select five years during this decade. For each year, find what countries had software

companies listed on NASDAQ. What does this list of countries say about the NASDAQ and about the international market during those years?

2. Examine the years 1999, 2000, 2001, and 2002 closely: Select four months in each year and compare the NASDAQ level for those months. What trends can you observe? How can you explain them?

This question deals with an important characteristic of software companies: their market value. It also, however, looks at the financial aspect of software development from both local and global viewpoints. The first part of the question asks the students to find out which countries played a major role in specific years. Such an examination may draw their attention to the fact that their local market is not the only player in this game. The second part of the question aims at improving students' ability to identify trends and patterns in data provided to them. It is important that these two messages are delivered to software engineers.

VI. Design Questions

In these questions, learners are asked to take an active role in the design process of the field of software engineering, a relatively young field that is still being shaped. Accordingly, the target of these tasks is to convey the message that, in the future, the learners may influence the way the field is shaped, its norms, its principles and the work habits of its practitioners.

Example 7: Lesson 1
The Nature of Software Engineering, Further-Review Task

Two case studies are presented. Then the following question is presented: Based on these two case studies, construct the principles of the ideal work place for software development.

This task is presented in the early stages of the course (Lesson 1). It is hoped that this mode of thinking will guide the students throughout the entire course. This message is further pursued in future lessons as the following task illustrates.

Example 8: Lesson 10
Learning Processes in Software
Engineering, Summary Question

Suppose you establish a software startup. Work on the following tasks:

1. *Describe the startup.*
2. *Lay out the basic activities you would set up in order to make it a learning organization.*
3. *Discuss what may happen if these activities are not set up when the startup is founded but rather a year later.*

This task asks the students to think as independent people, who may at some time in the future found their own company. It aims at conveying the ideas that there are decisions to be made prior to the establishment of a company, that such a construction process should be thoughtful, and that many of the decisions made at the early stages of the company might have a significant and direct influence on its future. The task achieves its goal by inviting the students to consider different approaches to dealing with a given situation, while exploring the different outcomes of each action.

VII. Scenario Analysis

The target of this kind of tasks is to let learners analyze situations they may encounter in software development processes. The underlying assumption is that the actual working on such tasks, as well as the class discussion that may follow it, can broaden the learners' perspective of possible approaches to specific situations in software development environments.

Example 9: Lesson 5
Code of Ethics of Software
Engineering, Preparation Task

Following are several cases related to software engineering. With respect to each scenario, express your opinion on the behavior described and explain how you would behave in such a case. Then, according to your decision, formulate one or more ethical norms that, in your opinion, should be included in the Software Engineering Code of Ethics. These norms should guide software developers in making their decisions in similar cases.

[The task includes several cases; for illustration purposes we present only one.]

Scenario One: Not Telling the Entire Truth
A programmer is asked to make a change in a software application used by an international bank. She performs all of the required tests. After all the tests passed, she recalls that one more test is required. This test does not pass. Since she does not have the time required for debugging, she submits her work and states that all the tests passed successfully.

As described above, the target of these tasks is to let students deal, during their studies, with situations they may encounter in the future. This kind of activity is further elaborated in the tenth kind of tasks, in which the students are asked to analyze scenarios that they have constructed.

VIII. Connection Questions

In these questions, learners are asked to discuss connections between different topics discussed in the course. The idea is to increase learners' awareness of such connections so that they will not perceive the different topics discussed in the course as isolated concepts. Indeed, the complexity that characterizes software development processes can be partially explained by the fact that the different factors involved in this process may have a mutual influence.

Example 10: Lesson 12
Software as a Business,
Preparation Questions

Suggest possible connections between e-commerce and the Software Engineering Code of Ethics.

Since there are so many ethical issues related to on-line communication, it is impossible to review them all in depth in one or two lessons. This question helps minimize the gap and, at the same time, enables students to consider the topic from the perspective of its connections to a topic that has been previously discussed in the course – the Software Engineering Code of Ethics. Students' work on this task serves as a basis for a subsequent class discussion.

IX. Research Oriented Questions

The aim of these questions is to let the students experience using some research tools they may employ in their future work for different purposes, such as information gathering and improving organizational processes.

Example 11: Lesson 3
Working in Software Teams,
Summary Question

Record one of your team meetings that is dedicated to solving a particular problem. Listen to the cassette and analyze the meeting: Did all participants contribute to the discussion? Did someone discourage the introduction of new ideas? At what points would you steer the meeting differently? Illustrate your analysis by quoting excerpts from the meeting.

Summarize: Did the meeting achieve its aims? Could it have been managed more efficiently? If so, how?

This question has several targets. First, it shows the students that it is possible to learn about processes within their teams and that careful examination of such processes can improve team management. Second, working on such a task highlights the idea that the effectiveness of meeting can be improved when the needed attention, that such an improvement requires, is given. Finally, the students experience using a simple tool that can be used also in other situations and for other purposes.

Example 12: Lesson 9
Program Comprehension,
Code Inspections, and Refactoring,
Summary Question

Write two computer programs that execute the same task such that the programming style of the first requires the addition of many comments in order to understand it, whereas the second program requires no comments (or almost no comments) for its comprehension.

a. *Give each program to a student/software engineer and ask them to explain the program they received. Observe and document the processes used by each. Draw appropriate conclusions.*

b. *Ask each of the two programmers to make the same modification in the program. Trace the change process in each case. What are your conclusions?*

c. *Select one or more qualitative research tools described in Lesson 4 - Software as a Product. Design a small-scale research outline that examines the influence of specific programming style guidelines on the way programmers develop a computer program. Conduct the research and describe your conclusions.*

This question is composed of two focused parts – (a) and (b) – and a more open part – (c). The first two parts aim at highlighting the influence of programming style on program comprehension processes. The third part requires the students to be creative and to plan a small research project for a specific target. It is hoped that such an experience will show the students, first, that there are cases in which a small-scale research is needed and, second, that they are equipped with the tools required to conduct such a research study.

X. Building Case Studies / Story Telling

These questions ask students to construct scenarios and case studies, based on their personal experience as well as on what has been learned and discussed in the course. The scope of the cases varies: from short and focused stories to vast narratives that encompass multiple aspects of software engineering. These tasks have several advantages. First, students must consider what is important, as well as less important, to include in the case study. Second, they must integrate different issues related to software engineering into a single story. Third, they must analyze what they have constructed, an activity that once again enhances their awareness of different topics related to software engineering. In what follows, we illustrate the application of these ideas with respect to stories of different scopes.

Example 13: Lesson 5
Software Engineering Code of Ethics, Intermediate-Stage Question

Suggest a situation in software development in which a team of software developers must make the decision whether or not to report to their management about a bug in a specific software tool they developed. What does the code of ethics say in such cases? How would you behave in such a case?

This task focuses on ethical issues. It asks the students to create a scenario that focuses on a particular case. It illustrates how small details determine the nature of the situation. When such a task is repeated with respect to different topics, this message is emphasized and highlighted.

Example 14: Lesson 5
Software Engineering Code of Ethics, Summary Question

Compose a story that raises ethical considerations. Interview software engineers about this case. Ask them to express their opinion and predicted behavior in such a case. Analyze their reactions. Are all of the reactions similar? How do they differ from each other and from your opinion? What do these reactions imply with respect to software development? What lessons will you take with you from this experience to your future development of software?

This task illustrates another way in which case studies can be used for educational purposes. Specifically, based on a story that the students develop, they carry out a small-scale research that explores different opinions related to software engineering processes.

Example 15: End of the Course Task, Case Study Construction and Analysis

At the end of the course, the students are asked to construct and analyze a case study following a process that guides them in their case-study construction. The process is outlined in the Appendix to this chapter. The target of this task is to integrate all of the material learned in the course and to enable the students to express their perspective on the variety of topics learned in the course.

FUTURE TRENDS

We now propose several suggestions for the continuation of the work presented in this chapter:

Evaluation: This chapter is organized by kinds of tasks. The actual influence of these tasks is now being examined in a qualitative research project that examines the multi-faceted contribution of these questions to students' awareness with respect to the different topics addressed in the course. In particular, we are exploring the development of this awareness, as well as its influence on students' perception of the discipline of software engineering.

Other categorizations: The tasks given to the students in the Human Aspects of Software Engineering course are presented in this chapter according to the kind of task the students are required to carry out. Naturally, there are other ways of categorizing the different tasks students work on during the course. One such categorization is by the learning target of the questions; another is by the mental processes employed when working on the tasks.

CONCLUSION

We conclude with some suggestions related to the application of the ideas presented in this chapter to other software engineering courses. In general, we propose that most kinds of tasks presented in this chapter can be applied in many software engineering courses.

We suggest that the tasks presented in this chapter, can contribute to students' professional skills while dealing with the challenges of the profession of software engineering. In particular, we suggest introducing questions of the kinds presented in this chapter in courses that:

- Aim at improving students' analytical skills, reflection processes and problem-solving abilities using a learning approach that enables the students to formulate their perspectives and explore resources on which to base their points of view.
- Aim at illustrating to students the multi-faceted nature of the profession of software engineering, in a way that guides them to seek for different points of view, controversial issues, and dilemmas and conflicts with which they will have to cope in the future.
- aim at basing the lessons on student interactions that encourage them to learn from their peers and experience teamwork and information sharing.

In our opinion, many of the courses taught in software engineering programs should target these issues. We hope that our contribution is be in the presentation of a collection of kinds of questions that can be used in order to achieve these goals.

NOTE

This chapter is dedicated to my colleague Jim Tomayko, my co-author of *Human Aspects of*

Software Engineering (2004), who passed away in January 2006.

REFERENCES

Cockburn, A. (2001). *Agile Software Development,* Addison-Wesley Pub Co.

Davis, R. B., Maher, C. A. and Noddings, N. (1990, eds.). Constructivist views on the teaching and learning of mathematics, *Journal for Research in Mathematics Education,* Monograph Number 4, The National Council of Teachers of Mathematics, Inc.

Hazzan, O. (2002). The reflective practitioner perspective in software engineering education, *The Journal of Systems and Software* **63**(3), pp. 161-171.

Kerth, N. (2001). *Project Retrospectives: A Handbook for Team Reviews,* Dorset House Publishing Company.

Piaget, J. (1977). Problems of Equilibration. In Appel, M. H and Goldberg, L. S. (1977). *Topics in Cognitive Development, Volume 1: Equilibration: Theory, Research and Application,* Plenum Press, NY, pp. 3-13.

Schön, D. A. (1983). *The Reflective Practitioner,* BasicBooks.

Schön, D. A. (1987). *Educating the Reflective Practitioner: Towards a New Design for Teaching and Learning in The Profession,* San Francisco: Jossey-Bass.

Smith, J. P., diSessa, A. A. and Roschelle, J. (1993). Misconceptions reconceived: A constructivist analysis of knowledge in transition, *The Journal of the Learning Sciences* **3**, pp. 115-163.

Tomayko, J. and Hazzan, O. (2004). *Human Aspects of Software Engineering,* Charles River Media.

APPENDIX – SIX STAGES OF CASE STUDY CONSTRUCTION

(Source: Tomayko and Hazzan, 2004, pp. 286-287)

Step 1. Select a topic: Think about a topic that you find interesting and relevant for you to discuss.

Step 2. Analyze the nature of the topic: In this stage, you are asked to check whether the topic you wish to focus on has enough heft to be at the center of a case study. Ask yourself questions such as:

- What software development activities are connected to the selected topic?
- Which players, that participate in software development environments, are connected to the topic?
- What human aspects of software engineering does the topic address?
- Is the topic connected to the individual in the team or to the team as an entity?

If your answers to the above questions indicate that the topic is indeed "rich" enough and can be connected to different issues in software development environments, it might be suitable as a central topic for a case study.

Step 3. Imagine possible situations: Envision at least two situations in software engineering in which the topic may be relevant. The idea is to see whether there are specific situations in software engineering in which the topic you wish to pursue has a significant expression.

Step 4. Write the case study: Start writing the selected case study. Try to make it as vivid as possible without forgetting to include the main issues you wish to address.

Step 5. Check the scope of the case study: After completing the first draft (and editing) of the case study, check whether other related topics can be added to the case. Make sure you do not change the focus of the case study. Then, check issues such as: Is the main message you wanted to convey in this case study reflected properly? Are the connections between the different topics addressed in the case study clear?

Step 6. Develop questions about the case study: Develop stimulating questions that can be explored with respect to the case study you just developed.

Chapter V
Speaking of Software:
Case Studies in Software Communication

Ann Brady
Michigan Technological University, USA

Marika Seigel
Michigan Technological University, USA

Thomas Vosecky
Michigan Technological University, USA

Charles Wallace
Michigan Technological University, USA

ABSTRACT

We describe our recent efforts to generate and use case studies to teach communication skills in software development. We believe our work is innovative in several respects. The case studies touch on rhetorical issues that are crucial to software development yet not commonly associated with the field of software engineering. Moreover, they present students with complex, problematic situations, rather than sanitized post hoc interpretations often associated with case study assignments. The case study project is an interdisciplinary collaboration that interweaves the expertise of software engineers and technical communicators. Our software engineering and technical communication curricula have been enhanced through this cross-fertilization.

OVERVIEW

We argue that the art of *communication*, in its oral and written forms, is given relatively little attention in software engineering education, despite its fundamental importance in software development. Two major problems appear to prevent a more thorough treatment of communication issues. First, although software engineers may be effective communicators, they typically do not have practice in articulating what it is that makes communication effective (or ineffective). That is, their knowledge remains at a tacit level, from which it is difficult to impart it to students. Second, part of what makes communication in the software workplace difficult is its intricacy and subtlety—"the devil is in the details". Students will not be convinced by toy examples; only realistic stories of software development will suffice. Yet the prospect of creating a communication setting of appropriate scale seems overwhelming.

Our ongoing interdisciplinary work seeks to address both of these problems. It utilizes the expertise of technical communicators, who are well versed in discussing and analyzing communication. Equipped with examples from software engineering, empirical techniques from ethnography, and analytical techniques from rhetoric, we have created *case studies* for teaching communication skills in software development, and we have used the case studies in upper-level courses in both software engineering and technical communication. Here we use the term "case study" not in its sense as a research tool in the social sciences, but rather in its sense as a *pedagogical* tool, currently used most prominently in law and business schools. Our case studies are based on the experiences of real software engineering students engaged in their capstone projects. The associated instructional materials touch on rhetorical issues not usually associated with software engineering: audience, active listening, critical analysis, timing, and planning. Moreover, they present students with complex, problematic situations, rather than sanitized *post hoc* interpretations often associated with case study assignments.

The case study project is an interdisciplinary collaboration that interweaves the expertise of software engineers and technical communicators. Our software engineering curriculum has been enhanced through this cross-fertilization—both by the insights into communication and by the qualitative methods employed in generating the cases. We report on the success of the project to date and describe some of the future directions we envision for this work.

MOTIVATION

We believe there is a significant gulf between the skills that students practice in academia and the skills they must use in the workplace. In this section, we show that practicing software developers acknowledge the importance of communication skills and expect new employees to have them. We then turn to the current state of software engineering education and comment on the status of communication skills in academia.

Communication in the Software Workplace

Within the lifespan of a single project, software engineers must engage with a wide range of stakeholders, with very different perspectives and goals (Poole, 2003). They must carefully elicit requirements from clients and keep them apprised of budget or scheduling changes. They must consult with end users to design products that provide both ease and value. They must also communicate within their development team, to maintain a clear vision of how to divide the labor and how to handle the project risks.

Stepping up from the level of individual projects to survey the software development landscape, we find an astounding variety of applications. No other engineered product has such a diverse set of potential uses. With this diversity of uses comes a diversity of stakeholders. In the span of a career, a software developer moves from project to project—and most likely from firm to firm—at each step negotiating a new application and a new set of stakeholders with widely varying knowledge, requirements, and communication styles.

Several studies point to deficiencies in requirements as the primary cause of large-scale project failures (Curtis, Krasner, & Iscoe, 1988; Davis, 1990; Glass, 1998). This can be traced to a lack of commitment and trust between customer and developer. Developers consider risks such as "failure to gain user commitment" and "lack of adequate user involvement" more important than such serious risks as "introduction of new technology" and "insufficient/inappropriate staffing" (Keil, Cule, Lyytinen, & Schmidt, 1998). This evidence indicates the need for improved communication during requirements elicitation and analysis.

Of course, communication issues are also a source of conflict within the development team. Demonstration of social skill sets—"the 'good communication skills' often referred to in job postings" (Reinsch & Shelby, 1997)—is now explicitly required of new workers (Muir, 2004). While intra-team conflicts are often viewed as management or organizational behavior issues, many researchers have identified them as inherently communicative (Putnam & Folger, 1988; Putnam & Poole, 1987; Schultz & Anderson, 1984). Regardless of whether the conflict is rooted in the actions of management, the behavior of individuals, or deficiencies in communication, improving communication skills is one way to avoid conflict in the first place, or resolve it should it occur. Discussing the skills students need to negotiate work conflicts early in their careers, Myers and Larson state that "[a] communicative understanding of conflict can facilitate students' transition to full-time employment by helping students to interpret the nature or types of conflicts employees experience in organizations" (Myers & Larson, 2005).

A survey of software engineering professionals (McMillan & Rajaprabhakaran, 1999) ranks four software engineering project features based on what they felt was most important for professional development. The first two, respectively, are "working with real users" and "developing a working prototype." This highlights the importance of client communication, essential to both these aspects of development. Student work often suffers when communication skills taught in class are not applied during their coursework both in communicating with their project teams and with their instructor (Liu, 2005).

Communication in a software setting is essentially problematic, for a number of reasons. Software development is complex, due not only to the functionality of the software itself, but also to the competing and often conflicting goals of different stakeholders. Software engineering is a nascent field, without a time-honored, universal lexicon. The wide range of application areas draws together stakeholders with different backgrounds and little in the way of a common vocabulary. Moreover, software developers work in a world of incomplete, imperfect information. While they can access the internals of the machine through the precision of computer languages, they must work through the less mechanical channel of human language to understand the needs and desires of other stakeholders. For these reasons, instruction in communication strategies requires grounding in realistic contexts that reflect and simulate these difficulties.

Communication in Software Engineering Education

We believe that the process of communicating about software is not given sufficient attention in software engineering education, given its importance and its difficulty. Instruction in communicating with other stakeholders and documenting software is typically the role of ancillary courses in technical communication, taught through departments outside of software engineering. While these courses offer an important introduction to effective means of workplace communication, a single class cannot provide the extensive practice in the variety of discipline-specific contexts needed to prepare software engineering students adequately.

The precision of programming languages and computer hardware is comforting to students and educators in the computing disciplines, but that very comfort can lull students away from looking at the human problems that motivate software development in the first place. The process of interacting with human stakeholders is often seen as "soft" material, not worthy of serious attention. Of the software engineering education contributions to the SIGCSE and CSEET conferences in recent years, only a handful of papers address issues of communication between humans in software development.

Part of the difficulty here is that the communicative skills that developers acquire on the job remain in a tacit form; by and large, there is no "explicit formulation of rules" (Freedman, 1993b). Addressing the gulf between the workplace and academia, Alred (Alred, 2006) suggests that "[t]he workplace requires practitioners to seek fundamentally different ways of responding to their contexts and exigencies—ways that do not require them, for example, to document either their intellectual processes or establish concurrence with scholarly or any other literature".

It is interesting to see how the issue of communication is treated in the *IEEE Software Body of Knowledge (SWEBOK)* (Abran, Moore, Bourque, & Dupuis, 2004). In the "Software Requirements" section, it states that "[o]ne of the fundamental tenets of good software engineering is that there be good communication between software users and software engineers". In the section on "Project management" – a "related discipline" outside of software engineering itself – it notes that "[c]ommunication management is also often mentioned as an overlooked but major aspect of the performance of individuals in a field where precise understanding of user needs and of complex requirements and designs is necessary".

Clearly, there is some ambivalence in the SWEBOK about the role of communication. On one hand, it does include language emphasizing the importance of communication in the software process. "Communication management" is even cited as an "overlooked" aspect. Yet it is not clear that the SWEBOK helps to raise the prominence of communication. Only communication between users and developers is included within the bounds of "software engineering"; all other types of communication (including intra-team communication) are relegated to an ancillary area. Locating communication outside of software engineering encourages the *status quo* of "outsourcing" communication to other departments, rather than dealing with it in the context of the software engineering curriculum.

VISION AND APPROACH

We have a vision of a new curriculum where communication is a core skill, tightly integrated with the other aspects of software engineering, rather than a stand-alone topic taught outside of the discipline. With such a curriculum, software engineering students will become not only creative designers and thoughtful analysts but also effective communicators. Empowering students to participate in active communication will make them more engaged in their profession and less prone to frustration and burnout. Furthermore, students with skills and interest in communication, who seek more than a cubicle-centered "programming" view of software development, will be attracted to the field. Margolis and Fisher indicate that many female students seek grounding in meaningful applications and become disillusioned with computer-centrism (Margolis & Fisher, 2002). Focusing on real software problems will likely attract those students who prefer "computing with a purpose".

To pursue this vision, we have assembled an interdisciplinary team of software engineers and technical communicators. We benefit from the experience our technical communicators have in preparing students for communication challenges. Here we explore the role of technical communication, rhetoric, and the value of case studies.

Technical Communication

The practice of technical writing can be traced from the fifth century BCE, through the Middle Ages, and into the Industrial Revolution (Tebeaux & Killingsworth, 1992). Its systematic instruction in the United States began after the Civil War (Connors, 2004). Histories of technical communication generally identify the Second World War as the birth of the profession, when the boom of wartime technologies triggered a corresponding boom in documentation that would facilitate dissemination and operation—and also necessitated a new class of workers to write and compile this documentation. Realizing that it was not profitable to hire engineers to both design and write, Westinghouse, General Motors, and General Electric developed their own in-house technical writing departments, and technical writing was finally recognized in the United States as a field of its own.

Early courses in technical communication were grounded in what has been called a "windowpane" view of language (Miller, 1979). According to this view, the technical communicator's role (whether that technical communicator is a professional in technical communication or a software developer who will work with technical communication genres as part of her profession) is to render technical information as clearly and transparently as possible. The problem with this view of technical communication is the implicit assumption that it is possible to attain a technical language that is universally clear and transparent. A corollary to this thesis is that any difficulties in deciphering such language are due to inadequacies of the reader or listener, not with the assumptions that underlie the presentation of the information. The windowpane view of technical communication assumes that meaning is transmitted unilaterally from sender to receiver rather than negotiated between them.

Particularly within the latter half of the twentieth century, technical communication scholars have argued for a more rhetorical and humanistic approach to teaching and practicing technical communication. For example, in her landmark article "A Humanistic Rationale for Technical Writing" (Miller, 1979), Miller argues that it is "the common opinion that [it] is a 'skills' course with little or no humanistic value is the result of a lingering but pervasive positivistic view of science... an efficient way of coercing minds to submit to reality". Consequently, students in technical communication courses tend to look upon writing as a "superfluous, bothersome, and usually irrelevant aspect of their technical work". As a corrective, Miller recommends that we "teach technical or scientific writing, not as a set of techniques for accommodating slippery words to intractable things, but as an understanding of how to belong to a community... to write well is to understand the conditions of one's own participation—the concepts, values, traditions and style which permit identification with that community and determine the success or failure of communication." Even more recently, scholars have begun to focus on genres surrounding software documentation and development, noting parallels between approaches to usability testing and research and a rhetorical view of communication. Like rhetorical approaches to communication, usability focuses on different types of audiences and the particular contexts within which they work and the purposes to which documentation will be put rather than positing a universal decontextualized user for whom expert, system knowledge must be "dumbed down" (Johnson-Eiola, 2001; Johnson, 1998).

Such a rhetorically grounded approach to technical communication, we believe, promises to make students more successful communicators when they enter the workplace. Rather than learning arhetorical, rote approaches to technical communication genres, students learn to strategically engage with and manipulate those genres according to the audiences, purposes, and contexts within which and with which they are working.

Rhetoric

In this project, we have a particular approach to communication grounded in theories and practices of rhetoric. While the term "rhetoric" has acquired a negative meaning of "[l]anguage that is elaborate, pretentious, insincere, or intellectually vacuous", we use an older definition: "[t]he art or study of using language effectively and persuasively" (Pickett, 2004). More precisely, we define rhetoric as *strategic communication*. Software developers are frequently confronted with challenges that can only be met through careful communication: for instance, understanding the typical use of a software product in the workplace, assessing user satisfaction with a prototype, or breaking the bad news about a missed deadline. Successful communication requires a strategy informed by an awareness of audience, a broad knowledge of potential genres, and sensitivity to the effects of style.

We see, in fact, a clean fit between rhetoric and software engineering. The software engineering student, like the rhetorician, can rely on the arts of knowing how to inquire, what questions to ask, in particular situations to make appropriate communications for a variety of audiences. When students are introduced to case studies, they are exposed to communication problems that can be analyzed and understood using these rhetorical principles.

Revealing to software engineering students the complexity of the rhetorical situation is the first step in teaching them to communicate strategically (Johnson, 1998). Software engineers produce much more than source code — design documentation, user guides, memos to management or other team members, to name just a few examples — and they must learn how to consider the broad contexts of use within which their products reside. For example, communication in a small start-up will be significantly different from that in a large corporation since institutions and disciplines constrain and define how it is carried

out. In a small, recently founded company, the communication system is likely to be organized in a "flat" manner; employees are likely to know one another and thus to communicate more directly and without regard to established protocols. Those working in larger and more established organizations may be required to communicate through a hierarchy of established channels. As another example, domestic communication practices will not necessarily work in international contexts, since cultures and historical legacies direct and shape organizational and stylistic conventions. Software engineering students who understand these subtleties are better prepared to work with fellow members of development teams as well as with both domestic and international stakeholders.

Rhetoric also offers software engineering students a practical understanding of communication as a *problem solving* process and gives them strategies for moving systematically toward a solution (Deili, 1988; Flower, 1998). While the term "problem" has a precise and time-honored meaning in the theory of computation, here we consider problems of a different sort—human-centered, not prone to mathematical formalization. Nevertheless, as software engineers venture into complicated contexts of communication, they can call upon a highly recognizable array of techniques from the problem-solving model. Specifically, rhetoric divides planning into stages: *invention, arrangement, style,* and *delivery*. This breakdown into stages is particularly useful for teaching students to engage in active listening and critical analysis.

The first stage of planning, invention, is perhaps the most important since it sets the requirements for the following three. It offers students a method for gathering information about how to communicate most effectively with particular audiences in specific contexts and is based on four sets of questions. The first question set focuses on audience. It poses questions about the characteristics of the stakeholders, about their attitudes toward the information that the students will communicate, and about the knowledge they might possess that could be useful in the development of the software. The second question set focuses on purpose. Here, students must consider what their aim is in communicating with their stakeholders—to learn, teach, inform, or persuade. Rhetoric also provides students with a way of knowing more than the needs of an audience and the problems of communicating with it. Problems do not exist in a vacuum but reside within given contexts that shape not only the problem, but the eventual solutions, as well. The next set of questions thus requires that student focus on the context in which the communication will occur and can suggest limitations to what the students intend to communicate, such as a short turn-around or steep learning curve. Answers to these questions can affect the way students organize their information or the format they chose to convey it. The final question set requires that students focus on themselves as communicators and how they aim to be perceived by their stakeholders—as problem solvers, investigators, facilitators, experts.

Decisions about the other three stages—arrangement, style, and delivery—are contingent on answers to questions posed in the first planning stage of invention, but are, nevertheless, themselves crucial to carrying out effective communication. The way that students arrange information, for instance, depends upon stakeholders' attitudes about the information and the students' purpose in conveying it. The style students choose to use—formal, informal, technical, colloquial—depends on both how they wish to be perceived, as well as their stakeholders' roles in the project. How students deliver the information—in an informal memo or more formal report—depends on the contexts in which users will apply the information.

To highlight the overlap and intersection of these stages, we use the metaphor of *communication cycles* (Johnson, 1998) to describe the various documents that record and communicate the software development process. For instance, a typical cycle would include several technical communication document genres that help to manage a project: an initial problem statement memo, followed by a project proposal, then a series of weekly progress reports that describe the successes and difficulties encountered as the project proceeds. Often, these exigencies will be cycled back to the problem statement and proposal, refining and adapting them in an iterative process. Finally, as the project comes to a close, participants generate a transmittal report and an oral presentation that explain the history and outcomes of the project to managers, clients, and teachers.

Case Studies

Typically, it is impractical to involve large numbers of students in real projects with real stakeholders. Students who do not participate in project-oriented courses get no exposure to the issues surrounding such communication, and those who do are thrust into a highly risky and sensitive situation with little previous guidance. Many in technical communication and software engineering have reported the value of students acquiring real-world experience in the workplace while at the same time lamenting the constraints: limited time and availability of internships, expense, and less than appropriate assignments once in the field (Blakeslee, 2001; Freedman, 1993a; Freedman, Adam, & Smart, 1994; Lave & Wenger, 1991).

These constraints can be relieved with the use of case studies in the classroom, where they can be guided by the instructor (Williams & Colomb, 1993). The use of case studies to simulate stakeholder interaction has a long history, and has been shown to be beneficial to both students and teachers (Christensen, 1987; Gale, 1993). Speaking from the perspective of business education, Fulmer claims that the case method helps to develop "skills of analysis, including learning how to ask the right questions, decision making, and persuasion" (Fulmer, 1992). The skills that Fulmer describes are clearly rhetorical skills.

Two reported deficiencies of case studies are their lack of immediacy and their failure to present compelling, realistic situations (Gale, 1993). While acknowledging the importance of case studies in pre-professional communications programs, Dorn's analysis of case studies from business education (Dorn, 1999) finds that case-based instruction may be of limited usefulness in the workplace: "[the cases] typically require students to respond to exceptional rhetorical situations when in reality the rhetorical situations writers usually face require more mundane and standardized types of discourse". For example, a common case study in technical communication focuses on the communication failures that led to the destruction of the space shuttle *Challenger* in 1986. While this is surely a compelling story, the circumstances are not likely to be encountered by many entry-level employees. Below, we describe a means to overcome these difficulties to create interesting cases that reflect the processes of undergraduate student projects.

CREATING THE CASES

The case studies we have assembled draw from ethnography and rhetoric—fields closely allied with technical communication. Here we explain how we found rich stories of communication close to home, and how we gathered and composed them.

Locating the Source

The goal of building case studies for use in teaching is often hampered by the secrecy surrounding most software development. While many of our students and most of our faculty have had experiences in industry- or government-sponsored development, the proprietary nature of this information has typically prevented them

from sharing their experiences. We do, however, have one valuable and readily available source: the students themselves. All Software Engineering students take the "Senior Design Project" capstone course. In this course, senior students develop real, practical software products intended for actual use in accordance with requirements from real clients and other stakeholders. These projects typically involve interaction with clients outside of the Computer Science department. The cases presenting these projects provide compelling, problematic examples of communication, and students can identify with them since they are grounded in the real experiences of fellow students.

Applying Ethnography to the Educational Sphere

Ethnography, as Beverly Moss explains, is "a qualitative research method that allows a researcher to gain a comprehensive view of the social interactions, behaviors, and beliefs of a community or social group. In other words, the goal…is to study, explore, and describe a group's culture" (Moss, 1992). We used some proven techniques from ethnography to create views of real software development settings. Our case studies, however, should not be mistaken for true ethnographical studies; since our resources were limited, we could not perform the years of fieldwork required of such endeavors.

Our method followed a qualitative case study approach, which attempts to "identify the important aspects or variables of the phenomenon" chosen for examination by "closely studying individuals, small groups, or whole environments" with the aim to identify avenues for further research (Lauer & Asher, 1988). In our work, that further research included the development of case studies based on our observations, and presented to other students as a means of simulating the conditions they will encounter later in their careers in computer science.

The desire to capture recurring patterns in software development problems has been expressed elsewhere in the software engineering literature. For instance, Sutcliffe et al. (A. G. Sutcliffe, Maiden, Minocha, & Manuel, 1988) propose that "if common abstractions in a new application domain could be discovered early in the requirements engineering (RE) process, then it may be possible to reuse generic requirements and link them to reusable designs. *This could provide a conduit for reusing the wealth of software engineering knowledge that resides in reusable component libraries*" (1073, italics ours). Put another way, individuals and the groups within which they work often create ways of coping with the uncertainties of the project design process, amassing a sizeable and valuable knowledge base as they do. Through our case studies we aim to capture that knowledge, reflected in the lived experience of one individual or group of individuals. Incorporating this knowledge and experience into pedagogical tools, our cases have the potential to instill that experience in others when used in the classroom.

Gathering the Data

As the students work on their Senior Design projects, significant case study data is accumulated: meeting minutes, email, reports for clients and for the Senior Design instructor, and documented code. Email is collected through *ad hoc* mailing lists, which the project teams use for communicating among themselves and with others. Furthermore, Senior Design students reflect on their daily results and then consolidate the information they have collected in one-page progress reports that they submit on a weekly basis to the instructor. Consequently, work on the case studies during the academic year is focused on data collection, organization and coding; summers are focused on case study construction.

To develop these first case studies, and pilot our approach, graduate students gathered written material (notes, meeting minutes, versions of the software, emails, and so forth) from the Senior Design students. Following standard practice in qualitative research (Agar, 1996; Kirsch & Sullivan, 1992; Lauer & Asher, 1988), the graduate students acted as participant observers during the majority of the students' meetings. As researchers, they made audio recordings, drew diagrams of where people sat and how they moved about the room, and recorded field notes for later reference. Following the suggestions of Emerson, Fretz, and Shaw, their field notes recorded fine details (Emerson, Fretz, & Shaw, 1995) for later recall, reconstruction, and analysis. Further, their notes focused on key events and incidents — such as dramatic and unexpected shifts in the client's requirements and expectations — and recorded stakeholders' reactions. These strategies brought the cases "to life" by including details and rich descriptions of action, thus capturing the visual and oral ambiance of the situation and giving that "you are there" feeling.

As the project came to a close, the graduate students also conducted semi-structured interviews with the Senior Design students and their clients. They used these interviews to triangulate early results as Hesse-Biber and Leavy recommend (Hesse-Biber & Leavy, 2005), and to support findings and "earn the confidence of the reader that the researchers have 'gotten it right'".

Constructing the Stories

To construct the case studies, the graduate students first assembled all the original material chronologically into one long summary account, with hyperlinks to the original documents, and then divided it into modules. They also developed question sets for each module to help students identify and examine the issues, as well as some password-protected teaching aids for the instructor giving background material and an "insider's view" of the situations. These were integrated into the final chronological version.

To develop the thematic version, the graduate students read through the chronological account. Relying on the grounded theory method (Strauss & Corbin, 1998), they started with a detailed, line-by-line analysis of the descriptions found in the transcripts. From this the graduate students generated initial categories, which focused on inherent meaning and details, aiming to identify central ideas of "what is going on here" and label them as emergent themes, often using terms taken from the words of the respondents themselves. These were then grouped into categories with explanatory and predictive potential. For example, one category they identified referred to the students' difficulties in learning and working with an unfamiliar programming language (Matlab). These instances were then abstracted and listed chronologically. Other themes were then identified and listed under their own headings. Comparing the content and frequency of interactions across categories, the graduate students began to see some explanatory power. For example, questions that arose in the "learning Matlab" category, yet were not answered in the "client interactions" category, stymied the students. These questions offer insight into why the project fell behind schedule. These comparisons also hold some measure of predictive power as well—a future interaction would likely follow the pattern of the past if no remediation was attempted.

Presenting the Stories

Our cases are presented in the style of the "realist tale" as described by Van Maanen (Van Maanen, 1988). These are "by far the most prominent, familiar, prevalent, and recognized form of ethnographic writing [which] push most firmly for the authenticity of the cultural representations conveyed by the text". Its typical form is a "documentary style focused on minute, but mundane details of everyday life". Such details are not random, but "accumulate" to make some important point; they "suggest intimacy and establish presence" and "draw in the audience". Our cases aim to present the participants' point of view through quotations, recordings, and other documentation, but also include their reflections. In light of our pedagogical goal, however, we as authors have "final word" on any depictions.

Our case studies consist of multimedia packages, combining text, audio and video material, to capture the real process of dealing with stakeholders. The cases are presented as hypertext documents. Apart from accessibility and portability, this electronic format allows us to embed links to the original documents instead of including them as an appendix. For example, the text of an email might be included in the scenario, but the attached document that came with it is left as a separate file. The student analyzing the case must open that file, much as if he or she had been the original recipient of the email. This action helps move the reader from passive observer to active participant, making the case more real and interesting.

The cases are expressed in plain language and mention specifics, preserving the vocabulary of the application domain to convey important contextual information that students might otherwise overlook. This encourages the kind of constructive questioning that fleshes out important details (A. Sutcliffe, 2003). In some instances, cases present examples of failures in communication, providing students the opportunity to reflect on what went wrong and suggest alternatives (Gale, 1993).

The presentation of the material has been designed so that information about the project requirements is imparted gradually. This simulates the problems of Senior Design students grappling with the issues of real clients. The raw materials of each case are organized into modules, representing periods of time in the project history, usually one week per module. These modules allow users to browse through stories, listen to audio clips, watch animations, and respond to questions that are specifically aimed toward provoking inquiry into a particular point in time, or a certain theme.

EXAMPLE: THE SEABASE CASE STUDY

We present examples of material from the "Seabase" case study, where Senior Design students (called the "CS team") worked with faculty and students in Mechanical Engineering to develop control software for a ship-based crane. The communication challenges in the project were significant: students had to learn the culture of mechanical engineers, as well as a new programming language, Matlab. As newcomers to a project that was already underway, they had to find their place in an established work environment that was foreign to them.

An excerpt from the Module C story is shown in Figure 1. The story document includes hyperlinks to three primary sources: the meeting minutes for the project team leaders, the risk document of the team, and email from a project advisor in Mechanical Engineering. The email reveals an interesting problem for the CS team: communications from the Mechanical Engineering faculty members that indicates differing expectations in what the challenging aspect of the project will be. Here, advisor Hank Taylor indicates that "the crane [controller] part is the 'biggest, nastiest'

part" and a side project to design a GUI for the crane controller is "the easiest part." In a meeting one week earlier, Nancy Smith had stated the opposite: "The GUI design is a good project for the CS team," and "working on only the crane controller would be 'too simple.'" The questions (shown in Figure 2) and instructor notes challenge the readers to use problem solving to resolve this disparity.

Figure 3 includes an excerpt from the Module E story that illustrates the notion of communication cycles. Two meetings occur in short order: first, an informal meeting of the team in which they prepare questions for Hank Taylor; then the meeting with Hank. There is a three-step process, in which the students formulate the questions, pose them, and finally unpack the answers later in Module F.

The Module E questions (shown in Figure 4) ask the readers to evaluate the effectiveness of this process: to what extent the students were able to articulate their needs and interpret Hank's responses. There are other links with wider scope. For instance, after listening to the discussion of the code from the model crane, the readers are asked to go back to documentation of this code that had been circulated earlier, and determine

Figure 1. Excerpt from Module C Story, Seabase case study

Module C Story

On Wednesday of the fourth week of the semester (Sept. 22) the leaders of the three crane project teams meet with Hank Taylor and Nancy Smith. They decide that since the "point of meeting is to get regular coordination of the teams, they will continue the meeting of team leaders on Wednesday from 12-1 on". Representing the CS Team are JoAnn, Ken and Bob; Matt and Ben come for the crane builders; and Jon is there to talk about the platform.

Minutes of Sept. 22 Crane Team Leaders meeting

The items on JoAnn's summary of the meeting are:

- The CS Team will work on crane, not on the platform, this term.
- In a discussion of scope of the CS Team's part, Hank says the crane part is the "biggest, nastiest part" and he thinks the GUI for the platform will take about an hour and is the "easiest part.

Figure 2. Module C Questions, Seabase case study

Module C Questions

1. Can you recap the project so far?
- What information has been conveyed?
- What questions remain about what has to be done?
- What would you do to answer those questions?
2. How would you characterize the interactions among Hank, Nancy, and the team members?
3. It's interesting that Hank says that the "crane part" is going to be "the biggest, nastiest part", and that the GUI design will be easiest. On the other hand, Nancy seems to be saying the opposite: the controller will not be very difficult, and the GUI will be more challenging.
- Why might they have such different opinions?
- How can the CS team resolve this difference?
4. The CS team attends a Team Leader meeting. What might be the value of this kind of meeting, instead of just meeting with Hank?
5. Critique the to-do list as given in the minutes.
- What purpose does it serve?
- Is there more information that you would add?
6. Critique the risk document, in a similar fashion.

Figure 3. Excerpt from Module E Story, Seabase case study

Module E Story

On Monday, Sept. 27, the CS team holds two meetings. The first is a "brainstorming what-to-do meeting" in the hall. Present are Ken Lundy, Bob Marin, JoAnn Durst, and Arnie. At this meeting they try to "get our heads straight about what we're doing and should be doing."

Minutes of Sept. 27 CS Team brainstorming meeting

After that, they meet with Hank Taylor to go over the code from the model crane in Albuquerque, a "code functionality meeting."

Minutes of Sept. code functionality meeting with CS Team and Hank

At the meeting with Hank Taylor, the purpose is to go over the code from the model crane in Albuquerque. (Listen in on the meeting as they dissect the code.)

There is also a lot of discussion about learning Matlab. (Listen to the discussion and follow along with the meeting minutes.)

Figure 4. Module E Questions, Seabase case study

Module E Questions

1. Discuss the outcome of each meeting.
- What conclusions did they reach?
- Could having roles (facilitator, agenda keeper, minute taker/poster, etc.) improve efficiency of meetings?
- If so, how should these jobs be distributed?
2. The term "big picture" arises twice: once at the brainstorming meeting, then later at the code functionality meeting. The CS team seems to want more of a "big picture" of the project, while (at least in the view of the CS team) Hank is encouraging them to "leap into coding".
- What additional "big picture" information might Hank be able to provide? What value (if any) would it be to the CS team?
- What (if anything) might the students gain from "leaping into coding"?
3. Did they resolve things they discussed at the "brainstorming meeting" by meeting with Hank? Which things were, which were not?
4. Look back at the "Function List." Does it make more or less sense now, based on the two meetings?
5. Look back at the Risk Document from Module C.
- Do you see any risks being played out?
- What are the students doing to mitigate them? Is it working?
- Are there any risks that should be added to or removed from the document?

Figure 5. Excerpt from Module E Instructor Notes, Seabase case study

Module E Instructor Notes

JoAnn mentions "requirements" twice in her email message:
- She makes a request for "crane requirements". It is interesting to look ahead and see when these requirements materialize.
- She makes this request so that the CS Team can write their requirements. The CS Team seems to have taken on the job of writing their own requirements. It is not clear who assigned them this task. It is probably worthwhile to discuss the problems with developers writing their own requirements.

whether the conversation helped to clarify the earlier documentation. Also, at the brainstorming meeting, it is determined that more requirements for the mechanical crane are needed; in the Instructor Notes (an excerpt of which is shown in Figure 5), readers are asked to look ahead in the story to discover when the requirements materialize.

EXAMPLE: THE SOILSIM CASE STUDY

We turn now to the "SoilSim" case study, where Senior Design students worked with an environmental scientist at a local research laboratory, to develop an educational simulation game about soil ecology for grade-school students. An excerpt from Module C story is shown in Figure 6. The students in the story were continuing a project that had been started by other students.

One student (Jacob) had done earlier work on the game, but the other two students in the team had to become familiar with both the basics of soil ecology and the code left behind by earlier teams. The team wrestled with understanding the ecological mechanisms involved in the problem, using documentation from earlier teams as well as Jacob's knowledge. Eventually, they realized that they needed some criteria for validating their simulation, and so turned to the scientist (Fritz). The story includes Jacob's email appeal for help, and audio clips of the subsequent discussion between Fritz and the team.

The questions and instructor notes shown in Figure 7 and Figure 8 focus on the second audio clip. The themes of interest here are the knowledge gap between client and developer (mitigated somewhat by Jacob's explanations to his teammates) and the risk of changing client

Figure 6. Excerpt from Module C Story, SoilSim case study

Module C Story
Dave appoints Jacob the team-client go-between and Jacob uses e-mail to contact Fritz about meeting with the team.

Fritz,
We were wondering if you could provide us with some sort of metric for testing, so we can verify that Soilsim is doing what it should be doing. Such as, if we add 10 worms to the simulation and a couple of spiders is the program behaving like it should be? We know how the program behaves in its current state, but we need some indicators to test for, to determine if it is behaving correctly. If you need to play around with the program a little to get us this information, we would be happy to meet with you and provide a copy of the program for you to take a look at. Let me know if you need any clarification on anything.
Thank you,   Jacob

Jacob, I'd be happy to provide you that information. The best way would be For me to see what the program is doing now, so if we could arrange a time next week that would work for me. -- Fritz.

On February 22, week 7 of the 14-week semester, Fritz and the team meet for the first time in the CS lab. This was an essential meeting for the team, markedly increasing productivity. Following is the audio recording of the meeting, presented as a chronological series of five clips.

Figure 7. Excerpt from Module C Questions, SoilSim case study

Module C Questions
Clip 2

1. Does a software engineer need to know biology in order to develop a biology-based project?
2. What kind of communication obstacles might develop in a cross-disciplinary team?
3. The team has been developing the project for nearly two months, yet this is the first time they have interacted with the client: what might be some implications?
4. What difficulties might a development team face if the overall product vision is not stable?
5. How might a back-and-forth vision-development communication process work?
6. The client has given a discipline-specific nuanced description of the C-N process, how does this differ from the initial overview Jacob gave the team at the beginning of the semester?

Figure 8. Excerpt from Module C Instructor Notes, SoilSim case study

Module C Instructor Notes
Clip 2

- The client asks the team about their biology background. They had basic biology in high school, but that's it. The client gives a systems analogy to assist them with a big-picture sense of the Carbon-Nitrogen cycle. This is a good place to discuss cross-disciplinary projects and the communication obstacles relative to such projects.
- The client is explaining the project to this semester's SoilSim team for the first time. The only explanation the team had up until now is the overview Jacob gave at the beginning of the semester. It might be interesting to compare and contrast the two versions and to discuss the implications of each version for project development.
- Interestingly, as the client develops his explanation of the project he seems, as well, to be expanding on his basic vision for the project. This is a place to discuss the value of a stable project outcomes vision and possible effects of fluctuating goals on project development.
- The team questions the client about the cycle and is offered a more detailed explanation. This may be a place to discuss the usefulness of back-and-forth developmental communication between the team and the client during which project vision can emerge and eventually become stable.

expectations (as evidenced implicitly by Fritz's comments during the meeting).

USING THE CASES

Our case studies have been used both within our software engineering curriculum and in a technical communication setting with a wide variety of students. The material appears to have not only the depth to recreate the complexity of communication in a software project, but also the breadth to connect with students outside of software engineering. We report on our findings here.

Technical Communication

We have used the Seabase case study in an interdisciplinary technical communication course that included computer science and software engineering students along with students majoring in engineering, business, and technical communication. The case was used over a two-and-a-half-week unit during summer 2006 and over a four-week unit during fall 2006. Students worked in interdisciplinary teams, each of which included a computer science or software engineering student. In class discussions, in memos, and in final reports, they analyzed how the various communication genres produced by the senior design group (such as requirements documents, risk documents, emails, timelines, meeting minutes, reports, and presentations) contributed to action or nonaction of project stakeholders and ultimately to the overall success or failure of the Seabase project. For example, one in-class exercise asked students to rewrite a set of meeting minutes taken from the case after extensive discussions about the purposes and audiences for these documents. Similarly, in their final reports, the teams of students not only analyzed the communication-related causes of the Seabase project's failure but also drew on their analyses to make recommendations that were designed to help fu-

ture senior design students and faculty improve their communication practices. The successful use of this case in a technical communication course demonstrates that the lessons that it teaches about communication and about working on interdisciplinary teams are applicable outside of, as well as within, the computer science classroom.

From written student comments and the analyses presented in their final reports, we conclude that students responded well to a rhetorical approach. They came away from the case study with a better understanding of the importance of a rhetorical—rather than rote—approach to problem solving and to communication cycles. The project particularly highlighted for students the importance of considering a document's various audiences—or stakeholders. In his reflections about the project, one student wrote, "Before this class I had simply written paper after paper without any thought as to who was reading it aside from the professor who assigned it. I feel that not only did I learn how to design a paper to fit a particular audience, I also learned to pick an audience and the importance of doing so."

Students particularly liked the fact that the case included the actual documents produced by the senior design group for the Seabase project: they were able to see how the documents' lack of rhetorical awareness (attention to factors of audience, purpose and context) significantly contributed to the project's ultimate failure. For example, in one final report students observed how the timeline produced by the CS team lacked dates and deliverables: "The biggest problem is that there are no dates at all on the timeline," they write. "The team has not worked out starting times, durations, and, most importantly, deadlines." The students reading the case study concluded that the document was produced in a rote manner, to satisfy a course requirement — without awareness that anyone would actually read it, use it, or modify it in the future. The student readers provided a revised timeline that included dates, deadlines, and deliverables, and specified which team members were responsible for which tasks. In a related example, students observed in class discussions how the risk document helped the senior design group to catalogue risks to the project as they occurred, but not to prevent or manage them.

The case also provides an excellent opportunity to encourage students to both discuss and experience communicating with stakeholders outside of one's discipline. For example, professors from the Mechanical Engineering department seemed to consistently underestimate the amount of work that the Computer Science students will need to put into the project. In the Module B, a mechanical engineering professor is quoted as saying that "working only on the crane controller would be 'too simple.'" In the next module, which is excerpted above in Figure 1, a different Mechanical Engineering professor gives an entirely opposite opinion (that the controller will be the hardest part). These two modules provide an excellent opportunity to discuss not only the importance of clarifying stakeholder roles and adequate documentation in reconciling conflicting claims such as these but also to discuss strategies for communicating across disciplines.

Although student response to the case in both the summer and fall sessions of this course was mostly positive, there were a couple of concerns that need to be addressed in future classes. First, students without experience in computer science were initially intimidated by the technical terminology that is employed throughout the case. Luckily, there were computer science and software engineering students in both sections of the course who helped to explain not only the terminology but also the level of knowledge about programs like Matlab that computer science students would likely have going into the project. As the case stands now, it would be difficult to teach without the help of students or an instructor with some expertise in the subject matter. As Schullery (1999) observes, "cases should [ideally] be applicable to all students in the class". But this lack

of technical information also had the unforeseen benefit of giving computer science and software engineering students a chance to explain technical information to people outside of their discipline, a skill that will certainly come in handy as they enter the workforce. These explanations could be formally built into the course. (For example, students could research an unfamiliar term and present a short "white paper" or similar document on the subject to the rest of the class.)

Studying the CS team's story was itself done in teams, which gave the case study readers a chance to apply immediately what they learned from analyzing the case. Some teams had to struggle with the very communication problems that the case highlighted — rote, formulaic approaches to document development, lack of respect for knowledge outside of one's discipline were especially in evidence. In particular, students often faced the prospect of their own skills being undervalued, the kind of power-based intra-team conflict described by Meyers and Larson (2005). For instance, in her evaluation of the project, one technical communication student wrote, "I did not like how my team functioned. Skills possessed by some were overlooked or not valued. The function of my team was to 'please the instructor' and not do good job working on the assignment." This is an issue that could be productively addressed in future courses: for example, students could discuss at the beginning of the project what skills they bring to the table and could clarify their own roles within the group.

Because much of the content of the case was specific to computer science and software engineering, some students lost interest in the case, particularly in the fall semester when the case took up four weeks of a fourteen-week course. Most students, however, seemed to find the case interesting and relevant for what it taught about project management (and about the management of senior design projects in particular), collaborative work, and rhetorical approaches to problem solving and to communication cycles.

While students in the class benefited from the computer science and software engineering students' insider knowledge of the case's subject matter, computer science and software engineering students left the class with concrete ideas for improving communications with stakeholders involved in their future projects. Finally, the case provides multiple opportunities to consider the challenges that women involved in male-dominated computer science and software engineering projects might face—particularly, gendered assumptions that women (even in leadership positions) should assume a secretarial role.

Software Engineering

We use the case studies in a software engineering course that focuses on requirements elicitation and analysis, usability, and testing. The course is a prerequisite for the Senior Design course and is therefore well placed to provide instruction on communication strategies. The curriculum includes a team project in which students design a prototypical user interface based on input from real people. One of the key assessment criteria for the project is the degree of attentiveness to their potential users, as reflected in the prototype.

We have used the case studies as preparation for this project; in particular, we have concentrated on the instances of direct communication between developer and client. The students worked both individually and in small teams on the case study material, both in and outside of class. One week of lecture time was devoted to the topic. We have evaluated the use of the Seabase case study in the fall 2006 offering of this course, using standard qualitative evaluation methods (Brown & Enos, 2002). Details can be found in an earlier paper (Brady, Seigel, Vosecky, & Wallace, 2007); here we summarize our conclusions.

Our analysis found that few students at the time of the pre-instruction evaluation had a concept of stakeholder that included more than the basics of developer, client and end user. Indeed, one of the sixteen students evaluated had a strong reaction *against* broadening the notion of stakeholder beyond "developer" and "client". When asked about the kinds of information that they would want to get from stakeholders, their answers did not extend beyond the basic notion of a list of desired features or services. This belies a simplistic view of clients and end users as nothing but sources of demands, rather than sources of useful background and prior experience. Likewise, individual students generally did not provide many ideas for getting information from stakeholders, though collectively there was a wide variety.

The post-instruction evaluation indicates that students gained a deeper awareness of the stakeholder concept, beyond their simple notion of "client and user". The evaluation also reveals a broader understanding of the issues at play when communicating with stakeholders: moving beyond the simple notion of "functional requirements" to issues of usability and project management. Students were able to suggest a broader set of potential methods to get information from stakeholders—that is, they became more creative problem solvers. Finally, the evaluation indicates that most students found their understanding of these concepts had changed—become more "detailed," "increased," become "fuller" or "broader"—as a result of instruction in the class.

The way in which the case study material is disclosed to the students can have profound effects on their attitude. Since only a week was devoted to the Seabase case, it was necessary to give the students access to the entire story, all at once. This particular Seabase story ends badly: the Senior Design team was unable to produce much by the end of the semester. (There is another case study that follows the successful efforts of a team that worked on Seabase one semester later.) Students following the case were able to "jump ahead" to the negative final results, and this clearly colored their opinion of the team's efforts. An easy cynicism emerged, and it was difficult to elicit any positive comments about how the Seabase project was conducted, even though there were clearly some good practices in place. A more effective teaching strategy, which we intend to use in the future, would impart the steps of the project more gradually, temporarily hiding the outcomes from the case study readers—just as they are hidden from the original project participants.

FUTURE DIRECTIONS

On one level, we see several ways in which our case study concept can be broadened and adapted for different uses. On a higher level, we hope that this work inspires further efforts across disciplines to strengthen the intrinsically interdisciplinary field of software engineering education.

Development and New Applications of Case Studies

Our case studies are publicly available, and we hope that the instructional material (questions and notes) surrounding them grow as more instructors use them. We hope to implement the case studies Website as a wiki in which instructors can contribute further questions and notes to the case studies. Our experience shows that the case studies also bring out issues that are not communication-related; it would be interesting to develop some of the other themes brought out in the case studies.

The case studies are necessarily complex and require time to study and understand. Currently, students see them relatively late in their undergraduate careers. It would be useful to introduce some of the themes earlier in the curriculum, but in a way that requires less of a time commitment. This has led us to the idea of drawing *scenarios* (Victor, 1999) from the case studies. Victor describes scenarios as like case studies in

the level of detail and in the lack of a "specific right answer" (100), but different in that they are smaller in scope and do not necessarily deal with real experiences. Our scenarios would have the advantage of coming from real software projects, but we would also have a certain "artistic license" to modify the stories in order to keep them succinct. One particular extension we have in mind is to dramatize some of the "scenes" from the case studies and put them in video form–what Victor calls "vignettes". This raises the possibility of interactive video, in which students can watch communication interchanges develop over time, then at certain points choose from a set of strategic options and watch the consequences of their choices.

Involving Students in Case Building

One issue that must be acknowledged is the time commitment involved in developing case studies. To pilot the methods, graduate students gathered material, acted as participant observers during meetings, and conducted semi-structured interviews with the students and their clients. At the end of the school year they wrote up the cases presented here. Fortunately, the students were funded through an NSF grant, but clearly this kind of support is not available to everyone who wishes to make case studies.

We have been testing procedures that will allow us to reduce the active role of the graduate students, thereby reducing cost and time commitments. We have introduced one undergraduate software engineering student to selected qualitative methods, and he has performed the actual observations and recording, under the supervision of a graduate student. Also, now that Senior Design students have been exposed to rhetorical principles through the case studies, the written reports that they produce as part of their projects can speak more directly to the communication issues we are interested in.

Interdisciplinarity: Encouraging Further Reciprocation

Software engineering is a field that draws from a wide range of disciplines. This project illustrates the benefits of reaching across disciplinary boundaries to bring outside knowledge into the software engineering curriculum (Brady, Johnson, & Wallace, 2006). For several decades, academic technical communicators have engaged in *extraction* and *incorporation*, the first stages of what Klein calls interdisciplinary exchange (Klein, 1990). That is, they have entered other disciplines (including software engineering), brought back important findings, and then applied them to technical communication practices and pedagogy. The result is a rich body of studies on communication and collaboration in real workplaces, as well as new ideas and best practices for interface design and composition. Our project represents the third stage of interdisciplinary exchange: *reciprocation*, in which technical communicators "give back", offering the fruits of their work to improve the field of software engineering.

To further this work and encourage others to engage in similar interdisciplinary efforts, we wish to build a community of software development stakeholders—both educators and practitioners—who understand one another's potential contributions and who are committed to the principle of integrating communication education into the software engineering curriculum. These stakeholders can describe the problems they encounter in teaching and employing communication, and the practices that they have found effective. Working as a group, we hope to explore how to extend current educational practices.

ONLINE CASE STUDIES

We have set up an online repository of case studies at www.speaksoft.mtu.edu/cases/. Currently the first-semester Seabase case and the SoilSim case are publicly available. Three more case studies will soon be added: the second (successful) semester of the Seabase project, the Java Logic Simulator project (interacting with a Computer Science professor to create an educational tool for circuit design), and the 3-D Maze project (interacting with another Computer Science professor to create a test platform for HCI research in three-dimensional interface navigation).

ACKNOWLEDGMENT

This work has been supported by NSF Award #CCF-0417548. We wish to thank our colleagues who helped design and implement the case studies: Anne Mareck, Leroy Steinbacher, Jon Woods, and Robert Johnson. We also deeply appreciate the participation of the Senior Design students whose projects we documented, and the students who used the case studies and participated in the evaluation. Finally, we thank our reviewers for their helpful comments.

REFERENCES

Abran, A., Moore, J. W., Bourque, P., & Dupuis, R. (Eds.). (2004). *Guide to the Software Engineering Body of Knowledge*. IEEE Computer Society.

Agar, M. (1996). *The Professional Stranger*. Academic Press.

Alred, G. J. (2006). Bridging Cultures: The Academy and the Workplace. *Journal of Business Communication, 43*, 79-88.

Blakeslee, A. M. (2001). Bridging the Workplace and the Academy: Teaching Professional Genres Through Classroom-Workplace Collaborations. *Technical Communication Quarterly, 10*(2), 169-192.

Brady, A., Johnson, R. R., & Wallace, C. (2006). The intersecting futures of technical communication and software engineering: Forging a multi-disciplinary alliance. *Technical Communication, 53*(3).

Brady, A., Seigel, M., Vosecky, T., & Wallace, C. (2007). *Addressing Communication Issues in Software Development: A Case Study Approach.* Paper presented at the Conference on Software Engineering Education and Training.

Brown, S., & Enos, T. (Eds.). (2002). *The Writing Program Administrator's Resource: A Guide to Reflective Institutional Practice.* Lawrence Erlbaum.

Christensen, C. R. (1987). *Teaching and the Case Method.* Harvard Business School.

Connors, R. J. (2004). The Rise of Technical Writing Instruction in America. In J. Johnson-Eiola & S. Selber (Eds.), *Central Works in Technical Communication* (pp. 4-19). Oxford University Press.

Curtis, B., Krasner, H., & Iscoe, N. (1988). A Field Study of the Software Design Process for Large Systems. *Communications of the ACM, 31*(11), 1268-1287.

Davis, A. (1990). *Software Requirements: Objects, Functions, and States.* Prentice Hall.

Deili, M. (1988). *A problem solving approach to usability testing.* Paper presented at the International Technical Communication Conference.

Dorn, E. M. (1999). Case Method Instruction in the Business Writing Classroom. *Business Communication Quarterly, 62,* 41-60.

Emerson, R. M., Fretz, R. I., & Shaw, L. L. (1995). *Writing Ethnographic Fieldnotes.* University of Chicago Press.

Flower, L. (1998). *Problem Solving Strategies for Writing in College and Community.* Harcourt Brace.

Freedman, A. (1993a). Show and Tell? The Role of Explicit Teaching in the Learning of New Genres. *Research in the Teaching of English, 27*(3), 222-251.

Freedman, A. (1993b). Show and Tell? The Role of Explicit Teaching in the Learning of New Genres. *Research in the Teaching of English, 27*(3), 222-251.

Freedman, A., Adam, C., & Smart, G. (1994). Wearing Suits to Class: Simulating Genres and Simulations as Genre. *Written Communication, 11*(2), 193-226.

Fulmer, W. E. (1992). Using Cases in Management Development Programmes. *Journal of Management Development, 11,* 33-37.

Gale, F. C. (1993). Teaching Professional Writing Rhetorically: The Unified Case Method. *Journal of Business and Technical Communication, 7*(2), 256-266.

Glass, R. L. (1998). *Software Runaways: Lessons Learned from Massive Software Project Failures.* Prentice Hall.

Hesse-Biber, S. N., & Leavy, P. (2005). Qualitative Research Inquiry. In *The Practice of Qualitative Research.* Sage.

Johnson-Eiola, J. (2001). Little Machines: Understanding Users; Understanding Interfaces. *ACM Journal of Computer Documentation, 25,* 119-127.

Johnson, R. R. (1998). *User-Centered Technology: A Rhetorical Theory for Computers and Other Mundane Artifacts.* SUNY Press.

Keil, M., Cule, P. E., Lyytinen, K., & Schmidt, R. C. (1998). A framework for identifying software project risks. *Communications of the ACM, 41*(1), 76-83.

Kirsch, G., & Sullivan, P. (1992). *Methods and Methodology in Composition Research.* Southern Illinois University Press.

Klein, J. T. (1990). *Interdisciplinarity.* Wayne University Press.

Lauer, J. M., & Asher, W. (1988). *Composition Research/Empirical Designs.* Oxford University Press.

Lave, J., & Wenger, E. (1991). *Situated Learning: Legitimate Peripheral Participation.* Cambridge University Press.

Liu, C. (2005). *Using issue tracking tools to facilitate student learning of communication skills in software engineering courses.* Paper presented at the Conference on Software Engineering Education & Training.

Margolis, J., & Fisher, A. (2002). *Unlocking the Clubhouse: Women in Computing.* MIT Press.

McMillan, W. W., & Rajaprabhakaran, S. (1999). *What leading practitioners say should be emphasized in students' software engineering projects.* Paper presented at the Conference on Software Engineering Education & Training.

Miller, C. R. (1979). A Humanistic Rationale for Technical Writing. *College English, 40,* 610-617.

Moss, B. J. (1992). Ethnography and Composition: Studying Language at Home. In G. Kirsch & P. Sullivan (Eds.), *Methods and Methodology in Composition Research.* Southern Illinois University Press.

Muir, C. (2004). Learning Soft Skills at Work: An Interview with Annalee Luhman. *Business Communication Quarterly, 67*(1), 99-101.

Myers, L. L., & Larson, R. S. (2005). Preparing Students for Early Work Conflicts. *Business Communication Quarterly, 68,* 306-317.

Pickett, J. P. (Ed.). (2004). *The American Heritage Dictionary of the English Language* (4th ed.). Houghton Mifflin.

Poole, W. G. (2003). *The softer side of custom software development: Working with the other players.* Paper presented at the Conference on Software Engineering Education and Training.

Putnam, L. L., & Folger, J. P. (1988). Communication, Conflict, and Dispute Resolution: The Study of Interaction and the Development of Conflict Theory. *Communication Research, 15,* 349-359.

Putnam, L. L., & Poole, M. S. (1987). Conflict and Negotiation. In F. M. Jablin, L. L. Putnam, K. H. Roberts & L. W. Porter (Eds.), *Handbook of Organizational Communication: An Interdisciplinary Perspective* (pp. 549-599).

Reinsch, L. N., & Shelby, A. N. (1997). What Communication Abilities Do Practitioners Need? *Business Communication Quarterly, 60*(4), 7-29.

Schultz, B., & Anderson, J. (1984). Training in the Management of Conflict: A Communication Theory Perspective. *Small Group Behavior, 15,* 333-348.

Strauss, A. L., & Corbin, J. M. (1998). *Basics of Qualitative Research: Techniques and Procedures for Developing Grounded Theory.* Sage.

Sutcliffe, A. (2003). *Scenario-based requirements engineering.* Paper presented at the IEEE International Conference on Requirements Engineering.

Sutcliffe, A. G., Maiden, A. M., Minocha, S., & Manuel, D. (1988). Supporting Scenario-Based Requirements Engineering. *IEEE Transactions on Software Engineering, 24*(12), 1072-1088.

Tebeaux, E., & Killingsworth, J. M. (1992). Expanding and Redirecting Historical Research in Technical Writing: In Search of Our Past. *Technical Communication Quarterly, 1*(2), 5-32.

Van Maanen, J. (1988). *Tales of the Field: On Writing Ethnography.* University of Chicago Press.

Victor, D. A. (1999). Using Scenarios and Vignettes in Cross-Cultural Business Communication Instruction. *Business Communication Quarterly, 62*(4), 99-103.

Williams, J. M., & Colomb, G. G. (1993). The Case for Explicit Teaching: Why What You Don't Know Won't Help You. *Research in the Teaching of English, 27*(3), 252-264.

Chapter VI
Novel Methods of Incorporating Security Requirements Engineering into Software Engineering Courses and Curricula

Nancy R. Mead
Software Engineering Institute, USA

Dan Shoemaker
University of Detroit Mercy, USA

ABSTRACT

This chapter describes methods of incorporating security requirements engineering into software engineering courses and curricula. The chapter discusses the importance of security requirements engineering and the relationship of security knowledge to general computing knowledge by comparing a security body of knowledge to standard computing curricula. Then security requirements is related to standard computing curricula and educational initiatives in security requirements engineering are described, with their results. An expanded discussion of the SQUARE method in security requirements engineering case studies is included, as well as future plans in the area. Future plans include the development and teaching of academic course materials in security requirements engineering, which will then be made available to educators. The authors hope that more educators will be motivated to teach security requirements engineering in their software engineering courses and to incorporate it in their curricula.

INTRODUCTION

Exploitable defects in software pose a threat to both our national security and our way of life. That is because our critical infrastructure is en-abled by information technology (PITAC, 2005). Nevertheless, even though software plays a pivotal role in ensuring every sector of our economy, the President's Information Technology Advisory Council (PITAC) found that "commonly used software engineering practices permit dangerous defects, which let attackers compromise millions of computers every year" (PITAC, 2005, p. 39).

Most defects are the result of programming or design errors (Jones, 2005). And such defects do not have to be identified or actively exploited in order to be a threat (Redwine, 2006). Yet, given that unfortunate fact, PITAC still found that "current commercial software engineering lacks the rigorous controls needed to [ensure defect free] products at acceptable cost" (PITAC, 2005, p. 39). And even worse, "In the future, the nation may face even more challenging problems as adversaries—both foreign and domestic—become increasingly sophisticated in their ability to insert malicious code into critical software" (Redwine, 2006, p. xiv).

In fiscal terms, the exploitation of defects costs the U.S. economy an average of $60 billion dollars per year (Newman, 2002). However, the real concern lies in the fact that the exploitation of a flaw in the software that underlies basic infrastructure services like power and communication could cause a significant national disaster. The Critical Infrastructure Taskforce sums up that likelihood in a single statement: "The nation's economy is increasingly dependent on cyberspace. This has introduced unknown interdependencies and single points of failure. A digital disaster strikes some enterprise every day, [and] infrastructure disruptions have cascading impacts, multiplying their cyber and physical effects" (Clark, 2002, p. 6).

The generally acknowledged solution to the problem of exploitable defects is more secure practice in every aspect of the acquisition, development, and sustainment of software and software artifacts. Nonetheless, "informed consumers have growing concerns about the scarcity of practitioners with requisite competencies to build secure software" (Redwine, 2006, p. xiii).

Because of the key importance of capable practitioners and the general lack of proper preparation, The National Strategy to Secure Cyberspace – Action/ Recommendation 2-14 has mandated the Department of Homeland Security (DHS) to "promulgate best practices and methodologies that promote integrity, security, and reliability in software code development, including processes and procedures that diminish the possibilities of erroneous code, malicious code, or trap doors that could be introduced during development" (NIAC, 2003, p. 35).

It would seem to be a simple task to "identify the necessary workforce competencies, leverage sound practices, and guide curriculum development for education and training relevant to software assurance" (Redwine, 2006, p. xiv.). However, the problem is that security is not a mature field, and so the teaching of security topics is done in a number of disjointed places within higher education. That includes "software engineering, systems engineering, information systems security engineering, safety, security, testing, information assurance, and project management" (Redwine, 2006, p. xiv).

Coherent knowledge about "software assurance processes and practices has yet to be integrated into the body of knowledge of the contributing disciplines" (Redwine, 2006, p. xiv). Too often, the result of this lack of integration is the graduation of a software engineering student who develops buggy code with weak security measures.

It is both impractical and impossible to simply drop the whole body of software assurance knowledge into a traditional computer curriculum. Therefore it is necessary to adopt a focused strategy and a clear starting point. One of the logical places to start the integration process is in an area that is vital to good security practice, but which is also well established and important to general development. That is security requirements engineering.

THE IMPORTANCE OF REQUIREMENTS ENGINEERING

It is well recognized that requirements engineering is critical to the success of any major development project (Addison, 2000; Carr, 2000; Hecht, 2000; Mead, 2006; Palyagar, 2004b). Several authoritative studies have shown that requirements engineering defects cost 10 to 200 times as much to correct once fielded than if they were detected during requirements development (Boehm, 2001). Other studies have shown that reworking requirements defects on most software development projects costs 40 to 50 percent of total project effort, and the percentage of defects originating during requirements engineering is estimated at more than 50 percent (McGibbon, 1999; Mead, 2005b). The total percentage of project budget due to requirements defects is 25 to 40 percent (McGibbon, 1999; Mead, 2005b).

A recent study found that the return on investment when security analysis and secure engineering practices are introduced early in the development cycle ranges from 12 to 21 percent, with the highest rate of return occurring when the analysis is performed during application design (Soo Hoo, 2001). Thus the costs of poor security requirements show that even a small improvement in this area would provide a high value. By the time that an application is fielded and in its operational environment, it is very difficult and expensive to significantly improve its security.

The Problem with Developing Security Requirements

Security requirements are often identified during the system life cycle. However, the requirements tend to be general specifications of the functions required, such as password protection, firewalls, and virus detection tools. Often the security requirements are developed independently of the rest of the requirements engineering activity and hence are not integrated into the mainstream of the requirements activities. As a result, security requirements that are specific to the system and that provide for protection of essential services and assets are often neglected.

In reviewing requirements documents, we typically find that security requirements, when they exist, are in a section by themselves and have been copied from a generic set of security requirements. The requirements elicitation and analysis that is needed to get a better set of security requirements seldom takes place.

Much of the study of requirements engineering research and practice has addressed the capabilities that the system will provide. So a lot of attention is given to the functionality of the system, from the user's perspective, but little attention is given to what the system should *not* do. In one discussion on requirements prioritization for a specific large system, ease of use was assigned a higher priority than security requirements. Security requirements were in the lower half of the prioritized requirements. This occurred in part because the only security requirements that were considered had to do with access control.

Current research recognizes that security requirements are negative requirements. Therefore, general security requirements, such as "The system shall not allow successful attacks," are generally not feasible because there is no consensus on ways to validate them other than to apply formal methods to the entire system, including COTS components. We can, however, identify the essential services and assets that must be protected. We are able to validate that mechanisms such as access control, levels of security, backups, replication, and policy are implemented and enforced. We can also validate that the system will properly handle specific threats identified by a threat model and correctly respond to intrusion scenarios.

If security requirements are not effectively defined, the resulting system cannot be effectively evaluated for success or failure prior to implementation. Security requirements are often missing in the requirements elicitation process and tend to be neglected subsequently. In addition to employing applicable software engineering techniques, the organization must understand how to incorporate the techniques into its existing software development processes (Linger, 1998). The identification of organizational mechanisms that promote or inhibit the adoption of security requirements elicitation can be an indicator of the security level of the resulting product.

RELATING SECURITY REQUIREMENTS PRACTICES TO CURRICULUM MODELS

Although data exists to support the benefit of requirements engineering in general, the data to specifically support the benefits of security requirements engineering is anecdotal. It is generally assumed that organizations could significantly improve the security of their systems by utilizing a systematic approach to security requirements engineering. Nevertheless, it was also felt that the first step in deciding how to integrate security requirements engineering into the bodies of knowledge of the contributing disciplines was to understand the precise relationship between security requirements practices and the curriculum models for each field. Thus a study was undertaken to specifically examine how security requirements might best fit into the curriculum requirements of all of the traditional computer disciplines. That effort was materially aided by the fact that the sponsoring societies of the three most influential areas in higher education had just finished their own comprehensive inventory of those curricula.

The Authoritative Baseline: CC2005

That study is the *Computing Curricula 2005: The Overview Report*, which is commonly called "CC2005." CC2005 is fully endorsed by each of the three bodies that prepared it, which are the ACM, the IEEE Computer Society, and the Association for Information Systems. The intention of CC2005 was to "offer society a practical vision of our shared field, of the various disciplines within it, and of the meaningful choices that face students, educators, and their communities. The goal of this report is to articulate the shared identity, the separate identities of each" (JTCC, 2005, p. 8). In that respect, CC2005 merges the recommendations for the content and focus of Computer Engineering, Computer Science, Information Systems, and Software Engineering curricula into a single authoritative digest.

To accomplish this, a working group of ACM, IEEE, and AIS experts reviewed the most current curriculum models for each of the participating disciplines. The group then "compared the contents [specified in the five model curricula] to one another, and synthesized what [they] believe to be the essential descriptive and comparative information" (JTCC, 2005, p. 5). That analysis produced 40 topic areas. These 40 topics are considered to be the complete set of curricular items appropriate for all five major computing disciplines. The report specifically states that "each one of the five discipline-specific curricula represents the best judgment of the relevant professional, scientific, and educational associations and serves as a definition of what these degree programs should be and do"(JTCC, 2005, p. 5).

In addition to the 40 topic areas, which in effect summarize all of the knowledge input to the teaching and learning process, CC2005 also provides a comparative view of the capabilities that might be expected from graduates of each degree program (JTCC, 2005). Thus, "besides summarizing what a student will study, [the report also]…summarizes the expectations for the student after graduation" (JTCC, 2005, p. 28). In some respects, the 60 capability goals were the greatest help, since they imply knowledge that would be necessary to produce a properly trained profession. By referencing those outcomes, it was possible to map a relationship between requirements of secure practice and the associated CC2005 curricular areas. It was also easier to see the places where essential knowledge capabilities are missing or where there was a misalignment between the capability areas and the aims of the discipline.

Comparison of Security Knowledge to General Computing Knowledge

We mapped the commonly recognized elements of secure practice to the CC2005 recommendations for three of the five disciplines (covered by the CC2005 analysis). Because of significant overlap with non-computing disciplines (JTCC, 2005, p.11)—computer engineering with electrical engineering and IT with business—we omitted the two disciplines that represent each end of the spectrum.

Using the expedient of characterizing the concentration of references by topic, the following eight CC2005 topic areas had a significant degree of required security knowledge associated with them (> 100 references): (1) Requirements, (2) Architecture, (3) Design, (4) Verification and Validation, (5) Evolution (e.g., maintenance), (6) Processes, (7) Quality, and (8) Project Management.

Using the same criterion, the following three CC2005 topic areas had moderate security content requirements (< 100): (1) Legal/Professional/ Ethics/Society, (2) Risk Management, and (3) Programming Languages. Finally, there is some requirement for security knowledge (< 10) in each of these thirteen areas: (1) Integrative Programming (integrated), (2) Information Systems Development, (3) Complexity, (4) Human Computer Interaction, (5) Operating Systems Principles & Design, (6) Operating Systems Configuration & Use, (7) Platform Technologies, (8) Algorithms, (9) Graphics and Visualization (conceptualiza-

tion), (10) Software Modeling and Analysis, (11) Database Practice, (12) Business Requirements, and (13) Engineering Economics for SW.

There is no apparent relationship between secure software assurance practice and (1) Management of Information Systems Organizations, (2) Systems Administration, (3) Systems Integration, (4) Mathematical Foundations, (5) Interpersonal Communication, (6) Organizational Theory, (7) Decision Theory, (8) Organizational Behavior, (9) Organizational Change Management, (10) General Systems Theory, (11) Business Models, and (12) Functional Business Areas.

In general these findings are no surprise, since the aim of any form of security is to foster secure practice in the *development* of software. Given that aim, the concentration of recommendations on the primary and supporting processes of the software life cycle and on project management should be expected. For the same reason, the areas of moderate coverage also contain no surprises except for the emphasis on the legal/professional/ethical and social aspects. The focus on knowledge in those areas might be indicative of the growing awareness that software vulnerabilities carry significant legal, social, and ethical implications.

The areas of "little" or "no" coverage tend to be the curricular elements that are particular to the specific disciplines in CC2005, computer science, software engineering and information systems. That tends to reinforce the conclusion that the main focus for security education ought to be on instilling best practice in software work rather than within the various academic studies of computing. Whether that implies a need for the further development of security knowledge is a matter of conjecture outside of the goals of our research. However, it does point to the fact that the current security knowledge would be best integrated into the places in each discipline where the elements of the software life cycle are introduced. In many higher education applications, those would be called the "core" areas rather than electives.

Another Way To Look at It: The Fit Between Security and Desired Outcomes

One of the more interesting aspects of the CC2005 report is the ranking by discipline of 60 fundamental competencies that might be expected of a computer graduate. The list is exhaustive, and because there is a difference in the type of employment for each discipline, there is a difference in what is expected. Thus there is a different set of presumed outcomes for computer scientists, software engineers, and IS workers. Nevertheless, one of the best ways of evaluating the usefulness and current application of the requirements of secure practice is to see just how well those match with the priority learning outcomes for each discipline.

The 60 expected capabilities are the direct consequence of the 40 learning topics. Therefore each outcome was parsed to determine which of the 40 topics could be specifically associated with it. Then, once the number of related topics was determined, the total references for each topic were compiled for the outcome.

For instance, if the outcome was to "design a user friendly interface," there are 255 common security topics associated with "design" and five references to "human/computer interfaces." That is the limit of topics that could reasonably be associated with interface design, and so the total number of security references for this outcome is 260. Since that is somewhere between moderate and good coverage based on the average number of references per topic, it might be said that there is a reasonable level of security knowledge involved in proper interface design.

Because employment expectations are different, each discipline within the CC2005 report had a different set of priority capabilities associated with it. Thus the capability requirements are different,

in the sense that each discipline assigns a different level of importance to each of the 60 outcomes. The CC2005 report uses six levels of importance to characterize potential expectations: "highest possible expectations," "highest expectations," "moderate expectations," "low expectations," "little expectations," and "no expectations."

We arrayed the desired outcomes for computer science, information systems, and software engineering into a single table and compared the relative level of outcome expectations for each. Not surprisingly, we found that the priority for the sixty outcomes is different for computer science, information systems, and software engineering work. Specifically, we found that secure software practice topics fit best with software engineering curricula and least with curricula associated with computer science programs. That is not surprising, since the intent of secure practice is to specify knowledge that practitioners can apply to real-world problems, and software engineering is probably the best aligned of the academic disciplines to that objective. The fact that information systems programs, which are also practitioner based, tend to score closer to software engineering in their relationship to secure practice reinforces this opinion.

Thus it would appear that the focus of secure practice is less academic than it is practitioner leaning. What that indicates is that it would be easier to introduce the current content into programs that are focused on applications and methods than ones in which principles and mathematical representation are the primary curricular focus. One other observation is that, although the "moderate expectations" category does not reflect priority areas of study in all of these disciplines, it is overwhelmingly the best aligned category for each discipline. What that might indicate is that, although secure software assurance is a legitimate area of study for all of these fields, it is not the highest priority in any of them. Only in the case of software engineering, whose curricular structure is life cycle based, is there consistent alignment above a moderate level of expectation between curricular outcomes and the knowledge elements associated with secure practice.

In terms of implementation, in each of these curricula, the practitioner orientation and the fact that security content is not the point of the field tends to indicate that the courses in which secure practice content would be most easily integrated would be those that are designed to provide students with knowledge about specific life cycle activities such as specification, design, and testing and assurance.

As a final note, the measurement process used in this study (a raw count) is inherently less accurate than expert contextual analysis of the meaning of each knowledge element. Therefore a more rigorous comparison should be undertaken to better characterize the functional relationship between the items in the CBK and the various curricular standards.

INCORPORATING SECURITY REQUIREMENTS ENGINEERING INTO MAINSTREAM ACADEMIA

Once we had better understood the relationship between the complete body of knowledge in security and the curricular recommendations for all computing disciplines, we were ready to tackle the question of how security requirements engineering is best presented in an academic setting.

The typical undergraduate curriculum does not provide much room for the addition of security requirements engineering practices other than as part of a project course that includes security requirements. There are, however, a number of ways that security requirements engineering methods could be incorporated into a software engineering curriculum (Mead, 2006). If an undergraduate project included requirements development, the students could be given an assignment to identify (and implement) security requirements along with other more traditional requirements. This would occur in the early part of the project. Alternatively, if the students did not develop the project's requirements, they could still be asked to recommend security requirements.

At the graduate (master's) level, it is much easier to see how security requirements might be addressed. This material could be part of a requirements course or a course on development of secure systems, with several lectures and an exercise or case study on security requirements. In a graduate level project course, the students would typically be developing requirements rather than developing software based on pre-existing requirements, so there would be opportunity to insert this methodology in such a course. In that instance the students would apply a method such as SQUARE as part of their requirements gathering process, and the instructor could grade the students on the quality of the security requirements and on the success of the implementation.

Another possibility is to incorporate the material into a course that is part of a security specialty within a graduate level program in software engineering or information systems. Typically there are several courses on information security, at least one of which deals with the development of secure software. Discussion of security requirements engineering could fit into a series of lectures and case studies. Eventually a half-semester or full-semester course could be devoted to security requirements engineering. This would also allow for a comparative study of various techniques that have been developed to support security requirements engineering.

Security Requirements Engineering Techniques

A report by Mead et al., which focuses on survivable requirements engineering, describes several requirements engineering techniques (Mead, 2003). In the course of assembling an elicitation framework and applying it to a software development effort, several effective approaches to security requirements engineering were identified, including

- Comprehensive, Lightweight Application Security Process—CLASP—is an activity-driven, role-based set of process components guided by formalized best practices. CLASP is designed to help software development teams build security into the early stages of existing and new-start software development life cycles in a structured, repeatable, and measurable way. CLASP is based on extensive field work by Secure Software employees in which the system resources of many development life cycles were decomposed to create a comprehensive set of security requirements. These resulting requirements form the basis of CLASP's Best Practices, which can enable organizations to systematically address vulnerabilities that, if exploited, can result in the failure of basic security services (e.g., confidentiality, authentication, and authorization). [http://www.owasp.org/index.php/Category:OWASP_CLASP_Project]
- Security Quality Requirements Engineering (SQUARE). This is a process aimed specifically at security requirements engineering. It is described in detail later in this chapter.
- Core security requirements artifacts (Moffett, 2004). This approach takes an artifact view and starts with the artifacts that are needed to achieve better security requirements. It provides a framework that includes both traditional requirements engineering approaches to functional requirements and an approach to security requirements engineering that focuses on assets and harm to those assets. "From requirements engineering it takes the concept of functional goals, which are operationalised into functional requirements, with appropriate constraints. From security engineering it takes the con-

cept of assets, together with threats of harm to those assets. Security goals aim to protect from those threats, and are operationalised into security requirements, which take the form of constraints on the functional requirements."
- Misuse/abuse cases. A security "misuse" case (Sindre, 2000; Alexander, 2003), a variation on a use case, is used to describe a scenario from the point of view of the attacker. Since use cases have proven useful in documenting normal use scenarios, they can also be used to document intruder usage scenarios, and ultimately to identify security requirements or security use cases. A similar concept has been described as an "abuse" case. One obvious application of a misuse case is in eliciting requirements. Since use cases are used successfully for eliciting requirements, it follows that misuse cases can be used to identify potential threats and to elicit security requirements. In this application, the traditional user interaction with the system is diagrammed simultaneously with the hostile user's interactions.

Another useful technique is attack trees for security requirements engineering (Ellison, 2003). Formal specification approaches to security requirements, such as Software Cost Reduction (SCR) (Heitmeyer, 2000) have also been useful.

INTEGRATING SECURITY REQUIREMENTS INTO STANDARD CURRICULA

A number of approaches can be used for integrating security requirements into standard curricula. At the National Institute of Informatics in Japan, the Top SE program [Honiden, 2007] includes security requirements engineering as part of its curriculum. The Top SE program includes discussion of misuse cases, TROPOS (Giorgini, 2007), and goal-driven requirements engineering (KAOS) (De Landtsheer, 2005). In addition there is a case study based on the Common Criteria.

Case studies for security requirements engineering and security engineering in general have been used at the International Institute of Information Technology, Hyderabad (Garg, 2006) as a means of bridging the industry/university gap.

The Networked Systems and Survivability (NSS) program at the Software Engineering Institute has, over three academic semesters, experimented with a novel technique to educate students on the development of security requirements engineering for software systems (Mead, 2006). In three separate course projects, thirteen students gained hands-on experience through case studies involving real-world software development projects. We present an expanded discussion of these case studies below.

A set of academic lectures has also been developed by the SEI for security requirements engineering and SQUARE. These are being piloted at University of Detroit Mercy and will be refined and made available to interested faculty elsewhere.

SQUARE CASE STUDIES

Using the Security Quality Requirements Engineering methodology (Mead, 2005a), the students were able to understand the importance of security requirements in software systems, as well as to improve the security foundation of the client projects with which they worked. In each study, the students were graduate students at Carnegie Mellon University. All were enrolled in an information security oriented curriculum, although their primary focus varied between security technology and information security policy.

Case Study Selection Process

The case study clients included industry and government projects. Specifically they included small to medium-size companies in the Pittsburgh area, a Department of Homeland Security project, and a Department of Defense project. Some of the considerations in project selection were (1) the ability to get access to key stakeholders in the organization, (2) projects that were a reasonable size for a one-semester project for a team of three to five students, (3) projects that were either new or major upgrades, although we did do some retrogressive analysis of existing projects, and (4) projects with a significant software development component. Note that clients were often concerned about the amount of time this would take, so we needed to be very sensitive to the need to manage meeting time and other client interactions. We also worked with a single point of contact on the client end so that we were not perceived as making constant demands on the time of large groups of staff members. We typically started with an overview briefing of the SQUARE process, identified key client participants, and then limited our interactions to only those participants until we were ready to report results.

Overview of the SQUARE Process

Security Quality Requirements Engineering is a model developed at Carnegie Mellon University by Nancy Mead of the Software Engineering Institute. The motivation behind SQUARE is to see whether good requirements engineering processes can be adapted specifically to the problem of identifying security requirements. If this can be done successfully, organizations will have the ability to identify security requirements up front rather than as an afterthought. The SQUARE process provides a means for eliciting, categorizing, and prioritizing security requirements for information technology systems and applications. Note that while there is nothing unique about the steps in the process, which have existed for many years in requirements engineering, we have seen relatively little evidence of their application to security requirements and even less on whether such a process is successful for developing security requirements.

Many of the existing methods that were described earlier fit nicely into the SQUARE process. These include misuse and abuse cases, attack trees, and formal methods. Others, such as the Common Criteria and SCR, suggest their own requirements engineering process. The SQUARE methodology seeks to build security concepts into the early stages of the development life cycle. The model may also be useful for documenting and analyzing the security aspects of fielded systems and could be used to steer future improvements and modifications to these systems.

The process is best applied by the project's requirements engineers and security experts in the context of supportive executive management and stakeholders. We believe the process works best when elicitation occurs after risk assessment (Step 4) has been done and when security requirements are specified prior to critical architecture and design decisions. Thus, critical business risks will be considered in the development of the security requirements.

The SQUARE steps are summarized below. A detailed discussion of SQUARE and how to apply it can be found in (Mead, 2005a).

Step 1: Agree on definitions
Input: Candidate definitions from IEEE and other standards

Techniques: Structured interviews, focus group
Participants: Stakeholders, requirements team

Output: Agreed-to definitions

Step 2: Identify security goals

Input: Definitions, candidate goals, business drivers, policies and procedures, examples

Techniques: Facilitated work session, surveys, interviews

Participants: Stakeholders, requirements engineer

Output: Goals

Step 3: Develop artifacts to support security requirements definition

Input: Potential artifacts (e.g., scenarios, misuse cases, templates, forms)

Techniques: Work session

Participants: Requirements engineer

Output: Needed artifacts: scenarios, misuse cases, models, templates, forms

Step 4: Perform risk assessment

Input: Misuse cases, scenarios, security goals

Techniques: Risk assessment method, analysis of anticipated risk against organizational risk tolerance, including threat analysis

Participants: Requirements engineer, risk expert, stakeholders

Output: Risk assessment results

Step 5: Select elicitation techniques

Input: Goals, definitions, candidate techniques, expertise of stakeholders, organizational style, culture, level of security needed, cost/benefit analysis, etc.

Techniques: Work session

Participants: Requirements engineer

Output: Selected elicitation techniques

Step 6: Elicit security requirements

Input: Artifacts, risk assessment results, selected techniques

Techniques: Accelerated Requirements Method (ARM), Joint Application Development (JAD), interviews, surveys, model-based analysis, checklists, lists of reusable requirements types, document reviews

Participants: Stakeholders facilitated by requirements engineer

Output: Initial cut at security requirements

Step 7: Categorize requirements as to level (system, software, etc.) and whether they are requirements or other kinds of constraints

Input: Initial requirements, architecture

Techniques: Work session using a standard set of categories

Participants: Requirements engineer, other specialists as needed

Output: Categorized requirements

Step 8: Prioritize requirements

Input: Categorized requirements and risk assessment results

Techniques: Prioritization methods such as AHP, Triage, Win-Win, etc.

Participants: Stakeholders facilitated by requirements engineer

Output: Prioritized requirements

Step 9: Requirements inspection

Input: Prioritized requirements, candidate formal inspection technique

Techniques: Inspection method such as Fagan, peer reviews, etc.

Participants: Inspection team

Output: Initial selected requirements, documentation of decision-making process and rationale

Novel Aspects of SQUARE Case Studies as a Learning Vehicle

In our academic case studies (Mead, 2006), the students had a variety of backgrounds. Some had a background in security and some had a background in software engineering or information technology. However, none of the students had experience in eliciting and documenting security requirements for software systems. It is also the case that they did not have experience working with methods, such as SQUARE, that were under development. The students therefore had to develop two products to complete their course requirements: (1) a document that was delivered to the client proposing security requirements and supporting artifacts for the client's project and (2) a process document delivered only to the faculty advisor. This second document described how the students went about applying each step in the process, whether it was easy or difficult to apply, and how it could be improved on. In other words, they were responsible for providing feedback to both the client and the faculty advisor for the purpose of improving the SQUARE process. To that end, the project provided them with a unique learning opportunity.

Evaluating the Work of the Students

It's always a challenge to find fair ways of evaluating the work of students who are working as a team but receive individual grades. The grading criteria that were used for the case study projects were as follows:

Client Satisfaction (25%)

- Quality of deliverables—reports, presentations, software, demonstrations.
- Significance of the team accomplishments.
- Quality of interactions with the client.
- How well client expectations were met.
- Effectiveness in solving the client's problem.
- Transparency—how easily the work products are understood.
- Ease of use and/or implementation of the work products.

Peer Evaluation (25%)

- Extent to which peers (team members) contributed to the overall project.
- Peer expectation management. (Did each team member meet the expectations of the team as a whole? Was the team kept informed? Did each team member share the workload? Was assistance provided to other team members?)
- "Free riding." (An individual team member who does not deliver work products as expected by the team or who does not participate in team activities will receive a measurably lower grade.)

Quality of the Deliverables—Reports, Presentations (30%)

- Significance of the accomplishments of the team.
- Creativity and elegance in the final product as delivered.
- Reports and presentations of high quality.
- Completeness of the final deliverables; all deliverables delivered as required.
- Adherence to the project plan as modified during the term.
- Proactively taking measures to ensure that the project is on track.
- Prompt submissions of weekly individual project status reports.

Project Management/Teamwork/etc. (15%)

- Advisor expectation management. (Was the faculty advisor kept informed? Were scheduled meetings and telecoms attended?)
- Client expectation management. (How well did the team *manage* the expectations of the client?)
- Team cohesion. (Did the team work together effectively? Did the team work to bring along the weaker members of the team? Did the team perform as a unit in public?)
- Communication and coordination. (Were communications made promptly and effectively?)

Other factors (5%)

- Personal growth of the team member.
- Extent to which the project fulfilled expectations of the MISM Program.
- Effort invested.

Students who met requirements—completed the work assigned to them, delivered acceptable products, participated in team meetings, advisor meetings, and client meetings, and received acceptable peer reviews—could expect to earn a B. Students who made less contribution than this, in terms of effort expended, failure to attend meetings, failure to deliver work products as promised, or inability to do the technical work, received a lower grade. Students who made a greater technical contribution to the accomplishments of the team, delivered superior products, took on extra work, and contributed constructively to meetings and to team interactions got a higher grade.

Assessment of the Benefits of This Approach

At present, we have only qualitative data confirming that the SQUARE approach is beneficial. Many of the students have gone on to positions in the security field and have indicated that the case study work was very useful to them. Here are comments from two students that we have stayed in touch with.

Hassan is with Ernst & Young: "The real-world experience I gained from the SQUARE project gave me the perfect set of information security project management and budgeting skills that were invaluable in my job at Ernst & Young."

Eric is working as a software engineer with the Space and Naval Warfare Systems Center (SPAWAR), San Diego: "While working on the SQUARE project with Dr. Mead, I took part in several in-depth case studies involving organizations of varying size and reputation. It was a wonderful opportunity to get a feel for how real companies develop and manage large IT projects. This insight, along with the security focus of SQUARE, allowed me to hit the ground running here at SPAWAR with the security projects we're developing. Overall it was an extremely valuable experience and I'm grateful that I was involved."

Also, we received the following testimonial from a client that was a subject of the study: "Our company operates in a lean, fast-paced, ever-changing environment, and I had some reserva-

tions as to how much time we could spend in accommodating the CMU graduate students' project goals and their busy schedules. I was impressed with how well we coordinated efforts in setting meeting dates, adhering to the schedule, and sharing information with minimal inconvenience to either side. Our company provided them with an opportunity to assess a many-faceted product, and they responded graciously by sharing the different techniques they used to analyze the security aspects of our application. Their results gave us insight that has since influenced our application development and configuration. It was a pleasure working with the three separate groups and their sponsor over the two-year period."

FUTURE PLANS

At present we are piloting workshop and academic course materials for security requirements engineering. This material will be made available to educators who wish to incorporate such topics into software engineering courses. In addition, we are doing further study of the coverage of the software assurance body of knowledge in standard software engineering curricula. As experience with these approaches grows, our plans include the gathering of more quantitative data to show the benefit of the approaches we have discussed here. It is our hope that in the future there will be more synergy between software assurance and software engineering education.

REFERENCES

Addison, T., & Vallabh, S. (2000). *Controlling Software Project Risks – an Empirical Study of Methods Used by Experienced Project Managers*. KPMG.

Alexander, I. (2003). Misuse cases: Use cases with hostile intent. *IEEE Software, 20*(1), 58-66.

Benzel, T. (1989). Integrating security requirements and software development standards. In *Proceedings of the 12th National Computer Security Conference* (pp. 435-458). Fort Meade, MD: National Computer Security Center.

Boehm, B., & Basili, V. (2001). Software defect reduction – Top 10 list. *IEEE Computer, 34*(1), 135-137.

Carr, J. J. (2000). Requirements engineering and management: The key to designing quality complex systems. *The TQM Magazine, 12*(6), 400-407.

Clark, R. A., & Schmidt, H. A. (2002). *A national strategy to secure cyberspace.* Washington, DC: The President's Critical Infrastructure Protection Board.

De Landtsheer, R., & van Lamsweerde, A. (2005). Reasoning about confidentiality at requirements engineering time. In *Proceedings of the 10th European Software Engineering Conference held jointly with 13th ACM SIGSOFT International Symposium on Foundations of Software Engineering* (pp. 41-49). New York, NY: ACM.

Ellison, R. J., & Moore, A. P. (2003). *Trustworthy refinement through intrusion-aware design* (Tech. Rep. No. CMU/SEI-2003-TR-002). Pittsburgh, PA: Software Engineering Institute, Carnegie Mellon University. Retrieved November 1, 2007 from http://www.sei.cmu.edu/publications/documents/03.reports/03tr002.html

Garg, K., & Varma, V. (2006). Security: Bridging the academia-industry gap using a case study. In *XIII Asia Pacific Software Engineering Conference Proceedings* (pp. 485-492). New York, NY: IEEE Computer Society Press.

Giorgini, P., Mouratidis, H., & Zannone, N. (2007). Modelling Security and Trust with Secure Tropos. *Integrating Security and Software Engineering: Advances and Future Visions*, 160-189. Hershey, PA: IGI Global.

Hecht, H., & Hecht, M. (2000). How reliable are requirements for reliable software? *Software Tech News, 3*(4). Retrieved May 31, 2007 from http://www.softwaretechnews.com

Heitmeyer, C., & Bharadwaj, R. (2000). Applying the SCR requirements method to the light control case study. *Journal of Universal Computer Science, 6*(7), 650-678.

Honiden, S., Tahara, Y., Yoshioka, N., Taguchi, K., & Washizaki, H. (2007). Top SE: Educating superarchitects who can apply software engineering tools to practical development in Japan. In *Proceedings of 29th International Conference on Software Engineering (ICSE'07)* (pp. 708-718). New York, NY: IEEE Computer Society.

Joint Taskforce for Computing Curricula (JTCC) 2004. (2004). *Software Engineering 2004: Curricular Guidelines for Undergraduate Programs in Software Engineering.* New York, NY: ACM and IEEE.

Joint Taskforce for Computing Curricula (JTCC) 2005. (2005). *Computing curricula 2005: The overview report.* New York, NY: ACM and IEEE.

Jones, C. (2005). *Software quality in 2005: A survey of the state of the art.* Marlborough, MA: Software Productivity Research.

Konieczka, S. (2003). Predictable releases: The key to quality software. Boulder, CO: SCM Labs, Inc. Retrieved November 1, 2007 from http://www.stickyminds.com/

Kuehl, C. S. (2001, October). *Improving system requirements quality through application of an operational concept process: An essential element in system sustainment.* Paper presented at NDIA 4th Annual Systems Engineering Conference, Dallas, TX. Retrieved November 2, 2007 from http://www.dtic.mil/ndia

Kumar, R. L. (2002). Managing risks in IT projects: An options perspective. *Information & Management, 40*(1), 63-74.

Lauesen, S., & Vinter, O. (2001). Preventing requirement defects: An experiment in process improvement. *Requirements Engineering, 6*(1), 37-50.

Linger, R. C., Mead, N. R., & Lipson, H. F. (1998). Requirements definition for survivable systems. In *Third International Conference on Requirements Engineering* (pp. 14-23). Los Alamitos, CA: IEEE Computer Society.

McGibbon, T. (1999). *A business case for software process improvement revised.* Washington, DC: DoD Data Analysis Center for Software (DACS).

Mead, N. R. (2003) *Requirements Engineering for Survivable Systems* (Tech. Rep. No. CMU/SEI-2003-TN-013). Pittsburgh, PA: Software Engineering Institute, Carnegie Mellon University. Retrieved November 2, 2007 from http://www.sei.cmu.edu/publications/documents/03.reports/03tn013.html

Mead, N. R., Hough, E. D., & Stehney, T. R. II. (2005a). *Security quality requirements (SQUARE) methodology* (Tech. Rep. No. CMU/SEI-2005-TR-009). Pittsburgh, PA: Software Engineering Institute, Carnegie Mellon University. Retrieved November 2, 2007 from http://www.sei.cmu.edu/publications/documents/05.reports/05tr009.html

Mead, N. R., & Stehney, T. R. II. (2005b, May). *Security quality requirements engineering (SQUARE) methodology.* Paper presented at the meeting of the Software Engineering for Secure Systems (SESS05), ICSE 2005 International Workshop on Requirements for High Assurance Systems, St. Louis, MO.

Mead, N. R., & Hough, E. D. (2006). Security requirements engineering for software systems: Case studies in support of software engineering education. In *Proceedings of the 19th Conference on Software Engineering Education and Training* (pp. 149-158). Los Alamitos, CA: IEEE Computer Society Press.

Moffett, J. D., Haley, C. B., & Nuseibeh, B. (2004). *Core Security Requirements Artefacts* (Technical Report 2004/23, ISSN 1744-1986). UK: The Open University. Retrieved November 2, 2007 from http://mcs.open.ac.uk/computing-tr/

National Infrastructure Advisory Council (NIAC). (2003). *National strategy to secure cyberspace.* Washington, DC: U.S. Department of Homeland Security.

Newman, Michael. (2002). *Software errors cost U.S. economy $59.5 billion annually.* Gaithersburg, MD: National Institute of Standards and Technology (NIST).

Palyagar, B. (2004). Measuring and influencing requirements engineering process quality. In *Proceedings of AWRE 04, 9th Australian Workshop on Requirements Engineering.* Retrieved November 2, 2007 from http://awre2004.cis.unisa.edu.au/

Palyagar, B. (2004). A framework for validating process improvements in requirements engineering. Retrieved November 2, 2007 from http://www.ics.mq.edu.au/~bpalyaga/papers/palyagar_b.pdf

President's Information Technology Advisory Committee (PITAC). (2005). *Cybersecurity: A crisis of prioritization.* Arlington, VA: Executive Office of the President, National Coordination Office for Information Technology Research and Development.

Redwine, S. T. (Ed.). (2006). *Software assurance: A guide to the common body of knowledge to produce, acquire and sustain secure software, version 1.1.* Washington, DC: U.S. Department of Homeland Security

Regnell, B., & Beremark, P. (1998). A market driven requirements engineering process – Results from industrial process improvement program. Retrieved November 2, 2007 from http://www.tts.lth.se/Personal/bjornr/Papers/CEIRE98-REJ.pdf

Sawyer, P., Sommerville, I., & Viller, S. (1997). Requirements process improvement through the phased introduction of good practice. *Software Process Improvement and Practice, 3*(1), 19-34.

Shoemaker, D., Mead, N. R., Drommi, A., Bailey, J., & Ingalsbe, J. (2007). SWABOK's fit to common curricular standards. In *Proceedings of the 20th Conference on Software Engineering Education*

and Training. Los Alamitos, CA: IEEE Computer Society Press.

Sindre, G., & Opdahl, A. (2000). Eliciting security requirements by misuse cases. In *Proceedings of TOOLS Pacific 2000* (pp. 120-130). Los Alamitos, CA: IEEE Computer Society Press.

Soo Hoo, K., Sudbury, A. W., & Jaquith, A. R. (2001). Tangible ROI through secure software engineering. *Secure Business Quarterly, 1*.

Zave, P. (1997). Classification of research efforts in RE. *ACM Computer Surveys, 29*(4), 315-321.

Section IV
Project-Based
Software Engineering

Chapter VII
The Software Enterprise:
Preparing Industry–Ready Software Engineers

Kevin A. Gary
Arizona State University, USA

ABSTRACT

"You can't teach experience" – but you can sure try. At the Polytechnic Campus of Arizona State University, we are developing a learning-by-doing approach for teaching software engineering called the Software Enterprise. The Capstone experience is extended to two one-year projects and serves as the primary teaching and learning vehicle for best practices in software engineering. Several process features are introduced in an attempt to make projects, or more importantly the experience gained from project work, more applicable to industry expectations. At the conclusion of the Software Enterprise students have an applied understanding of how to leverage software process as a tool for successful project evolution. This chapter presents the Software Enterprise, focusing the presentation on three novel aspects: a highly iterative, learner-centered pedagogical model, cross-year mentoring, and multiple projects as a novel means of sequencing learning objectives.

INTRODUCTION

Students must emerge from a "write-a-program-get-a-grade" mentality to a "follow-a-process-produce-a-deliverable" mentality (and eventually to "use-and-improve-processes-to-solve-customer-problems"). This evolution from learner to practitioner is a cultural mindset even at the personal level. Junior professionals are confronted with real-world situations immediately after graduating and entering the workforce. Professionalism challenges junior engineers in a different way than academic ethics. Junior professionals can gain professionalism through formal and informal mentoring relationships in professional settings such as internships, but we should not rely solely on industry to accept this burden; we must incorporate it into the learning environment.

The Software Enterprise, introduced four years ago in the Division of Computing Studies at Arizona State University's Polytechnic campus (ASU Poly), is our attempt at preparing new graduates for the software profession. In the model of a polytechnic, an increased emphasis is placed on hands-on practice over pure scientific study. The mechanism chosen for this approach is the Capstone project, which traditionally focuses on one or two semester projects required at the conclusion of the undergraduate degree program. The Capstone project, an inherited requirement from engineering disciplines, is often considered more a "rite of passage" than a teaching and learning opportunity. We contend the Capstone experience provides a great opportunity to be the primary teaching and learning model in software engineering. Our solution is a learn-by-doing model called the Software Enterprise.

The Software Enterprise is one part "evolution" and one part "revolution." It leverages some of the better practices we have seen from the multitude of Capstone software engineering projects published over the past decade. In particular, mentoring relationships within student teams are emphasized, as is a careful sequencing of course and project topics. The Software Enterprise also presents a novel pedagogical model geared to accelerate students' comprehension of software engineering. This combination of old and new is wrapped in an applied learning program so as to better prepare new graduates for the software engineering profession.

This chapter is organized as follows. The next section motivates the need for the Enterprise by discussing some perceived shortcomings of new computing graduates. The pedagogical innovation of the Enterprise is presented next, followed by a detailed description of how the pedagogy is implemented at ASU Poly. We conclude with an ongoing evaluation of the Enterprise and a summary.

BACKGROUND AND MOTIVATION

Software engineer ranks as one of the fastest growing occupations (U.S. BLS, 2007) with the highest median salary (Morsch, 2006). Unfortunately, many employers consider new graduates unproductive, while at the same time those graduates feel unprepared for that first job. Traditional computer science education is criticized as outdated, too theoretical, and too fractured. As educators, we should do a better job preparing new graduates for what lies ahead. We should expose students to the true nature of today's computing challenges, strive to ground students in fundamental theory, and provide them the modern tools a modern discipline requires.

The Software Enterprise uses a bottom-up approach to incorporating process best practices and process models via a multi-year Capstone experience. Example best practices include configuration management, unit testing, and code inspections for software development. By software process models we mean the incorporation of accepted process models as a mechanism for teaching and learning software construction, maintenance, and project management. The ability to identify issues, analyze risks, debate, create consensus, and work within a team are examples of managerial skills software engineers require perhaps more than other engineering disciplines due to the unique challenges in developing software products. We also contend there is more in the intersection of emphasizing process execution and project management skills than is given proper due. In other words, how does a learning facilitator demonstrate the need for process structure while at the same time mentor students on the judgment needed to know when to alter the current process instance to ensure project success?

The approach in the Software Enterprise is to provide a process structure, and then give teams "just enough rope" to resolve their own process-related issues. We do this in several ways. Traumatic "real-world events" are injected during project execution that force teams to exercise soft-skills while at the same time leveraging their process. Project teams force seniors to mentor juniors, providing a mentoring communication model. Students engage in reflective learning to identify the most appropriate process techniques and are asked to explain why they chose to employ these techniques over others available.

In our personal experience in industry and in discussions with industry advisors to our programs, a significant issue for employers hiring new graduates is that graduates are ill-equipped to practice the profession. Many students can manage to get good grades in software engineering classes, but when confronted with a software system of industry-level complexity, can they put that knowledge into practice? It is our opinion that often they cannot. We believe the culprit here is the traditional curricular pattern often adopted by software engineering programs shown in Figure 1.

The traditional model, following the general curricular patterns prescribed in the SE2004 guide (Association for Computing Machinery [ACM] & The Institute for Electrical and Electronic Engineers Computer Society [IEEE-CS], 2004) asks students to first take a breadth-oriented survey-of-the-field style course (or courses) that exposes them to a breadth of engineering practices and processes but typically lacks depth in any given area. The results are students who can recite the basic principles, but who lack the comprehension to apply them. These types of courses are then followed by courses that delve into a specific process topic in significant depth, for example a Software Design or a Software Quality Assurance course. These courses focus on deep skills development within the narrow process area. Students then complete the program with the capstone project, which asks them to apply this knowledge in a full semester project. This approach suffers from a "toy problem effect." Many students do

Figure 1. Traditional software engineering curricular pattern

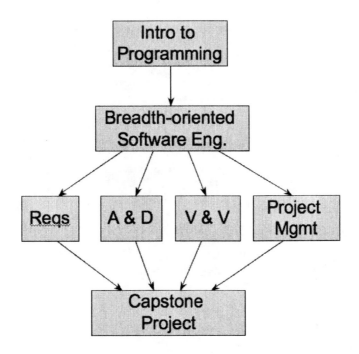

not get exposure to the full engineering process spectrum in a manner that allows them to apply the deeper skill sets they may have developed in a particular area. The results are students who can claim knowledge of a particular skill, but lack the context in which to apply this knowledge. A typical conversation an interviewer might have with a graduating student might be "well, yes I did a few use cases in my Software Requirements class, but no I have not done one of that size nor do I understand how to use that model to drive analysis and test planning."

THE SOFTWARE ENTERPRISE

We propose a new methodology for evolving a student's competencies from knowledge to comprehension to applied knowledge by co-locating lectures, problem-centered learning, and complex process planning activities in time. In other words, disseminate information, immediately follow with problem-centered learning techniques, and then ask the student teams to apply the knowledge within an ongoing project instance that follows a specified process. The result is a highly iterative methodology for evolving the student's competencies in a rapid fashion (Figure 2).

Contrast this model with the traditional software engineering instruction model shown in Figure 1.

We believe the Enterprise method of coupling disseminated knowledge to skills practice to incorporated process tasks leads to quicker comprehension and applied knowledge than the traditional model. We refer to this model as an "Iterative Instructor-facilitated, Learner-centered" model. Learners are responsible for individual study readings and exercises, for working individually or in small teams on problem-centered learning exercises, and for participating in complex projects under specified process roles (role playing). Instructors are responsible for disseminating knowledge via lectures and as a filter for reference content (research articles, industry publications, online searches, etc.). Instructors

Figure 2. Iterative instructor-facilitated learner-centered model © 2006 ASEE. Used with permission.

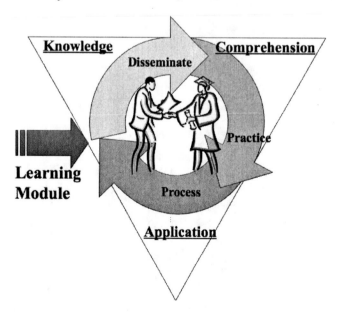

are responsible for crafting scripted exercises that allow for practice of specific skills. Instructors are also responsible for "coaching" teams and providing a context for projects. For example, the instructor serves the external roles of Senior Management and Technical Consultant for the current set of projects.

ENTERPRISE SEQUENCE IMPLEMENTATION

This section describes the implementation details used at ASU Polytechnic from student and faculty perspectives.

Student Curricular and Project Trajectories

The curricular topics covered in the Enterprise sequence are given in Table 1.

The Software Enterprise calls for two one-year projects that a student participates in sequentially. This sequence is shown in Table 2.

A student entering the Enterprise sequence begins by taking a Tools and Process course. In this course a student gains exposure to a set of tools that support the software process. This includes IDEs, data gathering and analysis tools (metrics), testing (unit, system, integration, and performance), build and deployment, and documentation. There is also a significant PSP component to train new students on how to account for time and defect injection rates. First semester students are currently asked to participate in requirements and design reviews plus prototype development during the second half (elaboration phase) of the Fall semester with the senior-level students (the first and third semester courses are scheduled at the same time).

The student's second semester (Spring Year 1 in Table 2) is spent in Construction and Transition. Students spend significant time developing the software according to specific project requirements. Students are also responsible for verification and validation activities against the requirements, and for transitioning activities such as packaging, deployment scripts, performance and scalability testing, and product documentation. Students are managed and mentored by students completing the fourth semester of the sequence. The completion of this semester also marks the completion of the student's first project.

In the third semester (Fall Year 2 in Table 2), a student begins a new project by starting with Inception and Elaboration. Students elicit requirements, create a vision document, document requirements, perform requirements analysis resulting in a logical model of the system, and construct an initial architecture realized both in code (User Interface and Architectural prototypes) and in an architecture description document. These artifacts serve as the input products for the Spring semester's Construction and Transition phases.

In the fourth and final semester (Spring Year 2 in Table 2) of the Enterprise sequence, a student serves as a process/project manager, quality assurance manager, or chief architect. As process manager, fourth semester students are responsible for process planning, process monitoring, and process changes. Fourth semester students are responsible for writing the test and deployment/release plans for their software products. Each student is responsible for one or more projects and one or more resources (the students in semester two). Fourth semester students are also responsible for ensuring the construction follows the architecture set forth in the Fall semester by the architecture document, or for managing changes to the architecture if they are desired.

Importantly, year 1 students act the learning role of mentors to year 2 students (i.e. seniors mentor juniors). This arrangement allows upperclassmen to mentor lower-division students in a highly interactive manner. For example, the Construction and Transition activities of second semester participants are planned, estimated, and tracked by fourth semester students. Year 2 students in the Enterprise also mentor in the sense they completed Year 1 and as such understand the exact situations these students face. Co-located weekly lab meetings facilitate collaborative and mentoring relationships.

The sequencing of topics and courses shown in Tables 1 and 2 is done for practical reasons. Course 1: Tools and Process, is a tool-centric course that indoctrinates first semester juniors

into the Enterprise. At this point in their academic careers, first semester juniors (in our program at least), have not relied heavily on tools and have not exercised the full range of software engineering activities, at least on a scalable team-oriented project. These students are given a light introduction to concepts and a heavy emphasis on tools. For example, build management is a topic covered using Apache's Ant tool (ant.apache.org). To most students at this level, a multiple (many) file,

Table 1. Software enterprise curricular topics

Course 1: Tools & Process	Course 2: Construction & Transition
Intro to PSP	GUI development
Using an IDE	Software Construction
Build Management	Unit Testing Concepts
Use case diagrams	Test-driven development
Unit testing	Defensive Programming
Functional testing	Refactoring
Metrics tools	Code Reviews
CM tool	Static/dynamic code analysis
	Configuration Management
	Professionalism & Ethics
Course 3: Inception & Elaboration	**Course 4: Process & Project Management**
Software Lifecycle Process	Software Development Planning
Requirements Engineering	Task Identification / WBS
Requirements Documentation	PERT, Critical Path Analysis
Requirements Elicitation	Task Scheduling / Gantt charts
Use Cases	Estimation
User Stories	Risk Management
Requirements Quality	Inspections
Requirements Analysis	Verification and Validation
RUP Analysis	Test Planning
Structured Analysis	Test Script Writing
Usability	Release Management
Requirements Management	Postmortem

Table 2. Software enterprise student participation trajectory

Year in Sequence	Project	Fall	Spring
Year 1 (Juniors)	1	Course 1	Course 2
Year 2 (Seniors/Graduates)	2	Course 3	Course 4

many package compilation and assembly process based on 3rd party components (jars) is a new experience, at least on a scalable level. Course 1 focuses on proficiency in Ant to complete "builds" and "deployments," even in lieu of a complete comprehension of component-based software engineering. Our objective is to get students to think in terms of building and deploying software instead of merely compiling and running it. This approach to Course 1 is out of practical necessity, and results in a situation where these students are gently brought into the projects; they are not turned loose from week 1. Note that most of the topics in Course 1 are revisited for greater conceptual depth later in the sequence.

Course 2 covers topics typically not included in traditional computing programs, but ones we believe essential to becoming a better programmer. The foundation of most topics in Course 2 comes from the Agile community, where code-level quality best practices are emphasized more than in other process models. Lectures in Course 2 cover conceptual foundations, while lab sessions put the concepts into practice. For example, the Configuration Management topic includes concepts like codeline quality thresholds, codeline branching patterns, and connections to release management; the lab has students create sandboxes, perform checkouts, updates, and merges. Course 2 students play the role of software developer, configuration manager, and build manager on project teams, so these concepts are put directly into practice. Whereas Course 1 gradually migrates students toward the pedagogical model shown in Figure 2, Course 2 follows it exactly.

Course 3 resembles requirements courses in many computing programs with any reasonable emphasis in software engineering; however the Enterprise course emphasizes the communication and understanding over specification. Significant time (more than half a semester) is spent on the convergent pipeline from business idea to requirements discovery to prioritized requirements identified through an iterative refinement process. The refinement process is particularly key, as teams are asked to repeatedly revisit requirements for clarity and maturity, expressed in terms of the quality attributes from the IEEE-830 standard (IEEE-CS 1998). Reflective learning is perhaps most important in this course, as students come to realize the process of eliciting and communicating requirements is not as simple as walking in and asking a project sponsor what they want.

Course 3 has the most curricular content, and the sheer breadth and depth of the material is challenging to cover for faculty and absorb for students. For students, this is their first exposure to a topic for which there is no concrete answer; requirements remain a primarily subjective process. This is particularly acute in the Enterprise due to the emphasis on communication (elicitation) and understanding (translation to architecture) over merely learning a set of specification notations and document formats. We also note, based on anecdotal observations and project grades, foreign students tend to struggle in such a course. We suggest this is due to the lecture-oriented push model prevalent in these cultures, and conclude that this makes such a course an even more important component of their educational experience.

By the time students reach Course 4, they are fully immersed in the Enterprise, meaning they are able to draw on the experiences of the previous 3 courses. They tend to be highly motivated to excel on their projects and take true ownership of the deliverables. Obstacles related to adapting to the pedagogical model are completely absent at this point, as students are now accustomed to rapid exposure and integration of new concepts. One common phenomenon in this course is students complain that they wish they knew of the techniques covered earlier, particularly in project management. Throughout the first 3 courses students organize team activities using a "common sense" approach, meaning they rely on ad hoc planning and monitoring techniques. This is done on purpose so that students understand the utility and importance of these techniques and the challenges in the job of a project manager. The goal is to combat the stereotype of a project manager's job as lacking in complexity, and "not as hard as the technical stuff." Course 4 students ultimately take ownership of the projects; while Course 3 tasks include identifying all stakeholders, Course 4 students are truly beholden to them.

Faculty Perspective and Logistical Issues

This section covers many of the important logistical considerations faculty face in the Software Enterprise.

Selecting a Process Lifecycle Model

The Software Enterprise uses a process *meta-model* to constrain process planning and process lifecycle model execution. The Software Enterprise constrains projects to use one process *meta-model* (a higher-order process model that may incorporate specific lifecycle models and process practices). This keeps major release points in synch across teams, and provides a basis for a higher-level of decision-making than exercised by projects constrained to a specific process lifecycle model. Process meta-models considered were the Personal/Team Software Process (PSP/TSP) (Humphrey 1997; Humphrey 2000), Agile methods specifically extreme programming (XP) (Beck 2000) the Rational Unified Process (RUP) (Krutchen 2000), and the Spiral/Theory-W model (Boehm et. al. 1998).

Our decision was to use the RUP as the process meta-model for the Software Enterprise. We do incorporate aspects of the Win-Win Spiral model where relevant, such as risk analysis, risk management, phase boundary planning, prototyping, and negotiation. Though "borrowing" activities from the Spiral model, the RUP model is used due to current tool support, availability of texts and other supporting materials, definition of a collaborative model with team roles, and inclu-

sion of a Transition (deployment) phase. It also helps that RUP's four phases line up better on semester boundaries than the reentrant nature of the Spiral model.

We decided against using Agile/XP methods at the process meta-model level. Logistically, students do not spend enough time on a single course to allow for the daily interactions needed for XP (Umphress, Hendrix, & Cross, 2002). More importantly, there is too much of a reliance on experience and constant integration to provide a suitable framework for student learning of software engineering in a project setting. Stated another way, many XP projects are successful due to the ability and experience of the engineers involved and their proximity to constantly collaborate. Students simply do not have the skill level or the consistent schedule needed to be successful with an Agile meta-model. However, many Agile methods, specifically XP, are very helpful in identifying practices useful during software construction, and we incorporate problem-centered learning modules based on these practices during the second semester (Construction & Transition) of the Enterprise sequence. Useful XP practices include refactoring, test-driven development, pair programming, metrics for evolution, configuration management, customer walkthroughs, frequent integration, and estimating velocity.

We also decided not to use the PSP/TSP at the software lifecycle level. After reviewing the textbook materials (Humphrey 1997; Humphrey 2000) and online materials (Carnegie Mellon 2005) for these processes and reviewing the literature for examples of their application for software engineering education (Borstler et. al. 2002; Hilburn & Humphrey, 2002; Sebern 2005), we considered them simply too burdensome to introduce at the lifecycle model level. The PSP/TSP lacks the flexibility of RUP and the Spiral model at the process meta-level. In addition, the method for employing it implies a take-it-or-leave-it approach. Because we could not decouple PSP/TSP activities from each other cleanly, we also did not employ individual PSP/TSP modules into the sequence in the same way as we employ XP practices discussed above. However, as we describe below, we eventually did find it important to leverage the PSP for first-year Enterprise participants.

Project Process Logistics

Projects proceed in iterations. Dates for iterations are set by the facilitator and typically run three weeks. Iterations are necessary to ensure there are well-defined synchronization and feedback points during project execution. Teams are required to indicate expectations for the iteration on a weekly status report, which includes progress on deliverables, schedule, and risks addressed. At the conclusion of an iteration teams are expected to revisit these expectations and indicate how well reality matched expectations, and do a simple causal analysis explaining any major deviations. This is a simple yet effective form of reflective learning.

The structure the Enterprise adopts is motivated by a need to give students enough process to guide them, while leaving certain details for teams to work out. This approach has worked for other project-oriented courses in the literature (Frailey, 2006; Umphress, Hendrix, & Cross, 2002). In particular, teams are presented best practices from a variety of software lifecycle models and asked to choose which ones they wish to apply for a given task. For example, SRS documents may or may not include use case analyses, user stories, or structured analysis artifacts such as structure charts or P-specs. Teams must submit a "rationale" document and give a presentation at the end of each phase that explains why they used particular techniques and did not use others. One may argue that in doing so we reduce the utility of the process model as a whole, and this may be the case. But we believe it is more important for students to assess best practices, exercise judgment in selecting practices, and reflect on the decisions than it is to prescribe practices by

rigidly adhering to a specific model. Instead of rote execution of a prescriptive process, teams must identify situations and determine the path that will lead to success. This mimics our understanding of industry best practices by incorporating a process framework but customizing best practices to the project instances.

This is a difficult approach to integrate into curricula for several reasons. Most process practices are fairly coupled to a specific process model, meaning you cannot mix and match best practices within other models easily. For example, RUP test case planning is use case driven. XP planning game estimation is tied to attributes sketched on user story cards. As a corollary, most software process-related teaching material presents best practices from the perspective of a specific process. We have not identified a text (we currently use (Leffingwell & Widrig 2003) for Inception and Elaboration, and (McConnell 2004) for Construction and Transition) that presents, in a suitable way, a detailed cross-section of best practices from all the major software process models.

Identifying Good Projects

A significant amount of prep work is required to identify good projects (and good project sponsors), and then match student teams to those projects. The ideal project for the Software Enterprise is one that (1) comes from off-campus, (2) sponsored by a project manager, (3) based technologically off an existing solution or set of solutions, and (4) vaguely defined. We arrived at these ideals through trial and error, and acknowledge these ideals are in fact idealistic; no single project ever fully attains them. These ideals are discussed next.

The best projects do not necessarily come from industry, but the best projects do come from off-campus. Some Enterprise projects have been sponsored off-campus by other academic institutions, most notably Mesa Community College and ASU's University Technology Office (located on a different campus). Several industry projects have chosen to meet primarily on-campus, often as the industry sponsor's excuse to "get out of the office." It is the student teams that need to be removed from their comfort zone. By conducting customer meetings at the customer site, student teams are much more cognizant of the business realities of the sponsoring organization, and as a result are better prepared and more professional. In a sense, it forces teams to act as service organizations (Poole, 2003). The Software Enterprise identifies project sponsors through personal industry contacts and industrial advisory boards. Only after off-campus sponsors are accounted for are on-campus sponsors considered.

The best projects are sponsored by project managers, especially those with limited software development expertise. Sponsors with significant technical expertise are often too eager to solve problems for the team, and also tend to not express requirements but instead define technical tasks. This is particularly evident in Course 3, where project teams are charged with eliciting requirements, prototyping, and defining architecture. These activities are amongst the most challenging to students. While certainly some benefit is gained from technical interaction with industry mentor types, too often these technologists become a solution crutch. Faculty members also make poor project sponsors, as they usually are interested in the learning objectives and assessment criteria of the projects. In short, they think they are teaching and grading the teams instead of sponsoring them. The situation is worse if the faculty member participates in the Enterprise in any fashion due to an inability, on both sides, to create distinct lines between student-faculty and team-sponsor interactions. Project managers who are not active technically (though manage technical projects) have worked best as they tend to follow a model of interaction that focuses on expectations, plans, risks, and progress on deliverables, and as such teams become accustomed to focusing their work the service they are to provide. Unfortunately,

at this time most Enterprise projects are sponsored by technologists, either from industry or academia.

The best projects leverage existing technologies. We have found that students are tremendously lacking in their ability to work, at an implementation level, with existing source code. The main reason for this is simple - they haven't been asked to yet. This is a larger problem for computing curricula. Students are not asked before the Enterprise to examine a large body of source code and understand its structure and style. Students are typically naïve about the scale of software systems, even ones they use every day. As an example, one in-class exercise asked students to estimate the lines of code in a specific software system they use almost every day. The system in question is about 2 million lines of code; more than half the class estimated 10 thousand lines or less, 2 less than one thousand. The Enterprise requires teams to leverage existing bodies of source code, often taken from previous solutions or from the open source community. Furthermore, most projects have a significant integration requirement, be it data or control integration. These projects are very useful for their realism as well as their technical characteristics.

The best projects are vaguely defined. The principal objective of Course 3 is to gain a shared understanding of the problem and solution spaces through elicitation, prototyping, and architecture. Giving projects that are too "canned" reduces the project to a big programming exercise, stripping the team of the need to experience how to perform an iterative refinement process. As Szyperski points out, stakeholders typically are better at expressing requirements as incremental extensions to systems with which they are already familiar (Szyperski, 2005). However, we do not want a system where the requirements are readily expressed by the customer; instead we want students to work at elicitation to draw those requirements out. On the other hand, giving projects that are too discovery oriented are typically overwhelming to students at this level as they require research and critical inquiry skills typically required of graduate students. Because the entry point for projects is Course 3, we look for projects where a sponsor has a concrete vision or idea, but has not gone down the path of fleshing the idea out or assigning resources to it. Sponsors write a short narrative "elevator pitch" regarding the project idea, and Enterprise faculty members engage in a brief give-and-take over email or the phone to determine whether the sponsor is at the right point for requirements elicitation.

Projects and potential sponsors are evaluated based on these attributes, though again no project has ever been able to address all of these perfectly. Often the burden is on the Enterprise facilitator to note beforehand where potential hurdles may arise, and attempt to navigate ways to clear them.

Supporting Heavily Tooled Environments

Professional software engineers rely heavily on tools to help with productivity and scalability. The Enterprise, mostly in Course 1, exposes students to tools in practical use. Table 3 below summarizes the tools used, their purpose, and some short comments on their utility in the Enterprise.

In many instances the specific tool chosen out of many options is not significant, assuming fundamental concepts taught in the classroom can be implemented by the tool. For example, though there are real practical differentiators to CM tools CVS, Subversion, and Jazz, each provide enough functionality to be applicable to Enterprise projects. Many of the tools selected are open source tools, done mostly for cost reasons but also in part because these tools are popular with Agile methodologies. A sensitive issue with open source tools is the level of support available, including documentation. On the positive side mature open source tools have mature communities willing and able to answer questions via online forums.

Another common issue is the need for project-specific or customer-mandated tools. Degree programs leveraging the Enterprise sequence all use Java as the required teaching language, though sponsors often identify other language needs and are accommodated by subsets of students (a common example is embedded systems projects in C). Project-specific tools are allowed if a justified need is presented. Customer-requested or mandated tools are trickier to deal with; often these requests are based on the customer's personal preferences or comfort and not on project requirements. At one time, teams were allowed to choose several of their own tools, such as CM repository, collaborative Websites, UML modeling, and office documents, but this situation was simply untenable to support and the policy was changed after the first year.

Putting the "Real" in Real-World Projects

Capstone courses provide an excellent opportunity for students to work on "real-world" projects. But what constitutes *real-world*? The complexity of the problem? Its scale? We contend it is more contextual, and we must teach students how to properly deal with change in this context. Students working in teams on class projects commonly react perturbed when unexpected events arise, and then expect the instructor to show lenience in assigned deadlines and grading criteria when they do occur. Unexpected events might include a server failure, a personal workstation crash, long lines in public computing facilities, group members getting sick, faculty members going on travel, sponsor unavailability, technical complexity, personality clashes on teams, misunderstood requirements, changing technologies; the list is endless. Showing leniency for these events sends the wrong message. The truth is, these things happen in real projects everyday. Co-workers become sick, antagonistic, or take new jobs; customers do not sit by the phone waiting to answer their

Table 3. Tools in use by the enterprise

Tool	Purpose	Comments
Eclipse/Jazz	IDE	Eclipse a major platform, Jazz built on Eclipse and freely available as a beta.
Ant	Build scripts	Open source standard, cross platform, Eclipse support. Considering maven.
Jira	Defect tracking	Vendor tool with reduced price for academic/bundled license w/ Confluence
CVS	Configuration management	Rudimentary but popular tool, considered Subversion, now using CM provided in Jazz
JUnit	Unit Test	Eclipse plugin available
SourceforgeMetrics	Metrics	metrics.sourceforge.net, Eclipse plugin
PMD	Static analysis	Eclipse plugin, highly customizable
iRise	Storyboards/UI prototypes	Vendor tool w/ free academic license, www.irise.com
MagicDraw	UML	Personal edition free for academic use, supports RUP analysis class stereotypes and is cross-platform.
MS Excel / Jira	Change Mgmt	Requirements often evolve through Confluence and Word versioning too.
MS Word	Documents	
Open Workbench	Project Management	Supports Work Breakdown Structures, PERT/Gantt Charts, Resource models
Coverlipse	Code coverage	Eclipse plugin
Checkclipse	Code style	Eclipse plugin
Jupiter	Code reviews	Eclipse plugin from University of Hawaii
Academus/Sakai	Course Mgmt	Portal interface supports team collaboration easier.
Confluence	Wiki	Organized around "spaces" makes team support easy.
Sticky notes	Elicitation	Brainstorming/Affinity processes, storyboarding

questions; stakeholders frequently change requirements, new technologies are announced daily, and computing facilities become unavailable. These unfortunate events that befall our students should be seen as learning opportunities in leveraging their process to work through these issues.

The Enterprise approach is simple to implement: deal with it. Successful teams find ways to work though issues, not use them as excuses and beg for mercy from their stakeholders. To that end not only is there a healthy dose of "tough love," but we often intentionally introduce disruptive events during projects and force students to solve them on-the-fly. Some examples of these events include:

- *Rotate team members.* Teams may exchange members once each semester. This exchange is made unannounced, and teams are typically given a short time (a few days) to transfer knowledge and tasks to other team members.
- *Cancel projects.* Projects that fall significantly behind or are judged to be on an unsuccessful track are cancelled. Team members are distributed to other projects.

- *Change requirements.* Requirements changes may be introduced by the customer at any time.
- *Change technologies.* Projects typically leverage open source technologies to complete project implementations. These technologies are subject to frequent change, and teams are asked to change with the technology.
- *Rotate team roles.* Though not as intrusive as switching team members, changing roles within a team tends to lead to greater intrateam chemistry.
- *Turnover between semesters.* A common issue with projects spanning more than one semester is student turnover. This is embraced as indicative of the "real world" where team member turnover is expected.

Certainly these types of issues tend to slow down and degrade the quality of the final software products produced. The benefit is that teams must rely on good process practices, organization, risk analysis, judgment, and collaboration to work through these problems.

Project Assessment

Student projects are graded on their ability to define a process, follow the process, and adapt to change. Grades are weighted for the sequence (particularly the second year) primarily on the ability to set, follow, and adapt activities within the context of a process, and only secondarily on the quality of deliverables produced. It is difficult to construct an assessment model based on these criteria. For one, it is difficult to directly measure the impact of one process model against another, particularly in a setting with naïve practitioners of the process (which by definition students typically are). Second, tracking process-related data on student projects can be a significant time burden for faculty. The validity of student process data gathering is another issue. While the PSP/TSP does emphasize aspects of data gathering and

data-driven process improvements, it still remains difficult to ask students to ascertain, for example, the impact of a particular configuration management policy on software quality. Additionally, students are grade-driven, so asking for honest reporting of process data when students are concerned about grade impacts often leads to optimistic reporting where sometimes the true nature of a team's situation is not revealed until the end of the semester. In our view, there are no easy answers to these issues.

Additionally, there are two key components of Enterprise projects that have an impact on assessment.

- Collaboration across academic years. As discussed previously, project teams consist of juniors and seniors collaborating on the same team. These teams also meet and work together on extended lab sessions once a week. The energy seniors devote to mentoring is included in the assessment of their final grade. This can be a point of contention with exceptionally talented students who have a tendency to work ahead of the rest of their team instead of pulling the team forward with them.
- Entire class is "the company." Student team projects are usually pitted against one another in a competition to show off the best resulting product in order to obtain the maximum grade. In the Enterprise all project teams are part of the same company, and the success of the company is as important, if not more important, than individual project success. Therefore a percentage of the final grade is influenced by how well all of the class projects perform, not just the project in which the team participates. This encourages teams to share lessons learned and sometimes resources across projects. This principle has been employed in other Capstone experiences (Coppit 2006; Turhan & Bener, 2007), though the principle differ-

ence is that in those projects a large class section participates on a single project as one company, whereas Enterprise students are one company executing many projects. We believe this more accurately recreates the pressures of software development and resource sharing at many software services shops.

EVALUATION

The Software Enterprise is currently in its fourth year; 82 different students have enrolled in at least one Enterprise course in the first three years and 43 students (30 new) are currently enrolled in Fall 2007. Due to the limited time it has been offered and the relatively low population, a statistically valid evaluation of student performance in meeting the overall objective of "industry preparedness" is not feasible at this time. However, we are in the progress of collecting longitudinal data and share what we have learned so far.

Several types of quantitative and qualitative assessment data are collected each year:

1. **Course assessments:** These are the standard rating-oriented course assessments performed for all courses at ASU. Students are asked to rate the quality of the learning experience as well as provide some qualitative feedback.
2. **Course survey:** An Enterprise-specific course survey is conducted at the end of each semester. Students are asked quantitative questions about the quality of the learning experience, as well as a self-assessment of expertise in course subject areas.
3. **Affinity process:** Students are posed context-free questions in small groups and organize responses in naturally forming clusters (the "affinity" for each other's responses). Interestingly, this process is also taught as part of requirements elicitation.

4. **Impending and recent graduates survey:** A survey of impending and recent graduates asked about perceptions they hold regarding the utility of their education with respect to their technical profession. The goal is to repeat this study for several years to accumulate trend data about the preparedness of our graduates.
5. Qualitative data is reflected in anonymous student write-in responses on surveys in 1 and 2, feedback from project sponsors, and input from two industry advisory councils.

The Affinity process (3) and course survey (2) are particularly useful in assessing the industry-preparedness perceptions of our students. The graduates survey (4) will be useful when results are complete.

Affinity process. An Affinity process is a method for obtaining unbiased results (Kawakita, 1982). The process is as follows:

1. Explain the process to participants
2. Pose question
3. Ask each participant to write down as many responses as possible (at least 10) regarding the question. Only one idea (preferably one word) should be written per post-it-note. Allow approximately 5 minutes for this phase.
4. Ask all participants to place all of their post-it-notes on the white board and to remain at the board as a group. Tell participants (without discussing it with each other) to cluster the ideas into coherent groups by physically moving post-it-note into close proximity with each other. Participants should consider all items on the board, not just ones they created. If a dispute exists (e.g., an idea ping pongs from one cluster to other, copy the idea onto another post-it-note and place in both clusters).

5. Ask participants, as a group, to name the clusters. They are encouraged to talk about the names in this phase. Write the name of each cluster on a post-it-note, place the post-it-note along with each cluster on the whiteboard, and circle the cluster.

6. Ask participants to individually multi-vote on importance of each named cluster using the voting stickers provided. Participants may vote many times for one cluster or may distribute their votes among many clusters.

7. Debrief participants regarding the choices made.

8. Collect post-it-notes from the whiteboard, placing the cluster name post-it-note on top of each topic group

The Affinity process was used as a means for evaluating what students thought were the most relevant concepts learned during a one-year experience on a project team. Affinity processes are conducted at the conclusion of each academic year, and for both year 1 and year 2 participants of the Enterprise. One of the three questions we ask students in this process is about their perceptions of skill needs for junior software engineers:

Q2: *What skills are most important to junior professionals?*

This question asks students to consider what skills they think they will need the most when they graduate. Interestingly, students adeptly responded with soft skills (e.g. "Proper attitude and personality" 43%) over technical skills (e.g. "Software skills" 19%).

This result is interesting in that it reflects undirected feedback regarding what skills students believe are most important to know as impending junior professionals, and students overwhelmingly recognize that soft skills will be a differentiator

when they take that first job. A report on our complete Affinity process results is available in our previous work (Gary et. al 2006).

A common problem with an Affinity study is an ability to align results longitudinally. While respondents may create similar clusters from year to year, they rarely create the exact same clusters, creating an issue as to how to normalize clusters for consistency.

Course survey. Students are asked to take an anonymous online survey after the each semester ends. The surveys ask students about the level of academic exposure they had to a particular Enterprise topic before starting the Enterprise, and the amount of professional benefit they expect to receive from exposure to the topic. Results are shown in Table 4.

These results reflect the responses of 29 students, and so are not statistically valid. It is interesting to observe anecdotally however, is that although students perceive a lot of professional benefit to most topics, their prior academic exposure is usually quite low.

The conclusion we draw from these studies is that the Enterprise includes industry-relevant topics. Anecdotally, industry partners believe both the topics and the pedagogy will produce better-prepared graduates. Additional anecdotal feedback from project sponsors and faculty colleagues at ASU suggest greater applied comprehension as well, as reflected in the depth and professionalism of the student teams and projects at year-end department-wide demonstration days. However, neither the studies nor the anecdotal feedback can determine at this time if greater applied knowledge results from the pedagogy. To this end, we are engaged in a longitudinal study (assessment technique number 4, first data collected December 2006) where we hope to show, over a period of time, greater industry preparedness of our graduates.

Table 4. Course survey results

Survey Results	Academic Exposure			Professional Benefit		
Topic Area	none	some	lot	lot	some	none
Code Reviews	57%	36%	8%	57%	43%	
CM	91%	9%		91%	9%	
Defensive Programming	36%	54%	9%	80%	20%	
IDEs (Eclipse)	15%	54%	31%	82%	9%	9%
Metrics	82%	9%	9%	40%	20%	40%
Refactoring	73%	27%	9%	82%	18%	
Deployment/Release Mgmt	92%	9%		67%	33%	
Unit Testing	36%	45%	18%	90%	10%	
Estimation	77%	23%		83%	17%	
Project Management	69%	23%	8%	77%	23%	
Quality Planning	57%	22%	22%	92%	8%	
Release Management	83%	17%		62%	23%	15%
Defect Tracking	67%	11%	22%	71%	29%	
Risk Management	53%	33%	13%	92%	8%	
Task Planning & Sequencing	53%	20%	27%	92%	8%	
Test Types (alpha, beta)	75%	8%	17%	50%	42%	8%
Analysis Modeling	75%	25%		57%	42%	

RELATED RESEARCH

Software engineering in higher education is maturing at a fast rate, even in the face of enrollment declines. The field has been very active over the past decade with new degree programs coming online (Bagert & Chenoweth, 2005), curricular recommendations (ACM & IEEE-CS, 2004), an availability of a body of knowledge (IEEE-CS, 2004), and a growing body of literature on software engineering pedagogy, much of it focused on project-oriented coursework. There are a large number of variations possible in software engineering projects, and the Software Enterprise both borrows and advocates practices taken from previous works at other academic programs, as described throughout the chapter. In this section we draw attention to project offerings particularly influential on the overall structure and implementation on the Enterprise.

Specific programs with exemplary project offerings that have had a deep influence on our evolution of the Software Enterprise include the Software Development Studio component of the Professional Master's program at Carnegie Mellon University (Tomayko 1996), the Software Development Laboratory at the Milwaukee School of Engineering (Sebern 2002), the Capstone projects at Auburn University (Umphress, Hendrix, & Cross, 2002), and the Capstone projects in the

Masters track at the University of West Florida (Wilde et. al, 2003).

The Software Development Studio at CMU (Tomayko 1996) is a seminal program in project-oriented software coursework. The Studio puts graduate students in a terminal degree program through a multi-semester project experience covering the full range of software process activities. The Studio motivated a precursor to the Enterprise called the Software Factory (Tvedt, Tesoriero, & Gary, 2001), which emphasized project engagement throughout the entire undergraduate experience. The Software Enterprise shares the multi-semester approach with an emphasis on soft-skill development with the Studio. The Enterprise, however, introduces the software phases in reverse order, and emphasizes soft-skills development through multi-year structured student collaborations. The Enterprise also introduces the sequence in the undergraduate, not graduate, program.

The reverse ordering of the process phases is also introduced by the Software Development Laboratory at MSOE. Sebern (Sebern 2002) acknowledges the difficulty newer students have grasping process and soft-skills concepts, and therefore students are led from "grave to cradle" through process phases. Unfortunately a further description of the utility of this approach is not provided. Sebern also discusses the issue of student turnover, or project continuity, and describes a pre-course for seniors preparing them for the project sequence. This course includes mentoring activities from project enrollees, shared advice on the project, and basic skills preparation. This is a model we are looking to replicate in our Year 1, first semester Tools offering.

(Umphress, Hendrix, & Cross, 2002) articulate the motivation for using the Capstone as a teaching and learning experience instead of a summative experience: "...Instructors expect them to integrate the technical skills they've learned in previous courses, learn to work synergistically as a team, plan and track their work, satisfy their customer – and produce sound software. Yet,

more often than not, projects so framed teach their participants yet another way not to develop software." We agree wholeheartedly. Further, our initial iterations of the Enterprise encountered some of the same concerns described in the paper – balancing workload, scaling of skills sets, responsibilities within a team – to which we responded by tightening certain parts of the process while leaving others intentionally open-ended. The result is our iteration-oriented RUP meta-model incorporating best practices along the way. This paper also influenced our thinking around using a process-oriented grading approach instead of a product-oriented one.

The University of West Florida project (Wilde et. al, 2003) was also influential in our thinking in that it emphasized software evolution as well as software process. The authors make a strong argument that it is difficult to learn concepts in evolution without putting them into practice, thereby applying that classroom-oriented instruction in these concepts will not necessarily translate to their successful implementation in a Capstone project. In other words, the only option here is to immediately apply the concepts in order to ground them. This is part of the foundation for our reasoning for the iterative delivery model in Figure 2. We wish however, that the authors also applied this approach to management topics, where instead they implemented a seminar-style format. In the Enterprise, management concepts are also introduced using the same pedagogical model, which is very effective in showing the value of these tools (work breakdown structures, critical path analysis, earned-value analysis, etc.).

Again, these are only a small cross-section of the large body of work now available on Capstone project implementations in software engineering. To a certain extent the Enterprise contributes its voice to the debates about the logistics of running such courses. On a larger level, the community now seems headed toward a larger discussion on the impact of software engineering education, what it is, where it has failed expectations, and what the major issues are to be addressed. A recent article (Lethbridge et. al 2007) articulates a number of open questions. As a Polytechnic and part of the only major research University in the nation's fifth largest metropolitan center, we are particularly interested in the research questions posed for communicating real-world industrial practices more effectively to students. The authors suggest that "hard-to-teach process concepts...can be learned reasonably well on the job, so increased emphasis in undergraduate programs may not be necessary." This conclusion is defeatist, and we do not think the academic community should punt the issue readily. To be fair, the authors present this question in the context of a larger discussion around the substantial issues in working with industry, and one cannot deny that there will always be things best learned "on the job." Yet as we said in the beginning, "You can't teach experience - but you can sure try." We should take these research questions as a challenge to produce graduates ready for the profession by leveraging successes from the past decade while addressing the shortcomings through innovative instruction. The Software Enterprise is one small step in this direction by promoting the Capstone as a teaching and learning vehicle using an iterative hands-on model that accelerates the student from concept to applied understanding.

SUMMARY

In our efforts to address the difficulties encountered in a Capstone project course, we asked how graduating students entering the marketplace gain the skills needed to become competent professionals. We identified some key characteristics then went about designing ways in which these experiences could be incorporated into our project course.

The result is a highly iterative, learner-centered pedagogical model where students are exposed to software engineering methods and tools via traditional lecture, practice them in learner-centered exercises, scale them up to large projects, and reflect on the viability of the methods and tools within the context of the software process. Prior, but not widely applied, innovations by fellow scholars in software engineering education are employed, namely emphasizing the ordering in which concepts are introduced and mentoring relationships. The Software Enterprise also contributes data points to existing avenues of evolution around software engineering project coursework, particularly in the areas of how to run project teams and select desirable project sponsors. A particular emphasis is placed in the Enterprise on process robustness, and on incorporating software development best practices from the Agile methodologies into the undergraduate curriculum.

The principal drawback to the Software Enterprise approach is the complexity of executing the highly iterative and integrated pedagogical model shown in Figure 2. The approach requires careful synchronization of course topics and project objectives, adaptation to project-specific obstacles, dealing with student team dynamics, identifying project sponsors and setting expectations, reviewing reams of project deliverables, teaching in non-mainstream computing material, and providing a heavily tooled environment.

The methodology also places a great burden on instructors-as-facilitators to lead students down the right path. Knowledge from disparate sources must be both filtered and aggregated; it must also be packaged for digestion in a practice-oriented, collaborative learning environment. Structured, hands-on exercises for problem-centered learning must be constructed. Facilitators must determine the correct amount of guidance and support to provide team projects that enable learning without causing projects to degenerate into a "thrashing" state, alienating students from finding the right path. Finally, instructors must rethink how learning is assessed, and how to assess the relative success of the Enterprise sequence.

Computer science, and software engineering by extension, has suffered from a perception that universities do not produce industry-ready graduates. We believe the Software Enterprise pedagogical approach facilitates applied comprehension. The Enterprise model fuses the best of the maturing work in software engineering education with a new delivery model for promoting understanding into practice. This approach is new and emerging, and we have had to make several adjustments and try several variations over the past four years. Now that we believe we have a stable platform, we are planning to undertake broader studies of the impact of the pedagogy, and are also examining the feasibility of extending the Software Enterprise model to non-capstone project courses, multidisciplinary projects, and non-software engineering concepts.

ACKNOWLEDGMENT

This work was supported by an Arizona Board of Regents Learner-Centered Education (LCE) grant.

REFERENCES

Association for Computing Machinery & Institute for Electrical and Electronic Engineers Computer Society (2004). *Software Engineering 2004 Curriculum Guidelines for Undergraduate Degree Programs in Software Engineering.* Joint Task Force on Computing Curricula.

Beck, K. (2000). *Extreme Programming Explained – Embrace Change,* Boston: Addison-Wesley.

Boehm, B., Egyed, A., Port, D., Shah, A., Kwan, J. & Madachy, R. (1998). A Stakeholder Win-win Approach to Software Engineering Education. *Annals of Software Engineering, 6,* 295-321.

Borstler, J., Carrington, D. Hislop, G., Lisack, S. Olsen, K. & Williams, L. (2002, Sept/Oct). Teaching PSP: Challenges & Lessons Learned. *IEEE Software 19(5),* 42-48.

Carnegie Mellon University (2005). *Academic PSP Material.* Retrieved January 4, 2008 from http://www.sei.cmu.edu/tsp/psp/download/academic.html.

Coppit, D. (2006). Implementing Large Projects in Software Engineering Courses. *Computer Science Education 16(1),* 53-73.

Frailey, D. (2006). Bringing realistic software engineering assignments to the software engineering classroom. Proceedings of CSEET'06: *The 19th Conference on Software Engineering Education and Training.* Ohau, HI.

Gary, K., Gannod, B. Gannod, G., Koehnemann, H., Lindquist, T., & Whitehouse, R. (2005). Work in progress – The Software Enterprise. Proceedings of FIE'05: *The Frontiers in Education Conference.* Indianapolis, IN.

Gary, K., Gannod, G., Koehnemann, H., & Blake, M.B. (2005). Educating Future Software Professionals on Outsourced Software Development. Proceedings of ASEE'05: *The National Conference of the American Society for Engineering Education.* Portland, OR.

Gary, K., Gannod, B., & Koehnemann, H. (2006). The Software Enterprise: Facilitating the Industry Preparedness of Software Engineers. Proceedings of ASEE'06: *The National Conference of the American Society for Engineering Education.* Chicago, IL.

Hilburn, T., & Humphrey, W. (2002, Sept/Oct). Teaching Teamwork. *IEEE Software 19(5),* 72-77.

Humphrey W.S. (1997). *Introduction to the Personal Software Process.* Boston: Addison-Wesley.

Humphrey W.S. (2000). *Introduction to the Team Software Process*. Boston: Addison-Wesley.

Institute for Electrical and Electronic Engineers Computer Society (1998). *IEEE Recommended Practice for Software Requirements Specifications*. (IEEE standard 830-1998). New York, NY.

Institute for Electrical and Electronic Engineers Computer Society (2004), *Guide to the Software Engineering Body of Knowledge (SWEBOK)*. Los Alamitos, CA.

Kawakita, J. (1982). *The Original KJ Method* (English). Tokyo: Kawakita Research Institute.

Kruchten, P. (2000). *The Rational Unified Process – An Introduction (2nd ed.)*. Boston: Addison-Wesley.

Leffingwell, D. & Widrig, D. (2003). *Managing Software Requirements: A Use Case Approach (2nd ed.)*. Boston: Addison-Wesley.

Lethbridge, T., Diaz-Herrera, J., LeBlanc, R., and Thompson, J.B. (2007). Improving software practice through education: Challenges and future trends. Proceedings of FOSE'07: *Future of Software Engineering*, special track at ICSE'07: *The 29th International Conference on Software Engineering*. Minneapolis, MN.

McConnell, S. (2004). *Code Complete 2 (2nd ed)*. Redmond WA: Microsoft Press.

Morsch, L. (2006). *What some fastest-growing jobs pay*. Retrieved January 4, 2008 from http://www.cnn.com/2006/US/Careers/01/26/cb.top.jobs.pay/index.html.

Poole, W.G. (2003). The softer side of customer software development: Working with the other players. Proceedings of CSEET'03: *The 16th Conference on Software Engineering Education and Training*. Madrid, Spain.

Sebern, M. (2002). The Software Development Laboratory: Incorporating industrial practice in an academic environment. Proceedings of CSEET'02: *The 15th Conference on Software Engineering Education and Training*. Covington, KY.

Sebern, M. (2005). Software Process: Applying industrial strength methods in engineering education. Proceedings of ASEE'05: *The National Conference of the American Society for Engineering Education*. Portland, OR.

Szyperski, C. (2005). The making of a software engineer: Challenges for the educator. Proceedings of ICSE'05: *The 27th International Conference on Software Engineering*. St. Louis, MO.

Tomayko, J.E. (1996). Carnegie Mellon's software development studio: a five year retrospective. Proceedings of CSEE'96: *The 9th Conference on Software Engineering Education*. Daytona Beach, FL.

Turhan, B. & Bener, A. (2007). A template for real world team projects for highly populated software engineering classes. Proceedings of ICSE'07: *The 29th International Conference on Software Engineering*. Minneapolis, MN.

Tvedt, J. Tesoriero, R., & Gary, K. (2001). The Software Factory: Combining undergraduate computer science and software engineering education. Proceedings of ICSE'01: *The 23rd International Conference on Software Engineering*. Toronto, CA.

Umphress, D., Hendrix, T., & Cross, J. (2002, Sept/Oct). Software Process in the Classroom: The Capstone Experience. *IEEE Software, 19(5)*, 78-81.

U.S. Bureau of Labor Statistics (U.S. BLS) (2007). *Economic and employment projections: 2006-2016*. Retrieved January 4, 2008 from http://www.bls.gov/news.release/ecopro.toc.htm.

Wilde, N., White, L.J., Kerr, L.B., Ewing, D.D., & Krueger, A. (2003). Some experiences with evolution and process-focused projects. Proceedings of CSEET'03): *The 16th Conference on Software Engineering Education and Training.* Madrid, Spain.

Chapter VIII
Teaching Software Engineering in a Computer Science Program Using the Affinity Research Group Philosophy

Steve Roach
The University of Texas at El Paso, USA

Ann Q. Gates
The University of Texas at El Paso, USA

ABSTRACT

This chapter describes a two-semester software engineering course that is taught in a computer science program at the University of Texas at El Paso. The course is distinguished from other courses in that it is based on the Affinity Research Group (ARG) philosophy that focuses on the deliberate development of students' team, professional and technical skills within a cooperative environment. To address the challenge of having to teach professional and team skills as well as software engineering principles, approaches, techniques, and tools in a capstone course, the authors have defined an approach that uses a continuum of instruction, practice, and application with constructive feedback loops. The authors hope that the readers will benefit from the description of the approach and how ARG components are incorporated into the course.

INTRODUCTION

The Computing Curricula 2001 (CC2001) project is the product of a joint effort by the Computer Society of the Institute for Electrical and Electronic Engineers (IEEE-CS) and the Association for Computing Machinery (ACM) with the goal of developing curricular guidelines for undergraduate programs in computing. CC2001 describes a set of recommendations for undergraduate programs in computer science (CS) and has had significant influences on curriculum development throughout the world (ACM, 2004). It includes the following statement with respect to the project component of a Computer Science Curriculum (CC2001, 2001, p. 45):

The course descriptions . . . offer several models for including project work in the curriculum. The first strategy is simply to include a project component as part of the required intermediate or advanced course that covers the core material on software engineering. This strategy is illustrated by the course CS292{C,W}. Software Development and Professional Practice, which includes a team project along with a significant amount of additional material. As long as students have sufficient time to undertake the design and implementation of a significant project, this approach is workable. The projects in such courses, however, tend to be relatively small in scale, simply because the time taken up by the software engineering material cuts into the time available for the project.

All accredited software engineering programs and almost all accredited CS programs in the United States have a capstone experience in the undergraduate curriculum (CC2001, 2001; EAC, 2007; CAC, 2007). Like many other CS programs, the CS program at the University of Texas at El Paso (UTEP) combines the project experience with an introduction to software engineering principles. The two-semester sequence is taken in the students' final year of study and focuses on fundamental software engineering topics while developing the students' communication and team skills, establishing a venue in which to engage in meaningful discussions about the Software Engineering Code of Ethics and Professional Practice (ACM/IEEE-CS, 1999), providing practical experience, and supporting faculty-student interaction.

Teaching a capstone course in a software engineering program, where students have had significant exposure to software engineering concepts prior to entering the course, and teaching a capstone in a CS program, where students

have usually had no prior software engineering courses, are manifestly different from each other. As noted in the CC2001 report, teaching the software engineering material and having students work together in a project setting is challenging. UTEP has met this challenge by developing a course that focuses on the practice of software engineering in a project that involves actual clients and the *deliberate* development of professional skills as espoused by the Affinity Research Group (ARG) model.

The primary goals of the UTEP course are to provide students with (a) a fundamental and functional understanding of the methods, tools, and techniques required of rigorous software engineering so that they can identify and adopt the practices needed in the workforce; (b) the experience of working with an actual client to develop a product so that they can learn to manage issues, such as incomplete, ambiguous, changing and inconsistent requirements, and to deal with time pressures; (c) the ability to apply software engineering principles to a software project; (d) the ability to prepare documentation in adherence to IEEE standards; and (e) the experience of working effectively in teams.

The UTEP approach is unique in that it uses the Affinity Research Group (ARG) model (Gates, 1999; Teller, 2001; Gates, 2007). The two principal tenants of the ARG model that apply to software development teams in the academic setting are the cooperative learning paradigm and the structured, intentional, and deliberate development of professional and technical skills. The ARG model has processes for evaluating work products and iteratively revising them. These processes have been adapted for use in the capstone project course.

In this chapter, we describe the techniques and approaches to teaching software engineering that we have developed and used for the past decade. Our philosophy, derived from the ARG model, is to focus on the development of each student.

BACKGROUND: THE AFFINITY RESEARCH GROUP MODEL

In 1995, the ARG model was developed at UTEP with the goal of involving undergraduates students from CS and electrical and computer engineering in research to improve recruitment, retention, and persistence of students, particularly female students and students from under-represented populations. UTEP is an urban university whose ethnic composition mirrors that of El Paso with an 80% Hispanic population. It is a commuter school, and a significant fraction of the undergraduate population is "first generation", i.e., the first generation in the family to acquire post-secondary education. In 1995, few students in CS were on campus other than to attend classes, and a low number of students continued to graduate school. With the introduction of ARGs, the culture in the CS department transitioned to one in which student-faculty interaction outside the classroom increased, a larger network of students formed study groups in their college careers, and students stayed on campus longer.

An ARG is a team of faculty mentor(s) and students who work together cooperatively to accomplish a research task. Team members have varying levels of expertise, capabilities, interests and skills; and they may have a variety of educational, cultural, and familial backgrounds. The ARG model embraces this diversity and exposes students to experiences that facilitate the development and transfer of knowledge and skills among members of the group. The ARG model joins two foundational ideas: interaction among students and faculty outside the classroom increases the likelihood of students persisting to graduation (Astin, 1985; Rodriguez, 1994, Tinto, 1993), and cooperative learning techniques maximize student learning and efficacy (Johnson, 1989). In addition, the model integrates best practices from a variety of sources in industry, research, and education. Using structured tasks and activities, students develop domain expertise, gain an understanding and appreciation of the research process and its practice, and acquire the skills that will make them effective leaders and successful in research, academia, and industry. The model has demonstrated success in increasing both the quality of undergraduate students' learning experiences and their participation in advanced studies.

A key element of the ARG model is the use of the cooperative learning paradigm (Johnson, 1989; Johnson, 1990; Johnson, 1991; Johnson, 1992a; Johnson, 1992b; Johnson, 1995). Cooperative groups create higher quality products, achieve mastery or competence of a task, develop a social network, and have increased self-esteem. Structured cooperative learning techniques are integrated into the routine functioning of the group. The mere formation of a group, as in traditional research groups, does not ensure that it will function cooperatively. As Johnson and colleagues note (Johnson, 1990, p. 4), "Cooperation is working together to accomplish shared goals. Within cooperative activities, individuals seek outcomes that are beneficial to themselves *and* beneficial to all other group members."

In an ARG, group members work together to maximize their own and each other's productivity and achievement. The ARG model ensures that structured cooperative learning techniques are part of the group's routine functioning. Because teaching and practicing professional skills are part of the research group activities, for example, students are able to learn skills from their groups and transfer them to other environments.

Five basic elements must be present for the group to truly function cooperatively: positive interdependence, face-to-face promotive interaction, individual and group accountability, professional skills development, and group processing. The ARG model incorporates all five by structuring them into weekly activities and in the group's day-to-day functioning.

- *Positive interdependence* is the situation where each team member's success depends on the success of the team as a whole. When positive interdependence is present, each member has a personal stake in the group's success and believes that the group values her or his contributions. An example of structuring positive interdependence in the classroom is to give students a grade based on the average of the individual scores of the group members on a quiz. In this situation, each team member becomes motivated to ensure the success of the other team members.

- *Face-to-face promotive interaction* occurs when students are situated so they can easily and comfortably talk to each other and actively seek participation from each other. The explicit goal in this sharing process is for members to help one another succeed and, therefore, help the group reach its goals. It is important to acknowledge and recognize each member's contribution, and a key skill is the proper use of constructive criticism, i.e., critiquing ideas and not the person. The practice of constructive critique is critical to the improvement of both the individual and the group, and it's important that students understand the need for and the role of critique in raising the quality of a product.

- *Individual and group accountability* is needed to ensure that individuals participate fully. One complaint that students, particularly high-achieving students, have with respect to working on teams is that the better students end up doing all the work and the weaker students share the grade. By structuring individual accountability in the groups, the faculty mentor ensures there are no "free rides". Each person must be responsible for tangibly contributing her or his fair share to the group. Likewise, the group as a whole is responsible for the group's smooth function and for delivering the required work. This is important when a large group is divided into smaller groups,

each with a given task. Constructing timelines and explicitly showing the dependencies among individual and group tasks are other effective techniques for structuring individual and group accountability.

- *Professional skills* are the skills needed to work with people in a business environment. They are the communication and interpersonal skills that facilitate working relationships. Professional skills are explicitly taught and practiced in activities designed around one or more technical topics such as critiquing a presentation, practicing active listening and asking questions. Fomenting effective professional skills makes for more productive and successful interaction among group members and is essential to the maintenance of positive interdependence.

- *Group processing* is the critical evaluation of the performance of the group. It consists of individuals assessing the quality of their contributions to the group as well as the group's considerations of its recent performance. Processing gives group members the opportunity to identify potential improvements for further work so that the individuals and the group's performance at a higher level. Group processing must be deliberately structured into activities.

BRIDGING THE GAP BETWEEN THE ABSTRACT AND CONCRETE

At UTEP, we face four significant hurdles to achieving the goals of the software engineering capstone course. Informal discussions with computer science faculty at other institutions indicate that these hurdles are not unique to our program.

1. Experienced instructors recognize that there is a gap between discussion of a technique in the classroom and endowing students

with the ability to apply the technique to real problems. Research supports the claim that application of concepts on real problems provides a bridge between abstract and concrete learning (Kurfiss, 1998) and that students learn best by doing, discussing, or taking action (American Psychological Association, 1992; McKeachie, 1986).

2. We have a CS, not a software engineering program. Students in the CS program (Parnas, 1999) are not well-versed in many aspects of large software system development or management. Few students entering the capstone course have developed or worked on software products larger than a few thousand lines of code. Generally, they lack understanding of and experience with project planning, requirements elicitation, requirements specification, modeling, development of test plans, documentation, and software maintenance; that is, they do not know the material that the course is designed to cover but that is needed in order to develop the software for the capstone project.

3. Few students have had the opportunity to work in software teams larger than two or three members and, thus, they lack the experience to work well in team situations. While students are regularly required to work in small groups throughout the curriculum, these groups are typically self-selected or unstructured.

4. Students lack adequate oral and written communication skills. Technical writing is difficult, and undergraduate students in particular need to practice this skill. Most good writers use an iterative process of writing, correcting, and rewriting in which the author strengthens the content, sharpens the focus, improves the organization, clarifies the point of view, and refines the tone (Hacker, 1991). Public speaking skills benefit from iterative refinement.

The UTEP software engineering course is structured as three hours of lecture per week for a 14-week semester. The ARG model makes extensive use of cooperative learning, and this is transferred to the course by using cooperative and problem based learning for one-third to two-thirds of the lecture time. Traditional lecture is used the rest of the time.

The ARG model stresses the development of each student's ability to assess her or his own contributions and capabilities as well as the ability to communicate professionally. In-class exercises focus not only on the application of software engineering techniques such as developing a test set to meet a test coverage criterium, but also on the assessment and critique of each student's and each team's work as well as the work of others. In class, we explicitly structure activities to facilitate students' learning and practice of giving and receiving constructive criticism.

In the ARG model, research team members are encouraged to become the team expert in a given subject. This expertise is used by the team as needed when the expert either produces a work product related to the area of expertise or trains other team members in the subject. This practice has been transferred to the capstone project by assigning team roles. The ARG model also stresses the development of each student. In the capstone course, leadership skills are developed in each team member by requiring each student to take the lead for several team deliverables (shown in Table 1), unlike many project teams where one student takes the lead for the duration of the project.

Students are assisted and evaluated by the Software Engineering Guidance Team, a team of faculty and graduate students who oversee the project. The faculty members are Certified Software Development Professionals (CSDP, 2007), and each have several years of industrial software development experience. Guidance Team members ensure individual accountability in part by interviewing individual students during group presentations and regularly assessing task assignments and work products produced by individuals during the semester.

Our approach to bridging the gap between abstract and concrete is to apply both lecture and practice repeatedly. We call our approach the Instruction-Practice-Application Continuum, which is described graphically in Figure 1. In this approach, as shown on the left side of the figure, classroom activities are used to introduce techniques, e.g., functional modeling, project planning, or software inspections. These activities include traditional lectures, problem-based instruction, and cooperative learning. Assessments such as home work, quizzes, exams, and in-class observations are used to determine how well students grasp the concepts in the academic setting. When necessary, topics are covered again in class.

In the case of the capstone experience, the task is to implement a solution to the problem around which the project is based. On the right side of Figure 1, the project is used to reinforce the concepts learned in class. In this setting, students work in teams to apply the techniques covered in lectures

to create project deliverables. The instructor assesses the deliverables and provides constructive feedback on drafts by conducting an informal walk-through of the deliverable with the team and asking questions; students improve deliverables based on the feedback and new knowledge gained. The purpose of the cycle on the left of the figure is to have students learn and apply new concepts to small problems assigned in class or as homework, while the cycle on the right moves the students toward higher-level thinking skills, such as analysis, synthesis, and evaluation (Bloom, 1956), by applying the newly learned material to the project. In this cycle, students produce work products such as models, requirements, documentation, design, test suites, and source code. These work products are reviewed by the course instructor and the Guidance Team, and frequently, the work products are returned to the students for further improvement. When problems are identified that are common across teams, these problems can be addressed in the lectures. In this way, the experience of the instructors is passed to the students in much the same way that experience is passed

Figure 1. Instruction-Practice-Application Continuum

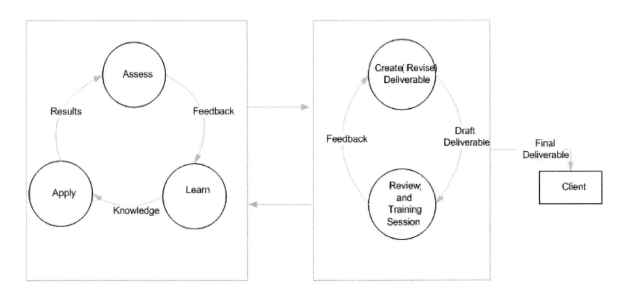

to apprentice tradesmen. Final versions of work products are delivered to the clients.

THE PROJECT

To address the issue of providing students with the experience of developing large software systems, the course requires that students construct software for a real client, someone who needs a software solution to a problem. Given the project's central role in the course, selection of the project is a key part of preparation for the course; however, the project is a means to an end. Our focus is on teaching students the methods that support building complex, reliable, and maintainable systems. The project gives them the opportunity to apply a process and practice process improvement.

Software engineering is about managing change, but students tend to have experience with requirements that do *not* change. What they need, then, is real-world experience where the customer may change the requirements during the project, may be unclear about their own needs, and are unsure about how to best solve their problem. Identifying and clarifying ambiguous, incomplete, and inconsistent requirements, as well as managing change, are an important part of the course. Students often lack experience in eliciting and specifying requirements, and the comment below from one of our clients supports the importance of defining a requirements process:

As the SCIMITAR project lead, I felt the students received a real-world immersion in the complexities of software development. They learned the importance of listening to the customer, developing requirements, and getting feedback from the customer. They also learned how difficult it is to really nail down those requirements, and how much it saves in the long run to do so. --Lon Anderson, Army Research Laboratory (L. Anderson, personal communication, 2003)

In addition to managing change in requirements and its impact on maintaining consistency, the students must learn to anticipate change in design. Indeed, the best way to appreciate designing for change is to have change looming during the design process, and then observe what happens to the design when change occurs.

Project Descriptions

There are endless possibilities for software engineering projects, and we are frequently approached by potential clients. To help us select appropriate projects, we consider the following requirements for projects:

- The client must truly want the software product. Involvement of the client is essential. Clients participate in interviews and demonstrations, and they are present for the final presentations each semester. They must be available to answer questions about the desired product during critical junctures of the two-semester course.

- The client must be willing to wait for two semesters or more to receive functional software. Two approaches can be used in this capstone course. One is the waterfall model and the other is an adaptation of the agile approach called Feature-Driven Development (FDD) (Coad,1999). The use of waterfall is intentional: Our students are familiar with coding, but not as familiar with the other aspects of software engineering. The original version of FDD is composed of five processes: develop an overall model, build a feature list, plan by feature, design by feature, and build by feature. The modified version of FDD (Rauda, 2005) uses the five processes, but modifies the internal tasks of the processes to meet the outcomes of the course.

- The project must have sufficient scope that it is infeasible for one or two students to complete the task in two semesters. This creates the positive interdependence that encourages teams to bond and work together.

- The project must be feasible, or it must be possible to set the scope of the project for the teams so that their part of the project is feasible.

Project clients have ranged from researchers in geology, agronomy, environmental sciences, and software engineering to project managers attempting to deliver software to customers in the U. S. Army, for the United States Geological Survey, and users of the geoinformatics grid (GEON, 2007). Here are some of the projects completed in the past several years.

- **PACES: Satellite Scene Viewer:** This project provided access to the Pan American Center for Earth and Environmental Studies (PACES) satellite image archive by integrating ENVI image processing and Oracle database management system software with graphical-user interfaces.
- **HATS GUI (Winter, 2006):** This project created a graphical user interface for the High-Assurance Transformation System (HATS) developed at Sandia National Laboratiories. The HATS GUI facilitated the creation and interpretation of transformation rules used to generate software for high-assurance applications.
- **Scene and Countermeasures Integration for Munition Interaction with Targets (SCIMITAR) (Anderson, 1999):** SCIMITAR is an analytical tool that evaluates munition interaction with ground platforms within a scene. SCIMITAR allows users to modify and analyze images by adding obscurants and target types onto the scene in order to analyze aimpoint probabilities and countermeasure effectiveness.
- **Gravity Data Repository and Processing System (GDRP) (GeoNet, 2007):** GDRP

is a web-based tool that provides general information about gravity measurements and presents a collection of tools for adding, accessing, visualizing, and manipulating data. The project was a coordinated effort with UTEP, Arizona State University, and U.S. Geological Survey.

Project Management

The end result of the project should be a software product or a prototype product. In order to produce a working piece of software, project management is essential. This is particularly relevant when managing several software teams simultaneously. While many resources are available to guide an instructor in basic software project management (Wysock, 2006; Whitehead, 2001; DeMarco, 1999; McConnell 1997), in this section we discuss aspects of project management specific to the academic capstone project.

Students in the UTEP course work in highly structured and managed project teams on all aspects of development: requirements elicitation, feasibility, modeling and analysis, prototyping, requirements specification, tracing, high-level and low-level designs, implementation, and testing. In addition, students submit formal documents (using IEEE standards when appropriate) including feasibility report, interview report, Software Requirements Specification (SRS), Software Design Document (SDD), test plan, testing defect report, and configuration management plan. Students participate in walkthroughs and inspections for designs and prototypes, and presentations of the software requirements and finished product are presented formally to the clients. Figure 2 shows a Gantt chart of the major deliverables for the two-semester course following a traditional academic year.

The verification and validation task includes paper prototype reviews, executable prototype reviews, inspections, walkthroughs, and structured testing. Clients and the Guidance Team are present for many of the reviews.

The Project Team

The CC2001 (2001, pp. 43-44) emphasizes the need for students to work in teams:

Few computer professionals can expect to work in isolation for very much of the time. Software projects are usually implemented by groups of people working together as a team. Computer science students therefore need to learn about the mechanics and dynamics of effective team participation as part of their undergraduate education. Moreover, because the value of working in teams (as well as the difficulties that arise) does not become evident in small-scale projects, students need to engage in team-oriented projects that extend over a reasonably long period of time, possibly a full semester or a significant fraction thereof.

Recruiters often tell us that they are looking for students with demonstrated abilities to work in teams. As educators, it is important for us to teach team skills and to structure teams in order to encourage the practice of professional skills that improve communication and accountability among members. To address the challenge of developing effective team skills, we use the ARG model, in particular, the cooperative paradigm, to build strong teams. This requires that facilitators build positive interdependence, encourage promotive interaction, structure individual accountability, teach team and professional skills, and discuss with the team what practices are--and are not--successful (Johnson,1992a; Scholtes, 1996). We strongly believe that these elements must be present in the teams we build for this course. Without the cooperative structure, inexperienced students will not work as a team; rather, they will merely be a collection of students.

Teams consist of five team members assigned by the Guidance Team. Teams persist across

Figure 2. Gantt Chart of course deliverables

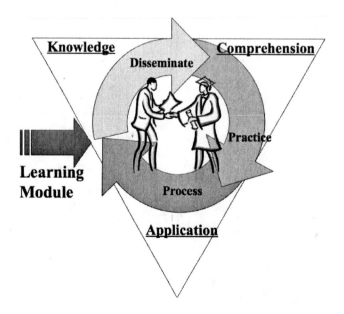

semesters. Students are assigned to positions on each team. The positions are:

- *Systems analyst.* The systems analyst is responsible for identifying the purpose of the system and the individual goals of the customer. The analyst must know the technology and be able to understand and respond to what is found in observing and talking with those who are commissioning a new system or will be the end users of it. This person needs considerable communication as well as generalization skills.
- *Systems architect.* The person in this position will define the computational components and the interactions among these components with respect to the specification. The architect must be able to deal with a large amount of technical detail while at the same time develop a superior view of the overall system.
- *Designer.* The designer must know the technology and be able to prepare detailed specifications and models of the new system by analyzing the requirements specification and high-level design document.

- *Lead programmer.* The lead programmer should have experience in code development in different programming paradigms. The lead programmer will manage the team that implements the code according to the specification and design. The person best suited for this job is someone who is willing to devote time to learn new technology, if necessary.
- *Verification and Validation (V & V) supervisor.* The V & V supervisor is in charge of developing and administering tests that are representative of the use of the system. This person is also responsible for configuration management, and verification and validation throughout all phases of development.

Team Selection

Some instructors feel that teams should be self-selected or homogenous (e.g., put all the "best" students on one team). We have tried these approaches, and they have not worked well. When everyone on the team thinks the same way, the team may stumble down a mutually agreed upon (but wrong) path, and students do not learn

Table 1. Deliverables by team role

Semester	Position	Deliverable
1	Systems analyst	Software Requirements Specification
	Systems architect	Feasibility report and final presentation
	Designer	Models, diagrams, and interface evaluation
	Lead Programmer	Interface prototype and tool support
	V & V	Tracing documents, test plan, and interview report.
2	Systems analyst	Final user-interface design and final presentation
	Systems architect	Architectural design document
	Designer	Detailed design document
	Lead Programmer	Code
	V & V	Tracing documents, configuration management and test plan

how to deal with and appreciate diverse ideas. A number of recruiters have told us that they recruit from different colleges and universities simply so their workforce will be educationally, and culturally diverse. We model this approach in our teams.

We assign students to five-member teams for an entire year, and it is rare that we remove a member from a team. Because of this, we are careful about the teams we create, and we expend substantial effort in selecting the members, considering four general areas: personality, position preference, experience, grade-point average, and project- and gender-specific issues. Students are given the position descriptions and the list of deliverables assigned for each position. They are asked to provide a résumé and write a letter of application in which they specify the three positions for which they feel most qualified or have the greatest interest. Our team assignment process includes steps such as evaluating students' letters of application and résumés, assessing dominant personality characteristics, and balancing the diversity of the teams with respect to gender, ethnicity, grades, and educational experiences.

We assess personality using the Shapes personality exercise (Bonura, 1998). This exercise is a modified form of the Myers Briggs personality type assessment. During the exercise, students select the personality "shape" with which they most identify. Students come to appreciate that not all of their fellow students identify with the same shape, and that there are strengths and needs associated with each of the shapes. On our teams, we strive to balance the four shapes on each team.

We attempt to balance the teams with respect to the experiences and academic achievements of the students. We ask that students report their cumulative and major grade point averages on their résumés. We also do a preliminary assessment of their writing abilities based on the letter of application. Our goal is to balance teams in terms of their academic histories. We attempt to have

several students with strong English skills or good academic records on each team. For particular projects, we also consider work experience and certain courses (such as database management) when assigning students to teams. We try to avoid assigning friends to the same team.

The gender-specific issues include assigning female students, when possible, to teams with at least one other female. Although not always necessary, the practice of having more than one female student on a team helps in situations when the female's opinions are ignored or not valued.

Development Professional Skills

Rather than assume that students know how to work effectively in teams by the mere fact that they are on a team, we deliberately teach students how to work in teams by describing how to conduct effective meetings, giving each student the opportunity to learn how to take a lead role, requiring students to analyze their teams' performance, and suggesting ways to improve individual participation and team effectiveness. Students are assigned specific positions on their team, and we use that position to assign the lead for different deliverables. The leader is responsible for ensuring the deliverable (refer to Table 1) is completed and that every team member contributes to each deliverable. This person is responsible for initiating the work (typically by calling a team meeting and setting the agenda for the meeting), monitoring task assignments, collecting finished products, and delivering the final version. Our goals in having rotating leads are to provide students with opportunities to practice task-planning strategies and to learn leadership skills. It has been our experience that some students who ordinarily would not choose to lead a team effort turn out to be good leaders and develop skills and exhibit talents that were previously unrecognized.

Other approaches to developing professional skills include using cooperative learning in the classroom and experience sharing, where a faculty or guest speaker discusses real-world experiences related to effective team behaviors. To encourage the development of basic leadership skills, we lecture on and model setting agendas, assigning roles in meetings, clarifying task assignments, reaching consensus, defining tasks and timelines, maintaining meeting minutes and checking on progress towards a goal. The agendas and minutes are used by the Guidance Team when assessing individual accountability.

Individual Accountability

We often hear from students that they do not like working in teams because some students do all the work and other students sit back and get a free ride. In class, it is not possible to fire a non-contributing team member. We can, however, structure the team so that it is difficult for inactive students to hide. We hold students accountable for their contribution to the team effort, and we use three essential tools for monitoring student participation: observation, self-assessment, and direct interview. Our formal and informal approaches to assessing the contributions that individuals make towards the team project give us a clear picture of the level of contributions made by each student, and we use these indicators to adjust individual grades for the group project.

The team notebook, which may include an individual engineering notebook, is updated weekly by students and contains meeting minutes, email exchanges, and draft work products. Reviews of these notebooks, which may be kept electronically (e.g., using WebCT), have frequently identified teams in conflict and instances of team members not performing to team expectations. These reviews can be used to identify problems in team functioning and allow the instructor to intervene when necessary. Informal approaches include observing students while they are working. The teaching assistants for the course are in frequent contact with students working in the laboratory,

and informally the TAs observe how project team members behave. To help with observation, a rubric is useful to tally particular behaviors exhibited by team members during meetings, e.g., seeking member participation, summarizing major points, or asking questions.

Students are required to self report their level of contribution. Some of these statements must be shared with (and signed by) other team members, and some are private between the student and the Guidance Team. In addition, members report on what is working well in the team and what needs to be improved.

During meetings between a team and the instructor, the instructor interviews each team member to assess the level of contribution. Exams are used to assess the level of competency with respect to given topics. Frequently, these exams expose weaknesses in students who have not participated in the development of a team's work products.

One further technique for assessing student performance on the team project is the interview at the final presentations. These presentations include members of the academic community outside the course, and questioning of individual students in this setting is highly effective in determining the familiarity with the course concepts as well as the level of contribution toward team success.

Team Issues

Frequently, students working in teams experience conflict, and not all students are equally adept at dealing with these situations, particularly those that result from clashing priorities and personalities (Scholtes, 1996). Significant challenges arise for the instructor of the project course when students are unable to resolve team issues on their own. In order for us to expect students to work on a team, we have to teach them *how* to resolve team conflicts. The process described by Johnson (Johnson, 2005) is generally more effective than ad hoc processes for conflict resolution.

The first step in assisting a team in resolving conflicts is to identify that a team has a problem. Frequently students will bring the problem to the attention of the instructor. To monitor teams who are not reporting difficulties, the Guidance Team looks at a number of indicators. For example, a lack of initiative shown in email trails or poor work delivered in rough drafts is an indication that a member of the team is not contributing. A series of work efforts not appearing in the final product or suggestions that appear in email, but not in work products may indicate team members are ignoring or discounting a team member.

Once a team issue is identified, the Guidance Team meets with the project team. In relatively simple cases, there may be a discussion of team skills and techniques for ensuring that communication is clear, for example summarizing the results of team meetings and emailing task assignments immediately after the meeting. Follow-up meetings can be used to assess the change in team functioning. In more complex cases, the process may entail a lengthier process that includes having team members voice their perceptions and emotions and having other team members paraphrase what their teammates have said. Paraphrasing forces a student to listen to and understand the position of the other students. Often, the students come away from such an experience with a new respect for and appreciation of their team mates. Complex cases usually require several guided meetings before the team is able to address issues on its own.

One source of team conflict is the case where we have highly motivated students mixed with less motivated students. While it is normal for lower-achieving students to become engaged and highly productive and valuable to project teams, it is not uncommon for teams to have one or two members who remain unmotivated and unproductive. In these cases, the Guidance Team negotiates grade and deliverable adjustments for individual students on the team.

In most cases, these simple interventions suffice. However, in more extreme cases, we have teams develop a code of conduct and identify their expectations for the course and project. In the most egregious cases, we have removed team members from a team and had that student report directly to the Guidance Team.

Written and Oral Communications Skills

In order to develop students' abilities to communicate technical concepts effectively, we use the Instruction-Practice-Apply Continuum shown in Figure 1. The process begins in the classroom. A common technique for ensuring individual accountability when using cooperative learning in class is to randomly select students to explain their group's solution to a given in-class problem. When students explain a solution, the faculty member can guide the student to a clear explanation by asking questions and helping the student rephrase statements.

Formal presentations are scheduled four times during the two semesters: a paper prototype presentation, a formal presentation of the SRS, an executable prototype presentation, and the final presentation. For each presentation, each student on the team is required to present some part of the product. The presentations are evaluated both on style and content by the Guidance Team and the clients. The rubric for evaluating students includes items such as use of visual aids, pace, eye contact, gender neutrality, ability to field questions, and use of language and terminology. The comments from the Guidance Team and clients are summarized and returned to the students. The common observation of the clients is that the final presentation is significantly better than the presentations from the first semester.

While all of our students have taken English writing classes prior to entering the capstone course, many of them have great difficulty with technical writing. Improving their abilities requires practice. The approach we take is to review student writing, make editorial comments, and have the students rewrite the work. Comments range from the correction of simple grammatical errors to explaining the grammar rules involved to issues related to content and structure. Common content problems include misuse of terms, sentences that imply a causal relationship that does not exist, factual errors, sentence fragments, and sentences that are incomprehensible. An example of a mistaken causal relationship is this statement: *Since V is developed using C++, most of us have experience using C++.* When shown this statement, most students agree that the dependent and independent clauses are not related.

Students in the course report that they realize that the criteria for written work include both technical content and grammatical composition. This and the requirement of revising drafts until they are acceptable, increases the students' level of effort in proof reading. When they believe that their writing has value to the client, the students are much more willing to spend the time producing higher quality work. Our experience has shown that students who rewrite documents to correct these errors are less likely to repeat them in the future.

Assessment and Evidence of Success

The structure of the course has been shaped by advice from alumni, recruiters, industry representatives, and academics from other institutions. In particular, we have evidence of the effectiveness of this course based on data collected from employers and alumni. The following correspondences were received from former students:

Working as a software engineer is like reliving your class times 10 and my grades are based on performance. I would like to talk to your class to show your students how all the material they are learning is relevant to the real world. Microsoft employee

I returned from an interview with Cisco Systems yesterday and I met a former student. She is now a team leader. She felt that your software engineering course was very helpful in her career and she wanted me to get this feedback to you. Interviewee at Cisco Systems

Wow, I never though I would see this SE stuff again…but, here I am beginning a huge project for the organization that I am in. Even though it's only me building the system, I figured that the only way to build something that would last is to go through all the steps that I learned in your class! I just thought you would like to hear that your class was so useful. Air Force officer

This course has changed my attitude toward groups. I saw how you structured the groups and instilled individual accountability so that each member contributed to the final product. Alum

The continued success of the course depends on making changes, and process improvement is structured in the course from three different perspectives—team, product, and course.

Team: In addition to team processing discussed earlier, the Guidance Team regularly requests teams to review their progress. This processing typically occurs after some major deliverable. Individuals on each team are asked to respond to the following questions:

- Did you complete your task on time?
- How did you encourage participation from another team member?
- What is working well in your team?
- What needs to be improved in your team?

The responses to these questions are consolidated, made anonymous, and shared with the team members. This process assists team members and the Guidance Team in identifying problems and reviewing with teams the skills that resolve them. The recurring themes, especially in the first semester, are centered on meetings and lack of commitment from all members.

Regarding meetings, the problems typically center on unproductive meetings, and length of meetings. The feedback in this area includes review of how to conduct effective meetings, e.g., setting an agenda, assigning roles such as time keeper and participation checker, creating action items, and checking status of previous action items. Students are also encouraged to consider the "100-mile rule," i.e., treat each meeting as though each member has travelled 100 miles to attend and, as a result, it's imperative to arrive on time and have a productive meeting (Scholtes, 1996).

The advice given to teams regarding lack of commitment centers on building positive interdependence and the importance of recognizing members' contributions to the project and valuing the opinions of others. Additional advice includes structuring individual accountability through task assignments and deadlines. The lead is encouraged to keep records of individual contributions and status through meeting minutes or e-mail exchanges. The following response to the question of "what worked well" reflects how one team improved from one semester to the next:

We worked horribly as a team last semester. This semester, however, we've come to terms with each member's benefits and weaknesses. Because we've learned to think as a team, we now act as one. It is much more evident that trusting of team members produces the desired results. Everyone is willing to spend as much time as necessary to produce what he/she needs to. By not wanting to let down the group, every member (including myself) works very hard to produce a team deliverable.

Another example of reflection from a team member is the following:

At the beginning of last semester when I looked at the names of my prospective team, I didn't know what to think, only one familiar name. Looking at this team now, we are really a "melting pot": one Taiwanese, one Hispanic/American, one Indian, one Mexican and one [anglo]. Who says that we can't all get along together? Each one of us had our own strengths and weaknesses in our abilities and our personalities. Miraculously, what I lacked, someone else had to offer. What someone else needed, I could help. This is the true definition of teamwork. And we made it work. I am truly enriched for this experience and I thank each one of you for that.

Product: Our assessment of the quality of the products produced by the students is part of the evaluations given during the final presentations each semester. These presentations are evaluated by the Guidance Team as well as the clients. Using these assessments, we have identified problems in the efficacy of the testing strategies and the specifications of pre- and post- conditions in the detailed designs.

Considering the student as a product, we look at Alumni Surveys to determine whether five years after graduation alumni believe that the program prepared them to work in teams, apply software engineering principles, model, and design. The survey results are given in Table 2. Recent focus group evaluations of alumni of the course support the ideas that the Affinity model assists students in dealing with conflict and improving their communications and presentation skills. One of the principal skills developed in the model is the ability to constructively critique other people's work and to accept constructive critique of their own work. The key factor is that the Affinity model has helped them develop the social and professional skills that allow them to interact productively with the other people with whom they work.

Course: With respect to the course, numerous changes have been made over the years, including introduction of new tools, improved tutorials on use of tools, and revised strategies for teaching concepts with which students have difficulties. An important method that we introduced for evaluating the course is the mapping of course outcomes to particular tasks or questions on tests, and assignments to determine the effectiveness of learning. For example, Table 3 shows a small subset of the course outcomes for the two-semester course and the corresponding ARG component that complement the outcome. The outcomes are given in two levels: Level 2 is Application and

Analysis. These are outcomes in which the student can apply the material in familiar situations, e.g., can work a problem of familiar structure with minor changes in the details. Level 3 is Synthesis and Evaluation. These are outcomes in which the student can apply the material in new situations. This is the highest level of mastery.

RELATED WORK

Since project and team experiences are embedded in most computer science and software engineer-

Table 2. Results of 2007 Alumni Survey (n=37)

Q17c: Prepared me to work in teams.	91.8% strongly agree or agree
Q17g: Developed ability to apply principles of software engineering.	97.3% strongly agree or agree
Q17h: Prepared to model real-world processes and objects.	81.0% strongly agree or agree
Q18: Have designed a system, component or process	91.9% yes
Q19: Quality of preparation for specific design task	29.4% excellent, 61.8% good, 8.8% below average

Table 3. Subset of course outcomes and corresponding ARG components

Course Outcome	Assessment	ARG Component Description
a. Apply techniques for eliciting requirements, including conducting interviews and developing a throw-away prototype.	Project: Interview, client interactions, and prototypes	Asking technical questions; Preparing presentations for prototype reviews
a. Analyze requirements to determine if they meet the attributes of well-written requirements.	Exams SRS Reviews	Peer evaluation of requirements, identifying common mistakes, SRS drafts
a. Exhibit responsible attitudes and work habits as individuals and groups, in accordance with professional software engineering codes of ethics.	Notebooks, team memos, presentation evaluations	Individual accountability in project work: preparing and documenting team meetings.
a. Assemble and present technical work orally.	Project presentations	Cooperative teams; delivering technical presentations; answering questions.
a. Develop effective techniques for collaboration and problem-solving within groups in order to create finished products of high quality.	Project Notebooks	Cooperative teams; professional and team skills; conflict resolution.
a. Conduct a technical review.	Prototype reviews, SRS reviews, design reviews, code reviews	Deliberate instruction in the skills needed to perform good reviews; professional presentation based on technical merit.
a. Compose technical documents that are grammatically correct and technically sound.	Project Documents	Perform good reviews; professional presentations.

ing undergraduate programs, it is no surprise that many faculty have encountered issues similar to the ones we encounter, and many of the approaches we suggest here are being used in other institutions. The use of cooperative and collaborative learning approaches, active learning, and pair programming facilitate the integration of teams where there are differences in the abilities of team members, assist team members in overcoming communications barriers, and help to motivate students in the team setting (Ellis, 2000; Aller, 2004; Doerschuk, 2004; Spickard-Prettyman, 2004; Mickle, 2004; Layman, 2005). Assessment of team projects is difficult and time-consuming, and most effective approaches include reviews and engineering notebooks (Meyer, 2005; Cooley, 2004). There are many ways to attempt to give academic projects a "real world" flavor by incorporating real clients (for example, see Ford 2004 and Bruhn 2004).

FUTURE TRENDS

The need for technology workers in the United States in the near future will continue to grow (Holahan, 2007; McGee, 2007a).The need for reliable software outstrips our ability to produce it. The President's Council of Advisors on Science and Technology (PCAST, 2007) reports on the importance of networking and information technology (NIT) systems connected with the physical world. These include embedded systems, engineered systems, and cyber-physical systems, e.g., home health-care devices, ground transportation monitoring, and environmental monitoring. The ability to design and develop safety-critical and secure NIT systems is a national priority. There will be a need to educate a workforce that can work in multidisciplinary environments with a strong understanding of security and verification. In addition, employers will continue to seek project management, communications, and team skills (McGee, 2007b). Team skills that include the ability to work with members

in different places, different time zones, and different cultures will become more common.

The trend towards distributed team development (see for example Ramesh 2002 and Duarte 2006) and multidisciplinary software development will continue. An example of this is the trend towards service orientation (SO), where applications are constructed from resources made available over the Internet as web or grid services. The term SO refers to the level of abstraction in which functionality is specified. In particular, SO is an approach for analysis, design, and development of modules that support principles such as reusability, loose coupling, abstraction, and separation of concerns (Erl, 2005). The more familiar term service-oriented architecture (SOA) is used to describe "the policies, practices, and frameworks that enable application functionality to be provided and consumed as sets of services" (Sprott, 2004).

There will be a need to integrate existing software services and components to rapidly produce software solutions. Application developers from business and scientific domains are using web services to implement systems based on the SOA paradigm. Web service technologies provide the necessary mechanisms to expose shareable resources (service-oriented modules that provide data and functionality) over the network and allow the resources to be consumed by users across heterogeneous platforms, enhancing interaction across organizations. The needed skills include the ability to specify functionality of services so that services can be advertised and discovered.

The Department of Labor's Bureau of Labor Statistics projects that over the 2004-2014 decade there will be increases of 46% for software engineers (Hecker, 2005). There is a strong need for software engineers who are familiar with software development tools such as automated testing tools and systems that assist developers in generating code from designs. The separation between CS and SE will increase, but the need for developers will require that we produce capable developers in CS programs.

CONCLUSION

The ARG model focuses on the development of the student. We use the cooperative learning and the development of skills by using the iterative feedback aspects of the ARG model to teach the software engineering capstone course. The course raises the level of our students to meet the needs and expectations of our constituents, the industry recruiters. The Instruction-Practice-Apply approach utilizes repeated application of software engineering techniques to a real-world problem and extensive interaction with experienced software engineers to teach students the practice of software engineering. As the ARG model suggests, we use structured and deliberate techniques to teach students how to work together to produce software engineering deliverables and resolve conflicts. Feedback from our industrial partners indicates that the team experience and the project are invaluable to our students. Feedback from our alumni and students indicate that theses experiences have a significant impact on their careers by preparing them for the workplace.

CC2001 (2001, p. 43) describes the importance of developing complementary curriculum, i.e., the constellation of skills that are taught through internship, such as the ability to write an effective résumé, manage time effectively, conduct library research, maintain professional responsibility, remain up current in the field, and engage in life-long learning. As described in this paper, it is clear that the UTEP SE approach provides the benefits of complementary curriculum by supporting the development of a set of transferable skills that enhance the students overall efficacy and ability to effectively contribute to the software engineering workforce.

ACKNOWLEDGMENT

This work was supported in part by the National Science Foundation (NSF) through grants DUE-0443061 and CNS-0540592. Any opinions, findings, and conclusions or recommendations expressed in the paper are those of the authors and do not necessarily reflect the views of the NSF.

REFERENCES

ACM/IEEE-CS Joint Task Force on Software Engineering Ethics and Professional Practices (1999). The ACM/IEEE Software Engineering Code of Ethics and Professional Practice. retrieved February 2007 from http://www.acm.org/about/se-code.

ACM Education Board (2004), *ACM Education Board Annual Report, Fiscal Year FY 2003.*

Aller, B. M., Kline, A. & Tsang, E. (2004). Work in Progress: Improving the senior capstone. In *Proceedings of the 334th ASEE/IEEE Frontiers in Education Conference* (pp. TCG/12-TCG/14).

American Psychological Association (1992). *Learner-Centered Psychological Principles: Guidelines for School Redesign and Reform.* Washington D.C.: American Psychological Association.

Anderson, L , Chenault, T., Churchman, J., & Homack, R. (1999). Scene and Countermeasure Integration for Munition Interaction with Targets Army Research Lab White Sands Missile Range NM Survivability/Lethality Analysis Directorate. Retrieved May 2007 from http://stinet.dtic.mil/oai/oai?&verb=getRecord&metadataPrefix=html&identifier=ADA368518

Astin, A. W. (1985). *Achieving Academic Excellence.* San Francisco: Jossey-Bass.

Bloom, B. (1956). *Taxonomy of Educational Objectives.* David McKay Company, Inc.

Bonura, S. & Hayman, B. (1998). *Shape Up! Resource Manual, Personality Styles and Human Interaction – Making Them Work for You!* Graphic Business Solutions, Inc: San Diego, CA.

Bruhn, R. & Camp, J. (2004). Creating corporate world experience in capstone courses. In *Proceedings of the 34th ASEE/IEEE Frontiers in Education Conference* (pp. T2G/1-T2G/6).

CAC (2007) *Computing Accreditation Commission Criteria for Accrediting Computing Programs*, Accreditation Board of Engineering Technology. Retrieved March 10, 2007, from http://www.abet.org/Linked%20Documents-UPDATE/Criteria%20and%20PP/C001%202006-07%20CAC%20Criteria%209-12-06.pdf

CC2001 (2001) *Computing Curricula 2001 Computer Science Volume*, Association of Computing Machinery. Retrieved October 2006 from http://www.sigcse.org/cc2001/.

Coad, P., Lefebvre, E. & De Luca, J. (1999). *Java Modeling in Color With UML: Enterprise Components and Process.* Prentice Hall International.

CSDP (2007) *IEEE Computer Society Certified Software Development Professional,* Retrieved May 1, 2007 from http://www.computer.org/portal/site/ieeecs/menuitem.c5efb9b8ade9096b8a9ca0108bcd45f3/index.jsp?&pName=ieeecs_level1&path=ieeecs/education/certification&file=index.xml&xsl=generic.xsl&

Cooley, W. (2004). Individual student assessment in team-based capstone design projects. In *Proceedings of the 34th ASEE/IEEE Frontiers in Education Conference* (pp. F1G-1-5).

DeMarco, T. & Lister, T. (1999). *Peopleware: Productive Projects and Teams Second Edition.* Dorset House Publishing Company, Inc.

Doerschuk, P. (2004). Incorporating team software development and quality assurance in software engineering education. In *Proceedings of the 34th*

ASEE/IEEE Frontiers in Education Conference (pp. F1C/7-F1C/12).

Duarte, D. & Snyder, N. T. (2006). *Mastering Virtual Teams: Strategies, Tools, and Techniques That Succeed,* Jossey-Bass.

Ellis, H. (2000). An Experience in Collaborative Learning: Observations of a Software Engineering Course. In *Proceedings of the 30th ASEE/IEEE Frontiers in Education Conference* (pp. T2C/1-T2C/6).

Engineering Accreditation Commission (EAC 2007). Criteria for accrediting engineering programs effective for the 2007-2008 accreditation cycle. Retrieved September 2007 from http://www.abet.org.

Erl, T. (2005). *Service oriented architecture: concepts, techniques, and design.* Prentice Hall.

Ford, R. & Lasher, W. (2004). Processes for ensuring quality capstone design. In *Proceedings of the 34th ASEE/IEEE Frontiers in Education Conference* (S2G/13-S2G/17).

Gates, A. Q., Delgado, N., & Mondragon, O. (2000). A structured approach for managing a practical software engineering course. In *Proceedings 30th ASEE/IEEE Frontiers in Education Conference* (pp. T1C/21 - T1C/26).

Gates, Q., Teller, P., Bernat, A., Delgado, N., & Della-Piana, C. (1999). Expanding participation in undergraduate research using the affinity research group model. *Journal of Engineering Education,* 88(4): 409-414.

GeoNet (2007). United States Gravity Data Repository System. Retrieved May 10, 2007 from http://paces.geo.utep.edu/gdrp/.

GEON (2007). GEON: the geosciences network. Retrieved November 2007 from: http://geongrid.org.

Gates, A.Q., Roach, S., Villa, E., & Kephart, K. (in press, 2007). *Affinity Research Groups: Creating and Maintaining Effective Research Teams.*

Hacker, D. (1991). *The Bedford Handbook for Writers*. Boston: Bedford Book of St. Martin's Press.

Hecker, D. E. (2005). Occupational Employment Projections to 2014. *Monthly Labor Review*. Department of Labor (pp. 70-101).

Holahan, C. (2007). The myth of high-tech outsourcing. *Business Week*, 4/24/07, retrieved on 4/2007 from http://www.businessweek. com/technology/content/apr2007/tc20070424_ 967747.htm?chan=top+news_top+news+index_ top+story.

Johnson, D., & Johnson, R. (1989). *Cooperation and competition: theory and research*. Edina, MN: Interaction Book Company.

Johnson, D., Johnson, R., & Holubec, E. (1990). *Circles of learning: cooperation in the classroom*. Edina, MN: Interaction Book Company.

Johnson, D., Johnson, R., & Smith, K. (1991). *Active learning: cooperation in the college classroom*. Edina, MN: Interaction Book Company.

Johnson, D., Johnson, R., & Holubec, E. (1992a). *Cooperation in the classroom*. Edina, MN: Interaction Book Company.

Johnson, D., Johnson, R., & Holubec, E. (1992b). *Advanced cooperative learning*. Edina, MN: Interaction Book Company.

Johnson, D., Johnson, R., & Holubec, E. (1994). *The nuts and bolts of cooperative learning*. Edina, MN: Interaction Book Company.

Johnson, D. & Johnson, R. (2005). *Teaching students to be peacemakers, 4th Edition*, Edina, MN: Interaction Book Company.

Kerth, N. L. (2001). *Software retrospectives: a handbook for team reviews*, Dorset House Publishing Company, Inc.

Kurfiss, J.G. (1998). *Critical thinking*. ASHE-ERIC Higher Education Report No. 2. Washington, D.C.: Association for the Study of Higher Education.

Layman, L., Willimas, L., Osborne, J., Berenson, S., Slaten, K. & Vouk, M. (2005). How and why collaborative software development impacts the software engineering course. In *Proceedings of the 35th ASEE/IEEE Frontiers in Education Conference* (pp. T4C/9-T4C/14).

McConnell, S. (1997). *Software project survival guide*. Microsoft Press.

McGee, M. K. (2007a). Bill to increase H1-B visa makes a comeback in congress. *InformationWeek*, retrieved 4/2007 from http://www.information-week.com/showArticle.jhtml;jsessionid=L5FSM T3UOTFHYQSNDLPSKHSCJUNN2JVN?artic leID=199101679&queryText=H-1B .

McGee, M. K. & Murphy, C. (2007b). In growing job market, IT pros get more for the soft skills. *InformationWeek* retrieved 10/07 from http://www.informationweek.com/story/show-Article.jhtml?articleID=202404815

McKeachie, W.J., Pintrich, P.R., Lin, Y.-G., & Smith, D.A.F. (1986). *Teaching and learning in the classroom: a review of the research literature*. Ann Arbor: National Center for Research to Improve Postsecondary Teaching and Learning, University of Michigan.

Mickle, M. H., Shuman, L., & Spring, M. (2004). Active learning courses on the cutting edge of technology. In *Proceedings of the 34th ASEE/ IEEE Frontiers in Education Conference* (pp. T2F/19-T2F/23).

Meyer, D. G. (2005). Capstone design outcome assessment: instruments for quantitative education. In *Proceedings of the 35th ASEE/IEEE Frontiers in Education Conference* (pp. F4D/7-F4D-11).

Parnas, D. L. (1999). Software engineering programs are not computer science programs. *IEEE Software*, 16 (6):19-30.

PCAST (2007). President's Council of Advisors on Science and Technology. *Leadership under challenge: information technology R&D in a competitive world: an assessment of the federal networking and information technology R&D program.* www.ostp.gov.

Ramesh, G. (2002). Managing global software projects: how to lead geographically distributed teams, manage processes and use quality models. McGraw-Hill Limited.

Rauda, L. G. (2005). A Feature-Driven Development approach for an undergraduate software engineering course. Master's Project, the University of Texas at El Paso, May 2007.

Rodriguez, C. (1994). Keeping minority undergraduates in science and engineering. Paper presented at the 19th Annual Conference of the Association for the Study of Higher Education, Tucson, Arizona.

Scholtes, P, Joiner, B. & Streibel, B. (1996). *The Team Handbook* 2nd Edition. Joiner Associates, Inc.

SE2004 (2004) *Curriculum Guidelines for Undergraduate Degree Programs in Software Engineering,* Association of Computing Machinery and IEEE Computer Society. Retrieved December 2006 from http://sites.computer.org/ccse/.

Spickard-Prettyman, S., Qammar, H., Broadway, F., Cheung, F.M. & Evans, E. (2004). The impact of vertical integration of design teams on the chemical engineering program. In the *Proceedings of the 34th ASEE/IEEE Frontiers in Education Conference* (T2G/15-T2G/19).

Sprott, D. & Wilkes, L. (2004). Understanding service-oriented architecture. *Microsoft Architect Journal.* Retrieved May 2007 from http://msdn2.microsoft.com/en-us/library/aa480021.aspx.

Teller, P. & Gates, A. Q. (2001). Using the affinity research group model to involve undergraduate students in computer science. *Journal of Engineering Education*, 549-555.

Tinto, V., Goodsell Love, A., & Russo, P. (1993). *Leaving college: rethinking the causes and curses of student attrition* (2 ed.). Chicago: The University of Chicago Press.

Whitehead, R. (2001). *Leading a software development team: a developer's guide to successfully leading people & projects,* Addison-Wesley.

Winter, V. (2006). *The high-assurance transformation system.* Retrieved December 2006 from http://faculty.ist.unomaha.edu/winter/HATS_Page/hats_index.html.

Whitehead, R. (2001). *Leading a software development team: a developer's guide to successfully leading people and projects,* Addison-Wesley.

Wysocki, R. (2006). *Effective software project management.* John Wiley & Sons.

Chapter IX
A Framework for Success in Real Projects for Real Clients Courses

David Klappholz
Stevens Institute of Technology, USA

Vicki L. Almstrum
The University of Texas at Austin, USA

Ken Modesit
Indiana University – Purdue University Ft. Wayne, USA

Cherry Owen
The University of Texas of the Permian Basin, USA

Allen Johnson
Huston-Tillotson University, USA

Steven J. Condly
HSA Learning & Performance Solutions, USA

ABSTRACT

In this chapter, we demonstrate the importance of Real Projects for Real Clients Courses (RPRCCs) in computing curricula. Based on our collective experience, we offer advice for setting up an effective support infrastructure for such courses. We discuss where and how to find clients, the types of projects that we have used, and how to form and train teams. We investigate the variety of standards and work products that we have used in our courses and explore issues related to assessment and evaluation. Finally, we consider the benefits of an RPRCC-centric approach to computing curricula.

A course is underway. Students are excited, engaged, eager to apply what they are learning, eager to communicate with one another about their project work, what they need to accomplish, and what they must find out from outside stakeholders. As a lovely bonus, the project the students are developing is more than a toy problem or a product that will gather dust on the back of the shelf — they are writing software that is useful and will be used.

This type of course exists and has been successful in many settings, including public and private institutions, small, medium, and large institutions, and Historically Black and Hispanic-Serving institutions (that is, the colleges and universities at which the co-authors teach). In this chapter, we promote the idea of Real Projects for Real Clients Courses (RPRCCs) and discuss key issues related to successfully planning for and executing them in a variety of settings.

INTRODUCTION

RPRCCs are courses in which students work in teams to develop real software for real clients, including faculty and staff from their own institutions, for-profit companies, not-for-profit organizations, and government agencies. To be "real," software must meet the needs of the client by solving a problem or providing a service for the client or the organization the client represents. RPRCCs are appropriate in all Computing Curricula 2005 (Joint IEEE CS/ACM Task Force, 2005) disciplines, that is, computer science (CS), information systems (IS), computer engineering (CE), software engineering (SE), and information technology (IT), which we refer to collectively as "computing disciplines" or simply as "computing." RPRCCs are also appropriate in the full range of post-secondary institutions, including community colleges, four-year colleges, and

universities, and can even be used at the secondary level.

This chapter explores the core issues covered in a taxonomy that has been developed by the co-authors over a number of years. The taxonomy, which delineates issues involved in designing and delivering RPRCCs, has been refined using feedback from participants in workshops and other conference activities (e.g., Almstrum, Klappholz, & Modesitt, 2007; Klappholz, Almstrum, & Modesitt, 2006). Appendix A gives the top two levels of the current version of the taxonomy.

In this chapter, we explore the following basic issues involved in developing and teaching an RPRCC:

* Client-related issues, including where to find them, how to vet them for appropriateness as clients, and how to manage client expectations;
* Project-related issues, including possible types of projects and how to vet projects for appropriateness;
* Team-related issues, including how to form teams and train them;
* Product-related issues, including standards and required work products; and
* Issues related to assessment and evaluation.

The full taxonomy details these and a large number of additional issues. Finally, in the Future Trends section, we argue for the notion of RPRCC-centric computing curricula, that is, curricula that include RPRCCs at multiple levels of the undergraduate program.

The experiences we discuss in this chapter can help readers understand the issues one must consider when planning the framework for an RPRCC. We sincerely hope that the ideas presented below will better equip instructors with all types of experience to plan and execute successful RPRCCs.

WHY RPRCCS?

Other than using real projects and real clients, how different is it to teach an RPRCC version of a course compared to a more traditional version of the same course? Several of us have observed that teaching an RPRCC probably takes more time than teaching a traditional version of the same course, especially if the instructor has never worked in a disciplined development environment. Certain aspects of teaching an RPRCC can be difficult to predict and control. An RPRCC requires a different style of planning (e.g., to find clients, determine teams, coordinate schedules, and manage client expectations) and a different style of oversight (e.g., to ensure that teams are making progress toward their goals). When starting to teach such a course, there is a sharp learning curve, making the first semester or two especially demanding and risky.

Why, then, should a computing instructor put in the added effort and a department expend the extra resources in order to offer RPRCCs? We argue that RPRCCs and RPRCC-centric curricula provide benefits to three constituencies: computing departments, computing students, and the IT/software development workforce. We discuss these issues below.

Benefits to the Department

The most straightforward benefit to computing departments that offer RPRCCs has to do with accreditation. In addition to the traditional set of technical skills, the new criteria from ABET, Inc., the recognized accreditor for U.S. college and university programs in applied science, computing, engineering, and technology include a second set of equally important professional skills, which are also essential aspects of RPRCCs. Shuman, Besterfield-Sacre, and McGourty (2005) divide these latter skills into *process skills*, which include communication, teamwork, ethics, and professionalism, and *awareness skills*, which include lifelong learning, a knowledge of contemporary issues, and engineering within a societal and global context.

A second potential benefit of RPRCCs is that using industrial clients can strengthen cooperation between educational institutions and industry. The close interaction can help students find placement in internships and post-graduation employment. The relationship can also support technology transfer and sharing of research results (Grisham, Krasner, & Perry, 2006).

Recruiting and retention are major concerns to most computing departments. Because students enrolled in RPRCCs tend to be strongly motivated by the mixture of real and theoretical skills inherent in these courses (Hogan, Smith, & Thomas, 2005), computing curricula that include RPRCCs may increase retention. RPRCCs early in the curriculum, for example at the pre-CS1 and secondary levels, may convince students with little or no programming background or who would otherwise never select a career in software development to consider a computing major.

The declining number of women in computing is disheartening when compared to increasing numbers of women in other areas of science and engineering. In 1985, 38% of B.S. degrees in CS were awarded to women. By 2003, their representation had shrunk to 28%. Because RPRCCs concentrate on interpersonal skills and because every community has potential RPRCC clients whose projects have social significance, the availability of RPRCCs can have a strong positive effect on efforts to recruit and retain women and members of under-represented minorities (Eisenman, 2001; Jessup, Sumner, & Barker, 2006; Margolis & Fisher, 2001; Norman & Keating, 1997; Schuhmann, 1992).

Benefits to Students

Individual students enrolled in RPRCCs and RPRCC-centric curricula can experience early opportunities for community service, added confidence in their own abilities, and a strong foundation for life-long employment. If an RPRCC uses not-for-profit or educational clients, this enables students to perform service to the community at the same time they are earning academic credit.

Many computing graduates report that what they learned as undergraduates did not prepare them sufficiently for the work they encountered after they entered the workforce (Fernandez & Tedford, 2006; Fernandez, Garcia, Camacho, & Evans, 2006). RPRCCs can help students gain confidence in their own skills as well as experience that will help them become productive more quickly once they enter the workforce.

RPRCCs instill a number of skills, especially business-related and inter-personal skills, which are among the most difficult to offshore (Aspray, Mayadas, & Vardi, 2006; Boehm, Abi-Antoun, Port, Kwan, & Lynch, 1999; Mitchell, 2006). While such skills can be taught as theoretical principles, most students will learn them in depth only by doing, that is, through active learning. Thus, the skills students practice while enrolled in RPRCCs form the basis for life-long careers for computing graduates wanting to work in countries that send work offshore.

RPRCCs fit snugly within the active learning genre, a type of learning that emphasizes student engagement in realistic problem solving, teamwork, and application of theory and principle (McKeachie, 1961). Courses that incorporate active learning into the curriculum have been shown to realize demonstrable improvements in student learning, achievement, and transfer in subjects as diverse as general science (Akinoglu & Tandogan, 2007), medicine (Frohna, Hamstra, Mullan, & Gruppen, 2007), nursing, (Bowles, 2006), business management (Zheng & Padmanabhan, 2006), statistics (Enders & Diener-West, 2006), entrepreneurship (Tan & Ng, 2006), and textiles (Kadolph, 2005). Interested readers can refer to the journal *Active Learning in Higher Education* (http://alh.sagepub.com/) for up-to-date research in this field.

Benefits to the IT/Software Development Workforce

RPRCCs provide both quantitative and qualitative benefits to the workforce. Statistics show that the current supply of computing graduates is not satisfying demand. The American Bureau of Labor Statistics (BLS) predicts that in the United States alone by 2014 there will be a total of 448,000 job openings in various aspects of IT and software development in response to industry growth and baby boomer retirement in spite of offshoring. In contrast, only 8,000 new research positions are predicted for computer and information scientists (Hecker, 2005; Vegso, 2006). Thus, if academia could produce sufficiently many new graduates to fill all of the projected openings, over 98% would be employed in some aspect of software development rather than in research. Students whose preparation includes the practical skills that RPRCCs are designed to instill in addition to the traditional theoretical background will be far better prepared to become productive members of the workforce soon after graduation.

The Standish Chaos reports (Standish Group, 1994, 2003), which outline reasons for software project cost and schedule overruns and outright cancellations after significant expenditure of time and resources, indicate that a major factor is a lack of certain skills, many of which are taught in RPRCCs. Starney (2006) has revealed three primary reasons for project failures: lack of requirements management, lack of risk management, and poor project planning. All of these skills are addressed in RPRCCs.

RPRCCs build skills above and beyond traditional academic computing skills, which cover only a fraction of the software development tasks that must be performed on typical projects. In addition to skills such as algorithm development and programming, project work requires skills inherent in RPRCCs, such as requirements engineering, analysis and design, testing, cost and effort estimation, scheduling, risk management, and overall project management. The ubiquity of software libraries and sophisticated middleware makes algorithm development a far less dominant aspect of the development process than it was 10 or 15 years ago.

WHY SO FEW RPRCCS?

Given these benefits, why do so many departments not include RPRCCs among their offerings? As we began our study of RPRCCs, we conjectured that a major reason is that many departments lack faculty with the background and confidence to teach such courses. Unlike technical computing courses, teaching RPRCCs requires skills that are difficult to learn by reading a textbook and solving sample problems. Rather, learning to teach RPRCCs requires practical experience with developing real software for real clients, experience typically acquired by working in industry, either as one's primary employment or through industrial faculty internships (e.g., http://www.boeing.com/companyoffices/pwu/fellowship/objective.html; Johnson, Powers, & Wagert, 1989). In our experience many computing faculty enter academia directly from graduate school without any detours for industry experience and are, therefore, ill-prepared to teach RPRCCs.

At the same time, industry folks coming to academia to teach RPRCCs can encounter challenges, although generally for different reasons. In one example, an instructor with over 30 years of industry and government experience taught a new RPRCC that had to be cancelled, with bad feelings all around. While the instructor did have the requisite software development skills, this individual lacked the teaching skills required to make the course interesting and successful for the students and the clients. On the other side of the pendulum, while working in industry one of our co-authors received special training in how to teach as part of the IBM University Programs in

Technical Education and was able to convert that experience into success in the classroom.

THE AUTHORS' SETTINGS

The details of a particular RPRCC depend on factors such as the course's desired outcomes, the preparation of students, and available resources. Before we address issues relating to clients, projects, teams, work products, and assessment, we describe the wide variety of settings in which we have taught RPRCCs at different levels of the computing curriculum.

The ideas in this chapter are drawn from close to 50 years of cumulative experience teaching RPRCCs. Students at our institutions have very different backgrounds and the resources available to instructors vary widely. This breadth of experience shows the broad range of possibilities and the different ways that RPRCCs can be realized in different settings. We have taught RPRCCs in computer science departments at the following types of post-secondary institutions in the United States:

- *A small private engineering school.* Students arrive well prepared, with overall SAT scores well above the national average. Nearly all entering CS freshmen have had at least one computing course in high school and quite a few students have done additional programming before entering the undergraduate program. In the past few years a handful of freshmen have entered with professional experience, mostly in Website design, and a small number have even had their own web design businesses.
- *A small Hispanic-Serving university.* Students may be admitted with low SAT scores and many enter with low math placement scores. Only a few of the students entering the CS major have had high school programming or other advanced placement

courses. Some students have been employed in industry, which has given them valuable project-work experience.

- *A small private Historically Black university.* Entering students have typically not had a programming course and may be weak in mathematics. Students are frequently admitted with low SAT scores, which can make it difficult for them to solve technical problems and design programs. Many students have family and job responsibilities as well as transportation problems, which makes it more difficult for them to schedule meetings and complete project work. As a partial solution to these problems, courses have been restructured to provide additional lab time for team meetings.

- *A medium-sized regional state university that is primarily a commuter campus.* Students are relatively well prepared, with mathematics as the most typical deficiency. Entering students have the highest SAT verbal and total scores of students in any program in the college and significantly exceed university and national norms. Most students have had some programming experience in high school, but may take a basic computing course (CS0) if they arrive without this experience. By the time they take the first of two required RPRCCs they are familiar with networks, databases, and architecture, as well as with technical writing. The program of study includes a new prerequisite of a non-computing course that emphasizes teamwork and leadership skills.

- *A large private research-oriented university.* The curriculum includes an elective two-semester introductory-level graduate SE RPRCC. Over three-quarters of the students in this course are recently-arrived Asian nationals, mostly Indian, but including many Chinese, Koreans, and Thais. About half of the students have some industry background.

- *A very large public state research university.* Over half of incoming students have had a computing course in high school, many have advanced placement credit, and about half have done web programming or created Websites. Only a few have professional experience. CS majors have among the highest average SAT scores in the university. The program does, however, include a significant number of weaker students who enjoy using computers and want to be CS majors.

Throughout the chapter, we embrace the diversity of our student populations and the great variety that characterizes RPRCCs at our different institutions. The courses in our examples include: several varieties of software engineering (SE) (e.g., a one-semester elective junior/senior-level course; a one-semester required course, and a two-semester required capstone sequence); a one-semester required sophomore/junior-level database course; a one-semester Information Systems Design course; a Senior Research course; and a required two-semester project-only capstone. In all of these courses, including those taught at levels as early as the sophomore year, students work on real projects for real clients.

Because of the diversity of our student populations, the educational goals for our various RPRCCs are significantly different in some respects. As a result our approaches to issues involved in designing and teaching RPRCCs have ranged from structured and prescriptive at one end of the spectrum to "seat of the pants" at the other end. The examples we include should give a sense of this range.

BUILDING THE CLIENT POOL

A planning challenge that can seem insurmountable to faculty members new to teaching an RPRCC is finding the clients who will form the backbone of the course (as well as the projects).

The first semester or two of teaching an RPRCC can be a challenge as the instructor builds up an initial pool of clients. After teaching RPRCCs once or twice, the pump is often sufficiently primed that past clients and new prospects initiate contact with the instructor well ahead of the time about being clients for the next RPRCC offering (Ecker, Caudill, Hoctor, & Meyer, 2004). Although outside forces can sometimes undermine an instructor's ability to recruit potential clients, for example when a bad economic climate forces willing potential clients to reprioritize how they spend their time, some instructors find that over time the bigger challenge is to hold the number of potential clients to a manageable number.

The process of building a client pool can build on experiences learned from others. After co-teaching the first semester of a two-semester graduate-level RPRCC during a sabbatical, one of the co-authors converted a required, junior-level DB course into an RPRCC. Emulating the approach used to seek clients for the graduate course, this instructor sent an email to faculty and staff explaining that students in the course would be doing real projects for real clients and inviting people to submit proposals and come to a meeting. For the first two years all clients were faculty and staff; after that, many new potential clients turned up thanks to word-of-mouth from previous clients or people who knew previous clients. In one example, a retiree sought a team to create a Website for a large not-for-profit, member-run yacht club. The Website incorporated five activities that had each been hand-run by different administrators. In the end, the client organization was very satisfied, even inviting the team to go for a sail and hiring some of the students to do more work on the Website.

In the next subsection, we explore general client characteristics, including potential sources of clients and how to vet potential clients for suitability. We also discuss the number of clients appropriate for an RPRCC and how to prepare them for what to expect.

Client Characteristics

Before the introduction of the PC in the early 1980s, only specialized individuals used computers and software, so sources of clients were very limited. Today everyone uses software, so almost anyone can serve as a client, either out of personal interest in a software application or as a representative of an organization's needs (Modesitt, Maxim, & Akingbehin, 1999). Even so, a careful client selection process that takes into consideration the educational goals of the particular RPRCC is invaluable in maximizing the likelihood of success for clients, students, the instructor, and the institution. In our settings, client sources have included: faculty in the same or another department; operational staff from academic departments; institutional administrators such as the president, provost, or registrar; members of the institutional IT office; other operational offices such as the library, career services, housing, or catering; student organizations; pre-secondary teachers, librarians, and educational specialists; staff of local and federal governmental agencies; employees of and volunteers with local not-for-profits; and employees of for-profit businesses.

In the remainder of this subsection, we discuss our experience in considering the following four general characteristics of potential clients:

- Their sophistication with respect to understanding software development and how to explain requirements.
- Their experience in this type of client role.
- Their physical location and ability to communicate by means other than face-to-face (e.g., email, telephone, on-line chat).
- Their schedule of availability for meeting with and conferring with a student team.

The continuum of sophistication runs from clients who are completely naïve in the ways of software development to those who are extremely savvy. Examples of the former are faculty members outside of the computing department, pre-college personnel, and representatives of not-for-profits. The latter group includes members of the computing department, members of the department's Professional Advisory Board (PAB), and employees of the institutional IT department.

Naïve clients typically have a problem they believe can be solved by software, but do not know precisely what the software can or should do and how it should look to the user. Boehm et al. (1999) refers to this as the IKIWISI (I'll know it when I see it) effect. While savvy clients are better able to delineate their needs and communicate those needs to the team, a savvy client may inadvertently detract from what students learn about requirements engineering by providing too much information too easily. In addition, teams working with naïve clients are more likely to understand the team's obligation to learn about the client's domain, rather than expecting the client to know about computing and software development.

The prior experience individuals have serving as a client in an RPRCC can have an enormous impact on their appropriateness as clients, regardless of their sophistication with respect to software development methods. An experienced client is more likely to understand the flow of the semester, the guidelines for what the team should produce at each step along the way, and the importance of allowing the team to make mistakes and recover. An experienced client understands the importance of being frank with the team about how well the developing product meets client expectations and that keeping quiet in order to "protect" the team does students a disservice in the long run.

The physical proximity of potential clients to campus can affect their effectiveness as clients. Progress reports, final demonstrations, and other meetings often involve travel for the student team or the client. If the client is located off-campus, it might be difficult for the student team to arrange transportation to reach the client site. At the same time, many instructors feel on-site meetings are vital for helping students better understand the client's needs. Working with off-site clients is typical of real world software development and, particularly if clients are remote, can expose student teams to issues such as communicating across time zones and using tools such as video, telephone, and on-line conferencing. However, instructors new to RPRCCs will probably find it easier to work with clients close to home. As the instructor gains confidence with logistics, using off-campus clients becomes more viable.

Constraints on a client's schedule can affect their suitability as a client. For example, if the client is a classroom teacher, the team may have to arrange to meet during a fixed planning period, after the school day ends, or on weekends. The client's travel commitments can be an issue, though modern technology makes it possible to hold geographically distributed meetings if the client can make time for them. In one RPRCC, a client was married in mid-semester and was unavailable for a month. Because the team did not think to ask and the client did not realize it was necessary to tell them, the students and the instructor learned a good lesson in risk management.

While most clients will have domain knowledge in the area of the proposed project, this is not an absolute requirement. Several of us have experience with clients who were not subject-matter experts, yet supported their teams in completing a successful project. In such cases, the clients either interacted with domain experts or put the teams in contact with the domain experts. To complement this, team members (usually) had the insight to understand what they did not know and what to ask of domain experts. Where domain knowledge was lacking, the client and team used other means, such as research, to obtain the necessary information. In other words, a success-oriented attitude often trumps domain knowledge and is a vital characteristic in clients. Our advice is to consider course goals and student characteristics in deciding whether to use clients who lack direct knowledge about the proposed software's domain.

Vetting Clients

As RPRCC instructors approach prospective clients, they are asking the client to give an informed opinion about whether or not they wish to assume the role. To support this, the instructor must provide information about the course, the project, the pros and cons of participating, samples from previous projects, and contact information from previous clients. The instructor must also make clear the importance of having the client remain actively involved in the project throughout the semester.

In the end, it is the RPRCC instructor's job to decide whether an individual who has offered to be a client is viable for that role. If the RPRCC instructor already knows the potential client, the decision is often easy. In other situations, the instructor must become acquainted with the potential client, whether face-to-face, by phone, or by email, and then decide. Sometimes it may be necessary to seek references from mutual acquaintances or others who are familiar with the potential client.

Types of Client Organizations

In this subsection we explore the types of organizations from which one or more of us has drawn clients for the RPRCCs we have taught. As appropriate, we discuss advantages and tradeoffs associated with each type of organization.

Clients drawn from the institution at which the RPRCC is being taught can be a comfortable choice for those new to teaching RPRCCs, especially when the individual is already an acquaintance. On-campus clients can often more easily arrange to meet with students than can off-site clients. While the pool of faculty and staff from outside of the computing department are generally

somewhat naïve about software development, they are invariably bright people who have interesting problems to solve. Using institutional staff from departments such as the sponsored research office, institutional police and security, the library, the Provost's office, or the graduate school can build good will and garner benefits for faculty, departments, and students alike. Another on-campus option is student organizations. For example, the Student Technology Assistant program was an outgrowth of campus involvement with the Teaching Learning Technology Roundtable at the University of Michigan–Dearborn (TLT Group, 2007).

In an RPRCC with a service-learning focus, the instructor is likely to want teams to work on software that benefits society in some way. ABET-CAC accreditation criteria (ABET, Inc. 2007) require programs to include social and ethical issues in computing. Service projects for non-profit agencies can help students understand these issues through first hand experience. Werner and MacLean (2006) discuss the use of community service projects in computer-related courses. Clients can be recruited from educational institutions and from not-for-profits, including local organizations such as nature centers and national organizations like Habitat for Humanity. Finding candidate clients at such organizations can be as simple as talking to family, friends, and acquaintances or methodically contacting promising sources, such as elementary or middle schools, local museums, and parks departments. School enrichment programs can offer contacts with innovative educators anxious to provide children with engaging educational software.

Government agencies, in particular city and county governments, can be a good source of clients and can enable students to work on significant problems, for example global warming or energy conservation (see American College & University Presidents Climate Commitment, 2007, for a coalition of institutions devoted to such issues). Public utility projects can provide an interesting challenge for RPRCCs, as such projects are often targeted for a harsher environment than an office setting. For example, in a project for a Water Quality Department, students developed embedded software for a hand-held device. A benefit of working for governmental agencies is that the students, the department, and the institution can gain widespread favorable publicity.

If an RPRCC is to produce software for for-profit businesses, potential clients can be drawn from among alumni, graduate students, and industrial advisors who have business connections. While relationships with industry can reap benefits for the RPRCC instructor and the department, political concerns may render it desirable for the instructor to have some experience at running RPRCCs prior to recruiting industry clients. For students, who may be seeking internships or full-time employment, clients drawn from business can lead to rewarding contacts. In addition to the regular client tasks, clients from for-profit businesses can often double as mentors thanks to experience with issues such as budget, schedule, deadlines, deliverables, quality, iterative development, communication skills, requirements, risk assessment, and testing.

If the department has one, the PAB can be a useful source of clients (Modesitt, 2005, 2006). Because PAB members are often eager to work with students who may one day become employees, they have a vested interest in successful projects. PAB members are also in a unique position to offer a wide variety of real problems for student teams. As an added benefit, PAB clients can serve a double purpose because accreditation organizations such as the Computing Accreditation Commission (CAC) of ABET encourage departments to utilize PABs.

How Many Clients are Sufficient?

The number of clients required to run an RPRCC depends on how the RPRCC is organized. If each team is to do a unique project, and each client

is to represent a single project, then the number of clients must equal the number of teams. A variation practiced by some of us is to offer more project options than the number of teams. With an excess of options, each team is more likely to end up matched with a project that suits its members well. A downside to this strategy is that some clients may not be matched with a team, an outcome that should be discussed in the process of managing the client's expectations (see the next subsection).

At times, a client may ask to propose multiple projects. If the client truly has time to act as the client for multiple projects, then the instructor can make do with fewer clients than teams. If the projects are completely distinct, then client interactions with each team can be relatively independent. If the client proposes a larger project, then different components can be assigned to different teams and integrated later, with the client meeting as appropriate with the separate teams or the combined team. We do not, however, recommend that clients work with multiple teams if they have never served in this role before.

Preparing the Potential Client for What to Expect

During the process of recruiting prospective clients, the instructor must provide clear information about what the role entails, both risks and rewards. A good starting point can be a flyer or webpage that introduces the course, the role of the client, the rhythm of the activities in the course, and the types of project that are appropriate. This information can also be communicated via telephone or email, either personal or broadcast.

The introductory information supplied to potential clients should include:

- An indication that this is a quest for clients who have project ideas that could be developed by a team of students.

- A broad description of the type(s) of software that a student team is typically able to develop in the allotted time.
- Samples of previous successful projects developed by student teams in earlier offerings of the course at this or other institutions (and perhaps a description of some of the twists and turns on the path to success).
- A list of earlier clients, which may very well include some that the prospective client knows personally.
- A rough estimate of the time and effort investment typically required of a client.
- The general timeline for the RPRCC, including dates when the client will need to be available to meet with the team, review documents, and attend presentations.
- The need, in some situations, for student access to workspace at the client's site or to a development environment similar to the target environment.
- Information that the prospective client must provide to the instructor to support the decision-making process.

Candidate clients should be encouraged to ask questions by email, by phone, or in person, whichever is most convenient. If the match-up seems promising, the instructor should arrange for a meeting to further explore the potential relationship.

Once the instructor has agreed to take on a particular client, the client must generate a brief description (for many of us, no more than a half page in length) for the proposed project. While many clients are able to capture the project ideas on their own, some instructors find it helps to work directly with clients and possibly with other critical stakeholders to refine the rough description or even to generate ideas. Developing the rough description of the requirements requires a delicate balance. The description must give a fair idea of the project without encroaching on the requirements engineering the team should

perform to iteratively refine the rough statement and detail what the software should do to satisfy the stakeholders.

DEVELOPING THE PROJECT OPTIONS

There is a strong relationship between the process of recruiting clients and the task of determining the projects that will be available to the teams. Whatever the project types allowed for a specific RPRCC, they must align well with the goals for the course. Some instructors want students to gain experience doing new development from scratch. Others want students to experience the advantages and disadvantages of doing enhancement projects. For SE RPRCCs and capstones, many instructors want student teams to identify the best solution from across the entire spectrum of possibilities. This latter approach mimics a software development workplace where developers work with the client to determine the type of development that best satisfies the client's needs at an acceptable cost.

With stronger students, many of us have teams go through the entire software development life cycle in a single semester, from requirements engineering to implementation, testing, and deployment. When teams encounter unforeseen difficulties, they can confer with various stakeholders to prioritize features and, if necessary, scale back plans for the functionality that can be achieved in the given timeframe. An approach that can help weaker students complete a significant piece of work or stronger students attack a truly challenging project is to limit the tasks the team must complete during the semester to performing requirements analysis and constructing a prototype. In our experience, many clients can be satisfied even if the team's final results fall short of fully functional industrial-strength software. For-profit clients often find it useful to have student developers perform this early step in the development process; later, software development professionals or students in a subsequent RPRCC can implement the product and test it, often with considerable net financial savings to the client organization.

In this section we discuss categories of projects, from custom development at one end of the spectrum to research-oriented projects at the other. We also explore considerations for vetting projects, including project demands, academic challenges, and post-delivery considerations.

Project Categories

Our collective experience includes a broad variety of project types: custom software designed and implemented from scratch; projects to enhance results from earlier offerings; applications that tie together multiple open-source or Commercial-Off-The-Shelf (COTS) products with "glue code;" tailoring open-source or COTS products that approximate the client's needs; and projects that contribute to independent research and development (IRAD).

In a custom development project, the team begins by developing requirements based on what might be a fairly vague problem statement. For weaker students enrolled in a one-semester RPRCC, this type of project may be too demanding. In a two-semester sequence, the work can be split, for example with the first semester devoted to requirements engineering and design and the second to implementation and testing. Another approach when working with weaker students is to accept only smaller projects, while a third is to allow larger projects that can be partitioned into easily integrated modules or packages. While the latter approach makes it possible for multiple teams to work on different modules in parallel with one another, the instructor must consider client capacity for working with multiple teams and may have to guide the process of partitioning the project and planning for incremental integration.

Having teams enhance software produced by others can be an especially valuable experience. Studies have shown that in industry an average 60% of the work is maintenance and enhancement (Hanna, 1993; Glass, 2001), with initial job assignments for many software developers focused on these tasks. Enhancement projects arise for a variety of reasons: perhaps an earlier team had to scale back from the original requirements; it may be the next step in an iterative development plan for a project too large for a one-semester course; or the client may have gained insights for how to expand a product or make it more useful. In a later RPRCC, possibly one devoted to learning maintenance and enhancement skills, such a project can be continued by a different team. In any case, the new team must use the documentation and other artifacts produced by the original development team, so the experience is likely to teach them the importance of readable project artifacts and well-documented code. In getting started on an enhancement project, the team must review the artifacts from the existing version(s) of the application to understand the requirements and possible solutions that were tried. Generally, the team's task will include updating and extending the artifacts, although some teams decide to start over from scratch rather than modifying earlier work. In the latter case, the team should be required to justify starting over with a reason other than NIH (Not Invented Here). In one enhancement project, a team worked for a humanities professor to modify a database with the full corpus of the medieval French poet who was this professor's research focus. Two earlier teams had worked on this project in the context of a DB RPRCC. After the first class presentation by the latest team, the instructor realized that the software, including the DB schema, was poorly documented. The task for the newest team then became to document the schema in an acceptable fashion, rather than trying to correct all the existing software defects. This experience gave the entire class a good lesson in prioritizing and re-scoping.

COTS-intensive projects tend not to require much, if any, from-scratch programming. Having teams work on such projects can be a real challenge, especially for the novice RPRCC instructor, because the projects may involve considerations alien to those without relevant experience (Boehm, Port, Yang, Bhuta, & Abts, 2003; Boehm, Yang, Bhuta, & Port, 2005; Franch & Port, 2005). Moreover, for some RPRCCs, COTS-intensive projects may be incompatible with the learning goals if, for example, the instructor wants students to do full-fledged object-oriented analysis and design. COTS-intensive projects can help students master the type of risk management that requires them to determine which artifacts to produce on the principle that "if it's risky not to do it, then do it; if it's risky to do it (e.g., because it takes valuable time from more urgent activities), then don't do it."

IRAD projects can be an exciting, and at times unsettling, addition to the spectrum of project types. IRAD projects tend to be exploratory, often providing the client with proof of concept and a better understanding of the problem. For IRAD projects, it may be difficult to predict the final work products from the beginning and, in fact, the final work products might be no more than a report, a trade study, a demonstration, or a rough prototype. In one such project, the client was a research scientist from an institute that focuses on accessibility issues. The team developed a prototype for a new screen reader component to give users with vision limitations a no-cost open-source alternative to the expensive commercial screen reader. One student from the original team continued to develop this project over several semesters, with the end result being a solid prototype that has attracted attention from users and researchers across the world.

PROJECT VETTING BY INSTRUCTOR

In this subsection we discuss issues that an instructor must consider in determining whether the demands of a particular project are appropriate for their setting. These include the scale and scope of the project in terms of complexity and duration, the academic challenges inherent in a project, and post-release issues such as ownership and maintenance of the resulting product.

Assessing Project Demands

Several factors come into consideration in understanding the likely level of effort required by a particular project. For all RPRCCs, one consideration is the skill set students must have or acquire to complete the project. For projects that involve technologies or skills new to most or all of the team members, another factor is the likelihood of a steep learning curve. For projects that are to be partitioned among a number of teams, an additional issue is how easily the project can be partitioned into reasonable units, and even whether a reasonable partitioning is possible at all.

Some of us do no more than an informal assessment of project complexity, based on past experience with software development and with earlier RPRCCs we have taught. Often, a short description is enough to give us a feeling for whether a project is a good match with the educational goals of the course, the students' abilities, and the duration of the RPRCC. Others of us prefer a more formal approach such as the one that Shelly, Cashman, and Rosenblatt (2008, p. 66) describe in the "Preliminary Investigation Overview" section of their textbook.

Client expectations for a project also have a bearing on whether a project is an appropriate choice. Williams, Bair, Borstler, Lethbridge, and Surendran (2003) estimate that only one in five student teams produce a professional-quality product. Software that must meet critical needs for the client organization in the near future is, therefore, almost certainly a poor choice.

Academic Challenges

Some of us prefer to offer projects from domains with which students are at least somewhat familiar. For weaker students a completely unfamiliar domain can slow the team down so much that they cannot make much progress in one semester, which can lead to a sense of failure. For stronger students, being faced with an unfamiliar domain offers the advantage of simulating reality, although students may initially reel at being faced with this unaccustomed challenge. While some of us expend considerable energy in assessing the scope of potential projects, others leave the bulk of the task of scoping and adjusting expectations to the team as part of their learning experience.

For any type of project, a key influence on the pace at which work can proceed is how familiar team members are with the tools or components that may be required, e.g. a DBMS or middleware. Some of us require students to use specific programming (or other) skills learned in earlier courses in their RPRCC projects, which can limit the types of projects that are appropriate. Others of us leave the choice of languages, tools, and components to the team as it develops an understanding of the client's domain and requirements, begins to develop a design, and communicates with the stakeholders who will host the completed software to determine the technologies they are willing and able to support.

For any type of project, one option is to have multiple teams work in parallel on different aspects of the same project or even on the entire project. Each team can work on one or more components of the project and integrate the full system later in the course. For example, when a 6th-grade teacher wanted a grading tool, one team focused on the front-end components (user interface and reports), while another team focused on back-end issues (DB and data analysis). The challenge with this approach is coordinating delivery schedules and integrating the completed components into a single product. A benefit of this approach is that it can stimulate teams to share ideas and review one another's work. However, integration should be done iteratively, rather than at the end as a big bang effort.

It is also possible to have multiple teams work independently on exactly the same project in parallel with one another, rather than on different aspects of the same project. While multiple attempts at accomplishing the client's goals may appear to increase the likelihood that at least one will succeed, this approach can put an unacceptably heavy demand on the client's time. One way around this is to require that all teams be represented at all client meetings. A downside to this approach, however, is that it can engender the sort of competition that tempts teams to undermine, rather than support, one another.

For novice RPRCC instructors, particularly those who do not have earlier experience working in industry, it is probably best to avoid having multiple teams work in parallel on the same project. The potential risks can be difficult to appreciate and deal with until an instructor has sufficient experience.

Issues Relating to the Delivered Product

Some of us accept only projects for which the client agrees to allow all artifacts produced by the team to be placed in the public domain. When projects are developed under an open-source agreement, future teams at the same or other institutions can extend them and learn from them. Others of us accept projects that obligate us, and sometimes the students, to sign contracts that restrict future uses of some or all resulting work products. If a project is being done for a for-profit business or university entity, then privacy, trade secrecy, and intellectual property issues may be important. In these instances, teams may be required to sign non-disclosure agreements and to keep in-progress work products securely under lock-and-key. Some of us do not mind constraints of this type, while others have avoided such situations.

A key issue that must be discussed with the client is post-delivery maintenance of software produced by student teams. Part of managing client expectations is to explain the likelihood that maintenance will be necessary in the future and to consider who will be responsible. In some cases, the client's organization assumes this responsibility. For example, the client for a Website developed for a Chinese charity was a former teaching assistant from the instructor's database course. For this project, the former TA was capable and willing to maintain the product after it was developed by the student team. Another solution is to have future student teams do maintenance, possibly as a part of their regularly scheduled project work. One of us has arranged to have maintenance tasks on past projects completed by students enrolled in independent study and student workers supported by a related grant. In other situations, all future maintenance will be the responsibility of a separate organization. Sun and Decker (2004) discuss tradeoffs among various options for who should handle maintenance, for example, the current team, a future team, or a separate support mechanism such as the client's IT organization. At some of our institutions, the IT department has been willing to maintain Websites developed for clients at the institution if the product was developed using COTS products already in use and if, in addition, testing shows that the product is of sufficient quality.

In some cases, a client proposes a project that is to be developed by multiple teams over multiple semesters. Each semester, one or more teams works to develop and deliver a component or increment of the project, which is then used as a foundation for a later class. Werner and MacLean (2006) describe one such project, a community service project that was expanded

over 5 semesters. One of us has experience with this in industry, where a company took a very methodical approach to having teams successively build up a complex project over several semesters. Another one of us has experienced this with several clients from educational settings. For example, one project, which was designed to help young children explore mathematical concepts such as combinatorics and recursion, was expanded and improved over seven semesters by eight different teams.

The long-term vision for software developed during RPRCCs varies widely. In some cases, any future maintenance is solely the responsibility of the client. This means that if problems are discovered or if there are changes to the hosting platform, operating system, or component COTS product (for example, if one of these is updated to a new, incompatible version), the client must find someone else (perhaps another RPRCC team) to update the product.

Another long-term consideration for products developed during an RPRCC is how (and if) they should be made available beyond the end of the course. One of us created an overall identity that spanned offerings to keep every project available as part of an instructor-maintained on-line repository. The repository included an underlying management system to support the course each semester and provide access to all work products under a uniform interface.

TEAM FORMATION AND PREPARATION

Before students can begin to work on their projects they must be assigned to teams. In this section we discuss factors influencing choice of team size, options for how to assemble teams, how to prepare students for teamwork, and approaches to matching teams to projects. At smaller institutions with small class sizes, team set-up is somewhat simpler because the instructor already knows the students well and there are fewer possible permutations. Yet a viable option is to set up teams that span multiple institutions (see, for example, Last, Almstrum, Erickson, Klein, & Daniels, 2000; Modesitt, 2004) or even multiple courses or departments at the same institution; however, we restrict our discussion to teams enrolled in a single course at the same institution.

Determining Team Size

Before deciding how to form teams, the RPRCC instructor must decide on team size. For the sake of discussion, we refer to teams of 2-3 students as small, teams in the 4-6 range as medium-sized, teams in the 7-10 range as large, and larger teams as super-sized. The lower and upper bounds on these team size designations are not intended to be precise.

Our experiences range across all of these possible sizes. One of us has observed that the way students in small teams share work is almost always acceptable to all, whereas with larger teams this is not always the case. Williams et al. (2003) have suggested using two-person teams for intensive training and XP pair-programming methods. Some of us deliberately use larger teams to ensure that students have the opportunity to understand the impact of team size on managing communication and other aspects of teamwork. Many published descriptions of RPRCC courses report that medium-sized teams work best (Ecker et al., 2004; Friedman, McHugh, & Deek, 2003; Koppelman & van Dijk, 2006; Kurtz, et al, 2007); this has been the rule for most of our settings, including the departments where two RPRCCs are required.

Larger teams can tackle significantly larger projects than can smaller teams. One approach is to divide large teams into smaller subteams, each of which executes a part of the overall project. There are many ways to divide responsibilities across subteams, for example according to component or according to phase (e.g. design, documentation,

verification & validation). Under either approach, one or more subteams can assume primary responsibility for full team tasks such as managing inter-team collaboration or integrating the various subteams' work products. With larger teams and larger products, students can practice skills beyond those required in smaller-scale software development. Two examples of RPRCCs in which multiple groups worked on various aspects of one project come from Fenwick and Kurtz (2005), where software development teams collaborated with Human Computer Interaction (HCI) teams, and Kurtz et al. (2007), where students from different universities worked on components of a very large project.

At the far end of the team-size spectrum is the super-sized team. A super-sized team will certainly have to be subdivided in some way, either by the team members themselves or by the instructor. Even with extensive industry experience, one of us has found that teaching an RPRCC with large or super-sized teams requires much more work by the instructor than using medium-sized teams. For instructors new to RPRCCs, particularly those without significant industry experience, it may be best to avoid using super-sized or large teams. Even for highly experienced instructors, it may be most effective to work up to larger-team skills using a stepwise approach. Students would first learn skills while working in a small or medium team, then in a later offering could work in a large or super-sized team. Because computing students can be resistant to learning skills other than programming and individual work, allowing them to acquire these additional skills in more gradual steps may be more effective. A stepwise approach also positions students to better understand and appreciate the differences when they encounter larger projects.

A final factor to consider in looking at team size is the overall number of teams that will result, given the RPRCC's enrollment. The total time required of the instructor for interacting with teams is a function of both the desired level of interaction and the number of teams. On the other hand, larger teams can require more work because of the need to manage and coordinate subteams (although in some circumstances, the teams themselves can take on much of this responsibility). In the end, the choice of team size depends on the goals of the RPRCC and the instructor's level of experience and comfort, as well as the individual team members.

Assembling Teams

Once team size is decided, the next issue is how to assemble teams. The major approaches are (1) the instructor assigns students to teams, (2) students form teams on their own, and (3) hybrid approaches that combine these two options. If students form their own teams, the instructor can vet each team to ensure an appropriate mix of skills, adjusting team composition if necessary. If the course is assigned teaching assistants, the TAs can be enlisted to propose a first cut at teams based on a pre-specified algorithm, with the instructor fine-tuning as needed. Cultural and language considerations can also play into team composition. For example, one of us who usually assigns teams has at times allowed self-selected teams that were totally Chinese, African, or Middle Eastern because it supported better communication among teams, a critical success factor. In this case, the teams were still required to balance team skills as described later in this section.

In a multi-staged two-semester approach to team formation, smaller teams go through all the steps required to create a platform-specific design during the first semester, then during the second semester carry out implementation, testing, installation, and user training. In one RPRCC sequence that uses this approach, students who enroll in the first semester are not required to enroll in the second. Because enrollment usually drops significantly from the first semester to the second semester, the number of teams also drops from the first semester to the second semester. In

most cases the projects that are carried through lose at least one or two team members between semesters, so some students must be reassigned to a new team. If a project has lost most of its team members, it is rarely carried through to the second semester. This potential outcome must be clearly explained up front to potential clients as part of expectations management.

A key question regarding team formation is how soon after the semester begins they should be formed. We have found that it is wise to wait with team formation until course registration has stabilized, assuming that the end of the drop/add period is not too far beyond the start of the course. While forming teams earlier can enable teams to start their project(s) earlier, this may require additional work if students are allowed to add or drop the course in the first few weeks (a problem that is less likely to occur if the RPRCC is a required course).

Once the work is underway, circumstances can arise well into the semester when it is necessary to realign teams, for example, if the institution allows late drops. Realignment can also be necessary if team members become uniformly dissatisfied with one team member's behavior or performance. It is prudent to publish a procedure that teams can use to bring grievances before the instructor so students understand the consequences of removing a team member from a team. In our experience, however, teams are generally able to work out such issues on their own.

Skills Needed within Teams

A team must possess a number of skills in order to succeed on a software development project. Among these are inter-personal communication skills, writing skills, problem-solving skills (e.g., for analysis and design), and technology skills. Different individuals will bring different strengths to the team, in part due to inherent talents. However, students' earlier experiences will also have a strong influence, for example, because of differences in the required or elective courses they have taken, the outside software projects with which they have been involved, and the employment or internship opportunities they have enjoyed.

Among the tools we have used to assess students' skills are the following:

- Survey instruments that list skills, including various programming languages and COTS products such as DB systems and middleware. Students respond by self-assessing each of these skills on a scale that ranges from zero to five.
- Personal data forms that solicit information such as courses taken, weekly schedule, on-campus vs. commuter status (to determine availability outside of class time), and computing equipment available at home.
- Formal resumes, in some cases prepared with the help of the Career Services department.
- Informal "about-me" reports.
- In-class interviews of each student, either by the instructor or by other students. The interview process can range from very informal to fairly formal to allow students to practice for future job interviews. Interview protocols can be adapted from ones provided by sources such as the department's PAB.
- Transcripts, which are typically legally available only to the instructor, not to TAs or other students.

In the real world of software development, project management generally assigns developers to teams based on matching skills to project needs. If the instructor assigns students to teams, it may be easier to balance the skill mix for each team to help ensure that every team can succeed on its project. Allowing students themselves to determine the teams may result in an uneven distribution of skills across the teams.

One of us starts the process of assigning students to teams by characterizing each student using these indicators:

1. Technology experience (based on a self-assessment survey).
2. Communication skills (based on grade point average (GPA) in humanities courses).
3. Problem-solving skills (based on GPA in computing and mathematics courses).
4. Drive to ensure the project will be successful (based on overall GPA).

This instructor sets up teams so that each is composed of at least two students with high self-reported technology experience, at least one student with strong communication skills, at least one student with strong problem-solving skills, and at least one student with strong drive. On occasion, the instructor allows self-selected groups of four or five students who offer a compelling argument that they should be allowed to form a team, for example because they have previously worked together on a successful project. In most cases the results have been very good.

Another instructor-driven approach to team formation sorts students according to information gathered via personal data collected early in the semester. One of us regularly uses this list of criteria, ordered from highest to lowest priority, to determine teams:

1. **Anti-affinity:** Who does not want to work with whom.
2. **Schedule (compatibility):** Based on general timing categories {morning, afternoon, early evening, late evening}, preferred days of the week, and full schedules as a final sanity check.
3. **Gender:** No gender should be represented by only one person in a group except in the case of strong mutual requests (that is, avoid teams with just one woman).
4. **Break up cliques:** No more than three mutual requests per team.
5. **Affinity:** Who wants to work with whom; worth more if a mutual request.

6. **Skill coverage in the group:** An ideal team assignment balances success-critical skills, including management, programming/technical, writing, SE and testing experience, and industry experience.

7. **Interview/travel plans:** No team should be composed of members who are all interviewing for jobs during the semester.

8. **Nearness to graduation:** Minimize the potential effect of "senioritis".

Is it essential to balance all teams according to all of these factors? For some of us, the results have been mixed. Some teams run into difficulties even though on paper there is a balance of strengths in each of the areas. Other teams seem weak from the start, but manage to dig up the skills and shine, even though the indicators would have predicted otherwise. Pre-planning can go only so far – the rest is up to the team.

Team Formation by Students

Students often prefer to form their own teams. One risk is that individuals who know few of the other students or are perceived to have weaker skills can end up feeling slighted. In one author's experience, allowing students to select their own teams is more successful among graduate students than undergraduates.

To support the self-selection process, students must first understand the roles needed to make a team successful as well as the responsibilities associated with each role. Among many others, these roles might include: team manager; client contact; documentation manager; programmer; configuration manager; and tester. Students should also learn about the risks associated with forming a team that lacks members able and willing to serve in one or more of the required roles. Students must receive sufficient information about other class members to be able to consider relevant factors such as skills and compatibility of weekly schedules. This information can be posted in an easily accessible spot, for example in the protected area of a course management tool such as Blackboard or WebCT.

To prepare for self-selection of teams, one of us provides students with a two-hour lecture on issues relating to roles and skill sets. Immediately after the lecture, students attend a half-hour "mixer" where they stand under a banner that identifies their preferred role. During the mixer, students begin to talk with others whom they have not previously met. Over the next week or so students form their own teams and inform the course staff of their decisions, with no fine-tuning by instructional staff.

Regardless of how strongly an instructor stresses the skills required for the different roles, some groups of students will still form teams based purely on friendship or compatibility of another sort. In one case, a group of students with English as a second language, all very recently arrived in the United States, decided to form a team because they preferred to communicate in their native language. While they all had strong technical skills, the team failed miserably in their project because none of them could communicate with the client well enough to perform essential requirements engineering activities.

Teaching Teamwork

Teamwork skills can be conveyed though lectures, readings, talks given by guest speakers, and collected reflections and examples (also referred to as organizational memory) from earlier offerings of the RPRCC. Some of us provide students with instruction on teamwork and other software development-related issues on an ongoing, or "just in time," basis. This subsection discusses a few of the topics that we cover.

Among the important team skills students can learn are how to be an effective facilitator for team meetings or team-client meetings, how to divide work among team members, and how to deal with problems such as conflict between team members and non-responsive clients. In courses where teams are expected to hold formal technical reviews of work products, they can receive training on these techniques. Outside guest speakers can help bring these topics to life. Examples of guest speakers we have used include the Human Resources specialist from a local company, representatives from the organizational leadership and supervision department at the university, and an industrial psychologist from the university's business school, who specializes in team dynamics.

Students often assume that they have far better communication skills than they actually do. Oral communication skills concern intra-team issues as well as team-client issues, especially if the client comes from a radically different professional background (Boehm et al., 1999). Many of us have found it useful to coach students to help them understand the importance of these skills and to develop and improve them. Presentation skills are another area where students can benefit from coaching. A lecture on presentations can cover the gamut from how to prepare effective materials to tricks for calming nerves.

Social interaction can be a powerful mechanism for strengthening teamwork. It can be helpful to require each team to invent a team name, set up a team Website, and use other approaches to establishing their team identity. As an example of encouraging team identity, one of us pays for mugs that display team symbols and presents these to team members and the client.

Several of us have been very successful in building up and using an organizational memory based on information from earlier RPRCC offerings. For example, while an area such as risk management may be easy to discuss in the abstract, learning to do it well requires practical examples and harsh experience. The RPRCC's organizational memory can be built up on a Website or wiki over time to delineate risks faced by earlier teams, how teams dealt with these risks successfully or unsuccessfully, and the consequences.

One contribution to organizational memory can be a collection of "lessons learned" that each team is required to include in its final report and that the instructor organizes over time. One of us uses such material in a two-stage process in which individual students first study the past lessons to identify trends and themes and suggest ways a team can avoid problems and repeat successes. The second stage takes place after the teams have been set up. Each team discusses their observations, perhaps during a meeting or via email, and then writes up its compiled observations as part of their first team status report. This has been an effective exercise for allowing students in a new team to learn from one another and gain early insights into the development process they will be following.

Another way to build up organizational memory is to create an archive of project artifacts from earlier offerings of the RPRCC. These can be a valuable resource for helping students come up to speed on both teamwork and other aspects of software development. For example, one of us asks each student to formally review the work products created by one or more previous teams as part of the process of becoming familiar with the course's overall standards and guidelines. The assignment can require students to compare and contrast different approaches to such issues as planning, design, documentation, verification and validation, and quality. These reviews can also feed into plans for enhancement projects for future offerings of the RPRCC by identifying maintenance needs and possible extensions for earlier projects.

Matching Teams with Projects

While teams may appreciate the opportunity to indicate their preferences among the project options in our offerings, either we as the instructor or the client typically makes the final decision. Some of us match teams with projects with no team input, based purely on intuition and experience. The rest of this subsection describes other approaches.

Some of us provide teams with information about the project options by means of detailed requests for proposals (RFPs), informal project sketches, or client presentations. Each team then responds by preparing a proposal that explains its qualifications for and its proposed approaches to their top project choices. The instructor can then use the proposals as input for assigning teams to projects.

If all of the clients in a particular offering understand software development, the instructor can invite the clients to indicate team preferences based upon the proposed approaches and team qualifications. If no two clients choose the same team, then all clients get their first choice; if there are conflicts or if one or more teams is not chosen by any client, the instructor typically makes the final decision, often in consultation with the clients. (Recall that in some of our offerings there are generally more project options than teams, so some projects are dropped, at least for the time being.)

STANDARDS AND WORK PRODUCTS

We require a wide variety of different work products associated with the product and process aspects of a project. Terminology varies from person to person and from institution to institution, in the professional world as well as in the academic world. For the purposes of this chapter, a *work product* is any item that must be produced by a team as part of its project obligation. Frequently encountered synonyms for work product are *deliverable, document,* and *artifact.* While code is considered by most to be a work product, a deliverable, and a project-generated artifact, it is generally not referred to as a document.

Specific requirements depend on course objectives, on the training that students have had before starting this offering, and on training provided during the course. Written guidelines and standards for work products can range from terse to elaborate, and each work product can be as terse or elaborate as risk management suggests is best for the specific project.

Any guidelines and standards must be clear enough to enable students to grasp what they are supposed to produce and the required quality levels. For our purposes, *standards* serve as a reference point against which work products can be evaluated, and *guidelines* specify how teams should carry out their tasks and submit the resulting work products. Regardless of the specific work products an instructor requires, some set of work products other than actual code is required in virtually all RPRCCs. Support for developing guidelines and standards can be found in textbooks such as the one from Pressman (2005), in the IEEE family of standards for software development (IEEE Software Engineering Standards Central, 2007), and in the scaffolding approach described by Hislop (2006).

Some of us have developed a set of customized standards that specify the content and layout of all work products to be produced during the course, as well as a schedule of delivery dates for each. For some of us, a client-team contract specifies the deliverables, either based on pre-established standards in the client's organization or on negotiations with the students. In other circumstances, we require each team to determine not only the process they will use but also the work products needed for successful execution of the project using that process. This approach can work well in capstone RPRCCs when students already have previous experience in SE principles and practices. In this situation, determining the process and work products can be seen as a vital part of the learning experience and one that is of critical importance in professional software development.

Scheduling Guidelines

A key aspect of planning for an RPRCC is to develop a scheduling framework to keep teams on track and working at a steady rate. This type of framework increases the probability of successful project completion in the available timeframe. In a fully structured approach, which is appropriate for students new to software development, the instructor sets a strict schedule of when major work products are due and the team has control over intermediate deadlines.

As students gain experience with software development methods, especially in their second or third RPRCC, the instructor can use an approach in which teams determine their own deadlines. In capstone courses, this can be an excellent tool for practice in setting and meeting deadlines. For this approach to work, the instructor must maintain regular contact with each team to ensure they are making progress and meeting deadlines. This can be accomplished through periodic written progress reports, formal face-to-face meetings, and informal discussions.

Additional Guidelines

Guidelines are useful for helping teams maintain consistency in their efforts and can also make the task of evaluating work products easier for both the instructor and the client. Providing students with formatting guidelines can help them learn to follow professional workforce practices and can introduce consistency that is useful in assessing and using the work products. Guidelines can specify methods for submitting work products, for example number of hardcopies or how to submit work products via electronic means (e.g. as email attachments, as a document with a specific name in a specific folder, or as a submission within a course management system such as WebCT or Blackboard).

A guideline about deadlines can indicate what teams must do to request an extension and any consequences, such as how the grading will be affected, if there are delays. A related guideline could explain what a team must do to re-scope their project if the instructor and client agree that this is acceptable.

Another guideline might concern who can see work products and when. For some courses, the Website or project directory will be accessible only by team members; at the other extreme, work products might be posted on a public team Website throughout the course, thereby allowing anyone on the Internet to view them. If there are security and privacy requirements for the project, the instructor and the team must take care to protect private information.

Configuration management of one type or another is essential for coordinating versions of work products and also adds important skills to students' toolsets. A guideline can be introduced to explain whether teams are required to use a specific configuration management tool, another tool of their choice, or a more informal method for keeping track of versions of work products. A related guideline can cover the use of defect tracking tools and what types of defects teams should be tracking and reporting.

Individual Work Products

Formal individual writing assignments can help students explore issues related to the on-going work, as well as encourage them to read selected articles relevant to the project work. Such assignments can provide students with the opportunity to reflect on the team's work and think through possible solutions to problems. These types of assignments can serve an important role in the course, both in getting students to think and helping the instructor to better monitor team dynamics and frustrations.

Several of us review project work completed by individual students to help in assigning individual grades. Individual assignments can also help students think about the project and reflect on how well it is progressing. An example of an individual work product, typically delivered to the instructor, but not to the client, is a notebook where the student records personal project activities, and which the instructor examines periodically, often at randomly chosen times. A variation on this idea is to require individual reports, say every two weeks, that list accomplishments for the previous period, goals for the next period, problems encountered, and possible solutions. (We discuss progress reports more in the next subsection.)

Team Work Products

Team work products include the final deliverables for the project as well as any intermediate documents that aid in organizing and analyzing work accomplished. If industrial-strength standards are used, one risk is that the number and volume of work products can quickly become unmanageable, even for a small project. The number of required work products must be weighed against the time a team can realistically be expected to spend in developing the work products. All of us prioritize and, in general, require only the minimum number likely to lead to a successful outcome. For example, an SE RPRCC might require teams to develop all of the various types of project and product artifacts listed in this subsection. For other offerings, especially early ones, teams may only be required to produce a small subset. In any offering, however, the instructor must be clear about the goals behind the documentation requirements. This can help avoid a situation where students develop a disdain for following guidelines and standards because they perceive (perhaps correctly) that the work demanded of them is far more heavyweight and time-consuming than is strictly required for the success of their project.

In general, the main purpose of all required work products should be to facilitate communication and keep the project work transparent to all stakeholders. The instructor and client must communicate to the team what is to be accomplished, and the team must communicate their understanding of what should be produced. The team must also communicate progress to all team members, to the instructor (for a grade), and to the client (for client satisfaction). Problems and solutions, as well as questions and answers, must be communicated throughout the project. The final deliverables must include all information the client and other stakeholders need in order to use the software product successfully and provide for its maintenance and possible enhancement. Teams should learn to always think about who will be using each specific artifact and include only information needed by – and understandable to – the relevant stakeholders.

Guidelines can be presented in the form of templates, examples of previous project artifacts, or descriptions of each work product's content and structure. It is vital for teams to receive periodic feedback so they can iteratively improve all deliverables. The rest of this subsection explores some of the specific work products we require in the RPRCCs we teach.

While a formal *project plan* might not be required for every project, some type of planning must take place before a project starts. Depending on the goals for the RPRCC, the written project plan can be a one-shot document that defines initial planning or a document that is frequently updated to reflect changes in planning.

Several of us require *periodic progress reports*, in the form of either a written document or a face-to-face meeting. The periodicity for these reports can be weekly, bi-weekly, or even monthly. Like an individual progress report, a team progress report usually records the previous period's progress, goals for the coming period, problems that have arisen, and possible solutions; some of us have teams combine the individual and team information into a single report. The progress report can facilitate dialog among team members, the instructor, and the client. The team can include questions for the instructor or the client, and either the instructor or the client can respond so that all team members see the answer. A benefit of written, as opposed to oral, progress reports is that they provide a chronological record of the entire project from beginning to end.

Most of us require that all client meetings be documented in *client meeting reports*. These reports can be part of the progress reports or can be separate documents. Client meeting reports should capture points of discussion and any decisions made during the meeting.

A *requirements document* is used to record the required features both of the product and, if specified by the client, of the process to be used in developing it. This document helps ensure that the right system is built. In some situations, some of us have allowed teams to forego a requirements document in favor of a well-documented GUI prototype.

A *design document* shows the structure of the application to be built. This document typically describes the high-level (architectural) and low-level designs of the projected software and may include both platform-independent and platform-dependent models, perhaps documented as dataflow or UML diagrams.

Prototyping allows students to explore alternative possibilities and learn to use new development tools. A prototype can focus on the entire product or on only a part, such as the GUI interface. Prototypes are often thrown away after the proposed product is better understood, but in some cases are given to the client to support work on future increments. The following quote from the original edition of Brooks' classic *The mythical man-month* (1975) reflects this situation well:

In most projects, the first system built is barely usable. It may be too slow, too big, awkward in use or all three. There is no alternative but to start again, smarting but smarter, and build a redesigned version in which these problems are solved. ... Where a new system concept or new technology is used, one has to build a system to

*throw away, for even the best planning is not so omniscient as to get it right the first time. The management question, therefore, is not **whether** to build a pilot system and throw it away. You **will** do that. The only question is whether to plan in advance to build a throwaway, or to promise to deliver the throwaway to customers...* (p. 116)

This is true of many student projects. As with real world clients, RPRCC clients often do not know what they want until they see it. Additionally, the technology used on a project might be new to both the client and the student team. Incremental prototypes can help the client better clarify project requirements and understand development options. Even if a team does not use the full prototyping approach, many software development process models encourage prototyping at various phases of the project. (Section 3.4 of Pressman (2005) gives a rationale for this type of iterative process.)

Testing, verification, and validation are closely related tasks but treated very differently in different RPRCCs. For example, some of us require a comprehensive *Verification and Validation Plan* that describes and specifies the timing for reviews of all types of project artifacts and the tests to be carried out at each stage of the development life cycle. Others of us include only functionality test planning, particularly if the offering is early in the curriculum. The instructor must guide teams to develop test plans that are suitable for the goals of the course, yet sufficiently limited in scope that the tests can be completed in the time available. A simple form of test plan lists each test with a unique test number, a description of the test, and a description of the expected test results. Once a test has been conducted, students should record the results and compare them with the expected results to demonstrate that the application is working as expected. Some of us require teams to describe all verification and validation work, including the test results, in a separate *Verification and Validation Report*.

Even if online help is available, many software products should include a *Users' Manual* and/or *Installation Manual*. If the application is well designed, these manuals can be very brief. The team should make the decision as to whether these manuals are needed in collaboration with the client.

Some of us require students to review one another's work, as both document and code reviews have been shown to improve the quality of software. Some of us require teams to complete a Formal Technical Review before the project work can progress from one step to the next in the development process.

Most of us require teams to give one or more *oral presentations*. A presentation can be a formal event to share information about the project with peers, the client, other stakeholders, or faculty from the department and institution. In some presentations, the team walks through a document or the product and receives feedback from the instructor and other students. A presentation can be part of the review of the final application or other deliverables and can also serve as a feedback session for further improvements of the product.

ASSESSMENT AND EVALUATION

Assigning individual grades to students who work and learn in teams can be challenging. Yet the positive effect of group participation on individual learning is very clear; Slavin (2005) gives strong evidence that working in cooperative groups and on teams has positive effects on individual student achievement, even when achievement is measured using conventional instruments such as quizzes. Indeed, mastery learning seems to thrive in a group dynamic, provided members of the group meet regularly (Bloom, Madaus, & Hastings, 1981).

This section provides a brief overview of various approaches to assessment and evaluation,

with an eye toward making clear the differences between assessment in RPRCCs and other types of courses. Additionally, we draw a distinction between assessments (which relate directly to the individual students or teams of students) and evaluations (which concern the course itself) (Linn, 1989; Voigt, 2007). We assess students and evaluate programs. Increasingly, accreditation bodies are tightening their requirements, leading to an increased focus on the role of high quality assessment and evaluation. In the following paragraphs, we discuss approaches to both in the context of RPRCCs. We distinguish between issues related to assessing individual student accomplishments and assessing the work of the team.

When students work in teams, performing assessment and evaluation is considerably more complex than it is in more traditional instructional settings. Some parts of an RPRCC, such as standard textbook-related content, are readily amenable to traditional assessments like quizzes, tests, and written exercises. Other aspects of RPRCCs, such as compliance with deadlines, communication with team members, and dealing with unanticipated problems, must be assessed differently. However assessment is conducted, the instructor must make expectations clear to students throughout the course, including how project-related performance is to be assessed (Deretchin, 2002). Since assessment in an RPRCC often differs dramatically from what students have experienced in other courses, the instructor must emphasize the assessment protocol clearly and from the beginning. For example, one of us gives a team the grade of incomplete if they shirk their responsibilities or if their client is dissatisfied. A team can make up the incomplete if they provide the client with something useful, which usually takes just a few more hours or days of work.

In addition to traditional course content, RPRCCs cover concepts and skills that are important in the workplace but often absent in computing discipline programs other than software engineering. The combination of content (e.g. SE, DBMS, or web programming) and project work common in many RPRCCs can make it challenging for an instructor to fit in all of the traditional content in addition to teamwork- and project-related knowledge and skills. Instructors can push the learning envelope by devising assessment and evaluation approaches that have the side effect of helping students learn more about course content (McMillan, 2001; Young & Marks-Maran, 2002). Some tools we have used in assessing non-traditional learning outcomes include individual journal entries, team progress reports, and one-minute papers (What did you learn today? What confused you?). The instructor can customize such assignments to ensure that they address course objectives. For example, if a course objective is for students to learn to apply time management skills, the instructor can have students explain what they have learned about time management, how they have handled time management problems, and how their thinking about time management has changed. Another assessment tool is Team-Based Learning (Michaelsen, 2002). In this two-stage approach to giving quizzes, individual students take a quiz, turn in the answers, then convene in their teams. Each team negotiates to create a group response to the same items and, by the end of the class meeting, the instructor reveals the correct responses. As follow up, each team submits a written discussion of why they chose the response they recorded. If the team disagrees with an answer from the key, they are encouraged to include an argument (ideally with evidence) for why they feel a different answer should be the correct one.

In the workplace, software developers provide management with periodic evidence of progress by means of status reports, time sheets, and similar tools. Most of us require this type of reporting from both individuals and teams when we teach SE and capstone RPRCCs. Some of us find that periodic written status reports are sufficient. Others hold weekly meetings with each team to elicit the information that would otherwise be included in a well-written report, which offers the added benefit of frequent contact. When requiring status reports, the requirements must outline exactly what the team is to report about its progress (Stein & Hurd, 2000); these reports can provide insights into what the students are learning. One of us schedules periodic project audits for each team, in which someone from outside of the team (generally the instructor or a teaching assistant) does a careful walkthrough of various aspects of the on-going project work, then meets with the team to go over the results and check current status.

In addition to instructor assessment of individuals and teams, Schmuck and Schmuck (1997) encourage having students assess one another. They state that assessments may carry more weight if they come from peers rather than from the resident expert or sage (i.e., the instructor). Some of us incorporate such assessments into overall student grades only after providing students with the opportunity to read and respond to their own assessments by peers. Others are wary of privacy issues, particularly if there are negative comments, so use other methods to share feedback with each student. To ensure the privacy of the comments, one of us summarizes the peer reviews for each student. While this is very time-consuming, it reaps rich rewards for the students.

The assessment approaches we have discussed thus far focus on process, one of the two major aspects of software development. The other aspect that must be assessed is the product itself, including documentation. A novel aspect of an RPRCC is that the client plays an involved, yet outside, role. Clients are in a unique position for giving informed feedback regarding the quality of the product. Some of us use this feedback as additional data in determining grades, accounting for a small part of the final grade (say 5%); others avoid asking clients for a direct contribution into the grade due to concerns about inconsistencies in applying the criteria. One of us asks the client to give an overall assessment by signing off on the final grade the instructor proposes for the team. If the client feels the grade is too high, this perception can lower the team members' grades. If the client is dissatisfied and refuses to sign off on the grade, this can result in an incomplete for the students on the team. On the other hand, because it is impossible to know whether a client is truly assessing the product or showing compassion for the students, some of us choose to use client assessment only indirectly. Some of us simply talk to the client informally to get a feel for how satisfied they are, with the grade influenced by client satisfaction.

The assessment scheme for the project portion of an RPRCC tends to be more holistic than that used in standard courses. RPRCC assessment schemes are generally broader than those used in more traditional instruction, which may be limited to one test per chapter, lab reports, or homework exercises. A special feature of assessment for RPRCCs is that they can involve incremental assessment of process and product, but should at the same time encourage and recognize continual improvement of most work products. Some of us maintain a portfolio for each team, tracking their progress in improving the work products based on feedback and continued work. This very rich form of assessment fits with the position of the psychometrics community that more and varied assessments produce a better and clearer picture of student learning than do occasional and uniform assessments (Ardovino, Hollingsworth, & Ybarra, 2000).

On the issue of evaluating instructional pedagogy, just as on the issue of assessment, RPRCCs present both greater challenges and richer opportunities. Some of the sources of input for evaluating an RPRCC include the instructor, teaching assistants, teammates, student peers, the intact team, peer teams, clients, departmental faculty, and representatives of PABs. When RPRCCs are first added to a curriculum they are typically subject to more scrutiny than may be the case for a more traditional new offering. Because of the novelty

of this approach and because this type of course involves individuals from outside of the classroom (i.e., the clients), there is good reason to question the validity and efficacy of the RPRCC and its results. In situations in which an RPRCC version of a topic is being taught in parallel with a more traditional version (usually as an experiment), it may be possible for the instructor to evaluate the RPRCC version by comparing performance results from traditional exams and assignments between the two. The teams' progress reports, final reports, and client communications can serve as data in forming an overall evaluation of the effectiveness of the RPRCC version. To add longitudinal data to the evaluation, instructors or departments can survey former students for their views about the skills they gained during their RPRCCs and other coursework. This type of data can carry particular weight with administrators, given that garnering alumni support is a vital strategy for many institutions.

Regardless of the source of the evaluation data, it is important for the instructor to consider whether they are engaging in *formative* or *summative* evaluation. The former guides day-to-day decisions and often involves minor adjustments to instruction, curriculum, and schedule. The latter is concerned with the RPRCC as a whole and might motivate wholesale changes if warranted by the collected data (Worthen & Sanders, 1988). The assignments given to assess student learning can be used in the evaluation process; however, the issue here is not whether a student has learned something, but whether some aspect of the course can be adjusted in order to maximize student learning or improve the deliverable for the client. Admittedly there is no shortcut to good assessment and evaluation, but quizzes, exercises, journal entries, reports, and the like can be used in a manner that coheres with the course objectives and allows instructors to judge learning and course efficacy.

FUTURE TRENDS

With increased emphasis on encouraging students, especially women and minorities, to study computing, we anticipate increasing interest in RPRCCs. For pre-college students to be attracted to computing, they (and their parents) must understand that computing is more than just programming (Morris, 2004; Supercomputing Online, 2007). The vast majority of students entering computing are likely to spend the bulk of their careers working in teams on real projects for real clients. How, then, can we be more honest in attracting students to computing than by offering RPRCCs and RPRCC-centric curricula?

There are many potential benefits to an RPRCC approach to computing education. Increasing the pipeline of students taking RPRCCs would benefit the computing workforce, which will otherwise be in danger, as documented in the figures cited earlier from the Bureau of Labor Statistics studies (Hecker, 2005, Vegso, 2006) and the Standish Chaos reports (Standish Group, 1994, 2003). An appropriate mix of clients and projects can facilitate the transfer of improved technology from the research community to the workplace by giving students the theoretical knowledge required to understand and apply breakthroughs as well as the skills to develop them. Finally, the choice of client can serve the greater good, for example through service to society in terms of pro bono for not-for-profit clients or enhanced rapport with members of the academic community and with local industry and government entities.

For all of these reasons, we expect to see a significant increase in RPRCC offerings. We also expect to see the introduction of RPRCC-centric curricula, i.e., programs of study that include multiple RPRCCs. One of the most exciting aspects of this vision is the prospect of including RPRCCs at all levels, starting early in the curriculum. In such a curriculum software development skills would be introduced in early offerings and then covered in more detail or more formally in one or more later courses. For example, a Website design RPRCC taught prior to or concurrently with CS1 could teach relatively informal requirements engineering and requirements documentation techniques. Implementation of the software could be carried out later by students in an advanced course, which could itself include instruction on more formal specification techniques.

Having a curriculum with multiple RPRCCs would support a spiral approach to teaching a variety of skills, many of which are easy to talk about in the abstract but difficult to learn and to perform. Examples of such skills are requirements engineering, risk management, cost and effort estimation, and project scheduling. This approach would also allow students to experiment with customizing their development processes to achieve an appropriate balance between lightweight (or agile) methods and more heavyweight methods (Boehm & Turner, 2004).

An RPRCC-centric program of study could introduce large-project skills in later courses. These skills could be taught in a capstone or as part of a separate (possibly elective) SE course late in the curriculum. In this way, students would learn skills needed for large projects only after they have a solid foundation and truly understand the need for small-project SE skills. At this point, students should also be better prepared intellectually to understand when and why large-project skills are needed.

All of these promising possibilities add urgency to the goal of assisting individuals new to RPRCCs as they plan for and deliver these courses for the first time. We are exploring the idea of a knowledge-based tool based upon the taxonomy of RPRCC issues (given in part in Appendix A), which can aid an RPRCC instructor in navigating the many decisions and challenges inherent in such courses. This would involve gathering information from experts on the many approaches to these factors so that over time novices could use the tool to figure out how to design a course that fits well with local needs.

CLOSING THOUGHTS

This chapter is far from exhaustive. For every idea we have shared, there are many more variants that we and others have tried. From the student's point of view, taking an RPRCC can run the range from fun and stimulating to difficult and frustrating. In response to students' laments about the workload and challenges, we often point out the value of using "war stories" from RPRCC experiences during employment interviews. A student's explanation of how they or their team overcame adversity on their project is far more likely to impress an interviewer than is a story about an individual programming or database assignment.

From the instructor's point of view, teaching RPRCCs can be challenging, exhausting, frustrating, rewarding, time-consuming … and exactly the type of experience students need to prepare them for their futures. The glowing feedback, experienced by all of us, that "This was the most useful course I took as an undergraduate" gives anecdotal evidence of the importance of RPRCCs.

As we continue to develop the RPRCC taxonomy, we plan to contribute to a repository of instructor-related, student-related, and client-related materials, each with variants appropriate to different educational goals and available resources. We hope that this chapter is a useful beginning.

REFERENCES

ABET, Inc. (2007). Item IV-17. *2007-2008 Criteria for Accrediting Computing Programs*. Available: http://www.abet.org/forms.shtml#For_Computing_Programs_Only

Akinoglu, O., & Tandogan, R. Ö. (2007). The effects of problem-based active learning in science education on students' academic achievement, attitude and concept learning. *Eurasia Journal of Mathematics, Science & Technology Education, 3*(1), 71-81.

Almstrum, V. L., Klappholz, D., & Modesitt, K. (2007, March). Workshop on planning and executing real projects for real clients courses. *Proceedings of the 38th SIGCSE Technical Symposium on Computer Science Education* (p. 582). Covington, KY.

American College & University Presidents Climate Commitment (2007). Program overview. Available: http://www.presidentsclimatecommitment.org/

Ardovino, J., Hollingsworth, J., & Ybarra, S. (2000). *Multiple measures: Accurate ways to assess student achievement*. Thousand Oaks, CA: Corwin Press.

Aspray, W., Mayadas, F., & Vardi, M. Y. (Eds). (2006). *Globalization and offshoring of software*. A Report of the ACM Job Migration Task Force. Available: http://www.acm.org/globalizationreport/

Bloom, G. S., Madaus, G. F., & Hastings, J. T. (1981). *Evaluation to improve learning*. New York: McGraw-Hill.

Boehm, B. W., Abi-Antoun, M., Port, D., Kwan, J., & Lynch, A. (1999). Requirements engineering, expectations management, and the two cultures. *Proceedings of the 4th IEEE International Symposium on Requirements Engineering* (pp. 14-22). Limerick, Ireland: IEEE.

Boehm, B. W., Port, D., Yang, Y., Bhuta, J., & Abts, C. (2003). Composable process elements for developing COTS-based applications. *ISESE 2003*, 8-17.

Boehm, B. W., & Turner, R. (2004). *Balancing agility and discipline: A guide for the perplexed*. Boston: Addison-Wesley.

Boehm, B. W., Yang, Y., Bhuta, J., & Port, D. (2005). Composable spiral processes for COTS-based application development. *Proceedings of the 4th International ICCBSS conference* (pp. 6-7), Bilbao, Spain: Springer.

Bowles, D. J. (2006). Active learning strategies … Not for the birds! *International Journal of Nursing Education Scholarship, 3*(1), 0-11.

Brooks, F. (1975). *The mythical man-month: Essays on software engineering.* Reading, MA: Addison-Wesley.

Deretchin, L. F. (2002). Making the grade. In P. Schwartz & G. Webb (Eds.), *Assessment: Case studies, experience and practice from higher education* (pp. 114-120). London: Kogan Page.

Ecker, P. S., Caudill, J., Hoctor, D., & Meyer, C. (2004). Implementing an interdisciplinary capstone course for associate degree Information Technology programs, *Proceedings of the 5th Conference on Information Technology Education* (pp. 60-65). Salt Lake City, UT.

Eisenman, R. (2001). Stimulating achievement among Hispanic college students. *Radical Pedagogy, 3*(2). Available: http://radicalpedagogy. icaap.org/content/issue3_2/eisenman.html

Enders, F. B., & Diener-West, M. (2006). Methods of learning in statistical education: A randomized trial of public health graduate students. *Statistics Education Research Journal, 5*(1), 5-19.

Fenwick, J. B., & Kurtz, B. L. (2005). Intra-curriculum software engineering education. *ACM SIGCSE Bulletin inroads, 36*(1). 540-544.

Fernandez, J. D., & Tedford, P. (2006). Evaluating computing education programs against real world needs. *Journal of Computing Sciences in Colleges, 21*(4), 259-265.

Fernandez, J. D., Garcia, M., Camacho, D., & Evans, A. (2006). Software engineering industry experience – the key to success. *Journal of Computing Sciences in Colleges, 21*(4), 230-236.

Franch, X., & Port, D. (2005). COTS-Based Software Systems. *Proceedings of the 4th International ICCBSS Conference* (LNCS 3412). Bilbao, Spain: Springer.

Friedman, R., McHugh, J. A., & Deek, F. P. (2003). NJIT's sandbox: An industry/education partnership for IT development. In *Proceedings of the 4th Conference on Information Technology Curriculum* (pp. 201-205). Lafayette, Indiana, USA.

Frohna, A. Z., Hamstra, S. J., Mullan, P. B., & Gruppen, L. D. (2006). Teaching medical education principles and methods to faculty using an active learning approach: The University of Michigan Medical Education Scholars Program. *Academic Medicine, 81*(11), 975-978.

Glass, R. L. (2001). Frequently forgotten fundamental facts about software engineering. *IEEE Software, 18*(3), 112 - 111.

Grisham, P. S., Krasner, H., & Perry, D. E. (2006). Data engineering education with real-world projects, *ACM SIGCSE Bulletin, 38*(2), pp. 64-68.

Hanna, M. (1993). Maintenance burden begging for a remedy. *Datamation*, April, 53-63.

Hecker, D. E. (2005). Occupational employment projections to 2014, Monthly Labor Review, Bureau of Labor Statistics, *128*(11), November 2005. Available: http://www.bls.gov/opub/mlr/2005/11/contents.htm

Hislop, G. W. (2006). Scaffolding student work in capstone design courses. *36th ASEE/IEEE Frontiers in Education Conference* (pp. T1A1-T1A4). San Diego, CA.

Hogan, J. M., Smith, G., & Thomas, R. (2005). Tight spirals and industry clients: The modern SE education experience. In *Proceedings of the 7th Australasian Conference on Computing Education - Volume 42* (pp. 217-222). A. Young & D. Tolhurst (Eds.), ACM International Conference Proceeding Series, vol. 106. Australian Computer Society, Darlinghurst, Australia.

IEEE Software Engineering Standards Central (2007). *Software Engineering Standards Over-*

view. Available: http://standards.ieee.org/software/overview.html

Jessup, E., Sumner, T., & Barker, L. (2006). Report from the trenches: Bringing more women to the study of computer science. Manuscript submitted for publication. Available: http://www.cs.colorado.edu/~jessup/SUBPAGES/PS/trenches.pdf

Johnson, A., Powers, C., & Wagert, S. (1989). EMCS implementation by IBM Advanced Workstation division. *Proceedings of GUIDE 75, Los Angeles, CA. Joint IEEE Computer Society/ACM Task Force on the "Model Curricula for Computing"*. Also available as IBM Technical Report TR51.0554, November, 1989.

Joint IEEE Computer Society/ACM Task Force on the "Model Curricula for Computing" (2005). *Computing Curricula Series.* Available: http://www.acm.org/education/curricula.html

Kadolph, S. J. (2005). Equipment experts: Enhancing student learning in textile science. *Clothing & Textiles Research Journal, 23*(4), 368-374.

Klappholz, D., Almstrum, V. L., & Modesitt, K. (2006, April). Workshop on real projects for real clients courses. *19th Conference on Software Engineering and Training*, Oahu, HI.

Koppelman, H., & van Dijk, B. (2006). Creating a realistic context for team projects in HCI, *Proceedings of the 11th Annual SIGCSE Conference on Innovation and Technology in Computer Science Education* (pp. 58-62). Bologna, Italy.

Kurtz, B. L., Fenwick, J. B., Ellsworth, C. C., Yuan, X., Steele, A., & Jia, X. (2007). Inter-university software engineering using web services. *ACM SIGCSE Bulletin inroads, 39*(1). 464-468.

Last, M., Almstrum, V., Erickson, C., Klein, B., & Daniels, M. (2000, June). An international student/faculty collaboration: The Runestone project. *ACM SIGCSE Bulletin inroads. 32*(3). 128-131.

Linn, R. L. (Ed.). (1989). *Educational Measurement* (3rd ed.). New York: American Council on Education and Macmillan Publishing.

Margolis, J., & Fisher, A. (2001). *Unlocking the clubhouse: Women in computing.* Cambridge, MA: MIT Press.

McKeachie, W. J. (1961). Understanding the learning process. *Journal of Engineering Education, 51*, 405-408.

McMillan, J. H. (2001). *Essential assessment concepts for teachers and administrators.* Thousand Oaks, CA: Corwin Press.

Michaelsen, L. K. (2002). Getting started with team-based learning. In L. K. Michaelsen, A. B. Knight, & L. D. Fink (Eds.), *Team-based learning: A transformative use of small groups* (pp. 27-50). Westport, CT: Praeger.

Mitchell, R. L. (2006). How not to get "offshored." *Computerworld Blogs.* March 31, 2006 http://www.computerworld.com/blogs/node/2150

Modesitt, K., Maxim, B., & Akingbehin, K. (1999). Just in Time Learning in software engineering. *The Journal of Mathematics and Science Teaching. 18*(3). 287-301.

Modesitt, K. (2004, September). The Distributed Development of Software Engineering Professionals. *International Colloquium on Engineering Education.* ASEE and Tsinghua University, Beijing, PRC.

Modesitt, K. (2005, October). W³ – Winning Three Times Over: Industry, University, Society. *ABET Annual Meeting on Accreditation, Innovation, and Improvement*, San Diego, CA, pp. 17-24.

Modesitt, K. (2006). A practical assessment guide to the use of Professional Advisory Boards. *Best Assessment Processes VIII of ABET*, Rose-Hulman Institute of Technology, February 27-28.

Morris, J. (2004). Programming doesn't begin to define computer science. *Pittsburgh Post-Gazette*. July 4, 2004. Retrieved June 6, 2007, from http://www.post-gazette.com/pg/04186/341012.stm

Norman, K. I., & Keating, J. F. (1997). Barriers for Hispanics and American Indians entering science and mathematics: Cultural dilemmas. *Association for the Education of Teachers in Science (AETS) Conference Proceedings* (pp. 448-464). Available: http://www.ed.psu.edu/ci/Journals/97pap22.htm

Pressman, R. S. (2005). *Software engineering: A practitioner's approach.* (6th ed.). New York: McGraw-Hill.

Schmuck, R. A., & Schmuck, P. A. (1997). *Group processes in the classroom* (7th ed.). Madison, WI: Brown & Benchmark.

Schuhmann, A. (1992). Learning to teach Hispanic students. In M. Dilworth (Ed.), *Diversity in teacher education – New expectations* (pp. 93-111). San Francisco: Jossey-Bass.

Shelly, G. B., Cashman, T. J., & Rosenblatt, H. J. (2008). *Systems analysis and design* (7th ed.). Boston: Thompson Course Technology.

Shuman, L. J., Besterfield-Sacre, M., & McGourty, J. (2005). ABET "professional skills" – Can they be taught? Can they be assessed? *The Journal of Engineering Education*, January 2005. Available: http://www.findarticles.com/p/articles/mi_qa3886/is_200501/ai_n9521126

Slavin, R. E. (2005). *Educational psychology: Theory and practice* (8th ed.). Boston: Allyn and Bacon.

The Standish Group. (1994). *The Standish Group Report – CHAOS 1994.* Standish Group International. Available: http://www.standishgroup.com/sample_research/chaos_1994_1.php

The Standish Group. (2003). *CHAOS Chronicles Version 3.0.* West Yarmouth, MA: The Standish Group.

Starney, K. (2006). Why do projects fail? *Cross-Talk: The Journal of Defense Software Engineering, 19*(6), 3. Available at http://www.stsc.hill.af.mil/crosstalk/2006/06/index.html

Stein, R.F., & Hurd, S. (2000). *Using student teams in the classroom: A faculty guide.* Boston: Anker Publishing.

Sun, N., & Decker, J. (2004). Finding an "ideal" model for our capstone experience. *Journal of Computing in Small Colleges, 20*(1), 211-219.

Supercomputing Online. (2007). Princeton professor foresees computer science revolution: An interview with Bernard Chazelle. Retrieved June 6, 2007, from http://www.supercomputingonline.com/article.php?sid=10496

Tan, S. S., & Ng, C. K. F. (2006). A problem-based learning approach to entrepreneurship education. *Education & Training, 48*(6), 416-428.

The TLT Group. (2007). Student Technology Assistant Programs. Available at http://www.tltgroup.org/programs/sta.html

Vegso, J. (2006). BLS IT workforce projections compared. *CRA Bulletin*, January 19, 2006. Available: http://www.cra.org/wp/index.php?cat=14

Voigt, W. P. (2007). *Quantitative research methods for professionals.* Boston: Allyn and Bacon.

Werner, M., & MacLean, L.M. (2006). Building community service projects effectively. *Journal of Computing Sciences in Colleges, 21*(6), 76-87.

Williams, J. C., Bair, B., Borstler, J., Lethbridge, T.C., & Surendran, K. (2003). Client sponsored projects in software engineering courses. *ACM SIGCSE Bulletin inroads, 35*(1). 401-402.

Worthen, B. R., & Sanders, J. R. (1988). *Educational evaluation: Alternative approaches and practical guidelines.* White Plains, NY: Longman.

Young, G., & Marks-Maran, D. (2002). But they looked great on paper. In P. Schwartz & G. Webb (Eds.), *Assessment: Case studies, experience and practice from higher education* (pp. 106-113). London: Kogan Page.

Zheng, Z. A., & Padmanabhan, B. (2006). Selectively acquiring customer information: A new data acquisition problem and an active learning-based solution. *Management Science, 52*(5), 697-712.

APPENDIX A: TOP TWO LEVELS OF RPRCC TAXONOMY

In this appendix we provide the top two levels of the current version of the draft RPRCC taxonomy. The taxonomy covers the large variety of issues relevant in Real Project for Real Client Courses (RPRCCs) and illustrates the potential diversity and robustness of RPRCCs. The taxonomy also demonstrates the broad set of issues that must be considered by any faculty member preparing to teach an RPRCC in order to tailor it to local needs and resource constraints.

I. COURSE

1. Course Profile
2. Professional topics covered in course
3. Other activities for learning software engineering principles
4. Course planning / flexibility ("reshuffling")
5. Support materials
6. Training students
7. Additional staff
8. Institutional memory
9. Showcasing projects (completed or in process)
10. Challenges
11. Other

II. TEAM

12. Team formation
13. Team style / organization
14. Matching teams with projects
15. Team-building and defining team operations
16. Communication considerations

III. CLIENT

17. Sources of clients
18. Client vetting by instructor
19. Preparing clients for their role
20. Legal issues

IV. PROJECT

21. Project types
22. Project vetting by instructor
23. Project proposals
24. Resource issues
25. Process guideline
26. Support tools
27. Work products / deliverables
28. Project-related activities
29. Project planning and tracking
30. Risk management of projects by students
31. Students using data from projects

V. ASSESSMENT & EVALUATION

32. Assessment during the academic term
33. Formal assessment of final work products
34. Evaluation of effectiveness and feedback on course

Chapter X
Experiences in Project–Based Software Engineering:
What Works, What Doesn't

Steven A. Demurjian
University of Connecticut, USA

Donald M. Needham
United States Naval Academy, USA

ABSTRACT

Project-based capstone software engineering courses are a norm in many computer science (CS) and computer science & engineering (CS&E) accredited programs. Such cap-stone design courses offer an excellent vehicle for educational outcomes assessment to support the continuous improvement process required for accreditation. A project-based software engineering capstone course near the end of a student's program can span the majority of CS and CS&E program objectives, providing a significant means to assess at-tainment of these objectives in a single course location. One objective of this chapter is to explore the role of a project-based, software engineering course in accreditation. An addi-tional objective is to relate over twelve combined years of experience in teaching such a course, and in the process, highlight what works and what does not. We candidly examine both the successes and the failures that we have encountered over the years, and provide a roadmap for other instructors and departments seeking to institute such courses.

INTRODUCTION

Since its early roots at the 1968 NATO conference in Garmisch Germany (Naur, Randell & Buxton, 1976), the software engineering discipline as has sought to use tools, techniques, and paradigms similar to those found in other engineering disci-plines in order to improve the quality and reduce the cost of software development. The seminal "No Silver Bullet" article by Brooks (1987) in part focuses on identifying the essence of what makes software development difficult and stresses that the ability to modify software so as to accom-modate evolving hardware requirements is one of the key aspects of understanding the inherent difficulties faced by software developers. Agile, lightweight methodologies such as Extreme Programming (Beck, 1999) emphasize customer involvement and promote team work in an effort to make the development process better suited to adapt to changing requirements. Of note with Beck's approach is the use of ad-hoc teams to resolve difficulties that arise during the development process. Software engineering educators have responded to these needs in part with the emergence of project-based software engineering capstone courses at the undergraduate level.

Such software engineering capstone courses are becoming a cornerstone of many computer science (CS) and computer science & engineering (CS&E) programs, and provide a means for practice-based exploration of large-scale projects in a team setting following current trends in software engineering course sequence design (Abran & Moore, 2004; Boehm, Kaiser & Port, 2000; LeBlanc & Sobel, 2004; Meyer, 2001; Shaw, 2000). Our approach to project-based software engineering capstone courses allows students to apply concepts and ideas garnered throughout their undergraduate program within a capstone experience near the end of their studies. For students, such courses can provide the opportunity to control the project topic, select teammates (to a limited degree), make critical decisions, and problem solve by applying coursework knowledge and their experiences. Project topics selected by our teams have run the gambit from standalone Java applications, automatic mixing machines that use windshield wiper motors and micro-processor controlled PVC pipes run via a web interface, to embedded system controllers for autonomous underwater vehicles. In such courses, instructors can serve as the mentor or project manager, overseeing the week-to-week schedule of deadlines, and arbitrating among team members when difficulties or clashes in personalities arise.

Project-based, software engineering capstone courses can also play a vital role in terms of ac-creditation. ABET, known prior to 2005 as the Accreditation Board for Engineering and Technology (ABET, 2007), has assumed accreditation over CS, CS&E, information technology, software engineering, and computer engineering programs. As part of ABET accreditation, departments must identify program objectives, and detail the program outcomes for each program; CS&E has outcomes that are influenced by engineering accreditation requirements, while CS outcomes have been influenced by computing accreditation requirements. Given a set of program outcomes, in order to support a continuous improvement process, it is necessary for departments to assess their programs on a regular basis. Since well-focused project-based software engineering courses can span nearly the entire curriculum in terms of topic coverage, they can serve as an ideal vehicle to accomplish this objective.

This chapter focuses primarily on CSE293, Capstone Project-Based Laboratory, in the Department of Computer Science & Engineering at the University of Connecticut (UConn). Experiences gained from a similar course, IC480, Computer Science Capstone, offered at the United States Naval Academy (USNA) are interleaved where they provide significant complementary or contrary perspectives. UConn's CSE293 was a new course developed during the Spring 2001 semester which we designed and instituted as part of our major curriculum changes for ABET 2000 accreditation. The course has been taught every semester at UConn since that time, with multiple sections by multiple instructors. The course philosophy of CSE293 is for the students (typically seniors near the end of their programs) to demonstrate the ability to work in a team with minimal or no guidance, where the team organizes, plans, designs, prototypes, and delivers a product according to milestones established (and known in advance) for the semester. Throughout the semester, the instructor delivers appropriate feedback to students in various mediums (oral, email, annotated documents, etc.), in response to assignment deliverables, presentations, individual/team meetings, and so on. The initial instructor of CSE293 developed baseline project assignment milestones which have evolved over the semesters into a generalized group of milestones organized on a course web page. This courseware has been used by different instructors over the years, and provides an organized and common means to deliver a consistent offering of CSE293.

The remainder of this chapter has five sections. First, background on accreditation is provided as a basis to later demonstrate the potential breadth of a project-based software engineering course in terms of assessment of program outcomes attainment. Then, the content, requirements, and projects for CSE293 as offered at UConn and IC480 as offered at USNA are presented. Next, self-assessments of CSE293 and IC480 are provided, with candid detailing of both successes and failures in delivering the course since its inception in Spring 2001. Then, future trends are discussed, with a focus on software engineering education and curricula, in general, and project-based software engineering courses, in particular. Finally, concluding remarks are presented.

BACKGROUND

Programs in CS and CS&E that are seeking to be accredited must satisfy stringent requirements for program educational objectives, and program outcomes and their assessment, as outlined by ABET (2007) which handles accreditation for applied science, computing, engineering, and technology programs. CS programs must satisfy Computing Accreditation Commission (CAC) requirements while CS&E programs must satisfy both CAC and Engineering Accreditation Commission (EAC) requirements. At the time of writing this paper, there are over 210 CS, and 11 CSE accredited programs.

Our concentration in this chapter emphasizes project-based software engineering and its critical role for CS and CS&E program outcomes and their assessment, since these are the two accredited programs at UConn. Table 1 gives the CS and CSE program outcomes from the criteria for accrediting programs for 2007-2008.

COURSE REQUIREMENTS AND PROJECTS

CSE293 Capstone Project-Based Laboratory is a three credit course taken at the end of an undergraduate's program, with two major prerequisites: an operating systems course (senior level as well, with many prerequisites such as computer architecture, introductory software engineering, and so on) and an initial laboratory course (digital hardware design, software engineering, networking, micro-processor, etc.). The CSE230 Introduction to Software Engineering course, required of all CS and CSE majors, is typically taken in the first semester of the junior year, and since 1990 has used the *Fundamentals of Software Engineering* (Ghezzi, Jazeyeri & Mandrioli, 2002) as its primary text. All of the material in this text is covered in one semester including: software qualities and principles, software design and specification, verification, the software process and management, and so on. This material is augmented with significant material on the UML and other special topics which vary by semester and instructor and typically include: software architectures, aspect-oriented software development, service-oriented computing, software reliability, etc. Students work both individually and in teams on instructor-directed design and programming projects throughout the semester.

The Naval Academy's software engineering prerequisite course is taken in the Fall of the senior year, which is the semester immediately preceding the capstone course. In this course, the students divide themselves into teams and are given a requirements document that includes an acceptance test plan for an instructor-determined

Table 1. CS and CSE program outcomes

CS Program Outcomes		CSE Program Outcomes	
CS-a	An ability to apply knowledge of computing and mathematics appropriate to the discipline.	CSE-a	An ability to apply knowledge of mathematics, science, and engineering.
CS-b	An ability to analyze a problem, and identify and define the computing requirements appropriate to its solution.	CSE-b	An ability to design and conduct experiments, as well as to analyze and interpret data.
CS-c	An ability to design, implement and evaluate a computer-based system, process, component, or program to meet desired needs.	CSE-c	An ability to design a system, component, or process to meet desired needs within realistic constraints such as economic, environmental, social, political, ethical, health and safety, manufacturability, and sustainability.
CS-d	An ability to function effectively on teams to accomplish a common goal.	CSE-d	An ability to function on multi-disciplinary teams.
CS-e	An understanding of professional, ethical, legal, security, and social issues and responsibilities.	CSE-e	An ability to identify, formulate, and solve engineering problems.
CS-f	An ability to communicate effectively with a range of audiences.	CSE-f	An understanding of professional and ethical responsibility.
CS-g	An ability to analyze the local and global impact of computing on individuals, organizations and society.	CSE-g	An ability to communicate effectively.
CS-h	Recognition of the need for, and an ability to engage in, continuing professional development.	CSE-h	The broad education necessary to understand the impact of engineering solutions in a global, economic, environmental, and societal context.
CS-i	An ability to use current techniques, skills, and tools necessary for computing practice.	CSE-i	A recognition of the need for, and an ability to engage in life-long learning.
CS-j	An ability to apply mathematical foundations, algorithmic principles, and computer science theory in the modeling and design of computer-based systems in a way that demonstrates comprehension of the tradeoffs involved in design choices.	CSE-j CSE-k	A knowledge of contemporary issues. An ability to use the techniques, skills, and modern engineering tools necessary for engineering practice.
CS-k	An ability to apply design and development principles in the construction of software systems of varying complexity.	CSE-l see notes	An ability to apply design and development principles in the construction of software systems of varying complexity.
		CSE-m see notes	An understanding of computer hardware and its relation to software design.

Notes:

1. Since CAC and EAC both use lower case letters for outcomes, we have added "CS-" and "CSE-" to preface CS and CSE program outcomes, respectively.

2. CS-j and CS-k are proposed by ABET-CAC.

3. EAC lists only CSE-a to CSE-k; UConn added CSE-l and CSE-m to reflect their practice and the overlap that exists between their CS and CS&E programs.

semester-long project. During this course the students attend lectures on the various phases of the software development life cycle, and develop, deliver and orally present and demonstrate milestones including a rapid prototype, specification/analysis, design, and testing. The final delivery milestone includes a presentation that demonstrates the degree to which each team meets the acceptance test plan given at the start of the course. The Naval Academy's capstone course is similar to UConn's CSE293 which is described in the following discussion.

The content of the UConn's CSE293 capstone course is reflected in its description:

This course is the second semester of the required major design experience. In one semester-long team project, students will propose, design, produce, and evaluate a software and/or hardware system. The project will culminate in the delivery of a working system, a formal public presentation, and written documentation. Oral and written progress reports are required.

In CSE293, the students organize their own teams, choose the project topic, determine team responsibilities, plan the prototyping schedule, and so on; the instructor is the project manager with the role of insuring that the project deadlines are met and that disputes among team members are resolved in a timely fashion. CSE293 is intended to demonstrate the ability of the students to work as a team with limited or minimal guidance. The course is offered in a section of up to 18 students organized into teams. Our one-semester capstone design course is consistent with other approaches (Ellis & Mitchell, 2004; Flener 2006).

In CSE293, the first half of the semester involves identifying the project topic (further discussed in the following sections), developing a comprehensive specification, performing a comprehensive and detailed design, and establishing milestones for prototyping deliverables and allocating work among teammates. Throughout each of these milestones, the instructor provides comments in different media (oral, email, written) to guide each team in a positive direction. The second half of the semester is for prototyping and assessment with multiple deliverables.

In terms of the course assignments, complete CSE293 details are available at http://www.engr.uconn.edu/~steve/Cse293/cse293.html and the specific course assignments are summarized in Table 2 and briefly reviewed below.

CSE293 meets formally once a week for a 2 hour block for a total of 14 weeks; the entire class

Table 2. CSE293 assignment description and timeline

Assignment	Due	Title	Description
1-Part I	Week 1	Establish Teams	Students are organized into teams of size four to six and informally discuss possible project topics.
1-Part II	Week 2	Preliminary Project Idea	Each team submits a 1-2 page project topic proposal for instructor critique. Team responds to critique, prepares a five page proposed project description, and presents their proposal. All presentations in the course are made to the instructor and the rest of the class.
2	Week 3	Specification and Software Quality Analyses	Teams submit a 10-12 page specification of their proposed project topic. Required sections are delineated by the instructor, and each student must identify the sections that they have written. In addition, each student selects two software characteristics (performance, reliability, reusability, etc.) and discusses the relevance/importance of the quality to their project topic and the way that it will be attained in their project topic.

continued on following page

Table 2. continued

3-Part I	Week 4	Revised Specification	Based on instructor comments, a revised and expanded/enhanced specification is due.
3-Part II	Week 5	Multi-Faceted Design	The design document requires the use of a design tool for UML and a detailed design organized into six tasks. Each student must be responsible for specific aspects of the design and must clearly identify their diagrams and documentation. The six tasks making contributing to the detailed design include: A. Entity Relationship Diagrams. B. Data-Flow Diagrams or UML Sequence Diagrams. C. Finite State Machines or UML Statechart Diagrams. D. UML Class/Object Diagrams. E. Petri Nets or UML Activity Diagrams. F. Three page summary document on the relationships and interplay of all of their diagrams from Tasks A to E.
3-Part III	Week 6	Revised Multi-Faceted Design	Based on instructor's critique for Assignment 3-Part II, the students are asked to revise their diagrams and written documentation.
4-Part I	Week 6	Prototyping Plan	Teams lay out a plan for implementing their project topic with prototype deliverables in the 9th, 12th, and 14th weeks. Plan describes the three prototypes, and the components and sub-components for each prototype.
4-Part II	Week 6	Management Plan	Teams complement the Assignment 4-Part I prototyping plan with a management plan that identifies the responsibilities of each team member for each sub-component, including a primary and backup individual per sub-component. Plan also identifies whether each sub-component is not-implemented (stub), partially implemented, or fully implemented for the respective prototypes.
4-Part III	Weeks 9, 12 and 14	Prototype Reports and Presentations	Teams provide deliverables for each prototype, including: A. Presentation of their progress/status including system demonstrations. B. Update of the prototype and management plan (what milestones did they hit/miss). C. Evaluation of the project status, and critique of teamwork experiences.
5	Last day of class	Realistic Issues for Product Development	Each student explores issues related to commercialization of their project by writing a 3 page analysis associated with issues such as: Funding, Commercialization, Intellectual Property, Social/Ethical/Legal, Software Licensing, Payment, HIPAA Security, or any other specific issues related to commercialization.
Final Project	Last day of class	Final Project Delivery	Industry managers in computing are invited and critique/provide input. The final submission has both team and individual parts. For the Team Submission, each team provides an overview of the project and its goals, a summary of changes since Assignment 3- Part III, a detailed user manual, etc. For the Individual Submission, there are team-assessments and self-assessments as well as student reflections on their accomplishments, what they have learned, and what they would change/do differently if they started the project again.

meets with the instructor each week for the first half of the semester. The instructor explains each deliverable assignment for the semester and acts as the project manager by providing oral and written feedback to each group. The first class is used to overview the course requirements, web site, and materials, and most importantly to organize the students into teams of four to six individuals (Assignment 1, Part I in Table 2). We typically have one or two teams that have pre-formed prior to the start of the class by students looking to work with one another, and the instructor forms the other teams. The teams that pre-form typically do quite a good job on their team projects since they are motivated to work together from the start. Since students predominately take CSE293 in their final semester, their backgrounds are very uniform in terms of prior courses, with slight variances. Consequently, there is no attempt to try to balance a team in terms of student skill sets. In terms of leadership, we allow the team and its dynamics to develop over the semester. Three days after the first class, each team is required to email a 1 to 2 page project proposal to the instructor, who provides feedback on its scope (to make sure that it is large enough) and offers other suggestions on possible problems, alternatives, etc. At USNA, we use a low-level rubric to assist in scoping the project by requiring each team to delineate at least one major and distinct focus area (grouping of functionality) per team member on the team. For example, a team of six will be required to have six major, distinct focus areas. Since we also require teams to turn in an acceptance test plan with their project proposal, each team's focus areas are further required to contain between five and eight itemized functional descriptions that map directly to the team's acceptance test plan. We have found that this primitive rubric is effective in guiding each team to a good starting point for their project proposal assignment so that the instructor can provide effective feedback.

At UConn, our objective is to choose a project scope that is significantly large from a specification and design perspective (the first half of the semester), which can then be narrowed for the implementation phase (the second half of the semester). Using this feedback, each team prepares a 10-15 minute presentation for the second class to the instructor and all other teams (Assignment 1, Part I in Table 2).

The initial specification (Assignment 2) is due at the third class (with instructor available to answer questions), and the instructor provides feedback to each team within 24 hours (typically annotated specification plus email). The course web page contains a detailed document discussing the specification content and process (along with samples from prior semesters). The specification is structured with specific sections including: introduction, operating environment, user, system, database interfaces, system operation, information, performance, and security; software qualities are given via Ghezzi, Jazeyeri & Mandrioli (2002) with the each student selecting two qualities and discussing their relevance, importance, and impact for their project. The revised specification (Assignment 3, Part I in Table 2) is due the 4th class and is based on these comments (with the instructor available to answer questions), with the initial multi-faceted design (Assignment 3, Part II in Table 2) of UML diagrams plus entity relationships due at the 5th class. Teams receive instructor feedback by the next day and prepare a revised design (Assignment 3, Part III in Table 2) along with a prototyping and management plan (Assignment 4, Parts I and II in Table 2) by the 6th class. This prototyping plan allows each team to scope the implementation down to a reasonable subset of the specification/design to deliver a solution in three increments (Assignment 4, Part III in Table 2) over the remainder of the semester (9th, 11th, and 14th classes). Each increment has a presentation, demonstration, and prototyping report; the final increment is more complete in all three and is often attended by industry personnel for more realistic feedback. For all of the assignments, there are multiple samples from past semester on the web page. The intent of all of the various milestones and associated presentations is to provide feedback to guide the students and allow the students to experience the successes and pitfalls of project development in a realistic setting. For each prototype, the team is asked to assess their prototyping/management plan in order to understand their progress and to re-plan for the remaining increments. The point of this reassessment is for the students to understand the difficulty in predicting and planning software increments prior to actually writing code.

In addition to the assignments shown in Table 2, each team must develop and deploy a project web page with all of these materials in electronic form, with each team member maintaining a blog of their activities throughout the semester. Students are required to use a UML tool (such as Borland's Together Architect or Eclipse plug in) for UML diagram development, and are encouraged to use an appropriate interactive development environment with source code control. Sample solutions for all course assignments and presentations are available on the course web page.

WHAT WORKS, WHAT DOESN'T

There are many efforts on project-based software engineering that relate lessons learned, including Flener (2006), who details his experiences in attempting to incorporate realism into the software engineering course with collected student comments on positive and negative experiences; Polack-Wahl (2006), who considers the impact of the type of project (instructor vs. industry vs. other) and student outcomes from the perspective of landing their first software engineering position; and, van der Duim, et al., (2007) which reports on experiences on multi-university team projects with conclusions that include real-life projects being too complex.

In this section, we report on our successes and failures in CSE293 in a number of different categories, ranging from external issues such as curriculum, accreditation and outcomes assessment, to internal issues such as project choice, team member backgrounds, and team size. We have found that the internal issues often have a strong potential for negative impact on both the students and the instructor. The remainder of this section discusses each of these issues in turn, and includes a candid assessment of our efforts as organized into two categories (what *Works* and what *Doesn't* work).

Accreditation and Outcomes Assessment

In terms of accreditation, project-based software engineering capstone courses (semester or year long) such as CSE293 provide an ideal opportunity to assess the attainment of program outcomes that cross the entire curriculum at the latter stage of a student's program (for both CS and CS&E programs). In accreditation, program outcomes assessment is intended to be a continuous improvement process that occurs each semester by identifying and assessing key courses against the program outcomes, CS-a to CS-k for CS programs and CSE-a to CSE-m for CS&E programs as discussed in the previous section. For example, at UConn, our CS program is assessed using five different categories of courses (software engineering, algorithms, ethics, programming languages and compilers, and capstone senior design in CSE293). CSE293 provides a means through which the students' deliverable work can be used to demonstrate significant contribution to outcomes CS-b to CS-k for CS programs and CSE-c to CSE-l for CS&E programs as outlined in Table 3.

As can be seen in Table 3, Course Assignments 2, 3, and 5 contribute quite heavily in the measuring attainment of both CS and CS&E program outcome assessments.

In summary, for both our CS and CS&E accredited programs, the ability of a capstone project-based software engineering course such as CSE293 to be used as the major outcomes assessment course for accreditation greatly facilitates the continuous evaluation process. For example, in analyzing CSE293 assessment measurements gathered during the Spring 2007 semester, we noticed that we lacked measurements for realistic issues as they arise in CS-e, CS-g, and CS-h of the CS program objectives and of CSE-f, CSE-h, CSE-i, and CSE-j of the CS&E program objectives. As a result of our evaluation process, Course Assignment 5 on Realistic Issues for Product

Table 3. Vehicles for measuring attainment of ABET program outcomes

ABET Program Outcomes	Vehicles for measuring attainment of ABET Program Outcomes
CS-b; CSE-e	Course Assignments 1 (Part II- Preliminary Project Idea) and 2 (Specification and Software Quality Analysis), along with Course Assignment 3 Part I require the student to analyze the problem and define its scope as part of the specification.
CS-c; CSE-e	Course Assignment 3 (Part II- Multi-Faceted Design and Part III- Revised Multi-Faceted Design) involve the design of a computer-based system.
CSE-e	Course Assignment 4 (Part I- Prototyping Plan and Part II- Management Plan and Part III – Prototype reports and Presentations) demonstrate to varying degrees an ability to identify, formulate and solve engineering problems.
CS-d; CSE-d	All course assignments require teamwork to a variety of degrees.
CSE-g	All course assignments require oral and written communication to the instructor. Prototype presentations are made to the entire class. For the final presentation, industry managers in computing are invited and critique/provide input.
CS-e; CSE-h	Course Assignment 5 (Realistic Issues for Product Development) explores realistic issues related to commercialization (e.g., professional, ethical, legal, security, social, global issues and responsibilities).
CS-f	All course assignments require oral and written communication to the instructor. Prototype presentations are to the entire class. For the final presentation, industry managers in computing are invited and critique/provide input.
CS-g; CSE-c, CSE-f	Course Assignment 5 (Realistic Issues for Product Development) explores realistic issues and constraints related to commercialization for local and global impact of computing on individuals, organizations and society, including ethical, legal, security and global policy issues.
CS-h; CSE-c CSE-i, CSE-j	Course Assignment 5 (Realistic Issues for Product Development) requires students to learn and research a topic (such as commercialization) that was likely not covered in depth in their program.
CS-i; CSE-k, CSE-l	Course Assignment 3 (Part II- Multi-Faceted Design and Part III- Revised Multi-Faceted Design) requires students to use current techniques (UML and other models) and associated tools for their design.
CS-j	When given feedback on their teams' initial and revised designs for Course Assignment 3 (Part II- Multi-Faceted Design and Part III- Revised Multi-Faceted Design), students must respond with revisions to the modeling and design of their systems.
CS-k	Course Assignment 3 (Part II- Multi-Faceted Design and Part III- Revised Multi-Faceted Design) demonstrate an ability to apply UML (and other models) to construct a solution for their project.

Development was added for subsequent offerings of this course. Overall, the issue of using the capstone course to measure attainment of program outcomes is in the *Works* category, although the danger exists for the capstone course to be saddled with gathering too many such measurements as we discuss in the following section.

As can be seen in Table 3, many program outcomes can be measured by capstone courses structured like CSE293. An unintended consequence of such a versatile (from an assessment perspective) course can be an undue burdening of the instructors teaching the course with the collection of a great deal of assessment data. To resolve this issue at USNA, the department's assessment committee compiled a matrix showing every possible program outcome that every course in the program could possibly measure. At a series of assessment-focused department meetings, the faculty members reviewed the matrix to ensure that each course in the program was indeed contributing to one or more outcomes, and modified the matrix to remove excessive redundancy (such as the same outcome being measured in too large a number of courses) as well as to evenly distribute the assessment workload across the curriculum. We sought to ensure that each program outcome was measured at least twice, and no more than four times throughout the program. This issue is definitely in the *Works* category as the process of analyzing our assessment matrix resulted in significant faculty buy-in to our approach to program assessment, and also served to streamline which of the possible program outcomes were measured in the various courses.

University-Wide Curriculum Goals

In Fall 2005, CSE293 was required to additionally count as a writing-course (W-course) so that it could be used to fulfill a university-wide writing continuum. A W-course requires that each student write a paper of at least 15 single spaced pages, and that these pages include both original pages and edited (revisions suggested by the instructor on English grammar, formatting, content, etc.). Students at UConn must take two W-courses to meet their general education requirements. For CS&E and computer engineering programs, the students meet this requirement without CSE293. For the CS program, CSE293 is vital. This has been a nightmare for CSE293, and has required the instructor to carefully partition every project so that each student's writing on each team can be tracked, even though only some of the students enrolled actually need CSE293 to count as a W-course. Further, there has been added documentation and revision cycles to attempt to get to the 15 pages early in the semester, since they must be

"edited" pages. Every student easily meets this goal by the end of the semester with final reports, user manuals, individual/team assessments, and so on. However, this approach is burdensome on the instructor. While CSE293 serves an exemplary role in outcomes assessment for accreditation, its role as a W-course for general education requirements is misplaced since CSE293 is taken too late in the program to be beginning to teach students about technical writing. We are currently discussing moving the W-course requirement to an earlier location in our program so as to allow students to take advantage of what they learn about technical writing, program documentation, etc., in subsequent courses. CSE293 as a W-course, while on the fence between *Works* and *Doesn't*, is clearly leaning towards *Doesn't*.

Courseware Sharing

CSE293 materials, as they appear on the web page, have been used by a number of faculty members since the inception of this course in Spring 2001. In the most recent semester (Spring 2007), the identical core of materials (course projects) was used, with the various instructors of the course making some interesting additions to their sections. In one section we added a fourth prototype deliverable, and found that this approach was not very successful since there was a limited time after spring break (seven weeks) and adding a fourth deliverable meant that there was only a very small potential for incremental functionality advancements for that deliverable. In another section we asked for self and team assessments related to each team's web site design for the course and the software development environment (SDE) used. For the SDE, we asked each student to detail the tools they used, how the tools were used, and if the student would use such tools again. Our analysis of the most recent offering of the course demonstrates that even though there are a core set of course assignments, there is enough versatility in the course to add to and otherwise customize the course based on the particular instructor's background and preferences. Courseware sharing also contributes to the continuous improvement process required by accreditation by supporting modifications to subsequent course offerings that incorporate both instructor and student feedback. Courseware sharing is definitely in the *Works* category.

Team Size

In the over 35 times that the authors have taught CSE293 or other similar team-based project courses, we have uniformly observed that teams of from four to six individuals work well, as has been noted by other efforts (Fleener, 2006). Teams of this size tend to allow students to undertake an adequately scoped project and to experience the critical personnel interactions that Brooks (1995) argues are inherent to large-scale commercial software development. A team size larger than six tends to introduce too many communication paths and typically requires another layer of management that is inappropriate given typical course constraints. A team size of less than four means that the loss of a team member due to illness, family situations, or senioritis, can significantly impact the team. What *Doesn't Work* in our experience are small teams of just two or three members, as the relatively small team size results in a variety of difficulties not typically experienced by larger teams. Small teams do not get as many opportunities to experience the full measure of personnel interactions that are inherent in larger teams. Small teams encounter greater bias while conducting peer evaluations (further discussed in the below sections). Further, small teams have greater difficulty meeting deadlines and objectives when they experience the literal, or figurative, loss of a team member. When one team member is unavailable, or doesn't carry their fair share of the workload, the loss of that team member represents a 33% loss of effort for a three person team or a 50% loss of effort for a two

person team. In such cases, it can be difficult for the remainder of the team to make up the workload difference without resorting to heroic efforts which are inappropriate, since this is, after all, an academic undertaking. In addition, if the rest of the class has larger team sizes of four to six students, the overall work done by the small two to three person groups tends to pale in comparison. This can lead to larger teams inferring that the larger teams had to do more work, and at the same time leaving the smaller teams thinking that the smaller teams had to put in more effort per-person than did students on the larger teams. To summarize what *Works*: We recommend balanced teams of four to six students in cases where students have generally similar academic backgrounds, projects are intended to be completed in a single semester, and peer assessments similar to those we discuss in the below Assessment/Individual Contribution section are used to help determine a student's individual grade for the course project.

Impact of Project Topic

Over the years, there have been many topics chosen by students that have been successfully completed by the teams while others teams have failed; likewise, topics selected from a list provided by the instructor have been successfully used by some teams while other teams have failed attempting the same topic. To summarize what *Works* are projects that teams undertake involving well-known, well-documented technologies that provide safe havens for technologically timid students, or conversely, project selections that involve innovative and cutting edge technologies that excite the more adventurous students. Successful teams that chose software-centric projects have typically included topics surrounding: web-based projects, stand alone Java/C++ projects, and database front ends. For example, a successful team's project was a United States Census browser that allowed users to make http queries against a massive database. Another example was a team that chose a web-based application for authors, reviewers, and editors to track submitted journal articles. In terms of innovation, hardware/software combination projects have included: an automatic mixing machine that used windshield wiper motors and PVC pipes controlled by a micro-processor and run via a web interface; a diagnostic system that ran on a laptop with a database and connected to a car's serial port for real-time analysis of an automobile's performance; model trains with embedded computers that support control and feedback sensors (termed digital trains) that are controllable through Java applications using serial connections; a multitude of single and multi-player web-based games; and robotics projects such as linking a robot to a PDA to a cell phone with a web-interface, and projects that link a robot with a web-controlled camera. What *Doesn't* work: Teams that fail do so for a variety of reasons that are in part due to their project selection. One failure characterization that seems to dominate is when teams choose obscure or antiquated hardware where documentation or hardware support is unavailable or outside the students' ability to acquire mastery over. For example, some team failures were attributed in part to their targeting of the Atari 800 computer platform. Other failures occurred when a team depended on the timing of commercial software releases that were promised by the company, but then didn't occur (if they did at all) until there were only a few weeks left in the semester. Interestingly, projects undertaken by teams that succeed one semester can fail for teams undertaking the same project in the next semester, even when both the teams have similar skill sets. For example, the requirements for the previously mentioned digital train system were instructor provided, and the first team to undertake the project was quite successful. However, teams in subsequent semesters using the same digital train requirements were much less successful. In retrospect, the follow-on digital train teams tended to choose the project topic because the team was unable to come up with their own project idea. Overall, success and failure often seems to depend more on team member buy-in to the project idea, rather than on the particular skills of the team members.

Year-Long Capstone Design

In many capstone-based software engineering courses, a two semester approach is promoted to provide adequate time for realistic experiences with the entire software engineering process (Bagert & Mengel, 2003; Clark, Davies & Skeers, 2005). In fact, at UConn and USNA, many of the non-computing engineering programs (e.g., mechanical, chemical, etc.), have a history of year-long projects. As an experiment under a Spring/Fall cycle, a year long project was instituted at UConn. In the Spring semester, CSEYYY (a predecessor of CSE293) was split into two groups: one group did one semester projects as usual. The second group defined two-semester projects that would continue in a sequence with CSE293. For example, three of the six groups in CSEYYY continued on with their project in the subsequent Fall semester in CSE293. This required maintaining two separate schedules and milestones (for one semester vs. two semester groups) and also providing additional work for the two-semester groups so as to define a larger-scale project for the two-semester sequence. This issue was definitely in the *Doesn't* work category at UConn; to say that it was a total failure would be an understatement. In Spring 2005, the three year-long groups had five, four, and four team members respectively. One group shrunk to two members who then switched projects. Another group, shrunk first from four to three members, and then to two over the last four weeks. The third group stayed intact, but had an overall implementation over the course of 15 weeks that was only incrementally better than a one semester project. The final grades that the students earned were the lowest that the instructor has ever given in a project-based course over his career at UConn (20 years with 18 project courses).

Although there are many examples of having two semester projects work (Bagert et al., 2003; Clark et al., 2005), we haven't experimented at UConn with year long projects since that time.

Our experiences at USNA with year-long (Fall/Spring) inter-disciplinary capstone projects (Needham, 2005) have been mixed. Some of these projects involved unmanned aerial vehicle (UAV) systems funded by a Department of Defense agency. The projects focused in part on determining what type of small unmanned flight-capable vehicles undergraduate-level groups could construct on limited budgets. An explicit requirement of the UAV teams was that they design, construct, and fly an UAV using commercial off the shelf software and components to the maximum extent possible. The computer science students on these inter-disciplinary teams (which also included aeronautical engineering students) did generally good jobs of software system design and prototyping in the fall semester, but fell victim to critical vendor-controlled software system upgrades that did not materialize (with severe negative impact on the resulting UAV systems).

Conversely, other multi-disciplinary teams have developed autonomous underwater vehicles (AUVs) for annual AUV competitions (AUVSI, 2007) jointly directed by the Association for Unmanned Vehicle Systems International and the Office of Naval Research and have met with great success. The computer science students on these teams (which also included mechanical, systems and ocean engineering students) under-took the year-long project as a two-course sequence, starting with an introductory instructor-driven project-based software engineering course the fall semester. In the fall course, multi-threaded prototype embedded system controllers were designed, constructed and tested through simulations. These software systems were developed with an eye towards software reusability since the AUSVI competition intentionally alters the competition parameters close to the competition date to force student teams to respond to changing environments. For the computer science students involved with our AUV teams, the initial software engineering course was followed by spring semester capstone courses in which the prototype software control systems were integrated with the physical systems constructed by the mechanical, systems and ocean engineering students. Most of the engineering students had only a rudimentary exposure to programming in C which was primarily focused on device driver development. Oddly, we encountered problems similar to those reported by Last, Hause, Daniels and Woodroffe (2002) in their exploration of virtual project teams in which team members were spread across continents (US, Sweden and the UK). We experienced a similar lack of programming language commonality (Java for the CS majors and C for the Systems Engineering majors), lack of motivation caused by some team members not knowing what other team members were doing, and an "us vs. them" mentality, even though the academic centers for our students were located just one building away from each other. Since our AUV teams had upwards of 10 students from various departments, a middle-tier management level was added part-way through the second semester of the sequence, one for software development and one for hardware construction.

This middle-tier management level addition greatly relieved many of the problems we experienced by instituting a single point of contact for communication both from and to the various subsets of the teams. On our most successful team, the middle-tier managers were roommates which likely enhanced the communications at their level. The success this team experienced further acknowledges the criticality of open lines of communication between team members. Over the years, AUV capstone project teams have met with various degrees of success, with the most fully operational resultant AUV systems typically participating in the ASUVI competition just one month after the respective spring semesters ended.

Assessment/Individual Contribution

A delicate aspect of teaching CSE293 is the requirement for each team member to perform confidential self and team-member assessments. As noted by Chrisman and Beccue (1987), Scott, Bisland, Tiehenor, and Cross (1994) and Wilkins and Lawhead (2000), individually assessing students within team settings present difficult problems that can be further complicated by the need for instructor intervention to resolve intra-team disputes. Over the years, we have tried different approaches as given in Table 4.

The first approach we tried, the "Letter Grade" technique from Table 4, resulted, with a few exceptions (less than seven out of more than 70 teams), in almost all students self-grading to an average of 90+ or higher for the semester and indicating that all team members deserve an A or A- at worst. This is often totally contrary to reality, particularly in terms of the grades that have been received by the students' respective course projects. We believe that this is a result of students' perceptions that if they finish the course project and it more or less "works", they deserve a high grade. A similar effect occurred when using the "Sums to One" approach in Table 4. Related examples occurred when each student was asked to identify his/her and teammates level of participation for each deliverable (e.g., specification, design,

etc.). Even though students are specifically told that not all students had to contribute equally to all deliverables, for four person teams, students usually indicated 25% effort per person per deliverable, for five person teams, 20%, and so on. In a few cases, the assessments were lopsided. For example, we had a case where for a team of six, five students indicated that the sixth student did not contribute equally and deserved a low grade; refreshingly, that sixth student concurred! There have also been dysfunctional teams where every team member criticized a different team member as not contributing, and teams that complained that the leader was too controlling.

Meaningful peer assessment has long been problematic in capstone courses. In efforts by Clark, et al. (2005), self and peer assessments were conducted in a formal business-oriented way with student supplied time sheets, detailed surveys, and grading formulas for instructors. In another effort (Ellis & Mitchell, 2004), surveys were used with the instructor making similar conclusions to our observations. In the following sections we discuss our approaches to strengthening the utility and impact of peer assessments.

At USNA, we instituted the rubric shown in Table 5 in pursuit of what we termed a Peer-Assessment-Multiplier for awarding individual students grades for team projects. During these assessments, each student circles a rating to in-

Table 4. Techniques for student assessments of self and team members

Description	Technique	Result
Letter Grade	Students assign a letter or numeric grade (0..100) to self and each of their teammates.	Unproductive. Almost all students self-graded to an average of 90+ or higher for the semester and indicated that all team members deserved an A or A- at worst
Sums to One	Students assign a fraction to self and team members where the fractions must sum to one.	Unproductive. Almost all students self-graded to a .25 for four person teams, .20 for five person teams, etc. Same net effect as Letter Grade above.
Descriptive Rubric	Students use a pre-defined descriptive rubric to assess self and team members.	Productive. Students rarely self-graded to a description that maximized their score, and few teams uniformly chose the highest descriptor for each team member.

dicate the degree to which the evaluating student feels that each team member fulfilled his/her responsibilities in completing the team-oriented project assignments. Students were advised that their rating of their team members should reflect each individual's level of participation, effort, and sense of responsibility, not his or her academic ability.

Students were given the rubric at the beginning of the semester so they knew how they would be assessed by their peers, and that the instructors would assign weights to the various ratings (such as 100 for an Excellent rating, 90 for Very Good, etc). The students were told that their specific ratings of their team members would remain confidential, but that they would be advised of their averaged peer assessment by the instructor at about 4 week intervals throughout the course. This is another area in which larger team sizes (four to six) work better than smaller team sizes (two to three), as it is more difficult to ensure such confidentiality within small teams. For even larger teams (more than six) we have found that students bring in additional influences that tend to reduce the utility of peer assessments. For ex-

ample, on the multi-disciplinary UAV and AUV teams discussed above, students from the same major tended to grade their fellow majors higher, primarily because they knew them better from having taken earlier classes together and they could better relate to the quality of the work done by students of the same major. With team sizes of four to six, we observed that there were generally less opportunities for such external influences to skew the peer assessments because the teams were comprised of either all the same major, or there were not enough students from each major to unduly the peer assessments.

In all cases, what noticeably improved the usefulness of the peer assessments was when we began informing the students that their own team-generated individual peer evaluation, as compared to their teams overall peer evaluation average, would impact each student's recorded team project grade. Our intentions were to use the peer assessment to award additional points to a team member whose peers felt was doing excellent work, and penalize poorly performing team members. For example, assume a team of four in which one team member's peer assess-

Table 5. Rubric for student assessments of self and team members

Rating	Description
Excellent	Consistently went above and beyond the call; nurtured teammates; routinely did far more than his/her assigned team responsibilities.
Very Good	Always did what he/she was supposed to do; very well prepared and very cooperative.
Good	Mostly did what he/she was supposed to do; acceptably prepared and cooperative.
Satisfactory	More often than not did what he/she was supposed to do, no more, no less; minimally prepared and cooperative.
Marginal	Sometimes failed to show up or complete assignments w/o valid reasons; rarely prepared.
Deficient	Often failed to show up or complete assignments w/o valid reasons; rarely prepared.
Grossly Unsat	Consistently failed to show up or complete assignments w/o valid reasons, unprepared.

ment rubric results average to Excellent, two team members average to Very Good, and one team member averages to Marginal. This gives a total of $100 + 90 + 90 + 60$, or 340 points, resulting in an overall team average of 85. Each student receives a peer-assessment-multiplier (here, 100/85, 90/85, 90/85 and 60/85) that is applied to their recorded final project grade that represents their individual, peer-assessed, accomplishments relative to the project. Continuing our example, assume a team has a final project score of 82%. In this case, the Excellent peer-rated student would receive (100/85)*82 or 96.4%, the two Very Good rated students would each receive an (90/85)*82 or 86.8%, and the Marginal student would receive a (60/85)*82 or 57.8% for their respective final project grades. It should be noted that the summation of the peer-assessment-multiplied final project scores remains the same ($96.4 + 86.8 + 86.8 + 57.8$ still average to 82), but the points have been re-distributed in a manner that rewards students that have been peer-assessed as carrying more than their share of the load. Further, team members that are shirking their responsibility are held accountable for their actions through a lower peer-assessment-multiplied final project score.

Most team members (over 88% in our analysis) perform at or near the team average and therefore experience minimal impact in terms of their project grade. We have found such peer-assessment to be a very effective technique, especially when applied early and at regular intervals throughout the semester. In particular, under-performing team members realize early on that their lack of commitment to the team project will impact their grade. This approach is quite useful in helping students acquire the ability to work well in the team environment. As a side note, we have also found that the Peer-Assessment-Multiplier approach serves as an excellent resource when students return to ask for letters of recommendation in their job searches. Although it would be inappropriate to disclose a student's multiplier, it can be quite useful as an aide in helping to recall

which students were the most effective in a team environment for semesters past.

The Peer-Assessment-Multiplier technique falls in the *Works* category, but there are a few caveats. Although the technique is not fool-proof (teams can still voluntarily pool their assessment grading and thereby render the technique useless, unpopular team members can be unfairly singled out, etc), our experiences have been that teams rarely want to freely carry the weight of an under-performer, and that (most) students are mature enough not to penalize a team member unfairly.

Non-Functioning Team Members

On very rare occasions, a team may have a team member that severely fails to fulfill his/her responsibilities towards the team project. At USNA, we sought to empower teams to handle such personnel issues at as low a level as possible, rather than have the instructor step in and act as arbitrator for every team difficulty encountered. Towards this end, we established the following Regulations for Ejecting Nonfunctioning Team Members:

1. **Warning Memo.** If the majority of a team determines that a member of the team is not fulfilling his/her responsibilities, they will send the member a formal warning memo, with a copy to the instructor. The memo must specifically state what the member has thus far failed to do in regard to meeting responsibilities as a team member, what the team member must do to correct the situation, must be dated, and must indicate that the member will be ejected from the team if the situation is not corrected within two weeks.

2. **Ejection Memo.** After a period of two weeks, if the individual has not taken appropriate steps to correct the situation, the team will send the individual a formal ejection memo, with a copy to the instructor. The instructor will formally meet with the team as a whole

to examine the situation and approve the ejection as appropriate, in which case the individual will be responsible for completing his or her own project.

3. **Relapse Memo.** If the individual temporarily corrects the lack of responsibility but then again relapses into being a nonfunctioning team member, no additional warning memos are necessary. The team may immediately follow the ejection memo steps delineated above.

We have used the above Regulations for Ejecting Nonfunctioning Team Members for over 50 teams with very good results. Cases in which the instructor had to step in as an arbitrator were greatly reduced, from a few every semester or so, down to the point where virtually no arbitration was required with the regulations in effect. In total, there were just four cases of warning memos being routed, with one of those cases continuing on to the ejection memo stage. The Regulations for Ejecting Nonfunctioning Team Members technique falls squarely into the *Works* category. Our approach encourages teams to resolve minor disputes at an appropriately low level, improves team communication, and encourages team members to actively participate in their team's project.

FUTURE TRENDS

Future trends in software engineering focus at the discipline, program, and instructor levels. Software engineering education is being influenced on both a national and international level by many different efforts. ABET has currently accredited 13 software engineering programs that meet its criteria. There are two major ongoing curriculum efforts: the Guide to Software Engineering Body of Knowledge (Abran & Moore, 2004), which is seeking to raise the software engineering profession to the level of other engineering disciplines in terms

of licensing and accreditation; and, Software Engineering 2004 (LeBlanc & Sobel, 2004), the curriculum guidelines for undergraduate degree programs in software engineering. Both of these efforts are the subject of much discussion in the literature: Simmons (2006) examined the need to address the world wide demand of software engineers as a result of outsourcing and US Department of Labor growth projections for the occupation; Thomson and Edwards (2006) reported on bridging the university/industry gap in software engineering education in the United Kingdom, and recommend the inclusion of best industry practices into curricula; and van Vliet (2005; 2006) identified the shortcomings of both SWEBOK and SE2004 in achieving real-world experiences, the dissimilarity between software engineering and other engineering disciplines, and the inaccuracy of project planning techniques. In addition, Bagert's (2004) work on a software engineering roadmap is an excellent summary of the issues including a discipline code of ethics, professional licensing (Texas and Canada), and accreditation (United States and Canada).

There are many novel efforts underway related to software engineering capstone courses such as CSE293. Bagert and Mengel (2003) discuss a standardized software process that is employed in their MSSE and BSCS programs that emphasizes a practice-based approach to software engineering education. Their undergraduate students take an initial software engineering course, followed by a senior-level product design course, and then a senior-level product implementation laboratory. This is similar to CSE293 in focus, but gives a full semester devoted to software design rather than the partial semester design focus of CSE293. Bernhart, Grechenig, Hetzl and Zuser (2006) have developed two courses in their quest to transition the software engineering knowledge requirements identified in SE2004 into actual software engineering course design. One is a project-based introductory software engineering course following an instructor dictated timeline; the second is a follow-on course in which students develop software systems based on their own timelines. This second course is similar to CSE293, with one interesting exception: the second course proposed by Bernhart et al. does not require the first course as a prerequisite. This is very different from CSE293 which requires a foundational knowledge of basic software engineering principals before students undertake the capstone project. Fenwick and Kurtz (2005) report on their efforts to have project-based software engineering experiences which involve teams that span multiple courses, and go so far as to involve freshman, sophomores, and juniors in a single project. Their approach essentially has the students in the lower level courses acting as contractors that deliver, for example, the database portion of the project to the students enrolled in the managerial-focused software engineering course. Daigle and Niccolai (1997) attempted a similar connection between a low level software engineering theory courses and senior level project courses. An advantage of both of these approaches is that the software engineering capstone students are relieved of some of the low level implementation concerns and are allowed to focus more on the analysis, design and management issues of the project. This is very different from the approach taken in CSE293 in which the teams have to build a project completely by themselves and from scratch. Ghezzi and Mandrioli (2005) propose knowledge skills and curricula requirements for software engineering education that are largely met by CESZZZ. Hazeyama (2005) reviews current practices in team-based software engineering and provides a paradigm to evaluate and assess these approaches. In particular, Hazeyama's proposal for assessment-based grading closely parallels the Peer-Assessment-Multiplier technique we discuss above. Van der Duim, Andersson and Sinnema (2007) propose seven best practices for software engineering education to enhance the

rigor and control of software engineering projects. However, they report difficulty in resolving what they term the "Free Riders" problem. This problem occurs with students that do not really contribute to the team's efforts, but hope to pass the course anyway by assuming that instructors do not have any real insight into individuals' efforts. We are confident that the Free Riders problem can be addressed using a combination of the Peer-Assessment-Multiplier and Regulations for Ejecting Nonfunctioning Team Members techniques we describe above.

CONCLUDING REMARKS

The main contribution of this chapter was to relate our experiences - what works and what doesn't, and discuss our experiences in relation to those of other educators. We detailed future trends in software engineering education at the discipline level (SWEBOK, SE2004, licensing, etc.) and novel approaches by individual educators in realizing practice-based experiences into the software engineering education process.

We reported on our successes and failures with UConn's Capstone Project-Based Laboratory, CSE293, with related experiences in similar courses at USNA. We found that team-oriented project-based software engineering capstone courses such as CSE293 provide a nearly ideal opportunity to assess the attainment of program outcomes in a manner that greatly facilitates the process of continuous evaluation. However, since such courses can be used to assess attainment of so many program outcomes, we have identified steps that can be taken to ensure that faculty teaching such courses are not overburdened with assessment data collection for either ABET-related or university-wide requirements.

We examined our development of a set of core capstone-oriented assignments for CSE293 to help standardize the capstone experience from semester to semester. Such core assignments must be developed with enough versatility in the course to allow instructors to add to and otherwise customize the course based on the particular instructor's background and preferences. Additionally, standardized core assignments can also contribute to the continuous improvement process required of accredited programs.

We discussed our experiences with various team sizes, and conclude that a targeted team size of four to six students provides suitable proportions with which to support appropriately scoped semester-long projects, withstand unforeseen team member losses, support confidential, and useful, peer evaluations and ensure that sufficient intra-team communication complexities are experienced by the team members.

In terms of project selection, we found that student-selected, instructor-scoped projects that involve well-known or emerging technologies work well. However, team members must conceptually buy-in to the basis behind the specific project proposed. Also, the team must take steps to avoid becoming constrained by commercially promised future software releases in order to complete their project. We have shown that year-long (as opposed to single-semester) inter-disciplinary capstone projects can work. We have discussed steps that can be taken concurrently across the involved departments to ensure that software and hardware being developed in different locations by different team subsets can be integrated at appropriate intervals throughout the year. Further, the design of software developed for such projects benefits from having paid careful attention to design reusability in order to gain the flexibility needed to overcome late term integration obstacles.

Key aspects of team-oriented software engineering capstone courses include the need for confidential self and team-member assessments as well as mechanisms for dealing with unco-operative team members. We present a rubric that culminates in a peer-assessment-multiplier for assigning individual student grades for team projects. We have shown how this multiplier can be used to reallocate a team's final project grade so that the peer-assessed hardest working team members are recognized, while also fairly dealing with underperforming team members. On very rare occasions, a team may have a team member that severely fails to fulfill his/her responsibilities towards the team project. To mitigate such situations, we presented our ejection regulations technique for empowering teams to handle such situations at the lowest possible level, much as they will need to do in industry.

In terms of future work, at USNA, in addition to our current ABET accredited CS program we have recently developed, offered and successfully undergone a pilot accreditation of our Information Technology (IT) program. As of the writing of this chapter there are currently only 5 ABET accredited IT programs in the country. For future offerings of our project-oriented software engineering capstone course, we plan on requiring our CS and IT majors to conduct their capstone projects within mixed teams that include proportionate numbers of both CS and IT majors. We are currently modifying our capstone course to accommodate the mixture of majors, and to ensure that the combined capstone course can provide measurements for the program outcomes assessments required by both programs in a manner similar to that in which CSE293 addresses both CS and CS&E program outcomes assessment.

For CSE293, we have also begun to explore different delivery mechanisms for the course. In an upcoming semester, we will be team teaching the course, with one instructor providing the overall guidance, and splitting the students into three sections (10 students and two teams per instructor) in order to provide more detailed interactions and guidance to each team through more contact hours with the instructor. This will allow one instructor to handle software/database focused projects, one instructor to handle software/web-based projects, and a third instructor to handle network/hardware based projects; each instructor will advise projects that are in their strength area.

Moreover, the CS and CSE students taking the course will be able to obtain advising tailored to their project domain.

REFERENCES

ABET (2007). *Leadership and Quality Assurance in Applied Science, Computing, Engineering, and Technology Education*. Retrieved December 18, 2007, from http://www.abet.org.

Abran, A., & Moore, J. W. (2004). *Guide to the Software Engineering Body of Knowledge*. IEEE Computer Board of Governors. Retrieved December 18, 2007, from ttp://www.swebok.org/

AUVSI (2007). *Association for Unmanned Vehicle Systems International*. Retrieved December 18, 2007, from http://www.auvsi.org.

Bagert, D., & Mengel, S. (2003). Using a Web-Based Project Process Throughout the Software Engineering Curriculum. *Proceedings of 25th International Conference on Software Engineering, ICSE 2003*, pp. 634-640.

Bagert, D. (2004). SEER: Charting a Roadmap for Software Engineering Education. *Proceedings of 17th Conference on Software Engineering Education and Training, CSEET 2004*, pp. 158-161.

Beck, K. (1999). Embracing Change with Extreme Programming, *IEEE Computer* 32(10), pp. 70-77.

Bernhart, M., Grechenig, T., Hetzl, J., & Zuser, W. (2006). Dimensions of Software Engineering Course Design. *Proceedings of 28th International Conference on Software Engineering, ICSE 2006*. pp. 667-672.

Boehm, B., Kaiser, G., & Port, D. (2000) A Combined Curriculum Research and Curriculum Development Approach for Software Engineering Education, *Conference on Software Engineering Education and Training*, 2000, p. 310.

Brooks, F. (1987). No Silver Bullet, *IEEE Computer* 20(4), pp. 10-19.

Brooks, F. (1995). *The Mythical Man-Month*, 2nd edition, Addison-Wesley Professional.

Chrisman, C., & Beccue, B. (1987) Evaluating students in system development group projects. *SIGCSE-Bulletin*, 19(1): pp. 366–373, 1987.

Clark, N., Davies, P., & Skeers, R. (2005). Self and Peer Assessment in Software Engineering Projects. *Proceedings of 7th Australasian Computing Education Conference, ACE 2005*, pp. 91-100.

Daigle, R. & Niccolai, M. (1997). Inter-Class Synergy by Design. In *Proceedings of the SIGCSE Conference on Computer Science Education (SIGCSE '97)*. New York, NY: ACM Press, pp. 92-95.

Ellis, H., & Mitchell, R. (2004). Self-Grading in a Project-Based Software Engineering Course. *Proceedings of 17th Conference on Software Engineering Education and Training, CSEET 2004*, pp. 138-143.

Fenwick, J., & Kurtz, B. (2005). Intra-curriculum software engineering education. *Proceedings of the 36th SIGCSE Technical Symposium on Computer Science Education, SIGCSE 2005*, pp. 540-544.

Flener, P. (2006). Realism in Project-Based Software Engineering Courses: Rewards, Risks, and Recommendations. *Proceedings. of 21st International Symposium on Computer and Information Sciences, ISCIS 2006*, pp. 1031-1039.

Ghezzi, C., Jazayeri, M., & Mandrioli, D. (2002). *Fundamentals of Software Engineering*. 2nd edition, Prentice Hall.

Ghezzi, C., & Mandrioli, D. (2005). The Challenges of Software Engineering Education. *Proceedings of 27th International Conference on Software Engineering, ICSE 2005*, pp. 637-638.

Hazeyama, A. (2005). State of the Survey on Team-based Software Engineering Project Course. *Proceedings of the 17th International Conference on Software Engineering and Knowledge Engineering, SEKE 2005*, pp. 430-435.

Last, M., Hause, L., Daniels, M., & Woodroffe, M. (2002). Learning from Students: Continuous Improvement in International Collaboration. *Proceedings of the Conference Integrating Technology into Computer Science Education, ITiCSE 2002*. ACM Press, New York, NY, pp. 136-140.

LeBlanc, R., & Sobel, A. (2004). Software Engineering 2004 Curriculum Guidelines for Undergraduate Degree Programs in *Software Engineering*, ACM, 2004. Retrieved December 18, 2007 from http://sites.computer.org/ccse/.

Meyer, B. (2001). Software Engineering in the Academy, *Computer*, 34(5), pp. 28-35.

Naur, P., Randell, B., & Buxton, J. (Eds.). (1976). *Software Engineering: Concepts and Techniques: Proceedings of the NATO Conferences*, Petrocelli-Charter, New York.

Needham, D. (2005). Interdisciplinary Teams for Software System Development. *Proceedings of the 2005 International Conference on Frontiers in Education: Computer Science & Computer Engineering, FECS 2005*, pp. 10-16.

Polack-Wahl, J. (2006). Lessons Learned From Different Types of Projects in Software Engineering. *Proceedings of the 2006 International Conference on Frontiers in Education: Computer Science & Computer Engineering, FECS 2006*, pp. 258-263.

Scott, T., Bisland, R., Tiehenor, L., & Cross, J. (1994). Team Dynamics in Student Programming Projects. *SIGCSE Bulletin* 26(1), pp. 111-115.

Shaw, M., Software Engineering Education: A Roadmap. *International Conference of Software Engineering - Future of SE Track, ICSE 2000*, pp. 371-380.

Simmons, D. (2006). Software Engineering Education in the New Millennium. *Proceedings of 30th Annual International Computer Software and Applications Conference, COMPSAC 2006*, pp. 46-47.

Thompson, J., & Edwards, H. (2006). Bridging the University/Industry Gap. *Proceedings of 28th International Conference on Software Engineering, ICSE 2006*, pp. 1011-1012.

van der Duim, L., Andersson J., & Sinnema M. (2007). Good Practices for Educational Software Engineering Projects. *Proceedings of 29th International Conference on Software Engineering, ICSE 2007*, pp. 698-707.

van Vliet, H. (2005). Some Myths of Software Engineering Education. *Proceedings of 27th International Conference on Software Engineering, ICSE 2005*, pp. 621-622.

van Vliet, H. (2006). Reflections on Software Engineering Education. *IEEE Software*, 24(3), pp. 55-61.

Wilkins, D., & Lawhead, P. (2000). Evaluating individuals in team projects. *SIGCSE-Bulletin*, 32(1), pp. 172–175.

Section V
Educational Technology

Chapter XI
Applying Blended Learning in an Industrial Context:
An Experience Report

Christian Bunse
International University in Germany, Germany

Christian Peper
Fraunhofer Institute Experimental Software Engineering, Germany

Ines Grützner
Fraunhofer Institute Experimental Software Engineering, Germany

Silke Steinbach-Nordmann
Fraunhofer Institute Experimental Software Engineering, Germany

ABSTRACT

With the rapid rate of innovation in software engineering, teaching and learning of new technologies have become challenging issues. The provision of appropriate education is a key prerequisite for benefiting from new technologies. Experience shows that typical classroom education is not as effective and efficient as it could be. E-learning approaches seem to be a promising solution but e-learning holds problems such as a lack of social communication or loose control on learning progress. This chapter describes a blended learning approach that mixes traditional classroom education with e-learning and that makes use of tightly integrated coaching activities. The concrete effects and enabling factors of this approach are discussed by means of an industrial case study. The results of the study indicate that following a blended learning approach has a positive impact on learning time, effectiveness and sustainability.

INTRODUCTION

Today, software systems are available for almost all aspects of human life, ranging from household appliances to transportation/logistics, communication and health. Although, this is good with respect to effort and costs, at the same time it increases the need for high quality systems. But, the development of high-quality software systems requires well-trained professionals using sophisticated tools and techniques. Unfortunately, transferring new techniques and tools from research into industrial practice is not easy. It may take years for a new, promising and even proven idea to become accepted as standard industrial practice. Software developers and organizations are regularly faced with technology decisions concerning the adoption of technology. Thus, technology adaptation and introduction requires adequate training (Lutz 2007), especially concerning development methodology and quality management.

Typically, the demand for training is based on the job- and activity profile of employees (i.e., developers are trained in technologies they are going to apply in their projects) or on the requirements of the applied curricula. Building a training program on the actual needs and requirements of its participants is a step into the right direction, since this overcomes the problems typically associated with static training programs concerning flexibility, timeliness, etc. (Singh 2003). However, even the most flexible training program (wrt. content) is of limited value if its transfer methodology (i.e., how the training should be performed) is not adapted in a way that ensures maximum sustainability.

According to (Wills 2006), "traditional" strategies, using classrooms and technology and topic experts (e.g., professionals or professors) are in broad use. Unfortunately, these strategies are not only cost- but also time-intensive. While this might be acceptable in a university context, companies, especially small and medium-sized enterprises that have tight development schedules and short software release rates, cannot afford such trainings. Developers participating in traditional training programs are not able to develop software at the same time (i.e., reduction of development time). E-learning has been advertised as one solution for this problem by allowing and actively supporting education at any time and at any place.

E-learning, which requires initial investments for preparing training media, is not "cheap". Companies offering such training activities therefore have to acquire a large audience in order to obtain a positive return on investment (Ochs & Pfahl 2002). However, a large audience bears the danger of generalization (i.e., the training material is not adapted towards the specific situation of its participants) and lacks in social communication (i.e., learning in isolation) (Stark & Schmidt 2002). Communication problems might be mitigated by providing online support, guidance, and discussion facilities, although these require extra resources and effort and thus, increase the need for an even larger audience. Another problem associated with large audiences is the varying level of experience and background knowledge of its participants (i.e., heterogeneity) (Bunse, Grützner, Peper & Steinbach-Nordmann 2005). Thus, cost efficiency and large audiences are like chasing one's own tail.

Traditional and e-learning both have their strengths and weaknesses. Combining them in so- called blended learning arrangements may outweigh the negative effects of both approaches, conserve the positive effects, and may even add additional value. Based on practical observations and experience with both "traditional" and e-learning, we propose a blended learning approach (Bunse, Grützner, Peper & Steinbach-Nordmann 2005) that mixes traditional classes and e-learning: E-learning is used to leverage knowledge and skills in the very beginning, followed by in-depth seminars for teaching advanced concepts as well as for performing group work, and practical exercises.

One important goal for developing and applying our approach has been the assurance of sustainable learning effects (Asian Development Bank 1997). In other areas of education and training (e.g., soft skills), coaching is an often used means for addressing this problem. Coaching is a technique for observing the current functioning, assessing the strengths and weaknesses, and developing measures for addressing needed changes. Transferred to the domain of technology education, coaching has to be integrated into the daily work of the trainees (i.e., be workflow-oriented) in order to obtain significant improvements. Therefore, our blended learning approach is enriched by a subsequent, workflow-oriented coaching process. To obtain evidence on the practicability and effectiveness of our approach, it has been applied in industrial training projects. The results show that especially its adaptivity towards the needs of participants and the coaching aspects are the most prominent benefits as perceived by the participants.

The remainder of this chapter is structured as follows. Section two introduces our blended learning strategy for teaching object-oriented development with UML. Section three describes major rationales for the product structure derived from market trends. Section four describes already existing experience on using our strategy in various application areas (e.g., for training students and professionals). In addition, it analyzes the effects of our approach on an objective basis and discusses how blended learning can improve software engineering education. Section five discusses the latest trend and directions in software engineering education. Finally, Section six provides a short summary and some conclusions.

BLENDED LEARNING IN SOFTWARE ENGINEERING EDUCATION

In general, blended learning uses a mixture of various teaching methods and media, to "get the right content in the right format to the right people at the right time". It therefore combines multiple delivery methods that complement each other (Singh 2003). As stated by the American Management Association (AMA), it "integrates seemingly opposite approaches … in order to achieve individual and organization (learning) goals". Besides traditional classroom trainings, possible elements of the blend include e-learning

modules and components (for example, assessments, simulations, resource collections, or online workbooks), virtual collaboration means (like email, communities of practice, online meetings, or e-mentoring facilities), or face-to-face methods (e.g., workshops, assignments for project team work, or coaching) (Rossett & Vaughan Frazee 2006, Singh 2003). With its advantages, especially in the field of (social) interaction and learning organization, the blended learning approach is increasingly penetrating teaching practice at universities (Jones & Northrop 2006a), training providers (Jones & Northrop 2006b), and industry (Lutz 2007 and Heidecke, Mayrhofer, Schiesser & Back 2007). Interestingly, there is a great variety concerning the methods applied in these domains. Methods range from educational games (Jain & Boehm, 2006), writing about a topic (Wang & Sorensen 2006), case studies (Burge & Troy 2006), project work (Frailey 2006) to simulations (Ubal, Cano, Petit & Sahuquillo 2006 as well as Fetaji & Fetaji 2006).

Interestingly, blended learning helps to overcome obstacles that prevent companies from using e-learning approaches to train their employees. According to market studies on e-learning potential (e.g. Ochs & Pfahl, 2002), the five most important resistance factors concerning e-learning are:

1. Insufficient qualification of personnel for e-learning-related tasks,
2. Low quality of the used software systems,
3. the overall quality of e-learning tools is seen to be unsatisfactory,
4. Existing tools are too expensive, and
5. The quality of contents is often seen to be inadequate to meet specific needs.

In addition, the study predicted an increased mid-term (i.e., 1-2 years, thus at present!) demand for service categories centered on e-learning (i.e., 43% for Web-based training, 61% for Web-based tutoring, and 58% for Web-based cooperative learning and problem solving).

Interestingly, the powers of resistance seem to be eliminated by blended learning programs, since these offer classroom trainings that fit exactly to the working context of the participants. An additional factor in this regard is that blended learning approaches (at least those presented in this chapter) allow using e-learning elements without requiring a special management system hosted on the training organization's platform. The increase in quality and thus, the mitigation of risk factors, is also indicated in the context of industrial case studies (i.e., successful certification of participants).

In summary, blended learning seems to be a valid approach for conducting effective and efficient trainings with sustainable effects. The blended learning approach presented in this chapter is based on the definition given in (Singh & Reed 2001): "Blended learning focuses on optimizing achievement of learning objectives by applying the "right" learning technologies to match the "right" personal learning style to transfer the "right" skills to the "right" person at the "right" time." This definition focuses on the learning objective and on the fact that many different personal learning styles need to be supported to reach a broad audience.

Ferreira, Fonseca, d'Alge and Montiero (2002) and Höhle and Cho (2000) have looked extensively into distance learning and how these courses are received and studied by their participants. They suggest that experience made in pure distance learning can be taken and applied to onsite combined learning courses, as that presented in this chapter. Following (Mühlhauser 2002) our approach is based on material that is used, updated and, most importantly of all, educates.

Our approach is based on standard definitions and approaches however the most important question is what are the concrete effects when applying the approach and what are its enabling factors. Thus, empirical evidence is needed.

Interestingly, previous research on case studies has not focused on blended learning (Solberg Søilen 2007). (Yildiz & Chang 2003) conclude that Web-based courses tend to be "richer and of more quality" than regular class room education. In contrast, (Mikulecky 1998) observed that students were able to generate more thoughtful responses in Web-based courses. Following (Solberg Søilen 2007) the three forms of interaction: learner-instructor, learner-content and learner-learner interaction are involved in interactive and blended learning. The case study presented in (Solberg Søilen 2007) confirms the importance of the interaction the student has with teacher and other student in addition to distance or e-learning. Our study supports this too and indicates that blended learning has a positive impact on learning time and, due to the integrated coaching measures, supports effective learning with sustainable results.

TEACHING OO-DEVELOPMENT WITH UML IN A BLENDED LEARNING APPROACH

Blended learning is a promising approach to facilitate software engineering education, given the need for training-on-the-job, the rapid change of technologies, and the diversity of application domains. In this section, we describe the application or instantiation of the general blended learning approach towards model-based and object-oriented development with UML.

Object-orientation and UML were chosen as training topics due to the growing popularity and distribution of the paradigm and its associated technologies in large parts of industry. Thus, in detail, there is a need for systematic education concerning sound OO analysis, design, and programming, as well as for model-based specifications and architectures using UML. Interestingly, the trend towards requesting e-learning facilities is increasing in parallel. This motivated the development of an integrated product known as "Blended learning OO & UML", which has already been successfully applied in academic and professional education.

In general, as discussed and outlined in section 2, blended learning proposes a mixture of learning activities comprising self-steered learning activities, cooperative and collaborative learning activities, learning activities supported by online tutors, social learning activities, and traditional classroom teaching activities. The approach has to address all these elements but, at the same time, needs to be flexible and adaptable towards different context requirements. This is comparable to the situation of software engineering technologies, which are unlikely to be transferred into practice in a monolithic style.

In summary, our approach establishes four modular learning product levels (see Figure 1). Each level integrates the respective lower level and supplements it with new activities in the teaching process. This modularity provides a maximum of flexibility for the design of educational programs and assures optimal appropriateness for the learners in specific programs. The following table (Table 1) provides a detailed description of each product level.

In general, the different program modules can be independently applied in concrete training activities. Since there are no silver-bullets, especially not in engineering education, simply using a pre-defined learning program or module will hinder obtaining sustainable effects. To create such effects, a program or module must thus be individually adapted to various context factors such as application domain (e.g., domain-specific examples and best-practices), skill level, etc. However, adaptation is neither easy nor cheap (e.g., adapting e-learning courses requires significant effort). Therefore, we defined in general that adaptation will focus on the classroom training aspects and use a standard e-learning course for creating a common understanding of the participants. The training material used in classroom training uses different modules that can be individually combined and/or exchanged. Thus, context-specific modules can be simply plugged into the training material. The underlying strategy (e-learning followed by classroom activities) requires the definition of a standard schema for actually conducting the training.

Figure 2 depicts the standard schema defined in the context of OO&UML. The schema transports the various contents of the product levels

Figure 1. Product levels

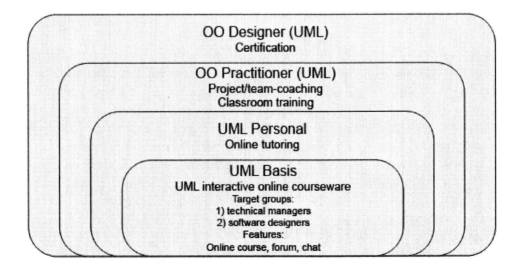

Table 1. Description of the product levels

Levels of the learning product	Description
UML Basis	"UML Basis", located at the lowest level, is centered around two Web-based trainings (WBT's), which target different groups: (1) "UML Interactive for Technical Managers" presents information on the origins, characteristics, and advantages of UML. It also presents a short overview of the different UML diagrams and available tool support. It enables the learner to make a decision concerning the use of UML in upcoming development. (2) "UML Interactive for Software Designers" provides additional learning content to enable learners to develop UML diagrams with good quality. Both WBTs are supported by an Internet forum granting synchronous and asynchronous communication opportunities. Here learners can ask questions or chat / discuss with peers.
UML Personal	"UML Personal" resides at the second level. In addition to "UML Basis", it provides support by online tutors. Tutors answer subject matter and organizational questions. In an extended version of the tutoring activities, tutors provide feedback on practical exercises That simulate real working tasks. They represent the third stage of knowledge transfer (i.e., in addition to examples and self-tests in the WBTs). Thus, tutors are able to evaluate acquired knowledge and skills as well as the individual learning behavior.
OO Practitioner (UML)	Learning activities added at the third level, "OO Practitioner (UML)", are classroom trainings and project coaching. Classroom trainings provide several topics from the field of object-oriented analysis, design, and implementation, and intensify object-oriented concepts, e.g., through exercises from the learners' application context. Topics are identified in advance, together with learners and their superiors. Subsequent to classroom trainings, project coaching (also known as action-learning) is offered. During the coaching phase, learners apply their acquired knowledge and skills in a real-world project supported by experts.
OO Designer (UML)	"OO Designer (UML)", at the top level, adds certification of learning activities. During certification, the learner has to either solve a complex exercise together with a peer or work on a long-term project within a team. Results are presented to and discussed with the tutors. Certification topics belong to the daily working routine of the learners.

to the learners. In the first phase, the educational program is designed and organized, integrating a detailed analysis of the learner's skills, educational needs, and learning environment. The method used to analyze these fields is the skill profiling and analysis method "QUALISEM-People"(de Haan, Waterson, Trapp & Pfahl, 2003), which assures that the content and instructional strategy of the program are defined based on objective information. This aims at increasing the acceptance level and thus the effectiveness of the learning program by satisfying objectively identified training needs. In the second phase, the educational program is launched. It starts with a kick-off workshop, which aims at learners as well as tutors getting to know each other and at explaining the organization of the program to the learners. This is followed by the online phase, in which the learners work with a Web-based training course of the UML Basis or the UML Personal level. The goal of the online learning phase is to reach an equal level of knowledge regarding the UML notation. This is a prerequisite for efficient teaching sessions in the subsequent classroom trainings, because the trainer can then concentrate on providing detailed advanced knowledge, such as object-oriented analysis, design, and programming from the product level OO Practitioner (UML). In the third phase, the knowledge acquired is transferred into practice. That is, the learners perform an object-oriented software development project. The tutors, now acting as coaches, support them in their efforts following the principles of scaffolding und fading. Eventually, the acquired knowledge is certified as having reached the highest product and thus education level OO Designer (UML).

OBSERVATIONS AND EXPERIENCES IN AN INDUSTRIAL SETTING

The blended learning approach presented here has been successfully tested both in academia and in industry and several experience reports have been published (Grützner & Bunse, 2002; Grützner, Steinbach-Nordmann, Ochs, & Bunse 2003; Bunse, Grützner, Peper, & Steinbach-Nordmann, 2005). With the intention of improving the blended learning arrangements and matching the industrial training programs with the needs of the participants, continuous evaluation was established. Concurrent to these evaluation activities, participants were questioned about their individual learning needs, their learning behavior, and their learning preferences. The questioning was divided into a pre-questionnaire (before the online learning in Phase I started) and a post-questionnaire at the end of Phase II.

Schedule of the Training Program

The blended learning approach had to be adapted to match the organizational needs of the enterprises. The education material for the workshops was adapted to match the specific needs of the domains and (as far as possible) the experience of the participants. For this purpose, the enterprises made some real-world material (documentations, source code, etc.) available that represented the specific application domain of the enterprise's business area. The course was concluded by a certification day where a complex and domain-specific exercise had to be autonomously solved by the participants in two- or three-person teams. All participants were still granted access to the online course after having finished the training part.

The Set-Up of the Case Study

To evaluate the impact and acceptance of the applied blended learning approach, we started some data collecting. We did not intend to test specified research hypotheses, but wanted to know more about the learning needs and preferences of the participants and how the training program could be improved.

In particular, we were looking for answers to the following questions:

Pre-Questionnaire:

(Q1) What are the individual starting points of participants regarding the training (e.g. experiences with UML, motivation, expectations, and individual time schedules)?

Figure 2. Product levels and phases

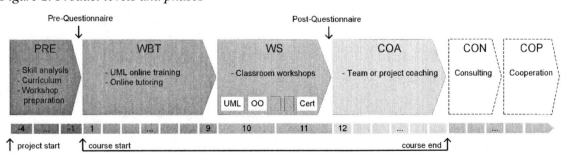

(Q2) How do participants prefer to learn?

Post-Questionnaire:

(Q3) How do participants evaluate the training measure and its elements (e.g., WBT, classroom training, training materials, and exercises)?

(Q4) How did participants use the Web-based training? Was it possible to integrate learning and working?

The pre-questionnaire preceded the training program and aimed at the collection of learning needs, preferences, and expectations regarding the upcoming training phase (cf. Table 2). The post-questionnaire was provided to the learners at the end of the certification day (cf. Table 3).

All participants were invited to fill out an on-line-questionnaire (see Table 2) at the beginning of Phase I (pre) and another printout questionnaire (see Table 3) at the end of Phase II (post).

Results of the Case Studies

A total of 42 employees (software developers, managers, persons in charge) at the age of 20-49 years attended the training program.

Group line-up of participants in the blended learning training in the industrial case study:

- **43% Software Developers** (others e.g., mechanical engineers)
- **85.71%** male
- range of age:
  - 20 - 29 years (28.6%)
  - **30 - 39 years (35.71%)**
  - 40 - 49 years (28.6%)

(missing to 100: no entry)

The return rate of questionnaires (28 pre/38 post) was quite satisfying, although the quantity of data and the group line-up do not allow any empirical generalization. Nevertheless, the results of the evaluation might give some interesting insights into the needs and expectations of learners and the usage of different elements of blended learning in an industrial context.

Pre-Questionnaire (N=28)

(Q1) What are the individual starting points of participants regarding the training?

Asked about the importance of a training program on object-oriented software development with UML for their future project work, almost half of the participants (48 %) replied that it is urgent to learn more about UML. Furthermore, asked about their individual goals and expectations concerning the training program (open question), the vast majority of answers provided (80%) could be summarized as 'be able to apply UML in future projects actively'.

When the participants were asked which element of the blended learning approach they would expect most of, they referred to classroom training, coaching, and the WBT in descending order.

When asked about which learning mode is most effective in their point of view, the participants decided in favor of more or less informal communication with their peers. Nearly at the same high level was classroom training involving a tutor who is also available after the training as a project coach (see Figure 5).

(Q2) How do participants prefer to learn? How do they integrate working and learning?

Except for one person, none of the participants (97.3%) had any experiences with any kind of e-learning resp. online training.

Post-Questionnaire (N=38)

Table 2. Pre-questionnaire: Prerequisites and learning needs

Question		Options
I. Personal Data		
1.1	Sex	*Male/Female*
1,2	Age	*<20, 20-29, 30-39, 40-49 years, 50-59, >60*
1.3	Position in company	*free text*
II. Individual Situation		
2.1	Which experience do you already have in working with UML?	*- None* *- I can understand some types of diagrams* *- I can understand all types of diagrams* *- I can create some types of diagrams* *- I can create all types of diagrams*
2.2	How urgently do you need the contents of the continuing education course for your daily work?	*(1) very urgently … (6) not at all*
2.3	How much time do you plan to invest into working with the Web-based Training "UML for Design Engineers"?	*Hours per week*
2.4	Do you expect that the work with the Web-based Training "UML for Design Engineers" can be integrated into your current daily work schedule?	*(1) well … (6) badly*
III. Advance Evaluation of the Continuing Education Course		
3.1	What is your personal goal for participating in the entire continuing education course?	*free text*
3.2	What are your expectations regarding the entire continuing education course?	*free text*
3.3	Which part of the continuing education course do you expect to be most beneficial for you?	*WBT, On-site training, Coaching*
IV. Media/Computer Usage Preferences		
4.1	What do you use the computer for (at work and at home)? <Information>, <Communication>, <Programming>, <Games>, <Entertainment>, <Continuing Education>, <Other>	*(1) very often … (6) very rarely*
4.2	Which type of e-learning programs do you already have experience with?	*- CBT (Computer-based training)* *- WBT (Web-based training)* *- E-Workshop* *- Professional online communities (newsgroups, blogs ....)* *- Other*
4.3	Which positive aspects do you associate with e-learning? (Please also answer this question if you have no experience yet with e-learning. The issue is your assessment at this point in time.)	*free text*
4.4	Which negative aspects do you associate with e-learning?	*free text*
V. Personal Learning Preferences		
5.1	What do you think are the best ways you can learn new, complex information? <By reading>, <By listening>, <Illustrated by images /graphics/animations>, <By acting>	*(1) best … (6) least*
5.2	What is your personal best way to obtain continuing education? <On-site training with trainer>, <Professional book>, <Journals, papers>, <Electronic learning material>, <Own research on WWW>, <Professional discussion/informal exchange with colleagues>	*(1) best … (6) least*

Table 3. Post-questionnaire: Assessment of satisfaction and learning behavior

Question	Options
Learning Behavior	
1. How much time did you invest into working with the Web-based Training (WBT)?	- More than planned - As planned - Less than planned - I did not plan any time period in advance
If you invested more or less time, what do you think are the reasons for this?	free text
2. How well were you able to integrate working with the WBT into your daily work?	Well, Not so well, Rather badly, Badly
Which factors were particularly beneficial, respectively detrimental, in this regard?	free text
3. How did you mostly work with the WBT? Please characterize your personal leaning situation with the help of the following categories (several answers are possible).	Online version, Printed version, At work, At home, On the road, During working hours, During spare time
Remarks	free text
Post-Evaluation of Education Course (Phase I-II)	
4. Which part of the continuing education course has fulfilled your expectations and goals best so far?	WBT, On-site training, The combination of WBT and on-site training (Blended Learning)
5. Which part of the continuing education course could you most easily do without?	WBT, On-site phase (training + certification), I don't want to do without anything.
6. How well did the following components of the WBT support you in understanding the study material? <The teaching texts of the WBT><The diagrams of the WBT><The animations of the WBT><The exercises of the WBT>	(1) very well, (2) well ... (6)
7. How well did the following components of the on-site phase support you in understanding the study material? <The explanations of the lecturer> <The presentation slides and the handout> <The exercises adapted to the domain> <Cooperation with colleagues> <The complex task during certification>	(1) very well, (2) well ... (6)
8. Has your basic attitude towards e-learning changed through your work with the WBT?	- No, I continue to think that e-learning is a good thing - No, I still do not think much of e-learning - Yes, it has improved, since: ... - Yes, it has gotten worse, since: ...
Personal Information	
9. Do you want to provide some personal information?	
<Sex> <Age> <Position in company>	Male, Female <20, 20-29, 30-39, 40-49 years, 50-59, >60 free text

(Q3) How do participants evaluate the training measure and its elements (e.g., WBT, classroom training, training materials, exercises)?

In the second questionnaire, the participants regarded classroom training as the most important learning mode in the blended learning program.

To explore which element of the training program did support their individual learning process most effectively, participants were asked to evaluate each element on a scale from 1 (= very good) to 6 (= inadequate).

When evaluating the elements of **Classroom Training,** participants were most satisfied with:

- Trainer instructions (1.6)
- Collaboration with colleagues (2)
- Domain-specific exercises (2.5)
- Training materials (2.7)

When evaluating the elements of **Web-based Training,** participants were most satisfied with:

- Illustrations (1.6)
- Texts (1.8)
- Exercises (2.1)
- Animations (2.1)

After the training, most of the participants (85 %) did not consider any of the parts dispensable.

The evaluation of training elements proves, that the existing learning preferences and habits of participants (classroom training and discussion with colleagues) lead to correspondent evaluation results: What was expected to be most effective before the training started was evaluated as the most effective way to learn after the training. But e-learning as the new learning mode seems to be highly accepted, too. The good evaluation of the Web-based training elements and the fact that none of the training parts is considered dispensable suggest that participants look at e-learning as a valuable addition to training. The latter also suggests that e-learning is not considered as a stand-alone training mode, but blended learning is an appreciated approach from the learners' point of view.

Figure 3. Perceived effectiveness of ways to learn (pre-questionnaire)

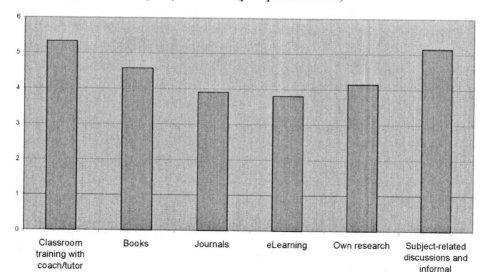

(Q4) How did participants use the Web-based training? Was it possible to integrate learning and working?

In an industrial training program, the participants are usually employees of an enterprise and have to continue their normal work during the course. Depending on the situation, it can be important not to disturb or interrupt a certain core working time. Therefore, the training program was designed with a Web-based training phase aimed at enabling learners to organize their learning activities in a flexible and individual way. Small learning units and the individual choice of content and learning time should guarantee that learning could be integrated more easily into day-to-day work than fixed training schedules. The estimated learning time for the whole Web-based training was 30-35 hours per participant. For evaluation purposes, it was of interest whether the estimated time slot was sufficient and whether participants were able to integrate working and learning activities.

When asked about their actual effort spent on the learning program compared to the estimated effort (30-35 hours), most of the participants answered that they spent less time than planned, nobody spent more time than planned, and five persons did not plan and, as a consequence, were not aware of time while learning (see Table 4).

The reasons for spending less time on learning were given in a freely edited list (open question):

- time pressure
- higher priorities (day-to-day business)
- skipping of redundancies
- waiving of well-known content
- supervisors restricted time resources

The success of integrating working and learning during the training was evaluated as very good by more than half of the participants. Three persons each evaluated the integration as poor, resp. really bad (see Table 5).

In an open question, participants were asked to name the reasons that encouraged resp. disabled the integration of working and learning activities. Table 6 illustrates which positive and negative influence factors were considered as positive resp. negative from the learners´ point of view.

The fact that the effort spent was less than planned, that the integration of learning and working was evaluated very positive, and the list of named influence factors suggest, that the concept of the blended learning program (modularity, small units, flexibility of time and space) supports the integration of learning activities into daily routines and tasks. All negative influence factors mentioned are environmental aspects, which have to be improved or optimized by measurements at the working place itself.

E-learning is often believed to happen in an employee's spare time. The results of the case study show that this assumption was not verified in our context (see Table 7). The participants learned predominantly at the work place during working hours in an online mode. Only six persons learned at home, 3 persons learned during their spare time, and nobody chose the opportunity of mobile learning. It is remarkable that more than 40% used the print-out version of the Web-based training (text + graphics). This effect may be explained by learners´ habits: Most of them responded in the pre-questionnaire that they consider reading journals and books the most effective way of learning.

Even though learning took place at work during working hours, learning did not conflict with day-day-to-tasks and the integration of working and learning was rated as very good. This may be explained by the individual learning schedule of each participant.

In order to get more information about the schedules, the access distribution was analyzed via logfile analysis.

Figure 4 shows the access distribution of the participants, whit the major part of the learning time being scheduled after about 4 p.m. Moreover, most of the time was scheduled on Fridays. Obviously, the flexibility of the online course was, in fact, used to optimize the coexistence of working and learning.

Lessons Learned

The previous section described the participants' experiences with the course. We will now switch to the perspective of the provider and discuss some qualitative experiences collected during (and further) case studies.

As argued, the adaptation of the workshop exercises and examples to a specific domain is an important success factor (keep in mind that the domain-specific exercises have been rated higher than all other training materials (Q3)). It is in the interest of both enterprise and teacher to keep effort and cost for this task as low as possible. In all previous projects, it was possible to agree on a certain effort for the adaptation, which was supported by suitable material from the enterprises. For a reasonable adaptation, some prerequisites turned out to be important: (a) The tutor preparing the material must be able to handle the application domain. This requirement is not trivial, because often a complete reverse engineering of the material has to be done: Often, you can only expect to be provided with C/Java source code or some textual documentation, from which a partial UML model has to be derived. (b) The

Table 4. Effort spent on the learning programme

More than planned	As planned	Less than planned	Did not plan
0 0%	8 21.0%	24 63.2%	5 13.1%

missing.: 1 (2.7%)

Table 5. Integration of learning and working activities

very good	ok	poor	really bad
20 52.6%	11 28.9%	3 7.9%	3 7.9%

missing.: 1 (2.7%)

Table 6. Factors influencing the integration of learning and working activities

Positive factors	Negative factors
- modularity of learning units - small units - commitment of supervisor - flexibility - homework	- noise, interruptions - day-to-day-business, short-term tasks - lack of organization (help needed) - slow data transfer - no Internet access

contact person in the enterprise should be able to select proper sources, i.e., he should already have some experience with the contents taught. (c) The participants should have enough time to become familiar with the selected original material.

The main target of an industrial technology transfer project is to provide the employees of an enterprise with the ability to apply certain knowledge to a given problem. In practice, the exact identification of the knowledge content and its application modalities are not as clear as might be expected.

The first reason for this is found in the different views of the involved people. We distinguish three roles in the context of an industrial project: Management is normally the project initiator and willing to invest into employees' education to achieve higher productivity. Therefore, it generally has high expectations concerning the outcome of the project. These might include increased usage of a certain technique or an expensive tool. The employees typically have different prior

experience and motivation in dealing with the new technology. Therefore, they often expect greatly different information from the knowledge content offered. The coach has to communicate this content to the employees, and keep in touch with management. Since management view and employee view usually differ, the coach becomes a moderator between these two parties. This also applies to the mediation between competitive groups of employees. Additionally, he might have his own academic interest, e.g., introducing a specific method, etc.

The second reason for the uncertainty regarding the content is the change of evidence over time. All project participants gain experience during the project. Therefore, the focus can move to knowledge details, which have turned out to be important for a successful application but were considered at the beginning.

In the blended learning approach we can distinguish several phases of project work: the self-organized occupation with the courseware or

Table 7. Learning with the Web based training

Where and how do participants learn with the Web-based training?	Responses (multiple answers)	
at work	29	(76.3%)
during working hours	28	(73.7%)
online	24	(63.1%)
print version (.pdf)	16	(42.1%)
at home	6	(15.8%)
spare time	3	(7.9%)
mobile	0	(0%)

Figure 4. Access distribution of participants as an indicator of online learning time

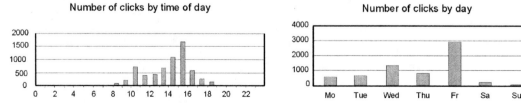

WBT (WBT), the classroom training workshops (WS), the coaching phase (COA), the consulting phase (CON), and the cooperation phase (COP). Some exemplary durations and coaching efforts for the first phases are shown in Figure 5a).

Figure 5b) also reflects the typical evolution of some characteristic parameters over the project's runtime (so far without empirical evidence). The bold curve shows how the main target, i.e., the ability of knowledge application, starts with some prior experience. This is improved by the WBT and workshops WS up to a sound and comparable, but theoretical knowledge level. It is subsequently transferred into practice by coaching (COA) and consulting (CON). Finally, it reaches a level of saturation. The project in this phase rather becomes a problem-oriented cooperation (COP) than a regular part of an education. The dashed line shows the accumulated project costs, which are also low at the beginning (only WBT licenses) and then increase because of the personnel-intensive workshops and coaching/consulting phases. Ideally, target and cost functions develop in the same way, so that all participants have a good feeling about the invested money and effort. When the costs continue to grow although the target function reaches the saturation level, consulting turns into cooperation and the education program can be declared as finished.

Scalability is one of the main advantages of the presented blended learning approach. It results directly from the close relation between target function and cost: the education can be customized to the enterprise's needs and financial situation simply by finishing the project after any phase. This design allows to initially agree on a small project containing only the early phases and to extend the project by additional phases if necessary and economically feasible. Thus, the early phases can work as a door opener for the consulting phase or even subsequent applied research projects.

There are some further aspects of a blended learning project that are important success factors and basically behave in a similar way: The social integration of the coach into the enterprise community is a prerequisite for the smooth transport of knowledge (in Q3, the trainer instructions have been evaluated best). If the coach is not accepted, the project will probably fail. The social integration usually starts at zero and is improved step by step during the use of the WBT (emails, forum), during the workshops (first personal contact), and in coaching meetings (intensive personal contact in small groups). It converges towards a project-specific maximum.

The adaptation of the knowledge content also starts at zero, already increasing a little bit

Figure 5. Expected development of project phases

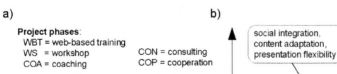
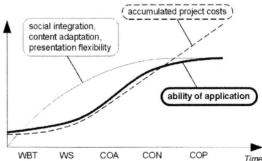

through first forum discussions during the WBT usage. The workshop typically considers domain-specific examples, the coaching introduces some superficial enterprise-specific problems (hours of preparation for the coach), and consulting brings up detailed problems (days of preparation). This ends in the cooperation phase, where the degree of adaptation cannot be further increased. The flexibility of the knowledge presentation is also zero for the WBT, since all material is presented in a standard form. For the workshops, this situation is slightly improved, but the coach still depends on a standard set of presentation slides and exercises. Since the effort available for preparation is significantly higher in subsequent phases, there is also much more room for selecting alternative approaches, discussions, etc.

Recommendations

The evaluations and observations presented in the previous sections can be summarized into several general consequences and recommendations:

- Even though e-learning and Web-based trainings aim to shorten learning time we point out that learning still needs time. This insight should be emphasized towards the enterprise management as often as possible to ensure adequate scheduling of the training.
- Let people choose their own learning mode and learning situation. We assume, that people are interested in flexible learning solutions and that they are capable of adapting a learning program to their individual context constraints in the most appropriate way (time, priorities of tasks).
- Combine e-learning resp. Web-based training with classroom training and coaching. Our experience is that individual learning via media (books, digital content) is an important issue. However, it is very content driven. To learn more about professional methodologies, participants should be en-

abled and encouraged to apply the knowledge they have learned and to learn what the effects in the real world are. This can be done in classroom trainings by using real-world tasks and materials or in real projects with the assistance of a coach.

- A social climate of confidence, with personal relationships between coach and employees (but also between coach and management), is very important. It should be deliberately developed during the project phases, e.g., by the following means:
  - Introduce the coach early, e.g., with personalized kick-off emails or even meetings with the WBT users.
  - Let the same person do the workshop and the subsequent coaching.
  - Do not change coaches.
  - Do not denigrate existing competencies, integrate them.
- The content should be adapted as early as possible. In the best case, you can take a concrete problem from the application environment as a reference example. However, this increases project costs early on.
- Do not stop the project too early, e.g., directly after the WBT. This leaves people alone with the mentioned content and application uncertainty.
- For the same reason, the project targets should be readjusted from time to time. Regular talks with the different participants help to reconcile their interests.
- Identify internal experts who can support and continue the knowledge transfer in the future.

FUTURE TRENDS

Teaching and learning object-oriented and model-based software development is a field in motion with a high innovation rate. Good examples are the recent advent of service orientation (i.e.,

SOA, SAC, SDO, BPEL, etc.) or the continuous evolvement of modeling languages such as UML. Concerning training and education, this creates special requirements. On the one hand, latest developments and findings have to be adequately reflected by constantly evolving training materials. On the other hand, new technologies are slowly penetrating the market, requiring training material for 'older' technologies, too. In the long run, this will definitively increase the size of the training material and will make maintenance a 'nightmare'. This becomes even worse when we think about document formats, multimedia technologies, etc. Interestingly, this is comparable to the situation of software legacy systems. Therefore, technological support is needed for facilitating the task of maintenance and development by providing means for managing complexity.

One idea to address this problem is single-source publishing (e.g., XML based) following a component- or service-oriented approach (i.e., a development methodology for training material). This allows creating individually combinable training modules with pre-defined adaptation spots that can be easily assembled into new trainings programs. Since all modules or documents are represented in a XML-based format, they can be easily mapped to different formats without the need to check for version numbers, operating systems, etc. (Thomas & Ras 2005).

Interestingly, this trend is in line with the technological trends in education in general. Currently, the original idea of e-learning is evolving from simple PowerPoint shows, via interactive training modules, towards collaborative learning and teaching. Major developments in these areas are the use of WIKIS, which allow people to teach each other and to share experience, Podcasts, Weblogs, and virtual learning environments (i.e., following the "Second life" idea). Another trend in this regard are Open Educational Resources and content sharing to make learning material freely available. In summary, it appears that tools to be used by many users without a lot of effort

for developing common solutions are of high importance. Standard authoring tools, although needed, are of less importance.

One reason for the technological developments might be the trend towards collaborative learning using supportive tools such as Weblogs, Wikis, or Communities. Thus, there is a clear trend towards personalized and user-centric learning with a specific focus on active and self-organized learners. At the same time the pressure to develop new learning platform or management systems seems to decrease.

Interestingly, the ideas of viewing the development of training material as a kind of 'engineering process' in order to obtain adaptable trainings combined with means for collaborative learning are already reflected in our blended learning arrangement. Tutoring, group work, online discussion, and coaching provide the basic means for collaborative learning. The modular structure, pre-defined variation points, and other adaptation mechanisms support complexity management and facilitate maintenance. In the future, we will use a single-source publishing approach based on XML technology that is currently being developed (Grützner, Thomas & Steinbach-Nordmann, 2006). This will again reduce maintenance effort and ensure tool/format independence.

SUMMARY AND CONCLUSION

The high innovation rate in software engineering technologies combined with the ever increasing pace of software development projects calls for highly motivated and trained developers. Thus, new and flexible teaching approaches are warranted to ensure effective technology transfer from academia into practice. In other words, training has to be performed in a way that is compatible with modern working styles and adaptable to the actual problem domain, while ensuring sustainable effects.

This chapter introduced a blended learning approach (i.e., a mixture of online training and traditional classroom education) enhanced by tightly integrated coaching activities. This approach was practically applied to train professional software developers in object-oriented software development with UML. In detail, the approach uses online training activities to create a common understanding and knowledge of the technology, classroom trainings for transferring application- and domain-specific knowledge, and coaching to ensure that the recently learned elements are correctly applied.

For successfully applying our approach in practice as well as for supporting others in their decision to adopt our results, it is important to evaluate the concrete effects of the approach and to critically reflect on the enabling factors, i.e., evidence is warranted. The second part of this chapter therefore presented an industrial case study to gain more insights into the learner's expectations, preferences and the integration of working and learning in an industrial setting. The results indicate that following a blended learning approach has a positive impact on learning time and, due to the integrated coaching measures, supports not only effective learning but also sustainable results. However, the limited amount of data-points does not allow generalizing the results. Thus, further additional studies are required.

REFERENCES

Rossett, A. & Vaughan Frazee, R. (2006). Blended Learning Opportunities. AMA Special Report. Retrieved October 24, 2007, from *http://www.amanet.org/blended/pdf/WhitePaper_BlendLearn.pdf*.

Asian Development Bank (1997). *Special Study of the Effectiveness and Impact of Training in Educational Projects*. Technical Report. Special Study Series Number 29), SST:INO 97023.

Burge, J. & Troy, D. (2006). Rising to the Challenge: Using Business-Oriented Case Studies in Software Engineering Education. *Proceedings of the Nineteenth Conference on Software Engineering Education & Training*. Turtle Bay, Hawaii.

Bunse, C., Grützner, I., Peper, C., Steinbach-Nordmann, S. (2005). Applying a Blended Learning Strategy for Software Engineering Education. *Proceedings of the 18th Conference on Software Engineering Education and Training (CSEE&T)*. Ottawa, Canada.

Collins, A., Brown, J. S. & Newman, S. E. (1990). Cognitive apprenticeship: teaching the crafts of reading, writing and mathematics. In: Resnick, L. B. (Ed.). *Knowing, learning and instruction: Essays in honor of Robert Glaser*. Hillsdale, N.J.: Lawrende Erlbaum.

de Haan, D., Waterson, P., Trapp, S. & Pfahl, D. (2003). Integrating needs assessment within next generation e-learning systems: Lessons learnt from a case study. *Proceedings of the IFIP OPEN WORKING CONFERENCE "eTRAIN 2003: E-Training Practices for Professional Organisations"*. Pori, Finland.

Ferreira, H.S., Fonseca, L.M.G., d'Alge, J.C.L., Montiero, A.M.V. (2002). New Approach on Teaching Geotechnology. *International Archives of Photogrammetry and Remote Sensing, and Spatial Information Science* San Jóse dos Campos, Brazil. Vol. XXXIV, Part 6, CVI.

Fetaji, B. & Fetaji, M. (2006). Software Engineering Java Educational Software and its Qualitative Research. *Proceedings of the IV International Conference on Multimedia and ICTs in Education m-ICTE 2006 "Current Developments in Technology-Asissted Education"*. Seville, Spain, Vol. 3.

Frailey, D. J. (2006). Bringing Realistic Software Engineering Assignments to the Software Engineering Classroom. *Proceedings of the Nineteenth Conference on Software Engineering Education & Training*. Turtle Bay, Hawaii.

Grützner, I. & Bunse, C. (2002). Teaching Object-Oriented Design with UML - A Blended Learning Approach. *Proceedings of the Sixth Workshop on Pedagogies and Tools for Learning Object-Oriented Concepts.* Held in conjunction with 16th European Conference for Object-Oriented Programming (ECOOP 2002), Malaga, Spain.

Grützner, I., Steinbach-Nordmann, S., Ochs, M. & Bunse, C. (2003). Der Baukasten Objektorientierte Software-Entwicklung: Berufliche Weiterbildung in der Software-Industrie. *Proceedings of the 6th International Conference on Information Management (Wirtschaftsinformatik).* Dresden, Germany (In German).

Grützner, I., Thomas, L., & Steinbach-Nordmann, S. (2006). Building re-configurable multilingual training media. *Proceedings of the IV International Conference on Multimedia and ICTs in Education m-ICTE 2006 "Current Developments in Technology-Asissted Education".* Seville, Spain, Vol. 3.

Heidecke, F., Mayrhofer, D., Schiesser, A. & Back, A. (2007). Organisation des Außendiensttrainings in der Pharma-Branche: Entwicklung eines Referenzmodells mittels Fallstudienforschung. In Breitner, M. H., Bruns, B. & Lehner, F. (eds.). *Neue Trends im E-Learning: Aspekte der Betriebswirtschaftslehre und Informatik.* Heidelberg: Physica (in German).

Höhle, J., Cho, K., 2000. Distance Learning and Exchange of Scientific Knowledge via Internet. *International Archives of Photogrammetry and Remote Sensing.* Amsterdam, Holland, Vol. XXXIII, Part B6. pp. 337-340.

Jain, A. & Boehm, B. (2006). SimVBSE: Developing a Game for Value-Based Software Engineering. *Proceedings of the Nineteenth Conference on Software Engineering Education & Training.* Turtle Bay, Hawaii.

Jones, S. & Northrop, M. (2006a). Blended Learning: the practicalities of implementation in a UK University. *Proceedings of the IV International Conference on Multimedia and ICTs in Education m-ICTE 2006 "Current Developments in Technology-Asissted Education".* Seville, Spain, Vol. 3.

Jones, S. & Northrop, M. (2006b). Implementation of a Blended Learning approach: Milestones, tractors and Crossroads. *Proceedings of the IV International Conference on Multimedia and ICTs in Education m-ICTE 2006 "Current Developments in Technology-Asissted Education".* Seville, Spain, Vol. 3.

Lutz, B. (2007). Training for Global Software Development in an International "Learning Network". *Proceedings of the International Conference on Global Software Engineering (ICGSE 2007).* Munich, Germany.

Mikulecky, L. (1998). Diversity, discussion, and participation: Comparing a Web-based and campus-based adolescent literature classes. *Journal of Adolescent & Adult Literacy,* 42(2), pp. 84-97.

Mühlhäuser, M., Trompler, C., 2002, Digital Lectures Halls Keep Teachers in the Mood and Learners in the Loop. *Proceedings of E-Learn 2002, Montreal, Canada. Association for the Advancement of Computing in Education (AACE).* pp. 714-721.

Ochs, M., & Pfahl, D. (2002) e-learning Market Potential in the German IT Sector: An explorative Study. Kaiserslautern, Germany: Fraunhofer IESE. Retrieved November 2, 2003 from *http://www.iese.fhg.de/market_survey.*

Singh, H. & Reed, C. (2001) *Achieving Success with Blended Learning.* Technical Report, Centra Software, 2001, Retrieved January 21, 2008, from: http://www.centra.com/download/whitepapers/blendedlearning.pdf

Singh, H. (2003). Building Effective Blended Learning Programs. *Journal on Educational Technology,* 43 (6), pp. 51-54.

Solberg Søilen, K. (2007). Using case studies in blended learning for increased interactivity and lower drop out rates. *19ᵗʰ Nordic Academy of Management Conference*. Bergen, Norway.

Stark, C.M. & Schmidt, K.J. (2002). Transitioning to e-Learning: A Case Study. *Proceedings of the 2002 eTEE Conference*. Davos, Switzerland.

Thomas L. & Ras E. (2005). Courseware Development Using a Single-Source Approach. *Proceedings of the World Conference on Education Multimedia, Hypermedia and Telecommunications.*

Ubal, R., Cano, J.-C., Petit, S. & Sahuquillo, J. (2006). RAC FP: A Training Tool to Work With Floating-Point Representation, Algorithms, and Circuits in Undergraduate Courses. *IEEE Transactions on Education*. 49 (3), pp. 321- 331.

Wang, A. I. & Sorensen, C.-F. (2006). Writing as a Tool for Learning Software Engineering. *Proceedings of the Nineteenth Conference on Software Engineering Education & Training*. Turtle Bay, Hawaii.

Wills, S. (2006). Strategic Planning for Blended e-learning. *Proceedings of the 7th International Conference on Information Technology Based Higher Education & Training*. Sydney, Australia.

Yildiz, Senem, Chang, Carrie (2003) Case Studies of Distance Students' Perceptions of Participation and Interaction in Three Asynchronous Web-based Conferencing Classes. *The U.S. Turkish Online Journal of Distance Education-TOJDE*. 4 (2).

Chapter XII
Integrated Software Testing Learning Environment for Training Senior-Level Computer Science Students

Daniel Bolanos
Universidad Autonoma de Madrid, Spain

Almudena Sierra
Universidad Rey Juan Carlos, Spain

ABSTRACT

Due to the increasingly important role of software testing in software quality assurance, during the last several years, the utilization of automated testing tools, and particularly those belonging to the xUnit family, has proven to be invaluable. However, as the number of resources available continues increasing, the complexity derived from the selection and integration of the most relevant software testing principles, techniques and tools into an adequate learning environment for training computer science students in software testing, increases too. In this chapter we introduce a experience of teaching Software Testing for a senior-level course. In the elaboration of the course a wide variety of testing techniques, methodologies and tools have been selected and seamlessly integrated. An evaluation of students performance during the three academic years that the course has been held show that students' attitudes changed with a high or at least a positive statistical significance.

INTRODUCTION

In this chapter we present a complete methodology for software testing training in the context of a laboratory course for senior-level computer science students. The intent of this work is to provide educators with a set of guidelines to effectively instruct computer science students on software testing. The goal is not only to incorporate specific software testing skills into students' curricula, but also to prepare the student with skills for independent lifelong learning on the topic. The designed course spans the whole software testing lifecycle, and includes teaching recommendations to address students' common difficulties and misconceptions, as well as techniques to evaluate Students' performance for every stage.

During three academic years (2003-2006, note that results for the ongoing academic year are not currently available) we have developed and improved a software testing learning environment that has been used to train senior-level students in the Department of Computer Science of Universidad Autonoma de Madrid (Spain). In this environment, students are instructed about the elaboration of the test plan, test cases design, testing automation by means of specific tools, reporting and interpreting test results and maintenance related issues. All of these tasks are carried out over a complete pre-existent software system that has been specifically developed for this purpose.

To evaluate the effectiveness of the approach we have carried out attitudinal surveys to students during the three years that the course has been offered. These surveys provided us with inestimable information about students' progress and perception on several aspects of the course. This information was used to find out which elements of the course were perceived by students as most useful, most difficult or most personally rewarding; and, of course, to improve the learning environment along the academic years. We have found that, thanks to their immersion in this testing environment, students understood the crucial importance of software testing across the software lifecycle. Also, they incorporated a complete testing methodology and a broad set of software testing tools into their previous knowledge.

The chapter is divided into the following sections: a background section in which previous work on the topic is discussed and compared to the proposed approach, a description of the software testing learning environment including teaching recommendations and a description of the students' performance evaluation method, an evaluation of the effectiveness of the approach and a final section with the conclusions and future work.

BACKGROUND

Due to the increasingly important role of software testing in software quality assurance, during the last years, the use of testing frameworks that assist the developer during the testing process, and particularly the use of those belonging to the xUnit family, has proven to be invaluable. The production of high-quality and bug-free software products and solutions has gained a crucial importance in the software development industry, always focused to meet the needs of its increasingly more demanding end-users. In the last few years, many software testing techniques and methodologies have emerged to address these challenges, some of them influenced by agile (Beck, K. et al., 2001) and particularly by Extreme Programming (XP) (Beck, K., 2000). These techniques provide a wide set of principles, practices and recommendations for all the tasks involved in the software testing process, from test case design to automation of functional tests. In this context, an overwhelming number of testing frameworks and tools have been developed and are available (many of them under open-source licenses) with the purpose of aiding the developer in testing every particular system aspect written in any programming language imaginable.

However, as the number of resources and techniques available continues increasing and demonstrating new benefits, the complexity derived from the selection and integration of the most relevant software testing principles, techniques and tools into an adequate learning environment for training computer science students in software testing, increases too. Though several interesting experiences have been reported, to collecting and integrating all of these continuously evolving sources of knowledge and experience into a methodology to effectively teach software testing, remains an unresolved issue. As we will see later on in this section, many experiences of taking software testing to the classroom have been reported. They are focused in a number of testing related topic like for example extreme programming, unit testing or pair programming. However, it seems like there have not been any experience of collecting and integrating the most relevant and successful techniques into the same course.

There have been numerous experiences bringing Extreme Programming principles to the classroom (Astrachan, O. Duvall, R.C. & Wallingford, E. 2001; Edwards, S. 2003; Kaufmann, R. & Janzen, D. 2003; Melnik, G. & Maurer, F. 2002; Mugridge, R. 2003; Müller, M. & Hagner, O. 2002; Müller, M. & Tichy, W. 2001; Reichlmayr, T. 2003; Shukla, A. & Williams, L. 2002; Tinkham, A. & Kaner, C. 2005) as well as other less specific like (Collofello, J. & Vehathiri, K., 2005) and (Astrachan, O., Duvall, R.C., & Wallingford, E., 2001). For example, in (Shukla, A., & Williams, L., 2002) a complete report of an undergraduate course on software testing focused on Test-Driven Development (also known as TDD and considered one of the most important aspects of Extreme Programming) is presented. The course was held during three academic years and, despite positive results in terms of students performance, a main problem was identified. The problem lies in the counterintuitiveness of TDD due to the fact that, according to this technique test cases need to be written before the code to test. This problem is especially significant in graduate and nearly-graduate students (for whom the course presented in this chapter is intended) who have already become established in the traditional "write the code and then test it" software testing strategy. In general, in the vast majority of these experiences a special need for coaching and

support for students has been detected due to the novelty of the topic and the large number of new concepts it involves. For this reason we decided to design an integrated learning environment in which students' progress is monitored through individualized tutoring during laboratory classes and the use of a centralized software repository where they store the work as they progressively complete it. In this respect the adoption of pair programming as the collaborative paradigm for the course has brought us the possibility of taking advantage of the benefits it provides to students when facing radically new software development related concepts and scenarios.

Pair programming is a software development model at the core of XP and is a kind of "collaborative programming". It consists of two programmers (two students), working side-by-side at one computer collaborating on the same design, algorithm, code or test. One person is the "driver", i.e. has control of the pencil/mouse/keyboard and is writing the design or code. The other person, the "observer," continuously and actively examines the work of the driver identifying tactical and strategic deficiencies in it (Williams, L., Kessler, R. A., Cunningham, W., & Jeffries, R. 2000). Despite cases of study (Müller, M., & Tichy, W. 2001) where pair programming has been shown to suffer from some waste of time and from an unclear division of work, we have chosen pair programming as the collaborative model during the laboratory course due to the following reasons:

- Pair pressure: pair programmers put pressure on each other. This is a form of positive pressure that leads students to keep each other focused and on-task (Williams, L. A., & Kessler, R. R. 2000).
- Pair programming has been shown to be beneficial independent of the developers' experience (Cockburn, A., & Williams, L. 2001). Note that our students do not have experience in formal software testing.

- Pair programming improves the success and morale of the students and increases satisfaction in the process (McDowell, C., Werner, L., Bullock, H., & Fernald, J. 2003).
- Pair programming increases confidence in the programming solutions
- Students are much less reliant on the teaching staff. When one partner doesn't know/understand something the other almost always does, therefore the teaching workload is reduced and lab consultation hours are very calm (McDowell, C., Werner, L., Bullock, H., & Fernald, J. 2002; Williams, L., & Kessler, R. 2000).Pair programming is much more productive when developers face unfamiliar problems than when facing familiar ones (Lui, K.M., & Chan, K. C.C. 2003). This is the case we are considering since students have no previous knowledge about the software system to test, nor experience using the testing tools introduced in the course.

THE SOFTWARE TESTING LEARNING ENVIRONMENT

The Course

The software testing course has been held during the second semester of the last three academic years (2003-2006) as a laboratory course in the senior-level Software Engineering subject at the Department of Computer Science of Universidad Autonoma de Madrid (Spain). At the beginning of the course students have intermediate Java programming skills and more than 100 hours of theoretical-practical software engineering training plus specific theoretical instruction in software testing fundamentals. This instruction comprised basically the following topics:

- Test design techniques: black box and white box.

- Integration strategies in structured programming languages: top-down, bottom-up, and sandwich.
- Integration strategies in object oriented programming languages.
- Test cases design.
- Testing across the software development lifecycle: unit, integration, system, acceptance, and regression testing
- Risk management during the test process.
- Test plan document elaboration guidelines.

Table 1 summarizes the most relevant features of the course.

The first day of the course students are grouped in pairs and informed about the work to do:

- Test plan documentation: scope, description of the integration strategy and techniques selected, assignment of responsibilities and resources, schedule, milestones, risk management, completion criteria, etc.
- Test development: test procedures, test scenarios, test cases and test source code.
- Test execution: execution of the software following the plans and reporting of failures and errors detected.
- Test reporting: final conclusions about the results obtained from the executed tests.

During the explanation teachers emphasize aspects related with the testing automation level, code coverage, test cases design and maintenance. Finally students are informed about the course evaluation procedures.

System to be Tested

A complete system has been developed by teachers with the sole purpose of being tested. The main advantage of this is that students have the same starting point what makes students' performance evaluation more straightforward. Due to the

Table 1. Summary of course details

Number of students	150 students divided into 5 groups with an average of 15 pairs of students and a dedicated teacher per group.
Qualification required	Last year undergraduate computer science students.
Programming language	Java JDK 1.5
Testing tools	JUnit 4.0, JFunc, HttpUnit, XMLUnit, JTestCase, JUnitReport, JUnitAddOns, and others.
Software configuration management tools	SVN 1.3 + TortoiseSVN
Software execution and deployment	Ant 1.6.5
Evaluation procedure	• Oral presentation. • Formal written report including the Test Plan, test cases design and test execution results and interpretation. • Software generated quality and completeness (only the software present in the repository is evaluated) • Practical examination.
Duration	8 Weeks

strict time constraints of the course as well as the broad software developing experience students acquired in previous years, we have not seen the necessity of spending time instructing students on development issues.

The developed system presents a very interesting set of features that makes the testing process very interesting from an educational point of view: multithreading, HTTP interface, file input/output, private methods, exception handling, XML documents generation and parsing, external configuration, etc. The system consists of 7 Java classes and about 1700 lines of code. However, no more than 200 lines shared out between a few selected methods are used for testing purposes. In order to delimit the range of results that can be potentially obtained from the testing process, as well as facilitating students' performance evaluation and making the testing process more rewarding, several failures affecting different parts of the system have been deliberately introduced. These failures have been carefully selected with the intention of being detected using different testing techniques and strategies: black box, white box (grey box), unit testing, integration testing,

functional testing, etc. Note that for obvious reasons the different failures introduced vary each academic year.

The system to be tested is named Road Information Server (RIS) and its aim is to serve XML documents via HTTP containing information about roads: traffic flow, presence of accidents in the road, weather forecast, etc. This information is taken by this module from the output of a hypothetical system named Road Observation and Information Providing System (ROIPS) from a data file (note that the format of this file is the only thing students need to know about the ROIP system) that acts as an interface between both systems. The RIS system is continuously reading the data from that file and generating XML documents containing the information requested via HTTP (GET method) by the clients. Since the information is published using HTTP the simplest way to interact with the system is from a conventional browser (this feature enables students to easily interact with the system). Figure 1 shows the system to be tested and its environment.

Elaboration of the Test Plan

Once the students understand the goals of the course and get familiarized with the system to test, they must start elaborating the test plan. This document is required to be formatted as a technical report, this point is the special interest because students are very close to finish their degree and need to be prepared for dealing with the document formatting standards used in the software development industry. This document must be realistic and include a schedule and milestones adjusted to the course length.

Unit Testing

Unit testing is one of the core practices of XP and consists of taking each class of an object oriented software system and testing it in isolation. Students are encouraged to select a bottom-up testing approach, i.e. testing the classes of the system first and then testing the sum of its classes. On such an approach, integration testing becomes much easier. Teachers also encourage students to put special emphasis on unit testing due to the following reasons:

- Unit testing implicitly involves a sort of documentation that provides students with a better understanding of modules, requirements and API's.
- Good unit tests are fundamental when doing regression tests.

Since Java is the programming language selected for the course, the tool selected to assist the unit testing process can't be other than JUnit. Many issues concerning test cases design and the right way to test an object in isolation need to be covered for an in-depth understanding of unit testing. In the following subsections we describe these issues in detail, providing some teaching recommendations obtained from our experience holding the course. However, note that some aspects, like test cases design, are not uniquely correlated with unit testing.

Test Cases Design

The first step when doing unit testing is to design the test cases, black box and white box techniques are both suitable for this purpose. Black box consists of testing whether the output of a function

Figure 1. Diagram of the system to be tested and its environment

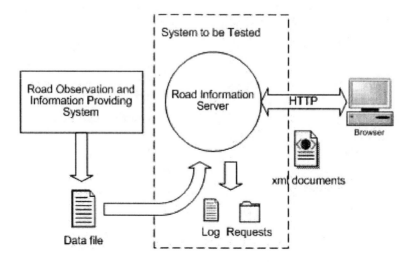

or method, given certain inputs, conforms to its functional specification. White box consists of analyzing the source code in order to guide the selection of test data. In this respect, students need to have good enough Java programming skills to throughfully understand the execution flow present in the methods' source code. It is important to balance the pairs when creating them at the beginning of the course; students with less Java programming skills must be paired with the more experienced ones. Test data must be appropriately selected to achieve an adequate coverage over the code to test. Students have to decide which coverage (statement, edge, branch or path) to use when testing each method and justify the decisions made. Also, students have to create flow graphs for each method and depict on them special situations derived from exception handling when it is the case. Note that only 6 methods of the whole system are selected to be tested, so the workload is assumable.

We have encountered difficulties among students to understand and appropriately set-up the context in which a method for a given test case must be called. There is a trend to conceive a method as an execution entity which results are only determined by the input parameters regardless the context in which the method is invoked. This problem is especially notorious when designing test cases under the white-box perspective. For this reason we have selected some methods which results are strongly influenced by events like the presence of a file in the file-system or the inner-state of the object in which the method is defined. Another important issue is to make students take into account all the factors involved in setting-up the method invocation context and to check all the observable results of its execution.

Testing in Isolation

Maybe the most difficult aspect when doing unit testing is to completely isolate a class from its collaborative classes. Usually an object makes use of other objects to carry out certain tasks beyond its own functionality. Obviously, the execution results (and so that the test results) of methods belonging to that object are going to be strongly determined by the inner-state of the object. Usually it is very difficult to set up domain state on such a way that it exposes the features to be tested. Even if we can do it, the written test will be probably very complex and difficult to understand and maintain. We can avoid these problems using Mock Objects (Mackinnon, T., Freeman, S., & Craig, P. 2000) that are a substitute implementation to emulate or instrument other domain code (in particular the collaborative classes). They should be simpler than the real code, not duplicate its implementation, and allow the developer to set up private state to aid in testing. Mock Objects are very useful, but to create them by hand may be tedious, therefore, students use a tool named JMock. JMock automatically generates the mock classes' source code from the original classes and presents a very intuitive interface with a very plain learning curve. In addition to the generation of the Mock Objects, a preliminary refactoring process is typically required, consisting in creating the factory methods in which the original objects will be replaced by mock objects. In the Source code listing 1, it is shown an example of a factory method that instantiates a collaborative class.

```
public class TargetClass() {
    protected CollabClass factory-
Method(){
    return new CollabClass();
  }
  ...
  }
```

Source Code Listing 1
Following this procedure, it is possible to test objects that inherit from the target class and override the factory method to replace the instantiation of the collaborative object with the instantiation

of the mock one. This can be seen in the Source code listing 2.

```
public void testTargetClassMethod {
// instantiation using mock objects
TargetClass targetInstance = new Tar-
getClass() {
    protected CollabClass
    factoryMethod {
      return new CollabClass();
    }
  }
  // test something
}
```

Source Code Listing 2

We have found that is very important to carefully select the code examples to which students must apply the Mock Objects technique so they can see a tangible benefit derived from its use. This way, applying Mock Objects becomes a very rewarding task rather than a nuisance. Otherwise they tend to consider the solution too complex in comparison to the problem to solve and it discourages them.

Testing Private Methods

Some TDD purists suggest that principles of encapsulation should never be violated for testing an object. Testing private methods (note that in the Java language as well as in other object oriented languages there are several access modifiers. In this respect, the qualifier private must not be interpreted literally but as "not belonging to the public interface of the class") means that you have to change your tests every time you change your private methods, and this becomes a barrier to refactoring and agile development. The reason is that, typically, private methods contain implementation details of the objects and therefore are more prone to suffer changes during the software maintenance process. We can consider, in the context of white-box testing technique, that a private method is implicitly tested by means of

testing the public methods that use it. However, sometimes it is not easy to obtain an acceptable coverage following this strategy. In these cases we may need to test private methods directly, so we include such an exercise in the laboratory course. The problem here is that private methods can't be called outside the class where they are defined and obviously the test code can't belong to the class to test. The best solution is to by-pass the Java Virtual Machine (JVM) encapsulation mechanism by using the Java Reflection API. This can be done using the classes included in the `java.lang.reflect` package or by means of the JUnit-addons library (available under an open source license). As can be seen in the Source code listing 3, calling a private method with the later is straightforward:

```
SomeClass returnValue = (SomeClass)Pr
ivateAccessor.invoke(
    instanceToTest,
    "methodToTest",
    new Class[]{ Class1, Class2},
    new Object[]{ param1, param2});
```

Source Code Listing 3

As a laboratory exercise, some private methods are selected; students must decide which of them should be tested and include the observed advantages and disadvantages of the decision taken in the documentation produced.

Testing Exceptions

Exceptions are a mechanism to handle unexpected or atypical situations during the execution of a program. Exception management code is responsible for the detection and handling of system conditions that could potentially lead to failure. As any other part of a software system, they must be tested. However this is probably one of the aspects of an object oriented programming language, which testing procedure has never been covered in detail in the available bibliography. There are a few recommendations on the topic; even frameworks like JUnit provide helper tools. However, we have observed a lack of an in-deep analysis in which students can rely to successfully proceed in most of the possible scenarios.

When testing exceptions, students use to consider them as an `if-else` block of code, where the `if` corresponds to the `try` sentence and the `else` corresponds to the `catch` sentence. This way, the testing procedure would consist in defining two test cases, one for each possible execution path. Nevertheless, there are a fair number of non trivial questions that arise among students when taking this procedure to practice. Should all the exceptions be tested following the same procedure? Should all the potentially thrown exceptions be tested? If not, what is the criteria to decide which of them should not? In the rest of this section we will try to shed some light on these questions.

The goal is to verify that exceptions are generated only when it's due, following this consideration it makes sense to classify them as expected or unexpected. Note that this classification does not attend to the exception itself but to the nature of the test cases designed for testing it.

Expected Exceptions

Expected exceptions refer to test cases in which the method-under-test execution context is set-up so an exception must be thrown. Testing them consists of invoking the throwing method with "exceptional" data and checking that the exception is actually thrown via an assertion. Testing this kind of exceptions can be done in JUnit 4.x using the annotation `@Test(expected=Ex pectedException.class)` when defining the test method. However, it presents a clear shortcoming, checking that the right exception has been produced is up to the framework and no extra verifications over the exception object itself can be done since it is not available in the

test method. For simplicity and generality the procedure shown in the Source code listing 4 has been proposed to students:

```
public void testSomeMethod () {
  try{
                instanceToTest.
methodToTest(params);
    fail("An exception was expected");
  } catch (ExpectedException e){
    // Execution control must reach
here
  }
}
```

Source Code Listing 4

With these code sentences we ensure that a failure will occur if the exception `ExpectedExcep tion` is not raised when invoking the method to test with the adequate parameters. We have observed among students a common misconception of expected exceptions. Sometimes, they include some test cases in which the concept of expected exceptions is extended to "testing the Java platform". For example, test cases are written which result in a method invoked over a non initialized object that produces a `NullPointerExcep tion` raised by the JVM. This kind of test cases doesn't make any sense because testing the JVM is obviously out of the scope of the test plan.

Unexpected Exceptions

Unexpected exceptions correspond to those unpredicted situations for which the system can not suggest any solution. This kind of exceptions is easy to test since JUnit automatically catches exceptions thrown by test methods and report them as errors (note the non trivial distinction between errors and failures in JUnit). While for unchecked exceptions (those who inherit from `RuntimeException`) nothing needs to be done, checked exceptions have to be declared in the throws clause of the test method definition.

```
public void testSomeMethod () throws
SomeCheckedException {
    // test something
}
```

Source Code Listing 5

Improving Maintainability

Nowadays, most of the activity and economic benefits of software enterprises come from maintenance related tasks. In fact, commonly in the vast majority of software projects, the maintenance life-cycle is much longer than the development one and so is the volume of resources dedicated to it. The interesting point here is that the larger the number of resources needed, the larger the potential for cost-effectiveness improvement and so must be the effort in teaching good practices on this topic.

During a maintenance stage in which the production code is being altered, regression tests need to be done with a very high periodicity and have to be as much automated as possible so they can be ran at a reasonable cost in resources. For this reason, it is necessary to train students in good testing practices that guarantee the production of not only maintainable test software but test software with a highly automated that can be effectively used in regression. In addition to some general recommendations, like minimizing the coupling between test code and production code and using auto-deployment scripts, students are trained in the use of an open source tool named JTestCase. This tool is very helpful assisting in the test cases design and execution tasks; it is basically a JUnit extension library that allows the test cases data to be separated from the test cases source code. This separation is provided by using XML data files to store test cases data in a very structured and readable fashion. To enhance maintainability even further, different XML files must be used to store test data belonging to different classes.

JTestCase also provides the API methods required to load this data into memory from the test code during the testing process. The main advantages that led us to recommend students the use of this library are two:

- It is possible to enlarge the test cases data set with only adding a new test case description to the XML files, and without modify and having to recompile the test source code.
- Developers who design test cases data sets don't need to know about the source code of the methods to test. Therefore a clear separation between the test cases design and execution roles is established.

Nevertheless, this library also presents some drawbacks we needed to deal with when designing the laboratory exercises in order not to increase excessively their complexity. For example, storing the parameters data of the methods to test in the XML files when they are instances of complex data types or user defined classes, may result in a very complex and tedious task (because they are not directly supported by the syntax JTestCase provides). Although this problem may be overcome using the JICE library, we considered it does not worth the time students spend to learn a new tool.

Another recommendation we do is to use the XML documents generated as part of the test cases design documentation (XML files are readable by both humans and machines) and therefore avoid duplicated information that is always hard to maintain.

Reporting and Interpreting Test Results

Once the test cases execution has been carried out using the corresponding Ant script, a fair amount of information summarizing the errors and failures detected is generated. The correct interpretation and understanding of this information is a key issue to locate and solve adequately the software defects found during the testing process. JUnit includes support for the presentation of test cases execution results in textual (standard output in the command window) or graphical form. However, in real applications for which thousands of test cases are typically developed, these methods of presenting the information are unreadable and impractical. To cope with this problem we have instructed students in the use of the JUnitReport tool, which allows the generation of hypertext browsable documents in HTML format containing the execution results for every particular executed test case. This tool is able to merge the individual XML files generated by the <junit> Ant task, and apply a stylesheet on the final document. JUnitReport is provided with the Ant release as an additional task but installation of external third party libraries is required. One important thing to point out is that both <junit> and <junitreport> tasks must be written in different targets inside the Ant script so the test case execution and results reporting tasks are not interdependent.

Another fundamental topic that must be covered is the correct interpretation of the obtained results. Usually, JUnit makes a distinction between errors and failures, however, this distinction is artificial, unuseful and usually a source of misunderstandings among students. This distinction does not provide clear information about the source of the software defects found. While failures relate to assertion methods that have not been satisfied, i.e. defects in the production code, errors reflect unanticipated situations that occurred during the test cases execution and could be caused by both defects in the production code or in the test code. This issue must be covered at the beginning of the course when the JUnit tool is introduced.

Integration Testing

Integration tests are centered on the collaboration of classes in a system. Once the different classes have shown to work well in isolation, is necessary to verify that they also work well when combined. When doing unit testing over a target class, students do a little refactoring process to replace domain objects with mock objects through the use of factory methods. After that, mock objects must be replaced progressively by the original ones. This can be done straightforward using the approach presented in (Wick, M., Stevenson, D., & Wagner, P. 2008). Students have to replace the factory method of the original target class with a new factory method that returns the actual object with which students wish to integrate. Note that this approach allows a step-by-step integration, i.e. if we replace factory methods one by one, we are adding the original classes to the integration test one-by-one. In comparison with unit tests, integration tests are more difficult to implement due to the complexity of setting up the domain in the right state to test a specific behavior. In integration tests lots of objects are involved while in unit tests only a few mock objects, plus the target object, are involved. Moreover, mock objects state is very easy to set up comparatively. Due to these difficulties, we have found that students need extra support and instruction to make integration testing successfully.

Functional Testing

The final step is to make functional tests over the system as a whole. For this purpose students are provided with a brief Software Requirements Document in which, for example, the syntax of the HTTP requests served by the system and the format of the XML documents returned are described. The goal is to make automated tests to verify that the system behavior meets the software requirements. Making functional tests from scratch over a distributed application with the only help of JUnit (note that despite its name JUnit is not exclusively attached to unit testing.) is a hard task. To cope with this difficulty we have introduced in the learning environment two interesting JUnit extension libraries (these two libraries as well as all the tools included in the learning environment described in this chapter are free-available open source tools) that facilitate this work: HttpUnit and XMLUnit. Note that despite their names, XMLUnit and HttpUnit are not unit testing tools but functional testing tools; nevertheless the "unit" prefix is an easy way to make these tools easily recognizable as belonging to the JUnit family. In one hand HttpUnit simplifies the interaction with a Web application by hiding all the HTTP protocol details from the developer. This tool basically emulates the functionality of a Web browser allowing the test code to navigate a Web application and retrieve its contents as a user would do by clicking links and reviewing documents using a conventional Web browser and the mouse. Once the test code is able to retrieve documents from the system, the next step is to validate the contents and structure of the documents retrieved to ensure they follow the specification contained in the Software Requirements Document. For this purpose, HttpUnit can be used in combination of XmlUnit. While the former is able to parse and validate the contents of HTML documents (like the title of the page, tables and forms present in it and even the correctness of the script code) the later is able to do XML documents validation.

Another interesting point when making functional tests is the possibility of allowing multiple failures, i.e. to allow more than one assert method to fail inside the same test method. JUnit typically stops the execution of a test method and continues with the execution of the next one when the first failure occurs. While this is convenient in the particular case of unit testing, in which after a failure happens the state of the object under test is potentially unpredictable, in functional tests is common to design a test case so it carries out a set of higher level operations that are often uncorrelated. In these cases, one failure may not affect the normal execution of the following operations and, since functional testing is usually a very time-consuming task, to be able to continue the testing process can save a lot of execution time. There is a specifically designed tool to overcome this drawback of JUnit when applied to functional

tests, its name is JFunc and was also incorporated to the testing environment.

In the following points we summarize some interesting issues we have observed during the three academic years the course have been held.

- The process of incorporating functional testing tools to the course involves a relatively long learning curve if is not accompanied by the adequate examples and instruction.
- Once the tools are effectively applied to the functional testing process, students realize the simplicity of the test code produced and the extensibility and generality of the solution. After an initial guided research effort followed by a posterior independent research effort, they incorporate to their curriculum a set of state-of-the-art functional testing tools that clearly improve the quality and the level of automation of the tests, as well as are very helpful in regression.
- Sometimes students need extra support to distinguish between the aspects of a Web document that must be tested and those that must not. While the contents and organization of the information contained are important, aspects like presentation and Web design elements are obviously out of the scope.
- The system to test produces dynamic documents, this is an interesting point because some dynamic contents we deliberately included, like time-stamps or auto-increment values, are by nature nearly impossible to test. In these cases, students are instructed to eliminate the validation of those values from the overall contents validation process.

Taking Advantage of Software Management Configuration Tools (SMC Tools)

Nowadays SMC tools are essential to track the evolution of the software under development and also represent the basic support for the collaborative work model of every software development team. For this reason, and in order to make the working environment as real as possible, we have considered a key issue to incorporate the use of a repository along the course. The version control system selected is SVN Subversion v1.3 (Subversion, 2000). This tool was originally created to replace CVS (Concurrent Version System) and presents some advantages over it, among them, its usage simplicity. Students interact with SVN by means of a Windows client named TortoiseSVN, which is integrated in the Windows Explorer contextual menu. The repository can also be accessed for reading purposes through a standard WEB browser using Apache authentication. Working with the repository using TortoiseSVN is a very easy task and only a few commands (import, checkout, commit …) and a basic knowledge about the work-cycle is necessary for students to get started. Each pair of students has a folder in the repository and a login/password to access it. The first day of the course students import the baseline software system to the corresponding work folder in the repository. At the end of every day in the course or after a major change has been made over the software contained in the local working folder, students are required to commit the changes to their personal folder in the repository. One common problem we have found is that some students can't clearly differentiate between software elements that must be stored in the repository (only those that evolve across the software life-cycle and can't be generated from others, as is the case of a .class file generated from a .java file) and those that must not. This concept is important because making a clear distinction between both kinds of elements prevents filling the repository with unuseful and redundant content and saves time in the interaction with it. For this purpose students are encouraged to define a "clean" task in the Ant script that allows deleting the compilation process results (binary files like .class and .jar) before committing to the repository.

The repository is also, indirectly, an excellent mechanism for teachers to track students' progress

and detect misconceptions in the early stages of the course, when these problems are more likely to happen and easier to deal with. We will cover this topic in more detail in the next point.

Students' Performance Evaluation

Students' performance evaluation along the course is based on the following:

- Oral presentations in which each student explains and defends the decisions made and justify the obtained results. A key aspect is the adequate defense of the testing process completion criteria and the testing techniques and strategies selected. Also students are required to make suggestion about how to improve the learning environment and how other parts of the system that remain out of the scope of the test plan could be tested.
- A formal written report including the Test Plan, test cases design as well as test execution results and interpretation: The goal is to get students used to write formal documents as close as possible to those used in real-world software companies.
- Software generated quality and completeness: At the end of the course, the test software contained in the students' folder in the repository is examined and evaluated in terms of readability, completeness, level of automation achieved, coverage over the production code, maintainability, etc. An existing tool designed for measuring the coverage achieved over the production code, which name is Cobertura (Cobertura, 2005), has been utilized for automatically measuring the coverage of students' generated test code and to compare it to the target coverage they described in the Test Plan. Another interesting point is the use of the repository to obtain feedback for evaluation purposes. By looking at the changes-log in the repository, it is possible to observe which versions

of which software elements and when were committed to the repository. This is very helpful for evaluating up to which extent the schedule students wrote in the Test Plan was met. This is an important issue because a last-year computer science student must demonstrate enough experience to accurately estimate time and resources to accomplish a task.

- A practical examination, in which the student is tested on skills that indicate a good level of understanding and handling of the tools used. In this respect students use to perform very well and, when asked, they show to be very capable of applying the tools to new scenarios.

In the vast majority of the cases students performed very well in the oral presentations and in the practical examination. Interestingly some students went beyond the scope of the course and incorporated new tools to the testing process, like it is the case of performance analysis tools. However after carefully examining the change-log of the working folder in the repository for each pair of students, it seems like some of them have troubles estimating the time needed to accomplish each task. We attribute it to the lack of experience taking to the practice the testing techniques introduced. We expect to get better performance in this respect in the following.

The final results indicate that about 85% of students (as an average of the three years in which the course has been held) completed the course satisfactory, being the average grade 7.5 out of 10. This percentage is very similar to the number of students who actually completed all the exercises comprised on the course. This, lead us to the conclusion that the learning environment success is guaranteed whenever the teachers get students enough involved on it.

EVALUATING THE EFFECTIVENESS OF THE APPROACH

To evaluate the impact of the course on students learning and attitudes we carried out a series of surveys. Surveys took place at the beginning and at the end of the course that has been held during the last three academic years. Despite the voluntary nature of the surveys, 93% of an average of 150 students per year completed them. It is important to note that students knew that their answers to the questions would have no effect in their grades. The purpose of the surveys was to evaluate whether students attitudes over relevant software testing topics covered during the course, changed accordingly with our previously stated hypotheses.

The attitude evaluation survey was designed in a similar fashion to the one presented in (Sitaraman, M., Long, T.J., Weide, B.W., Harner, E.J. & Wang, L. 2001). The survey consists on 18 statements. Each of them must be marked by students with one of six choices: strongly disagree (1), disagree (2), moderately disagree (3), moderately agree (4), agree (5) and strongly agree (6); where the number in brackets is the score associated to each choice. Table 2 contains 6 of the 18 sentences that compose the attitudinal survey. Note that each sentence is labeled with a word ("positive" or "negative") that refers to the expected trend for the sentence's results when comparing surveys at the beginning and end of the course.

Table 3 summarizes results from the sentences contained in Table 2. These results are obtained from 134 students of the course that was offered in the 2005-2006 academic year. The first column indicates the number of the sentence. The second and third columns indicate the average agreement scores for each sentence in the surveys taken at the beginning and at the end of the course respectively. The fifth column shows the P-value derived from one-sided paired t-tests on the raw data. These values are used to determine the statistical significance, which is contained in the sixth column.

CONCLUSSION AND FUTURE WORK

Looking at the overall results for the 2005-2006 course's surveys, we see that students' attitudes changed with a high or at least a positive statistical significance for 15 out of 18 sentences. Moreover, results associated to the sentences designed to evaluate the effectiveness of pair programming confirm initially stated hypotheses always with high statistical significance.

At the beginning of the course students are skeptical about the benefits of a formal software testing process when they realize the amount of work and time that such a process demands. However, we have found that the software testing environment presented here, change students' perception about the value of software testing to improve software reliability. Students see how to test an almost real application and we observe it really encourages them. During the years in which the course has been held, pair programming has demonstrated to be an effective collaborative work model, especially when two students with very different skills are grouped into the same pair. In this case, both members' skills converge to be at least equal to the higher one at the end of the course. After the training, students work was evaluated in terms of completeness, effectiveness, maintainability and level of automation, results show that more than 85 percent of students performed above the required level. This

Table 2. Attitudinal survey questions and expected trends

1.	To put a special effort in ensuring the software design quality plays a fundamental role in facilitating the software testing process. (positive)
1.	Software testing is an effective and powerful way to increase software reliability. (positive)
1.	Software testing process starts when all the source code is written and it is always the last stage of the software development life-cycle. (negative)
1.	Software testing is a very time consuming process. (positive)
1.	Software testing is a very repetitive and tedious task; however, no special skills are required to get satisfactory results. (negative)
1.	The best results you can find out once the software testing process is done, is that neither errors nor failures were found. (negative)

Table 3. Summary of attitudes changes

Sentence	Before	After	Difference	P-Value	Significant?
1	3.3	5.1	+1.8	< 0.01	High
2	4.5	5.3	+0.8	0.02	Yes
3	3.9	2.8	-1.1	< 0.01	High
4	4.1	4.5	+0.4	0.2	No
5	5.1	2.3	-2.8	<0.01	High
6	5.3	2.6	-2.7	<0.01	High

evaluation also shows that students usually have difficulties when doing integration tests. They don't know how to start the integration and how to progressively select new classes to be added to the integration test. Coaching is much needed at this point. Final evaluations also show that students are generally satisfied with their work and consider the methodology experimented to be useful in the long term.

Our current work and intention for the future is to update and enhance the learning environment by incorporating into it the most relevant software testing related trends and techniques among those that are continuously arising in the software testing world. In particular, we are currently working to incorporate into the course testing of database access and new ways to identify test anti-patterns.

REFERENCES

Astrachan, O., Duvall, R.C., & Wallingford, E. (2001). *Bringing Extreme Programming to the Classroom.* Presented at XPUniverse Conference'01, 2001.

Beck, K. et al. (2001). Agile Manifesto. Retrieved March 30th 2007, from http://agilemanifesto.org/

Beck, K. (2000). *Extreme Programming Explained: Embrace Change.* Addison Wesley.

Cobertura. (2005). Retrieved from http://cobertura.sourceforge.net/

Cockburn, A., & Williams, L. (2001) The costs and benefits of pair programming. In G. Succi and M. Marchesi (Eds.), *Extreme Programming examined* (pp. 223-243). Boston: Addison-Wesley.

Collofello, J. & Vehathiri, K. (2005). *An Environment for Training Computer Science Students on Software Testing.* Paper presented ad Frontiers in Education, 2005. FIE '05. 19-22 Oct. 2005, T3E-6- T3E-10.

Edwards, S. (2003). *Using Test-Driven Development in the Classroom: Providing Students with Automatic, Concrete Feedback on Performance.* Paper presented at International Conference on Education and Information Systems: Technology and Applications EISTA 2003, Orlando, FL, 2003.

Kaufmann, R., & Janzen, D. (2003). *Implications of test-driven development: a pilot study.* Paper presented at 18th annual ACM SIGPLAN conference on Object-oriented programming, systems, languages, and applications (OOPSLA 2003), Anaheim, CA, 2003.

Lui, K.M., & Chan, K. C.C. (2003). When Does a Pair Outperform Two Individuals?, *Lecture Notes in Computer Science,* Volume 2675, 225–233.

Mackinnon, T., Freeman, S., & Craig, P. (2000). *Endo-Testing: Unit Testing with Mock Objects.* Presented at eXtreme Programming and Flexible Processes in Software Engineering - XP2000.

McDowell, C., Werner, L., Bullock, H., & Fernald, J. (2002). *The Effects of Pair-Programming on Performance in an Introductory Programming Course.* Presented at 33rd SIGCSE technical-symposium on Computer science education. 2002, 38-42.

McDowell, C., Werner, L., Bullock, H., & Fernald, J. (2003). *The impact of pair programming on student Performance, perception and persistence.* Presented at Int.Conf. on Software Engineering (ICSE2003), 2003, 602-607.

Melnik, G., & Maurer, F. (2002) *Perceptions of Agile Practices: A Student Survey."* Paper presented at Agile Universe/XP Universe 2002, Chicago, IL, 2002.

Mugridge, R. (2003). *Challenges in Teaching Test Driven Development.* Paper presented at XP 2003, Genova, Italy, 2003.

Müller, M., & Hagner, O. (2002). Experiment about test-first programming *Software, IEE Proceedings* vol. 149, pp. 131-136.

Müller, M., & Tichy, W. (2001). *Case study: extreme programming in a university environment.* Paper presented at Software Engineering, 2001. ICSE 2001. Proceedings of the 23rd International Conference on, Toronto, Ontario, 2001.

Reichlmayr, T. (2003). *The agile approach in an undergraduate software engineering course project.* Paper presented at Frontiers in Education, 2003. FIE 2003. 33rd Annual, Boulder, CO, 2003.

Shukla, A., & Williams, L. (2002). *Adapting extreme programming for a core software engineering course.* Paper presented at 15th Conference on Software Engineering Education and Training, 2002. (CSEE&T 2002), Covington, KY, 2002.

Sitaraman, M., Long, T.J., Weide, B.W., Harner, E.J. & Wang, L. (2001). *A formal approach to component-based software engineering education and evaluation.* Paper presented at 23rd International Conference on Software Engineering. ICSE 2001.

Subversion. (2000). Retrieved from http://subversion.tigris.org/

Tinkham, A., & Kaner, C. (2005). *Experiences Teaching a Course in Programmer Testing.* Paper presented to Agile Conference, 2005. 24-29 July 2005, 298- 305.

Wick, M., Stevenson, D., & Wagner, P. (2008). *Using Testing and JUnit Across the curriculum.* Presented at 36th SIGCSE technical symposium on Computer science education, 2005, 236–240.

Williams, L., Kessler, R. A., Cunningham, W., & Jeffries, R. (2000). Strengthening the Case for Pair-Programming, *IEEE Software*, 17(4), 19-25.

Williams, L. A., & Kessler, R. R. (2000). *The Effects of 'Pair-Pressure' and 'Pair-Learning' on Software Engineering Education.* Presented at 13th Conference on Software Engineering Education and Training, March 2000, 59-65.

Williams, L., & Kessler, R. (2000). Experimenting with industry's pair programming model in the computer science Classroom. *Journal of Computer Science Education*, 10(4).

Section VI
Curriculum and Education Management

Chapter XIII
Software Engineering Accreditation in the United States

James McDonald
Monmouth University, USA

Mark J. Sebern
Milwaukee School of Engineering, USA

James R. Vallino
Rochester Institute of Technology, USA

ABSTRACT

This chapter provides a brief history of the accreditation of software engineering programs in the United States and describes some of the experiences encountered by programs in achieving their accreditation and by program evaluators in reviewing those programs. It also describes how the accredited programs have addressed the most difficult issues that they have faced during the accreditation process. The authors have served as leaders of the accreditation efforts at their own institutions and as ABET program evaluators at several other academic institutions that have achieved accreditation. The objective of this chapter is to provide those software engineering programs that will be seeking accreditation in the future with some of the experiences of those who are familiar with the process from both the programs' and the evaluators' points of view. Leaders of programs that are planning to request an accreditation review will be well prepared for that review if they combine the information contained in this chapter with the recommendations contained in Chapter XIX of this text.

INTRODUCTION

The history of software engineering education dates to the generally accepted origin of the software engineering discipline in 1968. This year is associated with the first NATO conference on software engineering in Garmisch, Germany. Tomayko (1998) points out, however, that the same year also marked what is apparently the first offering, by Douglas Ross at the Massachusetts Institute of Technology, of an academic course with the term "software engineering" in its title. For a variety of reasons, considerable time passed before courses with significant software engineering content became more common (Tomayko, 1998; Duggins 2002). Beginning in 1977, a number of graduate programs in software engineering were developed and began operation, including those at Seattle University, Texas Christian University, and the Wang Institute of Graduate Studies (Tomayko, 1998). At the undergraduate level, a number of computer science and computer engineering programs incorporated one or two courses in software engineering, typically taught using survey textbooks that offered reasonable breadth but relatively little depth. Although undergraduate software engineering programs began to emerge internationally as early as 1985 (Joint Task Force on Computing Curricula, 2004), it was not until 1996 that the Rochester Institute of Technology initiated what was to become, in 2003, one of the first four software engineering programs to receive accreditation in the United States; the other programs in this group were offered by Clarkson University, Milwaukee School of Engineering, and Mississippi State University.

While we recognize that software engineering programs in other countries have been accredited by accrediting agencies in those countries, this chapter addresses only the history and experiences of software engineering programs that have achieved accreditation in the United States. It is hoped that the material presented here will be of value to software engineering educators in both the United States and around the world.

ABET AND ENGINEERING PROGRAM ACCREDITATION

ABET, Inc., formerly known as the Accreditation Board for Engineering and Technology, is the recognized accreditation body in the United States for college and university programs in applied science, computing, engineering, and technology. It is a federation of professional and technical societies (28 at present) representing those fields. ABET accreditation activities are managed by four commissions; the two most directly related to software engineering are the Engineering Accreditation Commission (EAC) and the Computing Accreditation Commission (CAC). Like other engineering disciplines, software engineering falls under the EAC, while the CAC is responsible for computer science, information systems, and information technology. In possible contrast to some other disciplines, accreditation has historically been an expected attribute of United States engineering programs, and is thus an important concern for software engineering educators.

Each discipline has an associated "lead society", which is one of the member societies of ABET. This society has primary responsibility for defining discipline-specific accreditation criteria, as well as for selecting, training, and evaluating program evaluators. Initially, the lead society for software engineering was the Institute of Electrical and Electronic Engineers (IEEE), which prepared the original version of the software engineering program criteria (Engineering Accreditation Commission, 1999, p. 47), discussed later in this chapter.

With the integration of ABET and the Computing Sciences Accreditation Board (CSAB) in November 2001, CSAB took over the role of lead society for software engineering, and the IEEE became a "cooperating society." Unlike the IEEE and most other member societies of ABET, CSAB is not itself a membership society. Instead, the current members of CSAB are three other professional societies: the Association for Computing Machinery (ACM), the IEEE Computer Society (IEEE-CS), and the Association for Information Systems (AIS).

From the point of view of a software engineering program seeking initial accreditation, the process begins with a request for evaluation, which must be submitted by January of the year in which an evaluation visit is being requested. Since ABET policies require that a program have at least one graduate at the time of the evaluation visit, the request for evaluation is generally submitted in the year when the first graduates are anticipated.

Of course, the work of program and curriculum definition must begin much earlier. It is common for program faculty to attend ABET faculty workshops and to send representatives to training sessions for ABET program evaluators, in order to gain familiarity with the accreditation criteria, process, and practices. The program must also define its educational objectives and outcomes, discussed in more detail below.

Once the request for evaluation has been submitted, the next task is to complete the self-study report, which provides detailed data and evidence to show that the program meets the applicable accreditation criteria. The self-study report is based on an ABET-provided template (Engineering Accreditation Commission, 2007a) and must be submitted by the end of June during the year in which the request was made.

The evaluation visit takes place in the fall. The visiting team consists of a team chair (usually a member of the EAC) and at least one program evaluator (PEV) for each program to be evaluated. The minimum team size is three members (ABET, 2006, p. 8), so it is possible that two program evaluators may be assigned to a single program if no other program is being evaluated during the same visit. Prior to the visit, the program evaluator examines the self-study report and related materials such as student transcripts. Ongoing communication with the program leadership helps to resolve as many issues as possible before the team arrives on campus. During the visit, the evaluator interviews faculty members and students, examines additional materials such as examples of student work, evaluates facilities, and gathers any other necessary information.

During an exit session at the end of the visit, the accreditation team provides the institution with a summary of its evaluation. After the visit, the program has the opportunity to submit additional evidence, primarily to address any shortcomings that were identified during the visit. The team chair and program evaluators then prepare a draft statement of their findings, which is sent to the institution for comment. The final version of the statement incorporates any changes resulting from the institution's "due process" response and is sent to the EAC for final action during the summer after the visit. If accreditation is granted, it is common practice to extend accreditation retroactively to the prior year graduates, since it was their work and curriculum that were examined during the accreditation review.

CRITERIA FOR ACCREDITATION

The current engineering accreditation criteria (Engineering Accreditation Commission, 2007) are based on a major revision originally known as Engineering Criteria 2000 (often abbreviated as "EC2000" or "EC2K"). Prior versions of the criteria focused on detailed prescriptions and, in the view of many engineering educators, limited opportunities for flexibility and innovation. The revised criteria adopted an approach of setting general goals and assigning to individual programs the responsibility for demonstrating achievement of those goals through appropriate assessment and evaluation.

Each of the ABET criteria for accrediting baccalaureate-level engineering programs addresses a specific area of concern. During 2007, changes to the numbering and organization of the criteria were proposed, as indicated in Table 1; these changes will take effect for the 2008-2009 accreditation cycle.

Despite the change in organization, the content of each of the areas of concern has remained fairly

Table 1. Areas of concern covered in each ABET criterion

Area of Concern	Criterion (2007-2008)	Criterion (2008-2009)
Students	Criterion 1	Criterion 1
Program Educational Objectives	Criterion 2	Criterion 2
Program Outcomes	Criterion 3	Criterion 3
Continuous Improvement	Criteria 2-3	Criterion 4
Curriculum	Criterion 4	Criterion 5
Faculty	Criterion 5	Criterion 6
Facilities	Criterion 6	Criterion 7
Support	Criterion 7	Criterion 8
Program Criteria	Criterion 8	Criterion 9

stable from the introduction of the EC2000 criteria until the present time. The criteria are:

Students. For historical reasons, the criteria first address the relationship between an engineering program and its students, even though logically it would make more sense to begin with the program educational objectives and outcomes. Programs are required to evaluate students and monitor their progress, while providing both curricular and career advising. Specific note is made of the need for effective policies and procedures for the admission of transfer students, granting of transfer credit, and verification that all students meet all program requirements.

Program educational objectives. Since the initial introduction of the EC2000 criteria, there has been a continuing evolution and clarification of the terminology used to specify the results that an engineering program strives to achieve. By the current definition, the program educational objectives deal with the broad career and professional accomplishments for which graduates are being prepared. It is common for the program leadership and faculty to consult with employers and other stakeholders to ensure that the program objectives accurately reflect the environment in which the program's graduates will work. Since

these achievements relate to performance after graduation, the program's success in this regard cannot, in general, be determined until some time has passed. Even then, it may be difficult to assess the program's contribution to the individual graduate's success in meeting these longer-term objectives.

A program's educational objectives are expected to be consistent with its institutional mission and to communicate its specific goals to potential students and to the public at large. A typical program objective might be, "Graduates of the program are expected to obtain employment in the software development industry and/or to enter graduate school within six months after graduation."

Program outcomes. To complement the program educational objectives, programs are also required to define and assess program outcomes, which are narrower statements that describe the knowledge and skills expected of students at the time of graduation. The underlying assumption is that this knowledge and skill will provide the basis for achievement of the longer-term career and professional achievements. This criterion requires that a set of eleven specific outcomes be incorporated (often referred to as "a-k" because of the way they are enumerated), but programs are free to articulate additional outcomes. A typical outcome is: "By the time students have graduated from the program they must demonstrate the ability to apply knowledge of mathematics, engineering and science," which is outcome a) in the specific list of outcomes.

Historically, programs have been encouraged to formulate their own outcomes based on their specific program objectives. These program-specific outcomes are often designed to incorporate the "a-k" outcomes. For example, a software engineering program might adopt a program outcome related to designing software components and systems, implicitly referencing the "3(c)" outcome that deals with designing a system, component, or process within realistic constraints.

However, defining a complete set of program-specific outcomes can also mean extra work for the program in preparing for an accreditation visit, since it is then necessary to demonstrate student achievement of both the "a-k" and the additional "program-defined" outcomes. One alternative is to augment the standard "a-k" outcomes by articulating a small number of additional outcomes, if the program judges that the generic outcomes are not sufficient. The proposed 2008-2009 engineering criteria omit a previous requirement that the program must "formulate program outcomes" related to the program objectives, perhaps suggesting a shift away from program-specific outcomes.

Continuous improvement. The requirement for ongoing actions to improve the program, previously called out in the context of program objectives and outcomes, has become a separate criterion in the proposed 2008-2009 draft. Programs are required to show evidence for these actions, which are expected to be based on the results of assessment and evaluation processes called for in the criteria related to program objectives and program outcomes.

Curriculum. This section of the engineering criteria has two major parts. The first deals with minimum standards for curriculum content. The curriculum must include at least one year (typically 32 semester credits or 48 quarter credits) of college-level mathematics and basic sciences. At least some of the basic sciences course work must include experimental experience. A minimum of one and one-half years (48 semester credits or 72 quarter credits) of engineering topics is also required. The engineering topics consist of engineering sciences and engineering design. The curriculum is also required to incorporate a general education component that complements the technical content, but no quantitative specifications are mandated for this component.

One question for software engineering programs is whether some computer science content can be used to meet the "mathematics and basic science" requirement. This type of accounting seems quite reasonable, since the relationship between computer science and software engineering resembles that between, for example, physics of mechanics and mechanical engineering. In addition, many computer science topics are mathematical in nature. However, there is at present no explicit policy on this matter, so many programs have taken a defensive position that ensures the credit requirement is met using course content consistent with a more traditional definition of mathematics and basic science.

The second part of the curriculum criterion imposes a requirement that students be prepared for engineering practice through the curriculum and that this course work culminate in a major design experience that incorporates engineering standards and multiple realistic constraints. The requirement for a major design experience is often addressed by a "senior design project" course or course sequence.

Faculty. The criterion related to the program faculty addresses three primary concerns. First, the number of faculty members and their competencies must be sufficient to cover all curricular areas of the program, while also assuring that faculty members have time to advise and interact with students, support university service activities, continue their own professional development, and maintain links with practitioners and employers.

Second, the program faculty must be invested with sufficient authority to provide effective guidance for the program and to define and execute processes for assessment, evaluation, and continuous improvement of the program's objectives, outcomes, and curriculum.

Third, the criterion provides guidance for evaluating the competence of the faculty, citing factors such as education, diversity, engineering experience, teaching effectiveness, communication ability, scholarship, participation in professional societies, and professional engineering licensure. In addition to these traditional measures, the criterion also makes explicit the need for "enthusiasm for developing more effective programs" (Engineering Accreditation Commission, 2007, p. 3), perhaps recognizing the personal and communal investment that is required to institute and maintain effective assessment and improvement processes.

Facilities. Programs are required to ensure that classrooms, laboratories, and equipment are adequate and that they provide an atmosphere conducive to learning, foster student-faculty interaction, and support professional development and activities. Students must have opportunities to learn the use of modern engineering tools and adequate computing facilities must be available to support both students and faculty.

Support. Programs must have, and demonstrate that they have, the institutional support and financial resources needed to maintain the faculty and facilities. This criterion also explicitly requires adequate support personnel and institutional services. Specific mention is also made of the need for "constructive leadership" to assure the quality and continuity of the program.

Program Criteria. The general engineering accreditation criteria are intended to apply across widely disparate engineering disciplines. While this commonality and consistency is valuable, it is also understood that each discipline may have its own specific requirements. To address these issues, the engineering criteria incorporate sets of program-specific criteria, which are (at least nominally) limited to curricular topics and faculty qualifications. The applicability of a given set of program criteria is determined by the name of the program; for example, a program in "computer and software engineering" would be expected to meet the program criteria for both computer engineering and software engineering. When multiple sets of program criteria are applicable, overlapping requirements need only to be satisfied once. The program criteria for software engineering are discussed in the following section.

PROGRAM CRITERIA FOR SOFTWARE ENGINEERING

As noted above, program criteria are limited to curricular topics and faculty qualifications. The curriculum-related portion of the current software engineering program criteria (Engineering Accreditation Commission, 2007, p. 18) states two primary requirements.

First, the curriculum is required to provide breadth and depth across the range of engineering and computer science topics implied by the title and objectives of the program. Except in unusual cases (e.g., a program that focuses on applying software engineering to aeronautics or to financial modeling), this will normally imply compliance with an accepted "community" definition of the software engineering discipline. Two such definitions are given in the Guide to the Software Engineering Body of Knowledge (2004) and in the undergraduate software engineering curriculum guidelines prepared by the Joint Task Force on Computing Curricula (2004).

Second, the curriculum section of the program criteria for software engineering requires that the program demonstrate a number of specific student outcomes. While these mandated outcomes are not really "curricular topics", there is precedent for requirements of this type in the program criteria for many other disciplines (Engineering Accreditation Commission, 2007, pp. 5-18).

The software engineering program criteria require the program to demonstrate that graduates have the ability to analyze, design, verify, validate, implement, apply, and maintain software systems. Although the term "analyze" has a generic engineering meaning, in this context it is generally understood to refer to requirements analysis. Graduates must also be able to apply, in the context of complex software systems, discrete mathematics, probability, statistics, and relevant topics in computer science and supporting disciplines.

Additionally, the program must demonstrate that graduates have the ability to work in one or more significant application domains. In itself, this requirement does not dictate any particular curricular content, but it does imply some course-work or other experience beyond core software engineering and computer science topics. Some existing software engineering programs have chosen to require specific courses in one or more application domains such as embedded software, gaming software or web applications. Other programs have defined a set of elective course sequences, in a variety of areas, allowing students to choose according to their own interests. A few programs have adopted both of these strategies.

In regard to faculty qualifications, the current program criteria for software engineering do not impose any additional requirements. Effective for the 2001-2002 accreditation cycle, the program criteria were amended to require that "those faculty teaching core software engineering material have practical software engineering experience" (Engineering Accreditation Commission, 2000, p. 16), but that section was later deleted (Engineer-

ing Accreditation Commission, 2002, p. 22) with little public explanation for the change.

GROWTH OF ACCREDITED SOFTWARE ENGINEERING PROGRAMS

The first undergraduate program in software engineering in the United States was started in 1996 at Rochester Institute of Technology. Since that program took root and showed the viability of an undergraduate software engineering program, there has been a steady growth in the number of programs, with several new ones started each year. This has happened despite the general downturn in undergraduate computing program enrollments since 2000 (Computing Research News, 2007). There are currently 35 programs leading to an undergraduate degree in Software Engineering. Through the summer of 2007, fifteen of these programs have been accredited by ABET. The Rochester Institute of Technology program graduated its first class of baccalaureate-level software engineers in May 2001. The first four programs applying for accreditation had their campus visits in fall of 2002, and received accreditation approval in the summer of 2003. The EAC granted the Rochester Institute of Technology program an extended grandfathering which covered their May 2001 class. That gave the program the distinction of awarding the first ABET accredited BS in Software Engineering degrees. Figure 1 shows the growth in both the total number of undergraduate software engineering programs and the number of accredited programs.

CURRENTLY ACCREDITED PROGRAMS

Table 2 lists the fifteen software engineering programs accredited by ABET as of 2007. All

Figure 1. Number of undergraduate software engineering programs

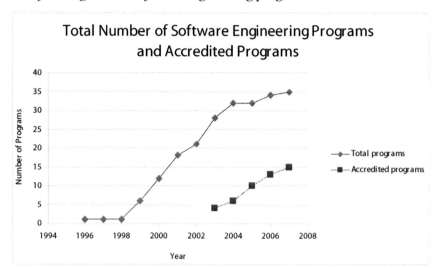

Table 2. Year when program was accredited

Name of Institution	Year Accreditation Awarded
Auburn University	2005
Clarkson University	2003
Embry-Riddle Aeronautical University (Florida)	2005
Fairfield University	2006
Florida Institute of Technology	2004
University of Michigan-Dearborn	2005
Milwaukee School of Engineering	2003
Mississippi State University	2003
Monmouth University	2005
Penn State University – Erie	2006
Rochester Institute of Technology	2003
University of Texas at Arlington	2004
University of Texas at Dallas	2006
Rose-Hulman Institute of Technology	2007
University of Wisconsin - Platteville	2007

of these programs award a Bachelor of Science degree in Software Engineering. The programs have a range of student populations from 30 to over 400.

EXPERIENCES OF PROGRAMS AND PROGRAM EVALUATORS

The authors have completed informal on-line surveys of both software engineering programs that have been accredited by ABET and the ABET program evaluators who have been involved in reviewing those programs. We have supplemented the data gathered in those surveys with our personal experiences as program evaluators and as program leaders to characterize the experiences of programs that have been accredited.

Both programs and program evaluators report that the programs that have been accredited have typically had little difficulty meeting the requirements of the **Facilities** and **Support** criteria. However, both programs and program evaluators report that several programs have had to take action, sometimes significant action, to meet the requirements of the **Students, Program Educational Objectives, Program Outcomes** and **Curriculum** criteria. Survey results indicate a few cases of disagreement, or even contention, between programs and program evaluators, specifically in the areas of faculty qualifications and curricular topics. The next two sections of this chapter highlight evaluation findings related to the criteria that have resulted in improvement actions by the software engineering programs and those criteria which have caused some tension between programs and their evaluators.

CRITERIA RESULTING IN IMPROVEMENT ACTIONS BY PROGRAMS

Many programs reported that they have adopted automated grade tracking and degree audit systems that are being used to replace some regular face-to-face student advising. This has made it more difficult to demonstrate that student progress is being properly evaluated and monitored by the faculty for conformance to program requirements as required by the **Students** criterion. A few programs found that they were not advising and monitoring their students carefully enough. This sometimes resulted in students not completing all of the courses required by the program, usually due to course substitutions that were done

without appropriate review. The programs that have had this problem have generally tightened their advising, monitoring and course substitution approval processes.

Most programs have had difficulty meeting the **Program Educational Objectives** criterion. These objectives represent achievements that students would be expected to reach after graduation. As such, the data are not under the program's direct control. One program commented:

"Assessing educational objectives is difficult. You must rely on outside information to get assessment data, and it is difficult to get enough results to make a reasonable measurement. Traditional alumni survey completion rates are very low and when the number of graduates is relatively low, it is difficult to get enough data from alumni survey results. Employer surveys are equally difficult to get unless you have dedicated employers that hire a large number of your graduates."

The **Program Educational Objectives** criterion requires a process, based on the needs of the program's constituents, in which the objectives are determined and an ongoing evaluation of the extent to which the objectives are being attained, the result of which must be used to improve the program.

Programs have sometimes created their **Program Educational Objectives** without the involvement of the program's constituencies or, in a few cases, without even explicitly defining those constituencies. To avoid this problem, successful programs have usually defined their constituents very explicitly in their self-study report. The constituents described are usually the program's students, the program's faculty and an industrial advisory committee representing potential employers of the program's alumni. Some programs have added parents of students, administrators of the institution and the state or region's economy. Reasonable and acceptable **Program Educational Objectives** have typically been created by first having the faculty draft a set of six to eight specific things that they would expect their graduates to achieve within a few years after graduation. Then these objectives are discussed with, and perhaps modified by, an industrial advisory committee, after forming such a committee if one doesn't already exist. A description of the interaction with constituents is documented and the objectives are published, usually in the institution's catalog, on the program's web site and in any materials being used to market the program. Some have developed employer surveys to get feedback on achievement of **Program Educational Objectives** and a few have modified the wording of their educational objectives to eliminate misunderstandings of the wording.

Most programs seeking initial accreditation have found it very difficult to measure achievement of their objectives by the time of the first evaluation visit, which usually occurs in the fall after the first alumni have graduated from the program. About the only thing the program can practically do within those few months is to informally speak with members of their industrial advisory board who may have hired the program's first graduates to get feedback on their opinions about the students' likelihood of meeting the objectives. Some programs have put off this step until several months after the visit and simply describe what the program is planning to do to evaluate achievement of the objectives.

In the period following the introduction of the EC2000 criteria, a common source of difficulty was confusion among program leaders and program faculty about the differences between educational objectives and program outcomes. Self study reports frequently made the objectives and the outcomes sound very similar to each other. Sometimes programs have used the same set of capabilities in describing the objectives and the outcomes and have simply grouped them in different ways. The intent of the ABET criteria is that the objectives and the outcomes are clearly different things. The easiest way to distinguish them from

each other are that the outcomes should be things that students are expected to achieve by the time they graduate while the objectives are career and professional accomplishments which they would be expected to achieve after graduation. As time has passed program leaders and faculty seem to have become more familiar with this distinction and the confusion has been diminishing.

Some programs and evaluators noted issues with the **Program Outcomes** criterion. One program, which was using student portfolios as the primary method for assessing outcomes, augmented their collection and evaluation of student portfolios based on suggestions made by the program evaluator. This augmentation involved developing very explicit instructions for students describing what they should include in their portfolios, how it should be organized and a rubric for use by the faculty describing how to evaluate the portfolio contents.

With regard to the specific "a-k" outcomes, some programs expressed difficulty sufficiently demonstrating achievement of: f) an understanding of professional and ethical responsibility; h) the broad education necessary to understand the impact of engineering solutions in a global, economic, environmental, and societal context; i) a recognition of the need for, and an ability to engage in life-long learning; and, j) a knowledge of contemporary issues. They have usually developed additional methods for measuring these outcomes and sometimes have developed new courses or added content to existing courses.

Some programs have had difficulty in complying with the requirements of the **Curriculum** criterion related to the culminating major design experience. This program component must provide a significant software engineering design experience to each student. In some cases this "capstone" experience may fall more into the realm of research than design or fail to incorporate appropriate engineering standards and constraints. Programs encountering this problem have had to develop methods to ensure that their projects have significant design content, that the work was clearly and completely documented, and that engineering standards and constraints were appropriately considered.

THE MOST DIFFICULT ISSUES

While the survey results indicated a good deal of agreement between program leaders and program evaluators, there were some exceptions. Specifically, there was some evidence, of inconsistency, and even some contention, related to faculty qualifications and curricular content.

Program leaders generally reported no problems related to faculty qualifications. However, several program evaluators expressed concerns regarding a low proportion of faculty with true breadth and depth of experience in software engineering. This issue seemed to arise primarily in software engineering programs housed in computer science departments. As one evaluator stated, "It is sometimes difficult to agree with established CS programs adding an SE program that they have sufficient breadth and stability in SE to satisfy the ABET criteria."

Another concern of some evaluators related to the isolation of some software engineering faculty members, who seemed to have little involvement with the software engineering practitioner community and with the software engineering education community.

PEVs noted a need for all faculty to be aware of and be involved with the ABET/EAC procedures and self-study preparation. The problem most frequently observed across all criteria has been defining appropriate and viable assessment and evaluation processes. Even when adequate processes have been defined, PEVs often identify problems with faculty compliance. To satisfy the requirements of outcomes assessment, the program faculty members must be committed to ongoing execution of the defined processes. Most programs and evaluators understood that

the **Outcomes Criterion** requires the direct measurement of student outcomes via capstone projects, portfolio evaluations or specific quiz or exam questions. However, almost all agreed that the overhead required to do this rigorously placed a high burden on the programs, particularly for programs that had decided to evaluate all outcomes and all students every year.

As noted previously, the software engineering **Program Criteria** require appropriate curricular content. Several evaluators commented that there were problems with programs' interpretations of the breadth and depth of software engineering material required to satisfy these criteria. They said that these problems have most frequently been seen when programs are developed from a base of a computer science or a computer engineering curriculum.

Two programs reported that they have had problems with a specific program evaluator's interpretation of the requirements related to **Program Criteria**. These evaluators, they say, were looking for coverage of a specific topic area, such as software evolution, as part of the maintenance activities which students are required to be able to do by the time they graduate according to this criterion.

In the case of programs that have had problems with curricular content, faculty members have sometimes felt that they were already covering many of the required software engineering topics. By requiring students to take specific existing computer science courses and adding a software engineering capstone course to the curriculum, they felt that they would meet the breadth and depth requirements.

The programs that have been most successful in satisfying the curriculum requirements of the program criteria have linked their curricula to accepted frameworks such as the Guide to the Software Engineering Body of Knowledge (2004) and Joint Task Force on Computing Curricula (2004) and have made these links explicit in their course syllabi, by describing which courses cover which topics outlined in those documents. The number of specific software engineering courses in these programs usually ranges from six to twelve. Typically those courses cover 50% to 80% of the topics specified in the referenced documents.

While the program criteria do require breadth and depth of software engineering content, it is not necessary that these topics be covered in specific "software engineering" courses. However, if this content is embedded in other (e. g., computer science) courses it must be very clear from the course syllabi and from the work done by students that the software engineering topics are, in fact, being covered. It is a common expectation that at least some of these courses employ textbooks that address a variety of advanced software engineering topics, and that they do not rely primarily on the small number of commonly used introductory software engineering textbooks.

IMPROVEMENTS MADE

The variety of improvements that have been made as a result of assessment and preparation for accreditation visits is extremely long. This section will summarize a subset of those with which the authors are familiar.

For the requirements related to **Students,** a few programs have found that they were not advising and monitoring their students carefully enough. This sometimes resulted in students not completing all of the courses required by the program, usually due to course substitutions that were done without appropriate review. The programs that have had this problem have typically tightened their advising and monitoring processes to insure that the problem does not happen in the future.

Several programs have formed new industrial advisory committees and gotten them deeply involved in helping to specify **Program Educational Objectives**. A few have developed employer surveys to get feedback on achievement of pro-

gram educational objectives and at least one has modified the wording of its objectives to eliminate misunderstandings of the wording. Based on our experience, with our own programs and with programs that we have evaluated, we believe that the greatest benefits to the programs have been the improved relationships between the programs and local industry that have resulted from the involvement of industrial advisory committees in the accreditation process.

In response to shortcomings identified in the **Program Outcomes** area and to the measurement of specific outcomes, many programs have modified the content of specific courses, usually with small changes to assure that prerequisite courses were meeting the expectations of instructors in later courses. Some programs have developed specific courses to assure that students were developing an understanding of professional and ethical responsibilities. Others have developed new methods and courses for assuring that students were receiving a broad education, recognizing the need to engage in life long learning and developing an understanding of contemporary issues. All of these improvements were made as direct results of measurements indicating that student learning results were below expectations for one or more of the specified outcomes.

To effectively demonstrate compliance with the requirements for a major design experience by the **Curriculum** criterion, some programs have provided additional encouragement for students to document their engineering processes, design approaches and their consideration of engineering standards and multiple practical constraints in their design projects.

To address shortcomings related to faculty experience and competencies to cover all curricular areas, as required by the **Faculty** criterion, a few programs have added one or more faculty members. Typically they have taken advantage of existing open positions or of planned retirements to add these resources. To strengthen faculty guidance and oversight, some programs have decided to encourage faculty member participation in workshops related to ABET accreditation and assessment.

To meet the **Program Criteria** requirements for curricular breadth and depth, a number of programs have modified their courses and their curricula to insure that adequate coverage of topics such as verification, validation and maintenance. Some have developed completely new courses to address missing content or to provide additional depth in certain areas.

While few of the programs from which data were collected reported unexpected benefits, those who have made improvements uniformly reported that the improvements made were beneficial and should have been made, with or without an accreditation process. In several cases program leaders agreed that the results of the accreditation review gave them leverage with both members of their faculty and with their institutions' administration to make appropriate improvements. And, finally, all agreed that having ABET accreditation gives credibility to their programs by certifying that their software engineering program is a real engineering program.

FUTURE DIRECTIONS

At the time this chapter was being written, there were 35 undergraduate software engineering programs being offered by colleges and universities in the United States. Fifteen of them have been accredited by ABET. It appears likely that most of the remaining programs, which are not yet accredited, will be seeking initial accreditation within the next few years.

Finally, the National Academy of Engineering has made a recommendation that the master's degree should become the first professional degree accepted for entry into the engineering profession. Currently, ABET allows only one degree level at each institution in each field of engineering to be accredited. If the master's degree becomes

the entry point into the engineering profession, that would imply a policy or practice change for ABET to allow accreditation at both the masters and bachelors level or to award accreditation primarily at the masters level. There are several good arguments for and against each of these proposals. Only time will tell if any change will be made and what form that change is likely to take.

REFERENCES

ABET. (2006). *Accreditation policy and procedure manual.* Baltimore, MD. ABET, Inc. Retrieved May 13, 2007, from http://abet.org/forms.shtml.

Computing Research News (2007), *2005-2006 Taulbe Survey*, May 2007.

Duggins, S. L., & Thomas, B. B. (2002). An historical investigation of graduate software engineering curricula. *Proceedings of the 15th Conference on Software Engineering Education and Training (CSEET'02),* Los Alamitos, CA, IEEE Computer Society Press.

Engineering Accreditation Commission. (1999). *Criteria for accrediting engineering programs: Effective for evaluations during the 2000-2001 Accreditation Cycle.* Baltimore, MD. ABET, Inc.

Engineering Accreditation Commission. (2000). *Criteria for accrediting engineering programs: Effective for evaluations during the 2001-2002 Accreditation Cycle.* Baltimore, MD. ABET, Inc.

Engineering Accreditation Commission. (2001). *Criteria for accrediting engineering programs: Effective for evaluations during the 2002-2003 Accreditation Cycle.* Baltimore, MD. ABET, Inc.

Engineering Accreditation Commission. (2002). *Criteria for accrediting engineering programs: Effective for evaluations during the 2003-2004 Accreditation Cycle.* Baltimore, MD. ABET, Inc.

Engineering Accreditation Commission. (2007). *Criteria for accrediting engineering programs: Effective for evaluations during the 2007-2008 Accreditation Cycle.* Baltimore, MD. ABET, Inc. Retrieved May 13, 2007, from http://abet.org/forms.shtml.

Engineering Accreditation Commission. (2007a). *Engineering self-study questionnaire.* Baltimore, MD. ABET, Inc. Retrieved May 13, 2007, from http://abet.org/forms.shtml.

Guide to the Software Engineering Body of Knowledge (2004), Bourque, P. and Dupuis, R., (Eds.), Los Alamitos, CA, IEEE Computer Society Press.

Joint Task Force on Computing Curricula. (2004). *Software Engineering 2004: Curriculum Guidelines for Undergraduate Degree Programs in Software Engineering.* IEEE Computer Society and Association for Computing Machinery.

Tomayko, J. E. (1998). Forging a discipline: An outline history of software engineering education. *Annals of Software Engineering 6(1998),* 3-18.

Chapter XIV
Software Engineering at Full Scale:
A Unique Curriculum

Jochen Ludewig
Universität Stuttgart, Germany

ABSTRACT

In 1996, a new Software Engineering curriculum was launched at Universität Stuttgart. It was based on many years of practical experience teaching computer science and also on experience in industry where most of our graduates will find jobs. While the topics of this curriculum are not very different from those of computer science, there is much more emphasis on problem solving, software construction, and project work. In 2009, our traditional curriculum leading to the so-called diploma (equivalent to a master's degree) will be replaced by a new curriculum according to the bachelor and master concept. This chapter describes both the old and the new curriculum, and discusses problems and achievements.

INTRODUCTION

Software engineering is usually taught as a special course for students studying computer science or engineering. But software engineering is not just a set of topics, as the SWEBOK (SWEBOK, 2004) suggests, but also, or primarily, a particular mindset, a way of thinking, very similar to the mindset engineers tend to have. One might say that you get a software engineer if you combine a computer science graduate's knowledge with the mental structure, the way of thinking, reasoning, and solving problems, of an engineer.

In order to educate such people, it is not enough to modify our CS programs by some cosmetic changes, a new lecture or a nice little project. We need a radical change. And we cannot pretend that our knowledge should be good enough for our students; we have to teach them what they need rather than teaching them what we like, because most people like to teach what they have taught all the time (Ludewig, Reißing, 1998). This paper describes such a new curriculum that was launched in 1996, and discusses our experience.

BACKGROUND

Traditionally, students of science and engineering in Germany finally receive a *diploma*, which is equivalent to a master's degree. Since there is no formal level below the diploma, there is no equivalent to the Bachelor's degree and, hence, no straightforward mapping between a curriculum in Germany and a curriculum in Great Britain or in the United States.

The Diploma curriculum is similar to what is called an integrated master's degree program in Great Britain, India and some other countries.

Though space does not allow for a detailed comparison, here are some significant differences:

- In Germany, three levels of school education are available, differing in their requirements and in their duration. The highest level leads to a final examination, the so-called "Abitur". One out of three young people actually pass this examination, usually at an age around 19. In most of the engineering studies including computer science and software engineering, those who hold an Abitur may enrol without entrance examinations. But many of them underestimate the difficulties they encounter at university. That is one of the reasons why many students fail soon after beginning.
- A complete curriculum consists of 9 semesters: 4 semesters for the "basic studies", another 4 for the "advanced studies", and one for the diploma thesis. Most students take more time, resulting in an average of some 12 semesters. Many students have a part-time job in industry, or even run a small business.

- Both written and oral examinations are offered once in every semester; there are no mid-term exams. Students may attend a lecture this year and take the examination next year or even later. If they fail, they are required to repeat the examination after another semester. If they do not pass in the second attempt, they have to leave.
- The curriculum of the basic studies (semesters 1 through 4) is fairly rigid because there is little choice for the students. Still, they may postpone lectures and examinations. Therefore, only a minority has actually finished all the examinations that constitute the so-called "Pre-diploma" (*Diplomvorprüfung*) after two years. The Pre-diploma is not a degree but only the entrance condition for the advanced studies. Though the Pre-diploma may at first sight resemble a bachelor's degree, it is in fact very different because it covers mainly fundamental topics like mathematics and theory.
- In the advanced studies, the students can arrange their schedule as they like. When they have met all requirements, they can start their diploma thesis, which is strictly limited to six months.

The effect of these differences is that our students must take full responsibility for themselves. If they fail to work continuously, they will drop out sooner or later, as more than 50 % actually do. Those who survive can usually handle common problems fairly well. Colleagues from abroad who come to Germany and teach at our university tend to find that the system is strange for them but works well for those who succeed.

Faculty members in Germany enjoy a constitutional freedom of teaching: While we have to teach, *we* decide *what* we teach. This freedom has a subtle influence on curricula: There are no standardized components like in the US, because any professor teaching e.g. the basic course "introduction to CS" can (and often will) change the content, the text book, and the exercises. When we design a new curriculum, we better make sure that we can actually implement it with the faculty that is around. If they do not like it, the curriculum will not work.

A few years ago, there was a political decision (the so called "Bologna agreement") to switch to the bachelor/master schedule; these changes will be discussed in the final part of this chapter.

Other changes take place as well. Traditionally, universities (like schools) were free for the students who had to pay a small administrational fee only. Now, they are charged in most states of our federal republic. Currently, charges are low compared to most universities in the world (around 1000 € per year), but this may be only the beginning. Private schools and universities do exist in Germany but are not relevant in a statistical sense. More than 96 % of all students attend one of the public universities; if only universities offering a Ph.D. are considered, it is more than 99 % (HRK, 2007).

CONCEPTS

When the Software Engineering curriculum (SEC) was designed in 1995 and 1996, little material was available. There was a guideline issued by the German CS society (Gesellschaft für Informatik, 1985); a new guideline was being prepared at that time. While the new guideline did not influence our curriculum, the curriculum had some impact on the guideline (Gesellschaft für Informatik, 1997; Mahn et al., 1999). Some of our concepts, in particular the large projects, have been successfully copied in other universities (cp. Bungartz, Bernreuther, 2006), but a complete university-level curriculum in software engineering has not yet been offered anywhere else in Germany.

In 1995, our department decided to have an evaluation of the CS curriculum including inter-

views with alumni. Many of them voted for better education in software engineering.

The SEC was launched in 1996. Since then, every year some 60 to 140 students were enrolled. In 1999, the SEC was evaluated by an international group of peers, with extremely positive results. Some minor changes were implemented shortly after. This paper refers to the SEC that has been applied since 2000.

The fundamental idea was to offer a curriculum that comprises most of the courses also contained in the CS curriculum, but far more project work of various types. The structure is very similar to an electrical engineering curriculum. (The author who designed the curriculum holds a diploma in electrical engineering.) This concept is often confused with an education covering both traditional engineering and CS, like the curriculum at MacMaster University in Hamilton, Ontario (Parnas, 1999). While their graduates *are* engineers in a traditional sense, our graduates should cooperate with other engineers, but not replace them. The similarity to other engineering studies lies in the practical, constructive approach: If you encounter a problem, solve it using a minimum of resources!

Many universities offer courses in software engineering as an add-on for CS students. But, despite SWEBOK, software engineering is not only a body of knowledge. Software engineering is a paradigm. If you put physicists into some courses on materials, they will still be physicists, not electrical engineers, because they have not enjoyed an engineer's education. Software engineering must be taught, and practiced, early.

Some time ago, when I talked to a student, I asked him if he was a CS student or an SE student. He said that he was a first year SE student. "Well, then you won't really feel a big difference, do you?" "Oh yes, I do", was his answer. "The CS students are those whose programs are unreadable."

COURSES

Students of Software Engineering share more than 50 % of their courses with CS students. They all have the usual courses on mathematics, theoretical computer science, programming languages, data base systems, etc. Figure 1 shows the complete SEC. Black lines under the boxes represent examinations, while dotted lines stand for the successful participation in exercises or small projects.

"L" stands for lecture, "E" for exercise, "P" for projects, "H" (hour) for anything else. The lesson is 45 min per week, but the usual format is a double pack. Therefore, "3L 1E", e.g., means three lectures plus one exercise, 90 min each, in two weeks.

Figure 1. Software Engineering curriculum

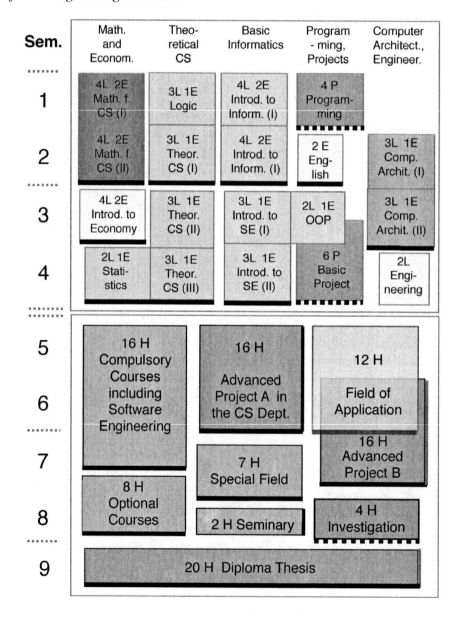

Here is a list of those components (courses) that were designed for, and are offered exclusively to, the Software Engineering students. They are discussed in detail in the following paragraphs.

a.   Programming lab (b (1st semester)
b.   Courses in English and economics
c.   Programming in the large ("Introduction to SE I" in Figure 1), including project-manager training using a project simulator (SESAM) (3rd semester)
d.   Programming in the small ("OOP" in Figure 1) (3rd semester)
e.   Formal methods ("Introduction to SE II" in Figure 1) (4th semester)
f.   First software project ("Basic project" in Figure 1) (4th semester)
g.   Lecture on advanced software engineering (5th semester)
h.   Large software project (5th and 6th semester)
i.   Large software project in an application area (6th and 7th semester)
j.   Project on problem analysis (8th semester)

All the lectures described below include exercises where small problems are discussed. The exercises are usually under the control of Ph.D. students (who are, in most cases, employees of the university). The volume is given in credit points. Our standard formula is 3 credit points per 2 lessons (= 2*45 min) per week for a full semester (15 weeks).

COURSE DETAILS

Programming Lab (1st Semester; 3 Credit Points)

Many students have written programs before they enter the university, while a few have not. Therefore, we have to teach programming, preferably using a language that is equally unknown to all the students. Currently, we teach Ada as the first programming language.

Programming is taught in the introductory course (where SE students are not separated from the CS students). The programming lab is directed towards *systematic* programming, with emphasis on style guides and other standards (e.g. for comments) that are to be observed. Our message is: The program that you build is not for you. It is for others who have to read and maintain it.

Until recently, we used to teach programming like most people do, i.e. bottom-up. Students learn some concepts of programming, like types and control structures. Then, they build a small program. From a software engineering point of view, that is wrong. Soon after, it takes us much effort to convince our students that large programs are not just multiples of small ones. The fact that software engineering is primarily concerned with complexity is not well integrated.

Therefore, we changed this course, starting with a fairly large software system. We use a program named AdaDoc, which generates HTML documents from Ada code. It is sufficiently large (2700 statements, 9341 non-comment source lines, more than 23 000 LOC altogether) to challenge the students. In order to modify this program, they have to understand it, though only partially. They easily learn to appreciate good style (egoless programming). The new course started only recently (in October 2007), but the first results are very promising. Students co-operate and learn from experience and understanding what used to be a boring, bureaucratical command.

Courses in English and Economics (3rd and 4th Semester; 6 Credit Points)

All our students (at least those who grew up in Germany) learned English in school. But some of them did not learn it very well. In order to make sure that our graduates can read English documents and communicate on an international level, we offer a course followed by a test (similar to a TOEFL). They also learn some economics because many of them will later be managers or run a software company.

Programming in the Large, Including Project Manager Training Using a Project Simulator (SESAM) (3rd Semester; 6 Credit Points)

The whole curriculum is project-driven. Therefore, the lecture on programming in the large covers a small project from planning and cost estimation all the way to testing, in order to equip our students for the larger projects (see d, g, h). Towards the end of this course, students practice software project management using a simulator that was developed in the department (SESAM; Drappa, Ludewig, 2000).

Programming in the Small (3rd Semester; 4 Credit Points)

Complementary to programming-in-the-large (b), students learn how to develop object-oriented systems using UML and Java.

First Software Project (4th Semester, 9 Credit Points)

In groups of three, students develop a mid-size program. All students start from the same (informal) specification. Some of the results are still in use, e.g. a tool for generating time shift diagrams.

Formal Methods (4th Semester; 5 Credit Points)

Students learn how to apply formal techniques for specification and verification; currently, they use Alloy as a specification language.

Lecture on Advanced Software Engineering (5th Semester; 6 Credit Points)

This lecture has two goals: Firstly, students should know more about software project management for mastering the problems of the large projects (see below). Secondly, some topics not strongly related to their project work like process assessment and improvement or ethics need to be addressed as well.

Much time is dedicated to discussion and motivation. Only if the students understand *why* good software engineering is desirable will they be able to convince their colleagues in industry.

Large Software Project (5th and 6th Semester; 24 Credit Points)

Research groups submit proposals for projects to the curriculum committee. These projects should not include research but serious software development. Most frequently, students develop some new tool or a new component for an existing tool. When a project has been accepted students can select it; but their freedom is limited by the condition that each project must have between six and twelve participants.

We require for each project certain roles to be provided by the research group: There must be a **professor** who will eventually examine the students; there is a **customer**, and there are (usually) two **supervisors** who will help the students when necessary. In order to avoid confusion, the customer must not serve as a supervisor; these roles are clearly separated. All responsibility rests with the students. Projects differ widely; in the Software Engineering group, all projects start with a bidding phase. If there are nine participants (the ideal size!), they form three competing companies. After talking to the customer, they will prepare a presentation, trying to win the project. Then the groups are merged and they all work together. (The research group is not involved except for the roles mentioned above.) They will elect a project manager and organize their work following the principles they have learned in their lectures and in the small project they have done before. While the project manager usually keeps his or her role, all other students take several positions; somebody may e.g. co-author the specification, implement parts of the system, and organize the reviews. This is left to the team. They have to document their effort, so they notice if somebody spends significantly less or more time on the project than others.

For ten to twelve months, the students spend much time together, and they experience all the problems and frustrations of real projects. This includes the effects of working in a fairly large group; while three people can cooperate without much organization, eight or ten can not. So they learn to appreciate good processes and sound project management. We try to make sure that they are eventually successful because we strongly believe that positive experience is much more effective than negative experience.

There is not just one "right solution". If it works and the documents are fairly complete and useful, it is fine. We found that a process with two passes is promising: They design and implement the core parts in about half of the time and then ask for feedback. Depending on the corrections and improvements that turn out to be necessary, they add some of the parts that are merely nice to have in the second pass.

Finally, the students will deliver a product to the customer. This final presentation tends to be quite an event. And most of the projects deliver software that is as good as, or even better than, software that is commercially available. Many of the systems are actually used and maintained afterwards.

The large projects include lectures and a seminary which addresses some more ambitious topics related to or beyond the project. We give marks on the project work (weight 0.5), the seminary (0.2), and the examination (0.3), resulting in one final mark. Nobody can pass who fails in the project work. We usually grade the project as a whole and apply corrections for those whose contributions were clearly above or below average.

In our (i.e. in the Software Engineering group's) projects, we tried various settings, depending on the task. Sometimes, we had customers from industry; sometimes we were the customers (asking for a new component for our SESAM system, see above). Our latest project (finished in November 2007) produced a new tool for glass box testing. This tool can collect, and visualize, several coverage metrics. The developers were required to develop software for the public domain; in the seminary, we discussed not only technical aspects of testing, but also questions concerning the licenses used in the public domain.

Large Software Project in an Application Area (6th and 7th Semesters)

Every student chooses an application area where he or she has to collect 18 credit points from written or oral examinations. We currently offer three such areas:

- Traffic systems (railway, air traffic, etc.)
- Industrial automation (including robotics and all the machines used in modern factories)
- Technology management (e.g. product engineering)

In this application area (i.e. in the department that sponsors the application area), students do not only attend lectures and are graded but also do their second large project. While these projects are formally just like the first ones, they tend to be more "realistic" because they take place in an environment where software engineering is not considered a primary goal and students cannot expect to get much support.

There is no particular reason to have just the application areas listed above; they (i.e. the departments) happened to be interested when we started and were able to offer projects for our students. We have to make sure that projects are sufficiently large; therefore, we did not yet extend the list (though other departments applied as well).

Small Project on Problem Analysis (8th Semester; 5 Credit Points)

In industry it is necessary to make decisions based on insufficient information. However, students do not like to express a definitive opinion. They would rather collect data in tables and charts and avoid taking a position. In this small project, we usually have a partner in industry where some question has to be answered, like "should we switch to a more complex tool for software configuration management?" or "is XP an attractive approach for our projects?" Then, three students analyse the situation, collect useful information on the problem, read the available books and papers, interview the stakeholders, and give a presentation on their final decision. Though this is only a small project, our experience is overwhelming. The students like it, and the companies like it even more.

Industrial Experience (3 Months, at Any Time)

Our students are required to spend at least three months in a company where software is developed. Only a few parameters are given, such as the minimum size of the company. The students have to deliver a report on their experience; the report is checked but not graded.

In most cases, our students learn that software engineering is not easy under the harsh conditions of industry. Some of the reports are more like horror tales. But the students recognize what is missing and they have a much better understanding of good software engineering afterwards. Reading their reports provides feedback for our lectures.

EXPERIENCE AND LESSONS LEARNED

After more than ten years, we have collected a large number of observations some of which are consistent with our expectations, while others are surprising.

Daring a Revolution

- Introducing a radically new curriculum is a very ambitious project that will fail in most circumstances. The hardest part is convincing the colleagues; they usually try to defend the status quo because any real change means either more work or less influence for somebody.
- Some of our new students expected a curriculum without mathematics and theory. They had to face the fact that SE is everything but just hacking.

Demand and Supply

- The demand for this curriculum has been steady for many years. Now, the number of new students is getting close to the numbers in CS. In 2007, for instance, there were 109 freshmen in CS and 89 in Software Engineering.
- Since the graduates hold a CS degree just like those who were in the CS program, they are hired like other CS graduates. (For several years, industry has been desperately looking for software people in Germany.) Those

in industry who know our program often ask for graduates who could contribute to software quality assurance and other fields where software engineering competence is essential.

Projects

- Large projects are highly attractive and often deliver very good results. Many professors are now keen on offering such projects because they know they get sound and really useful software. Most students like projects because they can demonstrate their abilities, learn a lot, and get much more satisfaction than from examinations. A large and useful project creates a win-win-situation.

- Supervising a project is hard work, even though we do not participate in the projects. Most effort is spent on checking interme-

diate results and for fire fighting when the project is in trouble. We want the students to ask for help if they need it; but they often do not recognize that they need it. Therefore, we have to watch their progress. Before a project is launched, the environment has to be set up because there is not enough time in the projects for evaluating and acquiring new tools, etc. On the other hand, we are not afraid of issuing tasks without foreseeing the solution. In engineering, there is not just one correct path. But any result can be checked for its qualities. It is not uncommon that students find solutions that the supervisors never thought of.

- Working in groups seems to have an effect on the individual marks. Our students are significantly more homogeneous than CS students in their examinations (Figure 2).

Figure 2. Average absolute deviation from the average number of points (written exams in programming languages and compiler construction, where both CS students and SE students participate)

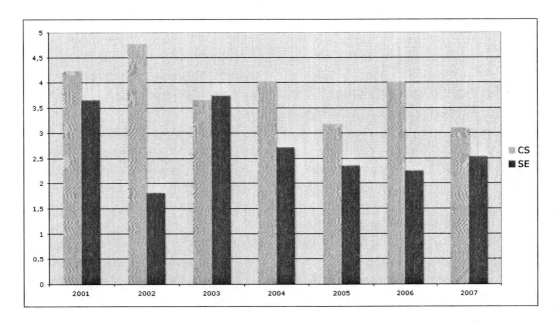

- Some of the students who are not doing very well in their exams show a great performance in projects. Our traditional criteria are biased towards scientific work, though most of our graduates will never do research but develop and maintain software systems and soon become managers.

- When students do real projects, there is a strong demand for lectures that address real problems. Students explicitly ask for hints (how to write specs, how to design software, etc.). Using one's own textbook (Ludewig, Lichter, 2007) is quite a relief in this situation, but its omissions are soon revealed. CS students who are usually not exposed to project work do not ask such questions.

- In every project, a certain style of cooperation and communication will emerge; we do not yet know which conditions determine this style (otherwise, we would like to influence it). The project manager is obviously important; but the students choose their project manager, we do not interfere.

- Any research group in the CS department may offer projects, i.e. act as a customer. But customers do not always appreciate good software engineering. This is not only true in industry but also within our university. We had several cases where the customer challenged planning and quality assurance in favour of fast progress in coding. Students have to learn that they must "sell" their approach well in order to avoid conflicts between tough deadlines and ambitious quality goals.

Soft Skills

- Soft skills, like giving presentations, negotiating changes or delays, or organizing groups, do not develop automatically when needed; they have to be taught. We offer a course on techniques for writing papers and giving presentations. We also use the semi-naries for coaching the presentation skills. Anything else is done within the projects.

- Industrial experience is very useful in any case: Students who find a company with high software engineering standards can see how it works. Others who get into an environment where little is known about software engineering will see what happens when people work on software unsystematically, without quality assurance, etc.

- We do not yet offer any other training courses, e.g. courses on group dynamics, mediation, or documentation. There is certainly a need for them, but not necessarily a demand. Students tend to spend their time only on activities that pay (in terms of credit points).

SWITCHING TO BACHELOR'S DEGREES

As mentioned in the beginning, our diploma will soon be abandoned, making way for bachelor's and master's degrees. While students starting in October 2008 will still follow the traditional schedule, those who enter in October 2009 will be in bachelor programs. Many universities have already switched to the new structures. (But new students prefer to enrol in other universities, demonstrating little confidence in the imported degrees.) In general, this is a revolution imposed from above, not supported by most of the faculty.

The Bologna agreement defined a total of 10 semesters. But most universities agreed upon a 6 plus 4 schedule, so we have to design a six-semester undergraduate course. Some professors believe that they can simply rearrange their curriculum because they expect the students, at least the good ones, to stay for the master's degree. But a majority of our students will leave as bachelors, because they are offered attractive jobs, their grants are discontinued, and they are fed up with taking

Figure 3. The future Software Engineering curriculum (bachelor level)

Sem. 1	4L 2E Math. f. CS (I)	3L 1E Logic & Discr. Struct.	4L 2E Introd. to Inform. (I)	2 P Pro- gram.	2 P Sw. Qual.
2	4L 2E Math. f. CS (II)	3L 1E Automata & Form. L.	4L 2E Introd. to Inform. (I)	3L 1E Introd. to SE (I)	
3	3L 1E Selectives (Cat. A)	3L 1E Algorithms & Comp.	4 P Basic Project	3L 1E OOP	3L 1E Computer Architecture
4	3L 1E Selectives (Cat. A)	3L 1E Selectives (Cat. A)	16 P	3L 1E Introd. to SE (II)	2 E Eng- lish / 2 H Gene- ral Skills
5	3L 1E Selectives (Cat. A)	3L 1E Safety & Security	Large Project, incl. Lectures and Seminary		
6	3L 1E Selectives (Cat. B)	3L 1E Selectives (Cat. C)	4 H Investi- gation	8 H Bachelor's Thesis	

exams all the time. Therefore, we have to make sure that a bachelor is not an incomplete master but a complete software engineer.

In 2007, we have reached an agreement upon the new Software Engineering undergraduate curriculum (SEUC, see Figure 3). A master's course is currently under construction; since Stuttgart is the capital of German car manufacturing, we might offer a degree with strong links to the car industry ("Automotive Software Engineering").

The catalogues mentioned at the left are A: programming languages, data base systems etc.; B: all areas represented by full professors in the department; C: all courses in the department.

IS IT STILL THAT DIFFERENT?

Since the gates of the SEC were opened in 1996, many universities all over the world have started, or improved, their software engineering programs. One might expect that the SEC is no longer a very special concept.

In fact, the SEC is obviously consistent with the goals and principles stated in the report by the IEEE CS & ACM Task Force (2004). But there are also differences, partially due to different traditions. The most important point seems to be the SEEK, the Software Engineering Education Knowledge. All entries in the list are highly attractive candidates for software engineering education. Still, we would not attempt to cover them all because we feel that we will never achieve completeness in any sense. We estimate one deep experience, even in a fairly small niche of software engineering, higher than any high-level overview. Our graduates are expected to solve problems they (and we) never heard of. We cannot equip them for their future challenges. But we can provide the experience that systematic work, continuous quality assurance, plus a fair portion of both knowledge and creativity do work. That is possibly the shortest description of our approach. We want to grow great software engineers (Brooks, 1987).

ENTERING THE AGE OF SPECIALISATION

Software engineering is a great area. Many of our heroes, like Dave Parnas, Barry Boehm, and Fred Brooks, are still around and still contribute. Which other field could offer almost the whole history in one conference room, as we saw in 1991 (Broy, Denert, 2002)?

But the pioneers give way to young experts. Since the field is large, there is not just one area of expertise, but many of them, say half a dozen or even a dozen. Software engineering in banks and insurance companies is not like software engineering in automotive systems. Therefore, there will be specialists on software in various application areas because these people differ in their goals, in their methods, in their languages and tools.

Specialisation is actually taking place but has hardly been reflected in books and magazines, and even less so in the education system. There are – at least – three reasons for this delay:

- There is no generally accepted taxonomy of the field. We do not know how to cut it into pieces.
- In most of these areas, we do not have the accumulated knowledge that would make up a scientific domain.

- Specialists who could teach in those areas do exist, but hardly within the universities. Most colleagues in the department will not like the idea of having several new professors who are not members of the CS community in a traditional sense.

Michael Jackson (1999) has pointed out that specialisation is very desirable. The IEEE CS & ACM Task Force (2004, 2.3.3) states: "Domain-specific techniques, tools, and components typically provide the most compelling software engineering success stories." But to date, things have not changed a lot. If private companies analysed their needs, they would certainly find that they should sponsor new professors in their particular fields. Maybe we should try to communicate this idea.

CONCLUSION

The SEC, started in 1996, has attracted more than 1000 students so far. Very few switched to CS later (which is comparatively easy). Many graduates have expressed their view that they have acquired very useful knowledge and experience. The curriculum has been influential in many other German universities, though nowhere else has a complete software engineering curriculum been established.

Very soon, the SEC will be replaced by an undergraduate course leading to a bachelor's degree. Most, though not all, features will survive. A master's degree offering some specialisation will soon be added.

REFERENCES

Brooks, F.P. (1987). No silver bullet – Essence and accidents of software engineering. *IEEE Computer, 20*(4), 10-19.

Broy, M., E. Denert (eds.) (2002). *Software pioneers: Contributions to software engineering.* Springer-Verlag, Berlin.

Bungartz, H.-J., & Bernreuther, M. (2006). First experiences with group projects in CSE Education. *Computing in Science and Engineering,* July 2006, 16-25.

Drappa, A., & J. Ludewig (2000). *Simulation in Software Engineering Training.* Proceedings of the 22nd ISCE, Limerick, Ireland, 199-208.

Gesellschaft für Informatik (1985). Ausbildung von Diplom-Informatikern an wissenschaftlichen Hochschulen. Empfehlung der GI vom 18. *März 1985, Informatik-Spektrum 8,* 164–165.

Gesellschaft für Informatik (1997). Lehrinhalte und Veranstaltungsformen im Informatikstudium, ergänzende Empfehlungen. Informatik Spektrum 20, Heft 5.

IEEE CS and ACM Joint Task Force on Computing Curricula (2004). Software Engineering 2004, Curriculum Guidelines for Undergraduate Degree Programs in Software Engineering. August 23, 2004.

Jackson, M. (1999). Specializing in software engineering. *IEEE Software, 16*(6), 119-121.

Ludewig, J., & Reißing, R. (1998). *Teaching what they need instead of teaching what we like* – the new Software Engineering curriculum at the University of Stuttgart. *Information and Software Technology, 40*(4), 239 - 244.

Ludewig, J., & Lichter, H. (2007). *Software engineering—Grundlagen, Menschen, Prozesse, Techniken.* dpunkt.verlag Heidelberg.

Mahn, A., et al. (1999). Empfehlungen der Gesellschaft für Informatik e.V. zur Stärkung der Anwendungsorientierung in Diplom-Studiengängen der Informatik an Universitäten, Informatik-Spektrum 22, 444-448.

Parnas, D. L. (1999). Software engineering programmes are not computer science programmes. *IEEE Software, 16*(6), 19-30. (Originally published in the Annals of Software Engineering, Vol. 6, April 1999, 19-37)

SWEBOK (2004). Software engineering body of knowledge. http://www.swebok.org/

HRK (2007). Hochschulkompass der HRK (Hochschulrektorenkonferenz). http://www.hochschulkompass.de/

Chapter XV
Continuous Curriculum Restructuring in a Graduate Software Engineering Program

Daniela Rosca
Monmouth University, USA

William Tepfenhart
Monmouth University, USA

Jiacun Wang
Monmouth University, USA

Allen Milewski
Monmouth University, USA

ABSTRACT

The development, maintenance and delivery of a software engineering curriculum present special challenges not found in other engineering disciplines. The continuous advances of the field of software engineering impose a high frequency of changes reflected in the curriculum and course content. This chapter describes the challenges of delivering a program meeting the needs of industry and students. It presents the lessons learned during 21 years of offering such a program, and dealing with issues pertaining to continuous curriculum and course content restructuring, the influence of the student body on the curriculum and course content. The chapter concludes with our recommendations for those who are seeking to create a graduate program in software engineering, with a special note on the situations where an undergraduate and graduate program will need to coexist in the same department.

INTRODUCTION

The objective of this chapter is to prepare those who are seeking to introduce a graduate program in software engineering (SE) for the challenges they will face. Towards that end, the lessons learned during 21 years of offering such a program at Monmouth University will be presented. As it will be demonstrated, the development, maintenance and delivery of a software engineering curriculum present special challenges not found in other engineering disciplines.

This chapter describes the challenges of delivering a program that meets the needs of industry and students in a highly dynamic field. The evolution of the curriculum induced by the domain's continuous advances and evolution in industry practice will be presented. The special meaning of continuous course content development in software engineering will be argued through issues pertaining to dated textbooks, ever-changing programming languages, operating systems, and software tools. The chapter will also present our experience in dealing with the diversity of the student body, and its influence on the curriculum and course content. The chapter will conclude with our recommendations for constructing a similar program, with a special emphasis on situations where an undergraduate and graduate program in software engineering will need to coexist in the same department.

BACKGROUND

Although software engineering was recognized as a field in 1968 at the NATO sponsored conference on the subject (Naur, 1968), it took universities and colleges a significant amount of time to respond to that fact. It was not until 1986 that Monmouth University (MU) started a graduate program dedicated to software engineering, which was offered by its Computer Science Department. In 1995 Monmouth created the first Software Engineering Department in United States. Now it is one of the pioneer universities offering a bachelor's degree in software engineering.

One motivation for creating a separate software engineering program and department was the awareness of the skills that industry would like students to have upon graduation, which are not stressed by most computer science curricula.

These skills include teamwork, communications, time management, engineering problem solving, quantitative and qualitative process management, reuse, requirements management, system architecture, testing and project management.

As one of the few universities with extensive and comprehensive experience in offering software engineering programs, we have learned much about providing such a program. With more and more undergraduate software engineering programs appearing, we feel it is beneficial to other institutions for us to share the problems encountered and lessons learned over the past 21 years. A summary of the problems encountered and the lessons learned are presented here:

- **Continuous curriculum restructuring.** One can expect to revisit the overall curriculum of the program every four to five years, in order to accommodate changes in industry practice and educational expectations. This is reflected also in the historical investigation of the graduate software engineering curriculum reported in (Duggins, 2002).
- **Continuous course content restructuring.** It is critically needed due to the dynamics of the field. The continuous development of course content implies also a continuous development of course projects, and dealing with dated textbooks, ever changing operating systems, programming languages and software tools.
- **Hiring and retaining faculty.** The need for new faculty to have a record of sustained scholarly accomplishments and industrial experience enforces great restrictions on the number of available candidates, as it was also notified by Glass (2003). Retaining faculty is complicated by the fact that in addition to performing their normal teaching duties SE faculty must continually keep up with changes in the field as a whole.
- **Influence of the diversity of the student body on the curriculum and course**

content. Issues raised by a diversity of educational backgrounds, employment status, educational goals, and communication skills introduce challenges that need to be dealt with by any software engineering program.

The remainder of the chapter discusses in detail the topics presented above. It begins with the presentation of the curriculum evolution over the history of our program. Then it discusses various issues involved in the continuous changes of the software engineering course content. The subsequent section outlines our experience in hiring and retaining the faculty, followed by a presentation of the student body influence of the diversity of the curriculum and course content. The chapter concludes with the presentation of our recommendations for those interested in starting a graduate program in software engineering, and future trends of the MU program. This discussion will emphasize the accommodation of an undergraduate and graduate program in software engineering in the same department.

CONTINUOUS CURRICULUM RESTRUCTURING

Over its short history, software engineering (SE) as a field has been a moving target. We have observed the introduction of the capability maturity model, the unified modeling language, personal and team software process, and corporate adherence to ISO Standards emerge as major forces within software engineering organizations. We have observed important changes in analysis and design with transitions from structured analysis and design ,to object-oriented analysis and design. Even the architectures being released today have shifted from client-server architectures to distributed architectures with the current trend being focused on service-oriented architectures.

A curriculum that addresses the skills and practices required by professionals in this field must continuously reinvent itself over time. The curriculum of Software Engineering changes with a frequency on the order of twice a decade as opposed to decades for engineering (Clough, 2005) and sciences (Stryer, 2003), in general. Just about every aspect of the software engineering curriculum is susceptible to change over a decade. In order to accommodate industry's needs and to keep pace with the advances of software engineering as a field, we have added or dropped courses, and added new tracks and programs. The decisions were made in the context of creating and maintaining a balance between the theory, technology and practical aspects of software engineering.

Changing the curriculum can not be performed in an ad hoc manner. We follow a well-defined process. First, the faculty discusses the need for change based on feedback from industry, students, and current publications. The acquisition of feedback is a continuous process that is assisted through an industry advisory board, alumni surveys, student exit interviews, student learning outcomes assessment, periodical evaluation of the program by an external reviewer who is a prominent figure in software engineering education, and attendance at professional meetings. We have established a set of learning outcomes that we monitor on a regular basis and we take into consideration when the need for a significant curriculum change is required.

Next, the program director writes a proposal identifying the new curriculum, and any additional courses that might be required. This effort includes writing a complete syllabus for each course that is introduced, modifying existing syllabi for courses with significant content changes, and a justification for each course that is dropped.

The proposal is put forth to the faculty in the department for comments. Comments include challenges to the changes in course content and discussion of the overall package. The syllabi for the various courses may undergo several iterations.

Once the proposal is approved within the department, the proposal is sent to the chairs meeting within the school. Often times, changes to the software curriculum may require changes in the course content of other departments (e.g., computer science and the business school). If significant push-back arises from the other departments within the school, the proposal is reconsidered by department.

At the school chairs meeting it can be decided that a stronger business case is required. An external body typically develops this business case. It is either a survey developed by an independent firm, or by an external industrial advisory committee. The business case reflects the needs and state of industry, which will attract new students.

After the eventual suggestions for change are incorporated into the proposal, it is submitted to the university graduate studies committee. Here the curriculum is evaluated in terms of its consistency with the University Policies applied to graduate programs. This includes establishing maximum class sizes, the number of contact hours, assignment of lab fees, and other factors.

Next we present the evolution of the Monmouth University's Graduate Software Engineering Curriculum. This evolution shows a gradual transition from a software engineering program created inside a Computer Science department, towards a program with engineering courses that span the entire software lifecycle. It incorporates the results of a strong collaboration between academia and industry (Powell, 1997).

The Initial Curriculum (1986)

The initial software engineering curriculum at Monmouth University consisted of 30 credits, with 6 core courses and 4 electives (see Figure 1). The core courses covered in detail only the implementation (in Ada) and project management aspects of the software lifecycle, due to the

limited availability of faculty with an appropriate background. The curriculum looked more like "a computer science curriculum with an engineering flavor" (Dart, 1997), covering classic computer science courses such as algorithms, operating systems, computer architecture and database management systems.

Students' practical training was accomplished in a 3-credit practicum course. This course consisted of a team project to develop a software system from initial requirements to the final, tested and documented product. The early curriculum was biased more on theoretical aspects (notice the heavy concentration on mathematical foundations of SE), with less exposure to specific SE technology and practice, as was very early recommended in (Ford, 1987).

1991 Curriculum Changes

This curriculum added a number of SE courses, including formal methods, formal specifications, software process and SE environments (see Figure 2). However, it still had a bias towards computer science, offering an artificial intelligence course, 4 courses of mathematical foundations and formal methods, and 4 courses in network technology, due to our geographic location in an area dominated by the telecommunications industry. It was similar to the First MSE model curriculum (Ardis, 1989a; Ardis 1989b) that recommended a set of 10-12 courses, which comprised 6 core courses, 3 or more electives and a two-semester practicum project. However, due to the lack of qualified faculty, the core courses offered were not able to cover the entire software lifecycle.

1995 Curriculum Changes

In 1995 the curriculum was substantially changed to include 36 credits, with 10 core and 2 elective courses (see Figure 3), in order to comply with the Software Engineering Institute model curriculum (Ardis, 1989) and the 1991 Computing

Figure 1. 1986 curriculum

Core Courses
(6 Courses = 18 Credits)
SE 501 Mathematical Foundation of Software Engineering I
(3 credits)
SE 505 Programming-in-the-large (3 credits)
SE 510 Computer Network Design (3 Credits)
SE 516 Software Engineering I (3 credits)
SE 518 Project Management (3 credits)
SE 525 System Project Implementation (3 credits)
Elective Courses
(4 Courses = 12 Credits)
SE 502 Mathematical Foundation of Software Engineering II
(3 Credits)
SE 506 Programming-in-the-small (3 credits)
SE 509 Programming Languages (3 Credits)
SE 511 Protocol Engineering (3 Credits)
SE 512 Algorithms Design and Analysis (3 Credits)
SE 514 Computer Architecture (3 Credits)
SE 515 Operating Systems Implementation (3 Credits)
SE 517 Software Engineering II (3 Credits)
SE 519 Database Management (3 Credits)

Figure 2. 1991 curriculum

Core Courses
(6 Courses = 18 Credits)
SE 501 Mathematical Foundation of Software Engineering I
(3 credits)
SE 505 Software System Design (3 credits)
SE 506 Formal Methods in Programming (3 credits)
SE 516 Software Engineering (3 credits)
SE 518 Project Management (3 credits)
SE 525 System Project Implementation (3 credits)

Elective Courses
(4 Courses = 12 Credits)
SE 502 Mathematical Foundation of Software Engineering II
(3 Credits)
SE 503 Intro. to Computer-Communication Networking
(3 Credits)
SE 509 Programming Languages (3 Credits)
SE 510 Computer Network Design (3 Credits)
SE 511 Protocol Engineering (3 Credits)
SE 519 Database Management (3 Credits)
SE 522 Software Engineering Environments (3 Credits)
SE 532 Software Process Quality (3 Credits)
SE 534 Formal Specifications of Software Systems
(3 Credits)
SE 536 Fundamentals of Computer Security (3 Credits)
SE 538 Advanced Topics in Networking Topology
(3 Credits)
SE 540 Introduction to Artificial Intelligence (3 Credits)

Figure 3. 1995 curriculum

Core Courses
(10 Courses = 30 Credits)
SE 501 Mathematical Foundation of Software Engineering I
(3 credits)
SE 504 Principles of Software Engineering (3 Credits)
SE 505 Software System Design (3 credits)
SE 506 Formal Methods in Software (3 credits)
SE 507 Software Systems Requirements (3 Credits)
SE 508 Software Implementation and Reuse (3 Credits)
SE 512 Software Testing and Quality (3 Credits)
SE 513 Software Systems Security (3 Credits)
SE 518 Software Project Management (3 credits)
SE 525 System Project Implementation (3 credits)
Advanced/Elective Specialization Tracks
(2-course track = 6 Credits)
Distributed Software Systems
SE 526 Networked Software Systems I
SE 527 Networked Software Systems II
Software Management
SE 531 Software Organization Management
SE 532 Software Quality Management
Information Systems
SE 541 Information Systems Architecture
SE 542 Information Systems Engineering
Real-Time Systems
SE 551 Real-Time Software Analysis & specification
SE 552 Real-Time Software Design & Implementation

Curriculum guidelines (Tucker, 1991; Ford 1991). That curriculum covered the entire software lifecycle in detail, by offering 3 new courses, specifically in requirements, implementation and reuse, and testing and quality. A former elective, software systems security, became a core course.

Having such a heavy core, this curriculum offered little flexibility for learning aspects of SE that students would be most interested in. Another major change was reflected in the introduction of several new courses that would form 6 credit elective specialization tracks: in distributed software systems, software management, information systems, and real-time sys-

tems. These tracks were introduced as a response to the needs and feedback from the local industry, and government collaborators (Powell,1997). The curriculum change was made possible by hiring faculty with both theoretical background and working experience in industry, supplemented with a substantial help from adjunct faculty with expertise in specialized areas of SE.

1996 Curriculum Changes

In 1996 minor changes were made in the curriculum. It remained a 36-credit program, with 9 core and 3 elective courses, which offered a bit more flexibility than the previous program. The curriculum covered all the aspects of the software lifecycle. The capstone course was either a 3-credit practicum, or 6-credits of thesis research. The introduction of a thesis option was made possible by attracting faculty with the desire to engage in research activities.

1998 Curriculum Changes

The 1998 curriculum represented another major change by providing for much more flexibility in a 36 credit program, with 5 core, 5 elective courses, and a 6-credit practicum or a 6-credit thesis (see Figure 4).

The recognition of the importance of exposure to practical experience in a software engineering program has lead to the increase of the practicum project from 3 to 6 credits, and to the introduction of term projects in most of the courses in the curriculum. This is similar to the recommendations of the First MSE curriculum (Ardis, 1989) of offering a two semester practicum and as much as 30% of the program be dedicated to project work.

The MU curriculum continued to follow the software life-cycle model, as opposed to the CMU Model (Garlan, 1995), which emphasized teaching "cross-cutting principles of software development" throughout the curriculum. As such, the CMU Model offered five core courses organized around modeling, methods of development, management, analysis and architecture. Also, they included a software development studio for the development of practice skills, during the entire duration of the program.

The 1998 MU curriculum has added a new course, The Process of Engineering Software, which largely follows Watts Humphrey's Personal Software Process (PSP) principles (Humphrey, 2005). The introduction of this course was justified by the need for graduates who are aware and have the necessary skills for predictably producing high quality systems, in a timely and cost effective manner, using reusable components as much as possible in their work. In spite of the

hard work necessary for the manual input of the data for the various forms and templates involved in the PSP, students have given us very positive feedback about the usefulness of the principles learned in this course. For alleviating the clerical work related to the manual input of data, we created a semi-automated tool to support the PSP process (Rosca, 2001). This tool was the result of a two-semester practicum project of one group of students.

Two of the former core courses, mathematical foundations of SE, and principles of SE, have been transformed into preparatory (bridge) courses (see Figure 4). Together with three other programming courses the "bridge" program is offered for students with an undergraduate major other than computer science, computer engineering, electrical engineering, or information systems. After taking the 15 credit preparatory courses and a one-semester project course, students can receive a certificate in software development if they don't wish to pursue a Master's program.

The elective courses included in this curriculum were necessary for completing a chosen specialization track, such as organizational management, telecommunications, embedded systems, and information systems. These 15-credit tracks were much more comprehensive than their counterparts in the 1995 curriculum. They comprise courses from other disciplines such as business, electrical engineering and computer science. However, students have been able to select elective courses across tracks if they didn't want to pursue a specialization. A brief description of the specialization tracks is given next.

The Organisational Management track prepares students to become software development managers or specialists in software process improvement. Topics of study include process improvement, quality management, organisational development and management, risk management and project planning and management.

Figure 4. 1998 curriculum

Preparatory Courses (15 Credits)
 CS 500 Program Development
 CS 503 Fundamental Algorithms I
 CS 505 Operating Systems
 SE 501 Mathematical Foundation of Software Engineering
 SE 504 Principles of Software Engineering
Core Courses (15 Credits)
 SE 500 The Process of Engineering Software
 SE 505 Software System Design
 SE 506 Formal Methods in Software
 SE 507 Software Systems Requirements
 SE 512 Software Testing and Quality
Capstone Course (6 credits) – Practicum/Thesis

Specialisation Tracks (15 Credits)

Organizational Management Track	Telecommunications Track
Required (9 Credits)	**Required Courses** (9 Credits)
SE 531 Software Organizational Management	EE 537 Wireless Communications
	SE 526 Network Software System I
SE 532 Software Quality Management	SE 527 Network Software System II
SE 518 Software Project Management	**Guided Electives** (6 Credits)
Guided Electives (6 Credits)	CS 526 Performance Evaluation
BM 525 Management of Human Resources	CS 535 Telecommunications
BM 565 Management of Technology	EE 505 Communications Technology
SE 560 Software Risk Management	EE 581 Data Networks
SE 565 Software Metrics	SE 513 Software System Security
	SE 598T Special Topics (Telecommunications)
Embedded Systems Track	**Information Management Track**
Required Courses (9 Credits)	**Required Courses** (9 Credits)
SE 526 Network Software System I	SE 541 Information Systems Architecture
SE 551 Real-Time Software Analysis and Spec.	SE 542 Information System Engineering
SE 552 Real-Time Software Design and Impl.	SE 518 Software Project Management
Guided Electives (6 Credits)	**Guided Electives** (6 Credits)
CS 525 Simulation	BM 520 Information System in Organisation
CS 526 Performance Evaluation	BM 565 Management of Technology
EE 509 Digital Signal Processing	BM 571 Introduction to US Health Care
SE 508 Software Implementation and Reuse	CS 517 Database Systems
SE 513 Software System Security	CS 530 Knowledge-Based Systems
SE 527 Network Software System II	SE 508 Software Implementation and Reuse
	SE 526 Network Software System I

The Telecommunications track prepares students to become specialists in telecommunications. Topics of study include networks, software systems security, and evaluation of telecommunications systems.

The Embedded Systems track prepares students to become specialists in embedded systems development. Topics of study include specification and analysis of embedded real-time systems requirements, design and implementation of embedded real-time software systems, performance evaluation of embedded real-time software systems, and development of real-time components.

The Information Management track prepares students to become chief information officers or specialists in information systems integration and development. Topics of study include information technology management, specification and analysis of information systems, evaluation of information systems, and development of information systems software components.

2002 Curriculum Change

In 2002, the only curriculum change was the addition of a new specialization track: the Management of Software Technology, offered in collaboration with the Monmouth University School of Business. The idea of this track grew out of the recognition that industry is outsourcing increasing amounts of software development. This track prepares students to be chief technology officers or specialists in the acquisition of software systems for businesses. Topics of study include assessing the impact that software can have on organizations, the development of requirements for system acquisition via purchase or outsourcing, the assessment of software technologies with regard to organizational needs, and implementing a controlled introduction of technology into an organization.

All the knowledge areas of the Software Engineering Body of Knowledge (SWEBOK)

project (Bourque, 2004) can be identified in this curriculum.

CONTINUOUS DEVELOPMENT OF COURSE CONTENT

Technologically, the computing field has undergone significant changes that have forced alterations in the material taught within Software Engineering courses. Since the inception of our SE Master's program, we have witnessed the widespread adoption of Object-Orientation (along with massive changes in techniques and methodologies), the phenomenal explosion of the World Wide Web, the emergence of Java, and the move of security requirements from corporate to consumer platforms, just to name a few of these changes. Therefore, the material covered within a curriculum that addresses the technological understanding required by professionals in this field, needs to be continuously updated over time.

This problem emerges in several different forms. In particular,

- Continuous course content changes
- Dated textbooks
- Operating system/programming language biases
- Continuous development of course projects

Each of these areas is discussed in greater detail in the paragraphs that follow.

Course Content Changes

One can expect to have to revise course material every year. This is necessary to accommodate technological changes and to incorporate new industrial practices. For example, since the inception of our program we have changed the programming languages taught in class from Ada, to C++ and

Java; in the requirements engineering course object-oriented analysis methods were added to the structured analysis methods (Rosca, 2000); in the design course a transition was made from structured design to object-oriented design, component-based design, and architectural design. In the testing course we have added segments on testing applications that are constructed using commercial off-the-shelf (COTS) components, using automated testing and test management tools. For project management more content was gradually introduced on the use of scheduling tools, such as MS project, risk simulators, like Risk+, and discussion of the use of buffer tasks in the planning of software development projects (McDonald, 2000). The burden of this continuous course creation or updating could be alleviated in the future by the curricular materials offered by the SWENET project (Lutz, 2003), created by the professionals in the SE community for the use of the community, at large.

The continuous revisions of course material constitutes a significant amount of work on the part of the faculty. In as little as three years, the changes within the field are significant enough that many courses have to be totally redesigned. The adoption of UML and its subsequent evolution has forced revisions in design diagrams, the vocabulary used to describe designs, and introduce new best practices.

Dated Textbooks

As technology changes and software engineering evolves, the ability of texts to keep up with these changes is severely stressed. An instructor will find himself or herself utilizing three or four texts in order to properly cover a topic area. Books will seemingly contradict each other, only because they were published two years apart. Often, a book that is only three years old will contain many concepts that have been already superseded or renamed. Many excellent textbooks have not been updated to use current representations, such as UML2, for example.

This forces faculty continuously research new and updated prints. The faculty has to take into consideration student feedback on the usefulness of the recommended textbooks. Some new textbooks might be already dated at the time of their publication.

Operating System/Programming Language Biases

Few topics seem to generate as much debate as the selection of which operating system (OS) or programming language should be the lingua franca for course work. It seems that everyone has an opinion or a realistic need to learn one environment over another. The selection of one environment over the other has significant impacts on the tools available for use by the instructor, the knowledge that the instructor has to bring into the classroom, and the equipment that must be maintained. In our case, over the years we have migrated from UNIX platforms, to Windows, and to dual-boot machines that run both Windows and Linux. Most of the students are familiar with both operating systems, since different instructors favor one OS over the other. They appreciate the flexibility offered by the dual-boot machines available in our labs.

The programming language debate is a little more problematic than OS preferences. Many of the students at the graduate level have jobs in which they work in C++, Java, or C#. The students often insist that the programming language that they use in the workplace be utilized in their courses. The problem is that choice of programming language can significantly impact what is appropriate content for a course. Designing C++ programs utilizes different patterns than those used in designing Java programs, since C++ programs must necessarily and explicitly manage memory. Historically, the choice of programming language has been made largely based on inputs from the market and external program reviewers. For example, at the time this paper was written, most courses use Java, with the exception of the real-time systems course which still uses C and C++.

Continuous Development of Course Projects

Faculty, students, and industry have universally recognized the need for hands-on experience (Ellis, 2000). Without practical training, students and industry complain that the material will be too theoretical and that graduates would have trouble applying the theory to real world projects. This has led us to incorporate projects into the majority of courses taught in the program, while maintaining a balance between the theoretical and practical aspects of the courses. The type of projects has changed over the years: we have started with stand-alone systems, to continue with distributed, web-based, service-oriented systems.

The program culminates with a two semester practicum, where students work in groups on all phases of a real-world project, starting with requirements elicitation, design, implementation, and testing. Unlike the course offered at University of Southern California by B. Boehm (Boehm, 2006), in our practicum there are no lectures, because it is assumed that students have already covered all software engineering core courses in the curriculum. Students need to follow a well defined software process, producing all the necessary documentation that covers the product life-cycle. Although the process is not prescribed by the instructor, as in (Germain, 2003), most of the students follow a heavy-weight type of process, such as UPEDU (Robillard, 2001). The students practice teamwork and communication skills, while working on a large-scale project proposed by a real client. The clients are either from our campus, or companies from the area surrounding the university. They are asked to provide comments and evaluate the deliverables, in addition to the instructor. The type of project proposals we

get from the industry partners points us to areas that need to be covered by the curriculum.

The course/term projects are administered at the beginning of the semester, and have a couple of milestones spread along the semester. The instructors check the documents and/or software applications delivered at each milestone and provide feedback to the students. The instructors provide the project statements. The members of the project teams are either established by the students, when they are not new to the program, or when no preferences are expressed, the instructor makes the choices. The teams have the authority to choose their leaders, and the role of each member.

The introduction of projects into a Software Engineering course encompasses its own set of difficulties. While a simple program for shuffling cards may suffice to teach students about algorithms and data structures in a programming course, software engineering has to deal with much larger problems in order to demonstrate the value and need for an engineering process. The result is that projects have to be big, but not so big that they cannot be performed within the confines of the course. Because the project has to be big, it has to be structured such that the students can incrementally develop it as the course unfolds.

As the course content, technology and available tools change, the course projects need to change too. We have found that the size issue can sometimes be addressed by partially completing the project before presenting it to the students. This might require the development of a set of requirements before introducing a larger project into a software design course, providing some economic or financial analyses before introducing a project into a software project management course, or developing requirements and code before introducing a project into a testing course. In any case such a strategy requires that the instructor spend significant time doing the background work and documenting the results of that work so that the students can make good use of it as they proceed with the next steps. This way the students are encouraged to concentrate on tasks for a specific project that are unique to the course in which the project is being used.

Hilburn (2006), who wants to develop a comprehensive case study along with education material that can be used throughout the curriculum, proposes another alternative. This way, students will use the output of one course project work in subsequent courses, and will be able to better understand the connections between the topics taught in different courses. Again, this approach requires more work for faculty while making it more difficult to adapt courses to technological advances.

DIFFICULTIES ATTRACTING AND RETAINING FACULTY

Software Engineers, even in difficult economic times, are a highly sought after commodity. It is extremely challenging for any software engineering program to both attract and retain their faculty, in USA or around the globe (Grant, 2000). We noticed that the stability of the faculty makes a program more attractive to prospective students.

It is very difficult to attract appropriate faculty, as it has been observed by Glass (2003). In particular, faculty members usually are acquired from computer science backgrounds and/or from industrial practice. The problem with faculty from computer science backgrounds is that their backgrounds are in computer science rather than software engineering. The problem with acquiring faculty from industry is that often they do not have documented credentials (a PhD degree) and a documented trace of their scholarly work.

With the need to continuously update course content and curricula, to keep up or advance the state of the field, the load on a faculty member in software engineering tends to be significantly greater than in some other academic areas. Given

that it is very difficult to hire faculty with the appropriate academic and industrial backgrounds, many of the hires are often non-tenure track. We are very fortunate to be positioned in a strong high tech industry area, with a steady supply of teachers with a very good industry experience, who are seeking to augment their income, are between jobs, or are retired.

A real solution for the administration is to provide competitive salaries and support consulting or research activities. This enables faculty to make up any shortfalls in salary and keep abreast of the industry needs and practices. With respect to this issue, MU offers faculty one day a week to spend on research or consulting activities. Also, MU has been successful in hiring excellent faculty with a PhD degree in areas other than computer science, with a strong industrial experience in software development.

We are aware that this solution might not be easy to implement at many universities, therefore we are suggesting another venue for attracting and retaining faculty: the creation of a research center or institute on campus. This way faculty with complementary expertise can collaboratively work on interesting, complex projects and create rich opportunities for research and publications. This allows faculty to keep current with the state of research and practice, feed this information into a curriculum that is up-to-date (Boehm, 2000), reduce the teaching load, and build a cohesive faculty community. MU has created the Rapid Response Institute, where faculty from the SE department works together with faculty and students from around the campus on research and applications for Homeland Security.

DIVERSITY OF THE STUDENT BODY

In the 21-year history of the software engineering program at MU we have observed increasing diversity within the student population. The diversity spans several dimensions: educational background, employment status, educational goals and native language. The successful program must address all these dimensions of diversity.

Educational Backgrounds

Consistent with the origins of the program, many students in the graduate program achieved undergraduate degrees in computer science. These students have strong programming skills, but very seldom have the engineering discipline that emphasizes understanding the problem to be solved, or the process to be followed. These students tend to immediately start coding once they receive a problem to be solved. Students asked on more than one occasion why it was necessary to design a program when they could write one faster.

We also have a large population of students that are coming into the graduate program from other engineering and non-engineering disciplines. These students usually are much more accepting of engineering processes, but have relatively weak programming skills and minimal knowledge about how computers function. To accommodate them we have had to incorporate a set of preparatory courses to provide the programming skills and computer knowledge necessary to succeed in the program.

Our program has already started receiving a new group of students. These students have undergraduate degrees in software engineering and already have a good understanding of engineering practices balanced with programming skills. At this point, our program had to address increasingly more advanced software engineering topics that may be beyond the knowledge of the other two groups of students. A detailed discussion of this topic is deferred to in the Future Trends section.

Employment Status

The employment status of students has significant impact on the program. It affects how long students are in the program, the effort that they put into assignments, their willingness to accept course material, and when classes are offered. It should be noted that (with a few exceptions) students entering into the program full-time usually find work at the end of their first year and become part-time students. The majority of our student population attends school part-time with full-time employment in the software industry. Most of our classes are offered in the early evening to accommodate them.

The fact that the average student is employed full-time and attends classes part-time means that they may be in the program for as long as 8 years. In fact, the population of students is much more stable than the curriculum. Some students have graduated on curriculums that have been replaced twice since they enrolled in the program.

Employment in the software industry has significant impact on the willingness of some students to accept the concepts taught in the classroom. These students have already acquired work habits that are not consistent with best practices. Students often state that they don't perform a particular engineering practice at work and that they don't see a need for it. Of course, many of these same students talk about how their projects at work tend to be chaotic. Other students report the difficulties they've encountered in trying to practice in their conservative organizations what they've learned in class. Either case tends to undermine the instructor in presenting new material in the classroom. Here is one of the situations where the instructor's industrial experience plays an important role in both selecting the material to be taught and in responding to student concerns regarding the usefulness of the topics learned in the real world.

Employed students also tend to focus on what they immediately need to succeed in today's workplace. There is often an insistence on learning a product (such as Oracle or Sybase) rather than the concepts (i.e., database principles). This emphasis on skill rather than knowledge runs counter to the goals of the program that are the development of software engineers who can lead their organizations into the future. We have included some of these products into our classrooms, but the main goals of the courses remain to teach the engineering principles of the field, which can be applied to a large number of products.

Students who are not employed in the industry have problems prioritizing the material being taught or placing it in the context of delivering a product. If they are required to know C++, they assume that all employers develop code in C++. They are often surprised when they get a job and discover that they will have to learn a new programming language. Students are occasionally concerned that courses cover many different methods and approaches to achieve a given goal rather than emphasize one method. They have to be taught to understand that the knowledge and skill they acquire in school will have to blend into whatever organization they join, and that they need to engage in a lifelong learning process that is inevitable in this dynamic field.

Educational Goals

It would be nice if all students entered the program with the desire and goal of becoming a software engineer and delivering a specific kind of product. However, the educational goals of the students range from wanting to know all about software and engineering, to the other extreme where they only want to get the credentials that will allow them to earn a higher salary. Our student body appears to be driven by a small number of educational goals, as we were able to derive from their application packages, advising sessions and an alumni survey. These are:

- Get the business and process knowledge that will allow them to manage software projects and people.
- Get the skills and knowledge that will allow them to be more productive in their chosen career.

- Start a career in which they can have a significant income
- Get a job in the software field that does not involve a lot of coding.

The major impact of these goals concerns the subject areas that interest the student. We have had to tailor our curriculum to respond to these different goals. We find a significant fraction of the students are very interested in the process, project management, and organizational management courses. Others find that the courses on requirements and software testing give them an entry point into a part of the software business that does not appear to require major coding efforts. Finally, the courses that emphasize specific types of software systems (real-time, information, and embedded systems) attract those students that are interested in gaining the particular knowledge and skills that will allow them to master their chosen field of work.

Communications Skills

There is significant diversity among our students in terms of their communication skills. However, communication skills are critical in software engineering, being considered as important as the technical skills (Teles, 2003; Lethbridge 2000). The average software engineering student will probably produce more documents and make more public presentations than the average English major. Communications have to be precise, unambiguous, complete, logically sound and well structured. Oral presentations have to convey complex information under time constraints. Students have to learn to gauge how much information is to be conveyed. This requires that they judge what their audience can be expected to know and what must be presented. Although typical undergraduate general education programs attempt to teach these skills most students who enter our graduate program require additional coaching and training in this area.

International students are often at a disadvantage due to the fact that English is their second language. This affects their writing ability where a weakness in vocabulary often prevents them from expressing themselves clearly and succinctly. It also undermines their confidence in public speaking due to concerns about their command of the language and fears that others will not understand them because of their accents. It can also severely limit their participation in class discussions.

International students are not the only ones with problems in communications. Many of the students, particularly those with computer science backgrounds, are not used to writing technical documents. While they may be good at writing code, they often have difficulties in expressing themselves succinctly in a written document.

The most direct approach to dealing with significant changes in the student population has been to adapt the curriculum and individual courses to meet the changing needs of our students. Employed students are encouraged to express their perspectives on the material so that their experiences can be shared with students that have yet not entered the field. In some classes, programming assignments can be written in Java or C++ depending upon the student's choice.

Another change has been the incorporation of more term papers into course work to allow students to get greater experience in writing. Papers are graded on technical content, structure, adherence to topic, and on the use of language. Corrections are suggested and students have a chance to resubmit corrected work. With respect to verbal communications, students are required to make oral presentations of their term projects. This way, until they reach the capstone project, students would have had the opportunity to exercise their communications skills several times. We have also observed significant progress in the communication skills and self-confidence of students when we created multicultural teams, and encouraged informal peer-mentoring. As one of our external program reviewers observed,

the oral communications skills of students significantly improved when they were repeatedly videotaped, and discussed the strengths and weaknesses of their recorded presentations with the instructor.

GUIDANCE ON STARTING AND MANAGING PROGRAMS

Based on the experience described above in starting and managing Monmouth University's software engineering program we would offer the following advice to academic departments that are considering a similar program:

1. Conduct research to determine the most current curriculum recommendations from the IEEE, ACM and other sources.
2. Find out, by participating in national groups and committees that develop those recommendations, what likely future changes might take place.
3. Enlist the academic institution's industrial advisory boards to determine how the general recommendations need to be tailored to suit the needs of local industry. The partnership with the local industry will bring multiple benefits, such as a good source of real world projects for courses, student placement for summer internships, industry guest lecturers for courses or a research seminar.
4. Form a Task Force with professors from both SE and CS departments to make sure the two departments will not conflict each other. Also invite an external reviewer who can offer concrete guidance, based on personal experiences in building such a program at another university.
5. Recruit full-time faculty who are competent to teach the required variety of courses and who have industrial experience in applying software engineering techniques in real

work environments. Don't expect this to be an easy task. You might need to manage the program initially with significant help from part-time faculty.

6. Expect that the curriculum will need to change with time to accommodate both changes in the discipline as well as changes in the needs of local employers.

7. Define a set of students learning outcomes that you will continuously monitor, and use the results to evaluate the need for improvements.

8. Periodically seek accreditation from a national board, or at least solicit a thorough review from an external evaluator, who is a prominent figure in the field. These efforts will ensure the quality of your curriculum.

9. If you intend to advertise your program to international students, make sure that you educate student's expectations regarding the research oriented or practical training oriented nature of the program.

10. If you intend to offer the program over multiple campuses, or on-line, you need to secure the equipment, technology and instructors qualified and willing to teach distance learning courses. Don't expect this to be an easy task, the instructor's effort to teach these courses might be considerably higher than teaching face-to-face courses.

FUTURE TRENDS

Having looked at the past, it is now appropriate to look to the future for our program. In particular, we recognized a need for another set of changes. The introduction of an undergraduate software engineering program had profound consequences on the graduate program, forcing severe changes in its curriculum. The redesigned curricula should allow the new graduates of the bachelor's degree in software engineering to have the opportunity of extending their knowledge and skills to new frontiers. In particular, we believe that while in the undergraduate program students should focus on the application level software development, at the graduate level they should focus on the enterprise and global levels. Also, we expect these students to show originality in the application of their knowledge and pursue research to push the boundaries of knowledge in the SE area of their choice (similar to the UK program reported in (Edwards, 2003)).

With this respect, in 2007 we modified our graduate program, such that the students with a bachelor's degree in SE will be required to take 5 core courses, 6 elective courses and a two-semester thesis. Up to 9 credits of core courses can be waived if equivalent courses have been completed as part of the students' Bachelor of Science in software engineering program. This would make our SE graduate program similar in structure to masters programs in electrical engineering, mechanical engineering, etc. throughout the United States (see Figure 5).

In particular, we moved a bridge course into a core course: former SE501 (Mathematical Foundations) is combined with former SE561(Formal Methods) into a new and augmented core course, SE561(Mathematical Foundations of Software Engineering). This course will include mathematical methods that a software engineer needs to master, such as graph theory, formal languages, logic, sets theory, etc.

Former SE565 and SE570, the requirements and design courses, have been changed to cover techniques at the global and enterprise levels of software development. Former SE575, the software verification and validation course, has been changed to cover verification, validation and maintenance techniques and tools. Former SE580 course will cover the team software process (Humphrey,1999) due to the recognition that the graduates will need to work in teams for most of their careers, and the feedback received from graduates.

Figure 5. 2007 curriculum

> **Core Courses(5 courses = 15 credits)**
> SE561 Mathematical Foundations of Software Engineering
> SE565 Software Systems Requirements
> SE570 Software System Design
> SE575 Software Verification, Validation and Maintenance
>
> **Electives(4 courses = 12 credits)**
> Choose two pairs of guided electives from among
>   SE601 Outsourcing: Specifications and Strategies
> and SE602 Technology assessment
>
>   SE620 Network Software Systems I
> and SE621   Network Software Systems II
>
>   SE625 Information Systems Architecture
> and SE626 Information Systems Engineering
>
>   SE630 Real-Time Software Analysis and Specifications
> and SE631 Real-Time Software Design and Implementation
>
>   SE637 Wireless Communications
> and SE638 Communications Systems
>
>   SE650 Software Project Management
> and SE651 Software Organization Management
>
> **Electives(2 courses = 6 credits)**
> Choose two guided electives from among
> SE601,SE602,SE603,SE605,SE610,SE611,SE615,SE620,SE625
> SE626,SE630,SE631,SE637,SE638,SE650,SE651,SE652,SE660,
> SE698,SE699,CS514,CS517,CS533,BM565
>
> **Thesis (6 credits)**
> Two semester Thesis:
>   SE690A: Thesis Research
> and   SE690B: Thesis Research

We have also made some changes in the bridge courses of our curriculum by adding two bridge-courses, SE510 (Object-oriented Analysis and Design) and SE515 (Disciplined Software Development). We strongly believe that all our students should know the basic analysis and design methods by the time they enter the graduate program. This would allow us to teach advanced methods for software analysis and design in the corresponding core courses (SE565 and SE570), instead of spending a considerable amount of time teaching basic knowledge. Also, we are strong believers of the engineering principles emphasized by a disciplined approach to developing programs, such as the Personal Software Process (PSP). We would like all our students to be familiar with these engineering techniques at the individual level, to be able to leverage them at the team level in the software process core course (SE580). This course will also introduce principles of agile software development.

We removed Operating Systems Concepts (CS505) from the curriculum since the material was covered in several other software engineering courses. We revised SE504 (Principles of Software Engineering) to focus on structured analysis and design methods while presenting the breadth of software engineering principles. This emphasis would allow us to focus on the modern object-oriented methods in the core analysis and design classes.

In the electives courses, we added a course on Secure Web Services Design (SE611) to develop a sequence of courses on security, together with SE610 (Software Systems Security). This sequence will cover both the theoretical and practical aspects of software systems security, given the ubiquity of security issues in today's systems.

Another future trend that we believe will induce major changes in the way we deliver our program will be determined by the increasingly mobile characteristic of the majority of our students, whom are working full-time and take the courses part-time. To allow them maximum flexibility, we might need to change our delivery mode to include more distance learning, maybe in the way The Open University in UK does (Quinn, 2006). At the moment we are experimenting with offering "hybrid courses" that are a combination of a traditional, face-to-face delivery, and distance learning that uses online curricular materials. This delivery mode saves students the travel time to campus, and also allows them to keep up to speed when they travel for business. Students are required to come to campus every other week, to meet with the instructor for a face-to-face class. If their grade falls below a certain threshold, they are required to come to class every week. This is

a new approach for us, and we don't have enough data yet for a thorough evaluation.

Another issue, that is beyond the scope of this paper though, is the awareness of the influence that the licensing of software engineers shall have on the design of the curriculum. However, the directions and discussions that are taking place with regard to licensing have to be followed so that appropriate changes can be implemented in the curriculum.

CONCLUSION

This chapter has presented the main problems and lessons learned from one of the oldest programs in software engineering in the USA. The evolution of the graduate curriculum over its 21 years of existence has been shown as an example for other colleges and universities considering the addition of a software engineering degree. We expect this evolution to continue in the future, as the SE field is a constant moving target.

We have argued that the continuous update of the course content has a special meaning in software engineering, due to the dynamics of the field. With this respect, we have shown the impact of the advances in the field on the textbooks used, the need for continuous reevaluation of the chosen programming language, operating system, or software tools used in class.

The chapter has shown the difficulties we have experienced in attracting and retaining the faculty over the years, due to the need of the new faculty to have both a record of scholarly accomplishments and industrial experience. The emphasis here is on the conjunction of these two requirements, which sets great restrictions on the pool of available candidates.

We explained how various issues related to the diversity of the student body influence the curriculum and course content. As such, the educational backgrounds, employment status, educational goals, and communications skills of the student body are challenges any software engineering program has to solve.

Based on our experience in dealing with these problems, we have offered some recommendations for those interested in starting a similar program, with an emphasis on the curriculum and course content issues that arise where an undergraduate and graduate program in software engineering coexist in the same department.

As a measure of success of our continuous efforts to improve, we have seen the program enrollment increasing steadily over the years. This is not a reason to rest, since the SE field will continue to evolve, and we will have to respond to new challenges.

REFERENCES

Ardis, M., & Ford, G. (1989). 1!989 SEI Report on Graduate Software Engineering Education (Tech. Rep. CMU/SEI-89-TR-21), Software Engineering Institute.

Ardis, M., & Ford,G. (1989). SEI Report on Graduate Software Engineering Education, *Proceedings of the Software Engineering Education Conference*, Springer-Verlag.

Boehm, B. (2006). Learning by Doing: Real-client Software Project Courses, *ASEE Tutorial 2006*, Retrieved from http://db-itm.shidler.hawaii.edu/cseet2006/Boehm%20ASEET.pdf .

Boehm, B., Kaiser, G., & Port, D. (2000). A Combined Curriculum Research and Curriculum Development Approach to Software Engineering Education, *Workshop on Developing Undergraduate Software engineering Programs*, *Proceedings of CSEE&T 2000*, 310-311

Bourque, P., & Dupuis, R. (2004). Guide to the Software Engineering Body of Knowledge – Final Version, SWEBOK, Feb. 2000, Retrieved from http://www.swebok.org/

Clough, G.W. (2005). Educating the Engineer of 2020: Adapting Engineering Education to the New Century. Washington, D.C.: National Academies Press, Retrieved from http://www.nap.edu.

Dart, P., Johnston, L., Schmidt, C., & Sonenberg, L. (1997). Developing an Accredited SE Program, *IEEE Software*, Nov/Dec, 66-70.

Duggins, S.L., & Thomas, B.B. (2002). An Historical Investigation of Graduate Software Engineering Curriculum, *Proceedings CSEE&T*, 78-87.

Ellis, H., McKim, J.C., & Younessi H. (2000). Issues Affecting Graduate and Postgraduate Software Engineering Curricula, Workshop on Developing Graduate and Postgraduate Software Engineering Courses, *Proceedings of CSEE&T 2000*, 190

Ford, G. (1991). 1991 SEI Report on Graduate Software Engineering Education, *Technical Report CMU/SEI-91-TR-2*, Software Engineering Institute, Carnegie Mellon University

Ford, G., Gibbs, N., & Tomayko, J. (1987). Software Engineering Education: An Interim Report from the Software Engineering Institute, Technical Report CMU/SEI-87-TR-8, Software Engineering Institute,

Garlan, D., Brown, A., Jackson, D., Tomayko, J., & Wing, J. (1995). The CMU Master of Software Engineering Core Curriculum, *Proceedings of CSEE&T 1995*, 65-86, Springer Verlag.

Germain, E., & Robillard, P. (2003). What Cognitive Activities are Performed in Student Projects?, *Proceedings of CSEE&T 2003*, 224-231

Glass, R. (2003). A Big Problem in Academic Software Engineering and a Potential Outside-the-Box Solution, *IEEE Software*, July/August,94-96.

Grant, D. (2000). Undergraduate Software Engineering Degrees in Australia, *Proceedings of CSEE&T 2000*, 308-309

Hiburn, T., Towhidnejad, M., Nangia, S., & Shen, L. (2006). A Case Study Project for Software Eductaion, *Proceedings FIE 2006*, M1F1-M1F5.

Humphrey, W. (1999). *Introduction to the Team Software Process*, Addison Wesley.

Humphrey, W. (2005). *A Discipline of Software Engineering*, Second Edition, Addison Wesley.

Lethbridge, T. (2000). What Knowledge is Important to a Software Professional?, *IEEE Computer*, 33(5), 44-50.

Lutz, M.J., Hilburn, T.B., Hislop, G., McCraken, M., & Sebern, M. (2003). The SWENET Project: bridging the gap from bodies of knowledge to curriculum development, *Proceedings FIE 2003*, vol.3, S3C-7.

McDonald, J. (2000). Teaching Software Project Management in Industrial and Academic Environments, *Proceedings of CSEE&T*, 151-160.

Naur, P., & Randall, B. (eds) (1968). Software Engineering: A report on a Conference Sponsored by the NATO Science Committee, NATO.

Powell, G., Diaz-Perrera, J., & Turner, D. (1997). Achieving Synergy in Collaborative Education. *IEEE Software*, Nov/Dec, 58-65.

Quinn, B., Barroca, L., Nuseibeh, B., Fernandez-Ramil, J., Rapanotti, L., Thomas, P., & Wermelinger, M. (2006). Learning Software Engineering at a Distance, IEEE Software, November/December, 36-43.

Robillard, P, Krutchen, P., & d'Astous, P. (2001) YOOPEEDOO (UPEDU): A Process for Teaching Software Process, *Proceedings of CSEE&T 2001*, 18-26

Rosca D. (2000). An Active/Collaborative Approach in Teaching Requirements Engineering, *Proceedings of FIE'00*, T2C9-12

Rosca, D., Li, C., Moore, K., Stephan, M., & Weiner, S. (2001). PSP-EAT – Enhancing a Personal Software Process Course, *Proceedings of FIE'01*, T2D18.

Stryer, L. (2005). Bio2010: Transforming Undergraduate Education For Future Research Biologists Washington, D.C.: National Academies Press, Retrieved from http://www.nap.edu.

Teles, V.M., & Oliveira C. (2003). Reviewing the Curriculum of Software Engineering Undergraduate Courses to Incorporate Communication and Personal Skills Teaching, *Proceedings CSEET 2003*, 158-165.

Tucker, A (Editor) et al. (1991). Report of the ACM/IEEE-CS Joint Curriculum Task Force. Retrieved from http://www.acm/education/curr91/homepage.html.

Chapter XVI
How to Create a Credible Software Engineering Bachelor's Program:
Navigating the Waters of Program Development

Stephen Frezza
Gannon University, USA

Mei-Huei Tang
Gannon University, USA

Barry J. Brinkman
Gannon University, USA

ABSTRACT

This chapter presents a case study in the development of a Software Engineering (SE) Bachelor's Degree program. It outlines issues in SE program development, various means to address those issues, and explains how the issues were addressed in the initial and ongoing development of an undergraduate SE program. By using SEEK and SWEBOK as requirements sources to define what an undergraduate software engineer needs to know, the authors walk through the creation of a sample curriculum at a small, comprehensive university in the United States. Both the current and initial curricula are presented. The article discusses many items to consider in the process of planning and launching a new BSSE program, such as accreditation, curriculum guidelines, sources of information, and potential problems.

INTRODUCTION

Software Engineering is one of the newer engineering disciplines to emerge. Starting with the coining of the 'Software Engineering' term in 1968 (Naur, 1969), there has been continual growth in interest in software engineering education. Initially, these efforts were primarily at the graduate level, serving software engineering practitioners with undergraduate degrees in Computer Science, Computer Engineering or other related fields. In 1998, in recognition of the needs of bachelors-level computing graduates, the Computer Society of the Institute for Electrical and Electronic Engineers (IEEE-CS) and the Association for Computing Machinery (ACM) established the Joint Task Force on Computing Curricula 2001 (CC2001) to undertake a major review of curriculum guidelines for undergraduate programs in computing (Diaz-Herrera, 2004). This and other efforts (EA, 2007; CEAB, 2006; ABET, 2005) added official recognition of the need for the establishment of effective undergraduate programs preparing students to become software engineers.

The underlying assumption is that creating a new degree program for a relatively new discipline (Software Engineering), in a professional area (Computing) that already has several well-established disciplines (Computer Science, Computer Engineering, Information Systems, etc.) necessarily comes with a number of significant development risks. This chapter takes the form of an extended experience report, in the hope of presenting an overview of these risks, and practical means to mitigate them. This work is primarily based on the authors' experience in developing a software engineering undergraduate program leading to a Bachelor of Science degree in Software Engineering (BSSE) at a small comprehensive university in the United States (Frezza, 2006). Effort has been made to generalize this experience, and include questions and issues encountered in other SE program development efforts, as well as raising issues that may be more critical in other organizational settings.

ISSUES IN SE PROGRAM DEVELOPMENT

Developing a new undergraduate program, particularly one like Software Engineering that does not have long-established definitions can be (and for us was) a delicate business. Among the key stakeholders for a new SE program, the requirements for what belongs in such a major may not be well understood, or easily communicated. In all, our program development effort was similar to many of our software development experiences, in that the requirements management activities were significant, messy, and working to resolve them early proved worthwhile. Our undergraduate software engineering program, at the time of writing, has been developed, launched, gone through several on-going outcomes reviews, and we are currently preparing our first accreditation self-assessment.

Based on our reflection on the issues we encountered, and our post-design assessments, some of the key issues we've found in developing a new SE program include:

- **Organization:** Determining where the program is housed or sponsored within the institution
- **Vision:** Defining the style, or professional focus of the program
- **Accreditation:** Applying international and national standards to ensure program quality
- **Curriculum:** Designing the academic plan for students to meet or exceed the vision, and
- **Finding help:** Locating contacts to support program development

Organization

Determining where an SE program is housed is important to its success. The issue centers on faculty ownership of the program, and administrative support for the students. Many SE programs are organized in the same academic housing as Computer Science programs, but this is not universally the case. At issue is the blend of CS, IS, and Engineering courses currently available, and ability to work with the faculty delivering these courses to be effective for the new program. While Software Engineering is normally classified as a computing sub-discipline, in many institutions computing disciplines may be in multiple departments scattered across multiple schools, or not. The character and ability of the various departments and schools to collaborate (*e.g.,* School of Engineering *vs.* School of Arts and Science, etc.) may not be easily navigated, and can delay program introduction.

The housing issue for a program is significant, as it can affect issues related to shared course content, accreditation, funding, hiring, tenure, and a plethora of other subtle and inter-related academic issues, not the least of which is the culture of the faculty leading the program. Mismatches can adversely affect program development, but more especially student learning and faculty retention issues.

While many programs are initially housed in an existing department structure, in several instances, sponsoring departments have been cross-department, or even cross-college arrangements. In some cases these more complex structures, created to launch the SE program, were later replaced. Factors that can affect complex administrative structures include growing enrollments, competition, budgets and funding, faculty issues and other sustainability factors. In some schools, the more complex structures proved workable, and have been maintained (e.g., Drexel). The common theme is the ability to gain sufficient institutional agreement for offering SE course and related program content.

In our case, this negotiation of where to house the program led to delaying the program launch by about a year. Our initial proposal was to run the new SE program with a systems orientation from the Electrical and Computer Engineering (ECE) department. What was at issue was the nature of software engineering – few faculty having significant experience beyond embedded software development, or exposure to the signifi-

cant and world-wide efforts to define software engineering as a discipline (Bourque, 2000). Locating authoritative guidelines as to what a software engineering undergraduate program should include was significant to this negotiation. Even with these guidelines, identifying the nature of our new SE program, and where it should be developed/housed was by no means a simple process.

Addressing this housing issue led to several surveys and presentations, using materials from conferences (Diaz-Herrera, 2001), ABET program-specific criteria (ABET, 2005), the Certified Software Development Professional (CSDP) effort (McConnell, 1999; IEEE CS, 2001), SWEBOK drafts (Abran, 2004), and the SE2004 drafts (Diaz-Herrera, 2004) to define software engineering for students, faculty and administrators. In particular, SE2004, SWEBOK, and ABET proved to be the most useful, and served as authoritative guidelines for our proposal development. At the end of these discussions, even though the program proposal originated from our ECE department, the strong computing focus of the SE program was deemed more suitable to be housed in the Computer and Information Science (CIS) department offering our computer science (CS) and management information systems (MIS) degree programs.

As the CIS department was housed in the same school as ECE, no administrative objections were encountered. The new task was to redevelop the program vision and program details with a team of primarily CIS faculty in a way that would succeed when the new program was launched and managed from the CIS department. The decision to house the program in a different department meant ECE relinquishing control on the proposal, the proposal champion working with a new department chair and new faculty partners. The benefit of this redevelopment work was the promise of building consensus around a shared vision from those who would ultimately deliver the program.

Vision

Following a well-documented SE best practice, identifying a coherent vision was a useful starting point, and our experience confirmed that it is a key factor for success in developing a Software Engineering undergraduate program. Within the vision for an academic program, one of the most fundamental issues is the judicious selection of the type, or character of the program that is desired. Notwithstanding other sources, at least six application models for software engineering have been identified (Jones, 2003):

- **Military:** Applications built according to military or US Department of Defense standards. This may include weapons systems, but also logistics and non-military systems that use military standards.
- **Systems:** Applications developed to control hardware devices such as computers, aircraft, telephone switches, and other physical devices and products, including embedded systems.
- **Commercial:** Applications for lease or sale to external customers, occasionally referred to as 'shrink-wrap' software. This category includes many personal computer applications, but also includes larger mainframe applications.
- **Outsourced:** Applications developed for a specific client company under a contract. Because of contractual obligations and the possibility of litigation, outsourced projects have some additional activities in comparison to in-house development.
- **Management Information Systems (MIS):** Applications built to control major business functions such as accounting, marketing, sales, and personnel. This category includes many traditional mainframe applications, but also the more recent client-server, multi-tiered and web-based applications.
- **End-user development:** Small applications that various kinds of knowledge workers—such as accountants, engineers, or project managers—build for personal use.

In developing a vision for a specific program, casting the nature of the program may be decided by other factors, such as faculty availability, skills, and influences from local and regional employers. These can, and should influence what a specific SE program graduate should be able to do. However, this 'local' approach can easily ignore the other external 'requirements' for a credible program.

There exist broad and relatively well-developed, and reasonably authoritative guidelines for what software engineers need to know (See the *Defining the BSSE Graduate* and *What Software Engineers Need to Know* subsections that follow). However, the context in which these skills are developed is also important, as these different application models have differences that can be significant in program delivery. These differences will typically show up in the determination of the content of required upper-level courses and elective courses.

Developing a vision is important in that the vision statement, once agreed to, serves as a useful guide in helping to sell the program to different academic and administrative stakeholders, as well as a useful reference during program design. Like most business exercises in vision, developing this as a shared vision, rooted in the realistic limitations of the organization will help reduce the risk of failure.

In our case, the decision to house the program in the CIS department led to a new shared vision for our SE program. The initial ECE-based proposal was based on a *systems* focus. With CIS faculty participation, the revised program proposal focused on delivering skills and knowledge for the *outsourced* and *MIS* categories. These represented trade-offs among the program developers, recognizing that the *outsourced/MIS* view would have distinctly different courses and flavor from the *systems* view. While different from the initial vision, this was a vision that was both legitimate, and would work well within the exiting department and course structures then in place. The tradeoffs allowed the new proposal to parallel the CS program more closely, but with the recognition that software engineering concepts needed to be integrated into courses taken jointly by CS and MIS students. Ultimately, this has proven to be useful in our situation, as the integration of software engineering concepts into early courses was easily negotiated, and continues to be well received.

Accreditation

In the US and many other countries, the use of the term "Engineering" in a program or degree title is necessarily accompanied by the requirement for some form of national accreditation which serves to ensure program quality. In the United States, ABET, Inc. (ABET, 2007) is responsible for the specialized accreditation of educational programs in applied science, computing, engineering, and technology. In Canada, the Canadian Engineering Accreditation Board (CEAB), serves as the accreditation body for engineering programs (CEAB, 2006), while Engineers Australia (EA) is responsible for this service in Australia (EA, 2007). This is an important initial consideration for creating a new program, because the nature of engineering accreditation generally brings with it required documentation processes, criteria and even academic culture that may be foreign to the institution or sponsoring department. Taking the time to become familiar with the processes and documentation needed is important, and in some instances may require hiring consultants to review academic proposals.

At the time of writing, 13 such programs were accredited in the United States (ABET, 2006), 12 in Canada (CEAB, 2006), and 18 in Australia (EA, 2007). To give a sampling of the breadth of universities that have chosen this route, these universities are listed in Figure 1. In our case, the goal was to create a program that would warrant including Gannon University in the list.

While not all programs require national accreditation, international guidelines exist (such as SE2004) to help ensure the quality of Software Engineering undergraduate programs. In our case, accreditation was a process new to the sponsoring department, but not to the school. Experience in applying the ABET criteria was easy to find, and the use of the EAC accreditation criteria (ABET, 2005) and the related SE2004 volume served as significant drivers in assessing the quality of the program proposal. This validation of the curriculum development process was extremely valuable in describing software engineering to program stakeholders, and served as a very useful means of assessing changes to the program (Frezza, 2006). These processes as we applied them are described in more detail in the pages that follow.

Curriculum Development

Ultimately one of the most critical portions of the program delivery is the curriculum employed by the program. The curriculum development process includes the development of the program objectives, as well as courses and course objectives. In most institutions, these are developed within the framework of institutional standards, as well as existing computing, mathematics, engineering and other courses that would also be taken by SE students. This key issue is discussed in much more detail in sections which follow.

Sources of Help and Advice

As in most engineering endeavors, one of the most useful sources of development information comes from others who have developed similar products (Kelley, 1999). These resources are particularly useful for helping to understand issues, avoid issues, or also experience to resolve issues as they are encountered in your program

Figure 1. Accredited software engineering related programs in the U.S., Canada, and Australia (current as of Sept. 2007)

US (*ABET*)	Canada (*CEAB*)	Australia (*EA*)
Auburn University	University of Calgary	Australian National University
Clarkson University	Carleton University	Curtin University of Technology
Embry-Riddle Aeronautical University, Daytona Beach	Concordia University	Flinders University
Fairfield University-School of Engineering	Lakehead University	Griffith University Nathan Campus
Florida Institute of Technology	McMaster University	La Trobe University (Bundoora campus)
University of Michigan-Dearborn	University of New Brunswick	Monash University
Milwaukee School of Engineering	University of Ottawa	Murdoch University
Mississippi State University	University of Waterloo	RMIT University
Monmouth University	University of Western Ontario	Swinburne University of Technology
Pennsylvania State University, Behrend College	École de technologie supérieure	University of Canberra
Rochester Institute of Technology	Laval	The University of Melbourne
University of Texas at Arlington	Polytechnique	The University of Newcastle
University of Texas at Dallas		The University of New South Wales
		The University of Queensland
		The University of Western Australia
		University of Southern Queensland
		University of Sydney
		University of Technology, Sydney

development. This is also a significant source of external expertise that can be used to help validate the program, such as a 'blue-ribbon' or other external panel that can validate or provide guidance to program development.

In our case, finding help in the form of the Working Group on Software Engineering and Education, and the more recent Software Engineering Program Leaders Association (SEPLA) proved to be extremely useful for helping find and share materials to explain the SE profession to various constituents (faculty, students, administrators), as well as provide useful market data and comparison programs. Various SEPLA members also volunteered, and provided input on various program proposals. The SEPLA listserv is available at sepla@listserv.butler.edu.

In our experience, the faculty development wherein we used authoritative guidelines to define Software Engineering for ourselves was absolutely essential. The need for this education came initially in response to addressing our organization issues. Our Accreditation goal dictated that ABET criteria needed to be considered, but the more extensive international guidelines (SWEBOK and SE2004) were more informative. The process of blending these viewpoints helped establish detailed 'requirements' for our BSSE program, as well as establish agreement on these requirements. This analysis work was crucial to the success of the program proposal process, and became central to developing the program outcomes, expectations, and ultimately its detailed design. Our particular blending is summarized in the *Defining the BSSE Graduate* and the *What Software Engineers Need to Know* sections that follow.

While the authoritative sources (ABET, SE2004 and SWEBOK) are all aimed at different target audiences, the definitions of software engineering they provide for these audiences are important. These definitions all speak directly to what the expectations would be for our BSSE graduates *after* the program was established, hopefully accredited, and they were well into their careers. Because the definitions were external, they carried significantly more weight than the viewpoint of any particular faculty member. These definitions, once blended, became central to developing the shared vision for our BSSE program as the program was developed, and has since continued to support outcomes assessment and program enhancement.

DEFINING THE BSSE GRADUATE

For the purposes of creating a quality, accreditable program, it is essential to define the desired knowledge and skills possessed by the BSSE graduates. One of the more useful forms for defining the desired knowledge and skills are the "outcomes" for the program. Outcomes relate to broadly defined skills, knowledge, and behaviors that students should acquire as they progress through the program (Wankat, 1993). If a graduate achieves all the program outcomes, this indicates that the student meets the program's stated educational objectives and is equipped to function as expected of a BSSE graduate.

To create an accreditable SE program, the program design must meet the established educational objectives and program criteria for a BSSE program. There are at least two primary sources for these objectives and criteria which define the minimal knowledge and skills for a BSSE graduate. In the US, the Engineering Accreditation Commission (EAC) provides two categories of objectives and criteria that apply to the design of engineering programs (ABET, 2005).The first category, the EAC Program

Educational Objectives, is a broader set which applies to all engineering programs. The second category provides each engineering discipline a unique set of program criteria specific to the discipline.

While these objectives and criteria are definitive for accreditation in the U.S., they do not provide as much detail as the SE2004 guidelines (Diaz-Herrera, 2004). The difficulty is that when comparing the SE2004 Student Outcomes (Diaz-Herrera, 2004) with the related EAC Program Educational Objectives (ABET, 2005) and EAC SE Program Criteria (ABET, 2005), there are noticeable gaps among them (Frezza, 2006). However, the superset of related SE skills indicates that a program should provide at least the following outcomes (Frezza, 2006):

- Show mastery of the software engineering knowledge and skills, and professional issues necessary to begin practice as a software engineer

- Demonstrate the ability to appropriately apply science, discrete mathematics, empirical techniques, probability and statistics and relevant topics in computer science and supporting disciplines to the development of complex software systems

- Work as an individual and as part of a multidisciplinary team to develop and deliver quality software artifacts

- Reconcile conflicting project objectives, finding acceptable compromises within limitations of cost, time, knowledge, existing systems and organizations

- Design appropriate solutions in one or more application domains using software engineering approaches that integrate ethical, social, legal and economic concerns

- Understand professional and ethical responsibility

- Demonstrate an understanding of and apply current theories, models, and techniques that provide a basis for problem identification

and analysis, software design, development, implementation, and documentation
- Demonstrate an understanding and appreciation for the importance of negotiation, effective work habits, leadership, and good communication with stakeholders in a typical software development environment
- Learn new models, techniques and technologies as they emerge and appreciate the necessity of such continuing professional development
- Obtain knowledge of contemporary issues
- Receive and internalize a broad education necessary to understand the impact of engineering solutions in a global, economic, environmental, and societal context

These program outcomes, which arguably must be met for a U.S.-based program, provide a useful definition of what the BSSE graduate should know and be able to do. Although important for defining and continually improving program effectiveness, the outcomes by themselves don't provide adequate detail about the specifics for "software engineering knowledge and skills". What specifically should we teach students? What should the courses contain? SE fortunately has other sources that define more specifically what students must know and be able to do.

WHAT SOFTWARE ENGINEERS NEED TO KNOW

In order to craft a credible Software Engineering curriculum that also paves the way to students' success in the workforce, we need to understand what knowledge students are expected to possess. Not only does this include knowledge that students fresh out of college are expected to know, but also knowledge that these students after a few years in the workforce are expected to hold. There are two primary sources for these requirements, SE2004 (Diaz-Herrera, 2004) and SWEBOK

(Abran, 2004), addressing aforementioned types of knowledge respectively.

- **SE2004 (Software Engineering 2004):** defines the body of knowledge that every software engineering degree graduate fresh out of college needs to know as the *Software Engineering Education Knowledge (SEEK)*.
- **SWEBOK (Guide to the Software Engineering Body of Knowledge):** characterizes the contents of software engineering discipline, i.e., the knowledge needed for the practice of software engineering after four years in the workforce.

Both of these documents carry with them extended development processes and improvements. In addition, both development efforts included significant efforts to ensure that the documents, and thus the educational patterns that might emerge from them, were not US-centric. The SE2004 effort, in particular, has been translated into Russian to support curricular development efforts in Central and Eastern Europe (Pavlov, 2006). At the time of this writing, new curriculum pilots based on SE2004 have been started in over 30 Central and Eastern European universities (Sobel, 2007).

SE2004

The Joint Task Force on Computing Curricula sponsored by the IEEE Computer Society and the Association of Computing Machinery Joint Task Force developed *Software Engineering 2004 (SE2004)* as curriculum guidelines for undergraduate degree programs in software engineering (Diaz-Herrera, 2004). SE2004 defines a detailed set of knowledge expected of a BSSE graduate as the *Software Engineering Education Knowledge (SEEK)*. SEEK is designed as a guide to support the development of undergraduate software engineering education curricula.

SEEK defines 10 education *knowledge areas* (*KAs*), each of which is recognized as a significant part of the body of knowledge that every bachelors-level software engineering graduate needs to know. A short description for each of the ten knowledge areas defined by SEEK (Diaz-Herrera, 2004) are listed below:

1. **Software evolution.** "Software evolution is the result of the ongoing need to support the stakeholders' mission in the face of changing assumptions, problems, requirements, architectures, and technologies." (Diaz-Herrera, 2004)

2. **Software process.** "Software process is concerned with knowledge about the description of commonly used software life-cycle process models and the contents of institutional process standards; definition, implementation, measurement, management, change and improvement of software processes; and use of a defined process to perform the technical and managerial activities needed for software development and maintenance." (Diaz-Herrera, 2004)

3. **Software verification and validation.** "Software verification and validation uses both static and dynamic techniques of system checking to ensure that the resulting program satisfies its specification and that the program as implemented meets the expectations of the stakeholders." (Diaz-Herrera, 2004)

4. **Software quality.** "Software quality is a pervasive concept that affects, and is affected by all aspects of software development, support, revision, and maintenance. It encompasses the quality of work products developed and/or modified … and the quality of the work processes used to develop and/or modify the work products." (Diaz-Herrera, 2004)

5. **Software design.** "Software design is concerned with issues, techniques, strategies, representations, and patterns used to determine how to implement a component or a system. The design will conform to functional requirements within the constraints imposed by other requirements such as resource, performance, reliability, and security." (Diaz-Herrera, 2004)

6. **Software management.** "Software management is concerned with knowledge about the planning, organization, and monitoring of all software life-cycle phases." (Diaz-Herrera, 2004)

7. **Computing essentials.** "Computing essentials includes the computer science foundations that support the design and construction of software products." (Diaz-Herrera, 2004)

8. **Software modeling and analysis.** "Modeling and analysis can be considered core concepts in any engineering discipline, because they are essential to documenting and evaluating design decisions and alternatives. Modeling and analysis is first applied to the analysis, specification, and validation of requirements." (Diaz-Herrera, 2004)

9. **Mathematical and engineering fundamentals.** "The mathematical and engineering fundamentals of software engineering provide theoretical and scientific underpinnings for the construction of software products with desired attributes." (Diaz-Herrera, 2004)

10. **Professional practice.** "Professional Practice is concerned with the knowledge, skills, and attitudes that software engineers must possess to practice software engineering in a professional, responsible, and ethical manner." (Diaz-Herrera, 2004)

Each knowledge area (KA) is further divided into smaller modules called *units*. The left column in Figure 2 lists the SEEK knowledge areas in light grey shades, and the knowledge units (KUs) defined for each KA in italics.

Each knowledge unit defined in SEEK is further divided into *topics*. Some topics are designated as 'essential', and constitute the core knowledge which is considered required for anyone to obtain a software engineering undergraduate degree. In its current (2004) revision, SE2004 defines 240 topics as essential that software engineers graduating from credible programs need to know (Diaz-Herrera, 2004). A summary of the number of units, topics, essential topics, and contact hours for essential topics are listed in Table 1.

The topic-level detail outlined in Table 1 can be a two-edged sword for program design. With the rigorous application of the topic-level information, those developing new software engineering programs may well find that the credit hours needed to cover the 'essential' units would be well beyond the ability to offer a program within most University constraints. Similarly, this 'essential' detail can be too detailed for effective course planning, and can obscure what units are more essential than others, particularly in the context of making a program unique to an institution (Frezza, 2003). Conversely, the detail facilitates definition of what is meant by particular knowledge units, and thus strongly facilitates measuring the completeness of a program, and clarity in communicating what constitutes a BSSE degree.

Besides the undergraduate education knowledge defined by SEEK, we also need to know about what kinds of knowledge are needed for the practice of software engineering in the workforce. The guide to the Software Engineering Body of Knowledge (SWEBOK) does just that.

SWEBOK

The IEEE Computer Society established a baseline for the body of knowledge and recommended practices for the field of software engineering in the Guide to the Software Engineering Body of Knowledge (SWEBOK) (Abran, 2004). SWEBOK characterizes the contents of software engineering discipline, *i.e.* the knowledge needed for the practice of software engineering after four years in the workforce, into ten Knowledge Areas (KAs). Each knowledge area is further divided into subareas, and each subarea is further divided into topics and subtopics. The right column in Figure 2 lists the SWEBOK knowledge areas in light grey shades, and the knowledge subareas defined for each KA in italics.

The KAs for both SEEK and SWEBOK are highlighted in light grey shades in Figure 2. The double arrowed lines given in Figure 2 outline the similarities, the dashed lines outline partial coverage, while KAs without links indicate the differences between SEEK and SWEBOK KAs. As you can see from the figure, for the first six SEEK knowledge areas (KA) each has a very related KA in SWEBOK as indicated by the double arrowed lines. Typically the KA in SWEBOK has a broader coverage in topics than the corresponding SEEK KA. However, the SEEK knowledge units listed in light grey are not covered by its knowledge area's corresponding SWEBOK KA, but are covered by the SWEBOK KA to which it is linked with solid lines. For example, SEEK unit *Software Configuration Management* in *Software Management* KA is covered by SWEBOK *Software Configuration Management* KA. SEEK unit *Product Assurance* in *Software Quality* KA is covered by SWEBOK subarea *Software Design Quality Analysis and Evaluation* in *Software Design* KA.

In addition to the closely related SEEK and SWEBOK KAs mentioned above, two SWEBOK KAs, each having significant overlap with but only partially covering its corresponding SEEK KA, are shown in dashed lines. SWEBOK KA *Software Requirements* only covers requirements related units in SEEK KA *Software Modeling and Analysis*, while *Software Construction* covers construction related units in *Computing Essentials*.

Noticeable unit differences between SEEK and SWEBOK are highlighted in reverse diagonal shades. Both *Mathematical and Engineering Fun-*

Figure 2. SE2004 SEEK knowledge areas and units vs. SWEBOK knowledge areas and subareas

SEEK Knowledge Areas and Units	SWEBOK Knowledge Areas and Subareas
Software Evolution	**Software Maintenance**
Evolution Processes	Software Maintenance Fundamentals
Evolution Activities	Key Issues in Software Maintenance
	Maintenance Process
	Techniques for Maintenance
Software Process	**Software Engineering Process**
Process Concepts	Process Implementation and Change
Process Implementation	Process Definition
	Process Assessment
	Process and Product Measurement
Software Verification and Validation	**Software Testing**
V&V Terminology and Foundations	Software Testing Fundamentals
Reviews	Test Levels
Testing	Test Techniques
Problem Analysis and Reporting	Test-related Measures
Human Computer User Interface Testing and	Test Process
Software Quality	**Software Quality**
Software Quality Concepts and Culture	Software Quality Fundamentals
Software Quality Standards	Software Quality Management Processes
Software Quality Processes	Practical Considerations
Process Assurance	
Product Assurance	
Software Design	**Software Design**
Design Concepts	Software Design Fundamentals
Design Strategies	Key Issues in Software Design
Architectural Design	Software Structure and Architecture
Human Computer Interface Design	Evaluation
Detailed Design	Software Design Notations
Design Support Tools and Evaluation	Software Design Strategies and Methods
Software Management	**Software Engineering Management**
Management Concepts	Initiation and Scope Definition
Project Planning	Software Project Planning
Project Personnel and Organization	Software Project Enactment
Project Control	Review and Evalution
Software Configuration Management	Closure
	Software Engineering Measurement
	Software Configuration Management
	Management of the SCM Process
	Software Configuration Identification
	Software Configuration Control
	Software Configuration Status Accouting
	Software Configuration Auditing
	Software Release Management and Delivery
Computing Essentials	**Software Construction**
Computer Science Foundations	Software Construction Fundamentals
Construction Technologies	Managing Construction
Construction Tools	Practical Considerations
Formal Construction Methods	
Software Modeling and Analysis	**Software Requirements**
Modeling Foundations	Software Requirements Fundamentals
Types of Models	Requirements Process
Analysis Fundamentals	Requirements Elicitation
Requirements Fundamentals	Requirements Analysis
Eliciting Requirements	Requirements Specification
Requirements Specification & Documentation	Requirements Validation
Requirements Validation	Practical Considerations
Mathematical and Engineering Fundamentals	**Software Engineering Tools and Methods**
Mathematical Foundations	Software Engineering Tools
Engineering Foundations for Software	Software Engineering Methods
Engineering Economics for Software	
Professional Practice	
Group Dynamics/psychology	
Communications Skills (specific to SE)	
Professionalism	

Table 1. Summary of SEEK knowledge areas, units and yopics

SEEK Knowledge Area	Units	Topics	Essential Topics	Essential Contact Hours
Computing Essentials	4	42	37	172
Mathematical and Engineering Fundamentals	3	22	19	89
Professional Practice	3	17	17	35
Software Modeling and Analysis	7	42	33	53
Software Design	6	37	31	45
Software Verification and Validation	5	30	28	42
Software Evolution	2	13	9	10
Software Process	2	14	13	13
Software Quality	5	28	25	16
Software Management	5	31	28	19
Total	**42**	**276**	**240**	**494**

damentals and *Professional Practice* SEEK KAs do not have corresponding SWEBOK KAs due to the educational nature and curricula development purpose of SEEK. As the SWEBOK focuses on the boundary of software engineering, hence non-software engineering-specific knowledge, such as the fundamental background required to acquire software engineering specific knowledge, was intentionally left out.

Another noticeable difference is in the SWE-BOK *Software Engineering Tools and Methods* KA as highlighted in dark grey shades. The *Software Engineering Tools* subarea is embodied inside the *Software Evolution, Software Process, Software Verification and Validation, Software Quality, Software Design, Software Management, Computing Essentials, Software Modeling and Analysis, Mathematical and Engineering Fundamentals* and *Professional Practice* topics in SEEK, as highlighted in dark grey shades.

Both SEEK and SWEBOK define the specific knowledge and skills required of a software engineer. For undergraduate software engineering graduates fresh out of college, the knowledge they attain comes from the courses they complete in their curricula, hence curricula plays an important role in deciding what knowledge students will posses when they graduate. While both SEEK and SWEBOK are designed as a guide/foundation for software engineering curricula development, SEEK is especially designed for undergraduate software engineering curricula development with detailed topics defined, and an expectation that accredited programs will reflect this set of knowledge and skills in their program.

SEEK provides description for each KA, but no descriptions are provided for the units and topics defined. This kind of set up could be hard for syllabus development as the contents which should be included for the name provided for units and topics could be open for interpretation.

With no reference materials provided, it could be difficult for faculty to find suitable textbooks or materials to cover the desired topics. On the other hand, SWEBOK provides detailed description and interesting discussion for each KA, subarea, topic and subtopic defined as well as links to books and articles.

STARTING THE PROCESS

The practical process of developing a vision for a specific instance of a Software Engineering program includes a number of concerns to be addressed, such as focus, style, leadership, and the requirements derived from the institutional strengths, weaknesses and opportunities. The experience of the authors is that of developing a program within the context of existing computing and engineering programs within the sponsoring institution, so issues concerning the creation of new academic structures will only be by inference.

Project Leadership

The immediate starting point is necessarily one of leadership – who will lead the project to define and launch the program. While this may seem trite, clearly defining the academic stakeholders is critically important, as the risks of not involving appropriate representation from related academic departments early in the program development are real, and have proven to be stumbling blocks to SE program development. As with any successful project, establishing executive sponsorship at various levels is key, as is communication with the executive sponsors and other stakeholders. One mechanism for supporting ongoing validation, communication and development of the program is a steering committee.

An effective program development steering committee should follow effective patterns within the institution, and typically is formed from department chairs, experienced faculty, external advisors, and anyone else deemed appropriate to the institution. This committee, whether formal or informal in its makeup, should necessarily include persons who have the authority to formally propose a new program within the institution. In some cases, this process may require cross-college cooperation, and thus may also include either academic deans or their representatives.

The steering committee should at minimum approve program development decisions, but may (as in our situation) be significantly more active in the development of the program details. Among these, determining the expected style of the program was a significant set of decisions. For example, in our case, the deliberate choice was to not require co-ops, and to not focus on one particular SE style, such as embedded systems, but rather allow styles and domains to be student-selected via the use of technical electives.

In our development process, the project started with one faculty project leader, and eventually formed a development committee after the housing (which department) issue was settled. In the case of Butler University in Indiana, the housing department was clear, and they developed an external advisory board consisting of local software industry leaders which helped significantly in crafting the program and building internal credibility (Henderson, 2003).

Capitalizing on Institutional Strengths

Each educational institution has its own set of distinguishing characteristics, including things like the faculty, teaching style(s), history, physical location, etc. Part of the success of a new program is its ability to realize these characteristics within the program in ways that strengthen the program, its appeal to students and its effectiveness for graduates.

In many cases, these institutional strengths are easily recognized, and involve institution-wide structures to support them. These structures can take on many forms: core curricula, freshmen sequences, service learning, marketing, development, alumni services, cooperative arrangements, etc. While many of these academic and non-academic features may also act as constraints, they are also what bring the institutions' unique stamp to the new program. Clearly identifying and celebrating these institutional strengths are significant for marketing the program, both internally and externally. Performing a formal Strengths, Weaknesses, Opportunities and Threats (SWOT) analysis may be useful.

One of the more common SE program development questions that hinges upon institutional strengths is that of requiring cooperative employment placements as part of the academic program. In some institutions, such as Rochester Institute of Technology (RIT) and Drexel University, this is an institutional strength, and is required of most programs. In other schools, required co-ops are common, and institutional support is readily available. Yet this is not the case in most institutions – neither the culture nor the academic structures support co-ops, so the decision to include a required co-op placement as part of the program design may involve significantly more cost to the program.

In our case, similar to that of Butler University, we developed our BSSE program in a 'liberal arts' institution, where the general education requirements included 36 semester hours of general education, and provides a significant institutional 'stamp' to the program. Similarly, there was no institutional support for required co-op placements, and despite the attraction of such an arrangement, it was deemed unfeasible by the development steering committee.

One of the more important institutional limitations to be negotiated is the availability of faculty resources; some institutions are very risk-adverse, and consequently are very reluctant to invest in new faculty positions for new programs until the enrollment proves the need. Other institutions are more accepting of risk, and are more tolerant of investment that will help distinguish a program, and ensure its early success.

In our case, after creating the initial academic plan, we projected the faculty resources needed to develop and sustain the new program. With an enrollment estimate, the request took the form of one new faculty member the year after the program launch, and another faculty member two years after launch if enrollment met or exceeded the estimates.

CURRICULUM CONSTRUCTION AND DESIGN

Students gain and build knowledge and skills from the courses they take while in college. Curriculum dictates what courses students in a specific program should take and the sequence of taking them. Hence curriculum plays an important role in determining what *knowledge and skills* students should possess when they graduate with a bachelor's degree. On the other hand, each course students take has a specific set of course objectives that students completing the course are expected to accomplish; curriculum also plays a determining role in what *program outcomes* will be achieved through the course outcomes. Furthermore, curriculum is the place where each institution showcases its strength, uniqueness and special program focus. So what courses should be included in an institution's BSSE curriculum? There is no one easy answer for that.

For the purpose of creating an accreditable program, where graduates meet or exceed expected program outcomes, in our experience, there are several factors to consider during the curriculum design and construction process.

1. Institutional/university strength and constraints

Each university/educational institution has its unique set of characteristics as discussed in the *Capitalizing on Institutional Strengths* subsection. No matter what the characteristics are, some (such as faculty, teaching style(s) and co-op arrangement) are great for marketing as the unique strength of the institution while others (such as core curricula, co-op requirement and freshmen sequences) can be considered as constraints for curriculum development.

In our case, our university mandates 36 credit hours of general education which ensures that every graduate achieves the university outcomes (Frezza, 2003). Although the number of credits required is mandated, every program does have the autonomy of restricting course(s) that students can select from each category to better suit the needs of each program. Furthermore, our SE program does not have co-op requirement which opens up credit hours for curriculum. On the other hand, if a co-op arrangement is instituted by the university, the number of credit hours required for the co-op arrangement would be a constraint for curriculum design.

An area where this can be significant is that of total credit hours – in our case, the Computer Science and other Engineering programs all require over 130 semester credits, so this afforded a bit of room in creating courses for the SE program. Many schools have very specific credit constraints that can make this more difficult, e.g., in the United States, many schools have 128 credit limits for bachelors degree programs. As in our case, using related programs in the school (such as EE or CS) as patterns can prove to be effective. Many of the patterns these existing programs have, such as when they take general education courses, the patterns for lab courses and lab credits, the patterns for co-ops, the patterns for common and discipline-specific courses can prove to be useful. In our case we used the CS degree as the pattern,

and reused as many of these courses as possible; by replacing some advanced mathematics courses with SE courses, this allowed us to create a program with essentially the same number of credit hours as the CS program.

2. SE program hosting department/college constraints

In addition to university/institutional constraints, program hosting department/college may have its own set of requirements (such as maximum reuse of faculty and existing courses offered, existing prerequisite structure, capstone project requirement, departmental outcomes, maximum number of credits required in a program) that need to be fulfilled.

In our case, the SE hosting department, CIS, expects the new SE program to be compatible with the existing CIS computing programs: computer science and management information systems. This is not only for the economic benefits of shared courses and faculty resources but also allows students to switch majors early in the program without much impact on required time to earn the degree (Frezza, 2003). Such a requirement leads to the mapping/compatibility analysis of existing CIS course offerings, prerequisite structure and the SE program vision. Since the SE program focuses on the *outsourced* and *MIS* categories, the CIS faculty felt the strong need of solid programming, systems, networking and computing background for SE students which in turn leads to the reuse of a great number of existing CIS courses. Specifically, SE and CS program students have almost identical courses for the first two years. However, such an arrangement also limits the number of credits available for Software Engineering specific courses that can be offered.

In addition, every CIS department graduate is expected to complete a capstone project and achieve a set of departmental outcomes. The capstone project, which integrates ethics and project management with a multi-disciplinary two semester long team project, mandates six credit hours of the senior year schedule. Although the set of departmental outcomes are not in the form of credit hours, it requires careful traceability analysis on the mappings of course outcomes to departmental outcomes. The analysis result could start the process of redefining current course content and outcomes, as well as creating new courses and the responsibility (assignment of departmental outcomes) of new courses.

3. Defined SE program outcomes

Besides the hosting departmental/college outcomes that need to be achieved, every SE program that hopes to be accredited should also fulfill the outcomes defined by its accreditation body. As discussed in the *Accreditation* subsection and *Defining the BSSE Graduate* section, every SE program needs to define its own set of program outcomes that can be related to the outcomes required by the accreditation body and specified in SE2004 (Diaz-Herrera, 2004). Both departmental outcomes and the defined SE outcomes will serve as targets for the courses designed into the BSSE curriculum.

In our case, we combined the generic CIS departmental outcomes with specific SE outcomes that then defined the BSSE program outcomes. A gap analysis was performed on the mapping of BSSE program outcomes to the eleven outcomes, the superset of ABET EAC, EAC SE and SE2004 outcomes, described in *Defining the BSSE Graduate* section. The result is shown in Table 2. The analysis goal was to make sure that every Gannon BSSE outcome maps to at least one generic SE outcome and every generic SE outcome maps to at least one Gannon BSSE outcome.

4. Outcomes to Courses: Applying ABET, SEEK and SWEBOK

The outcomes only convey what objectives should be achieved by the courses prescribed in a BSSE curriculum but not courses should be offered. One of the important goals in the design and construction of courses is to build up students' knowledge and skills through the curriculum. Both SE2004 and SWEBOK, described in *What Software Engineers Need to Know* section, define *Knowledge Areas* (KAs) and *topics* that are important to a software engineer. By identifying *Knowledge Areas* (KAs), *Knowledge Units* (KUs) and *topics* that need to be covered by courses, assigning them to courses, defining course outcomes, and mapping course outcomes to BSSE program outcomes, this not only ensures that every BSSE program outcome is covered by one or more courses, but also ensures that the important (essential) topics hand-picked by the SE program committee are covered by one or more courses. While most ABET program outcomes (A-K) and program criteria were well covered, issues regarding the minimal standards for science, mathematics, and the application of SE to some discipline needed specific inclusions in the program designs under consideration.

In our experience, SWEBOK proved to be invaluable in helping to define Knowledge Areas, subareas and topics to be covered by courses. Although SWEBOK is not designed specifically for undergraduate curriculum development and accreditation, we found it provided easy to understand, and more in-depth description of knowledge areas and topics than SE2004. In addition, it also provided useful references in building syllabi for new courses.

Since SE2004 SEEK and SWEBOK defined very similar *Knowledge Areas* (KAs), as discussed in *What Software Engineers Need to Know* section, it was not difficult for us to identify *Knowledge Areas* (KAs) that need to be covered by courses in SE curriculum. SE2004 SEEK defined very detailed topics for each KA, more specifically topics that are designated as *essential* should be covered by an accreditable SE curriculum. In an ideal world, we should be able to assign every essential topic or even non-

Table 2. Mapping of Gannon BSSE program outcomes to generic SE outcomes

9. Apply quantitative measures in the evaluation of software components and systems	8. Apply discrete mathematics and abstract structures to system development	7. Realize and manage high quality sw development lifecycle processes in one or more application domains	6. Maintain a comprehension of the changing technology and its ramifications	5. Demonstrate the ability to continue in professional development and expansion of their professional interests	4. Demonstrate effective verbal, written, and listening communication skills as required for professional, group, and team interactions	3. Comprehend ethical decisions and their ramifications as professionals.	2. Interface with business and analytical professionals to solve software or systems development problems	1. Apply problem solving strategies to software development	Gannon Software Engineering (BSSE) program outcomes 2006-7
x	x	x		x	x	x	x	x	Show mastery of the software engineering knowledge and skills, and professional issues necessary to begin practice as a software engineer
x	x	x						x	Ability to appropriately apply science, discrete mathematics, empirical techniques, probability and statistics and relevant topics in computer science and supporting disciplines to the development of complex software systems
		x			x		x		Work as an individual and as part of a multi-disciplinary team to develop and deliver quality software artifacts
x		x						x	Reconcile conflicting project objectives, finding acceptable compromises within limitations of cost, time, knowledge, existing systems and organizations
		x				x		x	Design appropriate solutions in one or more application domains using software engineering approaches that integrate ethical, social, legal and economic concerns
						x			Understanding of professional and ethical responsibility
x		x		x					Demonstrate an understanding of and apply current theories, models, and techniques that provide a basis for problem identification and analysis, software design, development, implementation, and documentation.
				x	x	x			Demonstrate an understanding and appreciation for the importance of negotiation, effective work habits, leadership, and good communication with stakeholders in a typical software development environment.
			x	x					Learn new models, techniques and technologies as they emerge and appreciate the necessity of such continuing professional development.
				x					Knowledge of contemporary issues
			x			x			Broad education necessary to understand the impact of engineering solutions in a global, economic, environmental, and societal context

essential ones defined in SEEK to courses in our SE curriculum. In reality, we had to operate under institutional and departmental constraints; those are 36 credits of general education requirement, remaining compatible to existing CS and MIS programs (maximum reuse of existing CIS courses), six credits of capstone project, and 135 maximum credits for the SE program.

Our program development model started with using an existing program (in this case, Computer Science) as the basis for the formulation. Instead of assigning all essential and even non-essential SEEK topics, KUs and KAs to whatever courses that we imagined as important for SE curriculum, we started with mapping these topics, KUs and KA's to existing computer science courses, related discipline and general education course contents. After such a mapping exercise, we were able to find the topics, KUs, KAs and even BSSE outcomes not covered by existing courses. This enabled us to revisit existing course contents and outcomes, and even allowed us the opportunity to reshape or redirect the contents and outcomes of existing courses, as well as facilitate the discussion to remove courses to make room for SE courses.

The mappings created were managed in a spreadsheet, much like requirements traceability lists, and showed that the 'requirements' coverage was incomplete. So there remained the question of whether we could cover the rest of essential topics, KUs and KAs reasonably by redesigning existing course offerings or whether new courses should be designed to serve this purpose.

In our case, we were not able to reasonably cover most of the essential topics, KUs, KAs and even BSSE outcomes by redesigning existing courses. Seven new SE specific courses: *Software Engineering Seminar, Requirements and Project Management, Formal Methods in Software Development, Software Architecture, Software Testing and Quality Assurance, Human Interface Design and Maintenance*, and *Personal Software Process*, totaling 19 credits, were created and offered by the CIS department. The initial cur-

riculum is presented in Figure 3, and the current (2007-8) curriculum is listed in Figure 4. Each SE student also needs to pick an application domain, consisting of nine credit hours of existing courses from various departments, to focus on. The math department also agreed to offer a new course – *Discrete Math 2* for our SE students. Even with the creation of these new courses, we still could not cover all the essential topics in SEEK due to the constraint of the maximum of 135 credits. The detailed examples of the mapping process can be found in (Frezza, 2003) and (Frezza, 2006).

Figure 3 presents the 135 credits initially proposed for the BSSE curriculum. These are organized by type, such as current Engineering and Computer and Information Science courses (51 credits), new Software Engineering courses (19 credits), Application Domain courses (9 credits), new and existing mathematics courses (15 credits), existing Science courses (8 credits), and existing liberal studies (general education) courses (36 credits).

5. New courses or reuse existing courses

In an ideal world where unlimited resources (faculty, budget, number of credits, etc.) are available, and no constraints are imposed for curriculum development, all new courses can be created specifically for an SE program. However, in reality, where multiple constraints exist and academic political issues are abundant, it's not always possible to create all the new courses a new SE program needs. In such a situation, a gap analysis on the mapping of existing course contents to SEEK topics, KUs, KAs and defined BSSE program outcomes could serve as the starting point for the discussion of redirecting current course contents, negotiating whether and what new courses to create, and where and how to run the new courses.

The discussions about old, revised and new courses were at times heated – for example, a more 'systems' or 'engineering' flavor to the course

Figure 3. Initial Gannon BSSE curriculum (as designed 2004)

FRESHMAN

Fall		Spring	
Introduction to Engineering	3	Software Engineering Seminar	1
Principles of Computing	3	PC – Database	1
Calculus I	3	Using UNIX	1
History of the West and World	3	Principles of Systems	3
College Composition	3	Intro. Programming & Lab	3
Sacred Scriptures	3	Calculus 2	3
		Critical Analysis & Comp.	3
		Introduction to Philosophy	3

SOPHOMORE

Fall		Spring	
Problem Solving with OOP	3	Intro Visual Programming	3
Intro. Networks	3	Data Structures	3
Discrete Mathematics 1	3	Adv. Object-Oriented Programming	3
Approved Science 1 & Lab	3	Computer Architecture	3
Theology Series II	3	Discrete Mathematics 2	3
		Philosophy Series II	3

JUNIOR

Fall		Spring	
Software Design and Test	3	Software Engineering	3
Personal Software Process	3	Database Management Systems	3
Formal Methods in Software Development	3	Distributed Programming	3
Probability & Statistics I	3	Software Architecture	3
Theology or Phil Series III	3	Requirements & Project Management	3
Application Domain 1	3		

SENIOR

Fall		Spring	
CIS Professional Seminar	1	Senior Design II	3
Senior Design I	3	Application Domain 3	3
Software Testing & Quality Assurance	3	Literature Series	3
Human Interface Design & Maintenance	3	Fine Art Series	3
Application Domain 2	3	Social Science, Humanities or Business Elective	3
Approved Science 2	3		
Approved Science 2 Lab	1		

Shading Key

Engineering, Computer and Information Science	51	Mathematics	15
Software Engineering (new)	19	Science	8
Application Domain	9	Liberal Studies	36

would have introduced discrete mathematics in the context of digital design, and then followed up with formal discrete mathematics course to fill out the KA. However, the 'MIS' vision prevailed, (and the desire to parallel the Computer Science program closely), and a *Discrete Mathematics 1,* followed by a *Discrete Mathematics 2* combination was agreed upon, followed up by a *Formal Methods in Software Development* course, offered by our department. For each of these courses, appropriate KA's were assigned to the mappings, as well as the subproject of getting our colleagues in the Math Department to support the approach. Such tradeoffs were not insignificant, but were guided by the needs as expressed in the traceability spreadsheet. The spreadsheet framed the problem; our particular resolution to the program vision (information systems) and organization issues (CIS department) guided the debate.

Similar issues surfaced around addressing the 'Computer Organization' requirements within the Computing Foundations KU, which could be implemented with a 'microprocessors course' or a 'computer architecture course' – neither of which would come from our department. Here the traceability showed the need for, and coverage within the spirit and letter of the requirements – but a choice/decision needed to be made. In this case, the previous 'Discrete 1 vs. Digital Logic' decision drove the issue. Only the 'Computer Architecture' remained as a viable choice, both because of the desire to parallel the CS program, and the fact that the architecture course accepted the *Discrete Mathematics 1* course as a prerequisite – whereas the microprocessor course did not.

In our case, the seven new SE specific courses fell logically on the shoulders of the hosting department, CIS, due the focus and skills of the department and faculty. We were able to negotiate with Math department to offer the new *Discrete Math 2* course due to its strong mathematics content. For domain related courses, we decided to reuse existing courses offered by various departments to offer students more domain specific

knowledge. Our current Software Engineering curriculum is presented in the Change Management section below.

Once the BSSE curriculum is developed, it is just a proposal – it serves as the guide and core for getting the agreement to launch the program, and ultimately for attracting students, staffing and running the courses that make up the program and continuing to improve the program to serve students' needs.

SELLING THE PROGRAM

During the early stages of conceiving and constructing the program, support must be obtained on several levels in order to reasonably proceed, and, ultimately, to launch a successful program.

Understanding the Student Market

One initial question which must be answered is whether there is and will be work for BSSE graduates. If this question is answered in the negative, there is little chance for program success since it will be extremely difficult to attract students to a program with bleak job prospects. According to the United States Bureau of Labor Statistics (U.S. Department of Labor, 2006a), computer software engineers in the United States held about 800,000 jobs in 2004. They are employed in a wide variety of industries, with employers ranging from startup companies to established industry leaders.

According to Bureau projections, computer software engineer will be one of the fastest-growing occupations through 2014 as businesses adopt and integrate new computer-based technologies. Jobs openings will be created both through employment growth and from the need to replace workers who retire or otherwise leave the occupation. Consulting opportunities for computer software engineers also should continue to grow.

Growth in the field will come from rapidly evolving technologies as well as new software needs driven by information security concerns.

With growing internationalization of software development, some countries will see more software development contracted out abroad. However, jobs in software engineering are less prone to being sent abroad because the occupation requires innovation and intense research and development. Most companies prefer to keep this function in-house whenever practical.

Since the BSSE is a relatively new major, it is often difficult to obtain accurate statistics which isolate the major. This is true when discussing starting salaries. Some basic information is available from the National Association of Colleges and Employers web site (National Association of Colleges and Employers, 2007) (more detailed information is available to members). This press release lists the average starting salary offer to recent bachelor's graduates in Management Information Systems/Business Data Processing as $46,966. The average offer for Computer Science graduates is listed as $52,177. The press release does not distinguish between types of job, nor does it list Software Engineering as a category of degree.

The United States Bureau of Labor Statistics (U.S. Department of Labor, 2006b), lists median salary data for computer software engineers in the United States, but the data is for the profession. As discussed below, most practicing software engineers do not have a degree in Software Engineering, so the data applies to anyone working as a software engineer, not just to those with a Software Engineering degree.

Given the promising employment outlook, a follow-up question is whether students are enrolling in BSSE programs. If we build it, will they come?

As with employment trends, it is difficult to obtain accurate enrollment statistics which apply specifically to the Software Engineering major. The Digest of Education Statistics, 2005 (National Center for Education Statistics, 2005), lists 163 students receiving a Bachelor's degree in Computer Software Engineering in 2003-04, while the 2004 Digest (National Center for Education Statistics, 2004), lists 121 students receiving a Bachelor's degree in Computer Software Engineering in 2002-03. These are the most recent official statistics generally available as of this writing. While these statistics indicate solid growth in the number of bachelor's degrees granted, the number of SE graduates is still extremely small when compared with the number of software engineers needed.

It is also difficult to obtain statistics for software engineering as a career preference. For example, the Post-Secondary Planning Survey Analysis, conducted by the National Research Center for College and University Admissions (NRCCUA) Career-Choice Preferences lists "Computer Sciences," "Information Technology," and several Engineering choices, but "Software Engineering" is not included as a separate choice (NRCCUA, 2007). The SAT survey of intended majors of college bound students in 2007 includes only the broad categories of "Computer and Information Sciences and Support Services" and "Engineering" (The College Board, 2007).

Based on the above numbers, it can be concluded that most practicing software engineers do not have a degree in Software Engineering, but rather in Computer Science or some other related discipline. The question is whether a traditional Computer Science degree program best prepares a student for today's typical software engineering jobs and future career need not be addressed; there is room for and need for both majors.

With promising employment and enrollment outlooks, a final general question is whether the market is already flooded with new BSSE programs. The brief, simple answer is "no" (or at least it was in 2002 and still is at the time of writing).

In 2003, there were 21 known programs in the United States offering some type of bachelor's degree in Software Engineering, with more being proposed (Bagert, 2003). As of January 1, 2007, there are at least 34 known BSSE programs in the U.S. 13 of which are accredited by ABET (ABET, 2006). Based on these numbers and the projected need for Software Engineers, it seems that many more programs with a Software Engineering focus are needed.

Building Additional Support

Once these initial questions are answered, support to proceed must be obtained from several groups. First, the affected faculty must support the program. If housed in a Computer Science program, one adjustment will be a shift in the focus of some upper division courses. The basics of programming, database, networking, operating systems, and computer architecture will be taught in both majors. However, Computer Science majors will then study topics such as analysis of algorithms, comparative programming languages, compilers, and formal languages. Software Engineers, on the other hand, with study topics such as software design and test, software architecture, requirements, project management, quality assurance, and human interface design.

For some faculty, this will be an issue. It will be seen as a move from a set of courses with technical, well-defined content to a set of courses with a more subjective content. If co-located with a Computer Science program, the split in focus and teaching assignment for upper division courses may fall naturally along the strengths and interests of the faculty and be seen as a positive. If not, some accommodation will need to be made for and by the faculty. This can often be accomplished by judicious distribution of the core set of courses. Regardless of initial reaction, recent downward trends in enrollment in Computer Science programs should provide motivation for faculty to support a program which will likely lead to an increase in enrollment.

Once the faculty is behind the concept of a Software Engineering program, the university administration must be convinced that launching the program is a good idea. While there are several factors involved, the overriding issue with the administration is likely to be economic: will the new program make money or lose money? For a university, the business case will boil down to whether revenue from increased enrollment will offset increased costs. The overall impact of the program proposal was the creation and staffing of seven new courses in software engineering; if offered annually, as was the plan, this defined the need for a new faculty member. In our case, we developed our proposal to feature launching the program first, and then adding the new faculty member in the second year in order to offset the economic impact.

Cost increase can vary greatly depending on factors discussed in preceding sections. If the program is housed in a department such as Computer Science, there can be much reuse of courses and faculty. As such, there will likely be little additional cost when the program is first launched. As the program moves into its third and fourth years, new upper division courses must be developed and taught. Part of this cost can be shifted by eliminating or reducing the frequency of current courses which are under-enrolled. Other costs are more than offset by the increase in enrollment.

A further advantage to the university is the visibility of offering a cutting-edge program. This will help attract both students and faculty. It will also bolster the overall image of the university. In our case, adding the SE program led to a change in the CS+SE enrollment trends – what had been on significant decline grew slightly and stabilized.

Finally, to be successful, the program must be attractive to both students and their parents. One major point, of course, is that Software Engineering is a promising career. The field provides an adequate number of jobs and good salaries. A degree in Software Engineering provides the right skill set for a student entering the job market, and degree in Software Engineering distinguishes the graduate from a graduate with a Computer Science degree. This can be highlighted by the admissions department as well as in any marketing provided by the university. One criticism of adding Software Engineering was the question of impact on Computer Science enrollment. In our case, there has been an impact on CS enrollment (and MIS for that matter). We have 'lost' students to SE from these programs, but we also found many new students who would have otherwise not applied to the university. For our (rather small) program, this has been averaging about 50% for the four years we have accepted students to the SE program. Over this period, about half of the new students who join the BS-SE would not have joined the university. For our department, this has resulted in a slight decline in CS undergraduates, but more recently it has also seen an increase in CS applicants, as well as a qualitative difference in those students who join the CS program – they are increasingly joining because they are genuinely interested in CS topics and approaches.

Finally, the entry in the university catalog for the new program becomes more important than for more established programs. In addition to just being a listing of required courses and their content, the catalog entries server as a marketing tool. A good entry will highlight the potential of the career path, the promise of the department to the students to deliver the appropriate courses and material, and the commitment of the university to support the new program.

LAUNCHING THE PROGRAM

Based on the plan initially proposed to and then approved by the university (Frezza, 2003), Gannon was able to launch the SE major with little impact on courses or faculty for the first two years. Based on the assessment of Gannon's strengths and those of the various departments as well as a review of

requirements imposed by the policies of both the university and college, the courses taken by SE majors in the first two years were already offered within the university. These courses consisted of Liberal Arts core courses taken by all Gannon students, CIS core courses already offered and taken by the CS and MIS majors at the university, and introductory science courses already offered to several majors. The only exception to this is the *Discrete Math 2* course taken second semester of sophomore year. The Math department was willing to develop and offer this course in the necessary time frame. By design, the first two years of the program had little immediate impact on course delivery or teaching load – only one new one-credit course was needed. Our internal goal of trying to reuse as many of the existing Computer Science curriculum courses and sequences as possible had the significant benefit of our being able to launch the program prior to searching for new faculty.

Adding New Faculty

Adding a new faculty member to the department proved to be significantly easy for our situation, as one of the proponents of the program (who was CSDP qualified), by mutual agreement, essentially transferred from the Electrical and Computer Engineering department. Finding a second qualified faculty member was not as easy. Finding a potential faculty member with a good academic background, worthwhile industry experience, an appropriate commitment to teaching and scholarship, who fits in the university/department culture and has not already taken on a higher-paying job in industry is a tall order.

While our experience has been somewhat limited, some of the problem areas have included recruitment of junior faculty; getting the right match for credentials, experience and fit have proven to be difficult. The typical Computer Science Ph.D. may not have any interest in 'core' software engineering topics; whereas Ph.D.'s from

Engineering or Information Science disciplines may not have any significant software development background. In any case, many typical Ph.D.s do not have either experience or education in SE 'special topics' areas such as project management, software maintenance or even requirements.

Additional issues abound when searching for seasoned faculty members – while they often have more project and teaching experience, they also have the potential for more (and more complex) issues in areas such as benefits and tenure. Such issues are often institutional, and flexibility may not be available.

Course Pilots

This particular facet of our program design did not eliminate the need for additional staffing, however. Based on our assessments, we would need a new faculty member in the second year of the program to teach the first round of the new SE courses, and if enrollment took off, in year three or four we would need another faculty member to help with the additional sections that would be needed in the introductory sequence. These points were very important to painting the financial picture to the university about the distribution of costs and risks in launching the program. Financially, the big impact would be in years two and four; academically, the real impact would begin in the third year of the program; a change-management plan was needed.

The plan was to hire a new (additional) SE-qualified faculty member in year two, and additionally to offer all of the new junior-level SE courses in advance. This latter plan was part of a (pedagogical) risk-management strategy so that the new faculty member and other department faculty members could pilot the new SE courses prior to the first wave of SE students entering the courses. The expanded department faculty would then offer each of the new SE courses one year in advance of the first wave of SE students – with

three semesters containing significant piloting of courses.

For the fall (piloting semester five) of their junior year, SE majors were scheduled to take three upper division SE-specific courses: *Software Design and Test*, *Personal Software Process*, and *Formal Methods in Software Development*. Of these, only one was new, as *Software Design and Test* was already a course offered and required of our CS majors and *Personal Software Process* was offered to our 1st-year graduate students. Hence neither of these courses needed significant modifications for the undergraduate BSSE population. The *Formal Methods* course was a different story – it was new to our faculty and needed to be developed and offered. Finding educational resources and faculty development seminars to support this course proved to be difficult. Developing this course offering required identifying and making decisions on course topics, approaches, tools, methodologies and textbooks that would work for our students.

During the next spring (piloting semester six), the impact intensified. The SE majors were scheduled to take two more new courses in the following year, so *Requirements and Project Management*, and *Software Architecture*, which were developed and offered in their pilot forms, knowing the regular group of majors would register in the following year. This additional workload was covered by the new faculty member.

The third year of the program (pilot for Semester seven) required the development and offering of two new undergraduate courses, both offered in the first semester: *Software Testing and Quality Assurance*, and *Human Interface Design and Maintenance*. These courses, along with the first regular offerings of the three fifth-semester SE-specific courses accounted for the additional time provided by the faculty hired at the beginning of the second year of the program.

In addition to the courses and faculty needed, two other factors needed to be considered. First, the university Admissions department needed to be involved in the process. The program needed to be advertised as much as possible, and admissions needed to understand the requirements for admission to the program. They also needed to place the incoming SE students in the proper courses for the freshman year.

Finally, the issue of transfer students, both internal and external, needed to be addressed. Since the program was phased-in over four years, for the first two years, we would be unable to accept upper division transfers (unless they were willing to stay an extra year) since the upper division courses were not available during those first two years. We did, in fact, accept one sophomore transfer the first year of the program and he was able to graduate with just one additional semester.

CHANGE MANAGEMENT

One important issue to address early in the program development is to plan for change. This begins with outcomes and measurement. We were fortunate that many of the processes that we required in this area were already largely in place. The CIS department already had outcomes defined for the CS and MIS majors and some measurement tools in place.

Further, the Electrical Engineering and Mechanical Engineering departments were ABET accredited. Concurrently with the launching of the SE major, the CIS department was preparing for ABET accreditation for the two existing majors, and the EE and ME departments were preparing to renew their accreditation. To aid in this process, an online course evaluation tool was prepared to gather information specifically required by the ABET process. (A university-wide course evaluation instrument had been in use for all courses for several years, but it did not gather all information required by ABET.) This tool was used from the beginning of the SE program.

Even though we are only about to begin our fourth year of the program, and the first time

the senior level courses will be offered, we have already made changes to the program. First, we realized that we had a hole in coverage in the operating systems area. To address this issue within faculty time and budget constraints, we added the full Operating Systems course to the list of required courses. To make room, we dropped an Introduction to Engineering course which had only partial content relevant to our needs. We moved the relevant content into pieces of existing courses where they fit the best.

One of the core Liberal Studies requirements is a basic business course. Many of our majors chose either Microeconomics or Macroeconomics. After two years of the program, we saw an opportunity to provide a business course more directly applicable to the SE majors. As such, we co-developed a course (*Project Economics*) with the business school which provides basic economics theory as well as the application of the theories in a project setting. This course is now the designated business course for SE majors.

Our current Software Engineering Curriculum (2007-8) is listed in Figure 4. Diagonal shading indicates reused Computer and Information Science courses. The darker grey shading indicates new courses developed for the Software Engineering major by the Computer and Information Science department. One of the seven originally proposed new Software Engineering courses (See Figure 3), the *Software Engineering Seminar*, was offered two times and it was determined that the course was not serving the needs of our software engineering students. Therefore, it was removed from the curriculum. As noted in a previous section, *Discrete Math 2* was developed by the Math department for our software engineering program. The remaining courses required for the software engineering major, including the application domain courses, are coded in Figure 4 as indicated by the shading key. These courses were already offered by various departments within the university, with the exception of *Project Economics* discussed above.

Figure 4. Current software engineering curriculum (2007-8)

FRESHMAN

Fall		Spring	
Principles of Computing	3	Using UNIX	1
PC – Database	1	Intro. Programming & Lab	3
Calculus I	3	Calculus 2	3
History of the West and World	3	Critical Analysis & Comp.	3
College Composition	3	Introduction to Philosophy	3
Sacred Scriptures	3	Approved Science 1 & Lab	4

SOPHOMORE

Fall		Spring	
Problem Solving with OOP	3	Data Structures	3
Intro. Networks	3	Adv. Object-Oriented Programming	3
Discrete Mathematics 1	3	Computer Architecture	3
Approved Science 2 & Lab	4	Database Management Systems	3
Project Economics	3	Discrete Mathematics 2	3
		Philosophy Series II	3

JUNIOR

Fall		Spring	
Software Design and Test	3	Software Engineering	3
Operating Systems	3	Visual Database Programming	3
Personal Software Process	3	Software Architecture	3
Formal Methods in Software Development	3	Requirements & Project Management	3
Probability & Statistics I	3	Application Domain 1	3
Theology Series II	3	Theology or Phil Series III	3

SENIOR

Fall		Spring	
CIS Professional Seminar	1	Senior Design II	3
Senior Design I	3	Distributed Programming	3
Software Testing & Quality Assurance	3	Application Domain 3	3
Human Interface Design & Maintenance	3	Literature Series	3
Application Domain 2	3	Fine Art Series	3
Social Science, Humanities or Business Elective	3		

Shading Key

Computer and Information Science	48	Mathematics	15
Software Engineering (new)	18	Science	8
Application Domain	9	Liberal Studies	36

CONCLUSION

This article does not address the relative merits of the education provided by a traditional Computer Science program compared with a Software Engineering program. It does seem that there is a need to provide the type of Software Engineering curriculum discussed in the article and that the curriculum can be provided along with, rather than instead of, a more traditional Computer Science curriculum. Programs have been and can be introduced at institutions with diverse size, diverse overall focus, diverse program style, and diverse strengths.

This article discusses many items to consider in the process of planning and launching a new BSSE program. Further, obtaining program accreditation is highly desirable, in some cases necessary. Understanding the steps required by the appropriate accrediting body to obtain accreditation is mandatory at some point in the program's lifecycle. Understanding the steps very early and accounting for them during program planning will help smooth the journey to accreditation.

REFERENCES

ABET Engineering Accreditation Commission (EAC) (2005). Criteria for Accrediting Engineering Programs, Effective for Evaluations during the 2006-7 Accreditation Cycle. Baltimore, MD. Retrieved May 28, 2007, from http://www.abet.org/forms.shtml.

ABET (2006). List of Accredited Programs in Software Engineering, October 1, 2006. Retrieved May 28, 2007, from http://www.abet.org/ABE-TWebsite.asp#area

ABET (2007). Home Page, Retrieved May 28, 2007, from http://www.abet.org/index.shtml

Abran, A., & Moore, J. (Eds.). (2004). Guide *to the Software Engineering Body of Knowledge,* *2004 Version*, IEEE Computer Society Press. Available at http://www.swebok.org.

Bagert, D., & Ardis, M. (2003, November). *Software Engineering Baccalaureate Programs In The United States: An Overview.* Proceedings of the Frontiers in Education Conference (FIE'03). Boulder, CO.

Bourque, P., Dupuis, R., Abran, A., Moore, J., & Tripp, L. (2000, August). *Developing Consensus on the Software Engineering Body of Knowledge.* Proceedings of the 2000 World Computer Congress, Beijing, China. Available at *http://www.gelog.etsmtl.ca/publications/pdf/535.pdf*

Canadian Council of Professional Engineers, Canadian Engineering Accreditation Board (2006). CEAB Accreditation Criteria and Procedures. Ottawa, Ontario, Canada. Retrieved October 26, 2007, from http://www.engineerscanada.ca/e/files/report_ceab.pdf

Diaz-Herrera, J. L., Hilburn, T., Hislop, G., Lutz, M., MacNeil, P.E., & McCracken, M. (2001, October). *Software Engineering Education Should Be Presented as A: Science, B: Engineering, C. Technology, D. None of the above, E. All of the above, Other.* Proceedings of the Frontiers in Education Conference (FIE'01), Reno, NV.

Diaz-Herrera, J. L., & Hilburn, T. (Eds.). (2004). *Software Engineering 2004 Curriculum Guidelines for Undergraduate Degree Programs in Software Engineering A Volume of the Computing Curricula Series.* Available at http://sites.computer.org/ccse

Engineers Australia (2007). Australian Professional Engineering Programs Accredited by Engineers Australia. Last updated 6 September 2007. Retrieved November 11, 2007 from http://www.engineersaustralia.org.au/education/program-accreditation/accredited-programs/accredited-programs_home.cfm

Frezza, S., Sasi, S., & Seol, J. (2003, November). *Report from the Trenches: Applying the SEEK to BSSE Program Development.* Proceedings of the Frontiers in Education Conference (FIE'03). Boulder, CO.

Frezza, S. T., Tang, M-H., & Brinkman, B. J. (2006). Creating an Accreditable Software Engineering Bachelor's Program. *IEEE Software,* 23(6), 27-35.

Henderson, P., Linos, P., & Tinsley, E. (2003). *Crafting an Undergraduate Software Engineering Program in a Liberal Arts Environment.* Unpublished extended abstract, Butler University, Indianapolis, IN.

IEEE Computer Society (2001). *The Certified Software Development Professional Program,* Available at http://www.computer.org/portal/pages/ieeecs/education/certification.

Jones, C. (2003). Variations in Software Development Practices. *IEEE Software,* 20(6), 22-27.

Kelley, R. E. (1999). How to be a Star Engineer, *IEEE Spectrum.* 36(10), 51-58.

McConnell, S., & Tripp, L. (1999). Professional Software Engineering: Fact or Fiction? *IEEE Software,* 16(6), 13-18.

National Association of Colleges and Employers (2007). *Higher Starting Salary Offers Reflect Positive Trend in Job Market for New College Graduates.* Press Release. Retrieved May 28, 2007, from http://www.naceweb.org/press/display.asp?year=2007&prid=256

National Center for Education Statistics (2004). Institute of Education Sciences, U. S. Department of Education. *Digest of Education Statistics, 2004.* Retrieved May 28, 2007, from http://nces.ed.gov/programs/digest/

National Center for Education Statistics (2005). Institute of Education Sciences, U. S. Department of Education. Digest of Education Statistics, 2005. Retrieved May 28, 2007, from http://nces.ed.gov/programs/digest/

National Research Center for College and University Admissions (2007). Post-Secondary Planning Survey Analysis, 2007-2008 Edition. Retrieved November 15, 2007, from http://www.nrccua.org/downloads/reports/survey_analysis.pdf

Naur, P. & Randell, B. (Eds.) (1969). *Software engineering: Report of a conference sponsored by the NATO Science Committee,* Garmisch, Germany, 7–11 October 1968, Brussels, Scientific Affairs Division, NATO.

Sobel, A. E. K., Bagert, D. J., Frezza, S. T., & Pavlov, V. L. (2007, October). Panel - *Assessing The Impact of the SE2004 Curriculum Guidelines,* presented at the Frontiers in Education Conference (FIE'07), Milwaukee, WI.

The College Board (2007). 2007 College Bound Seniors, Total Group Profile Report. Retrieved November 15, 2007, from http://www.collegeboard.com/prod_downloads/about/news_info/cbsenior/yr2007/national-report.pdf

U. S. Department of Labor, Bureau of Labor Statistics (2006a). *Occupational Outlook Handbook (OOH),* 2006-07 Edition. Retrieved May 28, 2007, from http://www.bls.gov/oco/

U. S. Department of Labor, Bureau of Labor Statistics (2006b). *Occupational Employment and Wages.* May 2006. Retrieved May 28, 2007, from http://www.bls.gov/oes/current/oes151032.htm

Wankat, P. & Oreovicz, F. (1993*). Teaching Engineering,* Upper Saddle River, NJ: McGraw Hill.

Section VII
Professional Practice

Chapter XVII
Ensuring Students Engage with Ethical and Professional Practice Concepts

J. Barrie Thompson
University of Sunderland, UK

ABSTRACT

The teaching and learning of aspects related to ethics and professional practice present significant challenges to both staff and students as these topics are much more abstract than say software design and testing. The core of this chapter is an in-depth examination of how ethics and professional practice can be addressed in a very practical manner. To set the scene and provide contextual information the chapter commences with information on an international model of professionalism, a code of ethics for Software Engineers, and different teaching and learning approaches that can be employed when addressing ethical issues. The major part of the chapter is then devoted to detailing a particular teaching and leaning approach, which has been developed at the University of Sunderland in the UK. Finally conclusions, views on the present situation and future developments, and details of outstanding challenges are presented.

INTRODUCTION

Software Engineers operate within a global market place where, for example, software can be specified in the USA, developed in India, and then used by individuals globally on the Internet. The systems that they produce provide solutions to problems across a wide range of areas from health care, through business, to all forms of transpor-

tation. Compared to what could be achieved just a few years ago the technical developments that software underpins can have far reaching implications on everyday life. Also, it must be noted that they support much of the world economy. However, these technical developments can also have a downside, raising significant social and ethical risks for individuals, organisations and society at large (ETHICOMP, 2004).

A major challenge for educators is to ensure that students do not just concentrate on the technical elements of Software Engineering. The students need to be prepared for their place as future professionals who can appreciate the wider issues associated with the systems for which they will have a responsibility. It is thus important that the students understand the need for professional practices and the roles that codes of ethics play in underpinning such practices. However, it is equally important to ensure that these "softer" subjects are treated in an engaging and meaningful manner that involves the students fully and interactively. Simply studying models of professionalism and codes of ethics in isolation can be, to say the least, a boring and unchallenging activity (both for the students and the academic staff).

The objectives of this chapter are firstly to provide some background and contextual information relating to an international model of professionalism relevant to professional practice in information technology and a code of ethics for Software Engineers. Then consideration will be given to different teaching and learning approaches that can be employed when addressing ethical issues. Following this, the major part of the chapter is devoted to presenting details of a particular teaching and learning approach, which has been developed at the University of Sunderland in the UK, and which is believed to:

- Give the students an understanding of the role and importance of codes of ethics and professional practice.
- Encourage students to engage and work together.
- Develop individual and group skills in the areas of analysis, appraisal, discussion, and presenting.
- Provide an environment in which the students can apply a code of ethics and professional practice to a realistic (though fictitious) situation.

- Encourage staff/student communication.
- Provide elements of: "fun" (yes, it does this), of competiveness, and real engagement.

The following two sections set the scene, by respectively, providing contextual information and examining teaching and leaning approaches. The next five sections then address, in detail, the approach adopted at Sunderland. The final section of the chapter is devoted to some conclusions, views on the present situation and future developments, and finally details of outstanding challenges.

BACKGROUND AND CONTEXTUAL INFORMATION

Since the mid 1990s there have been a number of initiatives relevant to professionalism within the wider Information and Communication Technology (ICT) sector. For example, during the 1990s the International Federation for Information Processing (IFIP), following encouragement from the World Trade Organisation, undertook activities related to defining international standards for professionals in the field of Information Technology. Whilst in the USA, during the same time-frame, the ACM and IEEE Computer Society worked together on a number of initiatives which would support the establishment of Software Engineering as a profession. The ACM and IEEE Computer Society initiatives concentrated on areas associated with Ethics and Professional Practices, Body of Knowledge and Recommended Practices, and Education.

A detailed account of the efforts of IFIP and those of the ACM and IEEE Computer Society and what has followed them can be found in a paper presented at the 2007 ETHICOMP conference (Thompson, 2007). Of particular relevance to this chapter are:

- A framework or meta model that was approved by IFIP in 1999 and which was defined in a document entitled "Harmonization of Professional Standards" (Mitchell, Juliff, & Turner, 1998) and

- The "Software Engineering Code of Ethics and Professional Practice" (SECEPP, 1999) produced under the auspices of the ACM and IEEE Computer Society.

With regard to the other ACM and IEEE Computer Society initiatives, the project that was concerned with defining a Body of Knowledge was completed by the IEEE Computer Society alone after a difference of views split the relationship (ACM, 2000). The resultant publication "Guide to the Software Engineering Body of Knowledge" (SWEBOK) appearing in 2004 (Bourque & Dupuis, 2004). However, the two societies subsequently worked together to produce the curriculum document "Software Engineering 2004, Curriculum Guidelines for Undergraduate Degree Programs in Software Engineering" (IEEE-CS & ACM, 2004).

IFIP's Professional Standards Framework

IFIP is a non-governmental, non-profit umbrella organisation for national societies working in the field of information processing. The federation is essentially a society of societies—included in its membership are the ACM, Australian Computer Society, British Computer Society, and IEEE Computer Society along with many others. IFIP has the mission to be the leading, truly international, apolitical organisation which encourages and assists in the development, exploitation and application of Information Technology for the benefit of all people. Technical work, which is the heart of IFIP's activity, is managed by a series of Technical Committees (TCs). Each of these is in turn responsible for a number of working groups (WGs).

During the 1990's, IFIP started to address issues that were related to the movement of Information Technology professionals from one country to another. A driver behind this was a view from the World Trade Organisation that the establishment of standards regarding the qualifications of professionals was very important in an era of international treaties that promoted free trade and the free movement of workers from one country to another. In 1997 a working party was created whose aim was to produce a document that would clearly set out the standards of tertiary education, experience or practice, ethics, and continuing education that a customer might expect from a practitioner offering services to the public. During 1998 a small writing party met and produced a draft standard entitled "Harmonization of Professional Standards" (Mitchell, Juliff, & Turner, 1998). This was subsequently presented in August 1999 to the IFIP Technical Committee on Education (TC3) and to a meeting of members of the TC3 Working Group that is concerned with Vocational Education and Training (WG3.4).

The main parts of the IFIP Professional Standards document are reproduced as Appendix 1 to this chapter and address the following six areas:

- Ethics of professional practice,
- Established body of knowledge,
- Education and training,
- Professional experience,
- Best practice and proven methodologies, and
- Maintenance of competence.

Within Working Group 3.4 it was felt that the most appropriate area within the field of Information Processing for consideration of professionalism was Software Engineering. Thus, starting in September 2000 a series of activities commenced that was undertaken over a two year period to promote the IFIP Professional Standards document and provide a forum for an analysis of its relevance to Software Engineering community. The overall reaction by the community was very encouraging—it was recognised that the IFIP document essentially defines a framework or meta model, which should assist advancing professional standards if it is used in a sensitive and appropriate manner. A summary of the work undertaken in promoting and evaluating document and the most significant outcomes were reported at the IFIP 2005 World Conference on Computers in Education (Thompson, 2005). That paper also details concerns associated with Software Engineering maturity in the areas of best practice and proven methodologies, maintenance of competence, and the educational support for these.

Software Engineering Code of Ethics and Professional Practice

The ACM and IEEE-CS collaboration with regard to Software Engineering started in 1993 with the creation of a Joint Steering Committee for "The Establishment of Software Engineering as a Profession". The committee's task was primarily to "establish the appropriate set(s) of criteria and norms for professional practice of software engineering upon which industrial decisions, professional certification and education curricula can be based." (ACM & IEEE-CS, 1999a). In 1998 the two organisations further formalised their co-operation with the creation of Software Engineering Coordinating Committee (SWECC) which was made responsible for co-ordinating, sponsoring and fostering all their various activities regarding Software Engineering (ACM & IEEE-CS, 1999b).

A major success resulting from the SWECC co-operation between the ACM and IEEE-CS was the production of the Software Engineering Code of Ethics and Professional Practice (SECEPP) by a task force led by Don Gotterbarn of East Tennessee State University.

The code is available in two forms - a short version which summarises aspirations at a high level of abstraction and a full version which has additional clauses (SECEPP, 1999). The latter provide examples and details of how the aspirations of the code should change the way people act as SE professionals. The current short version of the code (version 5.2) is reproduced in Appendix 2 to this chapter and addresses basic principles with regard to eight areas:

- Public,
- Client and Employer,
- Product,
- Judgement,
- Management, Profession,
- Colleagues, and
- Self

Perhaps of particular note is the ordering of these areas with "Public" first and "Self" last. The code in addition to being approved by both ACM and IEEE-CS (Gotterbarn, Miller, & Rogerson, 1999) has been widely adopted across the world (SECEPP, ud). In fact it appears to be one particular project that has been outstanding in the lack of criticism associated with it. A possible reason for this was that the task force which produced the code (consisting of a three-person Executive Committee and a general membership of 22 members) had a truly international composition.

TEACHING AND LEARNING APPROACHES

The importance of addressing ethical and professional issues in Software Engineering programmes is clearly recognised within the guiding principles for the Software Engineering volume of the Computing Curricula:

"The education of all Software Engineering students must include student experiences with the professional practice of Software Engineering. The professional practice of Software Engineering encompasses a wide range of issues and activities including problem solving, management, ethical and legal concerns..." (IEEE-CS & ACM, 2004, p. 10).

The particular issues associated with professionalism and ethics in the real world situations that Software Engineers operate in have been addressed in many papers and texts since the mid 1990s (e.g. Myers, Hall & Pitt, 1997, and Bott, 2005). Unfortunately, support for the teaching and learning related to the subject area is not so readily available as for other more technical subjects such as design and testing. A further problem is that the major Software Engineering textbooks tend to provide little more than passing references to professional and ethical issues. However, various teaching and leaning approaches have been addressed in depth in recent papers presented at the 2003 and 2004 Conferences on Software Engineering Education and Training (Towell, 2003, and Towell & Thompson, 2004). In addition, papers addressing teaching and learning approaches that relate to addressing professionalism and ethics, but to a wider computing audience, can be found in the proceedings of the Ethicomp Series of Conferences, The Ethicomp Journal and the Journal of Information Communication and Ethics in Society (further information on theses sources can be obtained from the Centre for Computing and Social Responsibility at De Montfort University (DMU, 2007)).

More plentiful sources of information on teaching and learning approaches are the various workshops and tutorials that have been held in conjunction with international conferences (e.g. Granger et al (1997), Gotterbarn & Miller (2001), Thompson & Towell (2004)). The latter of these events was held at the 2004 Conference on Software Engineering Education and Training and specifically addressed the teaching of ethics in Software Engineering programs. The operation and results of the workshop were subsequently reported in the 160th issue of the Forum

for Advancing Software engineering Education (FASE, 2004). During the workshop the commonest teaching techniques that were used when addressing ethics were identified as:

- Discussion of an instructor's personal experiences
- Discussion of current events
- Reviewing various codes of ethics such as the Software Engineering Code of Ethics and Professional Practice
- Using case studies to highlight particular ethical considerations.
- Using role-play to engage students in the exploration of ethical situations
- Using games such as Lockheed Martin's "The Ethics Challenge" (documented by Bekir, Cable, Hashimoto, & Katz, 2001)
- Employing Web-Based Learning Systems such as Walter Maner's Interactive Computer Ethics Explorer. (Maner, ud)

Further details of these approaches can be found in a paper by Towell, Thompson and Mc-Fadden (2004) which considered how to address professional standards within the Information Systems curriculum.

When it comes to delivery of ethical and professional related topics a major issue that instructors have to address is: whether the best approach is to have one or more very specific modules that address these areas or whether the topics should be treated throughout the curriculum and thus directly complement and support the other subject areas. Gotterbarn (2001) is a clear proponent of the pervasive approach, however this can present some real difficulties:

- The majority of the staff teaching the other subjects need themselves to believe in the importance of ethics and professionalism and they need to have the necessary knowledge to address the issues that are likely to be raised by the students.

- If the academic programme needs to be accredited (for example, by ABET in the USA or the British Computer Society in the UK) it can very hard to convince a visiting accreditation panel that these topics really are pervasive throughout the curriculum.

The pragmatic approach taken by many institutions, especially when accreditation is seen as a major requirement, is to simply have one or more explicitly titled modules that can easily be identified as addressing the relevant issues.

THE SUNDERLAND APPROACH: OVERVIEW

At the University of Sunderland we have employed a particular approach to addressing ethical and professional practice concepts within our masters level programmes in computing that combines several of the strategies listed in the previous section. These programmes cover a wide range of range of specialisms including a Masters in Software Engineering. A common module entitled Research, Ethical, Professional and Legal Issues forms a key part of each of these programmes and it is within this module that we address issues relating to professionalism, ethics and codes of practice. Here, I intend only to consider the activities that we undertake in lecture and tutorial sessions that are relevant to ethics and professional practice. Tutorials, in the Sunderland context, are formal timetabled sessions with a tutor and a relatively small group of students that usually involves practically orientated or discursive work. Details of the overall module, its learning outcomes and its operation can be found in a paper that was presented at the 2004 ETHICOMP Conference (Thompson & Edwards 2004). Nevertheless it is worth noting that in a single year the module has been studied by up to 300 masters level students on-campus by

direct instruction and by an equal number of off-campus students via distance learning materials. Many of the on-campus programmes have a high intake of overseas students and we have found the approach to be very effective no matter what the ethnic mix. The major element of assessment is a critical review paper that addresses a particular ethical, professional, or legal issue and what we do in class helps provide a contextual understanding to support this.

Our approach makes use of the following:

- A brainstorming session to identify current ethical challenges.
- Consideration of a number of very short situational case studies.
- Consideration of international developments
- Consideration of the IFIP model as a framework for professionalism.
- Consideration of the Software Engineering Code of Ethics and Professional Practice (SECEPP)
- A major class role play exercise that makes use of the SECEPP and a fictitious case study - "The Case of the Killer Robot" (Epstein, 1997).

The above will be considered in turn in the following four sections. What we believe is important is student engagement and mechanisms that will encourage them to work together in teams rather than as individuals. We try to minimise the amount of face to face classroom teaching that involves simply information transfer. Our strategy is to use the lecture sessions to cover major concepts, outline new activities, and provide feedback on previous activity. The real work is undertaken in much smaller tutorial sessions via truly active learning.

THE SUNDERLAND APPROACH: PREPARATORY WORK

When addressing the concept of ethics we try and keep things as straightforward as possible. We start by pointing out that there are great debates by philosophers concerning ethics and morality but that we will simply consider ethics to be the moral principles held by an individual or a group. Thus, given a set of ethics, an individual can decide whether they believe certain behaviour to be right or wrong. We expand on this by considering ethics in academic research (which students can usually directly relate to) and the role of ethical committees to vet research activities. From then we go on to consider the ethical use of computer-based information systems especially with regard to the handling of personal information. Here we can use the lecturer's own experiences and even those of some of the students themselves.

Our first tutorial exercise is aimed at developing student engagement and collecting as wide a set of views as possible. We issue the students with Post-Its and then ask each student to write on a Post-It what they consider to be a major ethical challenge in computing. The submissions are posted on the classroom wall and one or two students are charged with the task of organising the submissions into groupings. We get the students to view and consider what has been submitted, and we then follow this with a classroom discussion in which we attempt to expand on the issues raised.

Our next classroom exercise involves consideration of a set of mini-scenarios that were detailed in a paper "Can a Software Engineer Afford to be Ethical" (Langford, 1996). These cover elements of individual behaviour, "public" behaviour, company behaviour, and effects of acting unethically at work with regard to short term consequences, image, and the law. We issue the students with copies of the paper several days before the class, tell them to read it fully and consider whether or not the examples are still relevant today (the

paper being over 10 years old). The students have by then been organised into groups and they are told to discuss their individual findings with the other members of the group and come to a consensus opinion on each scenario prior to the class meeting. In the class itself we will get each group to present their findings on one particular scenario – each presentation is then followed by a class discussion. An alternative approach (if verbal student presentations present too much of a challenge) is, at the start of the session, to issue each group with one or two sheets of poster-sized paper and get the group to write up their findings on one particular scenario. These are then posted on the classroom wall, the students view them and then we debate each one. Once started, students will usually debate issues for a reasonable time – getting them to debate is usually not a challenge, although getting groups or individuals to do presentations often is! Hence the use of posters.

THE SUNDERLAND APPROACH: ADDRESSING DEVELOPMENTS AND A FRAMEWORK FOR PROFESSIONALISM

Our next step is to provide a wider contextual view for the role of ethics in computing and the developments there have been towards creating a professional discipline. As our exemplar we concentrate on the efforts that there have been with regard to Software Engineering. We cover both the developments in the USA during the 1990s and what IFIP was undertaking at the same time.

Developments in Professionalism

We often use the USA developments as an example of the problems and "politics" that can occur over a number of years:

- The creation in 1993 of the ACM and IEEE-CS Joint Steering Committee for "The Establishment of Software Engineering as a Profession" and the creation of task forces to address: Body of Knowledge and Recommended Practices, Ethics and Professional Practices, and Education. (ACM & IEEE-CS, 1999a).
- The 1998 further formal co-operation with the creation of Software Engineering Co-ordinating Committee (SWECC) (ACM & IEEE-CS, 1999b)
- The publication in 1999 of the Software Engineering Code of Ethics and Professional Practice (SECEPP, 1999).
- A revision of The Texas Engineering Practice Act that came into operation on January 1st 1999 (Texas Board of Professional Engineers, 1999) and which allowed the recognition of Software Engineering as a distinct engineering discipline and hence the licensing of such engineers.
- The withdrawal of the ACM from SWECC over the issue of licensing (ACM, 2000).
- The eventual publication in 2004 of " Guide to the Software Engineering Body of Knowledge" (SWEBOK) (Bourque & Dupuis, 2004) under the auspices of the IEEE Computer Society alone.
- The 2004 publication of the curriculum document "Software Engineering 2004, Curriculum Guidelines for Undergraduate Degree Programs in Software Engineering" (IEEE-CS & ACM, 2004) under the auspices of both organisations.
- The IEEE Computer Society's own effort to offer Certified Software Development Professional (CSPD) designation (Engel, 2006). This involves passing an examination that in turn is related to the SWEBOK.

This somewhat erratic progress can be used to develop classroom discussions and examine the motivators behind what has happened.

We also make clear that there are different models for regulating professional practices either by licensing or certification where:

- Licensing – is a mandatory process administered by a government authority
- Certification – is a voluntary process administered by the profession itself.

Again these can lead to discussions on the pros and cons of each model.

The IFIP Professional Standards Framework

We use the development of the IFIP Professional Standards framework (Mitchell, Juliff, & Turner, 1998) as an example of international cooperation and we highlight how, with regard to Software Engineering, the efforts by the ACM and IEEE-CS together or alone are populating the IFIP framework that consists of:

- Ethics of professional practice,
- Established body of knowledge,
- Education and training,
- Professional experience,
- Best practice and proven methodologies, and
- Maintenance of competence.

For example, both the SWEBOK and the Body of Knowledge defined within the Software Engineering 2004 curriculum document support the second element of the IFIP framework.

We also emphasise, as detailed in the IFIP Professional Standards document, the claimed benefits for internationally recognised standards (Mitchell, Juliff, & Turner, 1998):

- The public is assured that safety or economically critical work is performed by competent individuals regardless of where in the world those persons gained their qualifications and experience.

- A client is assured that a person who meets such international standards is competent to carry out tasks in documented specific areas regardless of where the work is done or the output of the work is used (subject to recognition of issues of culture and locale).
- Professionals are assured that their qualifications, if recognised in one country, will be accepted in other countries without re-examination (except possibly for being up-to-date).

Again, claims such as these can be used to spark classroom discussion. However, the group exercise that we normally set the students after introducing the framework is for each student group to be given a copy of the IFIP Professional Standards document, and then for each of the groups to select one or more professional occupations outside computing (medics, lawyers or whatever). They then have to see how well the framework fits the professions they have chosen. Results are reported via posters at the next tutorial and discussions are held on the findings. The professions that the students select are usually quite wide ranging and their investigations can produce surprising results – according to one particular set of students it is the profession of International Football (Soccer) Referees who best fit the framework!

THE SUNDERLAND APPROACH: CODES OF PRACTICE AND ROLE PLAY

The first element within the IFIP framework is the Ethics of Professional Practice. We spend some time considering this and the fact that a professional discipline, as well as being supported by a clearly defined body of knowledge and curricula

for appropriate academic programmes, needs also to have formally defined ethical policies and professional practices. We also highlight the fact that as stated in the IFIP document for ethical codes to be effective they must be compatible with the culture of the society in which the practitioner normally works.

In addition to considering the Software Engineering Code of Ethics and Professional Practice (SECEPP, 1999) we also look at codes that have been produced to meet the specific needs of individual organisations for example:

- The ACM's Code of Ethics and Professional Conduct (ACM, 1997) and
- The British Computer Society's Code of Conduct & Code of Good Practice (BCS, ud)

However, it is the Software Engineering Code of Ethics and Professional Practice that receives the greatest attention because of its international nature, its form (short and full) and the particular ordering of its principles as referred to earlier. We also support the sentiments expressed in the preamble to the full version of the code that:

"Because of their roles in developing software systems, software engineers have significant opportunities to do good or cause harm, to enable others to do good or cause harm, or to influence others to do good or cause harm. To ensure, as much as possible, that their efforts will be used for good, software engineers must commit themselves to making software engineering a beneficial and respected profession"

But to be realistic, simply looking at codes or comparing one code with another is not the most exciting activity on the planet! Also, it must be recognised that such activities are more likely to turn students away from considering professional issues rather than arousing their interest.

Our solution has been to facilitate consideration of a code of ethics by use of a case study coupled with role-play. The latter becomes a highlight in our tutorial activities and has been found to be an excellent mechanism for encouraging the students to work together. The case study we use is the fictitious "The Case of the Killer Robot" (Epstein, 1997). This is a purposefully exaggerated study and in the full form it is rather long. However, we make use of an abridged version that is freely available on the web for student use. The core of this case study consists of seven newspaper articles, one journal article and one magazine interview. It is centred on the situation where a robot operator at Cybernetics, Inc., is killed by an assembly line robot produced by another company Silicon Techtronics. The case is first made that the cause of the accident was poor quality software produced by a programmer at Silicon Technologies. However, as the case study progresses it becomes more obvious that there are many other people who could be held fully or partly responsible and that numerous ethical issues are involved.

We divide the students into teams and each team is allocated a selected character from the case study. One half of the team must produce the case for their character being responsible for (or contributing to) the death of the robot operator and the other half of the team must produce the opposing view. The team also has to show how the action of the character was in contravention of the principles detailed in the Software Engineering Code of Ethics and Professional Practice. Students are each given a copy of the abridged case study, and the Code of Ethics and Professional Practice. The teams then have a week to prepare, with their team members, for the Killer Robot Trial/Investigation.

THE SUNDERLAND APPROACH: THE KILLER TRAIL / INVESTIGATION

We normally divide the students into five teams and allocate to each team one of the main characters from the case study. The particular characters and their roles which we have decided to concentrate on are (Epstein, 1997):

- Randy Samuels, a programmer. He wrote the program code that caused the Robbie CX30 robot to oscillate wildly, killing its operator, Bart Matthews.
- Sam Reynolds, the CX30 Project Manager. He had a background in data processing but was put in charge of the Robbie project. Reynolds was committed to the waterfall model of development.
- Michael Waterson, the President and CEO of Silicon Techtronics. He placed Sam Reynolds in charge of Robbie CX30 project as a cost-saving measure.
- Cindy Yardley, a Silicon Techtronics employee and software tester. She admitted to faking software tests in order to save the jobs of her co-workers.
- Bart Matthews, a robot operator. The malfunctioning Robbie robot struck him dead.

These characters give us a good coverage of people at different levels within the case study from top management to the worker who is killed. As stated above, in the week before the trial/investigation half the members of each team must prepare the case for their character being held responsible (the prosecution case) and other members of the team member must prepare the opposing view (the case for the defence). In each case they should make reference as to how the character's actions have aligned or not aligned with the code of ethics.

For the actual Killer Robot Trail/Investigation the process that we adopt is to consider each character in a predetermined order. Members from the relevant team must present the case for their character being held responsible (the prosecution case) and then other team members must present the opposing view (the case for the defence). After each presentation there is a short time for questions from the remaining members of the class. Finally, once both presentations regarding the character have been completed, the relative level of blame or no blame associated with the character is voted on, by the reminder of the class, depending on the strength of the arguments. When voting, the voters are told that they must just consider the presentations concerning the characters in question and forget any views concerning their own case study character.

The blame/no blame voting is on a scale of +5 to –5 where +5 represents total blame (the character is the "Devil Incarnate") to –5 the character is blameless (totally pure). The scores are recorded by a member of staff using a blank version of the form shown in Appendix 3. Once all the characters have been considered, an average level of blame can be computed for each character by summing the products of the number of votes with level of blame value and then dividing this sum by the number of voters. An example set of values is also given in the Appendix.

Students really do get involved in this exercise. They usually need a little prompting from the members of staff to get the arguments going but once started it is often very difficult to stop them and at times one feels that opposing teams could almost come to blows. Of course, it always helps if there are one or two students who have previously been involved in amateur dramatics or like to watch courtroom dramas! "Reality" in some instances has been helped by having a female member of staff play the part of Bart Matthews' widow (Roberta) who sits at the back of the class weeping gently and calling out "Bart, Bart, why did you have to die".

The enthusiasm for the exercise has been demonstrated by the ways in which the students prepare their "prosecutions" and "defence" cases. They often augment the supplied material with additional information that they have generated themselves. An example of such is shown in Appendix 4 which is part of the case for the defence for Bart Matthews produced by a group of students following an MSc programme entitled "Electronic Commerce Applications". This clearly shows a really significant level of commitment to the exercise, which it must be noted is not part of the formal assessment for the module. It is there just for fun (and some learning as well).

THE SUNDERLAND APPROACH: REFLECTIONS

The module has run for many years at Sunderland and has undergone formal quality checks each year. The inputs to these have been student feedback, feedback from the staff involved in the teaching and the support work, comments from External Examiners, comments from visiting academics who have observed particular parts of the module, and student results. The main challenges that the members of staff supporting the module face is ensuring that the students do enter into the spirit of our approach and do engage in discussions. In the early years of running the module we relied to a great extent on student presentations to report group findings. However, we found that it was nearly always the same students who were prepared to present. Also, students whose first language was not English were clearly hesitant to take a leading role. With a move to using posters to communicate the groups' findings these problems have been greatly reduced. Once the main points have been posted up it is much easier to get the majority of the students to express their views, especially if the members of staff take the role of very proactive facilitators.

The Killer Robot exercise has proved to be a success on almost every occasion we have run it - sometimes much to the surprise of the staff themselves. Even in cases where almost all the students have been from overseas countries we have found that they are willing to enter fully into the spirit of things. In fact some of the most animated interactions have occurred in such situations. However, again much depends on the staff motivating the students, encouraging diverse views, and keeping the trial progressing as an enjoyable and fun activity. The only start-up problem we encounter time and time again, when the case study is issued, is getting the students to understand that their group is NOT playing the allocated character they are playing the members of the prosecution and defence teams for that character.

Obviously what can be achieved in the way of student interaction depends to a great extent on classroom situations. The arrangement at Sunderland is that all the students from different programmes undertaking one particular iteration of the module have lectures together. Since this can total well over one hundred students, any extended discussions can be somewhat limited within those sessions. Hence the interactive work must be mainly within the supporting tutorial sessions where there is typically one member of staff to 16/20 students. In many cases, due to rooming constraints, tutorial groups are doubled up with two members of staff and 35 to 40 students. However, we have found that this is a situation that can actually help discussions and interactions – the two members of staff can "play-off" against each other and this can encourage the students to become more involved. In situations where the total class size is much smaller a more interactive approach can be taken where the formal lecture sessions and the tutorials can blur together. We always try and adjust our approach so that it fits best with the total class size and the resources available (rooms and support staff).

Wherever possible the tutorial sessions are for the students for one particular programme. This means that the discussions and considerations can be directed to address the particular challenges that exist within the relevant sphere of application. In such situations we can collect data from the Killer Robot Trial/Investigation that reflect the views of students on particular programs. Table 1 shows the data collected from one such set of trials. The figures reflect the levels of blame voted by students from six different MSc programmes. These figures can then be used to initiate further discussions especially since they show clear differences in the views of students from different

Table 1. Results from a set of Killer Robot Trials/Investigations that took place during the 2003/2004 academic year

Character	Average Blame (negative values represent no blame scores)					
	ITM	SE	ECA	EC	CBIS	HIM
Randy Samuels	3.0	2.3	2.3	2.1	2.3	1.9
Sam Reynolds	1.6	1.6	3.4	2.5	2.1	2.4
Michael Waterson	2.7	3.6	1.7	3.7	3.7	2.8
Cindy Yardley	2.7	3.4	2.1	2.3	1.9	1.4
Bart Matthews	0.3	1.7	1.2	0.1	-0.9	-2.0

programmes (a pattern that has been replicated on almost every occasion the exercise has been run).

Scoring from 5 representing absolute blame to -5 no blame whatsoever.

The MSc programmes involved were: Information Technology Management (ITM), Software Engineering (SE), Electronic Commerce Applications (ECA), Electronic Commerce (EC), Computer Based Information Systems (CBIS), Health Information Management (HIM).

CONCLUSION, THE PRESENT, THE FUTURE, AND OUTSTANDING CHALLENGES

Experiences at Sunderland over a number of years have shown that our approach has generated an enthusiasm in many of the students, has encouraged them to consider wider issues, and become really involved in the activities undertaken. Certainly the staff believe that the objectives that were listed at the start of this chapter are being met. Also, the use of a proven framework for professionalism as produced by IFIP means that we have a mechanism for addressing developments in the field, see where they fit in the overall picture, and help students to identify outstanding challenges. As the Software Engineering profession matures, many more elements of the framework (for example aspects relating to best practices and continuous development) will become populated giving the staff and students further areas to explore and discuss.

Professional and international bodies have continued to address the challenge of the computing discipline's perceived immaturity. In the last five years there have been a number of particular efforts to address professionalism in the computing field. These have either addressed the needs of a particular set of practitioners (for example, the certification of Software Development Professionals (Engel, 2006), internation-

alisation issues (IFIP OECD WITSA, 2002), or particular national needs (for example to provide indemnity insurance for professionals (Avram, 2006)). Of particular note is an ambitious three-year managed programme entitled "Professionalism in IT" (BCS, 2006) that the British Computer Society (BCS) embarked on in 2005. This has as its overall objective "… increasing professionalism, to improve the ability of business and other organisations to exploit the potential of information technology effectively and consistently" (Hughes, 2006). Indications of the programmes worth are that it has led to a formal alliance between professional bodies, a major government agency, and industry-led bodies within the UK and interest in it has been expressed from Canada, Australia, and South Africa. Developments such as this will continue and there is a clear trend that professionalism is taking on a greater international dimension. However, this also means that there needs to be clear Frameworks of Understanding that will help comprehension of the particular situation in each country (Thompson, 2007).

Despite all the above, many academic challenges remain with regard to addressing ethics and professionalism. A survey undertaken in 2003, which was aimed at Software Engineering educators, indicated that in many institutions the teaching of ethics in the curriculum was largely ignored (Towell & Thompson, 2004). The situation may have improved by now – but by how much? It is often very difficult indeed to get those members of staff who are teaching technical subjects to recognise the importance of topics like ethics and professionalism. One often feels that if it were not for the demands of accrediting bodies, these subjects would be totally ignored. This is a situation that must surely change.

That there is an essential and continuing need to properly address ethical and professional issues both at undergraduate and postgraduate levels is clear from the reports that address the needs of industry. For example, the 2004 report "The Challenges of Complex IT Projects" highlighted at the head of its Executive Summary: "The levels of professionalism observed in software engineering are generally lower than those in other branches of engineering, although there are exceptions" (Royal Academy of Engineering, 2004). Thus there is much for the academics still to do.

Similarly the workshop on Teaching Ethics in Software Engineering Programmes, held during the 2004 Conference on Software Engineering and Training identified numerous academic challenges (FASE, 2004). I believe that those which deserve the greatest priority are:

- Ethics teaching must be directed at the needs of the students and be relevant to their discipline (a general ethics course given by staff who do not have a computing background is unlikely to be of use).
- All the staff teaching within a Software Engineering programme must themselves be capable of taking on the teaching of ethical and professional issues (and ideally should be members of a relevant professional body).
- Teaching must be sensitive to the "values" of different ethnic groups. This is especially important where programmes recruit students from overseas.
- Whether the subject should pervade the curriculum or be addressed in very specific modules? Does the need to convince an accrediting body that the subject is being explicitly addressed act against its spread across the curriculum?
- Ensuring that the relevant professional body and its code of conduct receive the same exposure as they would on a traditional engineering programme. In that way ethical values should pervade the curricula.

It will be interesting to see how these and other issues are addressed in the future and whether people-orientated aspects will become just as important in academic programmes as the technically orientated aspects.

ACKNOWLEDGMENT

Parts of this paper are developed from 2004 and 2007 ETHICOMP papers that addressed our Teaching at Sunderland, and Globalisation and the IT Professional (Thompson & Edwards, 2004) and (Thompson, 2007) respectively.

Also thanks to Nicola Upton (Electronic Commerce Applications student in 2003) for allowing the use of the material reproduced in Appendix 4.

REFERENCES

ACM (1997). *ACM Code of Ethics and Professional Conduct*. Retrieved November 19, 2003, from http://www.computer.org

ACM (2000). *A Summary of the ACM Position on Software Engineering as a Licensed Engineering Profession*. Report retrieved April 1, 2006, from http://www.acm.org/serving/se_policy/selep_main.html

ACM & IEEE-CS (1999a). *History of Joint IEEE Computer Society and ACM Steering Committee for the Establishment of Software Engineering as a Profession*. Retrieved September 1, 1999, from http://www.acm.org/serving/se/History.htm

ACM & IEEE-CS (1999b). *Software Engineering Co-ordinating Committee (SWECC)*. Information retrieved September 1, 1999, from http://www.acm.org/serving/se/

Avram, C. (2006). *The Australian Perspective*. Presentation at IFIP Workshop on Improving IT Practitioner Skills, August 25, 2006, (A part of the 19th IFIP World Computer Congress, August 20-25, 2006, Santiago, Chile,), Abstract and presentation retrieved October 3, 2006, from http://www. ifip.org/projects/IT-Pract-main.htm

BCS (ud). *Code of Conduct & Code of Good Practice.* Both retrieved November 19, 2003, from http://www.bcs.org.uk

BCS (2006). Professionalism in IT Programme, covered in a series of articles in the May 2006 issue of *IT NOW*, Swindon, UK: British Computer Society.

Bekir, N., Cable, V., Hashimoto, I., & Katz, S. (2001). *Teaching Engineering Ethics: A New Approach.* Proceedings of the 31st ASEE/IEEE Frontiers in Education Conference, October 10-13, 2001, Reno, NV, USA, Session T2G. Piscataway, NJ: IEEE.

Bott, F. (2005). *Professional Issues in Information Technology.* Swindon, UK: British Computer Society.

Bourque, P., & Dupuis, R. (Eds.). (2004). *Guide to the Software Engineering Body of Knowledge (SWEBOK).* Published by IEEE Computer Society. The guide itself along with details of its development and further information on the SWEBOK project can be retrieved from: http://www.swebok.org

DMU (2007). De Monfort University, Centre for Computing and Social Responsibility. Provides details of the proceedings of the Ethicomp Series of Conferences, The Ethicomp Journal, and the Journal of Information Communication and Ethics in Society, home page: http://www.ccsr.cse.dmu.ac.uk/

Engel, G. (2006). *IT Opportunities from the IEEE Computer Society.* Presentation at IFIP Workshop on Improving IT Practitioner Skills, August 25, 2006 (A part of the 19th IFIP World Computer Congress, Santiago, Chile, August 20-25, 2006), Abstract and presentation retrieved October 3, 2006, from: http://www.ifip.org/projects/IT-Pract-main.htm

Epstein R.A.G. (1997). *The Case of the Killer Robot,* New York: John Wiley and Sons. There are also freely available abridged web versions e.g. from the Online Ethics Center at Case Western Reserve University: http://onlineethics.org/cases/robot/robot.html

ETHICOMP (2004). *Introduction ETHICOMP 2004.* In proceedings of Seventh International ETHICOMP Conference (ETHICOMP 2004), April 14-16 2004, Syros, Greece, (pp. 3-4). Syros: University of the Aegean.

FASE (2004). Report on the CSEE&T 2004 Workshop: Teaching Ethics in Software Engineering Programs. *Forum for Advancing Software engineering Education (FASE), 14*(4), (Issue 160), April 2004.

Gotterbarn, D. (2001). Views expressed during tutorial: Software Engineering Ethics Training in Industry and Academe: Professionalism and the Software Engineering Code of Ethics, organised by Gotterbarn, D. and Miller, K. at Fourteenth Conference on Software Engineering Education & Training, February 19-21, 2001, Charlotte, North Carolina. See Gotterbarn and Miller (2001) for details of tutorial.

Gotterbarn, D., & Miller, K. (2001). Tutorial: *Software Engineering Ethics Training in Industry and Academe: Professionalism and the Software Engineering Code of Ethics.* In proceedings of Fourteenth Conference on Software Engineering Education & Training, February 19-21, 2001, Charlotte, North Carolina, (pp. 24). Los Alamitos, CA, IEEE-Computer Society.

Gotterbarn, D., Miller, K., & Rogerson, S. (1999). Computer Society and ACM Approve Software Engineering Code of Ethics, *Computer,* October, (pp. 84-88).

Granger, M. J., Currie Little, J., Adams, E. S., Björkman, C., Gotterbarn, D., Juettner, D.D., et al, (1997). *Using information technology to integrate social and ethical issues into the computer science and information systems curriculum.* Report of the Iticse '97 Working Group on Social and Ethical Issue in Computing Curricula, in supplemental proceedings SIGSE/SIGCUE ITiCSE'97, (pp. 38 – 50). New York: ACM Press,

Hughes, C. (2006). IT comes of age – professionalism in the industry. *The British Computer Society Annual Review 2006,* (pp.12-13), Swindon: British Computer Society.

IEEE-CS & ACM (2004). *Software Engineering 2004, Curriculum Guidelines for Undergraduate degree Programs in Software Engineering.* Published by IEEE-CS, and accessible from the education web-site for the ACM: http://www.acm. org/education/

Development of the volume is documented at the SE2004 site: http://sites.computer.org/ccse/

IFIP OECD WITSA (2002). Joint Working Conference "Meeting Global IT Skills Needs – The Role of Professionalism", October, 25-27, 2002, Woking, UK, retrieved February 1, 2005, from http://www.globalitskills.org/

Langford, D. (1996). *Can A Software Engineer Afford to be Ethical?,* Proceedings of the conference: Professional Awareness in Software Engineering (PASE'96), February 1-2, 1996, London. The conference papers were later published as edited chapters in the text: Myers C., Hall T. and Pitt D, (Eds.), (1997), *The Responsible Software Engineer,* London, Springer-Verlag.

Maner, W. (ud). *Interactive Computer Ethics Explorer (ICEE).* Web application retrieved February 1, 2004, from http://www.cs.bgsu.edu/maner/xx-icee/html/welcome.htm

Mitchell, I,. Juliff, P., & Turner, J. (1998). *Harmonization of Professional Standards.* International Federation of Information Processing, 1998, retrieved February 13, 2001, from

http://www.cet.sunderland.ac.uk/seis/icse-2001workshop/IFIPharmonisationDraft1998.

html Also available as an appendix to the paper *Evaluations of IFIP's Proposed Standards for Professionals* (Thompson, 2005), and from

http://www.ifip.or.at/minutes/C99/C99_harmonization.htm

Myers, C., Hal,l T., & Pitt, D. (1997). *The Responsible Software Engineer : Selected readings in IT Professionalism.* London, Springer-Verlag.

Royal Academy of Engineering (2004). *The Challenges of Complex IT Projects.* Report of a working group from The Royal Academy of Engineering and The British Computer Society, 2004, retrieved October 12, 2006, from http://www.bcs. org/upload/pdf/complexity.pdf

SECEPP (ud). Adopting the Software Engineering Code of Ethics and Professional Practice, details retrieved April 1, 2006, from http://csciwww.etsu. edu/gotterbarn/secepp/

SECEPP (1999). *Software Engineering Code of Ethics and Professional Practice.* Retrieved April 1, 2006 from http://www.acm.org/serving/se/code. htm Details of the code and its development can also be retrieved from http://csciwww.etsu.edu/ gotterbarn/secepp/page.asp?Name=Code

Texas Board of Professional Engineers (1999). Texas Engineering Practice Act, Revised 1st January 1999, Austin. Texas, 1999. Retrieved July 11, 2000, from http://www.main.org/peboard/law. pdf

Thompson, J. B. (2005, July). *Evaluations of IFIP's Proposed Standards for Professionals.* Paper presented at the 8th IFIP World Conference on Computers in Education, (WCCE 2005), July 4-7, 2005, University of Stellenbosch, Cape Town, South Africa, Session P10.3.

Thompson, J.B. (2007). *Globalisation and the IT Professional.* In proceedings of 9th International ETHICOMP Conference, March 27-29, 2007, Meiji University, Tokyo, (pp. 564-575). Tokyo: Global e-SCM Research Centre, Meiji University.

Thompson, J. B., & Edwards H. M. (2004). *Providing Graduate Computing Students with an Appreciation of Appropriate Ethical, Professional and Legal Issues*, In proceedings of Seventh International ETHICOMP Conference (ETHICOMP 2004), April 14-16, 2004, Syros, Greece, (pp. 839-853). Syros: University of the Aegean.

Thompson, J. B., & Towell, E. (2004). Workshop: *Teaching Ethics in Software Engineering Programmes*. In proceedings of 17th Conference on Software Engineering Education & Training (CSEE&T2004), March 1-3, Norfolk. USA, (pp. 162-164). Los Alamitos, CA: IEEE-Computer Society.

Towell, E. (2003). *Teaching Ethics in the Software Engineering Curriculum.* In proceedings of the Sixteenth Conference on Software Engineering Education & Training, March 20-22, Madrid, Spain, (pp. 150-157). Los Alamitos, CA: IEEE-Computer Society Press.

Towell, E., & Thompson, J. B. (2004). *A Further Exploration of Teaching Ethics in the Software Engineering Curriculum.* In proceedings of the Seventeenth Conference on Software Engineering Education & Training, March 1-3, Norfolk, USA, (pp. 39-49). Los Alamitos, CA: IEEE-Computer Society.

Towell, E. Thompson J. B. and McFadden K.L. (2004). Introducing and Developing Professional Standards in the Information Systems Curriculum. *Ethics and Information Technology*, (2004) 6, 291-299.

APPENDIX A

EXTRACTS FROM IFIP DOCUMENT: HARMONIZATION OF PROFESSIONAL STANDARDS

Drafted by Ian Mitchell, FNZCS, Peter Juliff, FACS and Joe Turner, FACM.

The Standard for Professional Practice in Information Technology

Ethics of Professional Practice

A code of ethics acknowledges the professional responsibilities of practitioners to society at large, members of the public, employers, contracting parties and fellow practitioners.

Codes of ethics have been published by many member societies and IFIP itself.

Every implementation of the standard must include a code of ethics.

Such a Code of Ethics must be compatible with the culture of the society in which the practitioner normally works.

Practitioners must operate in a manner compatible with the culture of the locale in which they are currently working and in which the product may be used.

Practitioners must publicly ascribe to the code of ethics published within the standard.

Established Body of Knowledge

Several IFIP member societies have published bodies of knowledge, some of which have gained wide acceptance. Such recognised bodies of knowledge are divided into many domains determined by the various services carried out by practitioners. The body of knowledge on which any implementation is based should include at least the common components of these but also ensure that each domain is complete in itself for the domains adopted locally.

Mastery of such a body of knowledge forms the basis of preparation for practice. A practitioner must demonstrate mastery of at least one such domain as well as all core components identified in the body of knowledge.

Practitioners must be aware of and have access to a well-documented current body of knowledge relevant to the domain of practice.

Education and Training

Most practitioners will enter the workforce with prior education and training which will commonly be a baccalaureate degree assessing the mastery of the body of knowledge.

Institutions offering such education and training should be prepared to openly compare themselves to internationally well-known and recognised peer institutions offering similar programmes.

It is recognised that this level of mastery may be achieved by various combinations of education and experience. Nevertheless a practitioner must be able to provide evidence of such mastery to practitioners who have met this standard.

The minimum level of mastery of the body of knowledge must be at the baccalaureate level.

Professional Experience

Experience builds on knowledge in many essential ways. Such as:

- It develops and improves practical skills and competencies.
- It provides understanding of task definition in the users' terms.
- It helps develop interpersonal skills that facilitate the communication and human interaction between all participants.
- As many approaches to problem solution are not readily scaleable experience over a wide variety of problem types and sizes is desirable before working in an unsupervised environment. Experience is generally required in assessing task complexity.
- Task management, overall project management and quality management generally require experience.

Other professions have clear requirements for experience before allowing their members to practice without supervision.

In addition to a demonstrated mastery of the body of knowledge a minimum of the equivalent of two years supervised experience is recommended before the practitioner operates unsupervised.

Best Practice and Proven Methodologies

Experienced practitioners have identified and documented many practices and methodologies the use of which generally leads to successful project outcomes. Where such best practice and proven methodologies are available the practitioner should use them unless a particular task has exceptional attributes.

Member societies drawing on all available international sources should encourage the documentation and promulgation of best practice and proven methodologies.

Practitioners should be familiar with current best practice and relevant proven methodologies.

Maintenance of Competence

To maintain demonstrated competence practitioners must be familiar with new developments in their domains of practice.

Such developments may be reflected in the body of knowledge, best practice and proven methodologies as well as in specific skills.

Familiarity with new developments may be obtained through formal education or peer interaction.

There may be assessment of current competence by formal examination, peer assessment or employer or client acknowledgement of successful work.

A practitioner should participate for at least the equivalent of 10 days per year in activities that contribute to maintaining competence. It is recognised that in different locations the opportunities for such ongoing development may vary.

The standard in each country or region must state how this requirement will be met and the role of the IFIP member society in monitoring this function.

Practitioners must be able to provide evidence of their maintenance of competence.

APPENDIX B

SOFTWARE ENGINEERING CODE OF ETHICS AND PROFESSIONAL PRACTICE

Produced by ACM/IEEE-CS Joint Task Force on Software Engineering Ethics and Professional Practices.

Copyright (c) 1999 by the Association for Computing Machinery, Inc. and the Institute for Electrical and Electronics Engineers, Inc.

Short Version

PREAMBLE

The short version of the code summarizes aspirations at a high level of the abstraction; the clauses that are included in the full version give examples and details of how these aspirations change the way we act as software engineering professionals. Without the aspirations, the details can become legalistic and tedious; without the details, the aspirations can become high sounding but empty; together, the aspirations and the details form a cohesive code.

Software engineers shall commit themselves to making the analysis, specification, design, development, testing and maintenance of software a beneficial and respected profession. In accordance with their commitment to the health, safety and welfare of the public, software engineers shall adhere to the following Eight Principles:

1. PUBLIC - Software engineers shall act consistently with the public interest.
2. CLIENT AND EMPLOYER - Software engineers shall act in a manner that is in the best interests of their client and employer consistent with the public interest.
3. PRODUCT - Software engineers shall ensure that their products and related modifications meet the highest professional standards possible.
4. JUDGMENT - Software engineers shall maintain integrity and independence in their professional judgment.
5. MANAGEMENT - Software engineering managers and leaders shall subscribe to and promote an ethical approach to the management of software development and maintenance.
6. PROFESSION - Software engineers shall advance the integrity and reputation of the profession consistent with the public interest.
7. COLLEAGUES - Software engineers shall be fair to and supportive of their colleagues.
8. SELF - Software engineers shall participate in lifelong learning regarding the practice of their profession and shall promote an ethical approach to the practice of the profession.

APPENDIX C

EXAMPLE COMPLETED KILLER CHARACTERS VOTING FORM

Character	Blame						No Blame					Average Vote
	5	4	3	2	1	0	1	2	3	4	5	
Randy Samuels	2	2	21	1	1	1						3.0
Sam Reynolds	3	3	5	7	5	5	3	2				1.6
Michael Waterson	2	5	12	4	1	4						2.7
Cindy Yardley	6	11	4	1	2	3	1	0	1	1		2.7
Bart Matthews	9	0	0	0	2	11	1	2	0	0	6	0.3

APPENDIX D

DEFENCE FOR THE ACCUSED: MR. BARTHOLOMEW MATHEWS

Ladies and gentlemen of the jury.......let me take you back to a beautiful, sunny May morning, May the 17th 1992 to be precise. A Sunday, you may recall? (the date was actually a Sunday, I checked on the net!)

Mr. Mathews had kindly agreed to go to work for the morning (Cybernetics Inc in Silicon Heights), much to the dismay and disappointment of his wife (Roberta Mathews) and their children (the children's names have remained anonymous for their protection). Mrs. Mathews had planned to take the family out for the day to the coast to celebrate the successful heart transplant of their youngest child. (You may have seen the recent story in the local press! – DONOR FOUND AT LAST!)

However, Mr. Mathews being such a devotee to the company went in to work all the same........little did he know it would be the last day of his life.

Now, some simpletons may speculate that Mr. Mathew's death was caused by mere human error. I am here today to relay the REAL turn of events to this disastrous and harrowing death. Ladies and gentlemen, I would like you to forget the propaganda and hype that you have read in the press and listen and judge for yourself that Mr. Bartholomew Mathew's death was NO ACCIDENT!

Today I would like to highlight three main areas that will demonstrate that the deceased is innocent of the charge.

1. Mr. Mathews was well respected within his profession
2. Operational flaws
3. Cover up

1. Mr. Mathews was well respected within his profession.

Firstly I would like to draw your attention to **Exhibit A: 'The reconstruction of what is now being labelled as 'The Killer Robot tragedy'**. This document has been written by Dr. Horace Gritty from the Department of Computer Science and Related Concerns at Silicon Valley, USA.

Despite Mrs. Mathews plans, Mr. Mathews went into work on that Sunday morning. The reason being?

Cybernetics had recently purchased a new Robot (the CX30) for their assembly line plant. Matthew's and the company were very excited as the manufacture of the machine had been remarkably speedy..... and they were keen to see what it could do....the robot was revolutionary and represented a gigantic step forward in terms of sophistication. Mr. Mathews was quick to recognise this fact and proceeded with placing the manual right next to where he was working. **Exhibit A: 'The reconstruction of what is now being labelled as 'The Killer Robot tragedy'**. The Killer Robot Interface list of events: *"a reference manual was open and was laid flat in the workstation reading/writing area".*

Thus, reiterating that Mr. Mathews took his work very seriously and always maintained the utmost professionalism.

Exhibit B: Software Engineering Code of Ethics and Professional Practice. *3.07 "Strive to fully understand the specifications for software on which they work"* (in this instance the machine).

Secondly, I would like to remind you of the Silicon Techtronics Annual Report for Shareholders, published last March. Which has a picture of a smiling Bart Matthews on its glossy front cover (unfortunately we were unable to obtain a copy). The deceased is shown operating the very same CX30 which carried out the deadly deed some two months after the photograph was taken. This assures us once more that Mr. Matthews was well regarded within Cybernetics Inc. as he managed to hit the front page, not page 2 or 3 but the front page of the report that was given to all stakeholders (some of which would have known Mr. Mathews personally). Why, then would anyone suggest that Mr. Mathews could be responsible for his own death?

2. Operational flaws.

I would now like to refer back to **Exhibit A: 'The reconstruction of what is now being labelled as 'The Killer Robot tragedy'**. I would firstly like to read a few extracts from this article for your interest.

"The Robbie Cx30 robot violates nearly every rule of interface design"

"The Robbie Cx30 operator interface violated each and every one of Shneiderman's rules. Several of these violations were directly responsible for the accident which ended in the death of the robot operator."

"console had a keyboard, but no mouse."

"Reading/writing area was quite a distance from the computer screen....This placed much strain on the operator's back and also caused excessive eye strain."

"There were many violations of consistency in the Robbie CX30 user interface."

"System must have been quite a mental strain on the operator".

"most actions are irreversible when the system is in an exceptional state, and this helped lead to the killer robot tragedy".

There are many more quotations of a similar nature. I think it would be fair to conclude that Dr Gritty is of the opinion that the design of the interface had a lot to do with the cause of death.

Dr Gritty's deductions once more suggest that the deceased was innocent of negligence.

I would also like to refer to **Exhibit c: The Silicon Valley Sentinel-Observer's article title 'Quality of operator training questioned'.**

In it Ruth Witherspoon (spokesperson for the 'justice for Randy Samuels' committee) explained that *"Bart Mathews was killed when exceptional condition 5.2.4.26 arose. This involved an exceptionally violent and unpredictable robot arm motion. This condition required operator intervention, namely the entering of the command codes mentioned in the document.....the program correctly set off this exceptional condition and the robot operator received due warning that something was wrong"*

So why didn't Mathews enter the command code? Could it be that:

- The manual was too far a distance from the interface?
  (I refer back to exhibit A)
- The command code was too difficult to enter in such a short time?
  Again, in exhibit a Dr Gritty states "...He tries "emergency abort" submenu...This involves SIX separate menu choices."
- Mr. Mathews did not notice the error message because there was no audio affect to remind the user to look at the interface?
  In Exhibit A: Dr Gritty proposes *"at 10.22 am "ROBOT DYNAMICS INTERITY ERROR- 45 appears on the screen. Bart Mathews does not notice this because there is no beep or audio effect such as occurs with every other error situation".* (Also indicating an inconsistency in the design-to make the machine un-user friendly). This is also a violation of **Software Engineering Code of Ethics and Professional Practice; Exhibit B:**
  1.03 *"Approve software only if they have a well-founded belief that it is safe, meets specifications, passes appropriate tests, and does not diminish quality of life, diminish privacy or harm the environment"*
- Insufficient training was the cause of the tragedy?
  In **Exhibit c: The Silicon Valley Sentinel-Observer's article title 'Quality of operator training questioned'** a robot operator form Cybernetics Inc was quoted as saying:
  "Neither I nor Bart Mathew's was ever trained to handle this sort of exceptional condition. I doubt that the Bart Matthews was ever trained to handle this sort of exceptional condition. I doubt that Bart Mathew's had any idea what he was supposed to do when the computer screen started flashing the error message on the screen". As it states in the **software engineering code of ethics and professional practice (Exhibit B)**
  1.04 *"Disclose to appropriate persons or authorities any actual or potential danger to the user, the public, or the environment, that the public, or the environment, that they reasonable believe*

to be associated with software or related documents."

Silicon Techtronics claims to provide 40 hours of operator training however Witherspoon recalls that the robot operators were given only 8 hours.

3. Cover up.

Could it be, that laying the blame on the deceased (who conveniently cannot defend himself)? Is a conspiracy theory to deter the public from other goings on within Silicon Techtronics?

I am not here to accuse but to speculate.

I find it funny that the description of the death was pacified by the tabloids. Mr. Mathews was in fact decapitated and not crushed as was first printed.

I also find it odd that the 'exceptional circumstances' were never pointed out to the robot operators.

SUMMARY

- Mr. Mathews went into work on his day off despite personal circumstances
- The manual was found open at the scene of the crime
- Mr. Mathews was placed on the front cover of Silicon Techtronics report to stakeholders
- The design of the Robot was unsafe.
- The robot operators were not trained sufficiently and were not aware of any 'exceptional circumstances'.
- Propaganda
- Exceptional circumstances were never pointed out.

Chapter XVIII
An International Perspective on Professional Software Engineering Credentials

Stephen B. Seidman
University of Central Arkansas, USA

ABSTRACT

This chapter provides an international perspective on professional software engineering credentials. It distinguishes between professional licensing, certification, and other forms of credentials. It compares and contrasts several major approaches to professional credentials: broad-based certifications, national examinations, and job frameworks. Examples of credentials in each category are discussed in detail. The chapter also discusses efforts to develop international standards for these credentials. The chapter concludes with a brief description of the current landscape of professional software engineering credentials.

INTRODUCTION

Professional credentials can be classified into two broad categories. Credentials in the first category confer a governmentally sanctioned professional status that carries specific rights and privileges. For example, in the United States, a state awards licenses to individuals who wish to practice any of a wide variety of professions, including medi-cine, engineering, accounting, and architecture. Practice in these professions is limited to those holding appropriate licenses. Practicing a profession without a license is subject to legal penalties, including fines and imprisonment. In the United Kingdom and Australia, chartered status for engineers, architects, and accountants carries similar rights, privileges, and restrictions. The requirements and processes associated with attaining and maintaining licensed or chartered status are statutory. Enforcement of these requirements and processes is the responsibility of a government agency, which may possibly delegate this responsibility to a professional society.

Professional certifications constitute the second category of credentials. They are sought by practitioners who seek to demonstrate mastery of a particular body of knowledge. It is important to distinguish between broad-based certifications and product-specific certifications. Broad-based certifications are based on bodies of knowledge that cover an entire professional discipline or a subspecialty within such a discipline. These certifications are generally awarded by professional societies. Examples of broad-based certifications include specialty certifications in medicine or law and financial certifications. In the computing domain, broad-based certifications are available for software engineers and security experts. By contrast, product-specific certifications are based on a specific product or product line, such as a medical device or an operating system. The manufacturers of the products or product lines usually award certifications tied to their products.

In general, candidates applying for a broad-based certification must meet specific education and experience requirements. A candidate's familiarity with a body of knowledge is generally assessed by examination, although some certification programs use peer review to assess knowledge and/or professional experience. Most certification programs require that a certificate holder demonstrate professional activity and continuing education in order to maintain certification. Broad-based certification programs are governed by national and international standards. Product-specific certifications generally use examinations to assess candidates' familiarity with the product and its use, and maintenance requirements are less commonly found.

Another approach to professional credentials is based on job frameworks, which organize the tasks performed by professionals in a domain into a multidimensional structure. The dimensions represent the skills performed by professionals and the ways and levels at which those skills are utilized in a specific job category. Several job frameworks for the information and communication technology (ICT) domain have recently been developed in Europe.

This chapter will describe the spectrum of software engineering professional credentials. It will give an overview of the historical and international background of software engineering licensing and certification. It will summarize and place in context some current licensing and certification efforts that relate to software engineering professionals. Examples presented will include:

- The IEEE Computer Society's Certified Software Development Professional (CSDP) certification
- The Australian Computer Society's approach to granting chartered status to software engineers
- The approaches to software engineering licensure taken by Texas and some Canadian provinces
- The Japanese program of information technology professional examinations
- The iSQI approach to certifying software testing professionals
- The UK's SFIA job framework and its relationship to other European job frameworks

The chapter will also discuss the ongoing effort to develop an ISO/IEC standard for programs certifying software engineering professionals.

PROFESSIONALISM AND LICENSURE

Until the nineteenth century, professional status was limited to clergy, medical doctors, and lawyers. Professional organizations controlled status in the professions, sometimes enforced by links to government (e.g., the state-controlled Church of England) and to academia (e.g., medicine and Church of England clergy).

Technological advancements associated with the Industrial Revolution created a need for new professional roles. While engineering had a long military tradition, the increased need for civilian applications of engineering (hence "civil engineering") greatly expanded the number of engineers. During the course of the nineteenth century, engineering gradually moved from an apprenticeship model toward an academic model. In the US, the Morrill Act of 1862 supported the establishment of state-funded engineering colleges. However, state licensure of professional engineers in the US was not required until 1907. Wyoming was the first US state to require licensure, which was rapidly taken up by the other states. In the United States, each state has established its own regulations and requirements for engineering licensure, although the educational and experience requirements are similar. Candidates must pass two examinations common to all states: Fundamentals of Engineering (FE), and Principles and Practice (PE). The first examination covers knowledge common to the traditional engineering disciplines (e.g. statics, mechanics, thermodynamics), while the second examination deals with advanced material specific to a particular engineering discipline (e.g. civil engineering, electrical engineering)

Other countries link engineering licensure to the accreditation of university engineering programs. For example, as in the United States, the engineering profession in Canada is regulated locally (at the provincial level), but candidates with a degree from an accredited engineering program and with appropriate professional experience do not have to take an examination. In the United Kingdom, a national organization (Engineering Council UK) is responsible for engineering professional qualifications. Applicants for chartered status (equivalent to licensure) must submit dossiers that show that they have degrees from accredited

engineering programs and appropriate professional experience. Two professional engineers in the appropriate discipline review the dossier and interview the applicant. The situation in Australia is similar to that in the UK, except that regulation is once again at the local (state) level. In Germany, the academic title "Diplomingenieur", currently awarded to graduates of engineering programs, is also regulated at the state level. The German higher education system has multiple tiers, and graduates of lower-tier programs must use an appropriate modification of the title. The situation in Austria is similar, though the regulation is at the national level.

The Bologna accord (Fuller, Pears, Amillo, Avram, & Mannila, 2006) is having an impact on engineering education in the European Union. In particular, all universities will have to move toward a common degree structure: three years for a first-cycle degree, two years for a second-cycle degree, followed by doctoral education. This change doesn't alter the fact that the higher educational systems of most European countries are regulated at the national or state level.

The status of software engineering as an engineering discipline has received much attention (Shaw, 1990). In recent years, the increasingly critical role played by software in all aspects of life has raised the question of licensing software engineers, especially those working on systems that have critical health or safety implications. In the United States, Texas is so far the only state to license software engineers. Two problems with including software engineering in the US engineering licensure system are (1) there is currently no PE examination for software engineering, and (2) the FE examination covers material not generally included in software engineering curricula. Bagert (2004) gives the context and history of software engineering licensure in the United States.

Other countries have found it easier to include software engineers in engineering licensure systems. Since the Canadian system does not use licensure examinations, it has proved easier to incorporate software engineering into this system. It's important to note that since "engineer" and "engineering" are trademarks owned by Engineers Canada, accredited software engineering programs in Canada are offered in colleges of engineering. The provinces of Ontario, Alberta, and British Columbia are already licensing software engineers. This situation has led to a dispute between two professional societies: Engineers Canada (the business name of the Canadian Council of Professional Engineers) and the Canadian Information Processing Society (CIPS). The CIPS perspective on the Canadian situation is given in documents that can be found on the CIPS Website (Van Dalen, 2003; Canadian Information Processing Society, 2007). The Engineers Canada perspective can be found in a paper on its Website (Engineers Canada, 2001).

In the UK, the British Computer Society (BCS) is a licensed member of Engineering Council UK, and its members are therefore eligible to apply for Chartered Engineer status. This means that graduates of BCS-accredited programs with appropriate experience can apply for chartered engineer status. In Australia, the Australian Computer Society and Engineers Australia have developed a joint approach to chartering software engineers. This success of this approach also depends on tight control of program accreditation.

It is interesting to consider the emergence of software engineering in the context of the historical development of new professions. Adams (2004) discusses software engineering from this perspective, with particular reference to the US, UK, and Canada.

BROAD-BASED PROFESSIONAL CERTIFICATIONS

A broad-based professional certification scheme is intended to recognize an individual's professional competence in a body of knowledge recognized by a community of professionals. Examples of such schemes include the Project Management Professional (www.pmi.org), board certifications for medical specialties (www.ambs.org), the Certified Financial Planner (www.cfp.net), and for software engineers, the IEEE Computer Society's Certified Software Development Professional (CSDP; www.computer.org/certification).

The IEEE Computer Society's CSDP certification scheme is an example of a broad-based software engineering certification. The origin of this scheme can be traced back for almost a decade. In 1998, the IEEE Computer Society began to consider the feasibility of certifying software engineering professionals. The first step in a formal investigation of this possibility was to gather input from the professional community. In 1999, the Society conducted a study that included surveys and discussions with potential certificate holders and with industry representatives. The results of this study indicated a strong interest in certification. In the following two years, the Computer Society worked with a major test development consultant to prepare a certification examination. The process included preparing a listing of task and knowledge statements. The statements were then distributed for validation to a group of software engineers, whose comments were used to produce a final version of the statements. It's important to observe that the knowledge statements are regarded as primary, with task statements explicitly mapped to knowledge statements. Furthermore, an appropriate knowledge level is assigned to each knowledge statement, using a taxonomy first proposed by Bloom (1984). Test specifications were then developed from information derived from the job analysis. The specifications became the blueprint for defining the final content of the examination and determining the content weights Test questions (items) were then prepared and evaluated by an independent group of software engineers. The consultant ensured that the examination was psychometrically valid and culturally appropriate. The approved items were then assembled into two examination forms, each containing 180 questions, in accordance with the test specifications. The assembled forms were given a final review by a test developer and by a group of software engineers, who reviewed potential problem items and made substitutions were necessary. In 2001, the approved test forms when pilot-tested by a group of software engineers selected to match the targets for education and experience. After further analysis, cut scores were determined and accepted by the IEEE Computer Society Professional Practices Committee (PPC), acting as the CSDP oversight committee. The second form of the exam was then statistically equated to the first, after which the examination was officially ready for release.

The CSDP examination has been given since 2002. It consists of 180 questions, to be completed in 3.5 hours. The examination is offered at testing centers in many countries. There are currently more than 700 CSDP certificate holders. These individuals reside in many countries, in all parts of the world. The IEEE Computer Society's PPC is currently revising the examination to bring its body of knowledge into conformance with the revision of the SWEBOK body of knowledge (see www.swebok.org). At the same time, the PPC is developing a new examination targeting recent university graduates. This certification will be called the Certified Software Development Associate (CSDA).

Another example of a professional certification scheme addressed to software engineers is operated by the International Software Quality Institute (iSQI), an independent nonprofit organization in Germany (with support from German national and state governments) that provides comprehensive services in the field of software quality. iSQI's primary mission is to coordinate industry and professional efforts to develop and implement software quality standards. Certification of software engineering professionals is an important part of iSQI's activities. Certification is offered in three software engineering profes-

sional specialties: software architecture, project management, and software testing. Each iSQI examination is administered by an examination board.

All examinations are offered at foundation level. The testing examination is also offered at an advanced level, and an expert-level certification is under development. Advanced-level examinations are anticipated for the other specialties as well. The foundation-level examinations are 90-minute multiple-choice examinations. The advanced-level testing examination consists of three 90-minute multiple-choice parts (Test Manager, Functional Tester, Technical Tester). The examinations are offered frequently at two sites in Germany. Training courses for prospective examination takers are provided by a number of organizations. The appropriate examination boards accredit organizations that provide training courses. The underlying bodies of knowledge and examination specifications can be inferred from the training course outlines found on the iSQI Website (www.isqi.org).

In general, any approach to professional certification can be described using three relatively independent dimensions: (D1) a characterization of the professional role that is to be certified, (D2) a list of the abilities and skills needed by a professional in that role, and (D3) a description of the certification process and its organization, including development, management, and maintenance. National and international standards for certification schemes require a given scheme to describe how it is organized along these dimensions. In the United States, such a standard has been developed by the National Commission for Certifying Agencies (NCCA) (National Commission for Certifying Agencies, 2003). A similar international standard, ISO/IEC Standard 17024 (International Organization for Standardization, 2003), has recently been adopted as a standard by the European Community. This model makes it possible to compare and contrast different approaches to professional certification.

For example, the CSDP certification scheme's position on dimension D1 comes from the fact that the examination is intended for software engineering professionals with four years of experience. Specifically, applicants must have a baccalaureate degree and 9000 hours of professional experience in six of eleven specified knowledge areas. Its position on dimension D2 comes from the examination's list of knowledge areas and the corresponding task and knowledge statements. Its position on D3 has been described above.

NATIONAL EXAMINATIONS

The certification schemes described above are organized and operated by professional societies. These can be contrasted with national examination schemes operated by a government agency.

An example of a national examination scheme is the Japanese government's Information Technology Engineers Examination. In 1969, Japan's Ministry of Economy, Trade and Industry (then called the Ministry of International Trade and Industry) established the Information Technology Engineers Examination as a national examination. In 1984, the Japan Information Processing Development Corporation (JIPDEC) was designated as the official examination administrator by METI, and the Japan Information Technology Engineers Examination Center (JITEC) was established to carry out the details of the administration. JITEC has responsibility for all certification activities, from acceptance of applications to maintenance of certification. In 2004, examination administration was transferred to the Information-technology Promotion Agency, JAPAN (IPA). An overview of the Japanese examination program is given in (Information-Technology Promotion Agency, 2004).

The first examinations offered were Class I Information Technology Engineer and Class II Information Technology Engineer. During its 35 years of operation, the examination has under-

gone numerous changes and revisions. In 1994, a major revision introduced many new examination categories. The most recent revision was made in 2001, which resulted in the following examination categories: fundamental information technology engineer, systems auditor, systems administrator, senior systems administrator, information systems security administrator, systems analyst, project manager, applications systems engineer, and technical engineer (network systems, database systems, systems management, embedded systems). Some of the examination categories correspond to engineers who play primary roles in software development: system analyst, application systems engineer, software design and development engineer, and fundamental information technology engineer.

The scope and skill standards for the examination are based on the opinions of experts from industry and academia. These standards are continuously reviewed to keep them consistent with changes in the information technology and information industries. At the same time, the examination categories are reviewed for their relevance to current trends in information technology as well as for consistency with past examinations. The scope of an examination includes the test specification and an outline of the examination. The skill standard for an examination provides context. It describes the activities and tasks of engineers employed in the relevant examination category, as well as outlining the underlying knowledge needed in this category. The body of knowledge for each category includes material from software engineering, information systems, and computer science.

There are no specific eligibility criteria for the examinations. The duration of each examination is one day. A morning session uses multiple-choice questions to test a candidate's familiarity with the required knowledge. An afternoon session uses case studies and essay questions to test a candidate's ability to apply and practice the knowledge. The case study and essay questions also serve as a way of assessing a candidate's past experience. The examination questions are developed by an examination committee, which comprises about 400 experts from industry and academia. Subcommittees are charged with question development, checking, and selection. Each subcommittee has independent authority to construct appropriate questions. In general, new questions are produced for each examination, but some knowledge questions may be modified for reuse. After the examination, candidates can bring question papers home to use for self-study and further education. The correct answers for some questions are made available, and examinees can obtain their scores on the examination. Transparency of the examination is therefore ensured in several ways: scope of examination, production of examination questions, availability of examination scores and sample question answers.

The Ministry of Economy, Trade, and Industry issues certificates to successful examinees. The certificates show the date of certification, but currently have no expiration date. From 1969 through 2004, 12,404,713 candidates took the examinations; certificates were awarded to 1,324,869 successful candidates. During its 35 years of existence, the Information Technology Engineers Examination has been able to adapt to the rapidly changing information technology environment. Its adaptability to the demands of the times has been a major factor in its success. Furthermore, nine Asian countries (India, Singapore, Korea, China, Philippines, Thailand, Vietnam, Myanmar, Taiwan) have recently agreed to accept the Japanese examination as a professional credential.

JOB FRAMEWORKS

Another approach to certifying the expertise of software engineering professionals is to place the tasks carried out by these professionals in a broader model of information technology pro-

fessional positions. Such a model is called a *job framework*. The pioneering job framework effort in the information technology arena is the *Skills Framework for the Information Age* (SFIA, www. sfia.org.uk). The SFIA framework was developed in the UK and first launched in 2000; version 3 of the framework was released in 2005 (Skills Framework for the Information Age, 2005). SFIA is a two-dimensional model; the dimensions represent the *skills* used by information and communication technology (ICT) professionals and the *levels* at which these skills are needed for a particular job. The skills are placed along the first dimension of the model; they are grouped into six categories, such as development or service provision. The second dimension of the model consists of seven levels of responsibility and accountability exercised by ICT professionals. The two dimensions of the model give rise to a matrix showing the complete set of skills used by ICT professionals. Each skill and level in the matrix corresponds to a professional position. The model gives descriptors that provide examples of typical tasks performed by professionals in that position.

For example, the SFIA 3.0 skill category "development" contains the subcategory "systems development". The skills associated with this subcategory include "database design", "programming/software development", and "systems testing". Four of the seven levels are used: "assist", "apply", "enable", and "ensure/advise". The descriptors for the levels used in this subcategory are given below.

- (Assist) Designs, codes, tests, corrects and documents simple programs and assists in the implementation of software which forms part of a properly engineered information or communications system.
- (Apply) Designs, codes, tests, corrects and documents moderately complex programs and program modifications from supplied specifications, using agreed standards and tools. Conducts reviews of supplied specifications, with others as appropriate.

- (Enable) Designs, codes, tests, corrects and documents large and/or complex programs and program modifications from supplied specifications using agreed standards and tools, to achieve a well-engineered result. Takes part in reviews of own work and leads reviews of colleagues' work.
- (Ensure, advise) Sets standards for programming tools and techniques, advises on their application and ensures compliance. Takes technical responsibility for all stages in the software development process. Prepares project and quality plans and advises systems development teams. Assigns work to programming staff and monitors performance, providing advice, guidance and assistance to less experienced colleagues as required.

The relationship of job frameworks to professional credentials is that an individual can be certified with respect to his or her level on one or more skills. For example, a software developer could be classified as Level 5 (ensure/advise) according to the description given above. An application for SFIA Level 5 certification would include documentation of appropriate education/training and work experience. Evaluation of an application would include a review of the applicant's credentials and face-to-face interviews by examiners who are already certified at that level.

More recently, the European Community has sponsored an informatics certification program (EUCIP, www.eucip.com) that is based on a job framework. EUCIP divides the informatics career space into a number of *elective profiles*. By February 2004, the following profiles were defined: Business Analyst, Information Systems Analyst, Software Developer, and Network Manager. Many more EUCIP profiles have since been defined (European Certification of Informatics Professionals, 2006). The structure of a profile includes a brief description of the tasks to be carried out by a person working in the corresponding job, a list of essential behavioral skills for that job,

a list of required detailed skills, and a matrix of accredited learning modules by which an individual can demonstrate that he or she has these skills. The EUCIP job framework is also two-dimensional; one dimension consists of the skills needed, while the other dimension indicates the skill level, classified as *deep* (sound competence and experience), *incisive* (concepts reinforced by experience), or *introductory* (some concepts, general smattering).

For example, the task description for a EUCIP Software Developer (European Certification of Informatics Professionals, 2004) includes sentences like "Defines detailed specifications and directly contributes to the efficient creation and/or modification of complex software systems using the proper standards and tools.", and "Constructs or modifies, tests, and corrects large and/or complex component modules from specifications." The corresponding behavioral skills are given by sentences like "The Software Developer role requires first of all a rational mental attitude capable of conceptual and analytical thinking, a high regard for detail and a persistent goal-oriented approach, leading to the result through structured solutions formulated in a flexible way." The detailed skills are organized by level. Examples include:

- Deep: "Use different programming design methods, such as object-oriented design, top-down design, structured programming", "Understand the use of objects and classes", "Apply the principles of software engineering."
- Incisive: "Gather and analyse user requirements", "Coordinate a software development project", "Reuse objects and code."

The list of learning modules for this profile (European Certification of Informatics Professionals, 2004, p.12) includes university program names (e.g. information systems, software engineering) and industry certificates (Microsoft, Oracle, Sun).

It's important to note that job frameworks are organized around *skills* and *skill levels*. This contrasts with the knowledge-based approach used by the CSDP certification scheme and the SWEBOK body of knowledge.

The SFIA and EUCIP job frameworks were designed to cover the entire spectrum of information technology careers. The extent of this coverage tends to make such frameworks a less than perfect fit for industrial sectors or firms with specific needs. Grant (2006) explores the tension between specific and industry-wide frameworks.

EFFORTS TO STANDARDIZE PROFESSIONAL CREDENTIALS

The increasing globalization of the software industry suggests that software engineers will increasingly need to move between countries. Such individuals will need a way of acquiring professional software engineering credentials that are portable across national borders. One possible approach would be for one country to enter into bilateral agreements with other countries for mutual recognition of professional credentials. Japan has done this for its examination scheme with other Asian countries. The problem with this approach is that the number of bilateral agreements quickly becomes very large, and managing a country-by-country equivalence matrix will become a large problem.

A simpler and more maintainable approach would be to create an international standard for software engineering certifications. The existence of such a standard would make it easier for software engineering professionals to establish the international validity of certifications awarded by a country or professional society. A subcommittee of the International Standardization Organization (ISO) began such an effort in Fall 2004. Specifically, the ongoing effort is taking place within a working group of ISO/IEC JTC1 SC7, which is charged with developing software and systems engineering standards. A working draft of the standard has already been prepared, and it is hoped that the standard will be in final form and approved as an international standard by 2008. A certification scheme claiming conformance with the proposed standard will need to demonstrate (1) that it incorporates the processes for certification of individuals included in the existing international standard (ISO/IEC 17024) and (2) that the body of knowledge used by the certification scheme can be mapped to the SWEBOK body of knowledge for software engineering (Software Engineering Body of Knowledge, 2004).

Regional approaches to standardization are also under consideration. Several European countries have created job frameworks for information technology. We have already discussed the SFIA and EUCIP job frameworks, but there have also been other efforts to create frameworks in Europe. For this reason, the European Union has been working on standardizing professional credentials in information technology. This ongoing effort is centered in the work of the European Centre for the Development of Vocational Training (known by the French acronym CEDEFOP, www.cedefop.europa.eu). This organization, created in 1975, is the European Union's reference center for vocational education and training. One example of CEDEFOP's efforts to establish European standards for information technology skills is a series of conferences dealing with "e-skills" issues in Europe. The most recent conference in this series took place in Thessaloniki in October 2006. The URL describing the conference is http://eskills.cedefop.europa.eu/conference2006. One of the background papers for this conference is a document (European Committee for Standardization, 2006) released in February 2006 that proposed a European meta-framework for information technology skills. The intention is that a European meta-framework would provide a structure that could be used to contrast and compare existing national job frameworks, such as the UK's SFIA, the German AITTS framework (Federal Ministry for Information and Research, 2003) and the one developed by the French IT industry organization CIGREF (Club Informatique des Grandes Entreprises Françaises, 2006).

SUMMARY AND FUTURE TRENDS

It is increasingly clear that software engineering professionals (and more generally information technology professionals) need professional credentials that are not tied to a particular manufacturer's products. Several different approaches to such credentials are possible.

Professional licensure or chartered status builds on a model that is well established in other professions. In this approach, a government awards or approves the award of a professional status to an individual, and this status carries rights and privileges established in law. In the United States, this is only available to software engineers in Texas, and it doesn't seem likely to spread quickly to other states. In Canada, this status is more easily obtained. In the United Kingdom and Australia, chartered status for software and/or information technology professionals has been successfully modeled on chartered status for engineers. It seems unlikely that this model will spread to many other countries.

Broad-based professional certifications are generally awarded by professional societies. These certification schemes are based on established bodies of knowledge and conform to an international standard for the operation of certification schemes. Such schemes have been established and successful for many years in other professional disciplines. They are relatively new to software engineering, but based on the experience of other disciplines, it can be expected that they will gradually come to play a significant role in demonstrating the professional competence of a software engineer. The popularity and portability of these certification schemes will be aided by the emergence of an international standard.

National examinations also have a role to play in demonstrating the competence of information technology professionals. They are most important in Japan, where such examinations have been offered for decades to millions of aspiring professionals. Japan offers its examinations in many Asian countries, and mutual recognition agreements are in place. Outside of Asia, national examinations play a smaller role, typically as a way of demonstrating competence for information technology professionals who cannot demonstrate appropriate academic experience.

Job frameworks are yet another way to demonstrate the competence of information technology professionals. They are particularly popular in Europe, where the European Union is working to develop a meta-framework that can serve as a regional standard against which national frameworks can be measured.

The importance of information and software technologies to society today is certain to expand still further in the future. Under these circumstances, it is likely that all of the approaches to professional certifications described above will continue to increase in popularity and acceptance.

ACKNOWLEDGMENT

I would like to thank the following individuals for the information they provided on software engineering credentialing efforts in Europe, Australia, and Japan: Juan Garbajosa, Bob Hart, Bernd Hindel, Hiroshi Mukaiyama.

REFERENCES

Adams, T. (2004). *Software engineering in Canada, the US, and the UK: inter-professional relations and the emergence of a new profession.* London, Ontario: University of Western Ontario, Workforce Aging in the New Economy.

Bagert, D. (2004). Licensing and certification of computer professionals. *Advances in Computers, 60*, 1-34.

Bloom, B. (1984). *Taxonomy of Educational Objectives*. Boston MA: Allyn and Bacon.

Canadian Information Processing Society. (2007). *Software engineering*. Retrieved January 15, 2007, from http://www.cips.ca.it/position/softeng

Club Informatique des Grandes Entreprises Françaises. (2006). *Our expectations regarding the European e-competence framework*. Paper presented at the European e-Skills 2006 Conference, Thessaloniki, Greece. Retrieved February 4, 2007 from http://eskills.cedefop.europa.eu/conference2006/presentations/PS1-2_Delafon.pdf.

Engineers Canada. (2001). *Accreditation of software engineering programs is good news*. Retrieved September 29, 2007, from http://www.engineerscanada.ca/e/pub_ceo_01_02.cfm

European Certification of Informatics Professionals. (2004). *EUCIP Software Developer: elective level profile specification*. Dublin, Ireland: EUCIP Ltd.

European Certification of Informatics Professionals. (2006). *Introduction to the EUCIP elective level, version 2.3*. Dublin, Ireland: EUCIP Ltd.

European Committee for Standardization. (2006). *CWA 15515, European ICT Skills Meta-Framework – State-of-the-Art Review, clarification of the realities, and recommendations for next steps*. Brussels, Belgium: European Committee for Standardization.

Federal Ministry for Information and Research (2003). *The German Advanced IT Training System: Concepts and Results*. Bonn, Germany: Federal Ministry for Information and Research.

Fuller, U., Pears, A., Amillo, J., Avram, C., & Mannila, L. (2006). A computing perspective on the Bologna process. *ACM SIGCSE Bulletin, 38(4)*, 142-158.

Grant, S. (2006). Frameworks of competence: common or specific.

presented at *TenCompetence Workshop on Learning Networks for Lifelong Competence Development*, March 20-21, 2006, Sofia, Bulgaria. Retrieved September 29, 2007 from http://hdl.handle.net/1820/836

Information-Technology Promotion Agency. (2004). *Japan Information-Technology Engineers Examination Handbook*. Tokyo, Japan: Japan Information-Technology Engineers Examination Center.

International Organization for Standardization. (2003). *ISO/IEC 17024: Conformity assessment – general requirements for bodies operating certification of persons*. Geneva, Switzerland: ISO Copyright Office.

National Commission for Certifying Agencies. (2003). *Standards for the Accreditation of Certification Programs*. Washington, DC: National Organization for Competency Assurance.

Shaw, M. (1990). Prospects for an emerging discipline of software. *IEEE Software, 7(6)*, 15-24.

Skills Framework for the Information Age. (2005). London, UK: *SFIA framework reference, version 3*. SFIA Foundation.

Software Engineering Body of Knowledge. (2004). Retrieved February 4, 2007 from http://www.swebok.org

Van Dalen, G. (2003). *Software engineer – are you licensed?* Retrieved February 4, 2007 from http://www.cips.ca/news/national/news.asp?aID=1731

362

Compilation of References

Abernethy, K., & Kelly, J. (2000). Technology transfer issues for formal methods of software specification. In S. A. Mengel & P. J. Knoke (Eds.), *Proceedings of the thirteenth conference on software engineering education and training* (pp. 23-31). Austin, TX: IEEE Computer Society.

ABET (2006). List of Accredited Programs in Software Engineering, October 1, 2006. Retrieved May 28, 2007, from http://www.abet.org/ABET Website.asp#area

ABET (2007). Home Page, Retrieved May 28, 2007, from http://www.abet.org/index.shtml

ABET (2007). *Leadership and Quality Assurance in Applied Science, Computing, Engineering, and Technology Education*. Retrieved December 18, 2007, from http://www.abet.org.

ABET Engineering Accreditation Commission (EAC) (2005). Criteria for Accrediting Engineering Programs, Effective for Evaluations during the 2006-7 Accreditation Cycle. Baltimore, MD. Retrieved May 28, 2007, from http://www.abet.org/forms.shtml.

ABET. (2006). *Accreditation policy and procedure manual.* Baltimore, MD. ABET, Inc. Retrieved May 13, 2007, from http://abet.org/forms.shtml.

Abran, A., & Moore, J. (Eds.). (2004). Guide *to the Software Engineering Body of Knowledge, 2004 Version,* IEEE Computer Society Press. Available at http://www.swebok.org.

Abran, A., & Moore, J. W. (2004). *Guide to the Software Engineering Body of Knowledge.* IEEE Computer Board of Governors. Retrieved December 18, 2007, from ttp://www.swebok.org/

Abran, A., Moore, J. W., Bourque, P., & Dupuis, R. (Eds.). (2004). *Guide to the Software Engineering Body of Knowledge.* IEEE Computer Society.

Accreditation Board for Engineering and Technology (2007). Item IV-17. *2007-2008 Criteria for Accrediting Computer Programs.* Available: http://www.abet.org/Linked%20Documents-UPDATE/Criteria%20and%20PP/A004%2007-08%20Accreditation%20Policy%20and%20Procedure%20Manual%2011-10-06.pdf

ACM & IEEE (2004) *Computing Curricula, Software Engineering 2004: Curriculum Guidelines for Undergraduate Degree Programs in Software Engineering.* IEEE Computer Society and Association for Computing Machinery. Piscataway, NJ: IEEE CS Press

ACM & IEEE (2005) *Computing Curriculum 2005: The Overview Report.* IEEE Computer Society and Association for Computing Machinery. Piscataway, NJ: IEEE CS Press

ACM & IEEE-CS (1999a). *History of Joint IEEE Computer Society and ACM Steering Committee for the Establishment of Software Engineering as a Profession.* Retrieved September 1, 1999, from http://www.acm.org/serving/se/History.htm

ACM & IEEE-CS (1999b). *Software Engineering Coordinating Committee (SWECC).* Information retrieved September 1, 1999, from http://www.acm.org/serving/se/

ACM (1997). *ACM Code of Ethics and Professional Conduct.* Retrieved November 19, 2003, from http://www.computer.org

ACM (2000). *A Summary of the ACM Position on Software Engineering as a Licensed Engineering Profession.* Report retrieved April 1, 2006, from http://www.acm.org/serving/se_policy/selep_main.html

Adams, T. (2004). *Software engineering in Canada, the US, and the UK: inter-professional relations and the emergence of a new profession.* London, Ontario: University of Western Ontario, Workforce Aging in the New Economy.

Addison, T., & Vallabh, S. (2000). *Controlling Software Project Risks – an Empirical Study of Methods Used by Experienced Project Managers.* KPMG.

Agar, M. (1996). *The Professional Stranger.* Academic Press.

Akinoglu, O., & Tandogan, R. Ö. (2007). The effects of problem-based active learning in science education on students' academic achievement, attitude and concept learning. *Eurasia Journal of Mathematics, Science & Technology Education, 3*(1), 71-81.

Alexander, I. (2003). Misuse cases: Use cases with hostile intent. *IEEE Software, 20*(1), 58-66.

Almstrum, V. L., Klappholz, D., & Modesitt, K. (2007, March). Workshop on planning and executing real projects for real clients courses. *Proceedings of the 38th SIGCSE Technical Symposium on Computer Science Education* (p. 582). Covington, KY.

Alred, G. J. (2006). Bridging Cultures: The Academy and the Workplace. *Journal of Business Communication, 43,* 79-88.

American College & University Presidents Climate Commitment (2007). Program overview. Available: http://www.presidentsclimatecommitment.org/

Andresen, L., Boud, D., & Cohen, H. (1995). Experience-based learning. In G. Foley (Ed.), *Understanding Adult Education and Training* (pp. 207-215). Sydney: Allen and Unwin.

Ardis, M. A., & Ford, G. A. (1989) *SEI Report on Graduate Software Engineering Education.* TR CMU/SEI-89-TR-21. Pittsburgh PA: Carnegie Mellon University.

Ardis, M., & Ford, G. (1989). 1!989 SEI Report on Graduate Software Engineering Education (Tech. Rep. CMU/SEI-89-TR-21), Software Engineering Institute.

Ardis, M., & Ford,G. (1989). SEI Report on Graduate Software Engineering Education, *Proceedings of the Software Engineering Education Conference,* Springer-Verlag.

Ardovino, J., Hollingsworth, J., & Ybarra, S. (2000). *Multiple measures: Accurate ways to assess student achievement.* Thousand Oaks, CA: Corwin Press.

Armarego, J. (2002). *Advanced Software Design: a case in problem-based learning.* Paper presented at the CSEET2002 15th Conference on Software Engineering Education and Training, Covington (Ke).

Armarego, J. (2004). *Student perceptions of quality learning: evaluating PBL in Software Engineering.* Paper presented at the Seeking Educational Excellence: 13th Teaching Learning Forum, Perth.

Armarego, J. (2005). *Educating agents of change.* Paper presented at the CSEE&T2005 18th Conference on Software Engineering Education and Training, Ottawa.

Armarego, J. (2007a). *Beyond PBL: preparing graduates for professional practice.* Paper presented at the CSEET2007: 20th Conference on Software Engineering Education & Training, Dublin.

Armarego, J. (2007b). *Deconstructing student attitude to learning: a case study in IT education.* Paper presented at the CSITed2007: Computer Science and IT Education Conference, Mauritius.

Armarego, J. (2007c). *Educating Requirements Engineers in Australia: effective learning for professional practice.* Unpublished PhD, University of South Australia, Adelaide.

Armarego, J., & Fowler, L. (2005). *Orienting students to Studio Learning.* Paper presented at the Proceedings of the 2005 ASEE/AaeE 4th Global Colloquium on Engineering Education, Sydney.

Armarego, J., Fowler, L., & Roy, G. G. (2001). *Constructing Software Engineering Knowledge: development of a learning environment.* Paper presented at the In search of a Software Engineering Profession: CSEE&T2001 14th Conference on Software Engineering Education and Training, Charlotte (NC).

Asian Development Bank (1997). *Special Study of the Effectiveness and Impact of Training in Educational Projects.* Technical Report. Special Study Series Number 29), SST:INO 97023.

Aspray, W., Mayadas, F., & Vardi, M. Y. (Eds). (2006). *Globalization and offshoring of software.* A Report of the ACM Job Migration Task Force. Available: http://www.acm.org/globalizationreport/

Association for Computing Machinery & Institute for Electrical and Electronic Engineers Computer Society (2004). *Software Engineering 2004 Curriculum Guidelines for Undergraduate Degree Programs in Software Engineering.* Joint Task Force on Computing Curricula.

Association for Computing Machinery & Institute for Electrical and Electronic Engineers Computer Society (2004). *Software Engineering 2004 Curriculum Guidelines for Undergraduate Degree Programs in Software Engineering.* Joint Task Force on Computing Curricula.

Astrachan, O., Duvall, R.C., & Wallingford, E. (2001). *Bringing Extreme Programming to the Classroom.* Presented at XPUniverse Conference'01, 2001.

AUVSI (2007). *Association for Unmanned Vehicle Systems International.* Retrieved December 18, 2007, from http://www.auvsi.org.

Avram, C. (2006). *The Australian Perspective.* Presentation at IFIP Workshop on Improving IT Practitioner Skills, August 25, 2006, (A part of the 19th IFIP World Computer Congress, August 20-25, 2006, Santiago, Chile,), Abstract and presentation retrieved October 3, 2006, from http://www.ifip.org/projects/IT-Pract-main.htm

Bach, J. (1997). SE education: we're on our own. *IEEE Software, 14*(6), 26,28.

Bach, J. (1999). Reframing requirements analysis. *IEEE Computer, 32*(2), 120-122.

Bagert, D. (2004). Licensing and certification of computer professionals. *Advances in Computers, 60,* 1-34.

Bagert, D. (2004). SEER: Charting a Roadmap for Software Engineering Education. *Proceedings of 17th Conference on Software Engineering Education and Training, CSEET 2004,* pp. 158-161.

Bagert, D. J. & Ardis, M. A. (2003). Software Engineering Baccalaureate Programs in The United States: An Overview. *Proceedings, Frontiers in Education Conference,* pp. S3C-1 to S3C-6. Piscataway, NJ: IEEE CS Press.

Bagert, D. J. & Chenoweth, S. V. (2005). Future Growth of Software Engineering Baccalaureate Programs in the United States, *Proceedings, ASEE Annual Conference.* Portland, Oregon.

Bagert, D. J., Hilburn T. B., Hislop, G. W., Lutz, M., McCracken, M. & Mengel, S. (1999). *Guidelines for Software Engineering Education Version 1.0* Technical Report CMUISEI-99-TR-032. Pittsburgh PA: Carnegie Mellon University.

Bagert, D., & Ardis, M. (2003, November). *Software Engineering Baccalaureate Programs In The United States: An Overview.* Proceedings of the Frontiers in Education Conference (FIE'03). Boulder, CO.

Bagert, D., & Mengel, S. (2003). Using a Web-Based Project Process Throughout the Software Engineering Curriculum. *Proceedings of 25th International Conference on Software Engineering, ICSE 2003,* pp. 634-640.

Baker, A., Navarro, E. O., & van der Hoek, A. (2003). Problems and programmers: An educational software engineering card game. In *Proceedings of the 2003 international conference on software engineering* (pp. 614-619). Portland, Oregon.

Banks, D. A. (2003). Belief, inquiry, argument and reflection as significant issues in learning about Information Systems development methodologies. In T. McGill (Ed.), *Current Issues in IT Education* (pp. 1-10). Hershey (PA): IRM Press.

Barrows, H. S., & Tamblyn, R. M. (1980). *Problem-based Learning, an Approach to Medical Education.* New York: Springer.

BCS (2006). Professionalism in IT Programme, covered in a series of articles in the May 2006 issue of *IT NOW*, Swindon, UK: British Computer Society.

BCS (ud). *Code of Conduct & Code of Good Practice.* Both retrieved November 19, 2003, from http://www.bcs.org.uk

Beck, K. (1999). Embracing Change with Extreme Programming, *IEEE Computer* 32(10), pp. 70-77.

Beck, K. (2000). *Extreme Programming Explained – Embrace Change,* Boston: Addison-Wesley.

Beck, K. et al. (2001). Agile Manifesto. Retrieved March 30th 2007, from http://agilemanifesto.org/

Beckman, K., Khajenoori, K., Coulter, N., & Mead, N. R. (1997). Collaborations: Closing the industry-academia gap. *IEEE Software, 14*(6), 49-57.

Bekir, N., Cable, V., Hashimoto, I., & Katz, S. (2001). *Teaching Engineering Ethics: A New Approach.* Proceedings of the 31st ASEE/IEEE Frontiers in Education Conference, October 10-13, 2001, Reno, NV, USA, Session T2G. Piscataway, NJ: IEEE.

Bentley, J. F., Lowry, G. R., & Sandy, G. A. (1999). *Towards The Compleat Information Systems Graduate: a Problem based Learning Approach.* Paper presented at the Proceedings of the 10th Australasian Conference on Information Systems.

Benzel, T. (1989). Integrating security requirements and software development standards. In *Proceedings of the 12th National Computer Security Conference* (pp. 435-458). Fort Meade, MD: National Computer Security Center.

Bernhart, M., Grechenig, T., Hetzl, J., & Zuser, W. (2006). Dimensions of Software Engineering Course Design. *Proceedings of 28th International Conference on Software Engineering, ICSE 2006.* pp. 667-672.

Biggs, J. (1999). *Teaching for Quality Learning at University: what the student does.* Buckingham (UK): Open University Press.

Blake, B. M. (2003). A student-enacted simulation approach to software engineering education. *IEEE Transactions on Education, 46*(1), 124-132.

Blakeslee, A. M. (2001). Bridging the Workplace and the Academy: Teaching Professional Genres Through Classroom-Workplace Collaborations. *Technical Communication Quarterly, 10*(2), 169-192.

Bloom, B. (1984). *Taxonomy of Educational Objectives.* Boston MA: Allyn and Bacon.

Bloom, B. S. (1956). *Taxonomy of Educational Objectives: the classification of educational goals Handbook 1: cognitive domain.* New York: David Mackay.

Bloom, G. S., Madaus, G. F., & Hastings, J. T. (1981). *Evaluation to improve learning.* New York: McGraw-Hill.

Boehm, B. (2006) Learning by Doing: Real-client Software Project Courses, *ASEE Tutorial 2006,* Retrieved from http://db-itm.shidler.hawaii.edu/cseet2006/Boehm%20ASEET.pdf .

Boehm, B. W., & Turner, R. (2004). *Balancing agility and discipline: A guide for the perplexed.* Boston: Addison-Wesley.

Boehm, B. W., Abi-Antoun, M., Port, D., Kwan, J., & Lynch, A. (1999). Requirements engineering, expectations management, and the two cultures. *Proceedings of the 4th IEEE International Symposium on Requirements Engineering* (pp. 14-22). Limerick, Ireland: IEEE.

Boehm, B. W., Port, D., Yang, Y., Bhuta, J., & Abts, C. (2003). Composable process elements for developing COTS-based applications. *ISESE 2003*, 8-17.

Boehm, B. W., Yang, Y., Bhuta, J., & Port, D. (2005). Composable spiral processes for COTS-based application development. *Proceedings of the 4th International ICCBSS conference* (pp. 6-7), Bilbao, Spain: Springer.

Boehm, B., & Basili, V. (2001). Software defect reduction – Top 10 list. *IEEE Computer, 34*(1), 135-137.

Boehm, B., Egyed, A., Port, D., Shah, A., Kwan, J. & Madachy, R. (1998). A Stakeholder Win-win Approach to Software Engineering Education. *Annals of Software Engineering, 6*, 295-321.

Boehm, B., Egyed, A., Port, D., Shah, A., Kwan, J. & Madachy, R. (1998). A Stakeholder Win-win Approach to Software Engineering Education. *Annals of Software Engineering, 6*, 295-321.

Boehm, B., Kaiser, G., & Port, D. (2000) A Combined Curriculum Research and Curriculum Development Approach to Software Engineering Education, *Workshop on Developing Undergraduate Software engineering Programs, Proceedings of CSEE&T 2000*, 310-311

Boehm, B., Kaiser, G., & Port, D. (2000) A Combined Curriculum Research and Curriculum Development Approach for Software Engineering Education, *Conference on Software Engineering Education and Training*, 2000, p. 310.

Borstler, J., Carrington, D. Hislop, G., Lisack, S. Olsen, K. & Williams, L. (2002, Sept/Oct). Teaching PSP: Challenges & Lessons Learned. *IEEE Software 19(5)*, 42-48.

Borstler, J., Carrington, D. Hislop, G., Lisack, S. Olsen, K. & Williams, L. (2002, Sept/Oct). Teaching PSP: Challenges & Lessons Learned. *IEEE Software 19(5)*, 42-48.

Bott, F. (2005). *Professional Issues in Information Technology*. Swindon, UK: British Computer Society.

Bourque, P., & Dupuis, R. (2004). Guide to the Software Engineering Body of Knowledge – Final Version, SWEBOK, Feb. 2000, Retrieved from http://www.swebok.org/

Bourque, P., & Dupuis, R. (Eds.). (2004). *Guide to the Software Engineering Body of Knowledge (SWEBOK)*. Published by IEEE Computer Society. The guide itself along with details of its development and further information on the SWEBOK project can be retrieved from: http://www.swebok.org

Bourque, P., Dupuis, R., Abran, A., Moore, J., & Tripp, L. (2000, August). *Developing Consensus on the Software Engineering Body of Knowledge*. Proceedings of the 2000 World Computer Congress, Beijing, China. Available at *http*://www.gelog.etsmtl.ca/publications/pdf/535.pdf

Bowles, D. J. (2006). Active learning strategies … Not for the birds! *International Journal of Nursing Education Scholarship, 3*(1), 0-11.

Brady, A., Johnson, R. R., & Wallace, C. (2006). The intersecting futures of technical communication and software engineering: Forging a multi-disciplinary alliance. *Technical Communication, 53*(3).

Brady, A., Seigel, M., Vosecky, T., & Wallace, C. (2007). *Addressing Communication Issues in Software Development: A Case Study Approach*. Paper presented at the Conference on Software Engineering Education and Training.

Brooks, F. (1975). *The mythical man-month: Essays on software engineering*. Reading, MA: Addison-Wesley.

Brooks, F. (1987). No Silver Bullet, *IEEE Computer* 20(4), pp. 10-19.

Brooks, F. (1995). *The Mythical Man-Month*; 2nd edition, Addison-Wesley Professional.

Brooks, F. P. (1986). *No silver bullet - essence and accidents of software engineering*. Paper presented at the Proceedings of Information Processing 86: the IFIP 10th World Conference, Amsterdam.

Brooks, F.P. (1987): No silver bullet – essence and accidents of software engineering. IEEE Computer, Vol. 20 (4), 10-19.

Brown, G., Bull, J., & Pendlebury, M. (1997). *Assessing Student Learning in Higher Education*. London: Routledge.

Brown, J. S., Collins, A., & Duguid, P. (1989). Situated cognition and the culture of learning. *Educational Researcher, 18*, 32-42.

Brown, S., & Enos, T. (Eds.). (2002). *The Writing Program Administrator's Resource: A Guide to Reflective Institutional Practice*. Lawrence Erlbaum.

Broy, M., E. Denert (eds.) (2002): Software Pioneers: Contributions to Software Engineering. Springer-Verlag, Berlin.

Bruner, J. S. (1967). *On knowing: Essays for the left hand*. Cambridge, Mass.: Harvard University Press.

Bungartz, H.-J., M. Bernreuther (2006): First Experiences with Group Projects in CSE Education. Computing in Science and Engineering, July 2006, 16-25.

Bunse, C., Grützner, I., Peper, C., Steinbach-Nordmann, S. (2005). Applying a Blended Learning Strategy for Software Engineering Education. *Proceedings of the 18th Conference on Software Engineering Education and Training (CSEE&T)*. Ottawa, Canada.

Burge, J. & Troy, D. (2006). Rising to the Challenge: Using Business-Oriented Case Studies in Software Engineering Education. *Proceedings of the Nineteenth Conference on Software Engineering Education & Training*. Turtle Bay, Hawaii.

Canadian Council of Professional Engineers, Canadian Engineering Accreditation Board (2006). CEAB Accreditation Criteria and Procedures. Ottawa, Ontario, Canada. Retrieved October 26, 2007, from http://www.engineerscanada.ca/e/files/report_ceab.pdf

Canadian Information Processing Society. (2007). *Software engineering*. Retrieved January 15, 2007, from http://www.cips.ca.it/position/softeng

Carnegie (2007) *The Carnegie Classification of Institutions of Higher Education*. Stanford, CA: The Carnegie Foundation for the Advancement of Teaching. Retrieved January 15, 2008 from http://www.carnegiefoundation.org/classifications/

Carnegie Mellon University (2005). *Academic PSP Material*. Retrieved January 4, 2008 from http://www.sei.cmu.edu/tsp/psp/download/academic.html.

Carnegie Mellon University (2005). *Academic PSP Material*. Retrieved January 4, 2008 from http://www.sei.cmu.edu/tsp/psp/download/academic.html.

Carr, J. J. (2000). Requirements engineering and management: The key to designing quality complex systems. *The TQM Magazine, 12*(6), 400-407.

Carr, W., & Kemmis, S. (1986). *Becoming Critical: education, knowledge and action research*. Lewes (UK): Falmer.

Chrisman, C., & Beccue, B. (1987) Evaluating students in system development group projects. *SIGCSE-Bulletin*, 19(1): pp. 366–373, 1987.

Christensen, C. R. (1987). *Teaching and the Case Method*. Harvard Business School.

Clark, N., Davies, P., & Skeers, R. (2005). Self and Peer Assessment in Software Engineering Projects. *Proceedings of 7th Australasian Computing Education Conference, ACE 2005*, pp. 91-100.

Clark, R. A., & Schmidt, H. A. (2002). *A national strategy to secure cyberspace*. Washington, DC: The President's Critical Infrastructure Protection Board.

Clough, G.W. (2005) Educating the Engineer of 2020: Adapting Engineering Education to the New Century. Washington, D.C.: National Academies Press, Retrieved from http://www.nap.edu.

Club Informatique des Grandes Entreprises Françaises. (2006). *Our expectations regarding the European e-competence framework*. Paper presented at the European e-Skills 2006 Conference, Thessaloniki, Greece. Retrieved February 4, 2007 from http://eskills.cedefop.europa.eu/conference2006/presentations/PS1-2_Delafon.pdf.

Cobertura. (2005). Retrieved from http://cobertura.sourceforge.net/

Cockburn, A. (2001). *Agile Software Development*, Addison-Wesley Pub Co.

Cockburn, A., & Williams, L. (2001) The costs and benefits of pair programming. In G. Succi and M. Marchesi (Eds.), *Extreme Programming examined* (pp. 223-243). Boston: Addison-Wesley.

Collins, A., Brown, J. S. & Newman, S. E. (1990). Cognitive apprenticeship: teaching the crafts of reading, writing and mathematics. In: Resnick, L. B. (Ed.). *Knowing, learning and instruction: Essays in honor of Robert Glaser.* Hillsdale, N.J.: Lawrende Erlbaum.

Collofello, J. & Vehathiri, K. (2005). *An Environment for Training Computer Science Students on Software Testing.* Paper presented ad Frontiers in Education, 2005. FIE '05. 19-22 Oct. 2005, T3E-6- T3E-10.

Collofello, J. S. (2000). University/industry collaboration in developing a simulation based software project management training course. In S. Mengel & P. J. Knoke (Eds.), *Proceedings of the thirteenth conference on software engineering education and training* (pp. 161-168). Austin, TX: IEEE Computer Society.

Computing Research News (2007), *2005-2006 Taulbe Survey,* May 2007.

Connors, R. J. (2004). The Rise of Technical Writing Instruction in America. In J. Johnson-Eiola & S. Selber (Eds.), *Central Works in Technical Communication* (pp. 4-19). Oxford University Press.

Coppit, D. (2006). Implementing Large Projects in Software Engineering Courses. *Computer Science Education 16(1),* 53-73.

Cowling, A.J. (1998). The First Decade Of An Undergraduate Degree Programme In Software Engineering. *Annals of Software Engineering,* 6(1-4), 61-90.

Cropley, D. H., & Cropley, A. J. (1998). *Teaching Engineering Students to be Creative - Program and Outcomes.* Paper presented at the Australasian Association of Engineering Education: 10th Annual Conference.

Curtis, B., Krasner, H., & Iscoe, N. (1988). A Field Study of the Software Design Process for Large Systems. *Communications of the ACM, 31*(11), 1268-1287.

Daigle, R. & Niccolai, M. (1997). Inter-Class Synergy by Design. In *Proceedings of the SIGCSE Conference on Computer Science Education (SIGCSE '97).* New York, NY: ACM Press, pp. 92-95.

Dantas, A. R., Barros, M. O., & Werner, C. M. L. (2004). A simulation-based game for project management experiential learning. In *Proceedings of the 2004 international conference on software engineering and knowledge engineering.* Banff, Alberta, Canada.

Dart, P., Johnston, L., Schmidt, C., & Sonenberg, L. (1997) Developing an Accredited SE Program, *IEEE Software,* Nov/Dec, 66-70.

Davis, A. (1990). *Software Requirements: Objects, Functions, and States.* Prentice Hall.

Davis, R. B., Maher, C. A. and Noddings, N. (1990, eds.). Constructivist views on the teaching and learning of mathematics, *Journal for Research in Mathematics Education,* Monograph Number 4, The National Council of Teachers of Mathematics, Inc.

Dawson, R. (2000). Twenty dirty tricks to train software engineers. In *Proceedings of the 22nd international conference on software engineering* (pp. 209-218): ACM.

de Haan, D., Waterson, P., Trapp, S. & Pfahl, D. (2003). Integrating needs assessment within next generation e-learning systems: Lessons learnt from a case study. *Proceedings of the IFIP OPEN WORKING CONFERENCE "eTRAIN 2003: E-Training Practices for Professional Organisations".* Pori, Finland.

De Landtsheer, R., & van Lamsweerde, A. (2005). Reasoning about confidentiality at requirements engineering time. In *Proceedings of the 10th European Software Engineering Conference held jointly with 13th ACM SIGSOFT International Symposium on Foundations of Software Engineering* (pp. 41-49). New York, NY: ACM.

Deili, M. (1988). *A problem solving approach to usability testing.* Paper presented at the International Technical Communication Conference.

Deretchin, L. F. (2002). Making the grade. In P. Schwartz & G. Webb (Eds.), *Assessment: Case studies, experience and practice from higher education* (pp. 114-120). London: Kogan Page.

Development of the volume is documented at the SE2004 site: http://sites.computer.org/ccse/

Dewey, J. (1916). *Democracy and education.* New York, NY: Macmillan.

Diaz-Herrera, J. L., & Hilburn, T. (Eds.). (2004). *Software Engineering 2004 Curriculum Guidelines for Undergraduate Degree Programs in Software Engineering A Volume of the Computing Curricula Series.* Available at http://sites.computer.org/ccse

Diaz-Herrera, J. L., Hilburn, T., Hislop, G., Lutz, M., MacNeil, P.E., & McCracken, M. (2001, October). *Software Engineering Education Should Be Presented as A: Science, B: Engineering, C. Technology, D. None of the above, E. All of the above, Other.* Proceedings of the Frontiers in Education Conference (FIE'01), Reno, NV.

DMU (2007). De Monfort University, Centre for Computing and Social Responsibility. Provides details of the proceedings of the Ethicomp Series of Conferences, The Ethicomp Journal, and the Journal of Information Communication and Ethics in Society, home page: http://www.ccsr.cse.dmu.ac.uk/

Dorn, E. M. (1999). Case Method Instruction in the Business Writing Classroom. *Business Communication Quarterly, 62,* 41-60.

Drappa, A., & Ludewig, J. (2000). Simulation in software engineering training. In *Proceedings of the 22nd international conference on software engineering* (pp. 199-208): ACM.

Drappa, A., J. Ludewig (2000): *Simulation in Software Engineering Training.* Proceedings of the 22nd ISCE, Limerick, Ireland, 199-208.

Dreyfus, H. L., & Dreyfus, S. E. (1986). *Mind over Machine.* New York: Free Press.

Duggins, S. L., & Thomas, B. B. (2002). An historical investigation of graduate software engineering curricula. *Proceedings of the 15th Conference on Software Engineering Education and Training (CSEET'02),* Los Alamitos, CA, IEEE Computer Society Press.

Duggins, S.L., & Thomas, B.B. (2002) An Historical Investigation of Graduate Software Engineering Curriculum, *Proceedings CSEE&T,* 78-87.

Ecker, P. S., Caudill, J., Hoctor, D., & Meyer, C. (2004). Implementing an interdisciplinary capstone course for associate degree Information Technology programs, *Proceedings of the 5th Conference on Information Technology Education* (pp. 60-65). Salt Lake City, UT.

Edwards, S. (2003). *Using Test-Driven Development in the Classroom: Providing Students with Automatic, Concrete Feedback on Performance.* Paper presented at International Conference on Education and Information Systems: Technology and Applications EISTA 2003, Orlando, FL, 2003.

Eisenman, R. (2001). Stimulating achievement among Hispanic college students. *Radical Pedagogy, 3*(2). Available: http://radicalpedagogy.icaap.org/content/issue3_2/eisenman.html

Ellis, H., & Mitchell, R. (2004). Self-Grading in a Project-Based Software Engineering Course. *Proceedings of 17th Conference on Software Engineering Education and Training, CSEET 2004,* pp. 138-143.

Ellis, H., McKim, J.C., & Younessi H. Issues Affecting Graduate and Postgraduate Software Engineering Curricula, Workshop on Developing Graduate and Postgraduate Software Engineering Courses, *Proceedings of CSEE&T 2000,* 190

Ellison, R. J., & Moore, A. P. (2003). *Trustworthy refinement through intrusion-aware design* (Tech. Rep. No. CMU/SEI-2003-TR-002). Pittsburgh, PA: Software Engineering Institute, Carnegie Mellon University. Retrieved November 1, 2007 from http://www.sei.cmu.edu/publications/documents/03.reports/03tr002.html

Emerson, R.M., Fretz, R.I., & Shaw, L.L. (1995). *Writing Ethnographic Fieldnotes.* University of Chicago Press.

Enders, F. B., & Diener-West, M. (2006). Methods of learning in statistical education: A randomized trial of public health graduate students. *Statistics Education Research Journal, 5*(1), 5-19.

Engel, G. (2006). *IT Opportunities from the IEEE Computer Society.* Presentation at IFIP Workshop on Improving IT Practitioner Skills, August 25, 2006 (A part of the 19th IFIP World Computer Congress, Santiago, Chile,

August 20-25, 2006), Abstract and presentation retrieved October 3, 2006, from: http://www.ifip.org/projects/IT-Pract-main.htm

Engel, G., & Roberts, E. (Eds.). (2001). *Computing Curricula 2001: Computer Science -- final report*: Joint Task Force on Computing Curricula, ACM and IEEE Computer Society.

Engineering Accreditation Commission. (1999). *Criteria for accrediting engineering programs: Effective for evaluations during the 2000-2001 Accreditation Cycle.* Baltimore, MD. ABET, Inc.

Engineering Accreditation Commission. (2000). *Criteria for accrediting engineering programs: Effective for evaluations during the 2001-2002 Accreditation Cycle.* Baltimore, MD. ABET, Inc.

Engineering Accreditation Commission. (2001). *Criteria for accrediting engineering programs: Effective for evaluations during the 2002-2003 Accreditation Cycle.* Baltimore, MD. ABET, Inc.

Engineering Accreditation Commission. (2002). *Criteria for accrediting engineering programs: Effective for evaluations during the 2003-2004 Accreditation Cycle.* Baltimore, MD. ABET, Inc.

Engineering Accreditation Commission. (2007). *Criteria for accrediting engineering programs: Effective for evaluations during the 2007-2008 Accreditation Cycle.* Baltimore, MD. ABET, Inc. Retrieved May 13, 2007, from http://abet.org/forms.shtml.

Engineering Accreditation Commission. (2007a). *Engineering self-study questionnaire.* Baltimore, MD. ABET, Inc. Retrieved May 13, 2007, from http://abet.org/forms.shtml.

Engineers Australia (2007). Australian Professional Engineering Programs Accredited by Engineers Australia. Last updated 6 September 2007. Retrieved November 11, 2007 from http://www.engineersaustralia.org.au/education/program-accreditation/accredited-programs/accredited-programs_home.cfm

Engineers Canada. (2001). *Accreditation of software engineering programs is good news.* Retrieved Sep-

tember 29, 2007, from http://www.engineerscanada.ca/e/pub_ceo_01_02.cfm

English, F. (1978). *Quality control in curriculum development.* Arlington (VA): American Association of School Administrators.

Entwistle, N. J., & Ramsden, P. (1983). *Understanding Student Learning.* London: Croom Helm.

Entwistle, N. J., & Tait, H. (1990). Approaches to learning, evaluations of teaching, and preferences for contrasting academic environments. *Higher Education, 19*, 169-194.

Entwistle, N. J., & Tait, H. (1995). Approaches to studying and perceptions of the learning environment across disciplines. *New directions for teaching and learning, 64*, 93-103.

Epstein R.A.G. (1997). *The Case of the Killer Robot*, New York: John Wiley and Sons. There are also freely available abridged web versions e.g. from the Online Ethics Center at Case Western Reserve University: http://onlineethics.org/cases/robot/robot.html

ETHICOMP (2004). *Introduction ETHICOMP 2004.* In proceedings of Seventh International ETHICOMP Conference (ETHICOMP 2004), April 14-16 2004, Syros, Greece, (pp. 3-4). Syros: University of the Aegean.

European Certification of Informatics Professionals. (2004). *EUCIP Software Developer: elective level profile specification.* Dublin, Ireland: EUCIP Ltd.

European Certification of Informatics Professionals. (2006). *Introduction to the EUCIP elective level, version 2.3.* Dublin, Ireland: EUCIP Ltd.

European Committee for Standardization. (2006). *CWA 15515, European ICT Skills Meta-Framework – State-of-the-Art Review, clarification of the realities, and recommendations for next steps.* Brussels, Belgium: European Committee for Standardization.

Fairley, R. (1986). *The role of academe in software engineering education.* Proceedings of the 1986 ACM Fourteenth Annual Conference on Computer Science. p. 39-52. New York: ACM Press.

FASE (2004). Report on the CSEE&T 2004 Workshop: Teaching Ethics in Software Engineering Programs. *Forum for Advancing Software engineering Education (FASE), 14*(4), (Issue 160), April 2004.

Favela, J., & Pena-Mora, F. (2001). An experience in collaborative software engineering education. *IEEE Software, 18*(2), 47-53.

Federal Ministry for Information and Research (2003). *The German Advanced IT Training System: Concepts and Results.* Bonn, Germany: Federal Ministry for Information and Research.

Felder, G. M., & Spurlin, J. (2005). Applications, reliability and validity of the Index of Learning Styles. *International Journal of Engineering Education, 21*(1), 1-3-112.

Felder, R. M. (1996). Matters of Style. *Prism: Journal of the American Society of Engineering Education, 6*(4), 18-23.

Felder, R. M., & Brent, R. (2005). Understanding student differences. *Journal of Engineering Education, 94*(1), 57-72.

Felder, R. M., & Silverman, R. L. (1988). Learning and teaching styles in engineering education. *Engineering Education, 78*(8), 674-681.

Fenwick, J. B., & Kurtz, B. L. (2005). Intra-curriculum software engineering education. *ACM SIGCSE Bulletin inroads, 36*(1). 540-544.

Fenwick, J., & Kurtz, B. (2005). Intra-curriculum software engineering education. *Proceedings of the 36th SIGCSE Technical Symposium on Computer Science Education, SIGCSE 2005*, pp. 540-544.

Fernandez, J. D., & Tedford, P. (2006). Evaluating computing education programs against real world needs. *Journal of Computing Sciences in Colleges, 21*(4), 259-265.

Fernandez, J. D., Garcia, M., Camacho, D., & Evans, A. (2006). Software engineering industry experience – the key to success. *Journal of Computing Sciences in Colleges, 21*(4), 230-236.

Ferrari, M., Taylor, R., & VanLehn, K. (1999). Adapting work simulations for schools. *The Journal of Educational Computing Research, 21*(1), 25-53.

Ferreira, H.S., Fonseca, L.M.G., d'Alge, J.C.L., Montiero, A.M.V. (2002). New Approach on Teaching Geotechnology. *International Archives of Photogrammetry and Remote Sensing, and Spatial Information Science* San Jóse dos Campos, Brazil. Vol. XXXIV, Part 6, CVI.

Fetaji, B. & Fetaji, M. (2006). Software Engineering Java Educational Software and its Qualitative Research. *Proceedings of the IV International Conference onMultimedia and ICTs in Education m-ICTE 2006 "Current Developments in Technology-Asissted Education".* Seville, Spain, Vol. 3.

Fishbein, M., & Ajzen, I. (1975). *Belief, attitude, intention, and behavior: An introduction to theory and research.* Reading, Mass.: Addison-Wesley.

Flener, P. (2006). Realism in Project-Based Software Engineering Courses: Rewards, Risks, and Recommendations. *Proceedings. of 21st International Symposium on Computer and Information Sciences, ISCIS 2006,* pp. 1031-1039.

Flower, L. (1998). *Problem Solving Strategies for Writing in College and Community.* Harcourt Brace.

Ford, G. & Gibbs, N. (1996) *A Mature Profession of Software Engineering.* Software Engineering Institute. Technical Report CMU/SEI-96-TR-04. Pittsburgh, PA: Carnegie Mellon University.

Ford, G. (1991) 1991 SEI Report on Graduate Software Engineering Education, *Technical Report CMU/SEI-91-TR-2,* Software Engineering Institute, Carnegie Mellon University

Ford, G. (1991a). The SEI Undergraduate Curriculum in Software Engineering. *Proceedings, 22nd SIGCSE Technical Symposium on Computer Science Education.* pp. 375–385 New York: ACM Press.

Ford, G. A. (1991b) *SEI Report on Graduate Software Engineering Education.* CMU/SEI-91-TR-2. Pittsburgh, PA: Carnegie Mellon University.

Ford, G., Gibbs, N., & Tomayko, J. (1987) Software Engineering Education: An Interim Report from the Software Engineering Institute, Technical Report CMU/SEI-87-TR-8, Software Engineering Institute,

Ford, Gary A. (1994). The Progress of Undergraduate Software Engineering Education. *SIGCSE Bulletin.* 26,4. New York: ACM Press.

Frailey, D. (2006). Bringing realistic software engineering assignments to the software engineering classroom. Proceedings of CSEET'06: *The 19th Conference on Software Engineering Education and Training.* Ohau, HI.

Frailey, D. (2006). Bringing realistic software engineering assignments to the software engineering classroom. Proceedings of CSEET'06: *The 19th Conference on Software Engineering Education and Training.* Ohau, HI.

Frailey, D. J. (2006). Bringing Realistic Software Engineering Assignments to the Software Engineering Classroom. *Proceedings of the Nineteenth Conference on Software Engineering Education & Training.* Turtle Bay, Hawaii.

Franch, X., & Port, D. (2005). COTS-Based Software Systems. *Proceedings of the 4th International ICCBSS Conference* (LNCS 3412). Bilbao, Spain: Springer.

Freed, G. (1992). *Fifth generation innovation.* Sydney: Australian Centre for Innovation and International Competitiveness, University of Sydney.

Freedman, A. (1993a). Show and Tell? The Role of Explicit Teaching in the Learning of New Genres. *Research in the Teaching of English, 27*(3), 222-251.

Freedman, A. (1993b). Show and Tell? The Role of Explicit Teaching in the Learning of New Genres. *Research in the Teaching of English, 27*(3), 222-251.

Freedman, A., Adam, C., & Smart, G. (1994). Wearing Suits to Class: Simulating Genres and Simulations as Genre. *Written Communication, 11*(2), 193-226.

Frezza, S. T., Tang, M-H., & Brinkman, B. J. (2006). Creating an Accreditable Software Engineering Bachelor's Program. *IEEE Software*, 23(6), 27-35.

Frezza, S., Sasi, S., & Seol, J. (2003, November). *Report from the Trenches: Applying the SEEK to BSSE Program Development.* Proceedings of the Frontiers in Education Conference (FIE'03). Boulder, CO.

Friedman, R., McHugh, J. A., & Deek, F. P. (2003). NJIT's sandbox: An industry/education partnership for IT development. In *Proceedings of the 4th Conference on Information Technology Curriculum* (pp. 201-205). Lafayette, Indiana, USA.

Frohna, A. Z., Hamstra, S. J., Mullan, P. B., & Gruppen, L. D. (2006). Teaching medical education principles and methods to faculty using an active learning approach: The University of Michigan Medical Education Scholars Program. *Academic Medicine, 81*(11), 975-978.

Fuller, U., Pears, A., Amillo, J., Avram, C., & Mannila, L. (2006). A computing perspective on the Bologna process. *ACM SIGCSE Bulletin, 38(4)*, 142-158.

Fulmer, W. E. (1992). Using Cases in Management Development Programmes. *Journal of Management Development, 11*, 33-37.

Gale, F. C. (1993). Teaching Professional Writing Rhetorically: The Unified Case Method. *Journal of Business and Technical Communication, 7*(2), 256-266.

Garg, K., & Varma, V. (2006). Security: Bridging the academia-industry gap using a case study. In *XIII Asia Pacific Software Engineering Conference Proceedings* (pp. 485-492). New York, NY: IEEE Computer Society Press.

Garlan, D., Brown, A., Jackson, D., Tomayko, J., & Wing, J. (1995) The CMU Master of Software Engineering Core Curriculum, *Proceedings of CSEE&T 1995*, 65-86, Springer Verlag.

Garlan, D., Gluch, D. P., & Tomayko, J. E. (1997). Agents of Change: Educating Future Leaders in Software Engineering. *IEEE Computer, 30*(11), 59-65.

Gary, K., Gannod, B. Gannod, G., Koehnemann, H., Lindquist, T., & Whitehouse, R. (2005). Work in progress – The Software Enterprise. Proceedings of FIE'05: *The Frontiers in Education Conference.* Indianapolis, IN.

Gary, K., Gannod, B. Gannod, G., Koehnemann, H., Lindquist, T., & Whitehouse, R. (2005). Work in progress – The Software Enterprise. Proceedings of FIE'05: *The Frontiers in Education Conference.* Indianapolis, IN.

Gary, K., Gannod, B., & Koehnemann, H. (2006). The Software Enterprise: Facilitating the Industry Preparedness of Software Engineers. Proceedings of ASEE'06: *The National Conference of the American Society for Engineering Education.* Chicago, IL.

Gary, K., Gannod, G., Koehnemann, H., & Blake, M.B. (2005). Educating Future Software Professionals on Outsourced Software Development. Proceedings of ASEE'05: *The National Conference of the American Society for Engineering Education.* Portland, OR.

Germain, E., & Robillard, P. (2003) What Cognitive Activities are Performed in Student Projects?, *Proceedings of CSEE&T 2003*, 224-231

Gesellschaft für Informatik (1985): Ausbildung von Diplom-Informatikern an wissenschaftlichen Hochschulen. Empfehlung der GI vom 18. März 1985, Informatik-Spektrum 8, 164–165.

Gesellschaft für Informatik (1997): Lehrinhalte und Veranstaltungsformen im Informatikstudium, ergänzende Empfehlungen. Informatik Spektrum 20, Heft 5.

Ghezzi, C., & Mandrioli, D. (2005). The Challenges of Software Engineering Education. *Proceedings of 27th International Conference on Software Engineering, ICSE 2005*, pp. 637-638.

Ghezzi, C., Jazayeri, M., & Mandrioli, D. (2002). *Fundamentals of Software Engineering.* 2nd edition, Prentice Hall.

Gibbons, A. S. (2001). Model-centered instruction. *Journal of Structural Learning and Intelligent Systems, 14*(4), 511-540.

Giorgini, P., Mouratidis, H., & Zannone, N. (2007). Modelling Security and Trust with Secure Tropos. *Integrating Security and Software Engineering: Advances and Future Visions*, 160-189. Hershey, PA: IGI Global.

Glass, R. (2003). A Big Problem in Academic Software Engineering and a Potential Outside-the-Box Solution, *IEEE Software*, July/August,94-96.

Glass, R. L. (1992). A comparative analysis of the topic areas of Computer Science, Software Engineering, and Information Systems. *Journal of Systems and Software, 25.*

Glass, R. L. (1995). *Software Creativity*: Prentice-Hall.

Glass, R. L. (1998). *Software Runaways: Lessons Learned from Massive Software Project Failures.* Prentice Hall.

Glass, R. L. (2001). Frequently forgotten fundamental facts about software engineering. *IEEE Software, 18*(3), 112 - 111.

Gnatz, M., Kof, L., Prilmeier, F., & Seifert, T. (2003). A practical approach of teaching software engineering. In P. J. Knoke, A. Moreno & M. Ryan (Eds.), *Proceedings of the sixteenth conference on software engineering education and training* (pp. 120-128). Madrid, Spain: IEEE.

Goold, A., & Horan, P. (2002). Foundation software engineering practices for capstone projects and beyond. In M. McCracken, M. Lutz & T. C. Lethbridge (Eds.), *Proceedings of the fifteenth conference on software engineering education and training* (pp. 140-146). Covington, KY, USA: IEEE.

Gorgone, J. T., Davis, G. B., Valacich, J. S., Topi, H., Feinstein, D. L., & Longenecker, H. E. (Eds.). (2002). *IS 2002: model curriculum for undergraduate degree programs in Information Systems.* Park Ridge (IL): ACM.

Gott, S. P., Hall, E. P., Pokorny, R. A., Dibble, E., & Glaser, R. (1993). A naturalistic study of transfer: adaptive expertise in technical domains. In D. K. Detterman & R. J. Sternberg (Eds.), *Transfer on Trial: intelligence, cognition and instruction* (pp. 258-288). Norwood (NJ): Ablex.

Gotterbarn, D. (2001). Views expressed during tutorial: Software Engineering Ethics Training in Industry and Academe: Professionalism and the Software Engineering

Code of Ethics, organised by Gotterbarn, D. and Miller, K. at Fourteenth Conference on Software Engineering Education & Training, February 19-21, 2001, Charlotte, North Carolina. See Gotterbarn and Miller (2001) for details of tutorial.

Gotterbarn, D., & Miller, K. (2001). Tutorial: *Software Engineering Ethics Training in Industry and Academe: Professionalism and the Software Engineering Code of Ethics.* In proceedings of Fourteenth Conference on Software Engineering Education & Training, February 19-21, 2001, Charlotte, North Carolina, (pp. 24). Los Alamitos, CA, IEEE-Computer Society.

Gotterbarn, D., Miller, K., & Rogerson, S. (1999). Computer Society and ACM Approve Software Engineering Code of Ethics, *Computer*, October, (pp. 84-88).

Granger, M. J., Currie Little, J., Adams, E. S., Björkman, C., Gotterbarn, D., Juettner, D.D., et al, (1997). *Using information technology to integrate social and ethical issues into the computer science and information systems curriculum.* Report of the Iticse '97 Working Group on Social and Ethical Issue in Computing Curricula, in supplemental proceedings SIGSE/SIGCUE ITiCSE'97, (pp. 38 – 50). New York: ACM Press,

Grant, D. (2000) Undergraduate Software Engineering Degrees in Australia, *Proceedings of CSEE&T 2000*, 308-309

Grant, S. (2006). Frameworks of competence: common or specific. Paper presented at *TenCompetence Workshop on Learning Networks for Lifelong Competence Development*, March 20-21, 2006, Sofia, Bulgaria. Retrieved September 29, 2007 from http://hdl.handle.net/1820/836

Grisham, P. S., Krasner, H., & Perry, D. E. (2006). Data engineering education with real-world projects, *ACM SIGCSE Bulletin, 38*(2), pp. 64-68.

Groth, D. P., & Robertson, E. L. (2001). It's all about process: Project-oriented teaching of software engineering. In D. Ramsey, P. Bourque & R. Dupuis (Eds.), *Proceedings of the fourteenth conference on software engineering education and training* (pp. 7-17). Charlotte, NC, USA: IEEE.

Grützner, I. & Bunse, C. (2002). Teaching Object-Oriented Design with UML - A Blended Learning Approach. *Proceedings of the Sixth Workshop on Pedagogies and Tools for Learning Object-Oriented Concepts.* Held in conjunction with 16th European Conference for Object-Oriented Programming (ECOOP 2002), Malaga, Spain.

Grützner, I., Steinbach-Nordmann, S., Ochs, M. & Bunse, C. (2003). Der Baukasten Objektorientierte Software-Entwicklung: Berufliche Weiterbildung in der Software-Industrie. *Proceedings of the 6th International Conference on Information Management (Wirtschaftsinformatik).* Dresden, Germany (In German).

Grützner, I., Thomas, L., & Steinbach-Nordmann, S. (2006). Building re-configurable multilingual training media. *Proceedings of the IV International Conference on Multimedia and ICTs in Education m-ICTE 2006 "Current Developments in Technology-Asissted Education".* Seville, Spain, Vol. 3.

Guide to the Software Engineering Body of Knowledge (2004), Bourque, P. and Dupuis, R., (Eds.), Los Alamitos, CA, IEEE Computer Society Press.

Guilford, J. P. (1967). *The Nature of Human Intelligence.* New York: McGraw-Hill.

Guindon, R. (1989). The process of knowledge discovery in system design. In G. Salvendy & M. J. Smith (Eds.), *Designing and Using Human-Computer Interfaces and Knowledge Based Systems* (pp. 727-734). Amsterdam: Elsevier.

Guindon, R. (1990). Knowledge exploited by experts during software systems design. *International Journal of Man-Machine Studies, 33*, 279-304.

Habermas, J. (1972). *Theory and Practice* (V. J, Trans.). London: Heinemman.

Halling, M., Zuser, W., Kohle, M., & Biffl, S. (2002). Teaching the unified process to undergraduate students. In M. McCracken, M. Lutz & T. C. Lethbridge (Eds.), *Proceedings of the fifteenth conference on software engineering education and training* (pp. 148-159). Covington, KY, USA: IEEE.

Hanna, M. (1993). Maintenance burden begging for a remedy. *Datamation*, April, 53-63.

Hannafin, M. J. (1997). *The case for grounded learning systems design: what the literature suggests about effective teaching learning and technology.* Paper presented at the Proceedings of ASCILITE '97, Perth.

Hayes, J. H. (2002). Energizing software engineering education through real-world projects as experimental studies. In M. McCracken, M. Lutz & T. C. Lethbridge (Eds.), *Proceedings of the fifteenth conference on software engineering education and training* (pp. 192-206). Covington, KY: IEEE.

Hazeyama, A. (2005). State of the Survey on Team-based Software Engineering Project Course. *Proceedings of the 17th International Conference on Software Engineering and Knowledge Engineering, SEKE 2005,* pp. 430-435.

Hazzan, O. (2002). The reflective practitioner perspective in software engineering education, *The Journal of Systems and Software* **63**(3), pp. 161-171.

Hecht, H., & Hecht, M. (2000). How reliable are requirements for reliable software? *Software Tech News, 3*(4). Retrieved May 31, 2007 from http://www.softwaretechnews.com

Hecker, D. E. (2005). Occupational employment projections to 2014, Monthly Labor Review, Bureau of Labor Statistics, *128*(11), November 2005. Available: http://www.bls.gov/opub/mlr/2005/11/contents.htm

Heidecke, F., Mayrhofer, D., Schiesser, A. & Back, A. (2007). Organisation des Außendiensttrainings in der Pharma-Branche: Entwicklung eines Referenzmodells mittels Fallstudienforschung. In Breitner, M. H., Bruns, B. & Lehner, F. (eds.). *Neue Trends im E-Learning: Aspekte der Betriebswirtschaftslehre und Informatik.* Heidelberg: Physica (in German).

Heitmeyer, C., & Bharadwaj, R. (2000). Applying the SCR requirements method to the light control case study. *Journal of Universal Computer Science, 6*(7), 650-678.

Henderson, P., Linos, P., & Tinsley, E. (2003). *Crafting an Undergraduate Software Engineering Program in a Liberal Arts Environment.* Unpublished extended abstract, Butler University, Indianapolis, IN.

Hesse-Biber, S. N., & Leavy, P. (2005). Qualitative Research Inquiry. In *The Practice of Qualitative Research.* Sage.

Hiburn, T., Towhidnejad, M., Nangia, S., & Shen, L. (2006). A Case Study Project for Software Eductaion, *Proceedings FIE 2006*, M1F1-M1F5.

Hilburn, T. (1999). PSP metrics in support of software engineering education. In H. Saiedian (Ed.), *Proceedings of the twelfth conference on software engineering education and training* (pp. 135-136). New Orleans, LA, USA: IEEE.

Hilburn, T., & Humphrey, W. (2002, Sept/Oct). Teaching Teamwork. *IEEE Software 19(5),* 72-77.

Hilburn, T., & Humphrey, W. (2002, Sept/Oct). Teaching Teamwork. *IEEE Software 19(5),* 72-77.

Hislop, G. W. (2006). Scaffolding student work in capstone design courses. *36th ASEE/IEEE Frontiers in Education Conference* (pp. T1A1-T1A4). San Diego, CA.

Hislop, G. W., Lutz, M. J., & Sebern, M. J. (2006). Sharing Software Engineering Curriculum Materials. *Proceedings, ASEE 2006.*

Hogan, J. M., Smith, G., & Thomas, R. (2005). Tight spirals and industry clients: The modern SE education experience. In *Proceedings of the 7th Australasian Conference on Computing Education - Volume 42* (pp. 217-222). A. Young & D. Tolhurst (Eds.), ACM International Conference Proceeding Series, vol. 106. Australian Computer Society, Darlinghurst, Australia.

Höhle, J., Cho, K., 2000. Distance Learning and Exchange of Scientific Knowledge via Internet. *International Archives of Photogrammetry and Remote Sensing.* Amsterdam, Holland, Vol. XXXIII, Part B6. pp. 337-340.

Holt, J., & Solomon, F. (1996). Engineering Education - the way ahead. *Australasian Journal of Engineering Education,, 7*(1), 1-22; 83-98.

Honiden, S., Tahara, Y., Yoshioka, N., Taguchi, K., & Washizaki, H. (2007). Top SE: Educating superarchitects who can apply software engineering tools to practical development in Japan. In *Proceedings of 29th International Conference on Software Engineering (ICSE'07)* (pp. 708-718). New York, NY: IEEE Computer Society.

HRK (2007): Hochschulkompass der HRK (Hochschulrektorenkonferenz). http://www.hochschulkompass.de/

http://www.cet.sunderland.ac.uk/seis/icse-2001workshop/IFIPharmonisationDraft1998.html Also available as an appendix to the paper *Evaluations of IFIP's Proposed Standards for Professionals* (Thompson, 2005), and from

http://www.ifip.or.at/minutes/C99/C99_harmonization.htm

Hughes, C. (2006). IT comes of age – professionalism in the industry. *The British Computer Society Annual Review 2006*, (pp.12-13), Swindon: British Computer Society.

Humphrey W.S. (1997). *Introduction to the Personal Software Process*. Boston: Addison-Wesley.

Humphrey W.S. (1997). *Introduction to the Personal Software Process*. Boston: Addison-Wesley.

Humphrey W.S. (2000). *Introduction to the Team Software Process*. Boston: Addison-Wesley.

Humphrey W.S. (2000). *Introduction to the Team Software Process*. Boston: Addison-Wesley.

Humphrey, W. (1999) *Introduction to the Team Software Process*, Addison Wesley

Humphrey, W. (2005) . *A Discipline of Software Engineering*, Second Edition, Addison Wesley.

IEEE Computer Society (2001). *The Certified Software Development Professional Program*, Available at http://www.computer.org/portal/pages/ieeecs/education/certification.

IEEE CS and ACM Joint Task Force on Computing Curricula (2004): Software Engineering 2004, Curriculum Guidelines for Undergraduate Degree Programs in Software Engineering. August 23, 2004.

IEEE Software Engineering Standards Central (2007). *Software Engineering Standards Overview*. Available: http://standards.ieee.org/software/overview.html

IEEE-CS & ACM (2004). *Software Engineering 2004, Curriculum Guidelines for Undergraduate degree Programs in Software Engineering*. Published by IEEE-CS, and accessible from the education web-site for the ACM: http://www.acm.org/education/

IFIP OECD WITSA (2002). Joint Working Conference "Meeting Global IT Skills Needs – The Role of Professionalism", October, 25-27, 2002, Woking, UK, retrieved February 1, 2005, from http://www.globalitskills.org/

Iivari, J. (1991). A paradigmatic analysis of contemporary schools of IS development. *European Journal of Information Systems, 1*(4), 249-272.

Information-Technology Promotion Agency. (2004). *Japan Information-Technology Engineers Examination Handbook*. Tokyo, Japan: Japan Information-Technology Engineers Examination Center.

Institute for Electrical and Electronic Engineers Computer Society (1998). *IEEE Recommended Practice for Software Requirements Specifications*. (IEEE standard 830-1998). New York, NY.

Institute for Electrical and Electronic Engineers Computer Society (2004), *Guide to the Software Engineering Body of Knowledge (SWEBOK)*. Los Alamitos, CA.

Institute for Electrical and Electronic Engineers Computer Society (1998). *IEEE Recommended Practice for Software Requirements Specifications*. (IEEE standard 830-1998). New York, NY.

Institute for Electrical and Electronic Engineers Computer Society (2004), *Guide to the Software Engineering Body of Knowledge (SWEBOK)*. Los Alamitos, CA.

International Organization for Standardization. (2003). *ISO/IEC 17024: Conformity assessment – general requirements for bodies operating certification of persons*. Geneva, Switzerland: ISO Copyright Office.

Jackson, M. (1999): Specializing in Software Engineering. IEEE Software, Vol. 16, No. 6, 119-121.

Jain, A. & Boehm, B. (2006). SimVBSE: Developing a Game for Value-Based Software Engineering. *Proceedings of the Nineteenth Conference on Software Engineering Education & Training*. Turtle Bay, Hawaii.

Jessup, E., Sumner, T., & Barker, L. (2006). Report from the trenches: Bringing more women to the study of computer science. Manuscript submitted for publication. Available: http://www.cs.colorado.edu/~jessup/SUB-PAGES/PS/trenches.pdf

Johnson, A., Powers, C., & Wagert, S. (1989). EMCS implementation by IBM Advanced Workstation division. *Proceedings of GUIDE 75, Los Angeles, CA. Joint IEEE Computer Society/ACM Task Force on the "Model Curricula for Computing"*. Also available as IBM Technical Report TR51.0554, November, 1989.

Johnson, R. R. (1998). *User-Centered Technology: A Rhetorical Theory for Computers and Other Mundane Artifacts*. SUNY Press.

Johnson-Eiola, J. (2001). Little Machines: Understanding Users; Understanding Interfaces. *ACM Journal of Computer Documentation, 25*, 119-127.

Joint IEEE Computer Society/ACM Task Force on the "Model Curricula for Computing" (2005). *Computing Curricula Series*. Available: http://www.acm.org/education/curricula.html

Joint Task Force on Computing Curricula. (2004). *Software Engineering 2004: Curriculum Guidelines for Undergraduate Degree Programs in Software Engineering*. IEEE Computer Society and Association for Computing Machinery.

Joint Taskforce for Computing Curricula (JTCC) 2004. (2004). *Software Engineering 2004: Curricular Guidelines for Undergraduate Programs in Software Engineering*. New York, NY: ACM and IEEE.

Joint Taskforce for Computing Curricula (JTCC) 2005. (2005). *Computing curricula 2005: The overview report*. New York, NY: ACM and IEEE.

Jones, C. (2003). Variations in Software Development Practices. *IEEE Software*, 20(6), 22-27.

Jones, C. (2005). *Software quality in 2005: A survey of the state of the art*. Marlborough, MA: Software Productivity Research.

Jones, S. & Northrop, M. (2006a). Blended Learning: the practicalities of implementation in a UK University. *Proceedings of the IV International Conference on Multimedia and ICTs in Education m-ICTE 2006 "Current Developments in Technology-Asissted Education"*. Seville, Spain, Vol. 3.

Jones, S. & Northrop, M. (2006b). Implementation of a Blended Learning approach: Milestones, tractors and Crossroads. *Proceedings of the IV International Conference on Multimedia and ICTs in Education m-ICTE 2006 "Current Developments in Technology-Asissted Education"*. Seville, Spain, Vol. 3.

Kadolph, S. J. (2005). Equipment experts: Enhancing student learning in textile science. Clothing & Textiles Research Journal, 23(4), 368-374.

Kaufmann, R., & Janzen, D. (2003). *Implications of test-driven development: a pilot study*. Paper presented at 18th annual ACM SIGPLAN conference on Object-oriented programming, systems, languages, and applications (OOPSLA 2003), Anaheim, CA, 2003.

Kawakita, J. (1982). *The Original KJ Method* (English). Tokyo: Kawakita Research Institute.

Kawakita, J. (1982). *The Original KJ Method* (English). Tokyo: Kawakita Research Institute.

Keil, M., Cule, P. E., Lyytinen, K., & Schmidt, R. C. (1998). A framework for identifying software project risks. *Communications of the ACM, 41*(1), 76-83.

Keirsey, D., & Bates, M. (1984). *Please Understand Me* (3 ed.): Prometheus Nemesis Book Company.

Keller, J. M. (1983). Motivational design of instruction. In C. M. Reigeluth (Ed.), *Instructional design theories and models: An overview of their current status*. Hillsdale, NJ: Erlbaum.

Kelley, R. E. (1999). How to be a Star Engineer, *IEEE Spectrum*. 36(10), 51-58.

Kerth, N. (2001). *Project Retrospectives: A Handbook for Team Reviews*, Dorset House Publishing Company.

Kirsch, G., & Sullivan, P. (1992). *Methods and Methodology in Composition Research*. Southern Illinois University Press.

Kirschner, P. A., Sweller, J., & Clark, R. E. (2006). Why minimal guidance during instruction does not work: An analysis of the failure of constructivist, discovery, problem-based, experiential, and inquiry-based teaching. *Educational Psychologist, 41*(2), 75-86.

Klappholz, D., Almstrum, V. L., & Modesitt, K. (2006, April). Workshop on real projects for real clients courses. *19th Conference on Software Engineering and Training*, Oahu, HI.

Klein, J. T. (1990). *Interdisciplinarity*. Wayne University Press.

Klemola, T., & Rilling, J. (2002). *Modeling comprehension processes in software development*. Paper presented at the Proceedings of the first IEEE Conference on Cognitive Informatics (ICCI'02), Calgary (Canada).

Knight, J. & Leveson, N. (2002). Should Software Engineers be Licensed? *Communications of the ACM*. 45(11), 87-90. New York: ACM Press.

Knoke, P. J. (1998). *Graduate SE Program Survey Results And Evaluation*, Forum for Advancing Software engineering Education (FASE), Vol. 8, No. 9. (electronic newsletter) <http://www.cs.ttu.edu/fase/v8n09.txt>

Knowles, M. (1984). *Andragogy in action: Applying modern principles of adult education*. San Francisco, CA: Jossey Bass.

Kolb, D. A. (1984). *Experiential Learning Experience as the Source of Learning and Development,* : Prentice-Hall.

Kolb, D. A. (1984). *Experiential learning: Experiences as the source of learning and development*. Englewood Cliffs, NJ, USA: Prentice-Hall International, Inc.

Kolb, D. A. (1995). *Learning style inventory: technical specifications*. Boston: McBer & Company.

Kolikant, Y. B. (2001). Gardeners and cinema tickets: High school students' preconceptions of concurrency. *Computer Science Education, 11*(3), 221-245.

Konieczka, S. (2003). Predictable releases: The key to quality software. Boulder, CO: SCM Labs, Inc. Retrieved November 1, 2007 from http://www.stickyminds.com/

Koppelman, H., & van Dijk, B. (2006). Creating a realistic context for team projects in HCI, *Proceedings of the 11th Annual SIGCSE Conference on Innovation and Technology in Computer Science Education* (pp. 58-62). Bologna, Italy.

Kornecki, A. J. (2000). Real-time computing in software engineering education. In S. A. Mengel & P. J. Knoke (Eds.), *Proceedings of the thirteenth conference on software engineering education and training* (pp. 197-198). Austin, TX, USA: IEEE.

Kornecki, A. J., Khajenoori, S., & Gluch, D. (2003). On a partnership between software industry and academia. In P. J. Knoke, A. Moreno & M. Ryan (Eds.), *Proceedings of the sixteenth conference on software engineering education and training* (pp. 60-69). Madrid, Spain: IEEE.

Kruchten, P. (2000). *The Rational Unified Process – An Introduction (2ⁿᵈ ed.)*. Boston: Addison-Wesley.

Kruchten, P. (2000). *The Rational Unified Process – An Introduction (2ⁿᵈ ed.)*. Boston: Addison-Wesley.

Kuehl, C. S. (2001, October). *Improving system requirements quality through application of an operational concept process: An essential element in system sustainment*. Paper presented at NDIA 4th Annual Systems Engineering Conference, Dallas, TX. Retrieved November 2, 2007 from http://www.dtic.mil/ndia

Kumar, R. L. (2002). Managing risks in IT projects: An options perspective. *Information & Management, 40*(1), 63-74.

Kurtz, B. L., Fenwick, J. B., Ellsworth, C. C., Yuan, X., Steele, A., & Jia, X. (2007). Inter-university software engineering using web services. *ACM SIGCSE Bulletin inroads, 39*(1). 464-468.

Langford, D. (1996). *Can A Software Engineer Afford to be Ethical?*, Proceedings of the conference: Professional Awareness in Software Engineering (PASE'96), February 1-2, 1996, London. The conference papers were later published as edited chapters in the text: Myers C., Hall T. and Pitt D, (Eds.), (1997), *The Responsible Software Engineer*, London, Springer-Verlag.

Last, M., Almstrum, V., Erickson, C., Klein, B., & Daniels, M. (2000, June). An international student/faculty collaboration: The Runestone project. *ACM SIGCSE Bulletin inroads. 32*(3). 128-131.

Last, M., Hause, L., Daniels, M., & Woodroffe, M. (2002). Learning from Students: Continuous Improvement in International Collaboration. *Proceedings of the Conference Integrating Technology into Computer Science Education, ITiCSE 2002.* ACM Press, New York, NY, pp. 136-140.

Lauer, J. M., & Asher, W. (1988). *Composition Research/ Empirical Designs*. Oxford University Press.

Lauesen, S., & Vinter, O. (2001). Preventing requirement defects: An experiment in process improvement. *Requirements Engineering, 6*(1), 37-50.

Lave, J. (1988). *Cognition in practice: Mind, mathematics, and culture in everyday life*. Cambridge, UK: Cambridge University Press.

Lave, J., & Wenger, E. (1991). *Situated Learning: Legitimate Peripheral Participation.* Cambridge University Press.

LeBlanc, R., & Sobel, A. (2004). Software Engineering 2004 Curriculum Guidelines for Undergraduate Degree Programs in *Software Engineering*, ACM, 2004. Retrieved December 18, 2007 from http://sites.computer. org/ccse/.

LeBlanc, R., & Sobel, A. E. K. (Eds.). (2004). *Software Engineering 2004: curriculum guidelines for undergraduate degree programs in Software Engineering.* Los Alamitos (CA): IEEE Computer Society Press.

Lee, D. M. S. (1999a). Knowledge/skill requirements and professional development of IS/IT workers: a summary of empirical findings from two studies. In *Panel on Workforce Needs in Information Technology, Computer Science and Telecommunications Board, National Academy of Sciences.* Milwaukee (WI).

Lee, D. M. S. (2004). Organizational entry and transition from academic study: examining a critical step in the professional development of young IS workers. In M. Igbaria & C. Shayo (Eds.), *Strategies for Managing IS/IT Personnel* (pp. 113-141). Hershey (PA): Idea Group.

Leffingwell, D. & Widrig, D. (2003). *Managing Software Requirements: A Use Case Approach (2nd ed.).* Boston: Addison-Wesley.

Leffingwell, D. & Widrig, D. (2003). *Managing Software Requirements: A Use Case Approach (2nd ed.).* Boston: Addison-Wesley.

Lethbridge, T. (2000) What Knowledge is Important to a Software Professional?, *IEEE Computer*, 33(5), 44-50.

Lethbridge, T. C. (2000). What knowledge is important to a software professional? *IEEE Computer, 33*(5), 44-50.

Lethbridge, T. C., Diaz-Herrera, J., LeBlanc, R. J., & Thompson, J. B. (2007). Improving software practice through education: Challenges and future trends. *In 2007 Future of Software Engineering. International Conference on Software Engineering.* pp. 12-28. Piscataway, NJ: IEEE CS Press.

Lethbridge, T., Diaz-Herrera, J., LeBlanc, R., and Thompson, J.B. (2007). Improving software practice through education: Challenges and future trends. Proceedings of FOSE'07: *Future of Software Engineering*, special track at ICSE'07: *The 29th International Conference on Software Engineering.* Minneapolis, MN.

Lethbridge, T., Diaz-Herrera, J., LeBlanc, R., and Thompson, J.B. (2007). Improving software practice through education: Challenges and future trends. Proceedings of FOSE'07: *Future of Software Engineering*, special track at ICSE'07: *The 29th International Conference on Software Engineering.* Minneapolis, MN.

Linger, R. C., Mead, N. R., & Lipson, H. F. (1998). Requirements definition for survivable systems. In *Third International Conference on Requirements Engineering* (pp. 14-23). Los Alamitos, CA: IEEE Computer Society.

Linn, R. L. (Ed.). (1989). *Educational Measurement* (3rd ed.). New York: American Council on Education and Macmillan Publishing.

Liu, C. (2005). *Using issue tracking tools to facilitate student learning of communication skills in software engineering courses.* Paper presented at the Conference on Software Engineering Education & Training.

LTSN. (2002). *Constructive alignment and why it is important to the learner,* from http://www.ltsneng.ac.uk/er/theory/constructivealignment.asp

Lubars, M., Potts, C., & Richer, C. (1993). *A review of the state of the practice in requirements modeling.* Paper presented at the International Symposium on Requirements Engineering, San Diego.

Ludewig, J., H. Lichter (2007): Software Engineering – Grundlagen, Menschen, Prozesse, Techniken. dpunkt. verlag Heidelberg.

Ludewig, J., R. Reißing (1998): *Teaching what they need instead of teaching what we like* – the new Software Engineering curriculum at the University of Stuttgart. Information and Software Technology 40 (4), 239 - 244.

Lui, K.M., & Chan, K. C.C. (2003). When Does a Pair Outperform Two Individuals?, *Lecture Notes in Computer Science*, Volume 2675, 225–233.

Lumsdaine, M., & Lumsdaine, E. (1995). Thinking preferences of engineering students: implications for curriculum restructuring. *Journal of Engineering Education, 84*(2), 193-204.

Lutz, B. (2007). Training for Global Software Development in an International "Learning Network". *Proceedings of the International Conference on Global Software Engineering (ICGSE 2007)*. Munich, Germany.

Lutz, M. J. & Naveda, J. F. (1997). The Road Less Traveled: A Baccalaureate Degree In Software Engineering.

Proceedings, SIGCSE Technical Symposium. p. 287-291. New York: ACM Press.

Lutz, M.J., Hilburn, T.B., Hislop, G., McCraken, M., & Sebern, M. (2003) The SWENET Project: bridging the gap from bodies of knowledge to curriculum development, *Proceedings FIE 2003*, vol.3, S3C-7.

Mackinnon, T., Freeman, S., & Craig, P. (2000). *Endo-Testing: Unit Testing with Mock Objects.* Presented at eXtreme Programming and Flexible Processes in Software Engineering - XP2000.

Mahn, A., et al. (1999): Empfehlungen der Gesellschaft für Informatik e.V. zur Stärkung der Anwendungsorientierung in Diplom-Studiengängen der Informatik an Universitäten, Informatik- Spektrum 22, 444-448.

Mahoney, M.S. (2004) Finding a History for Software Engineering. *IEEE Annals of the History of Computing.* p. 8-19. Piscataway, NJ: IEEE CS Press.

Maiden, N. A. M., & Gizikis, A. (2001). Where do requirements come from? *IEEE Software, 18*(5), 10-12.

Maiden, N. A. M., & Sutcliffe, A. G. (1992). Exploiting reusable specifications through analogy. *Communications of the ACM, 34*(5), 55-64.

Maner, W. (ud). *Interactive Computer Ethics Explorer (ICEE).* Web application retrieved February 1, 2004, from http://www.cs.bgsu.edu/maner/xxicee/html/welcome.htm

Mann, J. (1996). *The Role of Project Escalation in Explaining Runaway Information Systems Development Projects: A Field Study.* Georgia State University.

Margolis, J., & Fisher, A. (2001). *Unlocking the clubhouse: Women in computing.* Cambridge, MA: MIT Press.

Margolis, J., & Fisher, A. (2002). *Unlocking the Clubhouse: Women in Computing.* MIT Press.

McCalla, G. (2002). Software Engineering Requires Individual Professionalism. *Communications of the ACM.* 45(11), 98-101. New York: ACM Press.

McConnell, S. (2004). *Code Complete 2 (2nd ed).* Redmond WA: Microsoft Press.

McConnell, S., & Tripp, L. (1999). Professional Software Engineering: Fact or Fiction? *IEEE Software,* 16(6), 13-18.

McDonald, J. (2000). Teaching Software Project Management in Industrial and Academic Environments, *Proceedings of CSEE&T,* 151-160.

McDowell, C., Werner, L., Bullock, H., & Fernald, J. (2002). *The Effects of Pair-Programming on Performance in an Introductory Programming Course.* Presented at 33rd SIGCSE technical symposium on Computer science education. 2002, 38-42.

McDowell, C., Werner, L., Bullock, H., & Fernald, J. (2003). *The impact of pair programming on student Performance, perception and persistence.* Presented at Int.Conf. on Software Engineering (ICSE2003), 2003, 602-607.

McGibbon, T. (1999). *A business case for software process improvement revised.* Washington, DC: DoD Data Analysis Center for Software (DACS).

McKeachie, W. J. (1961). Understanding the learning process. *Journal of Engineering Education, 51,* 405-408.

McKim, J. C., & Ellis, H. J. C. (2004). Using a multiple term project to teach object-oriented programming and design. In T. B. Horton & A. E. K. Sobel (Eds.), *Proceedings of the seventeenth conference on software engineering education and training* (pp. 59-64). Norfolk, VA: IEEE.

McMillan, J. H. (2001). *Essential assessment concepts for teachers and administrators.* Thousand Oaks, CA: Corwin Press.

McMillan, W. W., & Rajaprabhakaran, S. (1999). *What leading practitioners say should be emphasized in students' software engineering projects.* Paper presented at the Conference on Software Engineering Education & Training.

Mead, N. R. (2003) *Requirements Engineering for Survivable Systems* (Tech. Rep. No. CMU/SEI-2003-TN-013). Pittsburgh, PA: Software Engineering Institute, Carnegie Mellon University. Retrieved November 2, 2007 from http://www.sei.cmu.edu/publications/documents/03.reports/03tn013.html

Mead, N. R., & Hough, E. D. (2006). Security requirements engineering for software systems: Case studies in support of software engineering education. In *Proceedings of the 19th Conference on Software Engineering Education and Training* (pp. 149-158). Los Alamitos, CA: IEEE Computer Society Press.

Mead, N. R., & Stehney, T. R. II. (2005b, May). *Security quality requirements engineering (SQUARE) methodology.* Paper presented at the meeting of the Software Engineering for Secure Systems (SESS05), ICSE 2005 International Workshop on Requirements for High Assurance Systems, St. Louis, MO.

Mead, N. R., Hough, E. D., & Stehney, T. R. II. (2005a). *Security quality requirements (SQUARE) methodology* (Tech. Rep. No. CMU/SEI-2005-TR-009). Pittsburgh, PA: Software Engineering Institute, Carnegie Mellon University. Retrieved November 2, 2007 from http://www.sei.cmu.edu/publications/documents/05.reports/05tr009.html

Melnik, G., & Maurer, F. (2002) *Perceptions of Agile Practices: A Student Survey."* Paper presented at Agile Universe/XP Universe 2002, Chicago, IL, 2002.

Meyer, B. (2001). Software Engineering in the Academy, *Computer,* 34(5), pp. 28-35.

Meyer, J. H. F., & Boulton-Lewis, G. M. (1997). *The association between university students' perceived influences on their learning and their knowledge, experience, and conceptions, of learning.* Paper presented at the Proceedings of the 7th European Conference for Research on Learning and Instruction, Athens.

Michaelsen, L. K. (2002). Getting started with team-based learning. In L. K. Michaelsen, A. B. Knight, & L. D. Fink (Eds.), *Team-based learning: A transformative use of small groups* (pp. 27-50). Westport, CT: Praeger.

Middendorf, J., & Pace, D. (1986). Decoding the disciplines: a model for helping students learn disciplinary ways of thinking. *New Directions for teaching and learning, 98,* 1-12.

Mikulecky, L. (1998). Diversity, discussion, and participation: Comparing a web-based and campus-based adolescent literature classes. *Journal of Adolescent & Adult Literacy, 42*(2), pp. 84-97.

Miller, C. R. (1979). A Humanistic Rationale for Technical Writing. *College English, 40*, 610-617.

Minor, O. (2004). *Theory and Practice in Requirements Engineering: an investigation of curricula and industry needs.* Unpublished Master, University of Koblenz-Landau, Koblenz (Germany).

Mitchell, I,. Juliff, P., & Turner, J. (1998). *Harmonization of Professional Standards.* International Federation of Information Processing, 1998, retrieved February 13, 2001, from

Mitchell, R. L. (2006). How not to get "offshored." *Computerworld Blogs.* March 31, 2006 http://www.computerworld.com/blogs/node/2150

Modesitt, K. (2004, September). The Distributed Development of Software Engineering Professionals. *International Colloquium on Engineering Education.* ASEE and Tsinghua University, Beijing, PRC.

Modesitt, K. (2005, October). W³ – Winning Three Times Over: Industry, University, Society. *ABET Annual Meeting on Accreditation, Innovation, and Improvement,* San Diego, CA, pp. 17-24.

Modesitt, K. (2006). A practical assessment guide to the use of Professional Advisory Boards. *Best Assessment Processes VIII of ABET,* Rose-Hulman Institute of Technology, February 27-28.

Modesitt, K. L., Bagert, D. J., Werth, L. & Knoke, P. J. (2000). *Annual Survey of International Software Engineering Academic Programs - Progress Report Number 2.* Forum for Advancing Software engineering Education (FASE), Vol. 10, No. 11. (electronic newsletter) <http://www.cs.ttu.edu/fase/v10n11.txt>

Modesitt, K., Maxim, B., & Akingbehin, K. (1999). Just in Time Learning in software engineering. *The Journal of Mathematics and Science Teaching. 18*(3). 287-301.

Moffett, J. D., Haley, C. B., & Nuseibeh, B. (2004). *Core Security Requirements Artefacts* (Technical Report 2004/23, ISSN 1744-1986). UK: The Open University. Retrieved November 2, 2007 from http://mcs.open.ac.uk/computing-tr/

Morris, J. (2004). Programming doesn't begin to define computer science. *Pittsburgh Post-Gazette.* July 4, 2004. Retrieved June 6, 2007, from http://www.post-gazette.com/pg/04186/341012.stm

Morsch, L. (2006). *What some fastest-growing jobs pay.* Retrieved January 4, 2008 from http://www.cnn.com/2006/US/Careers/01/26/cb.top.jobs.pay/index.html.

Morsch, L. (2006). *What some fastest-growing jobs pay.* Retrieved January 4, 2008 from http://www.cnn.com/2006/US/Careers/01/26/cb.top.jobs.pay/index.html.

Moss, B. J. (1992). Ethnography and Composition: Studying Language at Home. In G. Kirsch & P. Sullivan (Eds.), *Methods and Methodology in Composition Research.* Southern Illinois University Press.

Mugridge, R. (2003). *Challenges in Teaching Test Driven Development.* Paper presented at XP 2003, Genova, Italy, 2003.

Mühlhäuser, M., Trompler, C., 2002, Digital Lectures Halls Keep Teachers in the Mood and Learners in the Loop. *Proceedings of E-Learn 2002, Montreal, Canada. Association for the Advancement of Computing in Education (AACE).* pp. 714-721.

Muir, C. (2004). Learning Soft Skills at Work: An Interview with Annalee Luhman. *Business Communication Quarterly, 67*(1), 99-101.

Mulder, K. F. (2006). Engineering curricula in Sustainable Development: an evaluation of changes at Delft University of Technology. *European Journal of Engineering Education, 31*(2), 133-144.

Müller, M., & Tichy, W. (2001). *Case study: extreme programming in a university environment.* Paper presented at Software Engineering, 2001. ICSE 2001.

Proceedings of the 23rd International Conference on, Toronto, Ontario, 2001.

Müller, M., & Hagner, O. (2002). Experiment about test-first programming *Software, IEE Proceedings* vol. 149, pp. 131-136.

Myers, C., Hal,l T., & Pitt, D. (1997). *The Responsible Software Engineer : Selected readings in IT Professionalism*. London, Springer-Verlag.

Myers, L. L., & Larson, R. S. (2005). Preparing Students for Early Work Conflicts. *Business Communication Quarterly, 68*, 306-317.

National Association of Colleges and Employers (2007). *Higher Starting Salary Offers Reflect Positive Trend in Job Market for New College Graduates.* Press Release. Retrieved May 28, 2007, from http://www.naceweb.org/press/display.asp?year=2007&prid=256

National Center for Education Statistics (2004). Institute of Education Sciences, U. S. Department of Education. *Digest of Education Statistics, 2004.* Retrieved May 28, 2007, from http://nces.ed.gov/programs/digest/

National Center for Education Statistics (2005). Institute of Education Sciences, U. S. Department of Education. Digest of Education Statistics, 2005. Retrieved May 28, 2007, from http://nces.ed.gov/programs/digest/

National Center for Research on Evaluation, Standards, and Student Testing, Graduate School of Education & Information Studies, UCLA.

National Commission for Certifying Agencies. (2003). *Standards for the Accreditation of Certification Programs*. Washington, DC: National Organization for Competency Assurance.

National Infrastructure Advisory Council (NIAC). (2003). *National strategy to secure cyberspace*. Washington, DC: U.S. Department of Homeland Security.

National Research Center for College and University Admissions (2007). Post-Secondary Planning Survey Analysis, 2007-2008 Edition. Retrieved November 15, 2007, from http://www.nrccua.org/downloads/reports/survey_analysis.pdf

Naur, P. & Randell, B. (Eds.) (1969). *Software engineering: Report of a conference sponsored by the NATO Science Committee,* Garmisch, Germany, 7–11 October 1968, Brussels, Scientific Affairs Division, NATO.

Naur, P. & Randell, B. eds. (1969) *Software Engineering: Report on a Conference Sponsored by the NATO Science Committee, Garmisch, Germany, 7th to 11th October 1968.* Scientific Affairs Division, NATO.

Naur, P., & Randall, B. (eds) (1968). Software Engineering: A report on a Conference Sponsored by the NATO Science Committee, NATO.

Naur, P., Randell, B., & Buxton, J. (Eds.). (1976). *Software Engineering: Concepts and Techniques: Proceedings of the NATO Conferences*, Petrocelli-Charter, New York.

Navarro, E. O. (2005). *A survey of software engineering educational delivery methods and associated learning theories* (Technical Report No. UCI-ISR-05-5). Irvine, CA: University of California, Irvine.

Navarro, E. O. (2006). *SimSE: A software engineering simulation environment for software process education.* Ph.D. Dissertation, University of California, Irvine, Irvine, CA.

Navarro, E. O., & van der Hoek, A. (2005a). Design and evaluation of an educational software process simulation environment and associated model. In T. C. Lethbridge & D. Port (Eds.), *Proceedings of the eighteenth conference on software engineering education and training.* Ottawa, Canada: IEEE.

Navarro, E. O., & van der Hoek, A. (2005b). Scaling up: How thirty-two students collaborated and succeeded in developing a prototype software design environment. In T. C. Lethbridge & D. Port (Eds.), *Proceedings of the eighteenth conference on software engineering education and training.* Ottawa, Canada: IEEE.

Navarro, E. O., & van der Hoek, A. (2007). Comprehensive evaluation of an educational software engineering simulation environment. In H. Edwards & R. Narayanan (Eds.), *Proceedings of the twentieth conference on software engineering education and training.* Dublin, Ireland.

Needham, D. (2005). Interdisciplinary Teams for Software System Development. *Proceedings of the 2005 International Conference on Frontiers in Education: Computer Science & Computer Engineering, FECS 2005*, pp. 10-16.

Newman, Michael. (2002). *Software errors cost U.S. economy $59.5 billion annually*. Gaithersburg, MD: National Institute of Standards and Technology (NIST).

Nguyen, L., & Swatman, P. A. (2000). *Essential and incidental complexity in requirements models.* Paper presented at the Fourth International Conference on Requirements Engineering Education, Schaumburg (Il).

Norman, K. I., & Keating, J. F. (1997). Barriers for Hispanics and American Indians entering science and mathematics: Cultural dilemmas. *Association for the Education of Teachers in Science (AETS) Conference Proceedings* (pp. 448-464). Available: http://www.ed.psu.edu/ci/Journals/97pap22.htm

Nulden, U., & Scheepers, H. (2000). Understanding and learning about escalation: Simulation in action. In *Proceedings of the 3rd process simulation modeling workshop (prosim 2000)*. London, United Kingdom.

Ochs, M., & Pfahl, D. (2002) eLearning Market Potential in the German IT Sector: An explorative Study. Kaiserslautern, Germany: Fraunhofer IESE. Retrieved November 2, 2003 from *http://www.iese.fhg.de/market_survey*.

Ohlsson, L., & Johansson, C. (1995). A practice driven approach to software engineering education. *IEEE Transactions on Education, 38*(3), 291-295.

Oliver, R. W. (2000). *The coming biotech age: The business of bio material*. New York: McGraw-Hill.

Palyagar, B. (2004). A framework for validating process improvements in requirements engineering. Retrieved November 2, 2007 from http://www.ics.mq.edu.au/~bpalyaga/papers/palyagar_b.pdf

Palyagar, B. (2004). Measuring and influencing requirements engineering process quality. In *Proceedings of AWRE 04, 9th Australian Workshop on Requirements Engineering*. Retrieved November 2, 2007 from http://awre2004.cis.unisa.edu.au/

Parnas, D. L. (1999): *Software Engineering Programmes are not Computer Science Programmes*. IEEE Software, Vol. 16, No. 6, 19-30. (Originally published in the Annals of Software Engineering, Vol. 6, April 1999, 19-37)

Parnas, D. L. (2002). Licensing Software Engineers in Canada. *Communications of the ACM.* 45(11), 90-98. New York: ACM Press.

Parnas, D. L., & Clements, P. C. (1986). A rational design process: how and why to fake it. *IEEE Transactions on Software Engineering, 12*(2), 251-257.

Pfahl, D., Klemm, M., & Ruhe, G. (2000). Using system dynamics simulation models for software project management education and training. In *Proceedings of the 3rd process simulation modeling workshop (prosim 2000)*. London, United Kingdom.

Pfleeger, S. L. (1999). Albert Einstein and empirical software engineering. *IEEE Computer, 32*(10), 32-37.

Piaget, J. (1977). Problems of Equilibration. In Appel, M. H and Goldberg, L. S. (1977). *Topics in Cognitive Development, Volume 1: Equilibration: Theory, Research and Application*, Plenum Press, NY, pp. 3-13.

Pickett, J. P. (Ed.). (2004). *The American Heritage Dictionary of the English Language* (4th ed.). Houghton Mifflin.

Polack-Wahl, J. (2006). Lessons Learned From Different Types of Projects in Software Engineering. *Proceedings of the 2006 International Conference on Frontiers in Education: Computer Science & Computer Engineering, FECS 2006*, pp. 258-263.

Poole, W. G. (2003). *The softer side of custom software development: Working with the other players.* Paper presented at the Conference on Software Engineering Education and Training.

Poole, W.G. (2003). The softer side of customer software development: Working with the other players. Proceedings of CSEET'03: The 16th Conference on Software Engineering Education and Training. Madrid, Spain.

Powell, G., Diaz-Perrera, J., & Turner, D. (1997). Achieving Synergy in Collaborative Education. *IEEE Software*, Nov/Dec, 58-65.

President's Information Technology Advisory Committee (PITAC). (2005). *Cybersecurity: A crisis of prioritization*. Arlington, VA: Executive Office of the President, National Coordination Office for Information Technology Research and Development.

Pressman, R. S. (2005). *Software engineering: A practitioner's approach*. (6th ed.). New York: McGraw-Hill.

Putnam, L. L., & Folger, J. P. (1988). Communication, Conflict, and Dispute Resolution: The Study of Interaction and the Development of Conflict Theory. *Communication Research, 15*, 349-359.

Putnam, L. L., & Poole, M. S. (1987). Conflict and Negotiation. In F. M. Jablin, L. L. Putnam, K. H. Roberts & L. W. Porter (Eds.), *Handbook of Organizational Communication: An Interdisciplinary Perspective* (pp. 549-599).

Quinn, B., Barroca, L., Nuseibeh, B., Fernandez-Ramil, J., Rapanotti, L., Thomas, P., & Wermelinger, M. (2006) Learning Software Engineering at a Distance, IEEE Software, November/December, 36-43.

Redwine, S. T. (Ed.). (2006). *Software assurance: A guide to the common body of knowledge to produce, acquire and sustain secure software, version 1.1*. Washington, DC: U.S. Department of Homeland Security

Reeves, T. C. (1994). *Evaluating what really matters in computer-based education*, from http://www.medicine.mcgill.ca/ibroedu/review/Reeves Evaluating What Really Matters in Computer-Based Education.htm

Regnell, B., & Beremark, P. (1998). A market driven requirements engineering process – Results from industrial process improvement program. Retrieved November 2, 2007 from http://www.tts.lth.se/Personal/bjornr/Papers/CEIRE98-REJ.pdf

Reichlmayr, T. (2003). *The agile approach in an undergraduate software engineering course project*. Paper presented at Frontiers in Education, 2003. FIE 2003. 33rd Annual, Boulder, CO, 2003.

Reigeluth, C. M. (1997). Instructional theory, practitioner needs and new directions: some reflections. *Educational Technology, 37*(1), 42-47.

Reigeluth, C. M., & Rodgers, C. A. (1980). The elaboration theory of instruction: Prescriptions for task analysis and design. *NSPI Journal, 19*, 16-26.

Reinsch, L. N., & Shelby, A. N. (1997). What Communication Abilities Do Practitioners Need? *Business Communication Quarterly, 60*(4), 7-29.

Robillard, P, Krutchen, P., & d'Astous, P. (2001) YOOPEEDOO (UPEDU): A Process for Teaching Software Process, *Proceedings of CSEE&T 2001*, 18-26

Robillard, P. N. (1999). The role of knowledge in software development. *Communications of the ACM, 42*(1), 87-92.

Roblyer, M. D. (2005). *Integrating educational technology into teaching* (4th ed.). Upper Saddle River, NJ: Prentice Hall.

Rosca D. (2000). An Active/Collaborative Approach in Teaching Requirements Engineering, *Proceedings of FIE'00*, T2C9-12

Rosca, D., Li, C, Moore, K., Stephan, M., & Weiner, S. (2001) PSP-EAT – Enhancing a Personal Software Process Course, *Proceedings of FIE'01*, T2D18

Rossett, A. & Vaughan Frazee, R. (2006). Blended Learning Opportunities. AMA Special Report. Retrieved October 24, 2007, from *http://www.amanet.org/blended/pdf/WhitePaper_BlendLearn.pdf*.

Rothman, R., Slattery, J. B., Vranek, J. L., & Resnick, L. B. (2002). *Benchmarking and Alignment of Standards and Testing* (CSE Report No. 566). Los Angeles: Center for the Study of Evaluation,

Royal Academy of Engineering (2004). *The Challenges of Complex IT Projects*. Report of a working group from The Royal Academy of Engineering and The British Computer Society, 2004, retrieved October 12, 2006, from http://www.bcs.org/upload/pdf/complexity.pdf

Royce, W. W. (1970). *Managing the development of large software systems: concepts and techniques.* Paper presented at the IEEE WESCON.

Sawyer, P., & Kotonya, G. (2000). *SWEBOK: software requirements engineering knowledge area description* (Version 0.6 ed.): IEEE Computer Society/ACM.

Sawyer, P., Sommerville, I., & Viller, S. (1997). Requirements process improvement through the phased introduction of good practice. *Software Process Improvement and Practice, 3*(1), 19-34.

Schank, R. C. (1997). *Virtual learning.* New York, NY, USA: McGraw-Hill.

Schmuck, R. A., & Schmuck, P. A. (1997). *Group processes in the classroom* (7th ed.). Madison, WI: Brown & Benchmark.

Schön, D. (1987). *Educating the reflective practitioner.* San Francisco, CA, USA: Jossey-Bass.

Schön, D. A. (1983). *The Reflective Practitioner*, BasicBooks.

Schön, D. A. (1983). *The Reflective Practitioner: How Professionals Think in Action.* New York: Basic Books.

Schön, D. A. (1987). *Educating the Reflective Practitioner: Towards a New Design for Teaching and Learning in The Profession*, San Francisco: Jossey-Bass.

Schuhmann, A. (1992). Learning to teach Hispanic students. In M. Dilworth (Ed.), *Diversity in teacher education – New expectations* (pp. 93-111). San Francisco: Jossey-Bass.

Schultz, B., & Anderson, J. (1984). Training in the Management of Conflict: A Communication Theory Perspective. *Small Group Behavior, 15*, 333-348.

Scott, G., & Yates, W. (2002). Using successful graduates to improve the quality of undergraduate engineering programs. *European Journal of Engineering Education, 27*(4), 60-67.

Scott, T., Bisland, R., Tiehenor, L., & Cross, J. (1994). Team Dynamics in Student Programming Projects. *SIGCSEBulletin* 26(1), pp. 111-115.

Sebern, M. (2002). The Software Development Laboratory: Incorporating industrial practice in an academic environment. Proceedings of CSEET'02: *The 15th Conference on Software Engineering Education and Training.* Covington, KY.

Sebern, M. (2002). The Software Development Laboratory: Incorporating industrial practice in an academic environment. Proceedings of CSEET'02: *The 15th Conference on Software Engineering Education and Training.* Covington, KY.

Sebern, M. (2005). Software Process: Applying industrial strength methods in engineering education. Proceedings of ASEE'05: *The National Conference of the American Society for Engineering Education.* Portland, OR.

SECEPP (1999). *Software Engineering Code of Ethics and Professional Practice.* Retrieved April 1, 2006 from http://www.acm.org/serving/se/code.htm Details of the code and its development can also be retrieved from http://csciwww.etsu.edu/gotterbarn/secepp/page.asp?Name=Code

SECEPP (ud). Adopting the Software Engineering Code of Ethics and Professional Practice, details retrieved April 1, 2006, from http://csciwww.etsu.edu/gotterbarn/secepp/

Shackelford, R. (Ed.). (2005). *Computing Curricula 2005: the overview report*: The Joint Task Force for Computing Curricula 2005.

Sharp, H., & Hall, P. (2000). An interactive multimedia software house simulation for postgraduate software engineers. In *Proceedings of the 22nd international conference on software engineering* (pp. 688-691): ACM.

Shaw, M. (1990). Prospects for an emerging discipline of software. *IEEE Software, 7(6),* 15-24.

Shaw, M. (1990). Prospects for an Engineering Discipline of Software. *IEEE Software.* 7(6), 15-24. Piscataway, NJ: IEEE CS Press.

Shaw, M. (2000). *Software Engineering Education: A Roadmap. Proceedings of the Conference on The Future of Software Engineering.* 373-380.

Shaw, M., Software Engineering Education: A Roadmap. *International Conference of Software Engineering - Future of SE Track, ICSE 2000,* pp. 371-380.

Shelly, G. B., Cashman, T. J., & Rosenblatt, H. J. (2008). *Systems analysis and design* (7th ed.). Boston: Thompson Course Technology.

Shoemaker, D., Mead, N. R., Drommi, A., Bailey, J., & Ingalsbe, J. (2007). SWABOK's fit to common curricular standards. In *Proceedings of the 20th Conference on Software Engineering Education and Training.* Los Alamitos, CA: IEEE Computer Society Press.

Shukla, A., & Williams, L. (2002). *Adapting extreme programming for a core software engineering course.* Paper presented at 15th Conference on Software Engineering Education and Training, 2002. (CSEE&T 2002), Covington, KY, 2002.

Shuman, L. J., Besterfield-Sacre, M., & McGourty, J. (2005). ABET "professional skills" – Can they be taught? Can they be assessed? *The Journal of Engineering Education,* January 2005. Available: http://www.findarticles.com/p/articles/mi_qa3886/is_200501/ai_n9521126

Simmons, D. (2006). Software Engineering Education in the New Millennium. *Proceedings of 30th Annual International Computer Software and Applications Conference, COMPSAC 2006,* pp. 46-47.

Sindre, G., & Opdahl, A. (2000). Eliciting security requirements by misuse cases. In *Proceedings of TOOLS Pacific 2000* (pp. 120-130). Los Alamitos, CA: IEEE Computer Society Press.

Singh, H. & Reed, C. (2001) *Achieving Success with Blended Learning.* Technical Report, Centra Software, 2001, Retrieved January 21, 2008, from: http://www.centra.com/download/whitepapers/blendedlearning.pdf

Singh, H. (2003). Building Effective Blended Learning Programs. *Journal on Educational Technology, 43* (6), pp. 51-54.

Sitaraman, M., Long, T.J., Weide, B.W., Harner, E.J. & Wang, L. (2001). *A formal approach to component-based software engineering education and evaluation.* Paper

presented at 23rd International Conference on Software Engineering. ICSE 2001.

Skills Framework for the Information Age. (2005). London, UK: *SFIA framework reference, version 3.* SFIA Foundation.

Slavin, R. E. (2005). *Educational psychology: Theory and practice* (8th ed.). Boston: Allyn and Bacon.

Smith, J. P., diSessa, A. A. and Roschelle, J. (1993). Misconceptions reconceived: A constructivist analysis of knowledge in transition, *The Journal of the Learning Sciences 3,* pp. 115-163.

Sobel, A. E. K., Bagert, D. J., Frezza, S. T., & Pavlov, V. L. (2007, October). Panel - *Assessing The Impact of the SE2004 Curriculum Guidelines,* presented at the Frontiers in Education Conference (FIE'07), Milwaukee, WI.

Software Engineering Body of Knowledge. (2004). Retrieved February 4, 2007 from http://www.swebok.org

Solberg Søilen, K. (2007). USING CASE STUDIES IN BLENDED LEARNING FOR INCREASED INTERACTIVITY AND LOWER DROP OUT RATES. *19th Nordic Academy of Management Conference.* Bergen, Norway.

Soloman, B., & Felder, R. (1999). *Index of Learning Styles (ILS),,* from http://www2.ncsu.edu/unity/lockers/users/f/felder/public/ILSpage.html

Somekh, B. (1989). Action research and collaborative school development. In R. McBride (Ed.), *The Inservice Training of Teachers: some issues and perspectives.* Brighton: Falmer Press.

Soo Hoo, K., Sudbury, A. W., & Jaquith, A. R. (2001). Tangible ROI through secure software engineering. *Secure Business Quarterly, 1.*

Spiro, R. J., Feltovich, P. J., Jacobson, M., & Coulson, R. (1991). Cognitive flexibility, constructivism and hypertext: random access instruction for advanced knowledge acquisition in ill-structured domains. *Educational Technology, 31,* 24-33.

Stark, C.M. & Schmidt, K.J. (2002). Transitioning to e-Learning: A Case Study. *Proceedings of the 2002 eTEE Conference*. Davos, Switzerland.

Starney, K. (2006). Why do projects fail? *CrossTalk: The Journal of Defense Software Engineering, 19*(6), 3. Available at http://www.stsc.hill.af.mil/crosstalk/2006/06/index.html

Stein, R.F., & Hurd, S. (2000). *Using student teams in the classroom: A faculty guide*. Boston: Anker Publishing.

Stevens, S. M. (1989). Intelligent interactive video simulation of a code inspection. *Communications of the ACM, 32*(7), 832-843.

Strauss, A. L., & Corbin, J. M. (1998). *Basics of Qualitative Research: Techniques and Procedures for Developing Grounded Theory*. Sage.

Stryer, L. (2005) Bio2010: Transforming Undergraduate Education For Future Research Biologists Washington, D.C.: National Academies Press, Retrieved from http://www.nap.edu.

Subversion. (2000). Retrieved from http://subversion.tigris.org/

Sun, N., & Decker, J. (2004). Finding an "ideal" model for our capstone experience. *Journal of Computing in Small Colleges, 20*(1), 211-219.

Supercomputing Online. (2007). Princeton professor foresees computer science revolution: An interview with Bernard Chazelle. Retrieved June 6, 2007, from http://www.supercomputingonline.com/article.php?sid=10496

Sutcliffe, A. (2003). *Scenario-based requirements engineering*. Paper presented at the IEEE International Conference on Requirements Engineering.

Sutcliffe, A. G., Maiden, A. M., Minocha, S., & Manuel, D. (1988). Supporting Scenario-Based Requirements Engineering. *IEEE Transactions on Software Engineering, 24*(12), 1072-1088.

SWEBOK (2004): Software Engineering Body of Knowledge. http://www.swebok.org/

SWEBOK. (2004). *Guide to the Software Engineering Body of Knowledge*. Piscataway, NJ: IEEE CS Press.

Szyperski, C. (2005). The making of a software engineer: Challenges for the educator. Proceedings of ICSE'05: *The 27th International Conference on Software Engineering*. St. Louis, MO.

Szyperski, C. (2005). The making of a software engineer: Challenges for the educator. Proceedings of ICSE'05: *The 27th International Conference on Software Engineering*. St. Louis, MO.

Tan, S. S., & Ng, C. K. F. (2006). A problem-based learning approach to entrepreneurship education. *Education & Training, 48*(6), 416-428.

Tebeaux, E., & Killingsworth, J. M. (1992). Expanding and Redirecting Historical Research in Technical Writing: In Search of Our Past. *Technical Communication Quarterly, 1*(2), 5-32.

Teles, V.M., & Oliveira C. (2003). Reviewing the Curriculum of Software Engineering Undergraduate Courses to Incorporate Communication and Personal Skills Teaching, *Proceedings CSEET 2003*, 158-165.

Texas Board of Professional Engineers (1999). Texas Engineering Practice Act, Revised 1st January 1999, Austin. Texas, 1999. Retrieved July 11, 2000, from http://www.main.org/peboard/law.pdf

The College Board (2007). 2007 College Bound Seniors, Total Group Profile Report. Retrieved November 15, 2007, from http://www.collegeboard.com/prod_downloads/about/news_info/cbsenior/yr2007/national-report.pdf

The Standish Group. (1994). *The Standish Group Report – CHAOS 1994*. Standish Group International. Available: http://www.standishgroup.com/sample_research/chaos_1994_1.php

The Standish Group. (2003). *CHAOS Chronicles Version 3.0*. West Yarmouth, MA: The Standish Group.

The TLT Group. (2007). Student Technology Assistant Programs. Available at http://www.tltgroup.org/programs/sta.html

Thomas L. & Ras E. (2005). Courseware Development Using a Single-Source Approach. *Proceedings of the World Conference on Education Multimedia, Hypermedia and Telecommunications.*

Thomas, J. C., Lee, A., & Danis, C. (2002). Enhancing creative design via software tools. *Communications of the ACM, 45*(10), 112-115.

Thompson, J. B. (2005, July). *Evaluations of IFIP's Proposed Standards for Professionals.* Paper presented at the 8th IFIP World Conference on Computers in Education, (WCCE 2005), July 4-7, 2005, University of Stellenbosch, Cape Town, South Africa, Session P10.3.

Thompson, J. B., & Edwards H. M. (2004). *Providing Graduate Computing Students with an Appreciation of Appropriate Ethical, Professional and Legal Issues,* In proceedings of Seventh International ETHICOMP Conference (ETHICOMP 2004), April 14-16, 2004, Syros, Greece, (pp. 839-853). Syros: University of the Aegean.

Thompson, J. B., & Towell, E. (2004). Workshop: *Teaching Ethics in Software Engineering Programmes.* In proceedings of 17th Conference on Software Engineering Education & Training (CSEE&T2004), March 1-3, Norfolk. USA, (pp. 162-164). Los Alamitos, CA: IEEE-Computer Society.

Thompson, J., & Edwards, H. (2006). Bridging the University/Industry Gap. *Proceedings of 28th International Conference on Software Engineering, ICSE 2006*, pp. 1011-1012.

Thompson, J.B. (2007). *Globalisation and the IT Professional.* In proceedings of 9th International ETHICOMP Conference, March 27-29, 2007, Meiji University, Tokyo, (pp. 564-575). Tokyo: Global e-SCM Research Centre, Meiji University.

Tinkham, A., & Kaner, C. (2005). *Experiences Teaching a Course in Programmer Testing.* Paper presented to Agile Conference, 2005. 24-29 July 2005, 298- 305.

Tomayko, J. and Hazzan, O. (2004). *Human Aspects of Software Engineering*, Charles River Media.

Tomayko, J. E. (1996). Carnegie Mellon's software development studio: A five year retrospective. In *Proceedings of the ninth conference on software engineering education and training* (pp. 119-129). Daytona Beach, FL, USA: IEEE.

Tomayko, J. E. (1998). Forging a Discipline: An Outline History of Software Engineering Education. *Annals of Software Engineering*, 6(1-4), 3-18.

Tomayko, J.E. (1996). Carnegie Mellon's software development studio: a five year retrospective. Proceedings of CSEE'96: *The 9th Conference on Software Engineering Education.* Daytona Beach, FL.

Towell, E. (2003). *Teaching Ethics in the Software Engineering Curriculum.* In proceedings of the Sixteenth Conference on Software Engineering Education & Training, March 20-22, Madrid, Spain, (pp. 150-157). Los Alamitos, CA: IEEE-Computer Society Press.

Towell, E. Thompson J. B. and McFadden K.L. (2004). Introducing and Developing Professional Standards in the Information Systems Curriculum. *Ethics and Information Technology*, (2004) 6, 291-299.

Towell, E., & Thompson, J. B. (2004). *A Further Exploration of Teaching Ethics in the Software Engineering Curriculum.* In proceedings of the Seventeenth Conference on Software Engineering Education & Training, March 1-3, Norfolk, USA, (pp. 39-49). Los Alamitos, CA: IEEE-Computer Society.

Trauth, E. M., Farwell, D., & Lee, D. M. S. (1993). The IS expectation gap: industry expectation versus academic preparation. *MIS Quarterly, 17*, 293-307.

Tucker, A (Editor) et al.(1991) Report of the ACM/IEEE-CS Joint Curriculum Task Force. Retrieved from http://www.acm/education/curr91/homepage.html.

Turhan, B. & Bener, A. (2007). A template for real world team projects for highly populated software engineering classes. Proceedings of ICSE'07: *The 29th International Conference on Software Engineering.* Minneapolis, MN.

Turley, R. T. (1991). *Essential Competencies of Exceptional Professional Software Engineers*. Colorado State University, Fort Collins (CO).

Turley, R. T., & Bieman, J. M. (1995). Competencies of exceptional and non-exceptional software engineers. *Journal od Systems and Software, 28*(1), 19-38.

Tvedt, J. Tesoriero, R., & Gary, K. (2001). The Software Factory: Combining undergraduate computer science and software engineering education. Proceedings of ICSE'01: *The 23rd International Conference on Software Engineering.* Toronto, CA.

Tvedt, J. Tesoriero, R., & Gary, K. (2001). The Software Factory: Combining undergraduate computer science and software engineering education. Proceedings of ICSE'01: *The 23rd International Conference on Software Engineering.* Toronto, CA.

Tynjälä, P., Salminen, R., Sutela, T., Nuutinen, A., & Pitkänen, S. (2005). Factors related to study success in engineering education. *European Journal of Engineering Education, 30*(2), 221-231.

U. S. Department of Labor, Bureau of Labor Statistics (2006a). *Occupational Outlook Handbook (OOH)*, 2006-07 Edition. Retrieved May 28, 2007, from http://www.bls.gov/oco/

U. S. Department of Labor, Bureau of Labor Statistics (2006b). *Occupational Employment and Wages.* May 2006. Retrieved May 28, 2007, from http://www.bls.gov/oes/current/oes151032.htm

U.S. Bureau of Labor Statistics (U.S. BLS) (2007). *Economic and employment projections: 2006-2016.* Retrieved January 4, 2008 from http://www.bls.gov/news.release/ecopro.toc.htm.

Ubal, R., Cano, J.-C., Petit, S. & Sahuquillo, J. (2006). RAC FP: A Training Tool to Work With Floating-Point Representation, Algorithms, and Circuits in Undergraduate Courses. *IEEE Transactions on Education.* 49 (3), pp. 321- 331.

Umphress, D., Hendrix, T., & Cross, J. (2002, Sept/Oct). Software Process in the Classroom: The Capstone Experience. *IEEE Software, 19(5)*, 78-81.

Umphress, D., Hendrix, T., & Cross, J. (2002, Sept/Oct). Software Process in the Classroom: The Capstone Experience. *IEEE Software, 19(5)*, 78-81.

UWA. (1996). *Do male and female students differ in their preferred style of learning?* Perth: Institutional Research Unit, University of Western Australia.

Van Dalen, G. (2003). *Software engineer – are you licensed?* Retrieved February 4, 2007 from http://www.cips.ca/news/national/news.asp?aID=1731

van der Duim, L., Andersson J., & Sinnema M. (2007). Good Practices for Educational Software Engineering Projects. *Proceedings of 29th International Conference on Software Engineering, ICSE 2007*, pp. 698-707.

van Eck, R. (2006). Digital game-based learning: It's not just the digital natives who are restless. *Educause Review, 41*(2), 17-30.

Van Maanen, J. (1988). *Tales of the Field: On Writing Ethnography.* University of Chicago Press.

van Vliet, H. (2005). Some Myths of Software Engineering Education. *Proceedings of 27th International Conference on Software Engineering, ICSE 2005*, pp. 621-622.

van Vliet, H. (2006). Reflections on Software Engineering Education. *IEEE Software*, 24(3), pp. 55-61.

Vegso, J. (2006). BLS IT workforce projections compared. *CRA Bulletin*, January 19, 2006. Available: http://www.cra.org/wp/index.php?cat=14

Victor, D. A. (1999). Using Scenarios and Vignettes in Cross-Cultural Business Communication Instruction. *Business Communication Quarterly, 62*(4), 99-103.

Visser, W. (1992). Designers' activities examined at three levels: organisation strategies and problem-solving processes. *Knowledge-Based Systems, 5*(1), 92-104.

Voigt, W. P. (2007). *Quantitative research methods for professionals.* Boston: Allyn and Bacon.

Waks, L. J. (2001). Donald Schon's Philosophy of Design and Design Education. *International Journal of Technology and Design Education, 11*, 37-51.

Wang, A. I. & Sorensen, C.-F. (2006). Writing as a Tool for Learning Software Engineering. *Proceedings of the Nineteenth Conference on Software Engineering Education & Training.* Turtle Bay, Hawaii.

Wankat, P. & Oreovicz, F. (1993*). Teaching Engineering*, Upper Saddle River, NJ: McGraw Hill.

Waterman, R. H., Waterman, J. A., & Collard, B. A. (1994). Toward a career resilient workforce. *Harvard Business Review, 69,* 87-95.

Werner, M., & MacLean, L.M. (2006). Building community service projects effectively. *Journal of Computing Sciences in Colleges, 21*(6), 76-87.

White, J. & Simons, B. (2002). ACM's Position on Licensing of Software Engineers. *Communications of the ACM. 45*(11), 91-92. New York: ACM Press.

Wick, M., Stevenson, D., & Wagner, P. (2008). *Using Testing and JUnit Across the curriculum.* Presented at 36th SIGCSE technical symposium on Computer science education, 2005, 236–240.

Wilde, N., White, L.J., Kerr, L.B., Ewing, D.D., & Krueger, A. (2003). Some experiences with evolution and process-focused projects. Proceedings of CSEET'03): *The 16th Conference on Software Engineering Education and Training.* Madrid, Spain.

Wilde, N., White, L.J., Kerr, L.B., Ewing, D.D., & Krueger, A. (2003). Some experiences with evolution and process-focused projects. Proceedings of CSEET'03): *The 16th Conference on Software Engineering Education and Training.* Madrid, Spain.

Wilkins, D., & Lawhead, P. (2000). Evaluating individuals in team projects. *SIGCSE-Bulletin,* 32(1), pp. 172–175.

Williams, J. C., Bair, B., Borstler, J., Lethbridge, T.C., & Surendran, K. (2003). Client sponsored projects in software engineering courses. *SIGCSE Bulletin in roads, 35*(1). 401-402.

Williams, J. M., & Colomb, G. G. (1993). The Case for Explicit Teaching: Why What You Don't Know Won't Help You. *Research in the Teaching of English, 27*(3), 252-264.

Williams, L. A., & Kessler, R. R. (2000). *The Effects of 'Pair-Pressure' and 'Pair-Learning' on Software Engineering Education.* Presented at 13th Conference on Software Engineering Education and Training, March 2000, 59-65.

Williams, L., & Kessler, R. (2000). Experimenting with industry's pair programming model in the computer science Classroom. *Journal of Computer Science Education,* 10(4).

Williams, L., Kessler, R. A., Cunningham, W., & Jeffries, R. (2000). Strengthening the Case for Pair-Programming, *IEEE Software,* 17(4), 19-25.

Wills, S. (2006). Strategic Planning for Blended eLearning. *Proceedings of the 7th International Conference on Information Technology Based Higher Education & Training.* Sydney, Australia.

Winn, W., & Snyder, D. (1996). Cognitive perspectives in psychology. In D. H. Jonassen (Ed.), *Handbook of Research for Educational Communications and Technology* (pp. 112-142). New York: Simon & Schuster Macmillan.

Wohlin, C., & Regnell, B. (1999). Achieving industrial relevance in software engineering education. In H. Saiedian (Ed.), *Proceedings of the twelfth conference on software engineering education and training* (pp. 16-25): IEEE Computer Society.

Worthen, B. R., & Sanders, J. R. (1988). *Educational evaluation: Alternative approaches and practical guidelines.* White Plains, NY: Longman.

Yildiz, Senem, Chang, Carrie (2003) Case Studies of Distance Students' Perceptions of Participation and Interaction in Three Asynchronous Web-based Conferencing Classes. *The U.S. Turkish Online Journal of Distance Education-TOJDE.* 4 (2).

Young, G., & Marks-Maran, D. (2002). But they looked great on paper. In P. Schwartz & G. Webb (Eds.), *Assessment: Case studies, experience and practice from higher education* (pp. 106-113). London: Kogan Page.

Zave, P. (1997). Classification of research efforts in RE. *ACM Computer Surveys, 29*(4), 315-321.

Zheng, Z. A., & Padmanabhan, B. (2006). Selectively acquiring customer information: A new data acquisition problem and an active learning-based solution. *Management Science, 52*(5), 697-712.

Zuber-Skerritt, O. (1995). Models for action research. In S. Pinchen & R. Passfield (Eds.), *Moving On: creative applications of action learning and action research* (pp. 3–29). Mt Gravatt (Qld): Action Learning, Action Research and Process Management Assn, Inc.

Zweben, S. (2007). *2005-2006 Taulbee Survey.* Computing Research News. pp. 7-22.

Zywno, M., & Waalen, J. (2001). *The effect of hypermedia instruction on achievement and attitudes of students with different learning styles.* Paper presented at the Proceedings of the 2001 American Society for Engineering Education Annual conference and Exposition Session 1330.

About the Contributors

Heidi J. C. Ellis is an assistant professor in the Computer Science Department at Trinity College, Hartford, CT. Dr. Ellis is a member of the IEEE Computer Society and the IEEE Education Society and has been involved in the development of the Computer Society's Certified Software Development Professional exam. Dr. Ellis is currently involved in the Trinity humanitarian free and open source (H-FOSS) effort. She is also a member of the CONNJUR project, an open source integration environment for biomolecular NMR data analysis developed collaboratively with Dr. Michael Gryk at the University of Connecticut Health Center. Dr. Ellis' research interests include software engineering education, technology for learning and teaching, and tools for biological data processing and analysis. Professor Ellis graduated from the University of Connecticut in 1995 with a PhD in computer science and engineering with a focus on software engineering.

Steven A. Demurjian is a full professor of computer science & engineering at the University of Connecticut. Dr. Demurjian is a member of ACM, IEEE Computer Society, IFIP WG11.3 on Database Security, and was elected in 2007 as a member of the Connecticut Academy of Science & Engineering. Dr. Demurjian's research interests include: UML extensions for role-based (RBAC) and mandatory (MAC) access control with assurance and automatic generation of aspect-oriented software for security enforcement, RBAC and MAC models and security solutions for assurance in web-based and distributed computing environments, and design/code level reusability and refactoring for component-based systems. Dr. Demurjian has over 120 archival publications (book, journal articles, book chapters, and conference/workshop articles). Dr. Demurjian graduated from The Ohio State University in 1987 with a PhD in Computer and Information Sciences with a focus on database models and systems.

J. Fernando Naveda is co-founder and chair of the department of software engineering at Rochester Institute of Technology (RIT), where he has been since 1993. In 1986 he earned a PhD in computer science from the University of Minnesota, Twin Cities; and a bachelor's degree in computer systems engineering from Instituto Tecnológico y de Estudios Superiores de Monterrey, México, in 1975. In 1990 he was a visiting scientist at the Software Engineering Institute. An active member and volunteer with the IEEE Computer Society, Naveda currently serves as the vice-chair in the Educational Activities Board. He is the co-editor of the volume *IEEE Computer Society Real-World Software Engineering Problems – A Self-Study Guide for Today's Software Professional.*

* * *

Vicki L. Almstrum is a research fellow with the Department of Electrical and Computer Engineering at The University of Texas at Austin, where she is leading the process of introducing an international senior design option. In articles, panel discussions, working groups, websites, and other activities, Dr. Almstrum has been a strong proponent of computing education research as a viable field. Dr. Almstrum has 10 years experience teaching a 1-semester elective upper-level SE RPRCC with clients from not-for-profits and educational institutions. She has eight years of industry experience with standards, methodologies, and quality assurance for Motorola (in Arizona) and Philips Elektronikindustrier (in Sweden).

Jocelyn Armarego worked for 10 years in industry as a requirements engineer before joining the academic staff of first Curtin and then Murdoch Universities. This chapter reflects her interests in SE education (in particular issues of non-traditional learning and student approaches to learning), requirements engineering (how we do it, how we teach it) and alignment between formal education and professional practice. She has been involved with the development of model curricula for software engineering and is a member of Engineers Australia's National Committee on SE. She is currently participating in a research project investigating creativity in software development in a distributed environment.

Daniel Bolanos was born in Madrid (Spain), in 1980. He received a BS in computer science in 2002 and an MS in computer engineering in 2004, both from the Autonoma University of Madrid. Daniel has been an assistant teacher for 4 years at the Autonoma University of Madrid, teaching software engineering and software testing. In 2006 he joined the Center for Spoken Language Research at Boulder, Colorado, where he is currently finishing his PhD in speech processing. His research activity is mainly focused in large vocabulary speech recognition. However, he is actively involved in the development and analysis of new software testing techniques and strategies.

Ann Brady is an assistant professor of humanities and the director of the Scientific and Technical Communication Program at Michigan Technological University. Her research focuses on interdisciplinarity as it informs the theory and practice of technical communication. She received a PhD in rhetoric and professional communication from Miami University of Ohio.

Barry J. Brinkman is an assistant professor in the Computer and Information Science Department, Gannon University. He received a PhD in computer and information science from The Ohio State University. With 25 years in research and development at Battelle and Bell Laboratories, his current research interests are in the areas of computer and network security and computer science education. As an active practitioner, his experience included all aspects of software development, from high-level requirements definition to specification, design, implementation, testing and maintenance. He teaches a variety of topics, from introductory programming, to networking, operating systems, and distributed systems development. Dr. Brinkman is currently a member of the Association of Computing Machinery.

Christian Bunse is associate professor for software engineering at the School of Information Technology, International University in Bruchsal, Germany. Prior to this, he had been the head of the Component Engineering Department at the Fraunhofer Institute for Experimental Software Engineering (IESE) in Kaiserslautern. Before joining Fraunhofer, he was a faculty research assistant of the Software-Technology-Transfer-Initiative, University of Kaiserslautern, Germany. His research interests are in the area of model-based development, resource awareness and empirical software engineering. He is a member of the GI and the special interest groups on software engineering, software architecture, and automotive software engineering.

Steven J. Condly is senior associate at HSA Learning & Performance Solutions and was formerly visiting assistant professor of educational psychology at the University of Central Florida. His expertise and research interests fall in the area of identifying and analyzing psychological variables related to human learning, motivation, performance, and testing and assessment. He studies students at the high school and collegiate level as well as adults employed in work settings. His research on the role of incentives in workplace performance garnered him three separate national awards, including the American Society for Training and Development Research Award for Article of the Year.

Stephen T. Frezza, CSDP, earned his PhD, MS, and BS degrees in electrical engineering from the University of Pittsburgh. He is an associate professor and chair of the Computer and Information Science Department at Gannon University. As a Certified Software Development Professional (CSDP), he remains actively involved in developing practical industry-university projects and partnerships. He teaches a variety of software engineering topics, primarily in the area of requirements engineering, project management, software testing and embedded systems. His research interests are in the areas of software engineering education, automatic schematics generation, automated software testing, and the relationship between engineering and theology. Dr. Frezza is a member of the IEEE Computer Society, and the Association of Computing Machinery.

Kevin A. Gary, PhD, joined the Division of Computing Studies at Arizona State University as an assistant professor in 2004 after spending several years in industry architecting solutions for e-learning. Since joining the faculty at ASU, Dr. Gary has designed a capstone experience named the Software Enterprise that aims to better prepare new graduates in software engineering for industry. The Enterprise emerged from Dr. Gary's industry experience and mentorship of junior software engineers. Dr. Gary's research activities focus on software process and architecture, for open source and web-based software. Current research projects are in the areas of open source software for image-guided surgery (the Image-guided Surgery Toolkit [IGSTK], www.igstk.org), search technologies for the semantic web, and web analytics. Dr. Gary also remains active in his dissertation area, workflow and business process system architectures. Dr. Gary remains connected to the practice as co-director (with Dr. Harry Koehnemann) of the Distributed and Enterprise Applications Consortium (DEAC, deac.asu.edu), by actively consulting with companies in the Phoenix metro area, and by remaining abreast enterprise technologies for higher education.

Ann Gates was one of the original investigators in the development of the ARG model and continues to play a key role in its implementation and refinement. She has published with others over twenty papers on the model. In addition, she presented the model in panels and gave workshops. Ann is a member of the IEEE-Computer Society (IEEE-CS) Board of Governors (2004-2006); IEEE-CS, Educational Activities Board (1997-present); the National Academy of Engineering's Committee on Engineering Education (2002-2004); steering committee for the Frontiers in Education Conference (2000-2002; 2003-2005); IEEE-CS Certified Software Development Professional Certification Committee; and founding member of the Computing Alliance for Hispanic-Serving Institutions as well as the Academic Alliance for the

National Center for Women in Information Technology. In addition, she is a program evaluator for the Computing Accreditation Committee of ABET. She received her PhD in computer science from New Mexico State University.

Ines Grützner received her diploma in computer science and economics from Dresden University of Technology. She works as a scientist and project manager in the field of Software Engineering Education and Training as well as eGovernment at the Fraunhofer Institute for Experimental Software Engineering (IESE) in Kaiserslautern. Her research in eLearning is focused on the systematic, engineering-style development of online courses. She has led several projects targeted at the development of online courses on software engineering topics.

Orit Hazzan is an associate professor at the Department of Education in Technology and Science of the Technion – Israel Institute of Technology and she heads the computer science education track of the department. She is a co-author (with Jim Tomayko) of *Human Aspects of Software Engineering* (2004, Charles River Media). Currently, she writes (with Yael Dubinsky) her second book – *Agile Software Engineering* – to be published by Springer in 2008. Dr. Hazzan has 19 years of teaching experience in academia and industry (courses, workshops, lectures and conference presentations) and she is the author of about 100 journal and conference publications.

Gregory W. Hislop is a faculty member and former associate dean in the College of Information Science and Technology at Drexel University. He has played a central role in development, implementation, and revision of degree programs in software engineering, information systems, and information technology. He was one of the four leaders of the NSF SWENET project, which created an online repository of software engineering curricular materials. Prior to coming to Drexel, Dr. Hislop spent 18 years working in government and industry. His efforts encompassed technology planning and evaluation, software development and support, and development and delivery of technical education. His research interests include technology for learning and teaching, education in the computing disciplines, and design, evolution, and evaluation of software. He has delivered over 60 papers and presentations related to these areas in recent years.

Allen Johnson is interim chair of computer science at Huston-Tillotson University. Dr. Johnson has more than 35 years of experience developing computer systems and software in the industry. He is the chair of the Student and Academic Relations Committee of the Association of Software Testing and served on the advisory board for the UT Austin Software Engineering Institute's Software Project Management certificate program. In workshops and presentations, Dr. Johnson has been an advocate for the scholarship of teaching and learning. He has over 25 years of experience teaching one-semester courses at the graduate/senior/junior level, teaching computer science college-level courses for IBM and other corporations, and 48-week industry courses that involved clients from not-for-profits and industry.

David Klappholz is associate professor of computer science at Stevens Institute of Technology. He has 33 years of experience teaching computer science and has performed and supervised technology research on parallel computing and compiler technology (sponsored by organizations such as NSF, DOE, and IBM Research). Dr. Klappholz is an ABET program evaluator and has been involved in NSF-sponsored software process pedagogy research. He co-taught CS577, Barry Boehm's SE RPRCC at

USC, during a sabbatical in 2002 and has spent parts of the past five summers as a Visiting Researcher engaged in improving CS577. Dr. Klappholz has five years of experience teaching a sophomore/junior-level required DBMS RPRCC at Stevens, with mostly university faculty and staff as clients, but also with a few not-for-profit and industry clients who heard about the course by word of mouth.

Jochen Ludewig was born in 1947 in Hannover, Germany. He holds a diploma in electrical engineering from the Technical University of Hannover, and a postgraduate certificate in computer science from the Technical University of Munich. He holds a PhD from the TU Munich with a thesis on the specification of software for real time systems (1981). After five years at Brown Boveri Research in Baden, Switzerland, he became an associate professor at the Swiss Federal Institute (ETH) at Zurich. In 1988, he returned to Germany as a full professor of software engineering at the Universität Stuttgart. He has authored or co-authored eight books, including an introduction to computer science and a textbook on software engineering. He designed the software engineering curriculum launched in 1996 at the Universität Stuttgart, and supervised and improved it ever since.

James McDonald is associate professor and chair of the Department of Software Engineering, Monmouth University. He earned a bachelor's degree in electrical engineering from New Jersey Institute of Technology, an MSEE degree from Massachusetts Institute of Technology and a PhD from New York University. Dr. McDonald has an extensive industrial background in both software and electrical engineering. He has worked at AT&T, Bell Laboratories, Bellcore and Lucent Technologies. He is a senior member of the Institute of Electrical and Electronic Engineers (IEEE), the IEEE Computer Society, the Association for Computing Machinery (ACM) and the American Society for Engineering Education (ASEE). At Monmouth University he teaches courses on Project Management, Software Organization Management, Software Verification, Validation and Maintenance, a Software Engineering Practicum, Information Technology and other software engineering topics. He is serving as an ABET program evaluator for electrical, computer and software engineering programs.

Nancy R. Mead is a senior member of the technical staff in the Survivable Systems Engineering Group, which is part of the CERT Program at the Software Engineering Institute (SEI). Mead is also a faculty member in the Master of Software Engineering and Master of Information Systems Management programs at Carnegie Mellon University. Her research interests are in the areas of information security, software requirements engineering, and software architectures. Mead has more than 100 publications and invited presentations. She is a Fellow of the Institute of Electrical and Electronic Engineers, Inc. (IEEE) and the IEEE Computer Society and is also a member of the Association for Computing Machinery (ACM). Dr. Mead received her PhD in mathematics from the Polytechnic Institute of New York, and received a BA and an MS in mathematics from New York University.

Allen Milewski is currently an associate professor of software engineering at Monmouth University in West Long Branch, NJ, USA. His research interests combine studies of collaborative work and user interface design. Projects include team collaboration, global teamwork and cultural variation in social and cognitive processes. In addition, he has published in the area of user interface internationalization. Most recently, he has included the design of collaborative information systems for Homeland Security and Emergency Management use. He has more than 20 years of Industry experience in engineering.

Kenneth Modesitt, prior to his retirement in 2007, was professor and interim chair of computer science as well as associate dean for external partnerships and research at Indiana University – Purdue University Ft. Wayne. His areas of expertise include software engineering, expert systems, and distributed learning. He has used teams of students to develop software for real clients for over 20 years at four different universities. His experiences working for industry have had a major impact on his quest to bring "realism" to the classroom. These experiences began in 1963 at Control Data Corporation and have included software and management positions with Texas Instruments, Rockwell International, and Loral.

Emily Oh Navarro is a project scientist in the Department of Informatics of the Donald Bren School of Information and Computer Sciences at the University of California, Irvine. She completed her PhD in information and computer science at UCI in 2006, with her dissertation entitled, "SimSE: A Software Engineering Simulation Environment for Software Process Education." She also holds an MS in information and computer science from UCI, along with a BS in biological sciences, also from UCI. Emily's research is focused on developing game-based simulation tools for software engineering education. She is the lead developer on the SimSE project and has also contributed to the design and evaluation of Problems and Programmers, an educational software engineering card game.

Donald M. Needham is an associate professor of computer science at the United States Naval Academy. Dr. Needham is an ABET-CAC program evaluator and a member of the ACM and the IEEE Computer Society. His research interests include safety-critical software metrics as applied to software fault trees and software reuse within product lines. He has been funded by the Joint Technology Office, Naval Sea Command Systems, Electric Boat, Naval Research Lab and NASA and has published over 40 archival publications (book, journal articles, book chapters, and conference/workshop articles). Dr. Needham graduated from the University of Connecticut in 1997 with a PhD in computer science and engineering.

Cherry Owen is assistant professor of computer science in the Department of Mathematics and Computer Science in the College of Arts and Sciences at The University of Texas of the Permian Basin. She has 20 years of experience teaching computer science and mathematics as well as seven years experience as a systems analyst with Exxon Company, USA. She has been incorporating real projects into various courses whenever possible for the last ten years, with clients from industry, not-for-profits, and university faculty.

Christian Peper studied computer science and physics at Saarland University, Germany. In 1995, he joined the University of Kaiserslautern as a researcher working on reuse-oriented application of formal description techniques. Since 2003, he has been working for the Fraunhofer Institute for Experimental Software Engineering (IESE) in Kaiserslautern with a current focus on development and specification of adaptive component-oriented systems. Since 2004, he has also acted as a UML trainer and consultant in several industrial education and cooperation projects.

Steve Roach has been using cooperative learning and the ARG model in his courses and research since 1999. In 2002 and 2003, he chaired the IEEE CCSE Sub-Committee on Advanced Software Engineering Curricula. The CCSE is an international organization developing models of undergraduate and graduate software engineering programs. In 2003, he chaired the panel session "The Art of Getting Students to Practice Team Skills," at the 33rd ASEE/IEEE Frontiers in Education Conference (with E. Villa, J. Sullivan, R. Upchurch, and K. Smith). He is an IEEE-CS Certified Software Development Professional and a program evaluator for the Computing Accreditation Committee of ABET. He received a PhD in computer science from the University of Wyoming.

Daniela Rosca is currently an associate professor in the Software Engineering Department at Monmouth University, NJ, USA. Her main research interests span the areas of requirements engineering, business rules, dynamic workflow systems, and process modeling. Recently, she has been applying her expertise to various systems for Emergency Management. Prior to joining Monmouth University, Dr. Rosca was a senior member of technical staff at the Romanian Institute for Computers Research. She is the author of numerous research papers published in journals, books, and conference proceedings. Dr. Rosca has served as program committee member, session chair or organizer for several international conferences and workshops. She is a member of ACM.

Mark J. Sebern is a professor in the Electrical Engineering and Computer Science Department at the Milwaukee School of Engineering (MSOE). He was the founding program director of MSOE's undergraduate software engineering program, one of the first four to be accredited in the United States. Prior to joining MSOE, Dr. Sebern worked in industry for twenty years as a practicing computer and software engineer. His interests include software engineering process, software design and architecture, databases, web application frameworks, and embedded computer systems. Dr. Sebern leads MSOE's cooperative efforts with industry partners in the area of software process improvement, providing targeted training and coaching support to software development teams and managers. He has also served as an ABET program evaluator for computer engineering and software engineering programs.

Stephen B. Seidman is dean of the College of Natural Sciences and Mathematics at the University of Central Arkansas. He has held administrative and academic posts at New Jersey Institute of Technology, Auburn University, Colorado State University, and George Mason University. He received a PhD in mathematics from the University of Michigan. Seidman's research interests are in software architectures, formal methods, and computing education. He has been active in efforts to improve computing and software engineering education and professionalism, including service as the IEEE Computer Society's Vice-President for Educational Activities, as a member of the CSAB board of directors, and as a member of an ISO/IEC working group.

Marika Seigel is an assistant professor of rhetoric and technical communication at Michigan Technological University, where she teaches undergraduate and graduate courses in technical communication to students from a variety of disciplines. In addition to technical communication, her research interests include usability, gender studies, and rhetorics of science and technology. She received her bachelor's degree in English from the University of Michigan and her master's degree and PhD in English (with a focus in rhetoric and composition) from Penn State University.

Dan Shoemaker is the director of the Centre for Assurance Studies, which is a National Security Agency (NSA) Center of Academic Excellence in IA Education. He has been professor and chair of computer and information systems at the University of Detroit Mercy for the past 24 years. He has been involved in software engineering education since 1988. He also co-authored McGraw-Hill's current textbook on information assurance, "Information Assurance for the Enterprise". His research interests are in the areas of secure software assurance, information assurance and enterprise security architectures, IT governance and control and strategic software management and he has close to 50 publications and invited presentations in these areas. Dr. Shoemaker has a bachelor's degree and a PhD from the University of Michigan He has two master's degrees from Eastern Michigan University.

Almudena Sierra-Alonso received her PhD in computer science from Universidad Politécnica de Madrid, in 2000. She joined the Computer Science Department at the Carlos III University in 1995 where she was an assistant professor until 2000. Currently she is an associate professor in the Computer Science Department of the Rey Juan Carlos University. She teaches software engineering from 2000. She has published in areas like the knowledge engineering methodologies and the confluence of knowledge and software engineering, mainly in the requirements phase. Her current research focuses in software architecture: the transition from requirements to software architecture and how to model and manage the design decisions made during that transition in order to use them for future maintenance.

Silke Steinbach-Nordmann studied educational sciences, psychology, and sociology combined with German language and modern literature studies at Philipps University Marburg, Germany. Before she joined the Fraunhofer Institute for Experimental Software Engineering (IESE), she worked as a researcher at the University of Kaiserslautern in the field of adult education and vocational training. For more than ten years, she has taught trainings and lessons in adult education and at universities with a focus on educational aspects. Since 2000, she has been working at Fraunhofer IESE; in November 2007, she took over the role of department head in the Education and Training Department (EAT). Her research interests are in technology-enhanced learning, didactics in vocational training, human aspects in technology, and empirical studies in software engineering.

Mei-Huei Tang earned a PhD and MS in computer science from the State University of New York, University at Albany. She is currently an assistant professor in Computer and Information Science Department at Gannon University in Erie, Pennsylvania. She teaches a variety of computer science and software engineering courses, including advanced programming, software architecture, testing and quality assurance and formal methods. Her research interests include change impact analysis, object-oriented design, software metrics, software architecture, software reliability, software testing, and software engineering education. Dr. Tang is currently a member of the Association of Computing Machinery.

William Tepfenhart is author of several books on object orientation. He is currently an associate professor in the Software and Electrical Engineering Department, Monmouth University and director of the Master's Program in Software Engineering. He is the chief technical officer of the Rapid Response Institute at Monmouth University. His current line of research investigates the use of software solutions to enhance the effectiveness of collaboration among first responders during emergency situations. Prior to his entry to the academic world, he was employed as a developer and technologist at AT&T Laboratories where he worked on applications associated with the long distance network, establishment of engineering practices at a corporate level, and working with advanced object-oriented technologies.

J. Barrie Thompson is a national teaching fellow in the UK and is professor in applied software engineering in the School of Computing and Technology at the University of Sunderland, UK. His prime interests are educational, professional and ethical issues associated with Software Engineering. He promotes the development of innovative teaching approaches relevant to the needs of industry. He was a member of the Software Engineering curriculum steering committee representing IEEE Computer Society's Technical Committee for Software Engineering. Since January 2005 he has been the chair of IFIP Working Group 3.4, Professional and Vocational Education and Training. He is a member of the Editorial Advisory Board for the Journal of Information Communication and Ethics in Society and an associate editor for the International Journal of Information and Communication Technology Education. He also co-edits the on-line newsletter FASE (Forum for Advancing Software engineering Education).

James E. Tomayko was a teaching professor in Carnegie Mellon University's School of Computer Science for more than 16-year. At the same time, he served as a part-time senior member of the technical staff at the Software Engineering Institute. Dr. Tomayko's publications include *Software Engineering Education: SEI Conference on Software Engineering* (1991), published by Springer-Verlag; *Computers in Space: Journeys with NASA* (1994), *Computers Take Flight: A History of NASA's Pioneering Digital Fly-by-Wire Project* (2000) and *Human Aspects of Software Engineering* (2004, with Orit Hazzan). Dr. Tomayko died on January 2006 after a long illness. He was 56.

Will Tracz is a principal software engineer/application architect for the Global Combat Support System - AF (GCSS-AF) Application Integration department at Lockheed Martin IS&S in Endicott, NY responsible for investigating innovative applications of and evaluating technology for the GCSS-AF Architecture Integration Framework. Dr. Tracz is a member Lockheed Martin's Corporate Advanced Software Technology Focus Group. In addition, he was a co-PI on the Defense Advanced Research Projects Agency (DARPA) Dynamic Assembly of Systems for Adaptability, Dependability, and Assurance (DASADA) and Domain-Specific Software Architecture (DSSA) Programs. Dr. Tracz is a member of the RIT Software Engineering Advisory Board, the Software Engineering Institute Technical Advisory Group on Engineering and Method, and an IEEE TCSE Executive Committee Member at Large. In addition, he is the editor of the ACM SIGSOFT Software Engineering Notes, past chairman of the International Conference on Software Engineering sponsored by IEEE and ACM, and the author of over 100 technical reports and books on software engineering, software architectures, and software reuse.

James R. Vallino is an associate professor in the Department of Software Engineering at Rochester Institute of Technology. He was actively involved in the development of the software engineering program, the first undergraduate software engineering program in the United States. This involvement included bringing active learning and problem-based learning into the curriculum, developing an NSF CCLI-funded inter-disciplinary course sequence in real-time and embedded systems, and guiding the program through its ABET accreditation. Prior to RIT, Dr. Vallino had seventeen years of software development experience in industry, followed by his PhD studies in computer science at the University of Rochester. His research interests include pedagogy for software engineering education, software design, especially in the real-time and embedded systems area, and model-based development methodologies.

André van der Hoek is an associate professor in the Department of Informatics of the Donald Bren School of Information and Computer Sciences and a faculty member of the Institute for Software Research, both at the University of California, Irvine. He holds a joint BS and MS degree in business-oriented computer science from the Erasmus University Rotterdam, The Netherlands, and a PhD in computer science from the University of Colorado at Boulder. André's research focuses on understanding and advancing the role of design, coordination, and education in software. He has developed several configuration management systems, designed the widely-used xADL 2.0 architecture description language, and created novel educational software engineering approaches used at institutions across the world. André is the principal designer of the new B.S. in Informatics at UC Irvine and was honored, in 2005, as UC Irvine Professor of the Year for his outstanding and innovative educational contributions.

Thomas Vosecky is a PhD candidate in rhetoric and technical communication at Michigan Technological University, where he is currently involved in the development of a writing center for the MBA program in the School of Business and Economics. His research interests include the ancient Greek concept of techné (the capacity to make), research methods, and the case study as a means of simulating practical experience in the classroom. He has received a bachelor's degree in psychology from the University of Minnesota, Minneapolis, a master's degree in rhetoric and technical communication from Michigan Tech, and ASE automobile technician certification.

Charles Wallace is an associate professor of computer science at Michigan Technological University. He has been involved in the undergraduate software engineering degree program at Michigan Tech since its inception in 2004. His research and teaching interests lie in software requirements, documentation, verification, and usability. He holds a bachelor's degree in linguistics from the University of Pennsylvania, a master's degree in linguistics from the University of California, Santa Cruz, and a doctorate in computer science and engineering from the University of Michigan.

Jiacun Wang received a PhD in computer engineering from Nanjing University of Science and Technology (NUST), China, in 1991. He is currently an associate professor in the Software Engineering Department, Monmouth University, West Long Branch, NJ, USA. From 2001 to 2004, he was a member of scientific staff with Nortel Networks in Richardson, Texas. Prior to joining Nortel, he was a research associate of the School of Computer Science, Florida International University (FIU) at Miami. Prior to joining FIU, he was an associate professor at NUST. His research interests include software engineering, discrete event systems, formal methods, wireless networking, and real-time distributed systems. He authored Timed Petri Nets: Theory and Application (Norwell, MA: Kluwer, 1998), and published more than 50 research papers in journals and conferences. He is an Associate Editor of IEEE Transactions on Systems, Man and Cybernetics, Part C, and has served as program chair, special sessions chair or program committee member for many international conferences. Dr. Wang is a senior member of IEEE.

Index